Collins English Thesaurus

Published by Collins
An imprint of HarperCollins Publishers
Westerhill Road
Bishopbriggs
Glasgow G64 2QT
www.harpercollins.co.uk

This Edition 2014

10 9 8 7 6 5 4 3 2 1

ISBN 978-0-00-794288-6
ISBN 978-0-00-794289-3
ISBN 978-0-00-748743-1
ISBN 978-0-00-789684-4

www.collins.co.uk
www.collinsdictionary.com

Printed in Great Britain by Clays Ltd, St Ives plc

A catalogue record for this book is available from the British Library.

If you would like to comment on any aspect of this book, please contact us at the above address or online.
E-mail: dictionaries@harpercollins.co.uk

Acknowledgements
We would like to thank those authors and publishers who kindly gave permission for copyright material to be used in the Collins Corpus. We would also like to thank Times Newspapers Ltd for providing valuable data.

Contents

EDITORIAL STAFF

EDITORS
Lorna Gilmour

FOR THE PUBLISHERS
Morven Dooner
Elaine Higgleton
Lorna Knight

USING THIS THESAURUS

Main entry words	Main entry words are printed in bold type: **altogether**
Parts of speech	Parts of speech are shown (in small capitals) when the entry has more than one part of speech. Where a word has several senses for one part of speech, the senses are numbered: **abandon** *verb* **1**
Alternatives	Alternatives are introduced by an equals sign: = The key synonym for each sense is underlined, with other alternatives given in roman: **absorb 1** = <u>soak up</u>, suck up, receive, digest, imbibe **2** = <u>engross</u>, involve, engage, fascinate, rivet, captivate
Opposites	Opposites are introduced by an equals sign with a line through it ≠partially

ABBREVIATIONS USED IN THIS THESAURUS

AD	anno Domini
adj	adjective
adv	adverb
anat	anatomy
archit	architecture
astrol	astrology
Aust	Australia(n)
BC	before Christ
biol	biology
Brit	British
Canad	Canadian
chem	chemistry
C *of* E	Church of England
conj	conjunction
E	East
eg	for example
esp	especially
etc	et cetera
fem	feminine
foll	followed
geom	geometry
hist	history
interj	interjection
lit	literary
masc	masculine
med	medicine
NZ	New Zealand

a

abandon VERB **1** = leave, strand, ditch, forsake, run out on, desert, dump **2** = stop, give up, halt, pack in (*Brit. informal*), discontinue, leave off ≠ continue **3** = give up, yield, surrender, relinquish ≠ keep
• NOUN = recklessness, wildness ≠ restraint
abandonment = desertion, leaving, forsaking
abbey = monastery, convent, priory, nunnery, friary
abduct = kidnap, seize, carry off, snatch (*slang*)
abide VERB = tolerate, suffer, accept, bear, endure, put up with, take, stand
• PHRASES **abide by something** = obey, follow, agree to, carry out, observe, fulfil, act on, comply with
abiding = enduring, lasting, continuing, permanent, persistent, everlasting ≠ brief
ability **1** = capability, potential, competence, proficiency ≠ inability **2** = skill, talent, expertise, competence, aptitude, proficiency, cleverness
able = capable, qualified, efficient, accomplished, competent, skilful, proficient ≠ incapable
abnormal = unusual, different, odd, strange, extraordinary, remarkable, exceptional, peculiar ≠ normal
abnormality **1** = strangeness, peculiarity, irregularity, singularity **2** = anomaly, oddity, exception, peculiarity, deformity, irregularity
abolish = do away with, end, destroy, eliminate, cancel, get rid of, ditch (*slang*), throw out ≠ establish
abolition = eradication, ending, end, destruction, wiping out, elimination, cancellation, termination
abort **1** = terminate (*a pregnancy*), miscarry **2** = stop, end, finish, check, arrest, halt, cease, axe (*informal*)
abortion = termination, miscarriage, deliberate miscarriage
abound = be plentiful, thrive, flourish, be numerous, proliferate, be abundant, be thick on the ground
about PREPOSITION **1** = regarding, on, concerning, dealing with, referring to, relating to, as regards **2** = near, around, close to, nearby, beside, adjacent to, in the neighbourhood of
• ADVERB = approximately, around, almost, nearly, approaching, close to, roughly, just about
above **1** = over, upon, beyond, on top of, exceeding, higher than ≠ under **2** = senior to, over, ahead of, in charge of, higher than, superior to, more powerful than
abroad = overseas, out of the country, in foreign lands
abrupt **1** = sudden, unexpected, rapid, surprising, quick, rash, precipitate ≠ slow **2** = curt, brief, short, rude, impatient, terse, gruff, succinct ≠ polite
absence **1** = time off, leave, break, vacation, recess, truancy, absenteeism, nonattendance **2** = lack, deficiency, omission, scarcity, want, need, shortage, dearth
absent ADJECTIVE **1** = away, missing, gone, elsewhere, unavailable, nonexistent ≠ present **2** = absent-minded, blank, vague, distracted, vacant, preoccupied, oblivious, inattentive ≠ alert
• PHRASES **absent yourself** = stay away, withdraw, keep away, play truant
absolute **1** = complete, total, perfect, pure, sheer, utter, outright, thorough **2** = supreme, sovereign, unlimited, ultimate, full, unconditional, unrestricted, pre-eminent **3** = autocratic, supreme, all-powerful, imperious, domineering, tyrannical
absolutely = completely, totally, perfectly, fully, entirely, altogether, wholly, utterly ≠ somewhat
absorb **1** = soak up, suck up, receive, digest, imbibe **2** = engross, involve, engage, fascinate, rivet, captivate
absorbed = engrossed, lost, involved, gripped, fascinated, caught up, wrapped up, preoccupied
absorbing = fascinating, interesting, engaging, gripping, compelling, intriguing, enticing, riveting ≠ boring
absorption **1** = soaking up, consumption, digestion, sucking up **2** = immersion, involvement, concentration, fascination,

preoccupation, intentness

abstract ADJECTIVE = theoretical, general, academic, speculative, indefinite, hypothetical, notional, abstruse ≠ actual • NOUN = summary, résumé, outline, digest, epitome, rundown, synopsis, précis ≠ expansion • VERB = extract, draw, pull, remove, separate, withdraw, isolate, pull out ≠ add

absurd = ridiculous, crazy (*informal*), silly, foolish, ludicrous, unreasonable, irrational, senseless ≠ sensible

abundance = plenty, bounty, exuberance, profusion, plethora, affluence, fullness, fruitfulness ≠ shortage

abundant = plentiful, full, rich, liberal, generous, ample, exuberant, teeming ≠ scarce

abuse NOUN **1** = maltreatment, damage, injury, hurt, harm, exploitation, manhandling, ill-treatment **2** = insults, blame, slights, put-downs, censure, reproach, scolding, defamation **3** = misuse, misapplication • VERB **1** = ill-treat, damage, hurt, injure, harm, molest, maltreat, knock about *or* around ≠ care for **2** = insult, offend, curse, put down, malign, scold, disparage, castigate ≠ praise

abusive 1 = violent, rough, cruel, savage, brutal, vicious, destructive, harmful ≠ kind **2** = insulting, offensive, rude, degrading, scathing, contemptuous, disparaging, scurrilous ≠ complimentary

academic ADJECTIVE **1** = scholastic, educational **2** = scholarly, learned, intellectual, literary, erudite, highbrow, studious **3** = theoretical, abstract, speculative, hypothetical, impractical, notional, conjectural • NOUN = scholar, intellectual, don, master, professor, fellow, lecturer, tutor, acca (*Austral. slang*)

accelerate 1 = increase, grow, advance, extend, expand, raise, swell, enlarge ≠ fall **2** = expedite, further, speed up, hasten ≠ delay **3** = speed up, advance, quicken, gather momentum ≠ slow down

acceleration = hastening, hurrying, stepping up (*informal*), speeding up, quickening

accent NOUN = pronunciation, tone, articulation, inflection, brogue, intonation, diction, modulation • VERB = emphasize, stress, highlight, underline, underscore, accentuate

accept 1 = receive, take, gain, pick up, secure, collect, get, obtain **2** = acknowledge, believe, allow, admit, approve, recognize, yield, concede

acceptable = satisfactory, fair, all right, suitable, sufficient, good enough, adequate, tolerable ≠ unsatisfactory

acceptance 1 = accepting, taking, receiving, obtaining, acquiring, reception, receipt **2** = acknowledgement, agreement, approval, recognition, admission, consent, adoption, assent

accepted = agreed, common, established, traditional, approved, acknowledged, recognized, customary ≠ unconventional

access 1 = admission, entry, passage **2** = entrance, road, approach, entry, path, gate, opening, passage

accessible = handy, near, nearby, at hand, within reach, at your fingertips, reachable, achievable ≠ inaccessible

accessory 1 = extra, addition, supplement, attachment, adjunct, appendage **2** = accomplice, partner, ally, associate (*in crime*), assistant, helper, colleague, collaborator

accident 1 = crash, smash, wreck, collision **2** = misfortune, disaster, tragedy, setback, calamity, mishap, misadventure **3** = chance, fortune, luck, fate, hazard, coincidence, fluke, fortuity

accidental 1 = unintentional, unexpected, incidental, unforeseen, unplanned ≠ deliberate **2** = chance, random, casual, unplanned, fortuitous, inadvertent

accidentally = unintentionally, incidentally, by accident, by chance, inadvertently, unwittingly, randomly, haphazardly ≠ deliberately

acclaim VERB = praise, celebrate, honour, cheer, admire, hail, applaud, compliment • NOUN = praise, honour, celebration, approval, tribute, applause, kudos, commendation ≠ criticism

accommodate 1 = house, put up, take in, lodge, shelter, entertain, cater for **2** = help, support, aid, assist, cooperate with, abet, lend a hand to **3** = adapt, fit, settle, alter, adjust, modify, comply, reconcile

accommodating = obliging, willing,

kind, friendly, helpful, polite, cooperative, agreeable ≠ unhelpful
accommodation = housing, homes, houses, board, quarters, digs (*Brit. informal*), shelter, lodging(s)
accompaniment 1 = backing music, backing, support, obbligato 2 = supplement, extra, addition, companion, accessory, complement, decoration, adjunct
accompany 1 = go with, lead, partner, guide, attend, conduct, escort, shepherd 2 = occur with, belong to, come with, supplement, go together with, follow
accompanying = additional, extra, related, associated, attached, attendant, complementary, supplementary
accomplish = realize, produce, effect, finish, complete, manage, achieve, perform ≠ fail
accomplished = skilled, able, professional, expert, masterly, talented, gifted, polished ≠ unskilled
accomplishment 1 = achievement, feat, act, stroke, triumph, coup, exploit, deed 2 = accomplishing, finishing, carrying out, conclusion, bringing about, execution, completion, fulfilment
accord NOUN 1 = treaty, contract, agreement, arrangement, settlement, pact, deal (*informal*) 2 = sympathy, agreement, harmony, unison, rapport, conformity ≠ conflict
• PHRASES **accord with something** = agree with, match, coincide with, fit with, correspond with, conform with, tally with, harmonize with
accordingly 1 = consequently, so, thus, therefore, hence, subsequently, in consequence, ergo 2 = appropriately, correspondingly, properly, suitably, fitly
account NOUN 1 = description, report, story, statement, version, tale, explanation, narrative 2 = importance, standing, concern, value, note, worth, weight, honour
• PLURAL NOUN (*Commerce*) = ledgers, books, charges, bills, statements, balances, tallies, invoices
• VERB = consider, rate, value, judge, estimate, think, count, reckon
accountability = responsibility, liability, culpability, answerability, chargeability
accountable = answerable, subject, responsible, obliged, liable, amenable, obligated, chargeable
accountant = auditor, book-keeper, bean counter (*informal*)
accumulate = build up, increase, be stored, collect, gather, pile up, amass, hoard ≠ disperse
accumulation 1 = collection, increase, stock, store, mass, build-up, pile, stack 2 = growth, collection, gathering, build-up
accuracy = exactness, precision, fidelity, authenticity, correctness, closeness, veracity, truthfulness ≠ inaccuracy
accurate 1 = precise, close, correct, careful, strict, exact, faithful, explicit ≠ inaccurate 2 = correct, true, exact, spot-on (*Brit. informal*)
accurately 1 = precisely, correctly, closely, truly, strictly, exactly, faithfully, to the letter 2 = exactly, closely, correctly, precisely, strictly, faithfully, explicitly, scrupulously
accusation = charge, complaint, allegation, indictment, recrimination, denunciation, incrimination
accuse 1 = point a *or* the finger at, blame for, denounce, hold responsible for, impute blame to ≠ exonerate 2 = charge with, indict for, impeach for, censure with, incriminate for ≠ absolve
accustom = familiarize, train, discipline, adapt, instruct, school, acquaint, acclimatize
accustomed 1 = used, trained, familiar, given to, adapted, acquainted, in the habit of, familiarized ≠ unaccustomed 2 = usual, established, expected, common, standard, traditional, normal, regular ≠ unusual
ace NOUN 1 (*Cards, dice*) = one, single point 2 (*Informal*) = expert, star, champion, authority, professional, master, specialist, guru
• ADJECTIVE (*Informal*) = great, brilliant, fine, wonderful, excellent, outstanding, superb, fantastic (*informal*), booshit (*Austral. slang*), exo (*Austral. slang*), sik (*Austral. slang*), ka pai (*N.Z.*)
ache VERB = hurt, suffer, burn, pain, smart, sting, pound, throb
• NOUN = pain, discomfort, suffering, hurt, throbbing, irritation, tenderness, pounding
achieve = accomplish, fulfil, complete, gain, perform, do, get, carry out
achievement = accomplishment, effort,

feat, deed, stroke, triumph, coup, exploit
acid 1 = sour, tart, pungent, acerbic, acrid, vinegary ≠ sweet 2 = sharp, cutting, biting, bitter, harsh, barbed, caustic, vitriolic ≠ kindly
acknowledge 1 = admit, own up, allow, accept, reveal, grant, declare, recognize ≠ deny 2 = greet, address, notice, recognize, salute, accost ≠ snub 3 = reply to, answer, notice, recognize, respond to, react to, retort to ≠ ignore
acquaintance 1 = associate, contact, ally, colleague, comrade ≠ intimate 2 = relationship, connection, fellowship, familiarity ≠ unfamiliarity
acquire = get, win, buy, receive, gain, earn, secure, collect ≠ lose
acquisition 1 = acquiring, gaining, procurement, attainment 2 = purchase, buy, investment, property, gain, prize, asset, possession
acquit VERB = clear, free, release, excuse, discharge, liberate, vindicate ≠ find guilty
• PHRASES **acquit yourself** = behave, bear yourself, conduct yourself, comport yourself
act VERB 1 = do something, perform, function 2 = perform, mimic
• NOUN 1 = deed, action, performance, achievement, undertaking, exploit, feat, accomplishment 2 = pretence, show, front, performance, display, attitude, pose, posture 3 = law, bill, measure, resolution, decree, statute, ordinance, enactment 4 = performance, show, turn, production, routine, presentation, gig (*informal*), sketch
acting NOUN = performance, playing, performing, theatre, portrayal, impersonation, characterization, stagecraft
• ADJECTIVE = temporary, substitute, interim, provisional, surrogate, stopgap, pro tem
action 1 = deed, act, performance, achievement, exploit, feat, accomplishment 2 = measure, act, manoeuvre 3 = lawsuit, case, trial, suit, proceeding, dispute, prosecution, litigation 4 = energy, activity, spirit, force, vitality, vigour, liveliness, vim 5 = effect, working, process, operation, activity, movement, functioning, motion 6 = battle, fight, conflict, clash, contest, encounter, combat, engagement
activate = start, move, initiate, rouse, mobilize, set in motion, galvanize ≠ stop
active 1 = busy, involved, occupied, lively, energetic, bustling, on the move, strenuous ≠ sluggish 2 = energetic, quick, alert, dynamic, lively, vigorous, animated, forceful ≠ inactive 3 = in operation, working, acting, at work, in action, operative, in force, effectual
activist = militant, partisan
activity 1 = action, labour, movement, energy, exercise, spirit, motion, bustle ≠ inaction 2 = pursuit, project, scheme, pleasure, interest, hobby, pastime
actor *or* **actress** = performer, player, Thespian, luvvie (*informal*)
actual = real, substantial, concrete, definite, tangible
actually = really, in fact, indeed, truly, literally, genuinely, in reality, in truth
acute 1 = serious, important, dangerous, critical, crucial, severe, grave, urgent 2 = sharp, shooting, powerful, violent, severe, intense, fierce, piercing 3 = perceptive, sharp, keen, smart, sensitive, clever, astute, insightful ≠ slow
adamant = determined, firm, fixed, stubborn, uncompromising, resolute, unbending, obdurate ≠ flexible
adapt 1 = adjust, change, alter, modify, accommodate, conform, acclimatize 2 = convert, change, transform, alter, modify, tailor, remodel
adaptation 1 = acclimatization, naturalization, familiarization 2 = conversion, change, variation, adjustment, transformation, modification, alteration
add 1 = count up, total, reckon, compute, add up, tot up ≠ take away 2 = include, attach, supplement, adjoin, augment, affix, append
addict 1 = junkie (*informal*), freak (*informal*), fiend (*informal*) 2 = fan, lover, nut (*slang*), follower, enthusiast, admirer, buff (*informal*), junkie (*informal*)
addicted
• PHRASES **addicted to** = hooked on, dependent on, accustomed to (*slang*), habituated to
addiction = dependence, habit, obsession, craving, enslavement *with* ***to*** = love of, passion for, attachment to

addition NOUN 1 = extra, supplement, increase, gain, bonus, extension, accessory, additive 2 = inclusion, adding, increasing, extension, attachment, insertion, incorporation, augmentation ≠ removal 3 = counting up, totalling, adding up, computation, totting up ≠ subtraction • PHRASES **in addition to** = as well as, along with, on top of, besides, to boot, additionally, over and above, to say nothing of
additional = extra, new, other, added, further, fresh, spare, supplementary
address NOUN 1 = location, home, place, house, point, position, situation, site 2 = speech, talk, lecture, discourse, sermon, dissertation, homily, oration • VERB = speak to, talk to, greet, hail, approach, converse with, korero (*N.Z.*)
adept ADJECTIVE = skilful, able, skilled, expert, practised, accomplished, versed, proficient ≠ unskilled • NOUN = expert, master, genius, hotshot (*informal*), dab hand (*Brit. informal*)
adequate 1 = passable, acceptable, average, fair, satisfactory, competent, mediocre, so-so (*informal*) ≠ inadequate 2 = sufficient, enough ≠ insufficient
adhere to = stick to, attach to, cling to, glue to, fix to, fasten to, hold fast to, paste to
adjacent ADJECTIVE = adjoining, neighbouring, nearby ≠ far away • PREPOSITION *with* ***to*** = next to, touching, close to, neighbouring, beside, near to, adjoining, bordering on
adjoin = connect with *or* to, join, link with, touch on, border on
adjoining = connecting, touching, bordering, neighbouring, next door, adjacent, abutting
adjourn = postpone, delay, suspend, interrupt, put off, defer, discontinue ≠ continue
adjust 1 = adapt, change, alter, accustom, conform 2 = change, reform, alter, adapt, revise, modify, amend, make conform 3 = modify, alter, adapt
adjustable = alterable, flexible, adaptable, malleable, movable, modifiable
adjustment 1 = alteration, change, tuning, repair, conversion, modifying, adaptation, modification 2 = acclimatization, orientation, change, regulation, amendment, adaptation, revision, modification
administer 1 = manage, run, control, direct, handle, conduct, command, govern 2 = dispense, give, share, provide, apply, assign, allocate, allot 3 = execute, give, provide, apply, perform, carry out, impose, implement
administration 1 = management, government, running, control, handling, direction, conduct, application 2 = directors, board, executive(s), employers 3 = government, leadership, regime
administrative = managerial, executive, directing, regulatory, governmental, organizational, supervisory, directorial
administrator = manager, head, official, director, executive, boss (*informal*), governor, supervisor, baas (*S. African*)
admirable = praiseworthy, good, great, fine, wonderful, excellent, brilliant, outstanding, booshit (*Austral. slang*), exo (*Austral. slang*), sik (*Austral. slang*), ka pai (*N.Z.*) ≠ deplorable
admiration = regard, wonder, respect, praise, approval, recognition, esteem, appreciation
admire 1 = respect, value, prize, honour, praise, appreciate, esteem, approve of ≠ despise 2 = adore, like, love, take to, fancy (*Brit. informal*), treasure, cherish, glorify 3 = marvel at, look at, appreciate, delight in, wonder at, be amazed by, take pleasure in, gape at
admirer 1 = fan, supporter, follower, enthusiast, partisan, disciple, devotee 2 = suitor, lover, boyfriend, sweetheart, beau, wooer
admission 1 = admittance, access, entry, introduction, entrance, acceptance, initiation, entrée 2 = confession, declaration, revelation, allowance, disclosure, acknowledgement, unburdening, divulgence
admit 1 = confess, confide, own up, come clean (*informal*) 2 = allow, agree, accept, reveal, grant, declare, acknowledge, recognize ≠ deny 3 = let in, allow, receive, accept, introduce, take in, initiate, give access to ≠ keep out
adolescence = teens, youth, minority, boyhood, girlhood
adolescent ADJECTIVE 1 = young, junior,

teenage, juvenile, youthful, childish, immature, boyish **2** = teenage, young, teen (*informal*)
• NOUN = teenager, girl, boy, kid (*informal*), youth, lad, minor, young man

adopt **1** = take on, follow, choose, maintain, assume, take up, engage in, become involved in **2** = take in, raise, nurse, mother, rear, foster, bring up, take care of ≠ abandon

adoption **1** = fostering, adopting, taking in **2** = embracing, choice, taking up, selection, assumption, endorsement, appropriation, espousal

adore = love, honour, admire, worship, esteem, cherish, revere, dote on ≠ hate

adoring = admiring, loving, devoted, fond, affectionate, doting ≠ hating

adorn = decorate, array, embellish, festoon

adrift ADJECTIVE **1** = drifting, afloat, unmoored, unanchored **2** = aimless, goalless, directionless, purposeless
• ADVERB = wrong, astray, off course, amiss, off target, wide of the mark

adult NOUN = grown-up, mature person, person of mature age, grown *or* grown-up person, man *or* woman
• ADJECTIVE **1** = fully grown, mature, grown-up, of age, ripe, fully fledged, fully developed, full grown **2** = pornographic, blue, dirty, obscene, filthy, indecent, lewd, salacious

advance VERB **1** = progress, proceed, come forward, make inroads, make headway ≠ retreat **2** = accelerate, speed, promote, hasten, bring forward **3** = improve, rise, develop, pick up, progress, upgrade, prosper, make strides **4** = suggest, offer, present, propose, advocate, submit, prescribe, put forward ≠ withhold **5** = lend, loan, supply on credit ≠ withhold payment
• NOUN **1** = down payment, credit, loan, fee, deposit, retainer, prepayment **2** = attack, charge, strike, assault, raid, invasion, offensive, onslaught **3** = improvement, development, gain, growth, breakthrough, step, headway, inroads
• ADJECTIVE = prior, early, beforehand
• PHRASES **in advance** = beforehand, earlier, ahead, previously

advanced = sophisticated, foremost, modern, revolutionary, up-to-date, higher, leading, recent ≠ backward

advancement = promotion, rise, gain, progress, improvement, betterment, preferment

advantage **1** = benefit, help, profit, favour ≠ disadvantage **2** = lead, sway, dominance, precedence **3** = superiority, good

adventure **1** = venture, experience, incident, enterprise, undertaking, exploit, occurrence, caper **2** = excitement, action, passion, thrill, animation, commotion

adventurous = daring, enterprising, bold, reckless, intrepid, daredevil ≠ cautious

adversary = opponent, rival, enemy, competitor, foe, contestant, antagonist ≠ ally

adverse **1** = harmful, damaging, negative, destructive, detrimental, hurtful, injurious, inopportune ≠ beneficial **2** = unfavourable, hostile, unlucky **3** = negative, opposing, hostile, contrary, dissenting, unsympathetic, ill-disposed

advert (*Brit. informal*) = advertisement, notice, commercial, ad (*informal*), announcement, poster, plug (*informal*), blurb

advertise = publicize, promote, plug (*informal*), announce, inform, hype, notify, tout

advertisement = advert (*Brit. informal*), notice, commercial, ad (*informal*), announcement, poster, plug (*informal*), blurb

advice = guidance, help, opinion, direction, suggestion, instruction, counsel, counselling

advise **1** = recommend, suggest, urge, counsel, advocate, caution, prescribe, commend **2** = notify, tell, report, announce, warn, declare, inform, acquaint

adviser = counsellor, guide, consultant, aide, guru, mentor, helper, confidant

advisory = advising, helping, recommending, counselling, consultative

advocate VERB = recommend, support, champion, encourage, propose, promote, advise, endorse ≠ oppose
• NOUN **1** = supporter, spokesman, champion, defender, campaigner, promoter, counsellor, proponent **2** (*Law*) = lawyer, attorney, solicitor, counsel, barrister

affair **1** = matter, business, happening, event, activity, incident, episode, topic

2 = relationship, romance, intrigue, fling, liaison, flirtation, amour, dalliance
affect[1] 1 = influence, concern, alter, change, manipulate, act on, bear upon, impinge upon 2 = emotionally move, touch, upset, overcome, stir, disturb, perturb
affect[2] = put on, assume, adopt, pretend, imitate, simulate, contrive, aspire to
affected = pretended, artificial, contrived, put-on, mannered, unnatural, feigned, insincere ≠ genuine
affection = fondness, liking, feeling, love, care, warmth, attachment, goodwill, aroha (*N.Z.*)
affectionate = fond, loving, kind, caring, friendly, attached, devoted, tender ≠ cool
affiliate = associate, unite, join, link, ally, combine, incorporate, amalgamate
affinity 1 = attraction, liking, leaning, sympathy, inclination, rapport, fondness, partiality, aroha (*N.Z.*) ≠ hostility 2 = similarity, relationship, connection, correspondence, analogy, resemblance, closeness, likeness ≠ difference
affirm 1 = declare, state, maintain, swear, assert, testify, pronounce, certify ≠ deny 2 = confirm, prove, endorse, ratify, verify, validate, bear out, substantiate ≠ refute
affirmative = agreeing, confirming, positive, approving, consenting, favourable, concurring, assenting ≠ negative
afflict = torment, trouble, pain, hurt, distress, plague, grieve, harass
affluent = wealthy, rich, prosperous, loaded (*slang*), well-off, opulent, well-heeled (*informal*), well-to-do ≠ poor
afford 1 = have the money for, manage, bear, pay for, spare, stand, stretch to 2 = bear, stand, sustain, allow yourself 3 = give, offer, provide, produce, supply, yield, render
affordable = inexpensive, cheap, reasonable, moderate, modest, low-cost, economical ≠ expensive
afraid 1 = scared, frightened, nervous, terrified, shaken, startled, fearful, cowardly ≠ unafraid 2 = reluctant, frightened, scared, unwilling, hesitant, loath, disinclined, unenthusiastic 3 = sorry, apologetic, regretful, sad, distressed, unhappy ≠ pleased
after PREPOSITION = at the end of, following, subsequent to ≠ before
• ADVERB = following, later, next, succeeding, afterwards, subsequently, thereafter

RELATED WORD

prefix: post-
aftermath = effects, results, wake, consequences, outcome, sequel, end result, upshot
again 1 = once more, another time, anew, afresh 2 = also, in addition, moreover, besides, furthermore
against 1 = beside, on, up against, in contact with, abutting 2 = opposed to, anti (*informal*), hostile to, in opposition to, averse to, opposite to 3 = in opposition to, resisting, versus, counter to, in the opposite direction of 4 = in preparation for, in case of, in anticipation of, in expectation of, in provision for

RELATED WORDS

prefixes: anti-, counter-
age NOUN 1 = years, days, generation, lifetime, length of existence 2 = old age, experience, maturity, seniority, majority, senility, decline (*of life*), advancing years ≠ youth 3 = time, day(s), period, generation, era, epoch
• VERB 1 = grow old, decline, weather, fade, deteriorate, wither 2 = mature, season, condition, soften, mellow, ripen
aged = old, getting on, grey, ancient, antique, elderly, antiquated ≠ young
agency 1 = business, company, office, firm, department, organization, enterprise, establishment 2 (*Old-fashioned*) = medium, means, activity, vehicle, instrument, mechanism
agenda = programme, list, plan, schedule, diary, calendar, timetable
agent 1 = representative, rep (*informal*), negotiator, envoy, surrogate, go-between 2 = author, worker, vehicle, instrument, operator, performer, catalyst, doer 3 = force, means, power, cause, instrument
aggravate 1 = make worse, exaggerate, intensify, worsen, exacerbate, magnify, inflame, increase ≠ improve 2 (*Informal*) = annoy, bother, provoke, irritate, nettle, get on your nerves (*informal*) ≠ please
aggregate NOUN = total, body, whole, amount, collection, mass, sum, combination
• ADJECTIVE = collective, mixed, combined,

collected, accumulated, composite, cumulative
• VERB = combine, mix, collect, assemble, heap, accumulate, pile, amass

aggression 1 = hostility, malice, antagonism, antipathy, ill will, belligerence, destructiveness, pugnacity 2 = attack, campaign, injury, assault, raid, invasion, offensive, onslaught

aggressive 1 = hostile, offensive, destructive, belligerent, unfriendly, contrary, antagonistic, pugnacious, aggers (*Austral. slang*), biffo (*Austral. slang*) ≠ friendly 2 = forceful, powerful, convincing, effective, enterprising, dynamic, bold, militant ≠ submissive

agitate 1 = stir, beat, shake, disturb, toss, rouse 2 = upset, worry, trouble, excite, distract, unnerve, disconcert, fluster ≠ calm

agony = suffering, pain, distress, misery, torture, discomfort, torment, hardship

agree 1 = concur, be as one, sympathize, assent, see eye to eye, be of the same opinion ≠ disagree 2 = correspond, match, coincide, tally, conform 3 = suit, get on, befit

agreement 1 = treaty, contract, arrangement, alliance, deal (*informal*), understanding, settlement, bargain 2 = concurrence, harmony, compliance, union, agreeing, consent, unison, assent ≠ disagreement 3 = correspondence, similarity, consistency, correlation, conformity, compatibility, congruity ≠ difference

agricultural = farming, country, rural, rustic, agrarian

agriculture = farming, culture, cultivation, husbandry, tillage

ahead 1 = in front, in advance, towards the front, frontwards 2 = at an advantage, in advance, in the lead 3 = in the lead, winning, leading, at the head, to the fore, at an advantage 4 = in front, before, in advance, in the lead

aid NOUN = help, backing, support, benefit, favour, relief, promotion, assistance ≠ hindrance
• VERB 1 = help, support, serve, sustain, assist, avail, subsidize, be of service to ≠ hinder 2 = promote, help, further, forward, encourage, favour, facilitate, pave the way for

aide = assistant, supporter, attendant, helper, right-hand man, second

ailing 1 = weak, failing, poor, flawed, unstable, unsatisfactory, deficient 2 = ill, poorly, sick, weak, crook (*Austral. & N.Z. informal*), unwell, infirm, under the weather (*informal*), indisposed

ailment = illness, disease, complaint, disorder, sickness, affliction, malady, infirmity

aim VERB 1 = try for, seek, work for, plan for, strive, set your sights on 2 = point
• NOUN = intention, point, plan, goal, design, target, purpose, desire

air NOUN 1 = wind, breeze, draught, gust, zephyr 2 = atmosphere, sky, heavens, aerosphere 3 = tune, song, theme, melody, strain, lay, aria 4 = manner, appearance, look, aspect, atmosphere, mood, impression, aura
• PLURAL NOUN = affectation, arrogance, pretensions, pomposity, swank (*informal*), hauteur, haughtiness, superciliousness
• VERB 1 = publicize, reveal, exhibit, voice, express, display, circulate, make public 2 = ventilate, expose, freshen, aerate

RELATED WORD
adjective: aerial

airborne = flying, floating, in the air, hovering, gliding, in flight, on the wing

airing 1 = ventilation, drying, freshening, aeration 2 = exposure, display, expression, publicity, vent, utterance, dissemination

airplane (*U.S. & Canad.*) = plane, aircraft, jet, aeroplane, airliner

aisle = passageway, path, lane, passage, corridor, alley, gangway

alarm NOUN 1 = fear, panic, anxiety, fright, apprehension, nervousness, consternation, trepidation ≠ calmness 2 = danger signal, warning, bell, alert, siren, alarm bell, hooter, distress signal
• VERB = frighten, scare, panic, distress, startle, dismay, daunt, unnerve ≠ calm

alarming = frightening, shocking, scaring, disturbing, distressing, startling, horrifying, menacing

alcoholic NOUN = drunkard, drinker, drunk, toper, lush (*slang*), tippler, wino (*informal*), inebriate, alko *or* alco (*Austral. slang*)
• ADJECTIVE = intoxicating, hard, strong, stiff, brewed, fermented, distilled

alert ADJECTIVE 1 = attentive, awake,

vigilant, watchful, on the lookout, circumspect, observant, on guard ≠ careless **2** = quick-witted, bright, sharp
• NOUN = warning, signal, alarm, siren ≠ all clear
• VERB = warn, signal, inform, alarm, notify, tip off, forewarn ≠ lull

alien ADJECTIVE **1** = foreign, strange, imported, unknown, exotic, unfamiliar **2** = strange, new, foreign, novel, unknown, exotic, unfamiliar, untried ≠ similar
• NOUN = foreigner, incomer, immigrant, stranger, outsider, newcomer, asylum seeker ≠ citizen

alienate = antagonize, anger, annoy, offend, irritate, hassle (*informal*), estrange

alienation = estrangement, setting against, separation, turning away, disaffection, remoteness

alight[1] **1** = get off, descend, get down, disembark, dismount **2** = land, light, settle, come down, descend, perch, touch down, come to rest ≠ take off

alight[2] = lit up, bright, brilliant, shining, illuminated, fiery

align **1** = ally, side, join, associate, affiliate, cooperate, sympathize **2** = line up, order, range, regulate, straighten, even up

alike ADJECTIVE = similar, close, the same, parallel, resembling, identical, corresponding, akin ≠ different
• ADVERB = similarly, identically, equally, uniformly, correspondingly, analogously ≠ differently

alive **1** = living, breathing, animate, subsisting, existing, functioning, in the land of the living (*informal*) ≠ dead **2** = in existence, existing, functioning, active, operative, in force, on-going, prevalent ≠ inoperative **3** = lively, active, vital, alert, energetic, animated, agile, perky ≠ dull

all PRONOUN **1** = the whole amount, everything, the total, the aggregate, the totality, the sum total, the entirety, the entire amount **2** = every, each, every single, every one of, each and every
• ADJECTIVE = complete, greatest, full, total, perfect, entire, utter
• ADVERB = completely, totally, fully, entirely, absolutely, altogether, wholly, utterly

allegation = claim, charge, statement, declaration, accusation, assertion, affirmation

allege = claim, charge, challenge, state, maintain, declare, assert, uphold ≠ deny

alleged = claimed, supposed, declared, assumed, so-called, apparent, stated, described

allegiance = loyalty, devotion, fidelity, obedience, constancy, faithfulness ≠ disloyalty

allergic = sensitive, affected by, susceptible, hypersensitive

allergy = sensitivity, reaction, susceptibility, antipathy, hypersensitivity, sensitiveness

alleviate = ease, reduce, relieve, moderate, soothe, lessen, lighten, allay

alley = passage, walk, lane, pathway, alleyway, passageway, backstreet

alliance = union, league, association, agreement, marriage, connection, combination, coalition ≠ division

allied **1** = united, linked, related, combined, integrated, affiliated, cooperating, in league **2** = connected, linked, associated

allocate = assign, grant, distribute, designate, set aside, earmark, give out, consign

allocation **1** = allowance, share, portion, quota, lot, ration **2** = assignment, allowance, allotment

allow VERB **1** = permit, approve, enable, sanction, endure, license, tolerate, authorize ≠ prohibit **2** = let, permit, sanction, authorize, license, tolerate, consent to, assent to ≠ forbid **3** = give, provide, grant, spare, devote, assign, allocate, set aside **4** = acknowledge, accept, admit, grant, recognize, yield, concede, confess
• PHRASES **allow for something** = take something into account, consider, plan for, accommodate, provide for, make provision for, make allowances for, make concessions for

allowance **1** = portion, lot, share, amount, grant, quota, allocation, stint **2** = pocket money, grant, fee, payment, ration, handout, remittance **3** = concession, discount, reduction, repayment, deduction, rebate

all right **1** = satisfactory, O.K. *or* okay (*informal*), average, fair, sufficient, standard, acceptable, good enough ≠ unsatisfactory **2** = well, O.K. *or* okay (*informal*), whole, sound, fit, safe, healthy, unharmed ≠ ill

ally NOUN = partner, friend, colleague, associate, mate, comrade, helper, collaborator, cobber (*Austral. & N.Z. old-fashioned informal*), E hoa (*N.Z.*) ≠ opponent
• PHRASES **ally yourself with something** *or* **someone** = unite with, associate with, unify, collaborate with, join forces with, band together with

almost = nearly, about, close to, virtually, practically, roughly, just about, not quite

alone ADJECTIVE **1** = solitary, isolated, separate, apart, by yourself, unaccompanied, on your tod (*slang*) ≠ accompanied **2** = lonely, abandoned, isolated, solitary, desolate, forsaken, forlorn, destitute
• ADVERB **1** = solely, only, individually, singly, exclusively, uniquely **2** = by yourself, independently, unaccompanied, without help, on your own, without assistance ≠ with help

aloud = out loud, clearly, plainly, distinctly, audibly, intelligibly

already = before now, before, previously, at present, by now, by then, even now, just now

also = and, too, further, in addition, as well, moreover, besides, furthermore

alter 1 = modify, change, reform, vary, transform, adjust, adapt, revise **2** = change, turn, vary, transform, adjust, adapt

alternate VERB **1** = interchange, change, fluctuate, take turns, oscillate, chop and change **2** = intersperse, interchange, exchange, swap, stagger, rotate
• ADJECTIVE = alternating, interchanging, every other, rotating, every second, sequential

alternative NOUN = substitute, choice, other (*of two*), option, preference, recourse
• ADJECTIVE = different, other, substitute, alternate

alternatively = or, instead, otherwise, on the other hand, if not, then again, as an alternative, as another option

although = though, while, even if, even though, whilst, albeit, despite the fact that, notwithstanding

altogether 1 = absolutely, quite, completely, totally, perfectly, fully, thoroughly, wholly **2** = completely, fully, entirely, thoroughly, wholly, in every respect ≠ partially **3** = on the whole, generally, mostly, in general, collectively, all things considered, on average, for the most part **4** = in total, in all, all told, taken together, in sum, everything included

always 1 = habitually, regularly, every time, consistently, invariably, perpetually, without exception, customarily ≠ seldom **2** = forever, for keeps, eternally, for all time, evermore, till the cows come home (*informal*), till Doomsday **3** = continually, constantly, all the time, forever, repeatedly, persistently, perpetually, incessantly

amass = collect, gather, assemble, compile, accumulate, pile up, hoard

amateur = nonprofessional, outsider, layman, dilettante, layperson, non-specialist, dabbler

amaze = astonish, surprise, shock, stun, alarm, stagger, startle, bewilder

amazement = astonishment, surprise, wonder, shock, confusion, admiration, awe, bewilderment

amazing = astonishing, surprising, brilliant, stunning, overwhelming, staggering, sensational (*informal*), bewildering

ambassador = representative, minister, agent, deputy, diplomat, envoy, consul, attaché

ambiguity = vagueness, doubt, uncertainty, obscurity, equivocation, dubiousness

ambiguous = unclear, obscure, vague, dubious, enigmatic, indefinite, inconclusive, indeterminate ≠ clear

ambition 1 = goal, hope, dream, target, aim, wish, purpose, desire **2** = enterprise, longing, drive, spirit, desire, passion, enthusiasm, striving

ambitious = enterprising, spirited, daring, eager, intent, enthusiastic, hopeful, striving ≠ unambitious

ambush VERB = trap, attack, surprise, deceive, dupe, ensnare, waylay, bushwhack (*U.S.*)
• NOUN = trap, snare, lure, waylaying

amend VERB = change, improve, reform, fix, correct, repair, edit, alter
• PLURAL NOUN (usually in *make amends*) = compensation, redress, reparation, restitution, atonement, recompense

amendment 1 = addition, change, adjustment, attachment, adaptation, revision, modification, alteration 2 = change, improvement, repair, edit, remedy, correction, revision, modification

amenity = facility, service, advantage, comfort, convenience

amid *or* **amidst** 1 = during, among, at a time of, in an atmosphere of 2 = in the middle of, among, surrounded by, amongst, in the midst of, in the thick of

ammunition = munitions, rounds, shot, shells, powder, explosives, armaments

amnesty = general pardon, mercy, pardoning, immunity, forgiveness, reprieve, remission (*of penalty*), clemency

among *or* **amongst** 1 = in the midst of, with, together with, in the middle of, amid, surrounded by, amidst, in the thick of 2 = in the group of, one of, part of, included in, in the company of, in the class of, in the number of 3 = between, to

amount NOUN = quantity, measure, size, supply, mass, volume, capacity, extent
• PHRASES **amount to something** 1 = add up to, mean, total, equal, constitute, comprise, be equivalent to 2 = come to, become, develop into, advance to, progress to, mature into

ample 1 = plenty of, generous, lavish, abundant, plentiful, expansive, copious, profuse ≠ insufficient 2 = large, full, extensive, generous, abundant, bountiful

amply = fully, completely, richly, generously, abundantly, profusely, copiously ≠ insufficiently

amuse 1 = entertain, please, delight, charm, cheer, tickle ≠ bore 2 = occupy, interest, involve, engage, entertain, absorb, engross

amusement 1 = enjoyment, entertainment, cheer, mirth, merriment ≠ boredom 2 = diversion, fun, pleasure, entertainment 3 = pastime, game, sport, joke, entertainment, hobby, recreation, diversion

amusing = funny, humorous, comical, droll, interesting, entertaining, comic, enjoyable ≠ boring

anaesthetic NOUN = painkiller, narcotic, sedative, opiate, anodyne, analgesic, soporific
• ADJECTIVE = pain-killing, dulling, numbing, sedative, deadening, anodyne, analgesic, soporific

analogy = similarity, relation, comparison, parallel, correspondence, resemblance, correlation, likeness

analyse 1 = examine, test, study, research, survey, investigate, evaluate, inspect 2 = break down, separate, divide, resolve, dissect, think through

analysis = examination, test, inquiry, investigation, interpretation, breakdown, scanning, evaluation

analytical *or* **analytic** = rational, organized, exact, precise, logical, systematic, inquiring, investigative

anarchy = lawlessness, revolution, riot, disorder, confusion, chaos, disorganization ≠ order

anatomy 1 = structure, build, make-up, frame, framework, composition 2 = examination, study, division, inquiry, investigation, analysis, dissection

ancestor = forefather, predecessor, precursor, forerunner, forebear, antecedent, tupuna *or* tipuna (*N.Z.*) ≠ descendant

ancient 1 = classical, old, former, past, bygone, primordial, primeval, olden 2 = very old, aged, antique, archaic, timeworn 3 = old-fashioned, dated, outdated, obsolete, out of date, unfashionable, outmoded, passé ≠ up-to-date

and 1 = also, including, along with, together with, in addition to, as well as 2 = moreover, plus, furthermore

anecdote = story, tale, sketch, short story, yarn, reminiscence, urban myth, urban legend

angel 1 = divine messenger, cherub, archangel, seraph 2 (*Informal*) = dear, beauty, saint, treasure, darling, jewel, gem, paragon

anger NOUN = rage, outrage, temper, fury, resentment, wrath, annoyance, ire ≠ calmness
• VERB = enrage, outrage, annoy, infuriate, incense, gall, madden, exasperate ≠ soothe

angle 1 = gradient, bank, slope, incline, inclination 2 = intersection, point, edge, corner, bend, elbow, crook, nook 3 = point of view, position, approach, direction, aspect, perspective, outlook, viewpoint

angry = furious, cross, mad (*informal*),

outraged, annoyed, infuriated, incensed, enraged, tooshie (*Austral. slang*), off the air (*Austral. slang*) ≠ calm

angst = anxiety, worry, unease, apprehension ≠ peace of mind

anguish = suffering, pain, distress, grief, misery, agony, torment, sorrow

animal NOUN **1** = creature, beast, brute **2** = brute, devil, monster, savage, beast, bastard (*informal, offensive*), villain, barbarian
• ADJECTIVE = physical, gross, bodily, sensual, carnal, brutish, bestial

animate ADJECTIVE = living, live, moving, alive, breathing, alive and kicking
• VERB = enliven, excite, inspire, move, fire, stimulate, energize, kindle ≠ inhibit

animated = lively, spirited, excited, enthusiastic, passionate, energetic, ebullient, vivacious ≠ listless

animation = liveliness, energy, spirit, passion, enthusiasm, excitement, verve, zest

announce = make known, tell, report, reveal, declare, advertise, broadcast, disclose ≠ keep secret

announcement **1** = statement, communication, broadcast, declaration, advertisement, bulletin, communiqué, proclamation **2** = declaration, report, reporting, revelation, proclamation

annoy = irritate, trouble, anger, bother, disturb, plague, hassle (*informal*), madden ≠ soothe

annoying = irritating, disturbing, troublesome, maddening, exasperating ≠ delightful

annual **1** = once a year, yearly **2** = yearlong, yearly

annually **1** = once a year, yearly, every year, per year, by the year, every twelve months, per annum **2** = per year, yearly, every year, by the year, per annum

anomaly = irregularity, exception, abnormality, inconsistency, eccentricity, oddity, peculiarity, incongruity

anonymous **1** = unnamed, unknown, unidentified, nameless, unacknowledged, incognito ≠ identified **2** = unsigned, uncredited, unattributed ≠ signed

answer VERB = reply, explain, respond, resolve, react, return, retort ≠ ask
• NOUN **1** = reply, response, reaction, explanation, comeback, retort, return, defence ≠ question **2** = solution, resolution, explanation **3** = remedy, solution

anthem = song of praise, carol, chant, hymn, psalm, paean, chorale, canticle

anthology = collection, selection, treasury, compilation, compendium, miscellany

anticipate **1** = expect, predict, prepare for, hope for, envisage, foresee, bank on, foretell **2** = await, look forward to, count the hours until

anticipation = expectancy, expectation, foresight, premonition, prescience, forethought

antics = clowning, tricks, mischief, pranks, escapades, playfulness, horseplay, tomfoolery

antique NOUN = period piece, relic, bygone, heirloom, collector's item, museum piece
• ADJECTIVE = vintage, classic, antiquarian, olden

anxiety = uneasiness, concern, worry, doubt, tension, angst, apprehension, misgiving ≠ confidence

anxious **1** = eager, keen, intent, yearning, impatient, itching, desirous ≠ reluctant **2** = uneasy, concerned, worried, troubled, nervous, uncomfortable, tense, fearful ≠ confident

apart **1** = to pieces, to bits, asunder **2** = away from each other, distant from each other **3** = aside, away, alone, isolated, to one side, by yourself **4** *with* ***from*** = except for, excepting, other than, excluding, besides, not including, aside from, but

apartment **1** (*U.S.*) = flat, room, suite, penthouse, crib **2** = rooms, quarters, accommodation, living quarters

apathy = lack of interest, indifference, inertia, coolness, passivity, nonchalance, torpor, unconcern ≠ interest

apiece = each, individually, separately, for each, to each, respectively, from each ≠ all together

apologize = say sorry, express regret, ask forgiveness, make an apology, beg pardon

apology NOUN = regret, explanation, excuse, confession
• PHRASES **apology for something** *or* **someone** = mockery of, excuse for, imitation of, caricature of, travesty of, poor

substitute for
appal = horrify, shock, alarm, frighten, outrage, disgust, dishearten, revolt
appalling 1 = horrifying, shocking, alarming, awful, terrifying, horrible, dreadful, fearful ≠ reassuring 2 = awful, dreadful, horrendous
apparatus 1 = organization, system, network, structure, bureaucracy, hierarchy, setup (*informal*), chain of command 2 = equipment, tackle, gear, device, tools, mechanism, machinery, appliance
apparent 1 = seeming, outward, superficial, ostensible ≠ actual 2 = obvious, marked, visible, evident, distinct, manifest, noticeable, unmistakable ≠ unclear
apparently = seemingly, outwardly, ostensibly
appeal VERB = plead, ask, request, pray, beg, entreat ≠ refuse
• NOUN 1 = plea, call, application, request, prayer, petition, overture, entreaty ≠ refusal 2 = attraction, charm, fascination, beauty, allure ≠ repulsiveness
• PHRASES **appeal to someone** = attract, interest, draw, please, charm, fascinate, tempt, lure
appealing = attractive, engaging, charming, desirable, alluring, winsome ≠ repellent
appear 1 = look (like *or* as if), seem, occur, look to be, come across as, strike you as 2 = come into view, emerge, occur, surface, come out, turn up, be present, show up (*informal*) ≠ disappear
appearance 1 = look, form, figure, looks, manner, expression, demeanour, mien (*literary*) 2 = arrival, presence, introduction, emergence 3 = impression, air, front, image, illusion, guise, façade, pretence
appease 1 = pacify, satisfy, calm, soothe, quiet, placate, mollify, conciliate ≠ anger 2 = ease, calm, relieve, soothe, alleviate, allay
appendix = supplement, postscript, adjunct, appendage, addendum, addition
appetite 1 = hunger 2 = desire, liking, longing, demand, taste, passion, stomach, hunger ≠ distaste
applaud 1 = clap, encourage, praise, cheer, acclaim ≠ boo 2 = praise, celebrate, approve, acclaim, compliment, salute, commend, extol ≠ criticize
applause = ovation, praise, cheers, approval, clapping, accolade, big hand
appliance = device, machine, tool, instrument, implement, mechanism, apparatus, gadget
applicable = appropriate, fitting, useful, suitable, relevant, apt, pertinent ≠ inappropriate
applicant = candidate, claimant, inquirer
application 1 = request, claim, appeal, inquiry, petition, requisition 2 = effort, work, industry, trouble, struggle, pains, commitment, hard work
apply VERB 1 = request, appeal, put in, petition, inquire, claim, requisition 2 = be relevant, relate, refer, be fitting, be appropriate, fit, pertain, be applicable 3 = use, exercise, carry out, employ, implement, practise, exert, enact 4 = put on, work in, cover with, lay on, paint on, spread on, rub in, smear on
• PHRASES **apply yourself to something** = work hard at, concentrate on, try at, commit yourself to, buckle down to (*informal*), devote yourself to, be diligent in, dedicate yourself to
appoint 1 = assign, name, choose, commission, select, elect, delegate, nominate ≠ fire 2 = decide, set, choose, establish, fix, arrange, assign, designate ≠ cancel
appointed 1 = decided, set, chosen, established, fixed, arranged, assigned, designated 2 = assigned, named, chosen, selected, elected, delegated, nominated 3 = equipped, provided, supplied, furnished, fitted out
appointment 1 = selection, naming, election, choice, nomination, assignment 2 = job, office, position, post, situation, place, employment, assignment 3 = meeting, interview, date, arrangement, engagement, fixture, rendezvous, assignation
appraisal = assessment, opinion, estimate, judgment, evaluation, estimation
appreciate 1 = enjoy, like, value, respect, prize, admire, treasure, rate highly ≠ scorn 2 = be aware of, understand, realize, recognize, perceive, take account of, be sensitive to, sympathize with ≠ be unaware of 3 = be grateful, be obliged,

be thankful, give thanks, be indebted, be in debt, be appreciative ≠ be ungrateful for **4** = increase, rise, grow, gain, improve, enhance, soar ≠ fall

appreciation **1** = admiration, enjoyment **2** = gratitude, thanks, recognition, obligation, acknowledgment, indebtedness, thankfulness, gratefulness ≠ ingratitude **3** = awareness, understanding, recognition, perception, sympathy, consciousness, sensitivity, realization ≠ ignorance **4** = increase, rise, gain, growth, improvement, escalation, enhancement ≠ fall

apprehension **1** = anxiety, concern, fear, worry, alarm, suspicion, dread, trepidation ≠ confidence **2** = arrest, catching, capture, taking, seizure ≠ release **3** = awareness, understanding, perception, grasp, comprehension ≠ incomprehension

apprentice = trainee, student, pupil, novice, beginner, learner, probationer ≠ master

approach **VERB** **1** = move towards, reach, near, come close, come near, draw near **2** = make a proposal to, speak to, apply to, appeal to, proposition, solicit, sound out, make overtures to **3** = set about, tackle, undertake, embark on, get down to, launch into, begin work on, commence on • **NOUN** **1** = advance, coming, nearing, appearance, arrival, drawing near **2** = access, way, drive, road, passage, entrance, avenue, passageway **3** *often plural* = proposal, offer, appeal, advance, application, invitation, proposition, overture **4** = way, means, style, method, technique, manner

appropriate **ADJECTIVE** = suitable, fitting, relevant, to the point, apt, pertinent, befitting, well-suited ≠ unsuitable • **VERB** **1** = seize, claim, acquire, confiscate, usurp, impound, commandeer, take possession of ≠ relinquish **2** = allocate, allow, budget, devote, assign, designate, set aside, earmark ≠ withhold **3** = steal, take, nick (*slang, chiefly Brit.*), pocket, pinch (*informal*), lift (*informal*), embezzle, pilfer

approval **1** = consent, agreement, sanction, blessing, permission, recommendation, endorsement, assent **2** = favour, respect, praise, esteem, acclaim, appreciation, admiration, applause ≠ disapproval

approve **VERB** = agree to, allow, pass, recommend, permit, sanction, endorse, authorize ≠ veto • **PHRASES** **approve of something** *or* **someone** = favour, like, respect, praise, admire, commend, have a good opinion of, regard highly

apt **1** = appropriate, fitting, suitable, relevant, to the point, pertinent ≠ inappropriate **2** = inclined, likely, ready, disposed, prone, liable, given, predisposed **3** = gifted, skilled, quick, talented, sharp, capable, smart, clever ≠ slow

arbitrary = random, chance, subjective, inconsistent, erratic, personal, whimsical, capricious ≠ logical

arbitration = decision, settlement, judgment, determination, adjudication

arc = curve, bend, bow, arch, crescent, half-moon

arcade = gallery, cloister, portico, colonnade

arch¹ **NOUN** **1** = archway, curve, dome, span, vault **2** = curve, bend, bow, crook, arc, hunch, sweep, hump • **VERB** = curve, bridge, bend, bow, span, arc

arch² = playful, sly, mischievous, saucy, pert, roguish, frolicsome, waggish

archetypal = typical, standard, model, original, classic, ideal, prototypic *or* prototypical

architect = designer, planner, draughtsman, master builder

architecture **1** = design, planning, building, construction **2** = construction, design, style **3** = structure, design, shape, make-up, construction, framework, layout, anatomy

archive **NOUN** = record office, museum, registry, repository • **PLURAL NOUN** = records, papers, accounts, rolls, documents, files, deeds, chronicles

arctic (*Informal*) = freezing, cold, frozen, icy, chilly, glacial, frigid

Arctic = polar, far-northern, hyperborean

ardent **1** = enthusiastic, keen, eager, avid, zealous ≠ indifferent **2** = passionate, intense, impassioned, lusty, amorous, hot-blooded ≠ cold

area **1** = region, quarter, district, zone, neighbourhood, locality **2** = part, section, sector, portion **3** = realm, part,

department, field, province, sphere, domain
arena 1 = ring, ground, field, theatre, bowl, pitch, stadium, enclosure 2 = scene, world, area, stage, field, sector, territory, province
argue 1 = quarrel, fight, row, clash, dispute, disagree, squabble, bicker 2 = discuss, debate, dispute 3 = claim, reason, challenge, insist, maintain, allege, assert, uphold
argument 1 = reason, case, reasoning, ground(s), defence, logic, polemic, dialectic 2 = debate, questioning, claim, discussion, dispute, controversy, plea, assertion 3 = quarrel, fight, row, clash, dispute, controversy, disagreement, feud ≠ agreement
arise 1 = happen, start, begin, follow, result, develop, emerge, occur 2 (*Old-fashioned*) = get to your feet, get up, rise, stand up, spring up, leap up 3 = get up, wake up, awaken, get out of bed
aristocrat = noble, lord, lady, peer, patrician, grandee, aristo (*informal*), peeress
aristocratic = upper-class, lordly, titled, elite, gentlemanly, noble, patrician, blue-blooded ≠ common
arm[1] = upper limb, limb, appendage
arm[2] VERB = equip, provide, supply, array, furnish, issue with, deck out, accoutre
• PLURAL NOUN = weapons, guns, firearms, weaponry, armaments, ordnance, munitions, instruments of war
armed = carrying weapons, protected, equipped, primed, fitted out
armour = protection, covering, shield, sheathing, armour plate, chain mail, protective covering
armoured = protected, mailed, reinforced, toughened, bulletproof, armour-plated, steel-plated, ironclad
army 1 = soldiers, military, troops, armed force, legions, infantry, military force, land force 2 = vast number, host, gang, mob, flock, array, legion, swarm
aroma = scent, smell, perfume, fragrance, bouquet, savour, odour, redolence
around PREPOSITION 1 = surrounding, about, enclosing, encompassing, framing, encircling, on all sides of, on every side of 2 = approximately, about, nearly, close to, roughly, just about, in the region of, circa (*used with dates*)
• ADVERB 1 = everywhere, about, throughout, all over, here and there, on all sides, in all directions, to and fro 2 = near, close, nearby, at hand, close at hand
arouse 1 = stimulate, encourage, inspire, prompt, spur, provoke, rouse, stir up ≠ quell 2 = inflame, move, excite, spur, provoke, stir up, agitate 3 = awaken, wake up, rouse, waken
arrange 1 = plan, agree, prepare, determine, organize, construct, devise, contrive, jack up (*N.Z. informal*) 2 = put in order, group, order, sort, position, line up, organize, classify, jack up (*N.Z. informal*) ≠ disorganize 3 = adapt, score, orchestrate, harmonize, instrument
arrangement 1 *often plural* = plan, planning, provision, preparation 2 = agreement, contract, settlement, appointment, compromise, deal (*informal*), pact, compact 3 = display, system, structure, organization, exhibition, presentation, classification, alignment 4 = adaptation, score, version, interpretation, instrumentation, orchestration, harmonization
array NOUN 1 = arrangement, show, supply, display, collection, exhibition, line-up, mixture 2 (*Poetic*) = clothing, dress, clothes, garments, apparel, attire, finery, regalia
• VERB 1 = arrange, show, group, present, range, display, parade, exhibit 2 = dress, clothe, deck, decorate, adorn, festoon, attire
arrest VERB 1 = capture, catch, nick (*slang, chiefly Brit.*), seize, detain, apprehend, take prisoner ≠ release 2 = stop, end, limit, block, slow, delay, interrupt, suppress ≠ speed up 3 = fascinate, hold, occupy, engage, grip, absorb, entrance, intrigue
• NOUN 1 = capture, bust (*informal*), detention, seizure ≠ release 2 = stoppage, suppression, obstruction, blockage, hindrance ≠ acceleration
arresting = striking, surprising, engaging, stunning, impressive, outstanding, remarkable, noticeable ≠ unremarkable
arrival 1 = appearance, coming, arriving, entrance, advent, materialization 2 = coming, happening, taking place, emergence, occurrence, materialization 3 = newcomer, incomer, visitor, caller, entrant

arrive 1 = come, appear, turn up, show up (*informal*), draw near ≠ depart 2 = occur, happen, take place 3 (*Informal*) = succeed, make it (*informal*), triumph, do well, thrive, flourish, be successful, make good
arrogance = conceit, pride, swagger, insolence, high-handedness, haughtiness, superciliousness, disdainfulness ≠ modesty
arrogant = conceited, proud, cocky, overbearing, haughty, scornful, egotistical, disdainful ≠ modest
arrow 1 = dart, flight, bolt, shaft (*archaic*), quarrel 2 = pointer, indicator, marker
arsenal = armoury, supply, store, stockpile, storehouse, ammunition dump, arms depot, ordnance depot
art 1 = artwork, style of art, fine art, creativity 2 = skill, craft, expertise, competence, mastery, ingenuity, virtuosity, cleverness
article 1 = feature, story, paper, piece, item, creation, essay, composition 2 = thing, piece, unit, item, object, device, tool, implement 3 = clause, point, part, section, item, passage, portion, paragraph
articulate ADJECTIVE = expressive, clear, coherent, fluent, eloquent, lucid ≠ incoherent
• VERB 1 = express, say, state, word, declare, phrase, communicate, utter 2 = pronounce, say, talk, speak, voice, utter, enunciate
artificial 1 = synthetic, manufactured, plastic, man-made, non-natural 2 = insincere, forced, affected, phoney *or* phony (*informal*), false, contrived, unnatural, feigned ≠ genuine 3 = fake, mock, imitation, bogus, simulated, sham, counterfeit ≠ authentic
artillery = big guns, battery, cannon, ordnance, gunnery
artistic 1 = creative, cultured, original, sophisticated, refined, aesthetic, discerning, eloquent ≠ untalented 2 = beautiful, creative, elegant, stylish, aesthetic, tasteful ≠ unattractive
as CONJUNCTION = when, while, just as, at the time that
• PREPOSITION 1 = in the role of, being, under the name of, in the character of 2 = in the way that, like, in the manner that 3 = since, because, seeing that, considering that, on account of the fact that
ashamed 1 = embarrassed, sorry, guilty, distressed, humiliated, self-conscious, red-faced, mortified ≠ proud 2 = reluctant, embarrassed
ashore = on land, on the beach, on the shore, aground, to the shore, on dry land, shorewards, landwards
aside ADVERB = to one side, separately, apart, beside, out of the way, on one side, to the side
• NOUN = interpolation, parenthesis
ask 1 = inquire, question, quiz, query, interrogate ≠ answer 2 = request, appeal to, plead with, demand, beg 3 = invite, bid, summon
asleep = sleeping, napping, dormant, dozing, slumbering, snoozing (*informal*), fast asleep, sound asleep
aspect 1 = feature, side, factor, angle, characteristic, facet 2 = position, view, situation, scene, prospect, point of view, outlook 3 = appearance, look, air, condition, quality, bearing, attitude, cast
aspiration = aim, plan, hope, goal, dream, wish, desire, objective
aspire to = aim for, desire, hope for, long for, seek out, wish for, dream about, set your heart on
ass 1 = donkey, moke (*slang*) 2 = fool, idiot, twit (*informal*, *chiefly Brit.*), oaf, jackass, blockhead, halfwit, numbskull *or* numskull, dorba *or* dorb (*Austral. slang*), bogan (*Austral. slang*)
assassin = murderer, killer, slayer, liquidator, executioner, hit man (*slang*), hatchet man (*slang*)
assassinate = murder, kill, eliminate (*slang*), take out (*slang*), terminate, hit (*slang*), slay, liquidate
assault NOUN = attack, raid, invasion, charge, offensive, onslaught, foray ≠ defence
• VERB = strike, attack, beat, knock, bang, slap, smack, thump
assemble 1 = gather, meet, collect, rally, come together, muster, congregate ≠ scatter 2 = bring together, collect, gather, rally, come together, muster, amass, congregate 3 = put together, join, set up, build up, connect, construct, piece together, fabricate ≠ take apart
assembly 1 = gathering, group, meeting, council, conference, crowd,

congress, collection, hui (*N.Z.*), runanga (*N.Z.*) **2** = putting together, setting up, construction, building up, connecting, piecing together

assert VERB **1** = state, argue, maintain, declare, swear, pronounce, affirm, profess ≠ deny **2** = insist upon, stress, defend, uphold, put forward, press, stand up for ≠ retract
• PHRASES **assert yourself** = be forceful, put your foot down (*informal*), put yourself forward, make your presence felt, exert your influence

assertion **1** = statement, claim, declaration, pronouncement **2** = insistence, stressing, maintenance

assertive = confident, positive, aggressive, forceful, emphatic, insistent, feisty (*informal, chiefly U.S. & Canad.*), pushy (*informal*) ≠ meek

assess **1** = judge, estimate, analyse, evaluate, rate, value, check out, weigh up **2** = evaluate, rate, tax, value, estimate, fix, impose, levy

assessment **1** = judgment, analysis, evaluation, valuation, appraisal, rating, opinion, estimate **2** = evaluation, rating, charge, fee, toll, levy, valuation

asset NOUN = benefit, help, service, aid, advantage, strength, resource, attraction ≠ disadvantage
• PLURAL NOUN = property, goods, money, funds, effects, capital, riches, finance

assign **1** = give, set, grant, allocate, give out, consign, allot, apportion **2** = select for, post, commission, elect, appoint, delegate, nominate, name **3** = attribute, credit, put down, set down, ascribe, accredit

assignment = task, job, position, post, commission, exercise, responsibility, duty

assist **1** = help, support, aid, cooperate with, abet, lend a helping hand to **2** = facilitate, help, further, serve, aid, forward, promote, speed up ≠ hinder

assistance = help, backing, support, aid, cooperation, helping hand ≠ hindrance

assistant = helper, ally, colleague, supporter, aide, second, attendant, accomplice

associate VERB **1** = connect, link, ally, identify, join, combine, attach, fasten ≠ separate **2** = socialize, mix, accompany, mingle, consort, hobnob ≠ avoid
• NOUN = partner, friend, ally, colleague, mate (*informal*), companion, comrade, affiliate, cobber (*Austral. & N.Z. old-fashioned informal*), E hoa (*N.Z.*)

association **1** = group, club, society, league, band, set, pack, collection **2** = connection, union, joining, pairing, combination, mixture, blend, juxtaposition

assorted = various, different, mixed, varied, diverse, miscellaneous, sundry, motley ≠ similar

assume **1** = presume, think, believe, expect, suppose, imagine, fancy, take for granted ≠ know **2** = take on, accept, shoulder, take over, put on, enter upon **3** = simulate, affect, adopt, put on, imitate, mimic, feign, impersonate **4** = take over, take, appropriate, seize, commandeer ≠ give up

assumed = false, made-up, fake, bogus, counterfeit, fictitious, make-believe ≠ real

assumption **1** = presumption, belief, guess, hypothesis, inference, conjecture, surmise, supposition **2** = taking on, managing, handling, shouldering, putting on, taking up, takeover, acquisition **3** = seizure, taking, takeover, acquisition, appropriation, wresting, confiscation, commandeering

assurance **1** = promise, statement, guarantee, commitment, pledge, vow, declaration, assertion ≠ lie **2** = confidence, conviction, certainty, self-confidence, poise, faith, nerve, aplomb ≠ self-doubt

assure **1** = convince, encourage, persuade, satisfy, comfort, reassure, hearten, embolden **2** = make certain, ensure, confirm, guarantee, secure, make sure, complete, seal **3** = promise to, pledge to, vow to, guarantee to, swear to, confirm to, certify to, give your word to

assured **1** = confident, certain, positive, poised, fearless, self-confident, self-assured, dauntless ≠ self-conscious **2** = certain, sure, ensured, confirmed, settled, guaranteed, fixed, secure ≠ doubtful

astonish = amaze, surprise, stun, stagger, bewilder, astound, daze, confound

astounding = amazing, surprising, brilliant, impressive, astonishing, staggering, sensational (*informal*), bewildering

astute = intelligent, sharp, clever, subtle, shrewd, cunning, canny, perceptive

≠ stupid
asylum 1 (*Old-fashioned*) = mental hospital, hospital, institution, psychiatric hospital, madhouse (*informal*) 2 = refuge, haven, safety, protection, preserve, shelter, retreat, harbour
athlete = sportsperson, player, runner, competitor, sportsman, contestant, gymnast, sportswoman
athletic ADJECTIVE = fit, strong, powerful, healthy, active, trim, strapping, energetic ≠ feeble
• PLURAL NOUN = sports, games, races, exercises, contests, sporting events, gymnastics, track and field events
atmosphere 1 = air, sky, heavens, aerosphere 2 = feeling, character, environment, spirit, surroundings, tone, mood, climate
atom = particle, bit, spot, trace, molecule, dot, speck
atrocity 1 = act of cruelty, crime, horror, evil, outrage, abomination 2 = cruelty, horror, brutality, savagery, wickedness, barbarity, viciousness, fiendishness
attach 1 = affix, stick, secure, add, join, couple, link, tie ≠ detach 2 = ascribe, connect, attribute, assign, associate
attached ADJECTIVE = spoken for, married, partnered, engaged, accompanied
• PHRASES **attached to** = fond of, devoted to, affectionate towards, full of regard for
attachment 1 = fondness, liking, feeling, relationship, regard, attraction, affection, affinity, aroha (*N.Z.*) ≠ aversion 2 = accessory, fitting, extra, component, extension, supplement, fixture, accoutrement
attack VERB 1 = assault, strike (at), mug, ambush, tear into, set upon, lay into (*informal*) ≠ defend 2 = invade, occupy, raid, infringe, storm, encroach 3 = criticize, blame, abuse, condemn, knock (*informal*), put down, slate (*informal*), have a go (at) (*informal*)
• NOUN 1 = assault, charge, campaign, strike, raid, invasion, offensive, blitz ≠ defence 2 = criticism, censure, disapproval, abuse, bad press, vilification, denigration, disparagement 3 = bout, fit, stroke, seizure, spasm, convulsion, paroxysm
attacker = assailant, assaulter, raider, intruder, invader, aggressor, mugger
attain 1 = obtain, get, reach, complete, gain, achieve, acquire, fulfil 2 = reach, achieve, acquire, accomplish
attempt VERB = try, seek, aim, struggle, venture, undertake, strive, endeavour
• NOUN 1 = try, go (*informal*), shot (*informal*), effort, trial, bid, crack (*informal*), stab (*informal*) 2 = attack
attend VERB 1 = be present, go to, visit, frequent, haunt, appear at, turn up at, patronize ≠ be absent 2 = pay attention, listen, hear, mark, note, observe, heed, pay heed ≠ ignore
• PHRASES **attend to something** = apply yourself to, concentrate on, look after, take care of, see to, get to work on, devote yourself to, occupy yourself with
attendance 1 = presence, being there, attending, appearance 2 = turnout, audience, gate, congregation, house, crowd, throng, number present
attendant NOUN = assistant, guard, servant, companion, aide, escort, follower, helper
• ADJECTIVE = accompanying, related, associated, accessory, consequent, resultant, concomitant
attention 1 = thinking, thought, mind, consideration, scrutiny, heed, deliberation, intentness 2 = care, support, concern, treatment, looking after, succour, ministration 3 = awareness, regard, notice, recognition, consideration, observation, consciousness ≠ inattention
attic = loft, garret, roof space
attitude 1 = opinion, view, position, approach, mood, perspective, point of view, stance 2 = position, bearing, pose, stance, carriage, posture
attract 1 = allure, draw, persuade, charm, appeal to, win over, tempt, lure (*informal*) ≠ repel 2 = pull, draw, magnetize
attraction 1 = appeal, pull (*informal*), charm, lure, temptation, fascination, allure, magnetism 2 = pull, magnetism
attractive 1 = seductive, charming, tempting, pretty, fair, inviting, lovely, pleasant ≠ unattractive 2 = appealing, pleasing, inviting, tempting, irresistable ≠ unappealing
attribute VERB = ascribe, credit, refer, trace, assign, charge, allocate, put down
• NOUN = quality, feature, property,

character, element, aspect, characteristic, distinction
audience 1 = spectators, company, crowd, gathering, gallery, assembly, viewers, listeners 2 = interview, meeting, hearing, exchange, reception, consultation
aura = air, feeling, quality, atmosphere, tone, mood, ambience
austerity 1 = plainness, simplicity, starkness 2 = asceticism, self-discipline, sobriety, puritanism, self-denial
authentic 1 = real, pure, genuine, valid, undisputed, lawful, bona fide, dinkum (*Austral. & N.Z. informal*), true-to-life ≠ fake 2 = accurate, legitimate, authoritative
authenticity 1 = genuineness, purity 2 = accuracy, certainty, validity, legitimacy, faithfulness, truthfulness
author 1 = writer, composer, novelist, hack, creator, scribbler, scribe, wordsmith 2 = creator, father, producer, designer, founder, architect, inventor, originator
authoritarian ADJECTIVE = strict, severe, autocratic, dictatorial, dogmatic, tyrannical, doctrinaire ≠ lenient
• NOUN = disciplinarian, dictator, tyrant, despot, autocrat, absolutist
authoritative 1 = commanding, masterly, imposing, assertive, imperious, self-assured ≠ timid 2 = reliable, accurate, valid, authentic, definitive, dependable, trustworthy ≠ unreliable
authority 1 *usually plural* = powers that be, government, police, officials, the state, management, administration, the system 2 = prerogative, influence, power, control, weight, direction, command, licence, mana (*N.Z.*) 3 = expert, specialist, professional, master, guru, virtuoso, connoisseur, fundi (*S. African*) 4 = command, power, control, rule, management, direction, mastery
authorize 1 = empower, commission, enable, entitle, mandate, accredit, give authority to 2 = permit, allow, grant, approve, sanction, license, warrant, consent to ≠ forbid
automatic 1 = mechanical, automated, mechanized, push-button, self-propelling ≠ done by hand 2 = involuntary, natural, unconscious, mechanical, spontaneous, reflex, instinctive, unwilled ≠ conscious
autonomous = self-ruling, free, independent, sovereign, self-sufficient, self-governing, self-determining
autonomy = independence, freedom, sovereignty, self-determination, self-government, self-rule, self-sufficiency, home rule, rangatiratanga (*N.Z.*) ≠ dependency
availability = accessibility, readiness, handiness, attainability
available = accessible, ready, to hand, handy, at hand, free, to be had, achievable ≠ in use
avalanche 1 = snow-slide, landslide, landslip 2 = large amount, barrage, torrent, deluge, inundation
avant-garde = progressive, pioneering, experimental, innovative, unconventional, ground-breaking ≠ conservative
avenue = street, way, course, drive, road, approach, route, path
average NOUN = standard, normal, usual, par, mode, mean, medium, norm
• ADJECTIVE 1 = usual, standard, general, normal, regular, ordinary, typical, commonplace ≠ unusual 2 = mean, middle, medium, intermediate, median ≠ minimum
• VERB = make on average, be on average, even out to, do on average, balance out to
• PHRASES **on average** = usually, generally, normally, typically, for the most part, as a rule
avert 1 = ward off, avoid, prevent, frustrate, fend off, preclude, stave off, forestall 2 = turn away, turn aside
avoid 1 = prevent, stop, frustrate, hamper, foil, inhibit, avert, thwart 2 = refrain from, bypass, dodge, eschew, escape, duck (out of) (*informal*), fight shy of, shirk from 3 = keep away from, dodge, shun, evade, steer clear of, bypass
await 1 = wait for, expect, look for, look forward to, anticipate, stay for 2 = be in store for, wait for, be ready for, lie in wait for, be in readiness for
awake ADJECTIVE = not sleeping, sleepless, wide-awake, aware, conscious, aroused, awakened, restless ≠ asleep
• VERB 1 = wake up, come to, wake, stir, awaken, rouse 2 = alert, stimulate, provoke, revive, arouse, stir up, kindle
awaken 1 = stimulate, provoke, alert, stir up, kindle 2 = awake, wake, revive, arouse, rouse

award NOUN = prize, gift, trophy, decoration, grant, bonsela (*S. African*), koha (*N.Z.*)
• VERB **1** = present with, give, grant, hand out, confer, endow, bestow **2** = grant, give, confer

aware = informed, enlightened, knowledgeable, learned, expert, versed, up to date, in the picture ≠ ignorant

awareness
• PHRASES **awareness of** = knowledge of, understanding of, recognition of, perception of, consciousness of, realization of, familiarity with

away ADJECTIVE = absent, out, gone, elsewhere, abroad, not here, not present, on vacation
• ADVERB **1** = off, elsewhere, abroad, hence, from here **2** = aside, out of the way, to one side **3** = at a distance, far, apart, remote, isolated **4** = continuously, repeatedly, relentlessly, incessantly, interminably, unremittingly, uninterruptedly

awe NOUN = wonder, fear, respect, reverence, horror, terror, dread, admiration ≠ contempt
• VERB = impress, amaze, stun, frighten, terrify, astonish, horrify, intimidate

awesome = awe-inspiring, amazing, stunning, impressive, astonishing, formidable, intimidating, breathtaking

awful **1** = disgusting, offensive, gross, foul, dreadful, revolting, sickening, frightful, festy (*Austral. slang*), yucko (*Austral. slang*) **2** = bad, poor, terrible, appalling, foul, rubbish (*slang*), dreadful, horrendous ≠ wonderful, ka pai (*N.Z.*) **3** = shocking, dreadful **4** = unwell, poorly (*informal*), ill, terrible, sick, crook (*Austral. & N.Z. informal*), unhealthy, off-colour, under the weather (*informal*)

awfully **1** (*Informal*) = very, extremely, terribly, exceptionally, greatly, immensely, exceedingly, dreadfully **2** = badly, woefully, dreadfully, disgracefully, wretchedly, unforgivably, reprehensibly

awkward **1** = embarrassing, difficult, sensitive, delicate, uncomfortable, humiliating, disconcerting, inconvenient, barro (*Austral. slang*) ≠ comfortable **2** = inconvenient, difficult, troublesome, cumbersome, unwieldy, unmanageable, clunky (*informal*) ≠ convenient **3** = clumsy, lumbering, bumbling, unwieldy, ponderous, ungainly, gauche, gawky, unco (*Austral. slang*) ≠ graceful

axe NOUN = hatchet, chopper, tomahawk, cleaver, adze
• VERB **1** (*Informal*) = abandon, end, eliminate, cancel, scrap, cut back, terminate, dispense with **2** (*Informal*) = dismiss, fire (*informal*), sack (*informal*), remove, get rid of
• PHRASES **the axe** (*Informal*) = the sack (*informal*), dismissal, the boot (*slang*), termination, the chop (*slang*)

axis = pivot, shaft, axle, spindle, centre line

b

baas (*S. African*) = master, bo (*informal*), chief, ruler, commander, head, overlord, overseer

baby NOUN = child, infant, babe, bairn (*Scot.*), newborn child, babe in arms, ankle-biter (*Austral. slang*), tacker (*Austral. slang*)
• ADJECTIVE = small, little, minute, tiny, mini, wee, miniature, petite

back NOUN **1** = spine, backbone, vertebrae, spinal column, vertebral column **2** = rear ≠ front **3** = reverse, rear, other side, wrong side, underside, flip side
• ADJECTIVE **1** = rear ≠ front **2** = rearmost, hind, hindmost **3** = previous, earlier, former, past, elapsed ≠ future **4** = tail, end, rear, posterior
• VERB **1** = support, help, aid, champion, defend, promote, assist, advocate ≠ oppose **2** = subsidize, help, support, sponsor, assist

backbone **1** = spinal column, spine, vertebrae, vertebral column **2** = strength of character, character, resolution, nerve, daring, courage, determination, pluck

backer **1** = supporter, second, angel (*informal*), patron, promoter, subscriber, helper, benefactor **2** = advocate, supporter, patron, sponsor, promoter

backfire = fail, founder, flop (*informal*), rebound, boomerang, miscarry, misfire

background **1** = upbringing, history, culture, environment, tradition, circumstances **2** = experience, grounding, education **3** = circumstances, history, conditions, situation, atmosphere, environment, framework, ambience

backing **1** = support, encouragement, endorsement, moral support **2** = assistance, support, help, aid, sponsorship, patronage

backlash = reaction, response, resistance, retaliation, repercussion, counterblast, counteraction

backward **1** = underdeveloped, undeveloped **2** = slow, behind, retarded, underdeveloped, subnormal, half-witted, slow-witted

backwards *or* **backward** = towards the rear, behind you, in reverse, rearwards

bacteria = microorganisms, viruses, bugs (*slang*), germs, microbes, pathogens, bacilli

bad **1** = harmful, damaging, dangerous, destructive, unhealthy, detrimental, hurtful, ruinous ≠ beneficial **2** = poor **3** = unfavourable, distressing, unfortunate, grim, unpleasant, gloomy, adverse **4** = inferior, poor, inadequate, faulty, unsatisfactory, defective, imperfect, substandard, bush-league (*Austral. & N.Z. informal*), half-pie (*N.Z. informal*), bodger *or* bodgie (*Austral. slang*) ≠ satisfactory **5** = incompetent, poor, useless, incapable, unfit, inexpert **6** = grim, severe, hard, tough **7** = wicked, criminal, evil, corrupt, immoral, sinful, depraved ≠ virtuous **8** = naughty, defiant, wayward, mischievous, wicked, unruly, impish, undisciplined ≠ well-behaved **9** = rotten, off, rank, sour, rancid, mouldy, putrid, festy (*Austral. slang*)

badge **1** = image, brand, stamp, identification, crest, emblem, insignia **2** = mark, sign, token

badger = pester, harry, bother, bug (*informal*), bully, plague, hound, harass

badly **1** = poorly, incorrectly, carelessly, inadequately, imperfectly, ineptly ≠ well **2** = severely, greatly, deeply, seriously, desperately, intensely, exceedingly **3** = unfavourably, unsuccessfully

baffle = puzzle, confuse, stump, bewilder, confound, perplex, mystify, flummox ≠ explain

bag NOUN = sack, container, sac, receptacle • VERB **1** = get, land, score (*slang*), capture, acquire, procure **2** = catch, kill, shoot, capture, acquire, trap

baggage = luggage, things, cases, bags, equipment, gear, suitcases, belongings

baggy = loose, slack, bulging, sagging, sloppy, floppy, roomy, ill-fitting ≠ tight

bail NOUN (*Law*) = security, bond, guarantee, pledge, warranty, surety • PHRASES **bail out** = escape, withdraw, get away, retreat, make your getaway, break free *or* out ◆ **bail something** *or* **someone out** (*Informal*) = save, help, release, aid, deliver, recover, rescue, get out

bait NOUN = lure, attraction, incentive, carrot (*informal*), temptation, snare, inducement, decoy • VERB = tease, annoy, irritate, bother, mock, wind up (*Brit. slang*), hound, torment

baked = dry, desert, seared, scorched, barren, sterile, arid, torrid

bakkie (*S. African*) = truck, pick-up, van, lorry, pick-up truck

balance VERB **1** = stabilize, level, steady ≠ overbalance **2** = weigh, consider, compare, estimate, contrast, assess, evaluate, set against **3** (*Accounting*) = calculate, total, determine, estimate, settle, count, square, reckon • NOUN **1** = equilibrium, stability, steadiness, evenness ≠ instability **2** = stability, equanimity, steadiness **3** = parity, equity, fairness, impartiality, equality, correspondence, equivalence **4** = remainder, rest, difference, surplus, residue **5** = composure, stability, restraint, self-control, poise, self-discipline, equanimity, self-restraint

balcony **1** = terrace, veranda **2** = upper circle, gods, gallery

bald **1** = hairless, depilated, baldheaded **2** = plain, direct, frank, straightforward, blunt, rude, forthright, unadorned

ball = sphere, drop, globe, pellet, orb, globule, spheroid

balloon = expand, rise, increase, swell, blow up, inflate, bulge, billow

ballot = vote, election, voting, poll, polling, referendum, show of hands

ban VERB **1** = prohibit, bar, block, veto, forbid, boycott, outlaw, banish ≠ permit **2** = bar, prohibit, exclude, forbid, disqualify, preclude, debar, declare ineligible
• NOUN = prohibition, restriction, veto, boycott, embargo, injunction, taboo, disqualification, rahui (*N.Z.*) ≠ permission
band¹ **1** = ensemble, group, orchestra, combo **2** = gang, company, group, party, team, body, crowd, pack
band² = headband, strip, ribbon
bandage NOUN = dressing, plaster, compress, gauze
• VERB = dress, cover, bind, swathe
bandit = robber, outlaw, raider, plunderer, mugger (*informal*), looter, highwayman, desperado
bang NOUN **1** = explosion, pop, clash, crack, blast, slam, discharge, thump **2** = blow, knock, stroke, punch, bump, sock (*slang*), smack, thump
• VERB **1** = resound, boom, explode, thunder, thump, clang **2** = bump, knock, elbow, jostle **3** *often with **on*** = hit, strike, knock, belt (*informal*), slam, thump, clatter
• ADVERB = exactly, straight, square, squarely, precisely, slap, smack, plumb (*informal*)
banish **1** = exclude, ban, dismiss, expel, throw out, eject, evict **2** = expel, exile, outlaw, deport ≠ admit **3** = get rid of, remove
bank¹ NOUN **1** = financial institution, repository, depository **2** = store, fund, stock, source, supply, reserve, pool, reservoir
• VERB = deposit, keep, save
bank² NOUN **1** = side, edge, margin, shore, brink **2** = mound, banking, rise, hill, mass, pile, heap, ridge, kopje *or* koppie (*S. African*) **3** = mass
• VERB = tilt, tip, pitch, heel, slope, incline, slant, cant
bank³ = row, group, line, range, series, file, rank, sequence
bankrupt = insolvent, broke (*informal*), ruined, wiped out (*informal*), impoverished, in the red, destitute, gone bust (*informal*) ≠ solvent
bankruptcy = insolvency, failure, disaster, ruin, liquidation
banner = flag, standard, colours, placard, pennant, ensign, streamer
banquet = feast, spread (*informal*), dinner, meal, revel, repast, hakari (*N.Z.*)
bar NOUN **1** = public house, pub (*informal, chiefly Brit.*), counter, inn, saloon, tavern, canteen, watering hole (*facetious slang*) **2** = rod, staff, stick, stake, rail, pole, paling, shaft **3** = obstacle, block, barrier, hurdle, hitch, barricade, snag, deterrent ≠ aid
• VERB **1** = lock, block, secure, attach, bolt, blockade, barricade, fortify **2** = block, restrict, restrain, hamper, thwart, hinder, obstruct, impede **3** = exclude, ban, forbid, prohibit, keep out of, disallow, shut out of, blackball ≠ admit
barbarian **1** = savage, monster, beast, brute, yahoo, swine, sadist **2** = lout, yahoo, bigot, philistine, hoon (*Austral. & N.Z.*), cougan (*Austral. slang*), scozza (*Austral. slang*), bogan (*Austral. slang*), boor, vulgarian
bare **1** = naked, nude, stripped, uncovered, undressed, unclothed, unclad, without a stitch on (*informal*) ≠ dressed **2** = simple, spare, stark, austere, spartan, unadorned, unembellished, unornamented ≠ adorned **3** = plain, simple, basic, obvious, sheer, patent, evident, stark
barely = only just, just, hardly, scarcely, at a push ≠ completely
bargain NOUN **1** = good buy, discount purchase, good deal, steal (*informal*), snip (*informal*), giveaway, cheap purchase **2** = agreement, deal (*informal*), promise, contract, arrangement, settlement, pledge, pact
• VERB = negotiate, deal, contract, mediate, covenant, stipulate, transact, cut a deal
barge = canal boat, lighter, narrow boat, flatboat
bark¹ VERB = yap, bay, howl, snarl, growl, yelp, woof
• NOUN = yap, bay, howl, snarl, growl, yelp, woof
bark² = covering, casing, cover, skin, layer, crust, cortex (*Anatomy, botany*), rind
barracks = camp, quarters, garrison, encampment, billet
barrage **1** = bombardment, attack, bombing, assault, shelling, battery, volley, blitz **2** = torrent, mass, burst, stream, hail, spate, onslaught, deluge
barren **1** = desolate, empty, desert, waste ≠ fertile **2** (*Old-fashioned*) = infertile, sterile, childless, unproductive
barricade NOUN = barrier, wall, fence,

blockade, obstruction, rampart, bulwark, palisade
• **VERB** = bar, block, defend, secure, lock, bolt, blockade, fortify

barrier = barricade, wall, bar, fence, boundary, obstacle, blockade, obstruction

base[1] **NOUN 1** = bottom, floor, lowest part ≠ top **2** = support, stand, foot, rest, bed, bottom, foundation, pedestal **3** = foundation, institution, organization, establishment **4** = centre, post, station, camp, settlement, headquarters, starting point **5** = home, house, pad (*slang*), residence **6** = essence, source, basis, root, core
• **VERB 1** = ground, found, build, establish, depend, construct, derive, hinge **2** = place, set, post, station, establish, locate, install

base[2] = dishonourable, evil, disgraceful, shameful, immoral, wicked, sordid, despicable, scungy (*Austral. & N.Z.*) ≠ honourable

bash NOUN (*Informal*) = attempt, go (*informal*), try, shot (*informal*), bid, crack (*informal*), stab (*informal*)
• **VERB** (*Informal*) = hit, beat, strike, knock, smash, belt (*informal*), slap, sock (*slang*)

basic ADJECTIVE 1 = fundamental, main, essential, primary, vital, principal, cardinal, elementary **2** = vital, needed, important, key, necessary, essential, primary, crucial **3** = essential, key, vital, fundamental ≠ secondary **4** = main, key, essential, primary **5** = plain, simple, classic, unfussy, unembellished
• **PLURAL NOUN** = essentials, principles, fundamentals, nuts and bolts (*informal*), nitty-gritty (*informal*), rudiments, brass tacks (*informal*)

basically = essentially, mainly, mostly, principally, fundamentally, primarily, at heart, inherently

basis 1 = arrangement, way, system, footing, agreement **2** = foundation, support, base, ground, footing, bottom, groundwork

bask = lie, relax, lounge, sprawl, loaf, lie about, swim in, sunbathe, outspan (*S. African*)

bass = deep, low, resonant, sonorous, low-pitched, deep-toned

batch = group, set, lot, crowd, pack, collection, quantity, bunch

bath NOUN = wash, cleaning, shower, soak, cleansing, scrub, scrubbing, douche
• **VERB** = clean, wash, shower, soak, cleanse, scrub, bathe, rinse

bathe 1 = swim **2** = wash, clean, bath, shower, soak, cleanse, scrub, rinse **3** = cleanse, clean, wash, soak, rinse **4** = cover, flood, steep, engulf, immerse, overrun, suffuse, wash over

baton = stick, club, staff, pole, rod, crook, cane, mace, mere (*N.Z.*), patu (*N.Z.*)

batter = beat, hit, strike, knock, bang, thrash, pound, buffet

battery = artillery, ordnance, gunnery, gun emplacement, cannonry

battle NOUN 1 = fight, attack, action, struggle, conflict, clash, encounter, combat, biffo (*Austral. slang*) ≠ peace **2** = conflict, campaign, struggle, dispute, contest, crusade **3** = campaign, drive, movement, push, struggle
• **VERB 1** = wrestle, war, fight, argue, dispute, grapple, clamour, lock horns **2** = struggle, work, labour, strain, strive, toil, go all out (*informal*), give it your best shot (*informal*)

battlefield = battleground, front, field, combat zone, field of battle

batty = crazy, odd, mad, eccentric, peculiar, daft (*informal*), touched, potty (*Brit. informal*), off the air (*Austral. slang*), porangi (*N.Z.*)

bay[1] = inlet, sound, gulf, creek, cove, fjord, bight, natural harbour

bay[2] = recess, opening, corner, niche, compartment, nook, alcove

bay[3] **VERB** = howl, cry, roar (*used of hounds*), bark, wail, growl, bellow, clamour
• **NOUN** = cry, roar (*used of hounds*), bark, howl, wail, growl, bellow, clamour

bazaar 1 = market, exchange, fair, marketplace **2** = fair, fête, gala, bring-and-buy

be = be alive, live, exist, survive, breathe, be present, endure

beach = shore, coast, sands, seaside, water's edge, seashore

beached = stranded, grounded, abandoned, deserted, wrecked, ashore, marooned, aground

beacon = signal, sign, beam, flare, lighthouse, bonfire, watchtower

bead = drop, tear, bubble, pearl, dot, drip, blob, droplet

beam VERB 1 = smile, grin **2** = transmit,

show, air, broadcast, cable, send out, relay, televise **3** = radiate, flash, shine, glow, glitter, glare, gleam
• NOUN **1** = ray, flash, stream, glow, streak, shaft, gleam, glint **2** = rafter, support, timber, spar, plank, girder, joist **3** = smile, grin

bear VERB **1** = carry, take, move, bring, transfer, conduct, transport, haul ≠ put down **2** = support, shoulder, sustain, endure, uphold, withstand ≠ give up **3** = display, have, show, hold, carry, possess **4** = suffer, experience, go through, sustain, stomach, endure, brook, abide **5** = bring yourself to, allow, accept, permit, endure, tolerate **6** = produce, generate, yield, bring forth **7** = give birth to, produce, deliver, breed, bring forth, beget **8** = exhibit, hold, maintain **9** = conduct, carry, move, deport
• PHRASES **bear something out** = support, prove, confirm, justify, endorse, uphold, substantiate, corroborate

bearer 1 = agent, carrier, courier, herald, envoy, messenger, conveyor, emissary **2** = carrier, runner, servant, porter

bearing NOUN **1** *usually with **on** or **upon*** = relevance, relation, application, connection, import, reference, significance, pertinence ≠ irrelevance **2** = manner, attitude, conduct, aspect, behaviour, posture, demeanour, deportment
• PLURAL NOUN = way, course, position, situation, track, aim, direction, location

beast 1 = animal, creature, brute **2** = brute, monster, savage, barbarian, fiend, swine, ogre, sadist

beastly = unpleasant, mean, awful, nasty, rotten, horrid, disagreeable ≠ pleasant

beat VERB **1** = batter, hit, strike, knock, pound, smack, thrash, thump **2** = pound, strike, hammer, batter, thrash **3** = throb, thump, pound, quake, vibrate, pulsate, palpitate **4** = hit, strike, bang **5** = flap, thrash, flutter, wag **6** = defeat, outdo, trounce, overcome, crush, overwhelm, conquer, surpass
• NOUN **1** = throb, pounding, pulse, thumping, vibration, pulsating, palpitation, pulsation **2** = route, way, course, rounds, path, circuit
• PHRASES **beat someone up** (*Informal*) = assault, attack, batter, thrash, set about, set upon, lay into (*informal*), beat the living daylights out of (*informal*)

beaten 1 = stirred, mixed, whipped, blended, whisked, frothy, foamy **2** = defeated, overcome, overwhelmed, cowed, thwarted, vanquished

beautiful = attractive, pretty, lovely, charming, tempting, pleasant, handsome, fetching ≠ ugly

beauty 1 = attractiveness, charm, grace, glamour, elegance, loveliness, handsomeness, comeliness ≠ ugliness **2** = good-looker, lovely (*slang*), belle, stunner (*informal*)

because CONJUNCTION = since, as, in that
• PHRASES **because of** = as a result of, on account of, by reason of, thanks to, owing to

beckon = gesture, sign, wave, indicate, signal, nod, motion, summon

become 1 = come to be, develop into, be transformed into, grow into, change into, alter to, mature into, ripen into **2** = suit, fit, enhance, flatter, embellish, set off

becoming 1 = flattering, pretty, attractive, enhancing, neat, graceful, tasteful, well-chosen ≠ unflattering **2** = appropriate, seemly, fitting, suitable, proper, worthy, in keeping, compatible ≠ inappropriate

bed 1 = bedstead, couch, berth, cot, bunk, divan **2** = plot, area, row, strip, patch, ground, land, garden **3** = bottom, ground, floor **4** = base, footing, basis, bottom, foundation, underpinning, groundwork, bedrock

before PREPOSITION **1** = earlier than, ahead of, prior to, in advance of ≠ after **2** = in front of, ahead of, in advance of **3** = in the presence of, in front of **4** = ahead of, in front of, in advance of
• ADVERB **1** = previously, earlier, sooner, in advance, formerly ≠ after **2** = in the past, earlier, once, previously, formerly, hitherto, beforehand

RELATED WORDS
prefixes: ante-, fore-, pre-

beforehand = in advance, before, earlier, already, sooner, ahead, previously, in anticipation

beg 1 = implore, plead with, beseech, request, petition, solicit, entreat **2** = scrounge, bum (*informal*), touch (someone) for (*slang*), cadge, sponge on (someone) for, freeload (*slang*), seek charity, solicit charity ≠ give

beggar = tramp, bum (*informal*), derelict, drifter, down-and-out, pauper, vagrant, bag lady (*chiefly U.S.*), derro (*Austral. slang*)

begin 1 = start, commence, proceed ≠ stop 2 = commence, start, initiate, embark on, set about, instigate, institute, make a beginning 3 = start talking, start, initiate, commence 4 = come into existence, start, appear, emerge, arise, originate, come into being 5 = emerge, start, spring, stem, derive, originate ≠ end

beginner = novice, pupil, amateur, newcomer, starter, trainee, apprentice, learner ≠ expert

beginning 1 = start, opening, birth, origin, outset, onset, initiation, inauguration ≠ end 2 = outset, start, opening, birth, onset, commencement 3 = origins

behave 1 = act 2 *often reflexive* = be well-behaved, mind your manners, keep your nose clean, act correctly, conduct yourself properly ≠ misbehave

behaviour 1 = conduct, ways, actions, bearing, attitude, manner, manners, demeanour 2 = action, performance, operation, functioning

behind PREPOSITION 1 = at the rear of, at the back of, at the heels of 2 = after, following 3 = supporting, for, backing, on the side of, in agreement with 4 = causing, responsible for, initiating, at the bottom of, instigating 5 = later than, after
• ADVERB 1 = after, next, following, afterwards, subsequently, in the wake (of) ≠ in advance of 2 = behind schedule, delayed, running late, behind time ≠ ahead 3 = overdue, in debt, in arrears, behindhand
• NOUN (*Informal*) = bottom, butt (*U.S. & Canad. informal*), buttocks, posterior

being 1 = individual, creature, human being, living thing 2 = life, reality ≠ nonexistence 3 = soul, spirit, substance, creature, essence, organism, entity

beleaguered 1 = harassed, troubled, plagued, hassled (*informal*), badgered, persecuted, pestered, vexed 2 = besieged, surrounded, blockaded, beset, encircled, assailed, hemmed in

belief 1 = trust, confidence, conviction ≠ disbelief 2 = faith, principles, doctrine, ideology, creed, dogma, tenet, credo 3 = opinion, feeling, idea, impression, assessment, notion, judgment, point of view

believe 1 = think, judge, suppose, estimate, imagine, assume, gather, reckon 2 = accept, trust, credit, depend on, rely on, have faith in, swear by, be certain of ≠ disbelieve

believer = follower, supporter, convert, disciple, devotee, apostle, adherent, zealot ≠ sceptic

bellow VERB = shout, cry (out), scream, roar, yell, howl, shriek, bawl
• NOUN = shout, cry, scream, roar, yell, howl, shriek, bawl

belly = stomach, insides (*informal*), gut, abdomen, tummy, paunch, potbelly, corporation (*informal*), puku (*N.Z.*)

belong = go with, fit into, be part of, relate to, be connected with, pertain to

belonging = fellowship, relationship, association, loyalty, acceptance, attachment, inclusion, affinity

belongings = possessions, goods, things, effects, property, stuff, gear, paraphernalia

beloved = dear, loved, valued, prized, admired, treasured, precious, darling

below PREPOSITION 1 = under, underneath, lower than 2 = less than, lower than 3 = subordinate to, subject to, inferior to, lesser than
• ADVERB 1 = lower, down, under, beneath, underneath 2 = beneath, following, at the end, underneath, at the bottom, further on

belt 1 = waistband, band, sash, girdle, girth, cummerbund 2 = conveyor belt, band, loop, fan belt, drive belt 3 (*Geography*) = zone, area, region, section, district, stretch, strip, layer

bemused = puzzled, confused, baffled, at sea, bewildered, muddled, perplexed, mystified

bench NOUN 1 = seat, stall, pew 2 = worktable, stand, table, counter, trestle table, workbench
• PHRASES **the bench** = court, judges, magistrates, tribunal, judiciary, courtroom

benchmark = reference point, gauge, yardstick, measure, level, standard, model, par

bend VERB = twist, turn, wind, lean, hook, bow, curve, arch
• NOUN = curve, turn, corner, twist, angle, bow, loop, arc

beneath PREPOSITION **1** = under, below, underneath, lower than ≠ over **2** = inferior to, below **3** = unworthy of, unfitting for, unsuitable for, inappropriate for, unbefitting
• ADVERB = underneath, below, in a lower place

RELATED WORD
prefix: sub-

beneficial = favourable, useful, valuable, helpful, profitable, benign, wholesome, advantageous ≠ harmful

beneficiary **1** = recipient, receiver, payee **2** = heir, inheritor

benefit NOUN **1** = good, help, profit, favour ≠ harm **2** = advantage, aid, favour, assistance
• VERB **1** = profit from, make the most of, gain from, do well out of, reap benefits from, turn to your advantage **2** = help, aid, profit, improve, enhance, assist, avail ≠ harm

benign **1** = benevolent, kind, kindly, warm, friendly, obliging, sympathetic, compassionate ≠ unkind **2** (*Medical*) = harmless, innocent, innocuous, curable, inoffensive, remediable ≠ malignant

bent ADJECTIVE **1** = misshapen, twisted, angled, bowed, curved, arched, crooked, distorted ≠ straight **2** = stooped, bowed, arched, hunched
• NOUN = inclination, ability, leaning, tendency, preference, penchant, propensity, aptitude
• PHRASES **bent on** = intent on, set on, fixed on, predisposed to, resolved on, insistent on

bequeath **1** = leave, will, give, grant, hand down, endow, bestow, entrust **2** = give, accord, grant, afford, yield, lend, pass on, confer

berth NOUN **1** = bunk, bed, hammock, billet **2** (*Nautical*) = anchorage, haven, port, harbour, dock, pier, wharf, quay
• VERB (*Nautical*) = anchor, land, dock, moor, tie up, drop anchor

beside PREPOSITION = next to, near, close to, neighbouring, alongside, adjacent to, at the side of, abreast of
• PHRASES **beside yourself** = distraught, desperate, distressed, frantic, frenzied, demented, unhinged, overwrought

besides PREPOSITION = apart from, barring, excepting, other than, excluding, as well (as), in addition to, over and above
• ADVERB = also, too, further, otherwise, in addition, as well, moreover, furthermore

besiege **1** = harass, harry, plague, hound, hassle (*informal*), badger, pester **2** = surround, enclose, blockade, encircle, hem in, shut in, lay siege to

best ADJECTIVE = finest, leading, supreme, principal, foremost, pre-eminent, unsurpassed, most accomplished
• NOUN = finest, top, prime, pick, flower, cream, elite, crème de la crème (*French*)
• ADVERB = most highly, most fully, most deeply

bestow = present, give, award, grant, commit, hand out, lavish, impart ≠ obtain

bet VERB = gamble, chance, stake, venture, hazard, speculate, wager, risk money
• NOUN = gamble, risk, stake, venture, speculation, flutter (*informal*), punt, wager

betray **1** = be disloyal to, dob in (*Austral. slang*), double-cross (*informal*), stab in the back, be unfaithful to, inform on *or* against **2** = give away, reveal, expose, disclose, uncover, divulge, unmask, let slip

betrayal = disloyalty, sell-out (*informal*), deception, treason, treachery, trickery, double-cross (*informal*), breach of trust ≠ loyalty

better ADVERB **1** = to a greater degree, more completely, more thoroughly **2** = in a more excellent manner, more effectively, more attractively, more advantageously, more competently, in a superior way ≠ worse
• ADJECTIVE **1** = well, stronger, recovering, cured, fully recovered, on the mend (*informal*) ≠ worse **2** = superior, finer, higher-quality, surpassing, preferable, more desirable ≠ inferior

between = amidst, among, mid, in the middle of, betwixt

RELATED WORD
prefix: inter-

beverage = drink, liquid, liquor, refreshment

beware **1** = be careful, look out, watch out, be wary, be cautious, take heed, guard against something **2** = avoid, mind

bewilder = confound, confuse, puzzle, baffle, perplex, mystify, flummox, bemuse

bewildered = confused, puzzled, baffled, at sea, muddled, perplexed, at a loss, mystified

beyond 1 = on the other side of 2 = after, over, past, above 3 = past 4 = except for, but, save, apart from, other than, excluding, besides, aside from 5 = exceeding, surpassing, superior to, out of reach of 6 = outside, over, above

bias NOUN = prejudice, leaning, tendency, inclination, favouritism, partiality ≠ impartiality
• VERB = influence, colour, weight, prejudice, distort, sway, warp, slant

biased = prejudiced, weighted, one-sided, partial, distorted, slanted

bid NOUN 1 = attempt, try, effort, go (*informal*), shot (*informal*), stab (*informal*), crack (*informal*) 2 = offer, price, amount, advance, proposal, sum, tender
• VERB 1 = make an offer, offer, propose, submit, tender, proffer 2 = wish, say, call, tell, greet 3 = tell, ask, order, require, direct, command, instruct

bidding = order, request, command, instruction, summons, beck and call

big 1 = large, great, huge, massive, vast, enormous, substantial, extensive ≠ small 2 = important, significant, urgent, far-reaching ≠ unimportant 3 = powerful, important, prominent, dominant, influential, eminent 4 = grown-up, adult, grown, mature, elder, full-grown ≠ young 5 = generous, good, noble, gracious, benevolent, altruistic, unselfish, magnanimous

bill[1] NOUN 1 = charges, rate, costs, score, account, statement, reckoning, expense 2 = act of parliament, measure, proposal, piece of legislation, projected law 3 = list, listing, programme, card, schedule, agenda, catalogue, inventory 4 = advertisement, notice, poster, leaflet, bulletin, circular, handout, placard
• VERB 1 = charge, debit, invoice, send a statement to, send an invoice to 2 = advertise, post, announce, promote, plug (*informal*), tout, publicize, give advance notice of

bill[2] = beak, nib, neb (*archaic*, *dialect*), mandible

bind VERB 1 = oblige, make, force, require, engage, compel, constrain, necessitate 2 = tie, join, stick, secure, wrap, knot, strap, lash ≠ untie
• NOUN (*Informal*) = nuisance, inconvenience, hassle (*informal*), drag (*informal*), spot (*informal*), difficulty, bore, dilemma, uphill (*S. African*)

binding = compulsory, necessary, mandatory, obligatory, irrevocable, unalterable, indissoluble ≠ optional

binge (*Informal*) = bout, spell, fling, feast, stint, spree, orgy, bender (*informal*)

biography = life story, life, record, account, profile, memoir, CV, curriculum vitae

bird = feathered friend, fowl, songbird

RELATED WORDS

adjective: avian
male: cock
female: hen
young: chick, fledg(e)ling, nestling
collective nouns: flock, flight
habitation: nest

birth 1 = childbirth, delivery, nativity, parturition ≠ death 2 = ancestry, stock, blood, background, breeding, pedigree, lineage, parentage

RELATED WORD

adjective: natal

bit[1] 1 = slice, fragment, crumb, morsel 2 = piece, scrap 3 = jot, iota 4 = part

bit[2] = curb, check, brake, restraint, snaffle

bite VERB = nip, cut, tear, wound, snap, pierce, pinch, chew
• NOUN 1 = snack, food, piece, taste, refreshment, mouthful, morsel, titbit 2 = wound, sting, pinch, nip, prick

biting 1 = piercing, cutting, sharp, frozen, harsh, penetrating, arctic, icy 2 = sarcastic, cutting, stinging, scathing, acrimonious, incisive, virulent, caustic

bitter 1 = resentful, angry, offended, sour, sore, acrimonious, sullen, miffed (*informal*) ≠ happy 2 = freezing, biting, severe, intense, raw, fierce, chill, stinging ≠ mild 3 = sour, sharp, acid, harsh, tart, astringent, acrid, unsweetened ≠ sweet

bitterness 1 = resentment, hostility, indignation, animosity, acrimony, rancour, ill feeling, bad blood 2 = sourness, acidity, sharpness, tartness, acerbity

bizarre = strange, unusual, extraordinary, fantastic, weird, peculiar, eccentric, ludicrous ≠ normal

black 1 = dark, raven, ebony, sable, jet, dusky, pitch-black, swarthy ≠ light 2 = gloomy, sad, depressing, grim, bleak, hopeless, dismal, ominous ≠ happy 3 = terrible, bad, devastating, tragic, fatal, catastrophic, ruinous, calamitous **4** = wicked, bad, evil, corrupt, vicious, immoral, depraved, villainous ≠ good **5** = angry, cross, furious, hostile, sour, menacing, moody, resentful ≠ happy

blackmail NOUN = threat, intimidation, ransom, extortion, hush money (*slang*) • VERB = threaten, squeeze, compel, intimidate, coerce, dragoon, extort, hold to ransom

blame VERB **1** = hold responsible, accuse, denounce, indict, impeach, incriminate, impute ≠ absolve **2** = attribute to, credit to, assign to, put down to, impute to **3** (used in negative constructions) = criticize, condemn, censure, reproach, chide, find fault with ≠ praise • NOUN = responsibility, liability, accountability, onus, culpability, answerability ≠ praise

bland **1** = dull, boring, plain, flat, dreary, run-of-the-mill, uninspiring, humdrum ≠ exciting **2** = tasteless, insipid, flavourless, thin

blank ADJECTIVE **1** = unmarked, white, clear, clean, empty, plain, bare, void ≠ marked **2** = expressionless, empty, vague, vacant, deadpan, impassive, poker-faced (*informal*) ≠ expressive • NOUN **1** = empty space, space, gap **2** = void, vacuum, vacancy, emptiness, nothingness

blanket NOUN **1** = cover, rug, coverlet **2** = covering, sheet, coat, layer, carpet, cloak, mantle, thickness • VERB = coat, cover, hide, mask, conceal, obscure, cloak

blast NOUN **1** = explosion, crash, burst, discharge, eruption, detonation **2** = gust, rush, storm, breeze, puff, gale, tempest, squall **3** = blare, blow, scream, trumpet, wail, resound, clamour, toot • VERB = blow up, bomb, destroy, burst, ruin, break up, explode, shatter

blatant = obvious, clear, plain, evident, glaring, manifest, noticeable, conspicuous ≠ subtle

blaze VERB **1** = burn, glow, flare, be on fire, go up in flames, be ablaze, fire, flame **2** = shine, flash, beam, glow, flare, glare, gleam, radiate • NOUN **1** = inferno, fire, flames, bonfire, combustion, conflagration **2** = flash, glow, glitter, flare, glare, gleam, brilliance, radiance

bleach = lighten, wash out, blanch, whiten

bleak **1** = dismal, dark, depressing, grim, discouraging, gloomy, hopeless, dreary ≠ cheerful **2** = exposed, empty, bare, barren, desolate, windswept, weather-beaten, unsheltered ≠ sheltered **3** = stormy, severe, rough, harsh, tempestuous, intemperate

bleed **1** = lose blood, flow, gush, spurt, shed blood **2** = blend, run, meet, unite, mix, combine, flow, fuse **3** (*Informal*) = extort, milk, squeeze, drain, exhaust, fleece

blend VERB **1** = mix, join, combine, compound, merge, unite, mingle, amalgamate **2** = go well, match, fit, suit, go with, correspond, complement, coordinate **3** = combine, mix, link, integrate, merge, unite, amalgamate • NOUN = mixture, mix, combination, compound, brew, union, synthesis, alloy

bless **1** = sanctify, dedicate, ordain, exalt, anoint, consecrate, hallow ≠ curse **2** = endow, give to, provide for, grant for, favour, grace, bestow to ≠ afflict

blessed = holy, sacred, divine, adored, revered, hallowed, sanctified, beatified

blessing **1** = benefit, help, service, favour, gift, windfall, kindness, good fortune ≠ disadvantage **2** = approval, backing, support, agreement, favour, sanction, permission, leave ≠ disapproval **3** = benediction, grace, dedication, thanksgiving, invocation, commendation, consecration, benison ≠ curse

blight NOUN **1** = curse, suffering, evil, corruption, pollution, plague, hardship, woe ≠ blessing **2** = disease, pest, fungus, mildew, infestation, pestilence, canker • VERB = frustrate, destroy, ruin, crush, mar, dash, wreck, spoil, crool *or* cruel (*Austral. slang*)

blind **1** = sightless, unsighted, unseeing, eyeless, visionless ≠ sighted **2** *often with to* = unaware of, unconscious of, ignorant of, indifferent to, insensitive to, oblivious of, unconcerned about, inconsiderate of ≠ aware **3** = unquestioning, prejudiced, wholesale, indiscriminate, uncritical, unreasoning, undiscriminating

blindly **1** = thoughtlessly, carelessly, recklessly, indiscriminately, senselessly,

heedlessly **2** = wildly, aimlessly
blink VERB **1** = flutter, wink, bat **2** = flash, flicker, wink, shimmer, twinkle, glimmer
• PHRASES **on the blink** (*Slang*) = not working (properly), faulty, defective, playing up, out of action, malfunctioning, out of order
bliss **1** = joy, ecstasy, euphoria, rapture, nirvana, felicity, gladness, blissfulness ≠ misery **2** = beatitude, blessedness
blister = sore, boil, swelling, cyst, pimple, carbuncle, pustule
blitz = attack, strike, assault, raid, offensive, onslaught, bombardment, bombing campaign
bloc = group, union, league, alliance, coalition, axis
block NOUN **1** = piece, bar, mass, brick, lump, chunk, hunk, ingot **2** = obstruction, bar, barrier, obstacle, impediment, hindrance
• VERB **1** = obstruct, close, stop, plug, choke, clog, stop up, bung up (*informal*) ≠ clear **2** = obscure, bar, obstruct **3** = shut off, stop, bar, hamper, obstruct
blockade = stoppage, block, barrier, restriction, obstacle, barricade, obstruction, impediment
bloke (*Informal*) = man, person, individual, character (*informal*), guy (*informal*), fellow, chap
blonde *or* **blond** **1** = fair, light, flaxen **2** = fair-haired, golden-haired, tow-headed
blood **1** = lifeblood, gore, vital fluid **2** = family, relations, birth, descent, extraction, ancestry, lineage, kinship
bloodshed = killing, murder, massacre, slaughter, slaying, carnage, butchery, blood-letting
bloody **1** = cruel, fierce, savage, brutal, vicious, ferocious, cut-throat, warlike **2** = bloodstained, raw, bleeding, blood-soaked, blood-spattered
bloom NOUN **1** = flower, bud, blossom **2** = prime, flower, beauty, height, peak, flourishing, heyday, zenith **3** = glow, freshness, lustre, radiance ≠ pallor
• VERB **1** = flower, blossom, open, bud ≠ wither **2** = grow, develop, wax **3** = succeed, flourish, thrive, prosper, fare well ≠ fail
blossom NOUN = flower, bloom, bud, efflorescence, floret
• VERB **1** = bloom, grow, develop, mature **2** = succeed, progress, thrive, flourish, prosper **3** = flower, bloom, bud
blow[1] VERB **1** = move, carry, drive, sweep, fling, buffet, waft **2** = be carried, flutter **3** = exhale, breathe, pant, puff **4** = play, sound, pipe, trumpet, blare, toot
• PHRASES **blow something up** **1** = explode, bomb, blast, detonate, blow sky-high **2** = inflate, pump up, fill, expand, swell, enlarge, puff up, distend **3** = magnify, increase, extend, expand, widen, broaden, amplify ♦ **blow up** **1** = explode, burst, shatter, erupt, detonate **2** (*Informal*) = lose your temper, rage, erupt, see red (*informal*), become angry, hit the roof (*informal*), fly off the handle (*informal*), go crook (*Austral. & N.Z. slang*), blow your top
blow[2] **1** = knock, stroke, punch, bang, sock (*slang*), smack, thump, clout (*informal*) **2** = setback, shock, disaster, reverse, disappointment, catastrophe, misfortune, bombshell
bludge (*Austral. & N.Z. informal*) = slack, skive (*Brit. informal*), idle, shirk
blue ADJECTIVE **1** = depressed, low, sad, unhappy, melancholy, dejected, despondent, downcast ≠ happy **2** = smutty, obscene, indecent, lewd, risqué, X-rated (*informal*) ≠ respectable
• PLURAL NOUN = depression, gloom, melancholy, unhappiness, low spirits, the dumps (*informal*), doldrums
blueprint **1** = scheme, plan, design, system, programme, proposal, strategy, pattern **2** = plan, scheme, pattern, draft, outline, sketch
bluff[1] NOUN = deception, fraud, sham, pretence, deceit, bravado, bluster, humbug
• VERB = deceive, trick, fool, pretend, cheat, con, fake, mislead
bluff[2] NOUN = precipice, bank, peak, cliff, ridge, crag, escarpment, promontory
• ADJECTIVE = hearty, open, blunt, outspoken, genial, ebullient, jovial, plain-spoken ≠ tactful
blunder NOUN = mistake, slip, fault, error, oversight, gaffe, slip-up (*informal*), indiscretion ≠ correctness
• VERB **1** = make a mistake, blow it (*slang*), err, slip up (*informal*), foul up, put your foot in it (*informal*) ≠ be correct **2** = stumble, fall, reel, stagger, lurch

blunt ADJECTIVE **1** = frank, forthright, straightforward, rude, outspoken, bluff, brusque, plain-spoken ≠ tactful **2** = dull, rounded, dulled, edgeless, unsharpened ≠ sharp
• VERB = dull, weaken, soften, numb, dampen, water down, deaden, take the edge off ≠ stimulate

blur NOUN = haze, confusion, fog, obscurity, indistinctness
• VERB **1** = become indistinct, become vague, become hazy, become fuzzy **2** = obscure, make indistinct, mask, obfuscate, make vague, make hazy

blush VERB = turn red, colour, glow, flush, redden, go red (as a beetroot), turn scarlet ≠ turn pale
• NOUN = reddening, colour, glow, flush, pink tinge, rosiness, ruddiness, rosy tint

board NOUN **1** = plank, panel, timber, slat, piece of timber **2** = council, directors, committee, congress, advisers, panel, assembly, trustees **3** = meals, provisions, victuals, daily meals
• VERB = get on, enter, mount, embark ≠ get off

boast VERB **1** = brag, crow, vaunt, talk big (*slang*), blow your own trumpet, show off, be proud of, congratulate yourself on, skite (*Austral. & N.Z. informal*) ≠ cover up **2** = possess, exhibit
• NOUN = bragging ≠ disclaimer

bob = bounce, duck, hop, oscillate

bodily = physical, material, actual, substantial, tangible, corporal, carnal, corporeal

body **1** = physique, build, form, figure, shape, frame, constitution **2** = torso, trunk **3** = corpse, dead body, remains, stiff (*slang*), carcass, cadaver **4** = organization, company, group, society, association, band, congress, institution **5** = main part, matter, material, mass, substance, bulk, essence **6** = expanse, mass, sweep
RELATED WORDS
adjectives: corporal, physical

bog = marsh, swamp, slough, wetlands, fen, mire, quagmire, morass, pakihi (*N.Z.*)

bogey = bugbear, bête noire, horror, nightmare, bugaboo

bogus = fake, false, artificial, forged, imitation, sham, fraudulent, counterfeit ≠ genuine

Bohemian ADJECTIVE *often not cap.* = unconventional, alternative, artistic, unorthodox, arty (*informal*), offbeat, left bank, nonconformist ≠ conventional
• NOUN *often not cap.* = nonconformist, rebel, radical, eccentric, maverick, hippy, dropout, individualist

boil[1] = simmer, bubble, foam, seethe, fizz, froth, effervesce

boil[2] = pustule, gathering, swelling, blister, carbuncle

bold **1** = fearless, enterprising, brave, daring, heroic, adventurous, courageous, audacious ≠ timid **2** = impudent, forward, confident, rude, cheeky, brazen, shameless, insolent ≠ shy

bolster = support, help, boost, strengthen, reinforce, shore up, augment

bolt NOUN **1** = pin, rod, peg, rivet **2** = bar, catch, lock, latch, fastener, sliding bar
• VERB **1** = lock, close, bar, secure, fasten, latch **2** = dash, fly **3** = gobble, stuff, wolf, cram, gorge, devour, gulp, guzzle

bomb NOUN = explosive, mine, shell, missile, device, rocket, grenade, torpedo
• VERB = blow up, attack, destroy, assault, shell, blitz, bombard, torpedo

bombard **1** = attack, assault, besiege, beset, assail **2** = bomb, shell, blitz, open fire, strafe, fire upon

bombardment = bombing, attack, assault, shelling, blitz, barrage, fusillade

bond NOUN **1** = tie, union, coupling, link, association, relation, connection, alliance **2** = fastening, tie, chain, cord, shackle, fetter, manacle **3** = agreement, word, promise, contract, guarantee, pledge, obligation, covenant
• VERB **1** = form friendships, connect **2** = fix, hold, bind, connect, glue, stick, paste, fasten

bonus **1** = extra, prize, gift, reward, premium, dividend **2** = advantage, benefit, gain, extra, plus, asset, icing on the cake

book NOUN **1** = work, title, volume, publication, tract, tome **2** = notebook, album, journal, diary, pad, notepad, exercise book, jotter
• VERB = reserve, schedule, engage, organize, charter, arrange for, make reservations
• PHRASES **book in** = register, enter

booklet = brochure, leaflet, hand-out, pamphlet, folder, mailshot, handbill

boom NOUN **1** = expansion, increase,

development, growth, jump, boost, improvement, upsurge ≠ decline 2 = bang, crash, clash, blast, burst, explosion, roar, thunder
• VERB 1 = increase, flourish, grow, develop, expand, strengthen, swell, thrive ≠ fall 2 = bang, roll, crash, blast, explode, roar, thunder, rumble

boon 1 = benefit, blessing, godsend, gift 2 = gift, favour

boost VERB = increase, develop, raise, expand, add to, heighten, enlarge, amplify ≠ decrease
• NOUN 1 = rise, increase, jump, addition, improvement, expansion, upsurge, upturn ≠ fall 2 = encouragement, help

boot = kick, punt, put the boot in(to) (*slang*), drop-kick

border NOUN 1 = frontier, line, limit, bounds, boundary, perimeter, borderline 2 = edge, margin, verge, rim
• VERB = edge, bound, decorate, trim, fringe, rim, hem

bore[1] = drill, mine, sink, tunnel, pierce, penetrate, burrow, puncture

bore[2] VERB = tire, fatigue, weary, wear out, jade, be tedious, pall on, send to sleep ≠ excite
• NOUN = nuisance, pain (*informal*), yawn (*informal*), anorak (*informal*)

bored = fed up, tired, wearied, uninterested, sick and tired (*informal*), listless, brassed off (*Brit. slang*), hoha (*N.Z.*)

boredom = tedium, apathy, weariness, monotony, sameness, ennui, flatness, world-weariness ≠ excitement

boring = uninteresting, dull, tedious, tiresome, monotonous, flat, humdrum, mind-numbing

borrow 1 = take on loan, touch (someone) for (*slang*), scrounge (*informal*), cadge, use temporarily ≠ lend 2 = steal, take, copy, adopt, pinch (*informal*)

boss NOUN = manager, head, leader, director, chief, master, employer, supervisor, baas (*S. African*)
• PHRASES **boss someone around** (*Informal*) = order around, dominate, bully, oppress, push around (*slang*)

bother VERB 1 = trouble, concern, worry, alarm, disturb, disconcert, perturb 2 = pester, plague, harass, hassle (*informal*), inconvenience ≠ help
• NOUN = trouble, problem, worry, difficulty, fuss, irritation, hassle (*informal*), nuisance, uphill (*S. African*) ≠ help

bottle shop (*Austral. & N.Z.*) = off-licence (*Brit.*), liquor store (*U.S. & Canad.*), bottle store (*S. African*), package store (*U.S. & Canad.*), offie *or* offy (*Brit. informal*)

bottle store (*S. African*) = off-licence (*Brit.*), liquor store (*U.S. & Canad.*), bottle shop (*Austral. & N.Z.*), package store (*U.S. & Canad.*), offie *or* offy (*Brit. informal*)

bottom NOUN 1 = lowest part, base, foot, bed, floor, foundation, depths ≠ top 2 = underside, sole, underneath, lower side 3 = buttocks, behind (*informal*), rear, backside, rump, seat, posterior
• ADJECTIVE = lowest, last ≠ higher

bounce VERB 1 = rebound, recoil, ricochet 2 = bound, spring, jump, leap, skip, gambol
• NOUN 1 = springiness, give, spring, resilience, elasticity, recoil 2 (*Informal*) = life, go (*informal*), energy, zip (*informal*), vigour, exuberance, dynamism, vivacity

bound[1] 1 = compelled, obliged, forced, committed, pledged, constrained, beholden, duty-bound 2 = tied, fixed, secured, attached, tied up, fastened, pinioned 3 = certain, sure, fated, doomed, destined

bound[2] 1 = surround, confine, enclose, encircle, hem in, demarcate 2 = limit, restrict, confine, restrain, circumscribe

bound[3] VERB = leap, bob, spring, jump, bounce, skip, vault
• NOUN = leap, bob, spring, jump, bounce, hurdle, skip, vault

boundary 1 = frontier, edge, border, barrier, margin, brink 2 = edges, limits, fringes, extremities 3 = dividing line, borderline

bounds = boundary, limit, edge, border, confine, verge, rim, perimeter

bouquet 1 = bunch of flowers, spray, garland, wreath, posy, buttonhole, corsage, nosegay 2 = aroma, smell, scent, perfume, fragrance, savour, odour, redolence

bourgeois = middle-class, traditional, conventional, materialistic, hidebound

bout 1 = period, term, fit, spell, turn, interval 2 = round, series, session, cycle, sequence, stint 3 = fight, match, competition, struggle, contest, set-to, encounter, engagement

bow[1] VERB = bend, bob, nod, stoop, droop, genuflect
• NOUN = bending, bob, nod, obeisance, kowtow, genuflection

bow[2] (*Nautical*) = prow, head, stem, fore, beak

bowels 1 = guts, insides (*informal*), intestines, innards (*informal*), entrails, viscera, vitals 2 = depths, hold, inside, deep, interior, core, belly

bowl[1] = basin, plate, dish, vessel

bowl[2] = throw, hurl, launch, cast, pitch, toss, fling, chuck (*informal*)

box[1] NOUN = container, case, chest, trunk, pack, package, carton, casket
• VERB = pack, package, wrap, encase, bundle up

box[2] = fight, spar, exchange blows

boxer = fighter, pugilist, prizefighter

boy = lad, kid (*informal*), youth, fellow, youngster, schoolboy, junior, stripling

boycott = embargo, reject, snub, black ≠ support

boyfriend = sweetheart, man, lover, beloved, admirer, suitor, beau, date

brace VERB 1 = steady, support, secure, stabilize 2 = support, strengthen, steady, reinforce, bolster, fortify, buttress
• NOUN = support, stay, prop, bolster, bracket, reinforcement, strut, truss

bracing = refreshing, fresh, stimulating, crisp, brisk, exhilarating, invigorating ≠ tiring

brain = intelligence, understanding, sense, intellect

brake NOUN = control, check, curb, restraint, constraint, rein
• VERB = slow, decelerate, reduce speed

branch 1 = bough, shoot, arm, spray, limb, sprig, offshoot 2 = office, department, unit, wing, chapter, bureau 3 = division, part, section, subdivision, subsection 4 = discipline, section, subdivision

brand NOUN 1 = trademark 2 = label, mark, sign, stamp, symbol, logo, trademark, marker
• VERB 1 = stigmatize, mark, expose, denounce, disgrace, discredit, censure 2 = mark, burn, label, stamp, scar

brash = bold, rude, cocky, pushy (*informal*), brazen, impertinent, insolent, impudent ≠ timid

brave ADJECTIVE = courageous, daring, bold, heroic, adventurous, fearless, resolute, audacious ≠ timid
• VERB = confront, face, suffer, tackle, endure, defy, withstand, stand up to ≠ give in to

bravery = courage, nerve, daring, pluck, spirit, fortitude, heroism, mettle ≠ cowardice

brawl NOUN = fight, clash, fray, skirmish, scuffle, punch-up (*Brit. informal*), fracas, altercation, biffo (*Austral. slang*)
• VERB = fight, scrap (*informal*), wrestle, tussle, scuffle

breach 1 = nonobservance, abuse, violation, infringement, trespass, transgression, contravention, infraction ≠ compliance 2 = opening, crack, split, gap, rift, rupture, cleft, fissure

bread 1 = food, fare, kai (*N.Z. informal*), nourishment, sustenance 2 (*Slang*) = money, cash, dough (*slang*)

breadth 1 = width, spread, span, latitude, broadness, wideness 2 = extent, range, scale, scope, compass, expanse

break VERB 1 = shatter, separate, destroy, crack, snap, smash, crush, fragment ≠ repair 2 = fracture, crack, smash 3 = burst, tear, split 4 = disobey, breach, defy, violate, disregard, flout, infringe, contravene ≠ obey 5 = stop, cut, suspend, interrupt, cut short, discontinue 6 = disturb, interrupt 7 = end, stop, cut, drop, give up, abandon, suspend, interrupt 8 = weaken, undermine, tame, subdue, demoralize, dispirit 9 = be revealed, be published, be announced, be made public, be proclaimed, be let out 10 = reveal, tell, announce, declare, disclose, proclaim, make known 11 = beat, top, better, exceed, go beyond, excel, surpass, outstrip
• NOUN 1 = fracture, opening, tear, hole, split, crack, gap, fissure 2 = interval, pause, interlude, intermission 3 = holiday, leave, vacation, time off, recess, awayday 4 (*Informal*) = stroke of luck, chance, opportunity, advantage, fortune, opening
• PHRASES **break off** = stop talking, pause ◆ **break out** = begin, start, happen, occur, arise, set in, commence, spring up ◆ **break something off** = detach, separate, divide, cut off, pull off, sever, part, remove ◆ **break something up** = stop, end, suspend, dismantle, terminate, disband, diffuse ◆ **break up** 1 = finish, be

suspended, adjourn **2** = split up, separate, part, divorce
breakdown = collapse
break-in = burglary, robbery, breaking and entering
breakthrough = development, advance, progress, discovery, find, invention, step forward, leap forwards
breast = bosom(s), front, chest, bust
breath = inhalation, breathing, pant, gasp, gulp, wheeze, exhalation, respiration
breathe **1** = inhale and exhale, pant, gasp, puff, gulp, wheeze, respire, draw in breath **2** = whisper, sigh, murmur
breathless **1** = out of breath, panting, gasping, gulping, wheezing, short-winded **2** = excited, curious, eager, enthusiastic, impatient, on tenterhooks, in suspense
breathtaking = amazing, exciting, stunning (*informal*), impressive, thrilling, magnificent, astonishing, sensational
breed NOUN **1** = variety, race, stock, type, species, strain, pedigree **2** = kind, sort, type, variety, brand, stamp
• VERB **1** = rear, tend, keep, raise, maintain, farm, look after, care for **2** = reproduce, multiply, propagate, procreate, produce offspring, bear young, bring forth young **3** = produce, cause, create, generate, bring about, arouse, give rise to, stir up
breeding = refinement, culture, taste, manners, polish, courtesy, sophistication, cultivation
breeze NOUN = light wind, air, draught, gust, waft, zephyr, breath of wind, current of air
• VERB = sweep, move briskly, pass, sail, hurry, glide, flit
brew VERB **1** = boil, make, soak, steep, stew, infuse (*tea*) **2** = make, ferment **3** = start, develop, gather, foment **4** = develop, form, gather, foment
• NOUN = drink, preparation, mixture, blend, liquor, beverage, infusion, concoction
bribe NOUN = inducement, pay-off (*informal*), sweetener (*slang*), kickback (*U.S.*), backhander (*slang*), enticement, allurement
• VERB = buy off, reward, pay off (*informal*), corrupt, suborn, grease the palm *or* hand of (*slang*)
bribery = corruption, inducement, buying off, payola (*informal*), palm-greasing (*slang*)
bridge NOUN = arch, span, viaduct, flyover, overpass
• VERB **1** = span, cross **2** = reconcile, resolve
brief ADJECTIVE = short, quick, fleeting, swift, short-lived, momentary, ephemeral, transitory ≠ long
• VERB = inform, prime, prepare, advise, fill in (*informal*), instruct, put in the picture (*informal*), keep (someone) posted
• NOUN = summary, résumé, outline, sketch, abstract, digest, epitome, rundown
briefing **1** = conference, priming **2** = instructions, information, priming, directions, preparation, guidance, rundown
briefly **1** = quickly, shortly, hastily, momentarily, hurriedly **2** = in outline, in brief, in a nutshell, concisely
brigade **1** = corps, company, force, unit, division, troop, squad, team **2** = group, band, squad, organization
bright **1** = vivid, rich, brilliant, glowing, colourful **2** = shining, glowing, dazzling, gleaming, shimmering, radiant, luminous, lustrous **3** = intelligent, smart, clever, aware, sharp, enlightened, astute, wide-awake ≠ stupid **4** = clever, smart, ingenious **5** = sunny, clear, fair, pleasant, lucid, cloudless, unclouded ≠ cloudy
brighten **1** = light up, shine, glow, gleam, lighten ≠ dim **2** = enliven, animate, make brighter, vitalize **3** = become brighter, light up, glow, gleam
brilliance *or* **brilliancy** **1** = cleverness, talent, wisdom, distinction, genius, excellence, greatness, inventiveness ≠ stupidity **2** = brightness, intensity, sparkle, dazzle, lustre, radiance, luminosity, vividness ≠ darkness **3** = splendour, glamour, grandeur, magnificence, éclat, illustriousness
brilliant **1** = intelligent, sharp, intellectual, clever, profound, penetrating, inventive, perspicacious ≠ stupid **2** = expert, masterly, talented, gifted, accomplished ≠ untalented **3** = splendid, famous, celebrated, outstanding, superb, magnificent, glorious, notable **4** = bright, shining, intense, sparkling, glittering, dazzling, vivid, radiant ≠ dark
brim NOUN = rim, edge, border, lip, margin, verge, brink
• VERB **1** = be full, spill, well over, run over

2 = fill, well over, fill up, overflow

bring VERB 1 = fetch, take, carry, bear, transfer, deliver, transport, convey 2 = take, guide, conduct, escort 3 = cause, produce, create, effect, occasion, result in, contribute to, inflict
• PHRASES **bring someone up** = rear, raise, support, train, develop, teach, breed, foster ◆ **bring something about** = cause, produce, create, effect, achieve, generate, accomplish, give rise to ◆ **bring something off** = accomplish, achieve, perform, succeed, execute, pull off, carry off ◆ **bring something up** = mention, raise, introduce, point out, refer to, allude to, broach

brink = edge, limit, border, lip, margin, boundary, skirt, frontier

brisk 1 = quick, lively, energetic, active, vigorous, bustling, sprightly, spry ≠ slow 2 = short, brief, blunt, abrupt, terse, gruff, brusque, monosyllabic

briskly = quickly, smartly, promptly, rapidly, readily, actively, efficiently, energetically

bristle NOUN = hair, spine, thorn, whisker, barb, stubble, prickle
• VERB 1 = stand up, rise, stand on end 2 = be angry, rage, seethe, flare up, bridle, see red

brittle = fragile, delicate, crisp, crumbling, frail, crumbly, breakable, friable ≠ tough

broad 1 = wide, large, ample, generous, expansive 2 = large, huge, vast, extensive, ample, spacious, expansive, roomy ≠ narrow 3 = full, general, comprehensive, complete, wide, sweeping, wide-ranging, thorough 4 = universal, general, common, wide, sweeping, worldwide, widespread, wide-ranging 5 = general, loose, vague, approximate, indefinite, ill-defined, inexact, unspecific

broadcast NOUN = transmission, show, programme, telecast
• VERB 1 = transmit, show, air, radio, cable, beam, send out, relay 2 = make public, report, announce, publish, spread, advertise, proclaim, circulate

broaden = expand, increase, develop, spread, extend, stretch, swell, supplement ≠ restrict

brochure = booklet, advertisement, leaflet, hand-out, circular, pamphlet, folder, mailshot

broekies (*S. African informal*) = underpants, pants, briefs, drawers, knickers, panties, boxer shorts, Y-fronts®, underdaks (*Austral. slang*)

broke (*Informal*) = penniless, short, ruined, bust (*informal*), bankrupt, impoverished, in the red, insolvent ≠ rich

broken 1 = interrupted, incomplete, erratic, intermittent, fragmentary, spasmodic, discontinuous 2 = imperfect, halting, hesitating, stammering, disjointed 3 = smashed, burst, shattered, fragmented, fractured, severed, ruptured, separated 4 = defective, not working, imperfect, out of order, on the blink (*slang*), kaput (*informal*)

broker = dealer, agent, trader, supplier, merchant, negotiator, mediator, intermediary

bronze = reddish-brown, copper, tan, rust, chestnut, brownish

brood NOUN 1 = offspring, issue, clutch, litter, progeny 2 = children, family, nearest and dearest, flesh and blood, ainga (*N.Z.*)
• VERB = think, obsess, muse, ponder, agonize, mull over, mope, ruminate

brook = stream, burn (*Scot. & Northern English*), rivulet, beck, watercourse, rill

brother 1 = male sibling 2 = monk, cleric, friar, religious

RELATED WORD

adjective: fraternal

brotherly = fraternal, friendly, neighbourly, sympathetic, affectionate, benevolent, kind, amicable

brown ADJECTIVE 1 = brunette, bay, coffee, chocolate, chestnut, hazel, dun, auburn 2 = tanned, bronze, tan, sunburnt
• VERB = fry, cook, grill, sear, sauté

browse 1 = skim, scan, glance at, survey, look through, look round, dip into, leaf through 2 = graze, eat, feed, nibble

bruise NOUN = discoloration, mark, injury, blemish, contusion
• VERB 1 = hurt, injure, mark 2 = damage, mark, mar, discolour

brush[1] NOUN 1 = broom, sweeper, besom 2 = conflict, clash, confrontation, skirmish, tussle 3 = encounter, meeting, confrontation, rendezvous
• VERB 1 = clean, wash, polish, buff 2 = touch, sweep, kiss, stroke, glance, flick, scrape, graze
• PHRASES **brush someone off**

(*Slang*) = ignore, reject, dismiss, snub, disregard, scorn, disdain, spurn ◆ **brush something up** *or* **brush up on something** = revise, study, go over, cram, polish up, read up on, relearn, bone up on (*informal*)

brush² = shrubs, bushes, scrub, undergrowth, thicket, copse, brushwood

brutal 1 = cruel, savage, vicious, ruthless, callous, sadistic, heartless, inhuman ≠ kind **2** = harsh, tough, severe, rough, rude, indifferent, insensitive, callous ≠ sensitive

brutality = cruelty, atrocity, ferocity, savagery, ruthlessness, barbarism, inhumanity, viciousness

bubble NOUN = air ball, drop, bead, blister, blob, droplet, globule
• VERB **1** = boil, seethe **2** = foam, fizz, froth, percolate, effervesce **3** = gurgle, splash, murmur, trickle, ripple, babble, burble, lap

bubbly 1 = lively, happy, excited, animated, merry, bouncy, elated, sparky **2** = frothy, sparkling, fizzy, effervescent, carbonated, foamy

buckle NOUN = fastener, catch, clip, clasp, hasp
• VERB **1** = fasten, close, secure, hook, clasp **2** = distort, bend, warp, crumple, contort **3** = collapse, bend, twist, fold, give way, subside, cave in, crumple

bud NOUN = shoot, branch, sprout, sprig, offshoot
• VERB = develop, grow, shoot, sprout, burgeon, burst forth

budding = developing, beginning, growing, promising, potential, burgeoning, fledgling, embryonic

budge 1 = move, stir **2** = dislodge, move, push, transfer, shift, stir

budget NOUN = allowance, means, funds, income, finances, resources, allocation
• VERB = plan, estimate, allocate, cost, ration, apportion

buff¹ ADJECTIVE = fawn, tan, beige, yellowish, straw-coloured, sand-coloured, yellowish-brown
• VERB = polish, smooth, brush, shine, rub, wax, brighten, burnish

buff² (*Informal*) = expert, fan, addict, enthusiast, admirer, devotee, connoisseur, aficionado, fundi (*S. African*)

buffer = safeguard, screen, shield, cushion, intermediary, bulwark

buffet 1 = smorgasbord **2** = snack bar, café, cafeteria, brasserie, refreshment counter

bug NOUN **1** (*Informal*) = illness, disease, virus, infection, disorder, sickness, ailment, affliction **2** = fault, error, defect, flaw, glitch, gremlin
• VERB **1** = tap, eavesdrop, listen in on **2** (*Informal*) = annoy, bother, disturb, irritate, hassle (*informal*), pester, vex, get on your nerves (*informal*)

build VERB = construct, make, raise, put up, assemble, erect, fabricate, form ≠ demolish
• NOUN = physique, form, body, figure, shape, structure, frame

building = structure, house, construction, dwelling, erection, edifice, domicile

build-up = increase, development, growth, expansion, accumulation, enlargement, escalation

bulge VERB **1** = swell out, project, expand, stick out, protrude, puff out, distend **2** = stick out, stand out, protrude
• NOUN **1** = lump, swelling, bump, projection, hump, protuberance, protrusion ≠ hollow **2** = increase, rise, boost, surge, intensification

bulk 1 = size, volume, dimensions, magnitude, substance, immensity, largeness **2** = weight, size, mass, heaviness, poundage **3** = majority, mass, most, body, best part, lion's share, better part, preponderance

bullet = projectile, ball, shot, missile, slug, pellet

bulletin = report, account, statement, message, communication, announcement, dispatch, communiqué

bully NOUN = persecutor, tough, oppressor, tormentor, bully boy, browbeater, coercer, ruffian
• VERB **1** = persecute, intimidate, torment, oppress, pick on, victimize, terrorize, push around (*slang*) **2** = force, coerce, browbeat, hector, domineer

bump VERB **1** = knock, hit, strike, crash, smash, slam, bang **2** = jerk, shake, bounce, rattle, jog, lurch, jolt
• NOUN **1** = knock, blow, impact, collision, thump **2** = thud, crash, knock, bang, smack, thump **3** = lump, swelling, bulge, hump, nodule, protuberance, contusion

bumper = exceptional, excellent, exo (*Austral. slang*), massive, jumbo (*informal*),

abundant, whopping (*informal*), bountiful
bunch NOUN 1 = group, band, crowd, party, team, gathering, gang, flock 2 = bouquet, sheaf 3 = cluster, clump
• PHRASES **bunch together** *or* **up** = group, mass, collect, assemble, cluster, huddle
bundle NOUN = bunch, group, collection, mass, pile, stack, heap, batch
• VERB = push, thrust, shove, throw, rush, hurry, jostle, hustle
• PHRASES **bundle someone up** = wrap up, swathe
bungle = mess up, blow (*slang*), ruin, spoil, blunder, botch, make a mess of, muff, crool *or* cruel (*Austral. slang*) ≠ accomplish
bungling = incompetent, blundering, clumsy, inept, cack-handed (*informal*), maladroit, ham-fisted (*informal*), unco (*Austral. slang*)
bunk *or* **bunkum** (*Informal*) = nonsense, rubbish, garbage (*informal*), hot air (*informal*), twaddle, moonshine, baloney (*informal*), hogwash, bizzo (*Austral. slang*), bull's wool (*Austral. & N.Z. slang*), kak (*S. African taboo slang*)
buoy = float, guide, signal, marker, beacon
buoyant ADJECTIVE = cheerful, happy, upbeat (*informal*), carefree, jaunty, chirpy (*informal*), light-hearted ≠ gloomy
• ADJECTIVE = floating, light
burden NOUN 1 = trouble, worry, weight, responsibility, strain, affliction, onus, millstone 2 = load, weight, cargo, freight, consignment, encumbrance
• VERB = weigh down, worry, load, tax, bother, handicap, oppress, inconvenience
bureau 1 = agency 2 = office, department, section, branch, station, unit, division, subdivision 3 = desk, writing desk
bureaucracy 1 = government, officials, authorities, administration, the system, civil service, corridors of power 2 = red tape, regulations, officialdom
bureaucrat = official, officer, administrator, civil servant, public servant, functionary, mandarin
burglar = housebreaker, thief, robber, pilferer, filcher, cat burglar, sneak thief
burglary = breaking and entering, housebreaking, break-in
burial = funeral, interment, obsequies, entombment, exequies
burn 1 = be on fire, blaze, be ablaze, smoke, flame, glow, flare, go up in flames 2 = set on fire, light, ignite, kindle, incinerate 3 = scorch, toast, sear, char, singe 4 = be passionate, be aroused, be inflamed 5 = seethe, fume, be angry, simmer, smoulder
burning 1 = intense, passionate, eager, ardent, fervent, impassioned, vehement ≠ mild 2 = blazing, fiery, smouldering, glowing 3 = flashing, blazing, flaming, gleaming, fiery 4 = crucial, important, pressing, significant, essential, vital, critical, acute
burrow NOUN = hole, shelter, tunnel, den, lair, retreat
• VERB 1 = dig, tunnel, excavate 2 = delve, search, probe, ferret, rummage, forage, fossick (*Austral. & N.Z.*)
burst VERB 1 = explode, blow up, break, split, crack, shatter, puncture, rupture 2 = rush, run, break, break out, erupt, spout, gush forth 3 = barge, charge, rush, shove
• NOUN 1 = rush, surge, outbreak, outburst, spate, gush, torrent, spurt 2 = explosion, crack, blast, bang, discharge
• ADJECTIVE = ruptured, flat, punctured, split, rent
bury 1 = inter, lay to rest, entomb, consign to the grave, inhume ≠ dig up 2 = hide, cover, conceal, stash (*informal*), secrete, stow away ≠ uncover 3 = sink, embed, immerse, enfold 4 = forget
bush NOUN = shrub, plant, hedge, thicket, shrubbery
• PHRASES **the bush** = the wilds, brush, scrub, woodland, backwoods, scrubland
business 1 = trade, selling, industry, manufacturing, commerce, dealings 2 = establishment, company, firm, concern, organization, corporation, venture, enterprise 3 = profession, work, job, line, trade, career, function, employment 4 = matter, issue, subject, point, problem, responsibility, task, duty 5 = concern, affair
businessman = executive, director, manager, merchant, capitalist, administrator, entrepreneur, tycoon
bust[1] = bosom, breasts, chest, front
bust[2] (*Informal*) VERB 1 = break, smash, split, burst, shatter, fracture, rupture 2 = arrest, catch, raid
• PHRASES **go bust** = go bankrupt, fail, be

ruined, become insolvent
bustle VERB = hurry, rush, fuss, hasten, scuttle, scurry, scamper ≠ idle
• NOUN = activity, to-do, stir, excitement, fuss, flurry, commotion, ado ≠ inactivity
bustling = busy, full, crowded, active, lively, buzzing, humming, swarming
busy ADJECTIVE **1** = active, industrious, rushed off your feet ≠ idle **2** = occupied with, working, engaged in, on duty, employed in, hard at work ≠ unoccupied **3** = hectic, full, exacting, energetic
•PHRASES **busy yourself** = occupy yourself, be engrossed, immerse yourself, involve yourself, absorb yourself, employ yourself, engage yourself
but CONJUNCTION = however, still, yet, nevertheless
• PREPOSITION = except (for), save, bar, barring, excepting, excluding, with the exception of
• ADVERB = only, just, simply, merely
butcher NOUN = murderer, killer, slaughterer, slayer, destroyer, executioner, cut-throat, exterminator
• VERB **1** = slaughter, prepare, carve, cut up, dress, cut, clean, joint **2** = kill, slaughter, massacre, destroy, cut down, assassinate, slay, liquidate
butt[1] **1** = end, handle, shaft, stock, shank, hilt, haft **2** = stub, tip, leftover, fag end (*informal*)
butt[2] = target, victim, dupe, laughing stock, Aunt Sally
butt[3] VERB = knock, push, bump, thrust, ram, shove, poke, prod
•PHRASES **butt in** **1** = interfere, meddle, intrude, heckle, barge in (*informal*), stick your nose in, put your oar in **2** = interrupt, cut in, break in, chip in (*informal*)
butt[4] = cask, barrel
butterfly
RELATED WORDS
young: caterpillar, chrysalis *or* chrysalid
enthusiast: lepidopterist
buy VERB = purchase, get, pay for, obtain, acquire, invest in, shop for, procure ≠ sell
• NOUN = purchase, deal, bargain, acquisition, steal (*informal*), snip (*informal*), giveaway
by PREPOSITION **1** = through, through the agency of **2** = via, over, by way of **3** = near, past, along, close to, closest to, neighbouring, next to, beside
• ADVERB = nearby, close, handy, at hand, within reach
bypass **1** = get round, avoid **2** = go round, circumvent, depart from, deviate from, pass round, detour round ≠ cross

C

cab = taxi, minicab, taxicab, hackney carriage
cabin **1** = room, berth, quarters, compartment **2** = hut, shed, cottage, lodge, shack, chalet, shanty, whare (*N.Z.*)
cabinet **1** = cupboard, case, locker, dresser, closet, press, chiffonier **2** *often cap.* = council, committee, administration, ministry, assembly, board
cad (*Old-fashioned, informal*) = scoundrel (*slang*), rat (*informal*), bounder (*Brit. old-fashioned slang*), rotter (*slang, chiefly Brit.*), heel
café = snack bar, restaurant, cafeteria, coffee shop, brasserie, coffee bar, tearoom, lunchroom
cage = enclosure, pen, coop, hutch, pound
cake = block, bar, slab, lump, cube, loaf, mass
calculated = deliberate, planned, considered, intended, intentional, designed, aimed, purposeful ≠ unplanned
calculating = scheming, sharp, shrewd, cunning, sly, devious, manipulative, crafty ≠ direct
calculation **1** = computation, working out, reckoning, estimate, forecast, judgment, result, answer **2** = planning, intention, deliberation, foresight, contrivance, forethought, premeditation
calibre *or* (*U.S.*) **caliber** **1** = worth, quality, ability, talent, capacity, merit, distinction, stature **2** = standard, level, quality, grade **3** = diameter, bore, gauge, measure
call VERB **1** = name, entitle, dub, designate, term, style, label, describe as **2** = cry, shout,

scream, yell, whoop ≠ whisper **3** = phone, telephone, ring (up) (*informal*, *chiefly Brit.*) **4** = hail, summon **5** = summon, gather, rally, assemble, muster, convene ≠ dismiss **6** = waken, arouse, rouse
• **NOUN** **1** = visit **2** = request, order, demand, appeal, notice, command, invitation, plea **3** (usually used in a negative construction) = need, cause, reason, grounds, occasion, excuse, justification **4** = attraction, pull (*informal*), appeal, lure, allure, magnetism **5** = cry, shout, scream, yell, whoop ≠ whisper
• **PHRASES** **call for someone** = fetch, pick up, collect ♦ **call for something** **1** = demand, order, request, insist on, cry out for **2** = require, need, involve, demand, occasion, entail, necessitate

calling = profession, trade, career, mission, vocation, life's work

calm **ADJECTIVE** **1** = cool, relaxed, composed, sedate, collected, dispassionate, unemotional, self-possessed ≠ excited **2** = still, quiet, smooth, mild, serene, tranquil, balmy, windless ≠ rough
• **NOUN** **1** = peacefulness, peace, serenity **2** = stillness, peace, quiet, hush, serenity, tranquillity, repose, peacefulness **3** = peace, calmness ≠ disturbance
• **VERB** **1** = soothe, quiet, relax, appease, still, allay, assuage, quieten ≠ excite **2** = placate, hush, pacify, mollify ≠ aggravate

camouflage **NOUN** **1** = protective colouring **2** = disguise, cover, screen, blind, mask, cloak, masquerade, subterfuge
• **VERB** = disguise, cover, screen, hide, mask, conceal, obscure, veil ≠ reveal

camp[1] = camp site, tents, encampment, bivouac, camping ground

camp[2] (*Informal*) = affected, mannered, artificial, posturing, ostentatious, effeminate

campaign **1** = drive, appeal, movement, push (*informal*), offensive, crusade **2** = operation, drive, attack, movement, push, offensive, expedition, crusade

canal = waterway, channel, passage, conduit, duct, watercourse

cancel **VERB** **1** = call off, drop, forget about **2** = annul, abolish, repeal, abort, do away with, revoke, eliminate
• **PHRASES** **cancel something out** = counterbalance, offset, make up for, compensate for, neutralize, nullify, balance out

cancellation **1** = abandonment **2** = annulment, abolition, repeal, elimination, revocation

cancer **1** = growth, tumour, malignancy **2** = evil, corruption, sickness, pestilence

candidate = contender, competitor, applicant, nominee, entrant, claimant, contestant, runner

cannabis = marijuana, pot (*slang*), dope (*slang*), grass (*slang*), hemp, dagga (*S. African*)

cannon = gun, big gun, field gun, mortar

canon **1** = rule, standard, principle, regulation, formula, criterion, dictate, statute **2** = list, index, catalogue, roll

canopy = awning, covering, shade, sunshade

cap **1** (*Informal*) = beat, top, better, exceed, eclipse, surpass, transcend, outstrip **2** = top, crown **3** = complete, crown

capability = ability, means, power, potential, capacity, qualification(s), competence, proficiency ≠ inability

capable **1** = able ≠ incapable **2** = accomplished, qualified, talented, gifted, efficient, competent, proficient ≠ incompetent

capacity **1** = ability, facility, gift, genius, capability, aptitude, aptness, competence *or* competency **2** = size, room, range, space, volume, extent, dimensions, scope **3** = function, position, role, post, office

cape = headland, point, head, peninsula, promontory

capital **NOUN** = money, funds, investment(s), cash, finances, resources, assets, wealth
• **ADJECTIVE** (*Old-fashioned*) = first-rate, fine, excellent, superb

capitalism = private enterprise, free enterprise, private ownership, laissez faire *or* laisser faire

capsule **1** = pill, tablet, lozenge **2** (*Botany*) = pod, case, shell, vessel, sheath, receptacle, seed case

captain **1** = leader, boss, master, skipper, head, chief **2** = commander, skipper

captivate = charm, attract, fascinate, entrance, enchant, enthral, beguile, allure ≠ repel

captive **ADJECTIVE** = confined, caged,

imprisoned, locked up, enslaved, incarcerated, ensnared, subjugated
• NOUN = prisoner, hostage, convict, prisoner of war, detainee, internee

captivity = confinement, custody, detention, imprisonment, incarceration, internment

capture VERB = catch, arrest, take, bag, secure, seize, collar (*informal*), apprehend ≠ release
• NOUN = arrest, catching, trapping, imprisonment, seizure, apprehension, taking, taking captive

car 1 = vehicle, motor, wheels (*informal*), auto (*U.S.*), automobile, jalopy (*informal*), motorcar, machine 2 (*U.S. & Canad.*) = (railway) carriage, coach, cable car, dining car, sleeping car, buffet car, van

cardinal = principal, first, leading, chief, main, central, key, essential ≠ secondary

care VERB = be concerned, mind, bother, be interested, be bothered, give a damn, concern yourself
• NOUN 1 = custody, keeping, control, charge, management, protection, supervision, guardianship 2 = caution, attention, pains, consideration, heed, prudence, vigilance, forethought ≠ carelessness 3 = worry, concern, pressure, trouble, responsibility, stress, anxiety, disquiet ≠ pleasure
• PHRASES **care for someone** 1 = look after, mind, tend, attend, nurse, minister to, watch over 2 = love, desire, be fond of, want, prize ♦ **care for something** *or* **someone** = like, enjoy, take to, relish, be fond of, be keen on, be partial to ♦ **take care of** 1 = look after, mind, watch, protect, tend, nurse, care for, provide for 2 = deal with, manage, cope with, see to, handle

career NOUN = occupation, calling, employment, pursuit, vocation, livelihood, life's work
• VERB = rush, race, speed, tear, dash, barrel (along) (*informal*, (*chiefly U.S. & Canad.*), bolt, hurtle

careful 1 = cautious, scrupulous, circumspect, chary, thoughtful, discreet ≠ careless 2 = thorough, full, particular, precise, intensive, in-depth, meticulous, conscientious ≠ casual 3 = prudent, sparing, economical, canny, provident, frugal, thrifty

careless 1 = slapdash, irresponsible, sloppy (*informal*), cavalier, offhand, neglectful, slipshod, lackadaisical ≠ careful 2 = negligent, hasty, thoughtless, unthinking, forgetful, absent-minded, remiss ≠ careful 3 = nonchalant, casual, offhand, artless, unstudied ≠ careful

caretaker = warden, keeper, porter, superintendent, curator, custodian, watchman, janitor

cargo = load, goods, contents, shipment, freight, merchandise, baggage, consignment

caricature NOUN = parody, cartoon, distortion, satire, send-up (*Brit. informal*), travesty, takeoff (*informal*), lampoon
• VERB = parody, take off (*informal*), mock, distort, ridicule, mimic, send up (*Brit. informal*), lampoon

carnage = slaughter, murder, massacre, holocaust, havoc, bloodshed, shambles, mass murder

carnival = festival, fair, fête, celebration, gala, jubilee, jamboree, revelry

carol = song, hymn, Christmas song

carp = find fault, complain, criticize, reproach, quibble, cavil, pick holes ≠ praise

carpenter = joiner, cabinet-maker, woodworker

carriage 1 = vehicle, coach, trap, gig, cab, wagon, hackney, conveyance 2 = bearing, posture, gait, deportment, air

carry VERB 1 = convey, take, move, bring, bear, transfer, conduct, transport 2 = transport, take, transfer 3 = transmit, transfer, spread, pass on 4 = win, gain, secure, capture, accomplish
• PHRASES **carry on** 1 = continue, last, endure, persist, keep going, persevere 2 (*Informal*) = make a fuss, misbehave, create (*slang*), raise Cain ♦ **carry something on** = engage in, conduct, carry out, undertake, embark on, enter into ♦ **carry something out** = perform, effect, achieve, realize, implement, fulfil, accomplish, execute

carry-on (*Informal, chiefly Brit.*) = fuss, disturbance, racket, commotion

carton = box, case, pack, package, container

cartoon 1 = drawing, parody, satire, caricature, comic strip, takeoff (*informal*), lampoon, sketch 2 = animation, animated

film, animated cartoon
carve **1** = sculpt, cut, chip, whittle, chisel, hew, fashion **2** = etch, engrave
cascade NOUN = waterfall, falls, torrent, flood, shower, fountain, avalanche, deluge
• VERB = flow, fall, flood, pour, plunge, surge, spill, tumble
case[1] **1** = situation, event, circumstance(s), state, position, condition, context, contingency **2** = instance, example, occasion, specimen, occurrence **3** (*Law*) = lawsuit, trial, suit, proceedings, dispute, action
case[2] **1** = cabinet, box, chest, holder **2** = container, carton, canister, casket, receptacle **3** = suitcase, bag, grip, holdall, portmanteau, valise **4** = crate, box **5** = covering, casing, shell, jacket, envelope, capsule, sheath, wrapper
cash = money, funds, notes, currency, silver, brass (*Northern English dialect*), dough (*slang*), coinage
cast NOUN **1** = actors, company, players, characters, troupe, dramatis personae **2** = type, sort, kind, style, stamp
• VERB **1** = choose, name, pick, select, appoint, assign, allot **2** = bestow, give, level, direct **3** = give out, spread, deposit, shed, distribute, scatter, emit, radiate **4** = throw, launch, pitch, toss, thrust, hurl, fling, sling **5** = mould, set, found, form, model, shape
caste = class, order, rank, status, stratum, social order
castle = fortress, keep, palace, tower, chateau, stronghold, citadel
casual **1** = careless, relaxed, unconcerned, blasé, offhand, nonchalant, lackadaisical ≠ serious **2** = chance, unexpected, random, accidental, incidental ≠ planned **3** = informal, leisure, sporty, non-dressy ≠ formal
casualty **1** = fatality, death, loss, wounded **2** = victim, sufferer
cat = feline, pussy (*informal*), moggy (*slang*), puss (*informal*), ballarat (*Austral. informal*), tabby

RELATED WORDS
adjective: feline
male: tom
female: tabby
young: kitten

catalogue *or* (*U.S.*) **catalog** NOUN = list, record, schedule, index, register, directory, inventory, gazetteer
• VERB = list, file, index, register, classify, inventory, tabulate, alphabetize
catastrophe = disaster, tragedy, calamity, cataclysm, trouble, adversity, fiasco
catch VERB **1** = capture, arrest, trap, seize, snare, apprehend, ensnare, entrap ≠ free **2** = trap, capture, snare, ensnare, entrap **3** = seize, get, grab, snatch **4** = grab, take, grip, seize, grasp, clutch, lay hold of ≠ release **5** = discover, surprise, find out, expose, detect, catch in the act, take unawares **6** = contract, get, develop, suffer from, incur, succumb to, go down with ≠ escape
• NOUN **1** = fastener, clip, bolt, latch, clasp **2** (*Informal*) = drawback, trick, trap, disadvantage, hitch, snag, stumbling block, fly in the ointment ≠ advantage
• PHRASES **catch on** **1** (*Informal*) = understand, see, find out, grasp, see through, comprehend, twig (*Brit. informal*), get the picture **2** = become popular, take off, become trendy, come into fashion
catching = infectious, contagious, transferable, communicable, transmittable ≠ non-infectious
category = class, grouping, heading, sort, department, type, division, section
cater
• PHRASES **cater for something** *or* **someone** **1** = provide for, supply, purvey **2** = take into account, consider, bear in mind, make allowance for, have regard for
cattle = cows, stock, beasts, livestock, bovines

RELATED WORDS
adjective: bovine
collective nouns: drove, herd

cause NOUN **1** = origin, source, spring, agent, maker, producer, root, beginning ≠ result **2** = reason, call, need, grounds, basis, incentive, motive, motivation **3** = aim, movement, principle, ideal, enterprise
• VERB = produce, create, lead to, result in, generate, induce, bring about, give rise to ≠ prevent
caution NOUN **1** = care, discretion, heed, prudence, vigilance, alertness, forethought, circumspection ≠ carelessness **2** = reprimand, warning, injunction, admonition

• **VERB** 1 = warn, urge, advise, alert, tip off, forewarn 2 = reprimand, warn, admonish, give an injunction to
cautious = careful, guarded, wary, tentative, prudent, judicious, circumspect, cagey (*informal*) ≠ careless
cavalry = horsemen, horse, mounted troops ≠ infantrymen
cave = hollow, cavern, grotto, den, cavity
cavity = hollow, hole, gap, pit, dent, crater
cease 1 = stop, end, finish, come to an end ≠ start 2 = discontinue, end, stop, finish, conclude, halt, terminate, break off ≠ begin
celebrate 1 = rejoice, party, enjoy yourself, carouse, live it up (*informal*), make merry, put the flags out, kill the fatted calf 2 = commemorate, honour, observe, toast, drink to, keep 3 = perform, observe, preside over, officiate at, solemnize
celebrated = renowned, popular, famous, distinguished, well-known, prominent, acclaimed, notable ≠ unknown
celebration 1 = party, festival, gala, jubilee, festivity, revelry, red-letter day, merrymaking 2 = commemoration, honouring, remembrance 3 = performance, observance, solemnization
celebrity 1 = personality, star, superstar, big name, dignitary, luminary, big shot (*informal*), V.I.P. ≠ nobody 2 = fame, reputation, distinction, prestige, prominence, stardom, renown, repute ≠ obscurity
cell 1 = room, chamber, lock-up, compartment, cavity, cubicle, dungeon, stall 2 = unit, group, section, core, nucleus, caucus, coterie
cement **NOUN** 1 = mortar, plaster, paste 2 = sealant, glue, gum, adhesive
• **VERB** = stick, join, bond, attach, seal, glue, plaster, weld
cemetery = graveyard, churchyard, burial ground, necropolis, God's acre
censor = expurgate, cut, blue-pencil, bowdlerize
censure **VERB** = criticize, blame, condemn, denounce, rebuke, reprimand, reproach, scold ≠ applaud
• **NOUN** = disapproval, criticism, blame, condemnation, rebuke, reprimand, reproach, stick (*slang*) ≠ approval
central 1 = inner, middle, mid, interior ≠ outer 2 = main, chief, key, essential, primary, principal, fundamental, focal ≠ minor
centre **NOUN** = middle, heart, focus, core, nucleus, hub, pivot, kernel ≠ edge
• **VERB** = focus, concentrate, cluster, revolve, converge
ceremonial **ADJECTIVE** = formal, public, official, ritual, stately, solemn, liturgical, courtly ≠ informal
• **NOUN** = ritual, ceremony, rite, formality, solemnity
ceremony 1 = ritual, service, rite, observance, commemoration, solemnities 2 = formality, ceremonial, propriety, decorum
certain 1 = sure, convinced, positive, confident, satisfied, assured ≠ unsure 2 = bound, sure, fated, destined ≠ unlikely 3 = inevitable, unavoidable, inescapable 4 = known, true, positive, conclusive, unequivocal, undeniable, irrefutable, unquestionable ≠ doubtful 5 = fixed, decided, established, settled, definite ≠ indefinite
certainly = definitely, surely, truly, undoubtedly, without doubt, undeniably, indisputably, assuredly
certainty 1 = confidence, trust, faith, conviction, assurance, sureness, positiveness ≠ doubt 2 = inevitability ≠ uncertainty 3 = fact, truth, reality, sure thing (*informal*), banker
certificate = document, licence, warrant, voucher, diploma, testimonial, authorization, credential(s)
certify = confirm, declare, guarantee, assure, testify, verify, validate, attest
chain **NOUN** 1 = tether, coupling, link, bond, shackle, fetter, manacle 2 = series, set, train, string, sequence, succession, progression
• **VERB** = bind, confine, restrain, handcuff, shackle, tether, fetter, manacle
chairman *or* **chairwoman** 1 = director, president, chief, executive, chairperson 2 = master of ceremonies, spokesman, chair, speaker, MC, chairperson
challenge **NOUN** 1 = dare, provocation, wero (*N.Z.*) 2 = test, trial, opposition, confrontation, ultimatum
• **VERB** 1 = dispute, question, tackle,

confront, defy, object to, disagree with, take issue with **2** = dare, invite, defy, throw down the gauntlet **3** = test **4** = question, interrogate

chamber **1** = hall, room **2** = council, assembly, legislature, legislative body **3** = room, bedroom, apartment, enclosure, cubicle **4** = compartment

champion NOUN **1** = winner, hero, victor, conqueror, title holder **2** = defender, guardian, patron, backer, protector, upholder
• VERB = support, back, defend, promote, advocate, fight for, uphold, espouse

chance NOUN **1** = probability, odds, possibility, prospect, likelihood ≠ certainty **2** = opportunity, opening, occasion, time **3** = accident, fortune, luck, fate, destiny, coincidence, providence ≠ design **4** = risk, speculation, gamble, hazard
• VERB = risk, try, stake, venture, gamble, hazard, wager

change NOUN **1** = alteration, innovation, transformation, modification, mutation, metamorphosis, difference, revolution **2** = variety, break (*informal*), departure, variation, novelty, diversion ≠ monotony **3** = exchange, trade, conversion, swap, substitution, interchange
• VERB **1** = alter, reform, transform, adjust, revise, modify, reorganize, restyle ≠ keep **2** = shift, vary, transform, alter, modify, mutate ≠ stay **3** = exchange, trade, replace, substitute, swap, interchange

channel NOUN **1** = means, way, course, approach, medium, route, path, avenue **2** = strait, sound, route, passage, canal, waterway **3** = duct, artery, groove, gutter, furrow, conduit
• VERB = direct, guide, conduct, transmit, convey

chant NOUN = song, carol, chorus, melody, psalm
• VERB = sing, chorus, recite, intone, carol

chaos = disorder, confusion, mayhem, anarchy, lawlessness, pandemonium, bedlam, tumult ≠ orderliness

chaotic = disordered, confused, uncontrolled, anarchic, tumultuous, lawless, riotous, topsy-turvy

chap (*Informal*) = fellow, man, person, individual, character, guy (*informal*), bloke (*Brit. informal*)

chapter **1** = section, part, stage, division, episode, topic, segment, instalment **2** = period, time, stage, phase

character **1** = personality, nature, attributes, temperament, complexion, disposition **2** = nature, kind, quality, calibre **3** = reputation, honour, integrity, good name, rectitude **4** = role, part, persona **5** = eccentric, card (*informal*), original, oddball (*informal*) **6** = symbol, mark, sign, letter, figure, device, rune, hieroglyph

characteristic NOUN = feature, mark, quality, property, attribute, faculty, trait, quirk
• ADJECTIVE = typical, special, individual, representative, distinguishing, distinctive, peculiar, singular ≠ rare

characterize = distinguish, mark, identify, brand, stamp, typify

charge VERB **1** = accuse, indict, impeach, incriminate, arraign ≠ acquit **2** = attack, assault, assail ≠ retreat **3** = rush, storm, stampede **4** = fill, load
• NOUN **1** = price, rate, cost, amount, payment, expense, toll, expenditure **2** = accusation, allegation, indictment, imputation ≠ acquittal **3** = care, trust, responsibility, custody, safekeeping **4** = duty, office, responsibility, remit **5** = ward, pupil, protégé, dependant **6** = attack, rush, assault, onset, onslaught, stampede, sortie ≠ retreat

charisma = charm, appeal, personality, attraction, lure, allure, magnetism, force of personality

charismatic = charming, appealing, attractive, influential, magnetic, enticing, alluring

charitable **1** = benevolent, liberal, generous, lavish, philanthropic, bountiful, beneficent ≠ mean **2** = kind, understanding, forgiving, sympathetic, favourable, tolerant, indulgent, lenient ≠ unkind

charity **1** = charitable organization, fund, movement, trust, endowment **2** = donations, help, relief, gift, contributions, assistance, hand-out, philanthropy, koha (*N.Z.*) ≠ meanness **3** = kindness, humanity, goodwill, compassion, generosity, indulgence, altruism, benevolence, aroha (*N.Z.*) ≠ ill will

charm NOUN **1** = attraction, appeal,

fascination, allure, magnetism ≠ repulsiveness **2** = talisman, trinket, amulet, fetish **3** = spell, magic, enchantment, sorcery, makutu (*N.Z.*)
• VERB **1** = attract, delight, fascinate, entrance, win over, enchant, captivate, beguile ≠ repel **2** = persuade, seduce, coax, beguile, sweet-talk (*informal*)

charming = attractive, pleasing, appealing, fetching, delightful, cute, seductive, captivating ≠ unpleasant

chart NOUN = table, diagram, blueprint, graph, plan, map
• VERB **1** = plot, map out, delineate, sketch, draft, tabulate **2** = monitor, follow, record, note, document, register, trace, outline

charter NOUN **1** = document, contract, permit, licence, deed, prerogative **2** = constitution, laws, rules, code
• VERB **1** = hire, commission, employ, rent, lease **2** = authorize, permit, sanction, entitle, license, empower, give authority

chase VERB **1** = pursue, follow, track, hunt, run after, course **2** = drive away, drive, expel, hound, send away, send packing, put to flight **3** = rush, run, race, shoot, fly, speed, dash, bolt
• NOUN = pursuit, race, hunt, hunting

chat VERB = talk, gossip, jaw (*slang*), natter, blather, blether (*Scot.*)
• NOUN = talk, tête-à-tête, conversation, gossip, heart-to-heart, natter, blather, blether (*Scot.*), korero (*N.Z.*)

chatter VERB = prattle, chat, rabbit on (*Brit. informal*), babble, gab (*informal*), natter, blather, schmooze (*slang*)
• NOUN = prattle, chat, gossip, babble, gab (*informal*), natter, blather, blether (*Scot.*)

cheap **1** = inexpensive, reduced, keen, reasonable, bargain, low-priced, low-cost, cut-price ≠ expensive **2** = inferior, poor, worthless, second-rate, shoddy, tawdry, tatty, trashy, bodger *or* bodgie (*Austral. slang*) ≠ good **3** (*Informal*) = despicable, mean, contemptible, scungy (*Austral. & N.Z.*) ≠ decent

cheat VERB = deceive, trick, fool, con (*informal*), mislead, rip off (*slang*), fleece, defraud
• NOUN = deceiver, sharper, shark, charlatan, trickster, con man (*informal*), double-crosser (*informal*), swindler, rorter (*Austral. slang*)

check VERB **1** *often with* ***out*** = examine, test, study, look at, research, investigate, monitor, vet ≠ overlook **2** = stop, limit, delay, halt, restrain, inhibit, hinder, obstruct ≠ further
• NOUN **1** = examination, test, research, investigation, inspection, scrutiny, once-over (*informal*) **2** = control, limitation, restraint, constraint, obstacle, curb, obstruction, stoppage

cheek (*Informal*) = impudence, nerve, disrespect, audacity, lip (*slang*), temerity, chutzpah (*U.S. & Canad. informal*), insolence

cheeky = impudent, rude, forward, insulting, saucy, audacious, pert, disrespectful ≠ respectful

cheer VERB **1** = applaud, hail, acclaim, clap ≠ boo **2** = hearten, encourage, comfort, uplift, brighten, cheer up, buoy up, gladden ≠ dishearten
• NOUN = applause, ovation, plaudits, acclamation
• PHRASES **cheer someone up** = comfort, encourage, hearten, enliven, gladden, gee up, jolly along (*informal*)
◆ **cheer up** = take heart, rally, perk up, buck up (*informal*)

cheerful **1** = happy, optimistic, enthusiastic, jolly, merry, upbeat (*informal*), buoyant, cheery ≠ sad **2** = pleasant ≠ gloomy

chemical = compound, drug, substance, synthetic substance, potion

chemist = pharmacist, apothecary (*obsolete*), dispenser

cherish **1** = cling to, prize, treasure, hold dear, cleave to ≠ despise **2** = care for, love, support, comfort, look after, shelter, nurture, hold dear ≠ neglect **3** = harbour, nurse, sustain, foster, entertain

chest **1** = breast, front **2** = box, case, trunk, crate, coffer, casket, strongbox

RELATED WORD
adjective: pectoral

chew = munch, bite, grind, champ, crunch, gnaw, chomp, masticate

chic = stylish, smart, elegant, fashionable, trendy (*Brit. informal*) ≠ unfashionable

chief NOUN = head, leader, director, manager, boss (*informal*), captain, master, governor, baas (*S. African*), ariki (*N.Z.*) ≠ subordinate
• ADJECTIVE = primary, highest, leading, main, prime, key, premier, supreme

≠ minor

chiefly **1** = especially, essentially, principally, primarily, above all **2** = mainly, largely, usually, mostly, in general, on the whole, predominantly, in the main

child **1** = youngster, baby, kid (*informal*), infant, babe, juvenile, toddler, tot, littlie (*Austral. informal*), ankle-biter (*Austral. slang*), tacker (*Austral. slang*) **2** = offspring

RELATED WORDS
adjective: filial
prefix: paedo-

childbirth = child-bearing, labour, delivery, lying-in, confinement, parturition

childhood = youth, minority, infancy, schooldays, immaturity, boyhood *or* girlhood

childish **1** = youthful, young, boyish *or* girlish **2** = immature, juvenile, foolish, infantile, puerile ≠ mature

chill VERB **1** = cool, refrigerate, freeze **2** = dishearten, depress, discourage, dismay, dampen, deject
• NOUN **1** = coldness, bite, nip, sharpness, coolness, rawness, crispness, frigidity **2** = shiver, frisson
• ADJECTIVE = chilly, biting, sharp, freezing, raw, bleak, chilly, wintry

chilly **1** = cool, fresh, sharp, crisp, penetrating, brisk, draughty, nippy ≠ warm **2** = unfriendly, hostile, unsympathetic, frigid, unresponsive, unwelcoming ≠ friendly

china[1] = pottery, ceramics, ware, porcelain, crockery, tableware, service

china[2] (*Brit. & S. African informal*) = friend, pal, mate (*informal*), buddy (*informal*), companion, best friend, intimate, comrade, cobber (*Austral. & N.Z. old-fashioned informal*), E hoa (*N.Z.*)

chip NOUN **1** = fragment, shaving, wafer, sliver, shard **2** = scratch, nick, notch **3** = counter, disc, token
• VERB **1** = nick, damage, gash **2** = chisel, whittle

choice NOUN **1** = range, variety, selection, assortment **2** = selection, preference, pick **3** = option, say, alternative
• ADJECTIVE = best, prime, select, excellent, exclusive, elite, booshit (*Austral. slang*), exo (*Austral. slang*), sik (*Austral. slang*)

choke **1** = suffocate, stifle, smother, overpower, asphyxiate **2** = strangle, throttle, asphyxiate **3** = block, clog, obstruct, bung, constrict, congest, stop, bar

choose **1** = pick, prefer, select, elect, adopt, opt for, designate, settle upon ≠ reject **2** = wish, want

chop = cut, fell, hack, sever, cleave, hew, lop

chore = task, job, duty, burden, hassle (*informal*), errand

chorus NOUN **1** = refrain, response, strain, burden **2** = choir, singers, ensemble, vocalists, choristers
• PHRASES **in chorus** = in unison, as one, all together, in concert, in harmony, in accord, with one voice

christen **1** = baptize, name **2** = name, call, term, style, title, dub, designate

Christmas = festive season, Noël, Xmas (*informal*), Yule (*archaic*), Yuletide (*archaic*)

chronicle VERB = record, tell, report, enter, relate, register, recount, set down
• NOUN = record, story, history, account, register, journal, diary, narrative

chuck (*Informal*) **1** = throw, cast, pitch, toss, hurl, fling, sling, heave **2** *often with* ***away*** or ***out*** = throw out, dump (*informal*), scrap, get rid of, ditch (*slang*), dispose of, dispense with, jettison **3** = give up *or* over, leave, abandon, cease, resign from, pack in **4** (*Austral. & N.Z. informal*) = vomit, throw up (*informal*), spew, heave (*slang*), puke (*slang*), barf (*U.S. slang*), chunder (*slang, chiefly Austral.*)

chuckle = laugh, giggle, snigger, chortle, titter

chum (*Informal*) = friend, mate (*informal*), pal (*informal*), companion, comrade, crony, cobber (*Austral. & N.Z. old-fashioned informal*), E hoa (*N.Z.*)

chunk = piece, block, mass, portion, lump, slab, hunk, nugget

churn **1** = stir up, beat, disturb, swirl, agitate **2** = swirl, toss

cinema **1** = pictures, movies, picture-house, flicks (*slang*) **2** = films, pictures, movies, big screen (*informal*), motion pictures, silver screen

circle NOUN **1** = ring, disc, hoop, halo **2** = group, company, set, club, society, clique, coterie
• VERB **1** = go round, ring, surround, enclose, envelop, encircle, circumscribe, circumnavigate **2** = wheel, spiral

circuit **1** = course, tour, track, route,

journey **2** = racetrack, course, track, racecourse **3** = lap, tour, revolution, orbit

circular ADJECTIVE **1** = round, ring-shaped **2** = circuitous, cyclical, orbital
• NOUN = advertisement, notice, ad (*informal*), announcement, advert (*Brit. informal*), press release

circulate **1** = spread, issue, publish, broadcast, distribute, publicize, disseminate, promulgate **2** = flow, revolve, rotate, radiate

circulation **1** = distribution, currency, readership **2** = bloodstream, blood flow **3** = flow, circling, motion, rotation **4** = spread, distribution, transmission, dissemination

circumstance **1** *usually plural* = situation, condition, contingency, state of affairs, lie of the land **2** *usually plural* = detail, event, particular, respect **3** *usually plural* = situation, state, means, position, station, status **4** = chance, the times, accident, fortune, luck, fate, destiny, providence

cite = quote, name, advance, mention, extract, specify, allude to, enumerate

citizen = inhabitant, resident, dweller, denizen, subject, townsman
RELATED WORD
adjective: civil

city = town, metropolis, municipality, conurbation
RELATED WORD
adjective: civic

civic = public, municipal, communal, local

civil **1** = civic, political, domestic, municipal ≠ state **2** = polite, obliging, courteous, considerate, affable, well-mannered ≠ rude

civilization **1** = society, people, community, nation, polity **2** = culture, development, education, progress, enlightenment, sophistication, advancement, cultivation

civilize = cultivate, educate, refine, tame, enlighten, sophisticate

civilized **1** = cultured, educated, sophisticated, enlightened, humane ≠ primitive **2** = polite, mannerly, tolerant, gracious, courteous, well-behaved, well-mannered

claim VERB **1** = assert, insist, maintain, allege, uphold, profess **2** = demand, call for, ask for, insist on
• NOUN **1** = assertion, statement, allegation, declaration, pretension, affirmation, protestation **2** = demand, application, request, petition, call **3** = right, title, entitlement

clamour = noise, shouting, racket, outcry, din, uproar, commotion, hubbub

clamp NOUN = vice, press, grip, bracket, fastener
• VERB = fasten, fix, secure, brace, make fast

clan **1** = family, group, society, tribe, fraternity, brotherhood, ainga (*N.Z.*), ngai (*N.Z.*) **2** = group, set, circle, gang, faction, coterie, cabal

clap = applaud, cheer, acclaim ≠ boo

clarify = explain, interpret, illuminate, clear up, simplify, make plain, elucidate, throw *or* shed light on

clarity **1** = clearness, precision, simplicity, transparency, lucidity, straightforwardness ≠ obscurity **2** = transparency, clearness ≠ cloudiness

clash VERB **1** = conflict, grapple, wrangle, lock horns, cross swords, war, feud, quarrel **2** = disagree, conflict, vary, counter, differ, contradict, diverge, run counter to **3** = not go, jar, not match **4** = crash, bang, rattle, jar, clatter, jangle, clang, clank
• NOUN **1** = conflict, fight, brush, confrontation, collision, showdown (*informal*) **2** = disagreement, difference, argument, dispute, dissent, difference of opinion

clasp VERB = grasp, hold, press, grip, seize, squeeze, embrace, clutch
• NOUN **1** = grasp, hold, grip, embrace, hug **2** = fastening, catch, grip, hook, pin, clip, buckle, brooch

class NOUN **1** = group, set, division, rank **2** = type, set, sort, kind, category, genre
• VERB = classify, group, rate, rank, brand, label, grade, designate

classic ADJECTIVE **1** = typical, standard, model, regular, usual, ideal, characteristic, definitive, dinki-di (*Austral. informal*) **2** = masterly, best, finest, world-class, consummate, first-rate ≠ second-rate **3** = lasting, enduring, abiding, immortal, undying, ageless, deathless
• NOUN = standard, masterpiece, prototype, paradigm, exemplar, model

classification = categorization, grading, taxonomy, sorting, analysis, arrangement

classify = categorize, sort, rank, arrange,

grade, catalogue, pigeonhole, tabulate
classy (*Informal*) = high-class, exclusive, superior, elegant, stylish, posh (*informal*, *chiefly Brit.*), up-market, top-drawer
clause = section, condition, article, chapter, passage, part, paragraph
claw NOUN 1 = nail, talon 2 = pincer
• VERB = scratch, tear, dig, rip, scrape, maul, mangulate (*Austral. slang*), lacerate
clean ADJECTIVE 1 = hygienic, fresh, sterile, pure, purified, antiseptic, sterilized, uncontaminated ≠ contaminated 2 = spotless, fresh, immaculate, impeccable, flawless, unblemished, unsullied ≠ dirty 3 = moral, good, pure, decent, innocent, respectable, upright, honourable ≠ immoral 4 = complete, final, whole, total, perfect, entire, decisive, thorough
• VERB = cleanse, wash, scrub, rinse, launder, scour, purify, disinfect ≠ dirty
cleanse = purify, clear, purge 1 = absolve, clear, purge, purify 2 = clean, wash, scrub, rinse, scour
clear ADJECTIVE 1 = comprehensible, explicit, understandable ≠ confused 2 = distinct ≠ indistinct 3 = obvious, plain, apparent, evident, distinct, pronounced, manifest, blatant ≠ ambiguous 4 = certain, sure, convinced, positive, satisfied, resolved, definite, decided ≠ confused 5 = transparent, see-through, translucent, crystalline, glassy, limpid, pellucid ≠ opaque 6 = unobstructed, open, free, empty, unhindered, unimpeded ≠ blocked 7 = bright, fine, fair, shining, sunny, luminous, cloudless, light ≠ cloudy 8 = untroubled, clean, pure, innocent, immaculate, unblemished, untarnished
• VERB 1 = unblock, free, loosen, extricate, open, disentangle 2 = remove, clean, wipe, cleanse, tidy (up), sweep away 3 = brighten, break up, lighten 4 = pass over, jump, leap, vault, miss 5 = absolve, acquit, vindicate, exonerate ≠ blame
clear-cut = straightforward, specific, plain, precise, black-and-white, explicit, definite, unequivocal
clearly 1 = obviously, undoubtedly, evidently, distinctly, markedly, overtly, undeniably, beyond doubt 2 = legibly, distinctly 3 = audibly, distinctly, intelligibly, comprehensibly
clergy = priesthood, ministry, clerics, clergymen, churchmen, the cloth, holy orders
clever 1 = intelligent, bright, talented, gifted, smart, knowledgeable, quick-witted ≠ stupid 2 = shrewd, bright, ingenious, resourceful, canny ≠ unimaginative 3 = skilful, talented, gifted ≠ inept
cliché = platitude, stereotype, commonplace, banality, truism, hackneyed phrase
client = customer, consumer, buyer, patron, shopper, patient
cliff = rock face, overhang, crag, precipice, escarpment, scar, bluff
climate = weather, temperature
climax = culmination, top, summit, height, highlight, peak, high point, zenith
climb VERB 1 = ascend, scale, mount, go up, clamber, shin up 2 = clamber, descend, scramble, dismount 3 = rise, go up, soar, ascend, fly up
• PHRASES **climb down** = back down, withdraw, yield, concede, retreat, surrender, give in, cave in (*informal*)
clinch 1 = secure, close, confirm, conclude, seal, sew up (*informal*), set the seal on 2 = settle, decide, determine
cling 1 = clutch, grip, embrace, grasp, hug, hold on to, clasp 2 = stick to, adhere to
clinical = unemotional, cold, scientific, objective, detached, analytic, impersonal, dispassionate
clip[1] VERB 1 = trim, cut, crop, prune, shorten, shear, snip, pare 2 (*Informal*) = smack, strike, knock, punch, thump, clout (*informal*), cuff, whack
• NOUN (*Informal*) = smack, strike, knock, punch, thump, clout (*informal*), cuff, whack
clip[2] = attach, fix, secure, connect, pin, staple, fasten, hold
cloak NOUN 1 = cape, coat, wrap, mantle 2 = covering, layer, blanket, shroud
• VERB 1 = cover, coat, wrap, blanket, shroud, envelop 2 = hide, cover, screen, mask, disguise, conceal, obscure, veil
clog = obstruct, block, jam, hinder, impede, congest
close[1] VERB 1 = shut, lock, fasten, secure ≠ open 2 = shut down, finish, cease 3 = wind up, finish, shut down, terminate 4 = block up, bar, seal ≠ open 5 = end, finish, complete, conclude, wind up,

terminate ≠ begin **6** = clinch, confirm, secure, conclude, seal, sew up (*informal*), set the seal on **7** = come together, join, connect ≠ separate
• NOUN = end, ending, finish, conclusion, completion, finale, culmination, denouement

close² **1** = near, neighbouring, nearby, handy, adjacent, adjoining, cheek by jowl ≠ far **2** = intimate, loving, familiar, thick (*informal*), attached, devoted, confidential, inseparable ≠ distant **3** = noticeable, marked, strong, distinct, pronounced **4** = careful, detailed, intense, minute, thorough, rigorous, painstaking **5** = even, level, neck and neck, fifty-fifty (*informal*), evenly matched **6** = imminent, near, impending, at hand, nigh ≠ far away **7** = stifling, oppressive, suffocating, stuffy, humid, sweltering, airless, muggy ≠ airy

closed **1** = shut, locked, sealed, fastened ≠ open **2** = shut down, out of service **3** = exclusive, select, restricted **4** = finished, over, ended, decided, settled, concluded, resolved, terminated

cloth = fabric, material, textiles

clothe = dress, array, robe, drape, swathe, attire, fit out, garb ≠ undress

clothes = clothing, wear, dress, gear (*informal*), outfit, costume, wardrobe, garments

clothing = clothes, wear, dress, gear (*informal*), outfit, costume, wardrobe, garments

cloud NOUN = mist, haze, vapour, murk, gloom
• VERB **1** = confuse, distort, impair, muddle, disorient **2** = darken, dim, be overshadowed

clout (*Informal*) VERB = hit, strike, punch, slap, sock (*slang*), smack, thump, clobber (*slang*)
• NOUN **1** = thump, blow, punch, slap, sock (*slang*), wallop (*informal*) **2** = influence, power, authority, pull, weight, prestige, mana (*N.Z.*)

clown NOUN **1** = comedian, fool, comic, harlequin, joker, jester, prankster, buffoon **2** = fool, idiot, twit (*informal, chiefly Brit.*), imbecile (*informal*), ignoramus, dolt, blockhead, dorba *or* dorb (*Austral. slang*), bogan (*Austral. slang*)
• VERB *usually with* ***around*** = play the fool, mess about, jest, act the fool

club NOUN **1** = association, company, group, union, society, lodge, guild, fraternity **2** = stick, bat, bludgeon, truncheon, cosh (*Brit.*), cudgel
• VERB = beat, strike, hammer, batter, bash, bludgeon, pummel, cosh (*Brit.*)

clue = indication, lead, sign, evidence, suggestion, trace, hint, suspicion

clump NOUN = cluster, group, bunch, bundle
• VERB = stomp, thump, lumber, tramp, plod, thud

clumsy = awkward, lumbering, bumbling, ponderous, ungainly, gauche, gawky, uncoordinated, unco (*Austral. slang*) ≠ skilful

cluster NOUN = gathering, group, collection, bunch, knot, clump, assemblage
• VERB = gather, group, collect, bunch, assemble, flock, huddle

clutch VERB **1** = hold, grip, embrace, grasp, cling to, clasp **2** = seize, catch, grab, grasp, snatch
• PLURAL NOUN = power, hands, control, grip, possession, grasp, custody, sway

clutter NOUN = untidiness, mess, disorder, confusion, litter, muddle, disarray, jumble ≠ order
• VERB = litter, scatter, strew, mess up ≠ tidy

coach NOUN **1** = instructor, teacher, trainer, tutor, handler **2** = bus, charabanc
• VERB = instruct, train, prepare, exercise, drill, tutor

coalition = alliance, union, association, combination, merger, conjunction, bloc, confederation

coarse **1** = rough, crude, unfinished, homespun, impure, unrefined, unprocessed, unpolished ≠ smooth **2** = vulgar, rude, indecent, improper, earthy, smutty, ribald, indelicate

coast NOUN = shore, border, beach, seaside, coastline, seaboard
• VERB = cruise, sail, drift, taxi, glide, freewheel

coat NOUN **1** = fur, hair, skin, hide, wool, fleece, pelt **2** = layer, covering, coating, overlay
• VERB = cover, spread, plaster, smear

coax = persuade, cajole, talk into, wheedle, sweet-talk (*informal*), prevail upon, entice, allure ≠ bully

cobber (*Austral. & N.Z. old-fashioned informal*) = friend, pal, mate (*informal*), buddy (*informal*), china (*Brit. & S. African informal*), best friend, intimate, comrade, E hoa (*N.Z.*)

cocktail = mixture, combination, compound, blend, mix

cocky *or* **cockie** (*Austral. & N.Z. informal*) = farmer, smallholder, crofter (*Scot.*), grazier, agriculturalist, rancher

code **1** = principles, rules, manners, custom, convention, ethics, maxim, etiquette, kawa (*N.Z.*), tikanga (*N.Z.*) **2** = cipher, cryptograph

coherent **1** = consistent, reasoned, organized, rational, logical, meaningful, systematic, orderly ≠ inconsistent **2** = articulate, lucid, comprehensible, intelligible ≠ unintelligible

coil **1** = wind, twist, curl, loop, spiral, twine **2** = curl, wind, twist, snake, loop, twine, wreathe

coin NOUN = money, change, cash, silver, copper, specie
• VERB = invent, create, make up, forge, originate, fabricate

coincide **1** = occur simultaneously, coexist, synchronize, be concurrent **2** = agree, match, accord, square, correspond, tally, concur, harmonize ≠ disagree

coincidence = chance, accident, luck, fluke, stroke of luck, happy accident

cold ADJECTIVE **1** = chilly, freezing, bleak, arctic, icy, frosty, wintry, frigid ≠ hot **2** = distant, reserved, indifferent, aloof, frigid, undemonstrative, standoffish ≠ emotional **3** = unfriendly, indifferent, frigid ≠ friendly
• NOUN = coldness, chill, frigidity, frostiness, iciness

collaborate **1** = work together, team up, join forces, cooperate, play ball (*informal*), participate **2** = conspire, cooperate, collude, fraternize

collaboration **1** = teamwork, partnership, cooperation, association, alliance **2** = conspiring, cooperation, collusion, fraternization

collaborator **1** = co-worker, partner, colleague, associate, team-mate, confederate **2** = traitor, turncoat, quisling, fraternizer

collapse VERB **1** = fall down, fall, give way, subside, cave in, crumple, fall apart at the seams **2** = fail, fold, founder, break down, fall through, come to nothing, go belly-up (*informal*)
• NOUN **1** = falling down, ruin, falling apart, cave-in, disintegration, subsidence **2** = failure, slump, breakdown, flop, downfall **3** = faint, breakdown, blackout, prostration

collar (*Informal*) = seize, catch, arrest, grab, capture, nail (*informal*), nab (*informal*), apprehend

colleague = fellow worker, partner, ally, associate, assistant, team-mate, comrade, helper

collect **1** = gather, save, assemble, heap, accumulate, amass, stockpile, hoard ≠ scatter **2** = assemble, meet, rally, cluster, come together, convene, converge, congregate ≠ disperse

collected = calm, cool, composed, poised, serene, unperturbed, unruffled, self-possessed ≠ nervous

collection **1** = accumulation, set, store, mass, pile, heap, stockpile, hoard **2** = compilation, accumulation, anthology **3** = group, company, crowd, assembly, cluster, assortment **4** = gathering **5** = contribution, donation, alms **6** = offering, offertory

collective **1** = joint, united, shared, combined, corporate, unified ≠ individual **2** = combined, aggregate, composite, cumulative ≠ separate

collide **1** = crash, clash, meet head-on, come into collision **2** = conflict, clash, be incompatible, be at variance

collision **1** = crash, impact, accident, smash, bump, pile-up (*informal*), prang (*informal*) **2** = conflict, opposition, clash, encounter, disagreement, incompatibility

colony = settlement, territory, province, possession, dependency, outpost, dominion, satellite state

colour *or* (*U.S.*) **color** NOUN **1** = hue, tone, shade, tint, colourway **2** = paint, stain, dye, tint, pigment, colorant
• VERB = blush, flush, redden

colourful **1** = bright, brilliant, psychedelic, variegated, multicoloured ≠ drab **2** = interesting, rich, graphic, lively, distinctive, vivid, picturesque ≠ boring

column 1 = pillar, support, post, shaft, upright, obelisk 2 = line, row, file, rank, procession, cavalcade

coma = unconsciousness, trance, oblivion, stupor

comb 1 = untangle, arrange, groom, dress 2 = search, hunt through, rake, sift, scour, rummage, ransack, forage, fossick (*Austral. & N.Z.*)

combat NOUN = fight, war, action, battle, conflict, engagement, warfare, skirmish ≠ peace
• VERB = fight, oppose, resist, defy, withstand, do battle with ≠ support

combination 1 = mixture, mix, blend, composite, amalgamation, coalescence 2 = association, union, alliance, coalition, federation, consortium, syndicate, confederation

combine 1 = amalgamate, mix, blend, integrate, merge ≠ separate 2 = join together, link, connect, integrate, merge, amalgamate 3 = unite, associate, team up, get together, collaborate, join forces, join together, pool resources ≠ split up

come VERB 1 = approach, near, advance, move towards, draw near 2 = arrive, turn up (*informal*), show up (*informal*) 3 = reach, extend, come up to, come as far as 4 = happen, fall, occur, take place, come about, come to pass 5 = be available, be made, be offered, be produced, be on offer
• PHRASES **come across as something** *or* **someone** = seem, look, seem to be, appear to be, give the impression of being ♦ **come across someone** = meet, encounter, run into, bump into (*informal*) ♦ **come across something** = find, discover, notice, unearth, stumble upon, chance upon = be obtained, be from, issue, emerge, flow, arise, originate, emanate

comeback 1 (*Informal*) = return, revival, rebound, resurgence, rally, recovery, triumph 2 = response, reply, retort, retaliation, riposte, rejoinder

comedian = comic, wit, clown, funny man, humorist, wag, joker, jester, dag (*N.Z. informal*)

comedy 1 = light entertainment ≠ tragedy, soapie (*Austral. slang*) 2 = humour, fun, joking, farce, jesting, hilarity ≠ seriousness

comfort NOUN 1 = ease, luxury, wellbeing, opulence 2 = consolation, succour, help, support, relief, compensation ≠ annoyance
• VERB = console, reassure, soothe, hearten, commiserate with ≠ distress

comfortable 1 = pleasant, homely, relaxing, cosy, agreeable, restful ≠ unpleasant 2 = at ease, happy, at home, contented, relaxed, serene ≠ uncomfortable 3 (*Informal*) = well-off, prosperous, affluent, well-to-do, comfortably-off, in clover (*informal*)

comforting = consoling, encouraging, cheering, reassuring, soothing, heart-warming ≠ upsetting

comic ADJECTIVE = funny, amusing, witty, humorous, farcical, comical, droll, jocular ≠ sad
• NOUN = comedian, funny man, humorist, wit, clown, wag, jester, dag (*N.Z. informal*), buffoon

coming ADJECTIVE = approaching, near, forthcoming, imminent, in store, impending, at hand, nigh
• NOUN = arrival, approach, advent

command VERB 1 = order, tell, charge, demand, require, direct, bid, compel ≠ beg 2 = have authority over, lead, head, control, rule, manage, handle, dominate ≠ be subordinate to
• NOUN 1 = order, demand, instruction, requirement, decree, directive, ultimatum, commandment 2 = domination, control, rule, mastery, power, government 3 = management, power, control, charge, authority, supervision

commander = leader, chief, officer, boss, head, captain, bass (*S. African*), ruler

commanding = dominant, controlling, dominating, superior, decisive, advantageous

commemorate = celebrate, remember, honour, recognize, salute, pay tribute to, immortalize ≠ ignore

commence 1 = embark on, start, open, begin, initiate, originate, instigate, enter upon ≠ stop 2 = start, open, begin, go ahead ≠ end

commend 1 = praise, acclaim, applaud, compliment, extol, approve, speak highly of ≠ criticize 2 = recommend, suggest, approve, advocate, endorse

comment VERB 1 = remark, say, note,

mention, point out, observe, utter **2** *usually with* ***on*** = remark on, explain, talk about, discuss, speak about, say something about, allude to, elucidate • NOUN **1** = remark, statement, observation **2** = note, explanation, illustration, commentary, exposition, annotation, elucidation

commentary 1 = narration, report, review, explanation, description, voice-over **2** = analysis, notes, review, critique, treatise

commentator 1 = reporter, special correspondent, sportscaster **2** = critic, interpreter, annotator

commercial 1 = mercantile, trading **2** = materialistic, mercenary, profit-making

commission VERB = appoint, order, contract, select, engage, delegate, nominate, authorize • NOUN **1** = duty, task, mission, mandate, errand **2** = fee, cut, percentage, royalties, rake-off (*slang*) **3** = committee, board, representatives, commissioners, delegation, deputation

commit 1 = do, perform, carry out, execute, enact, perpetrate **2** = put in custody, confine, imprison ≠ release

commitment 1 = dedication, loyalty, devotion ≠ indecisiveness **2** = responsibility, tie, duty, obligation, liability, engagement

common 1 = usual, standard, regular, ordinary, familiar, conventional, routine, frequent ≠ rare **2** = popular, general, accepted, standard, routine, widespread, universal, prevailing **3** = shared, collective **4** = ordinary, average, typical, dinki-di (*Austral. informal*) ≠ important **5** = vulgar, inferior, coarse, plebeian ≠ refined **6** = collective, public, community, social, communal ≠ personal

commonplace ADJECTIVE = everyday, common, ordinary, widespread, mundane, banal, run-of-the-mill, humdrum ≠ rare • NOUN = cliché, platitude, banality, truism

common sense = good sense, sound judgment, level-headedness, prudence, gumption (*Brit. informal*), horse sense, native intelligence, wit

communal = public, shared, general, joint, collective ≠ private

commune = community, collective, cooperative, kibbutz

communicate 1 = contact, talk, speak, make contact, get in contact **2** = make known, declare, disclose, pass on, proclaim, transmit, convey, impart ≠ keep secret **3** = pass on, transfer, spread, transmit

communication 1 = contact, conversation, correspondence, link, relations **2** = passing on, circulation, transmission, disclosure, imparting, dissemination, conveyance **3** = message, news, report, word, information, statement, announcement, disclosure

communism *usually cap.* = socialism, Marxism, collectivism, Bolshevism, state socialism

communist *often cap.* = socialist, Red (*informal*), Marxist, Bolshevik, collectivist

community = society, people, public, residents, commonwealth, general public, populace, state

commuter = daily traveller, passenger, suburbanite

compact[1] ADJECTIVE **1** = closely packed, solid, thick, dense, compressed, condensed, pressed together ≠ loose **2** = concise, brief, to the point, succinct, terse ≠ lengthy • VERB = pack closely, stuff, cram, compress, condense, tamp ≠ loosen

compact[2] = agreement, deal, understanding, contract, bond, arrangement, treaty, bargain

companion 1 = friend, partner, ally, colleague, associate, mate (*informal*), comrade, accomplice, cobber (*Austral. & N.Z. old-fashioned informal*) **2** = assistant, aide, escort, attendant

company 1 = business, firm, association, corporation, partnership, establishment, syndicate, house **2** = group, set, community, band, crowd, collection, gathering, assembly **3** = troop, unit, squad, team **4** = companionship, society, presence, fellowship **5** = guests, party, visitors, callers

comparable 1 = equal, equivalent, on a par, tantamount, a match for, proportionate, commensurate, as good as ≠ unequal **2** = similar, related, alike, corresponding, akin, analogous, of a piece, cognate

comparative = relative, qualified, by comparison
compare VERB = contrast, balance, weigh, set against, juxtapose
• PHRASES **compare to something** = liken to, parallel, identify with, equate to, correlate to, mention in the same breath as ◆ **compare with something** = be as good as, match, approach, equal, compete with, be on a par with, be the equal of, hold a candle to
comparison 1 = contrast, distinction, differentiation, juxtaposition 2 = similarity, analogy, resemblance, correlation, likeness, comparability
compartment 1 = section, carriage, berth 2 = bay, booth, locker, niche, cubicle, alcove, pigeonhole, cubbyhole
compass = range, field, area, reach, scope, limit, extent, boundary
compassion = sympathy, understanding, pity, humanity, mercy, sorrow, kindness, tenderness, aroha (*N.Z.*) ≠ indifference
compassionate = sympathetic, understanding, pitying, humanitarian, charitable, humane, benevolent, merciful ≠ uncaring
compatible 1 = consistent, in keeping, congruous ≠ inappropriate 2 = like-minded, harmonious, in harmony ≠ incompatible
compel = force, make, railroad (*informal*), oblige, constrain, coerce, impel, dragoon
compelling 1 = convincing, telling, powerful, forceful, conclusive, weighty, cogent, irrefutable 2 = pressing, binding, urgent, overriding, imperative, unavoidable, coercive, peremptory 3 = fascinating, gripping, irresistible, enchanting, enthralling, hypnotic, spellbinding, mesmeric ≠ boring
compensate 1 = recompense, repay, refund, reimburse, remunerate, make good 2 = make amends, make up for, atone, make it up to someone, pay for, do penance, cancel out, make reparation 3 = balance, cancel (out), offset, make up for, redress, counteract, counterbalance
compensation 1 = reparation, damages, recompense, remuneration, restitution, reimbursement 2 = recompense, amends, reparation, restitution, atonement
compete 1 = contend, fight, vie, challenge, struggle, contest, strive 2 = take part, participate, be in the running, be a competitor, be a contestant, play
competence 1 = ability, skill, talent, capacity, expertise, proficiency, capability ≠ incompetence 2 = fitness, suitability, adequacy, appropriateness ≠ inadequacy
competent 1 = able, skilled, capable, proficient ≠ incompetent 2 = fit, qualified, suitable, adequate ≠ unqualified
competition 1 = rivalry, opposition, struggle, strife 2 = opposition, field, rivals, challengers 3 = contest, event, championship, tournament, head-to-head
competitive 1 = cut-throat, aggressive, fierce, ruthless, relentless, antagonistic, dog-eat-dog 2 = ambitious, pushing, opposing, aggressive, vying, contentious, combative
competitor 1 = rival, adversary, antagonist 2 = contestant, participant, contender, challenger, entrant, player, opponent
compilation = collection, treasury, accumulation, anthology, assortment, assemblage
compile = put together, collect, gather, organize, accumulate, marshal, garner, amass
complacency = smugness, satisfaction, contentment, self-congratulation, self-satisfaction
complacent = smug, self-satisfied, pleased with yourself, resting on your laurels, contented, satisfied, serene, unconcerned ≠ insecure
complain = find fault, moan, grumble, whinge (*informal*), carp, groan, lament, whine
complaint 1 = protest, objection, grievance, charge 2 = grumble, criticism, moan, lament, grievance, grouse, gripe (*informal*) 3 = disorder, problem, disease, upset, illness, sickness, ailment, affliction
complement VERB = enhance, complete, improve, boost, crown, add to, set off, heighten
• NOUN 1 = accompaniment, companion, accessory, completion, finishing touch, rounding-off, adjunct, supplement 2 = total, capacity, quota, aggregate, contingent, entirety
complementary = matching,

companion, corresponding, compatible, reciprocal, interrelating, interdependent, harmonizing ≠ incompatible

complete ADJECTIVE 1 = total, perfect, absolute, utter, outright, thorough, consummate, out-and-out 2 = whole, full, entire ≠ partial 3 = entire, full, whole, intact, unbroken, faultless ≠ incomplete 4 = unabridged, full, entire 5 = finished, done, ended, achieved, concluded, fulfilled, accomplished ≠ unfinished 6 = perfect, finish off, round off, crown ≠ spoil
• VERB 1 = finish, conclude, end, close, settle, wrap up (*informal*), finalize ≠ start 2 = fill in, fill out

completely = totally, entirely, wholly, utterly, perfectly, fully, absolutely, altogether

completion = finishing, end, close, conclusion, fulfilment, culmination, fruition

complex ADJECTIVE 1 = compound, multiple, composite, manifold, heterogeneous, multifarious 2 = complicated, difficult, involved, elaborate, tangled, intricate, tortuous, convoluted ≠ simple
• NOUN 1 = structure, system, scheme, network, organization, aggregate, composite 2 (*Informal*) = obsession, preoccupation, phobia, fixation, fixed idea, idée fixe (*French*)

complexion 1 = skin, colour, colouring, hue, skin tone, pigmentation 2 = nature, character, make-up 3 = perspective, look, light, appearance, aspect, angle, slant

complexity = complication, involvement, intricacy, entanglement

complicate = make difficult, confuse, muddle, entangle, involve ≠ simplify

complicated 1 = involved, difficult, puzzling, troublesome, problematic, perplexing ≠ simple 2 = complex, involved, elaborate, intricate, convoluted, labyrinthine ≠ understandable

complication 1 = problem, difficulty, obstacle, drawback, snag, uphill (*S. African*) 2 = complexity, web, confusion, intricacy, entanglement

compliment NOUN = praise, honour, tribute, bouquet, flattery, eulogy ≠ criticism
• PLURAL NOUN 1 = greetings, regards, respects, good wishes, salutation ≠ insult 2 = congratulations, praise, commendation
• VERB = praise, flatter, salute, congratulate, pay tribute to, commend, extol, wax lyrical about ≠ criticize

complimentary 1 = flattering, approving, appreciative, congratulatory, commendatory ≠ critical 2 = free, donated, courtesy, honorary, on the house, gratuitous, gratis

comply = obey, follow, observe, submit to, conform to, adhere to, abide by, acquiesce with ≠ defy

component NOUN = part, piece, unit, item, element, ingredient, constituent
• ADJECTIVE = constituent, inherent, intrinsic

compose VERB 1 = put together, make up, constitute, comprise, make, build, form, fashion ≠ destroy 2 = create, write, produce, invent, devise, contrive 3 = arrange, make up, construct, put together, order, organize
• PHRASES **compose yourself** = calm, control, collect, quiet, soothe, pull yourself together

composed = calm, cool, collected, relaxed, poised, at ease, serene, sedate ≠ agitated

composition 1 = design, structure, make-up, organization, arrangement, formation, layout, configuration 2 = creation, work, piece, production, opus, masterpiece 3 = essay, exercise, treatise, literary work 4 = production, creation, making, fashioning, formation, putting together, compilation, formulation

compound NOUN = combination, mixture, blend, composite, fusion, synthesis, alloy, medley ≠ element
• ADJECTIVE = complex, multiple, composite, intricate ≠ simple
• VERB 1 = intensify, add to, complicate, worsen, heighten, exacerbate, aggravate, magnify ≠ lessen 2 = combine, unite, mix, blend, synthesize, amalgamate, intermingle ≠ divide

comprehend = understand, see, take in, perceive, grasp, conceive, make out, fathom ≠ misunderstand

comprehension = understanding,

grasp, conception, realization, intelligence, perception, discernment ≠ incomprehension

comprehensive = broad, full, complete, blanket, thorough, inclusive, exhaustive, all-inclusive ≠ limited

compress 1 = squeeze, crush, squash, press 2 = condense, contract, concentrate, shorten, abbreviate

comprise 1 = be composed of, include, contain, consist of, take in, embrace, encompass 2 = make up, form, constitute, compose

compromise NOUN = give-and-take, agreement, settlement, accommodation, concession, adjustment, trade-off ≠ disagreement
• VERB 1 = meet halfway, concede, make concessions, give and take, strike a balance, strike a happy medium, go fifty-fifty (*informal*) ≠ disagree 2 = undermine, expose, embarrass, weaken, prejudice, discredit, jeopardize, dishonour ≠ support

compulsive 1 = obsessive, confirmed, chronic, persistent, addictive, uncontrollable, incurable, inveterate 2 = fascinating, gripping, absorbing, compelling, captivating, enthralling, hypnotic, engrossing 3 = irresistible, overwhelming, compelling, urgent, neurotic, uncontrollable, driving

compulsory = obligatory, forced, required, binding, mandatory, imperative, requisite, de rigueur (*French*) ≠ voluntary

compute = calculate, total, count, reckon, figure out, add up, tally, enumerate

comrade = companion, friend, partner, ally, colleague, associate, fellow, co-worker, cobber (*Austral. & N.Z. old-fashioned informal*)

con (*Informal*) VERB = swindle, trick, cheat, rip off (*slang*), deceive, defraud, dupe, hoodwink
• NOUN = swindle, trick, fraud, deception, scam (*slang*), sting (*informal*)

conceal 1 = hide, bury, cover, screen, disguise, obscure, camouflage ≠ reveal 2 = keep secret, hide, disguise, mask, suppress, veil ≠ show

concede 1 = admit, allow, accept, acknowledge, own, grant, confess ≠ deny 2 = give up, yield, hand over, surrender, relinquish, cede ≠ conquer

conceive 1 = imagine, envisage, comprehend, visualize, think, believe, suppose, fancy 2 = think up, create, design, devise, formulate, contrive 3 = become pregnant, get pregnant, become impregnated

concentrate 1 = focus your attention on, focus on, pay attention to, be engrossed in, put your mind to, keep your mind on, apply yourself to, give your mind to ≠ pay no attention to 2 = focus, centre, converge, bring to bear 3 = gather, collect, cluster, accumulate, congregate ≠ scatter

concentrated 1 = condensed, rich, undiluted, reduced, evaporated, thickened, boiled down 2 = intense, hard, deep, intensive, all-out (*informal*)

concentration 1 = attention, application, absorption, single-mindedness, intentness ≠ inattention 2 = focusing, centring, consolidation, convergence, bringing to bear, intensification, centralization 3 = convergence, collection, mass, cluster, accumulation, aggregation ≠ scattering

concept = idea, view, image, theory, notion, conception, hypothesis, abstraction

conception 1 = idea, plan, design, image, concept, notion 2 = impregnation, insemination, fertilization, germination

concern NOUN 1 = anxiety, fear, worry, distress, unease, apprehension, misgiving, disquiet 2 = worry, care, anxiety 3 = affair, issue, matter, consideration 4 = care, interest, attentiveness 5 = business, job, affair, responsibility, task 6 = company, business, firm, organization, corporation, enterprise, establishment 7 = importance, interest, bearing, relevance
• VERB 1 = worry, trouble, bother, disturb, distress, disquiet, perturb, make anxious 2 = be about, cover, deal with, go into, relate to, have to do with 3 = be relevant to, involve, affect, regard, apply to, bear on, have something to do with, pertain to

concerned 1 = worried, troubled, upset, bothered, disturbed, anxious, distressed, uneasy ≠ indifferent 2 = involved, interested, active, mixed up, implicated, privy to

concerning = regarding, about, re, touching, respecting, relating to, on the subject of, with reference to

concession 1 = compromise, agreement, settlement, accommodation, adjustment, trade-off, give-and-take **2** = privilege, right, permit, licence, entitlement, indulgence, prerogative **3** = reduction, saving, grant, discount, allowance **4** = surrender, yielding, conceding, renunciation, relinquishment

conclude **1** = decide, judge, assume, gather, work out, infer, deduce, surmise **2** = come to an end, end, close, finish, wind up ≠ begin **3** = bring to an end, end, close, finish, complete, wind up, terminate, round off ≠ begin **4** = accomplish, effect, bring about, carry out, pull off

conclusion **1** = decision, opinion, conviction, verdict, judgment, deduction, inference **2** = end, ending, close, finish, completion, finale, termination, bitter end **3** = outcome, result, upshot, consequence, culmination, end result

concrete **1** = specific, precise, explicit, definite, clear-cut, unequivocal ≠ vague **2** = real, material, actual, substantial, sensible, tangible, factual ≠ abstract

condemn **1** = denounce, damn, criticize, disapprove, censure, reprove, upbraid, blame ≠ approve **2** = sentence, convict, damn, doom, pass sentence on ≠ acquit

condemnation = denunciation, blame, censure, disapproval, reproach, stricture, reproof

condition NOUN **1** = state, order, shape, nick (*Brit. informal*), trim **2** = situation, state, position, status, circumstances **3** = requirement, terms, rider, restriction, qualification, limitation, prerequisite, proviso **4** = health, shape, fitness, trim, form, kilter, state of health, fettle **5** = ailment, problem, complaint, weakness, malady, infirmity
• PLURAL NOUN = circumstances, situation, environment, surroundings, way of life, milieu
• VERB = train, teach, adapt, accustom

conditional = dependent, limited, qualified, subject to, contingent, provisional, with reservations ≠ unconditional

condone = overlook, excuse, forgive, pardon, turn a blind eye to, look the other way, make allowance for, let pass ≠ condemn

conduct VERB **1** = carry out, run, control, manage, direct, handle, organize, administer **2** = accompany, lead, escort, guide, steer, convey, usher
• NOUN **1** = management, running, control, handling, administration, direction, organization, guidance **2** = behaviour, ways, bearing, attitude, manners, demeanour, deportment
• PHRASES **conduct yourself** = behave yourself, act, carry yourself, acquit yourself, deport yourself, comport yourself

confer **1** = discuss, talk, consult, deliberate, discourse, converse **2** = grant, give, present, accord, award, hand out, bestow

conference = meeting, congress, discussion, convention, forum, consultation, seminar, symposium, hui (*N.Z.*)

confess **1** = admit, acknowledge, disclose, confide, own up, come clean (*informal*), divulge ≠ cover up **2** = declare, allow, reveal, confirm, concede, assert, affirm, profess

confession = admission, revelation, disclosure, acknowledgment, exposure, unbosoming

confidant *or* **confidante** = close friend, familiar, intimate, crony, alter ego, bosom friend

confide = tell, admit, reveal, confess, whisper, disclose, impart, divulge

confidence NOUN **1** = trust, belief, faith, dependence, reliance, credence ≠ distrust **2** = self-assurance, courage, assurance, aplomb, boldness, self-possession, nerve ≠ shyness **3** = secret
• PHRASES **in confidence** = in secrecy, privately, confidentially, between you and me (and the gatepost), (just) between ourselves

confident **1** = certain, sure, convinced, positive, secure, satisfied, counting on ≠ unsure **2** = self-assured, positive, assured, bold, self-confident, self-reliant, sure of yourself ≠ insecure

confidential **1** = secret, private, intimate, classified, privy, off the record, hush-hush (*informal*) **2** = secretive, low, soft, hushed

confine VERB **1** = imprison, enclose, shut up, intern, incarcerate, hem in, keep, cage **2** = restrict, limit
• PLURAL NOUN = limits, bounds, boundaries, compass, precincts, circumference, edge

confirm **1** = prove, support, establish,

back up, verify, validate, bear out, substantiate **2** = ratify, establish, sanction, endorse, authorize **3** = strengthen, establish, fix, secure, reinforce, fortify

confirmation **1** = proof, evidence, testimony, verification, ratification, validation, corroboration, authentication ≠ repudiation **2** = affirmation, approval, acceptance, endorsement, ratification, assent, agreement ≠ disapproval

confirmed = long-established, seasoned, chronic, hardened, habitual, ingrained, inveterate, dyed-in-the-wool

confiscate = seize, appropriate, impound, commandeer, sequester ≠ give back

conflict NOUN **1** = dispute, difference, opposition, hostility, disagreement, friction, strife, fighting ≠ agreement **2** = struggle, battle, clash, strife **3** = battle, war, fight, clash, contest, encounter, combat, strife ≠ peace
• VERB = be incompatible, clash, differ, disagree, collide, be at variance ≠ agree

conflicting = incompatible, opposing, clashing, contrary, contradictory, inconsistent, paradoxical, discordant ≠ agreeing

conform **1** = fit in, follow, adjust, adapt, comply, obey, fall in with, toe the line **2** = fulfil, meet, match, suit, satisfy, agree with, obey, abide by

confound = bewilder, baffle, confuse, astound, perplex, mystify, flummox, dumbfound

confront **1** = tackle, deal with, cope with, meet head-on **2** = trouble, face, perturb, bedevil **3** = challenge, face, oppose, tackle, encounter, defy, stand up to, accost ≠ evade

confrontation = conflict, fight, contest, set-to (*informal*), encounter, showdown (*informal*), head-to-head

confuse **1** = mix up with, take for, muddle with **2** = bewilder, puzzle, baffle, perplex, mystify, fluster, faze, flummox **3** = obscure, cloud, make more difficult

confused **1** = bewildered, puzzled, baffled, at sea, muddled, perplexed, taken aback, disorientated ≠ enlightened **2** = disorderly, disordered, chaotic, mixed up, jumbled, untidy, in disarray, topsy-turvy ≠ tidy

confusing = bewildering, puzzling, misleading, unclear, baffling, contradictory, perplexing ≠ clear

confusion **1** = bewilderment, doubt, uncertainty ≠ enlightenment **2** = disorder, chaos, turmoil, upheaval, muddle, shambles, commotion ≠ order

congestion = overcrowding, crowding, jam, clogging, bottleneck

congratulate = compliment, pat on the back, wish joy to

congratulations PLURAL NOUN = good wishes, greetings, compliments, best wishes, felicitations
• INTERJECTION = good wishes, greetings, compliments, best wishes, felicitations

congregation = parishioners, brethren, crowd, assembly, flock, fellowship, multitude, throng

congress **1** = meeting, council, conference, assembly, convention, conclave, hui (*N.Z.*), runanga (*N.Z.*) **2** = legislature, council, parliament, House of Representatives (*N.Z.*)

conjure VERB = produce, generate, bring about, give rise to, make, create, effect, produce as if by magic
• PHRASES **conjure something up** = bring to mind, recall, evoke, recreate, recollect, produce as if by magic

connect **1** = link, join, couple, attach, fasten, affix, unite ≠ separate **2** = associate, join, link, identify, lump together

connected = linked, united, joined, coupled, related, allied, associated, combined

connection **1** = association, relationship, link, bond, relevance, tie-in **2** = communication, alliance, attachment, liaison, affinity, union **3** = link, coupling, junction, fastening, tie **4** = contact, friend, ally, associate, acquaintance

conquer **1** = seize, obtain, acquire, occupy, overrun, annex, win **2** = defeat, overcome, overthrow, beat, master, crush, overpower, quell ≠ lose to **3** = overcome, beat, defeat, master, overpower

conquest **1** = takeover, coup, invasion, occupation, annexation, subjugation **2** = defeat, victory, triumph, overthrow, rout, mastery

conscience **1** = principles, scruples, moral sense, sense of right and wrong, still small voice **2** = guilt, shame, regret, remorse, contrition, self-reproach

conscious 1 *often with* **of** = aware of, alert to, responsive to, sensible of ≠ unaware 2 = deliberate, knowing, studied, calculated, self-conscious, intentional, wilful, premeditated ≠ unintentional 3 = awake, wide-awake, sentient, alive ≠ asleep

consciousness = awareness, understanding, knowledge, recognition, sensibility, realization, apprehension

consecutive = successive, running, succeeding, in turn, uninterrupted, sequential, in sequence

consensus = agreement, general agreement, unanimity, common consent, unity, harmony, assent, concord, kotahitanga (*N.Z.*)

consent NOUN = agreement, sanction, approval, go-ahead (*informal*), permission, compliance, assent, acquiescence ≠ refusal
• VERB = agree, approve, permit, concur, assent, acquiesce ≠ refuse

consequence 1 = result, effect, outcome, repercussion, issue, sequel, end result, upshot 2 = importance, concern, moment, value, account, weight, import, significance

consequently = as a result, thus, therefore, hence, subsequently, accordingly, for that reason, thence

conservation 1 = preservation, saving, protection, maintenance, safeguarding, upkeep, guardianship, safekeeping 2 = economy, saving, thrift, husbandry

conservative ADJECTIVE = traditional, conventional, cautious, sober, reactionary, die-hard, hidebound ≠ radical
• NOUN = traditionalist, reactionary, die-hard, stick-in-the-mud (*informal*) ≠ radical

Conservative ADJECTIVE = Tory, Republican (*U.S.*), right-wing
• NOUN = Tory, Republican (*U.S.*), right-winger

conserve 1 = save, husband, take care of, hoard, store up, use sparingly ≠ waste 2 = protect, keep, save, preserve

consider 1 = think, see, believe, rate, judge, suppose, deem, view as 2 = think about, reflect on, weigh, contemplate, deliberate, ponder, meditate, ruminate 3 = bear in mind, remember, respect, think about, take into account, reckon with, take into consideration, make allowance for

considerable = large, goodly, great, marked, substantial, noticeable, plentiful, appreciable ≠ small

considerably = greatly, very much, significantly, remarkably, substantially, markedly, noticeably, appreciably

consideration 1 = thought, review, analysis, examination, reflection, scrutiny, deliberation 2 = thoughtfulness, concern, respect, kindness, tact, considerateness 3 = factor, point, issue, concern, element, aspect 4 = payment, fee, reward, remuneration, recompense, tip

considering = taking into account, in the light of, bearing in mind, in view of, keeping in mind, taking into consideration

consist VERB
• PHRASES **consist in something** = lie in, involve, reside in, be expressed by, subsist in, be found *or* contained in
◆ **consist of something** = be made up of, include, contain, incorporate, amount to, comprise, be composed of

consistency 1 = agreement, regularity, uniformity, constancy, steadiness, steadfastness, evenness 2 = texture, density, thickness, firmness, viscosity, compactness

consistent 1 = steady, even, regular, stable, constant, persistent, dependable, unchanging ≠ erratic 2 = compatible, agreeing, in keeping, harmonious, in harmony, consonant, in accord, congruous ≠ incompatible 3 = coherent, logical, compatible, harmonious, consonant ≠ contradictory

consolation = comfort, help, support, relief, cheer, encouragement, solace, succour

console = comfort, cheer, soothe, support, encourage, calm, succour, express sympathy for ≠ distress

consolidate 1 = strengthen, secure, reinforce, fortify, stabilize 2 = combine, unite, join, merge, unify, amalgamate, federate

conspicuous = obvious, clear, patent, evident, noticeable, blatant, salient ≠ inconspicuous

conspiracy = plot, scheme, intrigue, collusion, machination

conspire 1 = plot, scheme, intrigue,

manoeuvre, contrive, machinate, plan 2 = work together, combine, contribute, cooperate, concur, tend

constant 1 = continuous, sustained, perpetual, interminable, unrelenting, incessant, ceaseless, nonstop ≠ occasional 2 = unchanging, even, fixed, permanent, stable, steady, uniform, invariable ≠ changing 3 = faithful, true, devoted, loyal, stalwart, staunch, trustworthy, trusty ≠ undependable

constantly = continuously, always, all the time, invariably, continually, endlessly, perpetually, incessantly ≠ occasionally

constituent NOUN 1 = voter, elector, member of the electorate 2 = component, element, ingredient, part, unit, factor
• ADJECTIVE = component, basic, essential, integral, elemental

constitute 1 = represent, be, consist of, embody, exemplify, be equivalent to 2 = make up, form, compose, comprise

constitution 1 = state of health, build, body, frame, physique, physical condition 2 = structure, form, nature, make-up, composition, character, disposition

constitutional = legitimate, official, legal, chartered, statutory, vested

constrain 1 = restrict, confine, curb, restrain, constrict, straiten, check 2 = force, bind, compel, oblige, necessitate, coerce, impel, pressurize

constraint 1 = restriction, limitation, curb, rein, deterrent, hindrance, check 2 = force, pressure, necessity, restraint, compulsion, coercion

construct 1 = build, make, form, create, fashion, shape, manufacture, assemble ≠ demolish 2 = create, make, form, compose, put together

construction 1 = building, creation, composition 2 (*Formal*) = interpretation, reading, explanation, rendering, inference

constructive = helpful, positive, useful, practical, valuable, productive ≠ unproductive

consult 1 = ask, refer to, turn to, take counsel, pick (someone's) brains, question 2 = confer, talk, compare notes 3 = refer to, check in, look in

consultant = specialist, adviser, counsellor, authority

consultation 1 = discussion, talk, council, conference, dialogue 2 = meeting, interview, session, appointment, examination, deliberation, hearing

consume 1 = eat, swallow, devour, put away, gobble (up), eat up 2 = use up, spend, waste, absorb, exhaust, squander, dissipate, expend 3 = destroy, devastate, demolish, ravage, annihilate, lay waste 4 *often passive* = obsess, dominate, absorb, preoccupy, eat up, monopolize, engross

consumer = buyer, customer, user, shopper, purchaser

consumption 1 = using up, use, loss, waste, expenditure, exhaustion, depletion, dissipation 2 (*Old-fashioned*) = tuberculosis, T.B.

contact NOUN 1 = communication, link, association, connection, correspondence 2 = touch, contiguity 3 = connection, colleague, associate, liaison, acquaintance, confederate
• VERB = get *or* be in touch with, call, reach, approach, write to, speak to, communicate with

contain 1 = hold, incorporate, accommodate, enclose, have capacity for 2 = include, consist of, embrace, comprise, embody, comprehend 3 = restrain, control, hold in, curb, suppress, hold back, stifle, repress

container = holder, vessel, repository, receptacle

contaminate = pollute, infect, stain, corrupt, taint, defile, adulterate, befoul ≠ purify

contamination = pollution, infection, corruption, poisoning, taint, impurity, contagion, defilement

contemplate 1 = consider, plan, think of, intend, envisage, foresee 2 = think about, consider, ponder, reflect upon, ruminate (upon), muse over, deliberate over 3 = look at, examine, inspect, gaze at, eye up, view, study, regard

contemporary ADJECTIVE 1 = modern, recent, current, up-to-date, present-day, à la mode, newfangled, present ≠ old-fashioned 2 = coexisting, concurrent, contemporaneous
• NOUN = peer, fellow, equal

contempt = scorn, disdain, mockery, derision, disrespect, disregard ≠ respect

contend 1 = argue, hold, maintain, allege, assert, affirm 2 = compete, fight, struggle, clash, contest, strive, vie, jostle

content[1] NOUN **1** = subject matter, material, theme, substance, essence, gist **2** = amount, measure, size, load, volume, capacity
• PLURAL NOUN = constituents, elements, load, ingredients

content[2] ADJECTIVE = satisfied, happy, pleased, contented, comfortable, fulfilled, at ease, gratified
• NOUN = satisfaction, ease, pleasure, comfort, peace of mind, gratification, contentment
• PHRASES **content yourself with something** = satisfy yourself with, be happy with, be satisfied with, be content with

contented = satisfied, happy, pleased, content, comfortable, glad, thankful, gratified ≠ discontented

contentious = argumentative, wrangling, bickering, quarrelsome, querulous, cavilling, disputatious, captious

contest NOUN **1** = competition, game, match, trial, tournament **2** = struggle, fight, battle, conflict, dispute, controversy, combat
• VERB **1** = compete in, take part in, fight in, go in for, contend for, vie in **2** = oppose, question, challenge, argue, debate, dispute, object to, call in *or* into question

contestant = competitor, candidate, participant, contender, entrant, player

context **1** = circumstances, conditions, situation, ambience **2** = frame of reference, background, framework, relation, connection

contingency = possibility, happening, chance, event, incident, accident, emergency, eventuality

continual **1** = constant, interminable, incessant, unremitting ≠ erratic **2** = frequent, regular, repeated, recurrent ≠ occasional

continually **1** = constantly, always, all the time, forever, incessantly, nonstop, interminably **2** = repeatedly, often, frequently, many times, over and over, persistently

continuation **1** = continuing, lasting, carrying on, keeping up, endurance, perpetuation, prolongation **2** = addition, extension, supplement, sequel, resumption, postscript

continue **1** = keep on, go on, maintain, sustain, carry on, persist in, persevere, stick at ≠ stop **2** = go on, progress, proceed, carry on, keep going **3** = resume, return to, take up again, proceed, carry on, recommence, pick up where you left off ≠ stop **4** = remain, last, stay, survive, carry on, live on, endure, persist ≠ quit

continuing = lasting, sustained, enduring, ongoing, in progress

continuity = cohesion, flow, connection, sequence, succession, progression

continuous = constant, extended, prolonged, unbroken, uninterrupted, unceasing ≠ occasional

contract NOUN = agreement, commitment, arrangement, settlement, bargain, pact, covenant
• VERB **1** = agree, negotiate, pledge, bargain, undertake, come to terms, covenant, make a deal ≠ refuse **2** = constrict, confine, tighten, shorten, compress, condense, shrivel **3** = tighten, narrow, shorten ≠ stretch **4** = lessen, reduce, shrink, diminish, decrease, dwindle ≠ increase **5** = catch, get, develop, acquire, incur, be infected with, go down with, be afflicted with ≠ avoid

contraction **1** = tightening, narrowing, shortening, constricting, shrinkage **2** = abbreviation, reduction, shortening, compression

contradict **1** = dispute, deny, challenge, belie, fly in the face of, be at variance with **2** = negate, deny, rebut, controvert ≠ confirm

contradiction **1** = conflict, inconsistency, contravention, incongruity **2** = negation, opposite, denial

contradictory = inconsistent, conflicting, opposed, opposite, contrary, incompatible, paradoxical

contrary ADJECTIVE **1** = opposite, different, opposed, clashing, counter, reverse, adverse, contradictory ≠ in agreement **2** = perverse, difficult, awkward, intractable, obstinate, stroppy (*Brit. slang*), cantankerous, disobliging ≠ cooperative
• NOUN = opposite, reverse, converse, antithesis

contrast NOUN = difference, opposition, comparison, distinction, foil, disparity, divergence, dissimilarity
• VERB **1** = differentiate, compare, oppose, distinguish, set in opposition **2** = differ, be

contrary, be at variance, be dissimilar
contribute VERB = give, provide, supply, donate, subscribe, chip in (*informal*), bestow
• PHRASES **contribute to something** = be partly responsible for, lead to, be instrumental in, be conducive to, help
contribution = gift, offering, grant, donation, input, subscription, koha (*N.Z.*)
contributor = donor, supporter, patron, subscriber, giver
contrive 1 = devise, plan, fabricate, create, design, scheme, manufacture, plot 2 = manage, succeed, arrange, manoeuvre
contrived = forced, planned, laboured, strained, artificial, elaborate, unnatural, overdone ≠ natural
control NOUN 1 = power, authority, management, command, guidance, supervision, supremacy, charge 2 = restraint, check, regulation, brake, limitation, curb 3 = self-discipline, self-restraint, restraint, self-command 4 = switch, instrument, button, dial, lever, knob
• PLURAL NOUN = instruments, dash, dials, console, dashboard, control panel
• VERB 1 = have power over, manage, direct, handle, command, govern, administer, supervise 2 = limit, restrict, curb 3 = restrain, limit, check, contain, curb, hold back, subdue, repress
controversial = disputed, contentious, at issue, debatable, under discussion, open to question, disputable
controversy = argument, debate, row, dispute, quarrel, squabble, wrangling, altercation
convene 1 = call, gather, assemble, summon, bring together, convoke 2 = meet, gather, assemble, come together, congregate
convenience 1 = benefit, good, advantage 2 = suitability, fitness, appropriateness 3 = usefulness, utility ≠ uselessness 4 = accessibility, availability, nearness 5 = appliance, facility, comfort, amenity, labour-saving device, help
convenient 1 = suitable, fit, handy, satisfactory 2 = useful, practical, handy, serviceable, labour-saving ≠ useless 3 = nearby, available, accessible, handy, at hand, within reach, close at hand, just round the corner ≠ inaccessible 4 = appropriate, timely, suitable, helpful
convention 1 = custom, practice, tradition, code, usage, protocol, etiquette, propriety, kawa (*N.Z.*), tikanga (*N.Z.*) 2 = agreement, contract, treaty, bargain, pact, protocol 3 = assembly, meeting, council, conference, congress, convocation, hui (*N.Z.*), runanga (*N.Z.*)
conventional 1 = proper, conservative, respectable, genteel, conformist 2 = ordinary, standard, normal, regular, usual 3 = traditional, accepted, orthodox, customary 4 = unoriginal, routine, stereotyped, banal, prosaic, run-of-the-mill, hackneyed ≠ unconventional
converge VERB = come together, meet, join, combine, gather, merge, coincide, intersect
• PHRASES **converge on something** = close in on, arrive at, move towards, home in on, come together at
conversation = talk, discussion, dialogue, tête-à-tête, conference, chat, gossip, discourse, korero (*N.Z.*)
RELATED WORD
adjective: colloquial
conversion 1 = change, transformation, metamorphosis 2 = adaptation, reconstruction, modification, alteration, remodelling, reorganization
convert VERB 1 = change, turn, transform, alter, transpose 2 = adapt, modify, remodel, reorganize, customize, restyle 3 = reform, convince, proselytize
• NOUN = neophyte, disciple, proselyte
convey 1 = communicate, impart, reveal, relate, disclose, make known, tell 2 = carry, transport, move, bring, bear, conduct, fetch
convict VERB = find guilty, sentence, condemn, imprison, pronounce guilty
• NOUN = prisoner, criminal, lag (*slang*), felon, jailbird
conviction 1 = belief, view, opinion, principle, faith, persuasion, creed, tenet, kaupapa (*N.Z.*) 2 = certainty, confidence, assurance, firmness, certitude
convince 1 = assure, persuade, satisfy, reassure 2 = persuade, induce, coax, talk into, prevail upon, bring round to the idea of
convincing = persuasive, credible, conclusive, telling, powerful, impressive, plausible, cogent ≠ unconvincing

cool ADJECTIVE **1** = cold, chilled, refreshing, chilly, nippy ≠ warm **2** = calm, collected, relaxed, composed, sedate, self-controlled, unruffled, unemotional ≠ agitated **3** = unfriendly, distant, indifferent, aloof, lukewarm, offhand, unenthusiastic, unwelcoming ≠ friendly **4** = unenthusiastic, indifferent, lukewarm, unwelcoming
• VERB **1** = lose heat, cool off ≠ warm (up) **2** = make cool, freeze, chill, refrigerate, cool off ≠ warm (up)
• NOUN **1** = coldness, chill, coolness **2** (*Slang*) = calmness, control, temper, composure, self-control, poise, self-discipline, self-possession

cooperate = work together, collaborate, coordinate, join forces, conspire, pull together, pool resources, combine your efforts ≠ conflict

cooperation = teamwork, unity, collaboration, give-and-take, combined effort, esprit de corps, kotahitanga (*N.Z.*) ≠ opposition

cooperative **1** = shared, joint, combined, collective, collaborative **2** = helpful, obliging, accommodating, supportive, responsive, onside (*informal*)

cope VERB = manage, get by (*informal*), struggle through, survive, carry on, make the grade, hold your own
• PHRASES **cope with something** = deal with, handle, struggle with, grapple with, wrestle with, contend with, weather

copy NOUN = reproduction, duplicate, replica, imitation, forgery, counterfeit, likeness, facsimile ≠ original
• VERB **1** = reproduce, replicate, duplicate, transcribe, counterfeit ≠ create **2** = imitate, act like, emulate, behave like, follow, repeat, mirror, ape

cord = rope, line, string, twine

cordon NOUN = chain, line, ring, barrier, picket line
• PHRASES **cordon something off** = surround, isolate, close off, fence off, separate, enclose, picket, encircle

core **1** = centre **2** = heart, essence, nucleus, kernel, crux, gist, nub, pith

corner NOUN **1** = angle, joint, crook **2** = bend, curve **3** = space, hideaway, nook, hide-out
• VERB **1** = trap, catch, run to earth **2** (usually with *market* as object) = monopolize, take over, dominate, control, hog (*slang*), engross

corporation **1** = business, company, concern, firm, society, association, organization, enterprise **2** = town council, council, municipal authorities, civic authorities

corps = team, unit, regiment, detachment, company, band, division, troop

corpse = body, remains, carcass, cadaver, stiff (*slang*)

correct ADJECTIVE **1** = accurate, right, true, exact, precise, flawless, faultless, O.K. *or* okay (*informal*) ≠ inaccurate **2** = right, standard, appropriate, acceptable, proper, precise **3** = proper, seemly, standard, fitting, kosher (*informal*) ≠ inappropriate
• VERB **1** = rectify, remedy, redress, right, reform, cure, adjust, amend ≠ spoil **2** = rebuke, discipline, reprimand, chide, admonish, chastise, chasten, reprove ≠ praise

correction **1** = rectification, improvement, amendment, adjustment, modification, alteration, emendation **2** = punishment, discipline, reformation, admonition, chastisement, reproof, castigation

correctly = rightly, right, perfectly, properly, precisely, accurately

correctness **1** = truth, accuracy, precision, exactitude, exactness, faultlessness **2** = decorum, propriety, good manners, civility, good breeding

correspond **1** = be consistent, match, agree, accord, fit, square, tally, conform ≠ differ **2** = communicate, write, keep in touch, exchange letters

correspondence **1** = communication, writing, contact **2** = letters, post, mail **3** = relation, match, agreement, comparison, harmony, coincidence, similarity, correlation

correspondent **1** = reporter, journalist, contributor, hack **2** = letter writer, pen friend *or* pen pal

corresponding = equivalent, matching, similar, related, complementary, reciprocal, analogous

corridor = passage, alley, aisle, hallway, passageway

corrupt ADJECTIVE **1** = dishonest, bent (*slang*), crooked (*informal*), fraudulent, unscrupulous, venal, unprincipled

≠ honest **2** = depraved, vicious, degenerate, debased, profligate, dissolute **3** = distorted, doctored, altered, falsified
• **VERB 1** = bribe, fix (*informal*), buy off, suborn, grease (someone's) palm (*slang*) **2** = deprave, pervert, subvert, debauch ≠ reform **3** = distort, doctor, tamper with

corruption 1 = dishonesty, fraud, bribery, extortion, venality, shady dealings (*informal*) **2** = depravity, vice, evil, perversion, decadence, wickedness, immorality **3** = distortion, doctoring, falsification

cosmetic = superficial, surface, nonessential

cosmic 1 = extraterrestrial, stellar **2** = universal, general, overarching

cosmopolitan = sophisticated, cultured, refined, cultivated, urbane, well-travelled, worldly-wise ≠ unsophisticated

cost NOUN 1 = price, worth, expense, charge, damage (*informal*), amount, payment, outlay **2** = loss, suffering, damage, injury, penalty, hurt, expense, harm
• **PLURAL NOUN** = expenses, spending, expenditure, overheads, outgoings, outlay, budget
• **VERB 1** = sell at, come to, set (someone) back (*informal*), be priced at, command a price of **2** = lose, deprive of, cheat of

costly 1 = expensive, dear, stiff, steep (*informal*), highly-priced, exorbitant, extortionate ≠ inexpensive **2** = damaging, disastrous, harmful, catastrophic, loss-making, ruinous, deleterious

costume = outfit, dress, clothing, uniform, ensemble, livery, apparel, attire

cosy 1 = comfortable, homely, warm, intimate, snug, comfy (*informal*), sheltered **2** = snug, warm, comfortable, sheltered, comfy (*informal*), tucked up **3** = intimate, friendly, informal

cottage = cabin, lodge, hut, shack, chalet, whare (*N.Z.*)

cough VERB = clear your throat, bark, hack
• **NOUN** = frog *or* tickle in your throat, bark, hack

council 1 = committee, governing body, board **2** = governing body, parliament, congress, cabinet, panel, assembly, convention, conference, runanga (*N.Z.*)

counsel NOUN 1 = advice, information, warning, direction, suggestion, recommendation, guidance **2** = legal adviser, lawyer, attorney, solicitor, advocate, barrister
• **VERB** = advise, recommend, advocate, warn, urge, instruct, exhort

count VERB 1 *often with* ***up*** = add (up), total, reckon (up), tot up, calculate, compute, tally, number **2** = matter, be important, carry weight, tell, rate, weigh, signify **3** = consider, judge, regard, deem, think of, rate, look upon **4** = include, number among, take into account *or* consideration
• **NOUN** = calculation, poll, reckoning, sum, tally, numbering, computation, enumeration
• **PHRASES count on** *or* **upon something** *or* **someone** = depend on, trust, rely on, bank on, take for granted, lean on, reckon on, take on trust

counter VERB 1 = oppose, meet, block, resist, parry, deflect, repel, rebuff **2** = retaliate, answer, reply, respond, retort, hit back, rejoin, strike back ≠ yield
• **ADVERB** = opposite to, against, versus, conversely, in defiance of, at variance with, contrariwise ≠ in accordance with

counterpart = opposite number, equal, twin, equivalent, match, fellow, mate

countless = innumerable, legion, infinite, myriad, untold, limitless, incalculable, immeasurable ≠ limited

country 1 = nation, state, land, commonwealth, kingdom, realm, people **2** = people, community, nation, society, citizens, inhabitants, populace, public **3** = countryside, provinces, sticks (*informal*), farmland, outback (*Austral. & N.Z.*), green belt, backwoods, bush (*N.Z. & S. African*) ≠ town **4** = territory, land, region, terrain

countryside = country, rural areas, outback (*Austral. & N.Z.*), green belt, sticks (*informal*)

county = province, district, shire

coup = masterstroke, feat, stunt, action, exploit, manoeuvre, deed, accomplishment

couple NOUN = pair, two, brace, duo, twosome
• **PHRASES couple something to something** = link to, connect to, pair with, unite with, join to, hitch to, yoke to

coupon = slip, ticket, certificate, token,

voucher, card
courage = bravery, nerve, resolution, daring, pluck, heroism, mettle, gallantry ≠ cowardice
courageous = brave, daring, bold, gritty, fearless, gallant, intrepid, valiant ≠ cowardly
courier 1 = messenger, runner, carrier, bearer, envoy 2 = guide, representative, escort, conductor
course NOUN 1 = route, way, line, road, track, direction, path, passage 2 = procedure, plan, policy, programme, method, conduct, behaviour, manner 3 = progression, order, unfolding, development, movement, progress, flow, sequence 4 = classes, programme, schedule, lectures, curriculum 5 = racecourse, circuit 6 = period, time, duration, term, passing
• VERB 1 = run, flow, stream, gush, race, speed, surge 2 = hunt, follow, chase, pursue
• PHRASES **of course** = naturally, certainly, obviously, definitely, undoubtedly, needless to say, without a doubt, indubitably
court NOUN 1 = law court, bar, bench, tribunal 2 = palace, hall, castle, manor 3 = royal household, train, suite, attendants, entourage, retinue, cortege
• VERB 1 = cultivate, seek, flatter, solicit, pander to, curry favour with, fawn upon 2 = invite, seek, attract, prompt, provoke, bring about, incite 3 = woo, go (out) with, date, take out, run after, walk out with, set your cap at
courtesy 1 = politeness, good manners, civility, gallantry, graciousness, affability, urbanity 2 = favour, kindness, indulgence
courtyard = yard, square, piazza, quadrangle, plaza, enclosure, cloister, quad (*informal*)
cove = bay, sound, inlet, anchorage
covenant = promise, contract, agreement, commitment, arrangement, pledge, pact
cover VERB 1 = conceal, hide, mask, disguise, obscure, veil, cloak, shroud ≠ reveal 2 = clothe, dress, wrap, envelop ≠ uncover 3 = overlay, blanket 4 = coat, cake, plaster, smear, envelop, spread, encase, daub 5 = submerge, flood, engulf, overrun, wash over 6 = travel over, cross, traverse, pass through *or* over 7 = protect, guard, defend, shield 8 = consider, deal with, investigate, describe, tell of 9 = report on, write about, commentate on, relate, tell of, narrate, write up 10 = pay for, fund, provide for, offset, be enough for
• NOUN 1 = protection, shelter, shield, defence, guard, camouflage, concealment 2 = insurance, protection, compensation, indemnity, reimbursement 3 = covering, case, top, coating, envelope, lid, canopy, wrapper 4 = bedclothes, bedding, sheets, blankets, quilt, duvet, eiderdown 5 = jacket, case, wrapper 6 = disguise, front, screen, mask, veil, façade, pretext, smoke screen
covering NOUN = cover, coating, casing, wrapping, layer, blanket
• ADJECTIVE = explanatory, accompanying, introductory, descriptive
covet = long for, desire, envy, crave, aspire to, yearn for, lust after, set your heart on
coward = wimp, chicken (*slang*), scaredy-cat (*informal*), yellow-belly (*slang*)
cowardly = faint-hearted, scared, spineless, soft, yellow (*informal*), weak, chicken (*slang*), fearful, sookie (*N.Z.*) ≠ brave
cowboy = cowhand, drover, rancher, stockman, cattleman, herdsman, gaucho (*S. American*)
crack VERB 1 = break, split, burst, snap, fracture, splinter 2 = snap, ring, crash, burst, explode, pop, detonate 3 (*Informal*) = hit, clip (*informal*), slap, smack, clout (*informal*), cuff, whack 4 = break, cleave 5 = solve, work out, resolve, clear up, fathom, decipher, suss (out) (*slang*), get to the bottom of 6 = break down, collapse, yield, give in, give way, succumb, lose control, be overcome
• NOUN 1 = break, chink, gap, fracture, rift, cleft, crevice, fissure 2 = split, break, fracture 3 = snap, pop, crash, burst, explosion, clap, report 4 (*Informal*) = blow, slap, smack, clout (*informal*), cuff, whack, clip (*informal*) 5 (*Informal*) = joke, dig, gag (*informal*), quip, jibe, wisecrack, witticism, funny remark
• ADJECTIVE (*Slang*) = first-class, choice, excellent, ace, elite, superior, world-class, first-rate
crackdown = clampdown, crushing, repression, suppression

cracked = broken, damaged, split, chipped, flawed, faulty, defective, imperfect

cradle NOUN 1 = crib, cot, Moses basket, bassinet 2 = birthplace, beginning, source, spring, origin, fount, fountainhead, wellspring
• VERB = hold, support, rock, nurse, nestle

craft 1 = vessel, boat, ship, plane, aircraft, spacecraft 2 = occupation, work, business, trade, employment, pursuit, vocation, handicraft 3 = skill, art, ability, technique, know-how (*informal*), expertise, aptitude, artistry

craftsman = skilled worker, artisan, master, maker, wright, technician, smith

cram 1 = stuff, force, jam, shove, compress 2 = pack, fill, stuff 3 = squeeze, press, pack in 4 = study, revise, swot, bone up (*informal*), mug up (*slang*)

cramp[1] = spasm, pain, ache, contraction, pang, stitch, convulsion, twinge

cramp[2] = restrict, hamper, inhibit, hinder, handicap, constrain, obstruct, impede

cramped = restricted, confined, overcrowded, crowded, packed, uncomfortable, closed in, congested ≠ spacious

crash NOUN 1 = collision, accident, smash, wreck, prang (*informal*), bump, pile-up (*informal*) 2 = smash, clash, boom, bang, thunder, racket, din, clatter 3 = collapse, failure, depression, ruin, downfall
• VERB 1 = fall, plunge, topple, lurch, hurtle, overbalance, fall headlong 2 = plunge, hurtle 3 = collapse, fail, go under, be ruined, go bust (*informal*), fold up, go to the wall, go belly up (*informal*)
• PHRASES **crash into** = collide with, hit, bump into, drive into, plough into

crate = container, case, box, packing case, tea chest

crater = hollow, hole, depression, dip, cavity

crave 1 = long for, yearn for, hanker after, want, desire, hope for, lust after 2 (*Informal*) = beg, ask for, seek, petition, pray for, plead for, solicit, implore

craving = longing, hope, desire, yen (*informal*), hunger, appetite, yearning, thirst

crawl VERB = creep, slither, inch, wriggle, writhe, worm your way, advance slowly ≠ run
• PHRASES **crawl to someone** = grovel, creep, fawn, toady, humble yourself

craze = fad, fashion, trend, rage, enthusiasm, vogue, mania, infatuation

crazed = mad, crazy, raving, insane, lunatic, berko (*Austral. slang*), off the air (*Austral. slang*), porangi (*N.Z.*)

crazy 1 (*Informal*) = ridiculous, absurd, foolish, ludicrous, senseless, preposterous, idiotic, nonsensical, porangi (*N.Z.*) ≠ sensible 2 = insane, mad, unbalanced, deranged, nuts (*slang*), crazed, demented, off the air (*Austral. slang*), out of your mind, porangi (*N.Z.*) ≠ sane 3 = fanatical, wild (*informal*), mad, devoted, enthusiastic, passionate, infatuated ≠ uninterested

cream NOUN 1 = lotion, ointment, oil, essence, cosmetic, paste, emulsion, salve 2 = best, elite, prime, pick, flower, crème de la crème (*French*)
• NOUN *or* ADJECTIVE = off-white, ivory, yellowish-white

creamy 1 = milky, buttery 2 = smooth, soft, velvety, rich

crease NOUN 1 = fold, line, ridge, groove, corrugation 2 = wrinkle, line, crow's-foot
• VERB 1 = crumple, rumple, fold, double up, corrugate 2 = wrinkle, crumple, screw up

create 1 = cause, lead to, occasion, bring about 2 = make, produce, invent, compose, devise, originate, formulate, spawn ≠ destroy 3 = appoint, make, establish, set up, invest, install, constitute

creation 1 = universe, world, nature, cosmos 2 = invention, production, achievement, brainchild (*informal*), concoction, handiwork, pièce de résistance (*French*), magnum opus 3 = making, generation, formation, conception, genesis 4 = setting up, development, production, institution, foundation, establishment, formation, inception

creative = imaginative, gifted, artistic, inventive, original, inspired, clever, ingenious

creativity = imagination, inspiration, ingenuity, originality, inventiveness, cleverness

creator 1 = maker, father, author, designer, architect, inventor, originator 2 *usually with cap.* = God, Maker

creature 1 = living thing, being, animal, beast, brute 2 = person, man, woman, individual, soul, human being, mortal
credentials 1 = qualifications, ability, skill, fitness, attribute, capability, eligibility, aptitude 2 = certification, document, reference(s), papers, licence, passport, testimonial, authorization
credibility = believability, reliability, plausibility, trustworthiness
credible 1 = believable, possible, likely, reasonable, probable, plausible, conceivable, imaginable ≠ unbelievable 2 = reliable, honest, dependable, trustworthy, sincere, trusty ≠ unreliable
credit NOUN 1 = praise, honour, recognition, approval, tribute, acclaim, acknowledgment, kudos 2 = source of satisfaction *or* pride, asset, honour, feather in your cap 3 = prestige, reputation, standing, position, influence, regard, status, esteem 4 = belief, trust, confidence, faith, reliance, credence
• VERB = believe, rely on, have faith in, trust, accept
• PHRASES **credit someone with something** = attribute to, assign to, ascribe to, impute to
creed = belief, principles, doctrine, dogma, credo, catechism, articles of faith
creek 1 = inlet, bay, cove, bight, firth *or* frith (*Scot.*) 2 (*U.S., Canad., Austral., & N.Z.*) = stream, brook, tributary, bayou, rivulet, watercourse, runnel
creep VERB = sneak, steal, tiptoe, slink, skulk, approach unnoticed
• NOUN (*Slang*) = bootlicker (*informal*), sneak, sycophant, crawler (*slang*), toady
• PHRASES **give someone the creeps** (*Informal*) = disgust, frighten, scare, repel, repulse, make your hair stand on end, make you squirm
crescent = meniscus, sickle, new moon
crest 1 = top, summit, peak, ridge, highest point, pinnacle, apex, crown 2 = tuft, crown, comb, plume, mane 3 = emblem, badge, symbol, insignia, bearings, device
crew 1 = (ship's) company, hands, (ship's) complement 2 = team, squad, gang, corps, posse 3 (*Informal*) = crowd, set, bunch (*informal*), band, pack, gang, mob, horde
crime 1 = offence, violation, trespass, felony, misdemeanour, misdeed, transgression, unlawful act 2 = lawbreaking, corruption, illegality, vice, misconduct, wrongdoing
criminal NOUN = lawbreaker, convict, offender, crook (*informal*), villain, culprit, sinner, felon, rorter (*Austral. slang*), skelm (*S. African*)
• ADJECTIVE 1 = unlawful, illicit, lawless, wrong, illegal, corrupt, crooked (*informal*), immoral ≠ lawful 2 (*Informal*) = disgraceful, ridiculous, foolish, senseless, scandalous, preposterous, deplorable
cripple 1 = disable, paralyse, lame, maim, incapacitate, weaken, hamstring 2 = damage, destroy, ruin, spoil, impair, put paid to, put out of action ≠ help
crippled = disabled, handicapped, paralysed, lame, incapacitated
crisis 1 = emergency, plight, predicament, trouble, deep water, meltdown (*informal*), dire straits 2 = critical point, climax, height, crunch (*informal*), turning point, culmination, crux, moment of truth
crisp 1 = firm, crunchy, crispy, crumbly, fresh, brittle, unwilted ≠ soft 2 = bracing, fresh, refreshing, brisk, invigorating ≠ warm 3 = clean, smart, trim, neat, tidy, spruce, well-groomed, well-pressed
criterion = standard, test, rule, measure, principle, gauge, yardstick, touchstone
critic 1 = judge, authority, expert, analyst, commentator, pundit, reviewer, connoisseur 2 = fault-finder, attacker, detractor, knocker (*informal*)
critical 1 = crucial, decisive, pressing, serious, vital, urgent, all-important, pivotal ≠ unimportant 2 = grave, serious, acute, precarious ≠ safe 3 = disparaging, disapproving, scathing, derogatory, nit-picking (*informal*), censorious, fault-finding, captious ≠ complimentary 4 = analytical, penetrating, discriminating, discerning, perceptive, judicious ≠ undiscriminating
criticism 1 = fault-finding, censure, disapproval, disparagement, stick (*slang*), flak (*informal*), bad press, character assassination 2 = analysis, assessment, judgment, commentary, evaluation, appreciation, appraisal, critique
criticize = find fault with, censure, disapprove of, knock (*informal*), condemn, carp, put down, slate (*informal*) ≠ praise
crook NOUN (*Informal*) = criminal, rogue, cheat, thief, shark, villain, robber, racketeer,

skelm (*S. African*)
• **ADJECTIVE** (*Austral. & N.Z. informal*) = ill, sick, poorly (*informal*), unhealthy, seedy (*informal*), unwell, queasy, out of sorts (*informal*)
• **PHRASES** **go (off) crook** (*Austral. & N.Z. informal*) = lose your temper, be furious, rage, go mad, lose it (*informal*), crack up (*informal*), see red (*informal*), blow your top

crooked **1** = bent, twisted, curved, irregular, warped, out of shape, misshapen ≠ straight **2** = deformed, distorted **3** = zigzag, winding, twisting **4** = at an angle, uneven, slanting, squint, awry, lopsided, askew, off-centre **5** (*Informal*) = dishonest, criminal, illegal, corrupt, unlawful, shady (*informal*), fraudulent, bent (*slang*) ≠ honest

crop **NOUN** = yield, produce, gathering, fruits, harvest, vintage, reaping
• **VERB** **1** = graze, eat, browse, feed on, nibble **2** = cut, trim, clip, prune, shear, snip, pare, lop
• **PHRASES** **crop up** (*Informal*) = happen, appear, emerge, occur, arise, turn up, spring up

cross **VERB** **1** = go across, pass over, traverse, cut across, move across, travel across **2** = span, bridge, go across, extend over **3** = intersect, intertwine, crisscross **4** = oppose, interfere with, obstruct, block, resist, impede **5** = interbreed, mix, blend, cross-pollinate, crossbreed, hybridize, cross-fertilize, intercross
• **NOUN** **1** = crucifix **2** = trouble, worry, trial, load, burden, grief, woe, misfortune **3** = mixture, combination, blend, amalgam, amalgamation **4** = crossroads, crossing, junction, intersection
• **ADJECTIVE** = angry, annoyed, put out, grumpy, short, ill-tempered, irascible, tooshie (*Austral. slang*), in a bad mood, hoha (*N.Z.*) ≠ good-humoured
• **PHRASES** **cross something out** *or* **off** = strike off *or* out, eliminate, cancel, delete, blue-pencil, score off *or* out

crouch = bend down, kneel, squat, stoop, bow, duck, hunch

crow = gloat, triumph, boast, swagger, brag, exult, blow your own trumpet

crowd **NOUN** **1** = multitude, mass, throng, army, host, pack, mob, swarm **2** = group, set, lot, circle, gang, bunch (*informal*), clique **3** = audience, spectators, house, gate, attendance
• **VERB** **1** = flock, mass, collect, gather, stream, surge, swarm, throng **2** = squeeze, pack, pile, bundle, cram **3** = congest, pack, cram

crowded = packed, full, busy, cramped, swarming, teeming, congested, jam-packed

crown **NOUN** **1** = coronet, tiara, diadem, circlet **2** = laurel wreath, trophy, prize, honour, garland, laurels, wreath **3** = high point, top, tip, summit, crest, pinnacle, apex
• **VERB** **1** = install, honour, dignify, ordain, inaugurate **2** = top, cap, be on top of, surmount **3** = cap, finish, complete, perfect, round off, put the finishing touch to, be the climax *or* culmination of **4** (*Slang*) = strike, belt (*informal*), bash, hit over the head, box, punch, cuff, biff (*slang*)
• **PHRASES** **the Crown** **1** = monarch, ruler, sovereign, emperor *or* empress, king *or* queen **2** = monarchy, sovereignty, royalty

crucial **1** (*Informal*) = vital, important, pressing, essential, urgent, momentous, high-priority **2** = critical, central, key, psychological, decisive, pivotal

crude **1** = rough, basic, makeshift **2** = simple, rudimentary, basic, primitive, coarse, clumsy, rough-and-ready **3** = vulgar, dirty, rude, obscene, coarse, indecent, tasteless, smutty ≠ tasteful **4** = unrefined, natural, raw, unprocessed ≠ processed

crudely **1** = roughly, basically **2** = simply, roughly, basically, coarsely **3** = vulgarly, rudely, coarsely, crassly, obscenely, lewdly, impolitely, tastelessly

cruel **1** = brutal, ruthless, callous, sadistic, inhumane, vicious, monstrous, unkind ≠ kind **2** = bitter, ruthless, traumatic, grievous, unrelenting, merciless, pitiless

cruelly **1** = brutally, severely, mercilessly, in cold blood, callously, monstrously, sadistically, pitilessly **2** = bitterly, deeply, severely, ruthlessly, mercilessly, grievously, pitilessly, traumatically

cruelty = brutality, ruthlessness, depravity, inhumanity, barbarity, callousness, spitefulness, mercilessness

cruise **NOUN** = sail, voyage, boat trip, sea trip
• **VERB** **1** = sail, coast, voyage **2** = travel

along, coast, drift, keep a steady pace
crumb 1 = bit, grain, fragment, shred, morsel 2 = morsel, scrap, shred, snippet, soupçon (*French*)
crumble 1 = disintegrate, collapse, deteriorate, decay, fall apart, degenerate, tumble down, go to pieces 2 = crush, fragment, pulverize, pound, grind, powder, granulate 3 = collapse, deteriorate, decay, fall apart, degenerate, go to pieces, go to wrack and ruin
crumple 1 = crush, squash, screw up, scrumple 2 = crease, wrinkle, rumple, ruffle, pucker 3 = collapse, sink, go down, fall 4 = break down, fall, collapse, give way, cave in, go to pieces 5 = screw up
crunch VERB = chomp, champ, munch, chew noisily, grind
• NOUN (*Informal*) = critical point, test, crisis, emergency, crux, moment of truth
crusade NOUN 1 = campaign, drive, movement, cause, push 2 = holy war
• VERB = campaign, fight, push, struggle, lobby, agitate, work
crush VERB 1 = squash, break, squeeze, compress, press, pulverize 2 = crease, wrinkle, crumple 3 = overcome, overwhelm, put down, subdue, overpower, quash, quell, stamp out 4 = demoralize, depress, devastate, discourage, humble, put down (*slang*), humiliate, squash
• NOUN = crowd, mob, horde, throng, pack, mass, jam, huddle
crust = layer, covering, coating, skin, surface, shell
cry VERB 1 = weep, sob, shed tears, blubber, snivel ≠ laugh 2 = shout, scream, roar, yell, howl, call out, exclaim, shriek ≠ whisper
• NOUN 1 = weep, sob, bawl, blubber 2 = shout, call, scream, roar, yell, howl, shriek, bellow 3 = appeal, plea
• PLURAL NOUN = weeping, sobbing, blubbering, snivelling
• PHRASES **cry off** (*Informal*) = back out, withdraw, quit, excuse yourself
cuddle VERB 1 = hug, embrace, fondle, cosset 2 = pet, hug, bill and coo
• PHRASES **cuddle up** = snuggle
cue = signal, sign, hint, prompt, reminder, suggestion
culminate = end up, close, finish, conclude, wind up, climax, come to a head, come to a climax
culprit = offender, criminal, felon, guilty party, wrongdoer, miscreant, evildoer, transgressor
cult 1 = sect, faction, school, religion, clique, hauhau (*N.Z.*) 2 = craze, fashion, trend, fad 3 = obsession, worship, devotion, idolization
cultivate 1 = farm, work, plant, tend, till, plough 2 = develop, establish, foster 3 = court, seek out, run after, dance attendance upon 4 = improve, refine
cultural 1 = ethnic, national, native, folk, racial 2 = artistic, educational, aesthetic, enriching, enlightening, civilizing, edifying
culture 1 = the arts 2 = civilization, society, customs, way of life 3 = lifestyle, habit, way of life, mores 4 = refinement, education, enlightenment, sophistication, good taste, urbanity
cultured = refined, intellectual, educated, sophisticated, enlightened, well-informed, urbane, highbrow ≠ uneducated
cunning ADJECTIVE 1 = crafty, sly, devious, artful, sharp, wily, Machiavellian, shifty ≠ frank 2 = ingenious, imaginative, sly, devious, artful, Machiavellian 3 = skilful, clever ≠ clumsy
• NOUN 1 = craftiness, guile, trickery, deviousness, artfulness, slyness ≠ candour 2 = skill, subtlety, ingenuity, artifice, cleverness ≠ clumsiness
cup 1 = mug, goblet, chalice, teacup, beaker, bowl 2 = trophy
cupboard = cabinet, press
curb VERB = restrain, control, check, restrict, suppress, inhibit, hinder, retard
• NOUN = restraint, control, check, brake, limitation, rein, deterrent, bridle
cure VERB 1 = make better, correct, heal, relieve, remedy, mend, ease 2 = restore to health, restore, heal 3 = preserve, smoke, dry, salt, pickle
• NOUN = remedy, treatment, antidote, panacea, nostrum
curiosity 1 = inquisitiveness, interest, prying, snooping (*informal*), nosiness (*informal*) 2 = oddity, wonder, sight, phenomenon, spectacle, freak, novelty, rarity
curious ADJECTIVE 1 = inquisitive, interested, questioning, searching, inquiring, meddling, prying, nosy (*informal*) ≠ uninterested 2 = strange, unusual, bizarre, odd, novel, rare,

extraordinary, unexpected
• ADJECTIVE ≠ ordinary
curl NOUN 1 = ringlet, lock 2 = twist, spiral, coil, kink, whorl 3 = crimp, wave, perm
• VERB 1 = twirl, turn, bend, twist, curve, loop, spiral, coil 2 = wind
curly = wavy, curled, curling, fuzzy, frizzy
currency 1 = money, coinage, legal tender, notes, coins 2 = acceptance, popularity, circulation, vogue, prevalence
current NOUN 1 = flow, course, undertow, jet, stream, tide, progression, river 2 = draught, flow, breeze, puff 3 = mood, feeling, spirit, atmosphere, trend, tendency, undercurrent
• ADJECTIVE 1 = present, fashionable, up-to-date, contemporary, trendy (*Brit. informal*), topical, present-day, in fashion ≠ out-of-date 2 = prevalent, common, accepted, popular, widespread, customary, in circulation
curse VERB 1 = swear, cuss (*informal*), blaspheme, take the Lord's name in vain 2 = abuse, damn, scold, vilify
• NOUN 1 = oath, obscenity, blasphemy, expletive, profanity, imprecation, swearword 2 = malediction, jinx, anathema, hoodoo (*informal*), excommunication 3 = affliction, plague, scourge, trouble, torment, hardship, bane
cursed = under a curse, damned, doomed, jinxed, bedevilled, accursed, ill-fated
curtail = reduce, diminish, decrease, dock, cut back, shorten, lessen, cut short
curtain = hanging, drape (*chiefly U.S.*), portière
curve NOUN = bend, turn, loop, arc, curvature
• VERB = bend, turn, wind, twist, arch, snake, arc, coil
curved = bent, rounded, twisted, bowed, arched, serpentine, sinuous
cushion NOUN = pillow, pad, bolster, headrest, beanbag, hassock
• VERB 1 = protect 2 = soften, dampen, muffle, mitigate, deaden, suppress, stifle
custody 1 = care, charge, protection, supervision, safekeeping, keeping 2 = imprisonment, detention, confinement, incarceration
custom 1 = tradition, practice, convention, ritual, policy, rule, usage, kaupapa (*N.Z.*) 2 = habit, way, practice, procedure, routine, wont 3 = customers, business, trade, patronage
customary 1 = usual, common, accepted, established, traditional, normal, ordinary, conventional ≠ unusual 2 = accustomed, regular, usual
customer = client, consumer, regular (*informal*), buyer, patron, shopper, purchaser
customs = import charges, tax, duty, toll, tariff
cut VERB 1 = slit, score, slice, slash, pierce, penetrate 2 = chop, split, slice, dissect 3 = carve, slice 4 = sever, cut in two 5 = shape, carve, engrave, chisel, form, score, fashion, whittle 6 = slash, wound 7 = clip, mow, trim, prune, snip, pare, lop 8 = trim, shave, snip 9 = reduce, lower, slim (down), diminish, slash, decrease, cut back ≠ increase 10 = abridge, edit, shorten, curtail, condense, abbreviate ≠ extend 11 = delete, take out, expurgate 12 = hurt, wound, upset, sting, hurt someone's feelings 13 (*Informal*) = ignore, avoid, slight, blank (*slang*), snub, spurn, cold-shoulder, turn your back on ≠ greet 14 = cross, bisect
• NOUN 1 = incision, nick, stroke, slash, slit 2 = gash, nick, wound, slash, laceration 3 = reduction, fall, lowering, slash, decrease, cutback 4 (*Informal*) = share, piece, slice, percentage, portion 5 = style, look, fashion, shape
cutback = reduction, cut, retrenchment, economy, decrease, lessening
cute = appealing, sweet, attractive, engaging, charming, delightful, lovable, winsome
cutting = hurtful, wounding, bitter, malicious, scathing, acrimonious, barbed, sarcastic ≠ kind
cycle = series of events, circle, revolution, rotation
cynic = sceptic, doubter, pessimist, misanthrope, misanthropist, scoffer
cynical 1 = sceptical, mocking, pessimistic, scoffing, contemptuous, scornful, distrustful, derisive ≠ trusting 2 = unbelieving, sceptical, disillusioned, pessimistic, disbelieving, mistrustful ≠ optimistic
cynicism 1 = scepticism, pessimism, misanthropy 2 = disbelief, doubt, scepticism, mistrust

d

dab VERB **1** = pat, touch, tap **2** = apply, daub, stipple
• NOUN **1** = spot, bit, drop, pat, smudge, speck **2** = touch, stroke, flick
daft (*Informal, chiefly Brit.*) **1** = stupid, crazy, silly, absurd, foolish, idiotic, witless, crackpot (*informal*), off the air (*Austral. slang*) **2** = crazy, mad, touched, nuts (*slang*), crackers (*Brit. slang*), insane, demented, deranged, off the air (*Austral. slang*), porangi (*N.Z.*)
dag NOUN (*N.Z. informal*) = joker, comic, wag, wit, comedian, clown, humorist, prankster
• PHRASES **rattle your dags** (*N.Z. informal*) = hurry up, get a move on, step on it (*informal*), get your skates on (*informal*), make haste
dagga (*S. African*) = cannabis, marijuana, pot (*slang*), dope (*slang*), hash (*slang*), grass (*slang*), weed (*slang*), hemp
daily ADVERB = every day, day by day, once a day
• ADJECTIVE = everyday, diurnal, quotidian
dam NOUN = barrier, wall, barrage, obstruction, embankment
• VERB = block up, restrict, hold back, barricade, obstruct
damage VERB = spoil, hurt, injure, harm, ruin, crush, devastate, wreck ≠ fix
• NOUN **1** = destruction, harm, loss, injury, suffering, hurt, ruin, devastation ≠ improvement **2** (*Informal*) = cost, price, charge, bill, amount, payment, expense, outlay
• PLURAL NOUN (*Law*) = compensation, fine, satisfaction, amends, reparation, restitution, reimbursement, atonement
damaging = harmful, detrimental, hurtful, ruinous, deleterious, injurious, disadvantageous ≠ helpful
dame = lady, baroness, dowager, grande dame (*French*), noblewoman, peeress
damn = criticize, condemn, blast, denounce, put down, censure ≠ praise
damned (*Slang*) = infernal, detestable, confounded, hateful, loathsome
damp ADJECTIVE = moist, wet, soggy, humid, dank, sopping, clammy, dewy ≠ dry
• NOUN = moisture, liquid, drizzle, dampness, wetness, dankness ≠ dryness
• VERB = moisten, wet, soak, dampen, moisturize
• PHRASES **damp something down** = curb, reduce, check, diminish, inhibit, stifle, allay, pour cold water on
dampen **1** = reduce, check, moderate, dull, restrain, stifle, lessen **2** = moisten, wet, spray, make damp
dance VERB **1** = prance, trip, hop, skip, sway, whirl, caper, jig **2** = caper, trip, spring, jump, bound, skip, frolic, cavort
• NOUN = ball, social, hop (*informal*), disco, knees-up (*Brit. informal*), discotheque, B and S (*Austral. informal*)
dancer = ballerina, Terpsichorean
danger **1** = jeopardy, vulnerability **2** = hazard, risk, threat, menace, peril, pitfall
dangerous = perilous, risky, hazardous, vulnerable, insecure, unsafe, precarious, breakneck ≠ safe
dangerously = perilously, alarmingly, precariously, recklessly, riskily, hazardously, unsafely
dangle **1** = hang, swing, trail, sway, flap, hang down **2** = wave **3** = offer, flourish, brandish, flaunt
dare **1** = risk doing, venture, presume, make bold (*archaic*), hazard doing **2** = challenge, provoke, defy, taunt, goad, throw down the gauntlet
daring ADJECTIVE = brave, bold, adventurous, reckless, fearless, audacious, intrepid, daredevil ≠ timid
• NOUN = bravery, nerve (*informal*), courage, spirit, bottle (*Brit. slang*), pluck, audacity, boldness ≠ timidity
dark ADJECTIVE **1** = dim, murky, shady, shadowy, grey, dingy, unlit, poorly lit **2** = black, brunette, ebony, dark-skinned, sable, dusky, swarthy ≠ fair **3** = evil, foul, sinister, vile, wicked, infernal **4** = secret, hidden, mysterious, concealed **5** = gloomy, sad, grim, miserable, bleak, dismal, pessimistic, melancholy ≠ cheerful
• NOUN **1** = darkness, shadows, gloom, dusk, obscurity, murk, dimness, semi-

darkness **2** = night, twilight, evening, evo (*Austral. slang*), dusk, night-time, nightfall

darken 1 = cloud, obscure, dim, overshadow, blacken ≠ brighten **2** = make dark, blacken

darkness = dark, shadows, shade, gloom, blackness, murk, duskiness

darling NOUN = beloved, love, dear, dearest, angel, treasure, precious, sweetheart
• ADJECTIVE = beloved, dear, treasured, precious, adored, cherished

dart = dash, run, race, shoot, fly, speed, spring, tear

dash VERB **1** = rush, run, race, shoot, fly, career, speed, tear ≠ dawdle **2** = throw, cast, pitch, slam, toss, hurl, fling, chuck (*informal*) **3** = crash, break, smash, shatter, splinter
• NOUN **1** = rush, run, race, sprint, dart, spurt, sortie **2** = drop, little, bit, shot (*informal*), touch, spot, trace, hint ≠ lot **3** (*Old-fashioned*) = style, spirit, flair, flourish, verve, panache, élan, brio

dashing 1 (*Old-fashioned*) = stylish, smart, elegant, flamboyant, sporty, jaunty, showy **2** = bold, spirited, gallant, swashbuckling, debonair ≠ dull

data = information, facts, figures, details, intelligence, statistics

date NOUN **1** = time, stage, period **2** = appointment, meeting, arrangement, commitment, engagement, rendezvous, tryst, assignation **3** = partner, escort, friend
• VERB **1** = put a date on, assign a date to, fix the period of **2** = become dated, become old-fashioned
• PHRASES **date from** *or* **date back to** (with a *time* or *date* as object) = come from, belong to, originate in, exist from, bear a date of

dated = old-fashioned, outdated, out of date, obsolete, unfashionable, outmoded, passé, old hat ≠ modern

daunting = intimidating, alarming, frightening, discouraging, unnerving, disconcerting, demoralizing, off-putting (*Brit. informal*) ≠ reassuring

dawn NOUN **1** = daybreak, morning, sunrise, daylight, aurora (*poetic*), crack of dawn, sunup, cockcrow **2** (*Literary*) = beginning, start, birth, rise, origin, emergence, advent, genesis
• VERB **1** = begin, start, rise, develop, emerge, unfold, originate **2** = grow light, break, brighten, lighten
• PHRASES **dawn on** *or* **upon someone** = hit, strike, occur to, register (*informal*), become apparent, come to mind, come into your head

day 1 = twenty-four hours **2** = daytime, daylight **3** = date **4** = time, age, era, period, epoch

daylight = sunlight, sunshine, light of day

daze VERB = stun, shock, paralyse, numb, stupefy, benumb
• NOUN (usually used in the phrase *in a daze*) = shock, confusion, distraction, trance, bewilderment, stupor, trancelike state

dazzle VERB **1** = impress, amaze, overwhelm, astonish, overpower, bowl over (*informal*), take your breath away **2** = blind, confuse, daze, bedazzle
• NOUN = splendour, sparkle, glitter, brilliance, magnificence, razzmatazz (*slang*)

dazzling = splendid, brilliant, stunning, glorious, sparkling, glittering, sensational (*informal*), virtuoso ≠ ordinary

dead ADJECTIVE **1** = deceased, departed, late, perished, extinct, defunct, passed away ≠ alive **2** = boring, dull, dreary, flat, plain, humdrum, uninteresting **3** = not working, useless, inactive, inoperative ≠ working **4** = numb, frozen, paralysed, insensitive, inert, deadened, immobilized, unfeeling **5** (usually used of *centre, silence,* or *stop*) = total, complete, absolute, utter, outright, thorough, unqualified **6** (*Informal*) = exhausted, tired, worn out, spent, done in (*informal*), all in (*slang*), drained, knackered (*slang*)
• NOUN = middle, heart, depth, midst
• ADVERB (*Informal*) = exactly, completely, totally, directly, fully, entirely, absolutely, thoroughly

deadline = time limit, cutoff point, target date *or* time, limit

deadlock 1 = impasse, stalemate, standstill, gridlock, standoff **2** = tie, draw, stalemate, impasse, standstill, gridlock, standoff, dead heat

deadly 1 = lethal, fatal, deathly, dangerous, devastating, mortal, murderous, malignant **2** (*Informal*) = boring, dull, tedious, flat, monotonous, uninteresting, mind-numbing, wearisome

deaf 1 = hard of hearing, without hearing, stone deaf 2 = oblivious, indifferent, unmoved, unconcerned, unsympathetic, impervious, unhearing

deal NOUN 1 (*Informal*) = agreement, understanding, contract, arrangement, bargain, transaction, pact 2 = amount, quantity, measure, degree, mass, volume, share, portion
• PHRASES **deal in something** = sell, trade in, stock, traffic in, buy and sell ◆ **deal something out** = distribute, give, share, assign, allocate, dispense, allot, mete out ◆ **deal with something** = be concerned with, involve, concern, touch, regard, apply to, bear on, pertain to ◆ **deal with something** *or* **someone** = handle, manage, treat, cope with, take care of, see to, attend to, get to grips with

dealer = trader, merchant, supplier, wholesaler, purveyor, tradesman

dear ADJECTIVE 1 = beloved, close, valued, favourite, prized, treasured, precious, intimate ≠ hated 2 (*Brit. informal*) = expensive, costly, high-priced, pricey (*informal*), at a premium, overpriced, exorbitant ≠ cheap
• NOUN = darling, love, dearest, angel, treasure, precious, beloved, loved one

dearly (*Formal*) 1 = very much, greatly, extremely, profoundly 2 = at great cost, at a high price

death 1 = dying, demise, end, passing, departure ≠ birth 2 = destruction, finish, ruin, undoing, extinction, downfall ≠ beginning
RELATED WORDS
adjectives: fatal, lethal, mortal

deathly = deathlike, white, pale, ghastly, wan, pallid, ashen

debacle *or* **débâcle** = disaster, catastrophe, fiasco

debate NOUN = discussion, talk, argument, dispute, analysis, conversation, controversy, dialogue
• VERB 1 = discuss, question, talk about, argue about, dispute, examine, deliberate 2 = consider, reflect, think about, weigh, contemplate, deliberate, ponder, ruminate

debris = remains, bits, waste, ruins, fragments, rubble, wreckage, detritus

debt NOUN = debit, commitment, obligation, liability
• PHRASES **in debt** = owing, liable, in the red (*informal*), in arrears

debtor = borrower, mortgagor

debut = entrance, beginning, launch, coming out, introduction, presentation, first appearance, initiation

decay VERB 1 = rot, spoil, crumble, deteriorate, perish, decompose, moulder, go bad 2 = decline, diminish, crumble, deteriorate, fall off, dwindle, lessen, wane ≠ grow
• NOUN 1 = rot, corruption, mould, blight, decomposition, gangrene, canker, caries 2 = decline, collapse, deterioration, failing, fading, degeneration ≠ growth

deceased = dead, late, departed, expired, defunct, lifeless

deceive = take in, trick, fool (*informal*), cheat, con (*informal*), mislead, dupe, swindle

decency 1 = propriety, correctness, decorum, respectability, etiquette 2 = courtesy, politeness, civility, graciousness, urbanity, courteousness

decent 1 = satisfactory, fair, all right, reasonable, sufficient, good enough, adequate, ample ≠ unsatisfactory 2 = proper, becoming, seemly, fitting, appropriate, suitable, respectable, befitting ≠ improper 3 (*Informal*) = good, kind, friendly, neighbourly, generous, helpful, obliging, accommodating 4 = respectable, pure, proper, modest, chaste, decorous

deception 1 = trickery, fraud, deceit, cunning, treachery, guile, legerdemain ≠ honesty 2 = trick, lie, bluff, hoax, decoy, ruse, subterfuge

decide 1 = make a decision, make up your mind, reach *or* come to a decision, choose, determine, conclude ≠ hesitate 2 = resolve, answer, determine, conclude, clear up, ordain, adjudicate, adjudge 3 = settle, determine, resolve

decidedly = definitely, clearly, positively, distinctly, downright, unequivocally, unmistakably

decision 1 = judgment, finding, ruling, sentence, resolution, conclusion, verdict, decree 2 = decisiveness, purpose, resolution, resolve, determination, firmness, forcefulness, strength of mind *or* will

decisive 1 = crucial, significant, critical,

influential, momentous, conclusive, fateful ≠ uncertain **2** = resolute, decided, firm, determined, forceful, incisive, trenchant, strong-minded ≠ indecisive

deck = decorate, dress, clothe, array, adorn, embellish, festoon, beautify

declaration **1** = announcement, proclamation, decree, notice, notification, edict, pronouncement **2** = affirmation, profession, assertion, revelation, disclosure, acknowledgment, protestation, avowal **3** = statement, testimony

declare **1** = state, claim, announce, voice, express, maintain, assert, proclaim **2** = testify, state, swear, assert, affirm, bear witness, vouch **3** = make known, reveal, show, broadcast, confess, communicate, disclose

decline VERB **1** = fall, drop, lower, sink, fade, shrink, diminish, decrease ≠ rise **2** = deteriorate, weaken, pine, decay, worsen, languish, degenerate, droop ≠ improve **3** = refuse, reject, turn down, avoid, spurn, abstain, say 'no' ≠ accept
• NOUN **1** = depression, recession, slump, falling off, downturn, dwindling, lessening ≠ rise **2** = deterioration, failing, weakening, decay, worsening, degeneration ≠ improvement

décor *or* **decor** = decoration, colour scheme, ornamentation, furnishing style

decorate **1** = adorn, trim, embroider, ornament, embellish, festoon, beautify, grace **2** = do up, paper, paint, wallpaper, renovate (*informal*), furbish **3** = pin a medal on, cite, confer an honour on *or* upon

decoration **1** = adornment, trimming, enhancement, elaboration, embellishment, ornamentation, beautification **2** = ornament, trimmings, garnish, frill, bauble **3** = medal, award, star, ribbon, badge

decorative = ornamental, fancy, pretty, attractive, for show, embellishing, showy, beautifying

decrease VERB **1** = drop, decline, lessen, lower, shrink, diminish, dwindle, subside **2** = reduce, cut, lower, moderate, weaken, diminish, cut down, shorten ≠ increase
• NOUN = lessening, decline, reduction, loss, falling off, dwindling, contraction, cutback ≠ growth

decree NOUN **1** = law, order, ruling, act, command, statute, proclamation, edict **2** = judgment, finding, ruling, decision, verdict, arbitration
• VERB = order, rule, command, demand, proclaim, prescribe, pronounce, ordain

dedicate **1** = devote, give, apply, commit, pledge, surrender, give over to **2** = offer, address, inscribe

dedicated = committed, devoted, enthusiastic, single-minded, zealous, purposeful, wholehearted ≠ indifferent

dedication **1** = commitment, loyalty, devotion, allegiance, adherence, single-mindedness, faithfulness, wholeheartedness ≠ indifference **2** = inscription, message, address

deduct = subtract, remove, take off, take away, reduce by, knock off (*informal*), decrease by ≠ add

deduction **1** = conclusion, finding, verdict, judgment, assumption, inference **2** = reasoning, thinking, thought, analysis, logic **3** = discount, reduction, cut, concession, decrease, rebate, diminution **4** = subtraction, reduction, concession

deed **1** = action, act, performance, achievement, exploit, feat **2** (*Law*) = document, title, contract

deep ADJECTIVE **1** = big, wide, broad, profound, yawning, bottomless, unfathomable ≠ shallow **2** = intense, great, serious (*informal*), acute, extreme, grave, profound, heartfelt ≠ superficial **3** = sound, profound, unbroken, undisturbed, untroubled **4** = absorbed, lost, gripped, preoccupied, immersed, engrossed, rapt **5** = dark, strong, rich, intense, vivid ≠ light **6** = low, booming, bass, resonant, sonorous, low-pitched ≠ high **7** = secret, hidden, mysterious, obscure, abstract, esoteric, mystifying, arcane **8** = far, a long way, a good way, miles, a great distance
• NOUN = middle, heart, midst, dead
• PHRASES **the deep** (*Poetic*) = the ocean, the sea, the waves, the main, the high seas, the briny (*informal*)

deepen **1** = intensify, increase, grow, strengthen, reinforce, escalate, magnify **2** = dig out, excavate, scoop out, hollow out

deeply = thoroughly, completely, seriously, sadly, severely, gravely, profoundly, intensely

de facto ADJECTIVE = actual, real, existing • ADVERB = in fact, really, actually, in effect, in reality

default VERB = fail to pay, dodge, evade, neglect • NOUN 1 (usually in phrase *by default* or *in default of*) = failure, neglect, deficiency, lapse, omission, dereliction 2 = nonpayment, evasion

defeat VERB 1 = beat, crush, overwhelm, conquer, master, rout, trounce, vanquish ≠ surrender 2 = frustrate, foil, thwart, ruin, baffle, confound, balk, get the better of • NOUN 1 = conquest, beating, overthrow, rout ≠ victory 2 = frustration, failure, reverse, setback, thwarting

defect NOUN = deficiency, failing, fault, error, flaw, imperfection • VERB = desert, rebel, quit, revolt, change sides

defence or (*U.S.*) **defense** NOUN 1 = protection, cover, security, guard, shelter, safeguard, immunity 2 = armaments, weapons 3 = argument, explanation, excuse, plea, justification, vindication, rationalization 4 = plea (*Law*), testimony, denial, alibi, rebuttal • PLURAL NOUN = shield, barricade, fortification, buttress, rampart, bulwark, fortified pa (*N.Z.*)

defend 1 = protect, cover, guard, screen, preserve, look after, shelter, shield 2 = support, champion, justify, endorse, uphold, vindicate, stand up for, speak up for

defendant = the accused, respondent, prisoner at the bar

defender 1 = supporter, champion, advocate, sponsor, follower 2 = protector, guard, guardian, escort, bodyguard

defensive 1 = protective, watchful, on the defensive, on guard 2 = oversensitive, uptight (*informal*)

defer = postpone, delay, put off, suspend, shelve, hold over, procrastinate, put on ice (*informal*)

defiance = resistance, opposition, confrontation, contempt, disregard, disobedience, insolence, insubordination ≠ obedience

defiant = resisting, rebellious, daring, bold, provocative, audacious, antagonistic, insolent ≠ obedient

deficiency 1 = lack, want, deficit, absence, shortage, scarcity, dearth ≠ sufficiency 2 = failing, fault, weakness, defect, flaw, drawback, shortcoming, imperfection

deficit = shortfall, shortage, deficiency, loss, arrears

define 1 = mark out, outline, limit, bound, delineate, circumscribe, demarcate 2 = describe, interpret, characterize, explain, spell out, expound 3 = establish, specify, designate

definite 1 = specific, exact, precise, clear, particular, fixed, black-and-white, cut-and-dried (*informal*) ≠ vague 2 = clear, black-and-white, unequivocal, unambiguous, guaranteed, cut-and-dried (*informal*) 3 = noticeable, marked, clear, decided, striking, particular, distinct, conspicuous 4 = certain, decided, sure, settled, convinced, positive, confident, assured ≠ uncertain

definitely = certainly, clearly, surely, absolutely, positively, without doubt, unquestionably, undeniably

definition 1 = description, interpretation, explanation, clarification, exposition, elucidation, statement of meaning 2 = sharpness, focus, clarity, contrast, precision, distinctness

definitive 1 = final, convincing, absolute, clinching, decisive, definite, conclusive, irrefutable 2 = authoritative, greatest, ultimate, reliable, exhaustive, superlative

deflect = turn aside, bend

defy = resist, oppose, confront, brave, disregard, stand up to, spurn, flout

degenerate VERB = decline, slip, sink, decrease, deteriorate, worsen, decay, lapse • ADJECTIVE = depraved, corrupt, low, perverted, immoral, decadent, debauched, dissolute

degrade = demean, disgrace, humiliate, shame, humble, discredit, debase, dishonour ≠ ennoble

degree = amount, stage, grade

delay VERB 1 = put off, suspend, postpone, shelve, defer, hold over 2 = hold up, detain, hold back, hinder, obstruct, impede, bog down, set back ≠ speed (up) • NOUN = hold-up, wait, setback, interruption, stoppage, impediment, hindrance

delegate NOUN = representative, agent, deputy, ambassador, commissioner, envoy, proxy, legate

• **VERB** 1 = entrust, transfer, hand over, give, pass on, assign, consign, devolve 2 = appoint, commission, select, contract, engage, nominate, designate, mandate

delegation 1 = deputation, envoys, contingent, commission, embassy, legation 2 = commissioning, assignment, devolution, committal

delete = remove, cancel, erase, strike out, obliterate, efface, cross out, expunge

deliberate **ADJECTIVE** 1 = intentional, meant, planned, intended, conscious, calculated, wilful, purposeful ≠ accidental 2 = careful, measured, slow, cautious, thoughtful, circumspect, methodical, unhurried ≠ hurried

• **VERB** = consider, think, ponder, discuss, debate, reflect, consult, weigh

deliberately = intentionally, on purpose, consciously, knowingly, wilfully, by design, in cold blood, wittingly

deliberation 1 = consideration, thought, reflection, calculation, meditation, forethought, circumspection 2 = discussion, talk, conference, debate, analysis, conversation, dialogue, consultation

delicacy 1 = fragility, flimsiness 2 = daintiness, charm, grace, elegance, neatness, prettiness, slenderness, exquisiteness 3 = difficulty 4 = sensitivity, understanding, consideration, diplomacy, discretion, tact, thoughtfulness, sensitiveness 5 = treat, luxury, savoury, dainty, morsel, titbit 6 = lightness, accuracy, precision, elegance, sensibility, purity, subtlety, refinement

delicate 1 = fine, elegant, exquisite, graceful 2 = subtle, fine, delicious, faint, refined, understated, dainty ≠ bright 3 = fragile, weak, frail, brittle, tender, flimsy, dainty, breakable 4 = skilled, precise, deft 5 = diplomatic, sensitive, thoughtful, discreet, considerate, tactful ≠ insensitive

delicious = delectable, tasty, choice, savoury, dainty, mouthwatering, scrumptious (*informal*), appetizing, lekker (*S. African slang*), yummo (*Austral. slang*) ≠ unpleasant

delight **NOUN** = pleasure, joy, satisfaction, happiness, ecstasy, enjoyment, bliss, glee ≠ displeasure

• **VERB** = please, satisfy, thrill, charm, cheer, amuse, enchant, gratify ≠ displease

• **PHRASES** **delight in** *or* **take (a) delight in something** *or* **someone** = like, love, enjoy, appreciate, relish, savour, revel in, take pleasure in

delightful = pleasant, charming, thrilling, enjoyable, enchanting, agreeable, pleasurable, rapturous ≠ unpleasant

deliver 1 = bring, carry, bear, transport, distribute, convey, cart 2 *sometimes with* ***up*** = hand over, commit, give up, yield, surrender, turn over, relinquish, make over 3 = give, read, present, announce, declare, utter 4 = strike, give, deal, launch, direct, aim, administer, inflict 5 (*Dated*) = release, free, save, rescue, loose, liberate, ransom, emancipate

delivery 1 = handing over, transfer, distribution, transmission, dispatch, consignment, conveyance 2 = consignment, goods, shipment, batch 3 = speech, utterance, articulation, intonation, elocution, enunciation 4 = childbirth, labour, confinement, parturition

delusion = misconception, mistaken idea, misapprehension, fancy, illusion, hallucination, fallacy, false impression

demand **VERB** 1 = request, ask (for), order, expect, claim, seek, insist on, exact 2 = challenge, ask, question, inquire 3 = require, want, need, involve, call for, entail, necessitate, cry out for ≠ provide

• **NOUN** 1 = request, order 2 = need, want, call, market, claim, requirement

demanding = difficult, trying, hard, taxing, wearing, challenging, tough, exacting ≠ easy

demise 1 = failure, end, fall, defeat, collapse, ruin, breakdown, overthrow 2 (*Euphemistic*) = death, end, dying, passing, departure, decease

democracy = self-government, republic, commonwealth

Democrat **ADJECTIVE** = left-wing, Labour

• **NOUN** = left-winger

democratic = self-governing, popular, representative, autonomous, populist, egalitarian

demolish 1 = knock down, level, destroy, dismantle, flatten, tear down, bulldoze, raze ≠ build 2 = destroy, wreck, overturn, overthrow, undo

demolition = knocking down, levelling, destruction, explosion, wrecking, tearing down, bulldozing, razing

demon 1 = evil spirit, devil, fiend, goblin, ghoul, malignant spirit, atua (*N.Z.*), wairua (*N.Z.*) 2 = wizard, master, ace (*informal*), fiend

demonstrate 1 = prove, show, indicate, make clear, manifest, testify to 2 = show, express, display, indicate, exhibit, manifest 3 = march, protest, rally, object, parade, picket, remonstrate, express disapproval, hikoi (*N.Z.*) 4 = describe, show, explain, teach, illustrate

demonstration 1 = march, protest, rally, sit-in, parade, picket, mass lobby, hikoi (*N.Z.*) 2 = display, show, performance, explanation, description, presentation, exposition 3 = indication, proof, testimony, confirmation, substantiation 4 = exhibition, display, expression, illustration

den 1 = lair, hole, shelter, cave, haunt, cavern, hide-out 2 (*Chiefly U.S.*) = study, retreat, sanctuary, hideaway, sanctum, cubbyhole

denial 1 = negation, contradiction, dissent, retraction, repudiation ≠ admission 2 = refusal, veto, rejection, prohibition, rebuff, repulse 3 = renunciation, giving up, rejection, abdication, repudiation, forswearing, disavowal, relinquishment

denomination 1 = religious group, belief, sect, persuasion, creed, school, hauhau (*N.Z.*) 2 = unit, value, size, grade

denounce 1 = condemn, attack, censure, revile, vilify, stigmatize 2 = report, dob in (*Austral. slang*)

dense 1 = thick, heavy, solid, compact, condensed, impenetrable, close-knit ≠ thin 2 = heavy, thick, opaque, impenetrable 3 = stupid (*Informal*), thick, dull, dumb (*informal*), dozy (*Brit. informal*), stolid, dopey (*informal*), moronic ≠ bright

density 1 = tightness, thickness, compactness, impenetrability, denseness 2 = mass, bulk, consistency, solidity

dent VERB = make a dent in, press in, gouge, hollow, push in
• NOUN = hollow, chip, indentation, depression, impression, pit, dip, crater, ding (*Austral. & N.Z. dated informal*)

deny 1 = contradict, disagree with, rebuff, negate, rebut, refute ≠ admit 2 = renounce, reject, retract, repudiate, disown, recant, disclaim 3 = refuse, forbid, reject, rule out, turn down, prohibit, withhold, preclude ≠ permit

depart 1 = leave, go, withdraw, retire, disappear, quit, retreat, exit ≠ arrive 2 = deviate, vary, differ, stray, veer, swerve, diverge, digress

department = section, office, unit, station, division, branch, bureau, subdivision

departure 1 = leaving, going, retirement, withdrawal, exit, going away, removal, exodus ≠ arrival 2 = retirement, going, withdrawal, exit, going away, removal 3 = shift, change, difference, variation, innovation, novelty, deviation, divergence

depend 1 = be determined by, be based on, be subject to, hang on, rest on, revolve around, hinge on, be subordinate to 2 = count on, turn to, trust in, bank on, lean on, rely upon, reckon on

dependent *or* (*U.S. sometimes*) **dependant** ADJECTIVE = reliant, vulnerable, helpless, powerless, weak, defenceless ≠ independent
• PHRASES **dependent on** *or* **upon** 1 = reliant on, relying on 2 = determined by, depending on, subject to, influenced by, conditional on, contingent on

depict 1 = illustrate, portray, picture, paint, outline, draw, sketch, delineate 2 = describe, present, represent, outline, characterize

deplete = use up, reduce, drain, exhaust, consume, empty, lessen, impoverish ≠ increase

deplore = disapprove of, condemn, object to, denounce, censure, abhor, take a dim view of

deploy (used of troops or military resources) = use, station, position, arrange, set out, utilize

deployment (used of troops or military resources) = use, stationing, spread, organization, arrangement, positioning, utilization

deport = expel, exile, throw out, oust, banish, expatriate, extradite, evict

depose = oust, dismiss, displace, demote, dethrone, remove from office

deposit NOUN 1 = down payment, security, stake, pledge, instalment, retainer, part payment 2 = accumulation, mass, build-up, layer 3 = sediment, grounds, residue,

lees, precipitate, silt, dregs
• VERB **1** = put, place, lay, drop **2** = store, keep, put, bank, lodge, entrust, consign

depot **1** = arsenal, warehouse, storehouse, repository, depository **2** (*Chiefly U.S. & Canad.*) = bus station, station, garage, terminus

depreciation = devaluation, fall, drop, depression, slump, deflation

depress **1** = sadden, upset, distress, discourage, grieve, oppress, weigh down, make sad ≠ cheer **2** = lower, cut, reduce, diminish, decrease, lessen ≠ raise **3** = devalue, depreciate, cheapen **4** = press down, push, squeeze, lower, flatten, compress, push down

depressed **1** = sad, blue, unhappy, discouraged, fed up, mournful, dejected, despondent **2** = poverty-stricken, poor, deprived, disadvantaged, run-down, impoverished, needy **3** = lowered, devalued, weakened, depreciated, cheapened **4** = sunken, hollow, recessed, indented, concave

depressing = bleak, sad, discouraging, gloomy, dismal, harrowing, saddening, dispiriting

depression **1** = despair, misery, sadness, dumps (*informal*), the blues, melancholy, unhappiness, despondency **2** = recession, slump, economic decline, stagnation, inactivity, hard *or* bad times **3** = hollow, pit, dip, bowl, valley, dent, cavity, indentation

deprivation **1** = lack, denial, withdrawal, removal, expropriation, dispossession **2** = want, need, hardship, suffering, distress, privation, destitution

deprive = dispossess, rob, strip, despoil, bereave

deprived = poor, disadvantaged, needy, in need, lacking, bereft, destitute, down at heel ≠ prosperous

depth **1** = deepness, drop, measure, extent **2** = insight, wisdom, penetration, profundity, discernment, sagacity, astuteness, profoundness ≠ superficiality **3** = breadth

deputy = substitute, representative, delegate, lieutenant, proxy, surrogate, second-in-command, legate

derelict ADJECTIVE = abandoned, deserted, ruined, neglected, discarded, forsaken, dilapidated
• NOUN = tramp, outcast, drifter, down-and-out, vagrant, bag lady, derro (*Austral. slang*)

descend VERB **1** = fall, drop, sink, go down, plunge, dive, tumble, plummet ≠ rise **2** = get off **3** = go down, come down, walk down, move down, climb down **4** = slope, dip, incline, slant
• PHRASES **be descended from** = originate from, derive from, spring from, proceed from, issue from

descent **1** = fall, drop, plunge, coming down, swoop **2** = slope, drop, dip, incline, slant, declivity **3** = decline, deterioration, degeneration **4** = origin, extraction, ancestry, lineage, family tree, parentage, genealogy, derivation

describe **1** = relate, tell, report, explain, express, recount, recite, narrate **2** = portray, depict **3** = trace, draw, outline, mark out, delineate

description **1** = account, report, explanation, representation, sketch, narrative, portrayal, depiction **2** = calling, naming, branding, labelling, dubbing, designation **3** = kind, sort, type, order, class, variety, brand, category

desert[1] = wilderness, waste, wilds, wasteland

desert[2] **1** = abandon, leave, quit (*informal*), forsake **2** = leave, abandon, strand, maroon, walk out on (*informal*), forsake, jilt, leave stranded ≠ take care of **3** = abscond

deserted **1** = empty, abandoned, desolate, neglected, vacant, derelict, unoccupied **2** = abandoned, neglected, forsaken

deserve = merit, warrant, be entitled to, have a right to, rate, earn, justify, be worthy of

deserved = well-earned, fitting, due, earned, justified, merited, proper, warranted

deserving = worthy, righteous, commendable, laudable, praiseworthy, meritorious, estimable ≠ undeserving

design VERB **1** = plan, draw, draft, trace, outline, devise, sketch, formulate **2** = create, plan, fashion, propose, invent, conceive, originate, fabricate **3** = intend, mean, plan, aim, purpose
• NOUN **1** = pattern, form, style, shape, organization, arrangement, construction

2 = plan, drawing, model, scheme, draft, outline, sketch, blueprint **3** = intention, end, aim, goal, target, purpose, object, objective

designate 1 = name, call, term, style, label, entitle, dub **2** = choose, reserve, select, label, flag, assign, allocate, set aside **3** = appoint, name, choose, commission, select, elect, delegate, nominate

designer 1 = couturier **2** = producer, architect, deviser, creator, planner, inventor, originator

desirable 1 = advantageous, useful, valuable, helpful, profitable, of service, convenient, worthwhile ≠ disadvantageous **2** = popular ≠ unpopular **3** = attractive, appealing, pretty, fair, inviting, lovely, charming, sexy (*informal*) ≠ unattractive

desire NOUN **1** = wish, want, longing, hope, urge, aspiration, craving, thirst **2** = lust, passion, libido, appetite, lasciviousness • VERB = want, long for, crave, hope for, ache for, wish for, yearn for, thirst for

despair NOUN = despondency, depression, misery, gloom, desperation, anguish, hopelessness, dejection • VERB = lose hope, give up, lose heart

desperate 1 = grave, pressing, serious, severe, extreme, urgent, drastic **2** = last-ditch, daring, furious, risky, frantic, audacious

desperately = gravely, badly, seriously, severely, dangerously, perilously

desperation 1 = misery, worry, trouble, despair, agony, anguish, unhappiness, hopelessness **2** = recklessness, madness, frenzy, impetuosity, rashness, foolhardiness

despise = look down on, loathe, scorn, detest, revile, abhor ≠ admire

despite = in spite of, in the face of, regardless of, even with, notwithstanding, in the teeth of, undeterred by

destination = stop, station, haven, resting-place, terminus, journey's end

destined = fated, meant, intended, certain, bound, doomed, predestined

destiny 1 = fate, fortune, lot, portion, doom, nemesis **2** *usually cap.* = fortune, chance, karma, providence, kismet, predestination, divine will

destroy 1 = ruin, crush, devastate, wreck, shatter, wipe out, demolish, eradicate **2** = slaughter, kill

destruction 1 = ruin, havoc, wreckage, demolition, devastation, annihilation **2** slaughter, extermination, eradication **3** = slaughter

destructive = devastating, fatal, deadly, lethal, harmful, damaging, catastrophic, ruinous

detach 1 = separate, remove, divide, cut off, sever, disconnect, tear off, disengage ≠ attach **2** = free, remove, separate, isolate, cut off, disengage

detached 1 = objective, neutral, impartial, reserved, impersonal, disinterested, unbiased, dispassionate ≠ subjective **2** = separate, disconnected, discrete, unconnected, undivided

detachment 1 = indifference, fairness, neutrality, objectivity, impartiality, coolness, remoteness, nonchalance **2** (*Military*) = unit, party, force, body, squad, patrol, task force

detail NOUN **1** = point, fact, feature, particular, respect, factor, element, aspect **2** = fine point, particular, nicety, triviality **3** (*Military*) = party, force, body, duty, squad, assignment, fatigue, detachment • VERB = list, relate, catalogue, recount, rehearse, recite, enumerate, itemize

detailed = comprehensive, full, complete, minute, particular, thorough, exhaustive, all-embracing ≠ brief

detain 1 = hold, arrest, confine, restrain, imprison, intern, take prisoner, hold in custody **2** = delay, hold up, hamper, hinder, retard, impede, keep back, slow up *or* down

detect 1 = discover, find, uncover, track down, unmask **2** = notice, see, spot, note, identify, observe, recognize, perceive

detective = investigator, cop (*slang*), private eye, sleuth (*informal*), private investigator, gumshoe (*U.S. slang*)

detention = imprisonment, custody, quarantine, confinement, incarceration ≠ release

deter 1 = discourage, inhibit, put off, frighten, intimidate, dissuade, talk out of **2** = prevent, stop

deteriorate = decline, worsen, degenerate, slump, go downhill ≠ improve

determination = resolution, purpose, resolve, dedication, fortitude, persistence,

tenacity, perseverance ≠ indecision
determine 1 = affect, decide, regulate, ordain 2 = settle, learn, establish, discover, find out, work out, detect, verify 3 = decide on, choose, elect, resolve 4 = decide, conclude, resolve, make up your mind
determined = resolute, firm, dogged, intent, persistent, persevering, single-minded, tenacious
deterrent = discouragement, obstacle, curb, restraint, impediment, check, hindrance, disincentive ≠ incentive
devastate = destroy, ruin, sack, wreck, demolish, level, ravage, raze
devastation = destruction, ruin, havoc, demolition, desolation
develop 1 = grow, advance, progress, mature, evolve, flourish, ripen 2 = establish, set up, promote, generate, undertake, initiate, embark on, cultivate 3 = form, establish, breed, generate, originate 4 = expand, extend, work out, elaborate, unfold, enlarge, broaden, amplify
development 1 = growth, increase, advance, progress, spread, expansion, evolution, enlargement 2 = establishment, forming, generation, institution, invention, initiation, inauguration, instigation 3 = event, happening, result, incident, improvement, evolution, unfolding, occurrence
deviant ADJECTIVE = perverted, sick (*informal*), twisted, warped, kinky (*slang*) ≠ normal
• NOUN = pervert, freak, misfit
device 1 = gadget, machine, tool, instrument, implement, appliance, apparatus, contraption 2 = ploy, scheme, plan, trick, manoeuvre, gambit, stratagem, wile
devil NOUN 1 = evil spirit, demon, fiend, atua (*N.Z.*), wairua (*N.Z.*) 2 = brute, monster, beast, barbarian, fiend, terror, swine, ogre 3 = person, individual, soul, creature, thing, beggar 4 = scamp, rogue, rascal, scoundrel, scallywag (*informal*), nointer (*Austral. slang*)
• PHRASES **the Devil** = Satan, Lucifer, Prince of Darkness, Mephistopheles, Evil One, Beelzebub, Old Nick (*informal*)
devise = work out, design, construct, invent, conceive, formulate, contrive, dream up
devoid *with* ***of*** = lacking in, without, free from, wanting in, bereft of, empty of, deficient in
devote = dedicate, give, commit, apply, reserve, pledge, surrender, assign
devoted = dedicated, committed, true, constant, loyal, faithful, ardent, staunch ≠ disloyal
devotee = enthusiast, fan, supporter, follower, admirer, buff (*informal*), fanatic, adherent
devotion NOUN 1 = love, passion, affection, attachment, fondness 2 = dedication, commitment, loyalty, allegiance, fidelity, adherence, constancy, faithfulness ≠ indifference 3 = worship, reverence, spirituality, holiness, piety, godliness, devoutness ≠ irreverence
• PLURAL NOUN = prayers, religious observance, church service, divine office
devour 1 = eat, consume, swallow, wolf, gulp, gobble, guzzle, polish off (*informal*) 2 = enjoy, take in, read compulsively *or* voraciously
devout = religious, godly, pious, pure, holy, orthodox, saintly, reverent ≠ irreverent
diagnose = identify, determine, recognize, distinguish, interpret, pronounce, pinpoint
diagnosis = identification, discovery, recognition, detection
diagram = plan, figure, drawing, chart, representation, sketch, graph
dialogue 1 = discussion, conference, exchange, debate 2 = conversation, discussion, communication, discourse
diary 1 = journal, chronicle 2 = engagement book, Filofax®, appointment book
dictate VERB = speak, say, utter, read out
• NOUN 1 = command, order, decree, demand, direction, injunction, fiat, edict 2 = principle, law, rule, standard, code, criterion, maxim
• PHRASES **dictate to someone** = order (about), direct, lay down the law, pronounce to
dictator = absolute ruler, tyrant, despot, oppressor, autocrat, absolutist, martinet
dictatorship = absolute rule, tyranny, totalitarianism, authoritarianism, despotism, autocracy, absolutism
dictionary = wordbook, vocabulary,

glossary, lexicon

die VERB **1** = pass away, expire, perish, croak (*slang*), give up the ghost, snuff it (*slang*), peg out (*informal*), kick the bucket (*slang*), cark it (*Austral. & N.Z. slang*) ≠ live **2** = stop, fail, halt, break down, run down, stop working, peter out, fizzle out **3** = dwindle, decline, sink, fade, diminish, decrease, decay, wither ≠ increase
• PHRASES **be dying for something** = long for, want, desire, crave, yearn for, hunger for, pine for, hanker after

diet[1] NOUN **1** = food, provisions, fare, rations, kai (*N.Z. informal*), nourishment, sustenance, victuals **2** = fast, regime, abstinence, regimen
• VERB = slim, fast, lose weight, abstain, eat sparingly ≠ overindulge

diet[2] *often cap.* = council, meeting, parliament, congress, chamber, convention, legislature

differ **1** = be dissimilar, contradict, contrast with, vary, belie, depart from, diverge, negate ≠ accord **2** = disagree, clash, dispute, dissent ≠ agree

difference **1** = dissimilarity, contrast, variation, change, variety, diversity, alteration, discrepancy ≠ similarity **2** = remainder, rest, balance, remains, excess **3** = disagreement, conflict, argument, clash, dispute, quarrel, contretemps ≠ agreement

different **1** = dissimilar, opposed, contrasting, changed, unlike, altered, inconsistent, disparate **2** = various, varied, diverse, assorted, miscellaneous, sundry **3** = unusual, special, strange, extraordinary, distinctive, peculiar, uncommon, singular

differentiate **1** = distinguish, separate, discriminate, contrast, mark off, make a distinction, tell apart, set off *or* apart **2** = make different, separate, distinguish, characterize, single out, segregate, individualize, mark off **3** = become different, change, convert, transform, alter, adapt, modify

difficult **1** = hard, tough, taxing, demanding, challenging, exacting, formidable, uphill ≠ easy **2** = problematical, involved, complex, complicated, obscure, baffling, intricate, knotty ≠ simple **3** = troublesome, demanding, perverse, fussy, fastidious, hard to please, refractory, unaccommodating ≠ cooperative

difficulty **1** = problem, trouble, obstacle, hurdle, dilemma, complication, snag, uphill (*S. African*) **2** = hardship, strain, awkwardness, strenuousness, arduousness, laboriousness

dig VERB **1** = hollow out, mine, quarry, excavate, scoop out **2** = delve, tunnel, burrow **3** = turn over **4** = search, hunt, root, delve, forage, dig down, fossick (*Austral. & N.Z.*) **5** = poke, drive, push, stick, punch, stab, thrust, shove
• NOUN **1** = cutting remark, crack (*slang*), insult, taunt, sneer, jeer, barb, wisecrack (*informal*) **2** = poke, thrust, nudge, prod, jab, punch

digest VERB **1** = ingest, absorb, incorporate, dissolve, assimilate **2** = take in, absorb, grasp, soak up
• NOUN = summary, résumé, abstract, epitome, synopsis, précis, abridgment

dignity **1** = decorum, gravity, majesty, grandeur, respectability, nobility, solemnity, courtliness **2** = self-importance, pride, self-esteem, self-respect

dilemma = predicament, problem, difficulty, spot (*informal*), mess, puzzle, plight, quandary

dilute **1** = water down, thin (out), weaken, adulterate, make thinner, cut (*informal*) ≠ condense **2** = reduce, weaken, diminish, temper, decrease, lessen, diffuse, mitigate ≠ intensify

dim ADJECTIVE **1** = poorly lit, dark, gloomy, murky, shady, shadowy, dusky, tenebrous **2** = cloudy, grey, gloomy, dismal, overcast, leaden ≠ bright **3** = unclear, obscured, faint, blurred, fuzzy, shadowy, hazy, bleary ≠ distinct **4** = stupid (*Informal*), thick, dull, dense, dumb (*informal*), daft (*informal*), dozy (*Brit. informal*), obtuse ≠ bright
• VERB **1** = turn down, fade, dull **2** = grow *or* become faint, fade, dull, grow *or* become dim **3** = darken, dull, cloud over

dimension **1** = aspect, side, feature, angle, facet **2** = extent, size

diminish **1** = decrease, decline, lessen, shrink, dwindle, wane, recede, subside ≠ grow **2** = reduce, cut, decrease, lessen, lower, curtail ≠ increase

din = noise, row, racket, crash, clamour, clatter, uproar, commotion ≠ silence

dine = eat, lunch, feast, sup

dinkum (*Austral. & N.Z. informal*) = genuine, honest, natural, frank, sincere, candid, upfront (*informal*), artless

dinner **1** = meal, main meal, spread (*informal*), repast **2** = banquet, feast, repast, hakari (*N.Z.*)

dip VERB **1** = plunge, immerse, bathe, duck, douse, dunk **2** = drop (down), fall, lower, sink, descend, subside **3** = slope, drop (down), descend, fall, decline, sink, incline, drop away
• NOUN **1** = plunge, ducking, soaking, drenching, immersion, douche **2** = nod, drop, lowering, slump, sag **3** = hollow, hole, depression, pit, basin, trough, concavity
• PHRASES **dip into something** = sample, skim, glance at, browse, peruse

diplomacy **1** = statesmanship, statecraft, international negotiation **2** = tact, skill, sensitivity, craft, discretion, subtlety, delicacy, finesse ≠ tactlessness

diplomat = official, ambassador, envoy, statesman, consul, attaché, emissary, chargé d'affaires

diplomatic **1** = consular, official, foreign-office, ambassadorial, foreign-politic **2** = tactful, politic, sensitive, subtle, delicate, polite, discreet, prudent ≠ tactless

dire = desperate, pressing, critical, terrible, crucial, extreme, awful, urgent

direct ADJECTIVE = quickest, shortest
• ADVERB **1** = straight, through ≠ circuitous **2** = first-hand, personal, immediate ≠ indirect **3** = clear, specific, plain, absolute, definite, explicit, downright, point-blank ≠ ambiguous **4** = straightforward, open, straight, frank, blunt, honest, candid, forthright ≠ indirect **5** = verbatim, exact, word-for-word, strict, accurate, faithful, letter-for-letter **6** = non-stop, straight
• VERB **1** = aim, point, level, train, focus **2** = guide, show, lead, point the way, point in the direction of **3** = control, run, manage, lead, guide, handle, conduct, oversee **4** = order, command, instruct, charge, demand, require, bid **5** = address, send, mail, route, label

direction NOUN **1** = way, course, line, road, track, bearing, route, path **2** = management, control, charge, administration, leadership, command, guidance, supervision
• PLURAL NOUN = instructions, rules, information, plan, briefing, regulations, recommendations, guidelines

directive = order, ruling, regulation, command, instruction, decree, mandate, injunction

directly **1** = straight, unswervingly, without deviation, by the shortest route, in a beeline **2** = immediately, promptly, right away, straightaway **3** (*Old-fashioned*) = at once, as soon as possible, straightaway, forthwith **4** = honestly, openly, frankly, plainly, point-blank, unequivocally, truthfully, unreservedly

director = controller, head, leader, manager, chief, executive, governor, administrator, baas (*S. African*)

dirt **1** = filth, muck, grime, dust, mud, impurity, kak (*S. African taboo slang*) **2** = soil, ground, earth, clay, turf, loam

dirty ADJECTIVE **1** = filthy, soiled, grubby, foul, muddy, polluted, messy, grimy, festy (*Austral. slang*) ≠ clean **2** = dishonest, illegal, unfair, cheating, crooked, fraudulent, treacherous, unscrupulous ≠ honest **3** = obscene, indecent, blue, offensive, filthy, pornographic, sleazy, lewd ≠ decent
• VERB = soil, foul, stain, spoil, muddy, pollute, blacken, defile ≠ clean

disability = handicap, affliction, disorder, defect, impairment, infirmity

disable = handicap, cripple, damage, paralyse, impair, incapacitate, immobilize, enfeeble

disabled = differently abled, physically challenged, handicapped, weakened, crippled, paralysed, lame, incapacitated ≠ able-bodied

disadvantage **1** = drawback, trouble, handicap, nuisance, snag, inconvenience, downside ≠ advantage **2** = harm, loss, damage, injury, hurt, prejudice, detriment, disservice ≠ benefit

disagree **1** = differ (in opinion), argue, clash, dispute, dissent, quarrel, take issue with, cross swords ≠ agree **2** = make ill, upset, sicken, trouble, hurt, bother, distress, discomfort

disagreement = argument, row, conflict, clash, dispute, dissent, quarrel, squabble ≠ agreement

disappear **1** = vanish, recede, evanesce

≠ appear 2 = pass, fade away 3 = cease, dissolve, evaporate, perish, die out, pass away, melt away, leave no trace

disappearance 1 = vanishing, going, passing, melting, eclipse, evaporation, evanescence 2 = flight, departure 3 = loss, losing, mislaying

disappoint = let down, dismay, fail, disillusion, dishearten, disenchant, dissatisfy, disgruntle

disappointment 1 = regret, discontent, dissatisfaction, disillusionment, chagrin, disenchantment, dejection, despondency 2 = letdown, blow, setback, misfortune, calamity, choker (*informal*) 3 = frustration

disapproval = displeasure, criticism, objection, condemnation, dissatisfaction, censure, reproach, denunciation

disapprove = condemn, object to, dislike, deplore, frown on, take exception to, take a dim view of, find unacceptable ≠ approve

disarm 1 = demilitarize, disband, demobilize, deactivate 2 = win over, persuade

disarmament = arms reduction, demobilization, arms limitation, demilitarization, de-escalation

disarming = charming, winning, irresistible, persuasive, likable *or* likeable

disarray 1 = confusion, disorder, indiscipline, disunity, disorganization, unruliness ≠ order 2 = untidiness, mess, chaos, muddle, clutter, shambles, jumble, hotchpotch ≠ tidiness

disaster 1 = catastrophe, trouble, tragedy, ruin, misfortune, adversity, calamity, cataclysm 2 = failure, mess, flop (*informal*), catastrophe, debacle, cock-up (*Brit. slang*), washout (*informal*)

disastrous 1 = terrible, devastating, tragic, fatal, catastrophic, ruinous, calamitous, cataclysmic 2 = unsuccessful

disbelief = scepticism, doubt, distrust, mistrust, incredulity, unbelief, dubiety ≠ belief

discard = get rid of, drop, throw away *or* out, reject, abandon, dump (*informal*), dispose of, dispense with ≠ keep

discharge VERB 1 = release, free, clear, liberate, pardon, allow to go, set free 2 = dismiss, sack (*informal*), fire (*informal*), remove, expel, discard, oust, cashier 3 = carry out, perform, fulfil, accomplish, do, effect, realize, observe 4 = pay, meet, clear, settle, square (up), honour, satisfy, relieve 5 = pour forth, release, leak, emit, dispense, ooze, exude, give off 6 = fire, shoot, set off, explode, let off, detonate, let loose (*informal*)
• NOUN 1 = release, liberation, clearance, pardon, acquittal 2 = dismissal, notice, removal, the boot (*slang*), expulsion, the push (*slang*), marching orders (*informal*), ejection 3 = emission, ooze, secretion, excretion, pus, seepage, suppuration 4 = firing, report, shot, blast, burst, explosion, volley, salvo

disciple 1 = apostle 2 = follower, student, supporter, pupil, devotee, apostle, adherent ≠ teacher

discipline NOUN 1 = control, authority, regulation, supervision, orderliness, strictness 2 = punishment, penalty, correction, chastening, chastisement, castigation 3 = self-control, control, restraint, self-discipline, willpower, self-restraint, orderliness 4 = training, practice, exercise, method, regulation, drill, regimen 5 = field of study, area, subject, theme, topic, course, curriculum, speciality
• VERB 1 = punish, correct, reprimand, castigate, chastise, chasten, penalize, bring to book 2 = train, educate

disclose 1 = make known, reveal, publish, relate, broadcast, confess, communicate, divulge ≠ keep secret 2 = show, reveal, expose, unveil, uncover, lay bare, bring to light ≠ hide

disclosure 1 = revelation, announcement, publication, leak, admission, declaration, confession, acknowledgment 2 = uncovering, publication, revelation, divulgence

discomfort 1 = pain, hurt, ache, throbbing, irritation, tenderness, pang, malaise ≠ comfort 2 = uneasiness, worry, anxiety, doubt, distress, misgiving, qualms, trepidation ≠ reassurance 3 = inconvenience, trouble, difficulty, bother, hardship, irritation, nuisance, uphill (*S. African*)

discontent = dissatisfaction, unhappiness, displeasure, regret, envy, restlessness, uneasiness

discontented = dissatisfied, unhappy, fed up, disgruntled, disaffected, vexed, displeased ≠ satisfied

discount NOUN = deduction, cut, reduction, concession, rebate
• VERB 1 = mark down, reduce, lower 2 = disregard, reject, ignore, overlook, discard, set aside, dispel, pass over

discourage 1 = dishearten, depress, intimidate, overawe, demoralize, put a damper on, dispirit, deject ≠ hearten 2 = put off, deter, prevent, dissuade, talk out of ≠ encourage

discourse 1 = conversation, talk, discussion, speech, communication, chat, dialogue 2 = speech, essay, lecture, sermon, treatise, dissertation, homily, oration, whaikorero (*N.Z.*)

discover 1 = find out, learn, notice, realize, recognize, perceive, detect, uncover 2 = find, come across, uncover, unearth, turn up, dig up, come upon

discovery 1 = finding out, news, revelation, disclosure, realization 2 = invention, launch, institution, pioneering, innovation, inauguration 3 = breakthrough, find, development, advance, leap, invention, step forward, quantum leap 4 = finding, revelation, uncovering, disclosure, detection

discredit VERB 1 = disgrace, shame, smear, humiliate, taint, disparage, vilify, slander ≠ honour 2 = dispute, question, challenge, deny, reject, discount, distrust, mistrust
• NOUN = disgrace, scandal, shame, disrepute, stigma, ignominy, dishonour, ill-repute ≠ honour

discreet = tactful, diplomatic, guarded, careful, cautious, wary, prudent, considerate ≠ tactless

discrepancy = disagreement, difference, variation, conflict, contradiction, inconsistency, disparity, divergence

discretion 1 = tact, consideration, caution, diplomacy, prudence, wariness, carefulness, judiciousness ≠ tactlessness 2 = choice, will, pleasure, preference, inclination, volition

discriminate VERB = differentiate, distinguish, separate, tell the difference, draw a distinction
• PHRASES **discriminate against someone** = treat differently, single out, victimize, treat as inferior, show bias against, show prejudice against

discriminating = discerning, particular, refined, cultivated, selective, tasteful, fastidious ≠ undiscriminating

discrimination 1 = prejudice, bias, injustice, intolerance, bigotry, favouritism, unfairness 2 = discernment, taste, judgment, perception, subtlety, refinement

discuss = talk about, consider, debate, examine, argue about, deliberate about, converse about, confer about

discussion 1 = talk, debate, argument, conference, conversation, dialogue, consultation, discourse, korero (*N.Z.*) 2 = examination, investigation, analysis, scrutiny, dissection

disdain NOUN = contempt, scorn, arrogance, derision, haughtiness, superciliousness
• VERB = scorn, reject, slight, disregard, spurn, deride, look down on, sneer at

disease = illness, condition, complaint, infection, disorder, sickness, ailment, affliction

diseased = unhealthy, sick, infected, rotten, ailing, sickly, unwell, crook (*Austral. & N.Z. informal*), unsound

disgrace NOUN 1 = shame, degradation, disrepute, ignominy, dishonour, infamy, opprobrium, odium ≠ honour 2 = scandal, stain, stigma, blot, blemish
• VERB = shame, humiliate, discredit, degrade, taint, sully, dishonour, bring shame upon ≠ honour

disgraceful = shameful, shocking, scandalous, unworthy, ignominious, disreputable, contemptible, dishonourable

disgruntled = discontented, dissatisfied, annoyed, irritated, put out, grumpy, vexed, displeased, hoha (*N.Z.*)

disguise NOUN = costume, mask, camouflage
• VERB = hide, cover, conceal, screen, mask, suppress, withhold, veil

disguised 1 = in disguise, masked, camouflaged, undercover, incognito 2 = false, artificial, forged, fake, mock, imitation, sham, counterfeit

disgust NOUN 1 = loathing, revulsion, hatred, dislike, nausea, distaste, aversion, repulsion ≠ liking 2 = outrage, shock, anger, hurt, fury, resentment, wrath, indignation
• VERB = sicken, offend, revolt, put off, repel, nauseate ≠ delight

disgusting 1 = sickening, foul, revolting, gross, repellent, nauseating, repugnant, loathsome, festy (*Austral. slang*), yucko (*Austral. slang*) 2 = appalling, shocking, awful, offensive, dreadful, horrifying

dish 1 = bowl, plate, platter, salver 2 = food, fare, recipe

dishonest = deceitful, corrupt, crooked (*informal*), lying, bent (*slang*), false, cheating, treacherous ≠ honest

disintegrate = break up, crumble, fall apart, separate, shatter, splinter, break apart, go to pieces

dislike VERB = hate, object to, loathe, despise, disapprove of, detest, recoil from, take a dim view of ≠ like
• NOUN = hatred, hostility, disapproval, distaste, animosity, aversion, displeasure, antipathy ≠ liking

dismal 1 = bad, awful, dreadful, rotten (*informal*), terrible, poor, dire, abysmal 2 = sad, gloomy, dark, depressing, discouraging, bleak, dreary, sombre ≠ happy 3 = gloomy, depressing, dull, dreary ≠ cheerful

dismantle = take apart, strip, demolish, disassemble, take to pieces *or* bits

dismay NOUN 1 = alarm, fear, horror, anxiety, dread, apprehension, nervousness, consternation 2 = disappointment, frustration, dissatisfaction, disillusionment, chagrin, disenchantment, discouragement
• VERB 1 = alarm, frighten, scare, panic, distress, terrify, appal, startle 2 = disappoint, upset, discourage, daunt, disillusion, let down, dishearten, dispirit

dismiss 1 = reject, disregard 2 = banish, dispel, discard, set aside, cast out, lay aside, put out of your mind 3 = sack, fire (*informal*), remove (*informal*), axe (*informal*), discharge, lay off, cashier, give notice to 4 = let go, free, release, discharge, dissolve, liberate, disperse, send away

dismissal = the sack, removal, notice, the boot (*slang*), expulsion (*informal*), the push (*slang*), marching orders (*informal*)

disobey 1 = defy, ignore, rebel, disregard, refuse to obey 2 = infringe, defy, refuse to obey, flout, violate, contravene, overstep, transgress

disorder 1 = illness, disease, complaint, condition, sickness, ailment, affliction, malady 2 = untidiness, mess, confusion, chaos, muddle, clutter, shambles, disarray 3 = disturbance, riot, turmoil, unrest, uproar, commotion, unruliness, biffo (*Austral. slang*)

disorderly 1 = untidy, confused, chaotic, messy, jumbled, shambolic (*informal*), disorganized, higgledy-piggledy (*informal*) ≠ tidy 2 = unruly, disruptive, rowdy, turbulent, tumultuous, lawless, riotous, ungovernable

dispatch *or* **despatch** VERB 1 = send, consign 2 = kill, murder, destroy, execute, slaughter, assassinate, slay, liquidate 3 = carry out, perform, fulfil, effect, finish, achieve, settle, dismiss
• NOUN = message, news, report, story, account, communication, bulletin, communiqué

dispel = drive away, dismiss, eliminate, expel, disperse, banish, chase away

dispense VERB 1 = distribute, assign, allocate, allot, dole out, share out, apportion, deal out 2 = prepare, measure, supply, mix 3 = administer, operate, carry out, implement, enforce, execute, apply, discharge
• PHRASES **dispense with something** *or* **someone** 1 = do away with, give up, cancel, abolish, brush aside, forgo 2 = do without, get rid of, dispose of, relinquish

disperse 1 = scatter, spread, distribute, strew, diffuse, disseminate, throw about 2 = break up, separate, scatter, dissolve, disband ≠ gather 3 = dissolve, break up

displace 1 = replace, succeed, supersede, oust, usurp, supplant, take the place of 2 = move, shift, disturb, budge, misplace

display VERB 1 = show, present, exhibit, put on view ≠ conceal 2 = expose, show, reveal, exhibit, uncover 3 = demonstrate, show, reveal, register, expose, disclose, manifest 4 = show off, parade, exhibit, sport (*informal*), flash (*informal*), flourish, brandish, flaunt
• NOUN 1 = proof, exhibition, demonstration, evidence, expression, illustration, revelation, testimony 2 = exhibition, show, demonstration, presentation, array 3 = ostentation, show, flourish, fanfare, pomp 4 = show, exhibition, parade, spectacle, pageant

disposable 1 = throwaway, nonreturnable 2 = available, expendable,

consumable
disposal NOUN = throwing away, dumping (*informal*), scrapping, removal, discarding, jettisoning, ejection, riddance
• PHRASES **at your disposal** = available, ready, to hand, accessible, handy, at hand, on tap, expendable
dispose VERB = arrange, put, place, group, order, distribute, array
• PHRASES **dispose of someone** = kill, murder, destroy, execute, slaughter, assassinate, slay, liquidate ◆ **dispose of something** 1 = get rid of, destroy, dump (*informal*), scrap, discard, unload, jettison, throw out *or* away 2 = deal with, manage, treat, handle, settle, cope with, take care of, see to
disposition 1 = character, nature, spirit, make-up, constitution, temper, temperament 2 = tendency, inclination, propensity, habit, leaning, bent, bias, proclivity 3 = arrangement, grouping, ordering, organization, distribution, placement
dispute NOUN 1 = disagreement, conflict, argument, dissent, altercation 2 = argument, row, clash, controversy, contention, feud, quarrel, squabble
• VERB 1 = contest, question, challenge, deny, doubt, oppose, object to, contradict 2 = argue, fight, clash, disagree, fall out (*informal*), quarrel, squabble, bicker
disqualify = ban, rule out, prohibit, preclude, debar, declare ineligible
disregard VERB = ignore, discount, overlook, neglect, pass over, turn a blind eye to, make light of, pay no heed to ≠ pay attention to
• NOUN = ignoring, neglect, contempt, indifference, negligence, disdain, disrespect
disrupt 1 = interrupt, stop, upset, hold up, interfere with, unsettle, obstruct, cut short 2 = disturb, upset, confuse, disorder, spoil, disorganize, disarrange
disruption = disturbance, interference, interruption, stoppage
disruptive = disturbing, upsetting, disorderly, unsettling, troublesome, unruly ≠ well-behaved
dissatisfaction = discontent, frustration, resentment, disappointment, irritation, unhappiness, annoyance, displeasure
dissatisfied = discontented, frustrated, unhappy, disappointed, fed up, disgruntled, displeased, unsatisfied ≠ satisfied
dissent = disagreement, opposition, protest, resistance, refusal, objection, discord, demur ≠ assent
dissident NOUN = protester, rebel, dissenter, demonstrator, agitator
• ADJECTIVE = dissenting, disagreeing, nonconformist, heterodox
dissolve 1 = melt, soften, thaw, liquefy, deliquesce 2 = end, suspend, break up, wind up, terminate, discontinue, dismantle, disband
distance 1 = space, length, extent, range, stretch, gap, interval, span 2 = aloofness, reserve, detachment, restraint, stiffness, coolness, coldness, standoffishness
distant 1 = far-off, far, remote, abroad, out-of-the-way, far-flung, faraway, outlying ≠ close 2 = remote 3 = reserved, withdrawn, cool, remote, detached, aloof, unfriendly, reticent ≠ friendly 4 = faraway, blank, vague, distracted, vacant, preoccupied, oblivious, absent-minded
distinct 1 = different, individual, separate, discrete, unconnected ≠ similar 2 = striking, dramatic, outstanding, noticeable, well-defined 3 = definite, marked, clear, decided, obvious, evident, noticeable, conspicuous ≠ vague
distinction 1 = difference, contrast, variation, differential, discrepancy, disparity, dissimilarity 2 = excellence, importance, fame, merit, prominence, greatness, eminence, repute 3 = feature, quality, characteristic, mark, individuality, peculiarity, distinctiveness, particularity 4 = merit, honour, integrity, excellence, rectitude
distinctive = characteristic, special, individual, unique, typical, peculiar, singular, idiosyncratic ≠ ordinary
distinctly 1 = definitely, clearly, obviously, plainly, patently, decidedly, markedly, noticeably 2 = clearly, plainly
distinguish 1 = differentiate, determine, separate, discriminate, decide, judge, ascertain, tell the difference 2 = characterize, mark, separate, single out, set apart 3 = make out, recognize, perceive, know, see, tell, pick out, discern
distinguished = eminent, noted, famous, celebrated, well-known, prominent,

esteemed, acclaimed ≠ unknown
distort 1 = misrepresent, twist, bias, disguise, pervert, slant, colour, misinterpret 2 = deform, bend, twist, warp, buckle, mangle, mangulate (*Austral. slang*), disfigure, contort
distortion 1 = misrepresentation, bias, slant, perversion, falsification 2 = deformity, bend, twist, warp, buckle, contortion, malformation, crookedness
distract 1 = divert, sidetrack, draw away, turn aside, lead astray, draw *or* lead away from 2 = amuse, occupy, entertain, beguile, engross
distracted = agitated, troubled, puzzled, at sea, perplexed, flustered, in a flap (*informal*)
distraction 1 = disturbance, interference, diversion, interruption 2 = entertainment, recreation, amusement, diversion, pastime
distraught = frantic, desperate, distressed, distracted, worked-up, agitated, overwrought, out of your mind
distress NOUN 1 = suffering, pain, worry, grief, misery, torment, sorrow, heartache 2 = need, trouble, difficulties, poverty, hard times, hardship, misfortune, adversity
• VERB = upset, worry, trouble, disturb, grieve, torment, harass, agitate
distressed 1 = upset, worried, troubled, distracted, tormented, distraught, agitated, wretched 2 = poverty-stricken, poor, impoverished, needy, destitute, indigent, down at heel, straitened
distressing = upsetting, worrying, disturbing, painful, sad, harrowing, heart-breaking
distribute 1 = hand out, pass round 2 = circulate, deliver, convey 3 = share, deal, allocate, dispense, allot, dole out, apportion
distribution 1 = delivery, mailing, transportation, handling 2 = sharing, division, assignment, rationing, allocation, allotment, apportionment 3 = spread, organization, arrangement, placement
district = area, region, sector, quarter, parish, neighbourhood, vicinity, locality
distrust VERB = suspect, doubt, be wary of, mistrust, disbelieve, be suspicious of ≠ trust
• NOUN = suspicion, question, doubt, disbelief, scepticism, mistrust, misgiving, wariness ≠ trust
disturb 1 = interrupt, trouble, bother, plague, disrupt, interfere with, hassle, inconvenience 2 = upset, concern, worry, trouble, alarm, distress, unsettle, unnerve ≠ calm 3 = muddle, disorder, mix up, mess up, jumble up, disarrange
disturbance 1 = disorder, fray, brawl, fracas, commotion, rumpus 2 = upset, bother, distraction, intrusion, interruption, annoyance
disturbed 1 (*Psychiatry*) = unbalanced, troubled, disordered, unstable, neurotic, upset, deranged, maladjusted ≠ balanced 2 = worried, concerned, troubled, upset, bothered, nervous, anxious, uneasy ≠ calm
disturbing = worrying, upsetting, alarming, frightening, distressing, startling, unsettling, harrowing
ditch NOUN = channel, drain, trench, dyke, furrow, gully, moat, watercourse
• VERB 1 (*Slang*) = get rid of, dump (*informal*), scrap, discard, dispose of, dispense with, jettison, throw out *or* overboard 2 (*Slang*) = leave, drop, abandon, dump (*informal*), get rid of, forsake
dive VERB 1 = plunge, drop, duck, dip, descend, plummet 2 = go underwater 3 = nose-dive, plunge, crash, swoop, plummet
• NOUN = plunge, spring, jump, leap, lunge, nose dive
diverse 1 = various, mixed, varied, assorted, miscellaneous, several, sundry, motley 2 = different, unlike, varying, separate, distinct, disparate, discrete, dissimilar
diversify = vary, change, expand, spread out, branch out
diversion 1 = distraction, deviation, digression 2 = pastime, game, sport, entertainment, hobby, relaxation, recreation, distraction 3 (*Chiefly Brit.*) = detour, roundabout way, indirect course 4 (*Chiefly Brit.*) = deviation, departure, straying, divergence, digression
diversity 1 = difference, multiplicity, heterogeneity, diverseness 2 = range, variety, scope, sphere
divert 1 = redirect, switch, avert, deflect, deviate, turn aside 2 = distract, sidetrack, lead astray, draw *or* lead away from 3 = entertain, delight, amuse, please, charm, gratify, beguile, regale

divide 1 = separate, split, segregate, bisect ≠ join 2 *sometimes with* ***up*** = share, distribute, allocate, dispense, allot, mete, deal out 3 = split, break up, come between, estrange, cause to disagree

dividend = bonus, share, cut (*informal*), gain, extra, plus, portion, divvy (*informal*)

divine ADJECTIVE 1 = heavenly, spiritual, holy, immortal, supernatural, celestial, angelic, superhuman 2 = sacred, religious, holy, spiritual, blessed, revered, hallowed, consecrated 3 (*Informal*) = wonderful, perfect, beautiful, excellent, lovely, glorious, marvellous, splendid
• VERB = guess, suppose, perceive, discern, infer, deduce, apprehend, surmise

division 1 = separation, dividing, splitting up, partition, cutting up 2 = sharing, sharing, distribution, assignment, rationing, allocation, allotment, apportionment 3 = disagreement, split, rift, rupture, abyss, chasm, variance, discord ≠ unity 4 = department, group, branch 5 = part, bit, piece, section, class, category, fraction

divorce NOUN = separation, split, break-up, parting, split-up, rift, dissolution, annulment
• VERB = separate, split up, part company, dissolve your marriage

dizzy 1 = giddy, faint, light-headed, swimming, reeling, shaky, wobbly, off balance 2 = confused, dazzled, at sea, bewildered, muddled, bemused, dazed, disorientated

do VERB 1 = perform, achieve, carry out, complete, accomplish, execute, pull off 2 = make, prepare, fix, arrange, look after, see to, get ready 3 = solve, work out, resolve, figure out, decode, decipher, puzzle out 4 = be adequate, be sufficient, satisfy, suffice, pass muster, cut the mustard, meet requirements 5 = produce, make, create, develop, manufacture, construct, invent, fabricate
• NOUN (*Informal, chiefly Brit. & N.Z.*) = party, gathering, function, event, affair, occasion, celebration, reception
• PHRASES **do away with something** = get rid of, remove, eliminate, abolish, discard, put an end to, dispense with, discontinue ◆ **do without something** *or* **someone** = manage without, give up, dispense with, forgo, kick (*informal*), abstain from, get along without

dock[1] NOUN = port, haven, harbour, pier, wharf, quay, waterfront, anchorage
• VERB 1 = moor, land, anchor, put in, tie up, berth, drop anchor 2 (*of spacecraft*) = link up, unite, join, couple, rendezvous, hook up

dock[2] 1 = cut, reduce, decrease, diminish, lessen ≠ increase 2 = deduct, subtract 3 = cut off, crop, clip, shorten, curtail, cut short

doctor NOUN = physician, medic (*informal*), general practitioner, medical practitioner, G.P.
• VERB 1 = change, alter, interfere with, disguise, pervert, tamper with, tinker with, misrepresent 2 = add to, spike, cut, mix something with something, dilute, water down, adulterate

doctrine = teaching, principle, belief, opinion, conviction, creed, dogma, tenet, kaupapa (*N.Z.*)

document NOUN = paper, form, certificate, report, record, testimonial, authorization
• VERB = support, certify, verify, detail, validate, substantiate, corroborate, authenticate

dodge VERB 1 = duck, dart, swerve, sidestep, shoot, turn aside 2 = evade, avoid, escape, get away from, elude 3 = avoid, evade, shirk
• NOUN = trick, scheme, ploy, trap, device, fraud, manoeuvre, deception

dodgy 1 (*Brit., Austral., & N.Z*) = nasty, offensive, unpleasant, revolting, distasteful, repellent, obnoxious, repulsive 2 (*Brit., Austral., & N.Z*) = risky, difficult, tricky, dangerous, delicate, uncertain, dicey (*informal, chiefly Brit.*), chancy (*informal*) 3 = second rate, poor, inferior, mediocre, shoddy, bush-league (*Austral. & N.Z. informal*), half-pie (*N.Z. informal*), bodger *or* bodgie (*Austral. slang*)

dog NOUN = hound, canine, pooch (*slang*), cur, man's best friend, kuri *or* goorie (*N.Z.*), brak (*S. African*)
• VERB 1 = plague, follow, trouble, haunt, hound, torment 2 = pursue, follow, track, chase, trail, hound, stalk
• PHRASES **go to the dogs** (*Informal*) = deteriorate, degenerate, be in decline, go downhill (*informal*), go down the drain, go to pot, go to ruin

RELATED WORDS

adjective: canine
female: bitch
young: pup, puppy
dogged = determined, persistent, stubborn, resolute, tenacious, steadfast, obstinate, indefatigable ≠ irresolute
dole NOUN = share, grant, gift, allowance, handout, koha (*N.Z.*)
• PHRASES **dole something out** = give out, distribute, assign, allocate, hand out, dispense, allot, apportion
dolphin
RELATED WORD
collective noun: school
domestic ADJECTIVE **1** = home, internal, native, indigenous **2** = household, home, family, private **3** = home-loving, homely, housewifely, stay-at-home, domesticated **4** = domesticated, trained, tame, pet, house-trained
• NOUN = servant, help, maid, daily, char (*informal*), charwoman
dominant 1 = main, chief, primary, principal, prominent, predominant, pre-eminent ≠ minor **2** = controlling, ruling, commanding, supreme, governing, superior, authoritative
dominate 1 = control, rule, direct, govern, monopolize, tyrannize, have the whip hand over **2** = tower above, overlook, survey, stand over, loom over, stand head and shoulders above
domination = control, power, rule, authority, influence, command, supremacy, ascendancy
don = put on, get into, dress in, pull on, change into, get dressed in, clothe yourself in, slip on *or* into
donate = give, present, contribute, grant, subscribe, endow, entrust, impart
donation = contribution, gift, subscription, offering, present, grant, hand-out, koha (*N.Z.*)
donor = giver, contributor, benefactor, philanthropist, donator ≠ recipient
doom NOUN **1** = destruction, ruin, catastrophe, downfall **2** = fate, fortune
• VERB = condemn, sentence, consign, destine
doomed = hopeless, condemned, ill-fated, fated, unhappy, unfortunate, cursed, unlucky
door = opening, entry, entrance, exit, doorway
dope NOUN **1** (*Slang*) = drugs, narcotics, opiates, dadah (*Austral. slang*) **2** (*Informal*) = idiot, fool, twit (*informal, chiefly Brit.*), dunce, simpleton, dimwit (*informal*), nitwit (*informal*), dumb-ass (*slang*), dorba *or* dorb (*Austral. slang*), bogan (*Austral. slang*)
• VERB = drug, knock out, sedate, stupefy, anaesthetize, narcotize
dorp (*S. African*) = town, village, settlement, municipality, kainga *or* kaika (*N.Z.*)
dose 1 = measure, amount, allowance, portion, prescription, ration, draught, dosage **2** = quantity, measure, supply, portion
dot NOUN = spot, point, mark, fleck, jot, speck, speckle
• VERB = spot, stud, fleck, speckle
• PHRASES **on the dot** = on time, promptly, precisely, exactly (*informal*), to the minute, on the button (*informal*), punctually
double ADJECTIVE **1** = matching, coupled, paired, twin, duplicate, in pairs **2** = dual, enigmatic, twofold
• VERB **1** = multiply by two, duplicate, increase twofold, enlarge, magnify **2** = fold up *or* over
• NOUN = twin, lookalike, spitting image, clone, replica, dead ringer (*slang*), Doppelgänger, duplicate
• PHRASES **at** *or* **on the double** = at once, now, immediately, directly, quickly, promptly, straight away, right away
◆ **double as something** *or* **someone** = function as, serve as
doubt NOUN **1** = uncertainty, confusion, hesitation, suspense, indecision, hesitancy, lack of conviction, irresolution ≠ certainty **2** = suspicion, scepticism, distrust, apprehension, mistrust, misgivings, qualms ≠ belief
• VERB **1** = be uncertain, be sceptical, be dubious **2** = waver, hesitate, vacillate, fluctuate **3** = disbelieve, question, suspect, query, distrust, mistrust, lack confidence in ≠ believe
doubtful 1 = unlikely, unclear, dubious, questionable, improbable, debatable, equivocal ≠ certain **2** = unsure, uncertain, hesitant, suspicious, hesitating, sceptical, tentative, wavering ≠ certain
doubtless = probably, presumably, most

likely
down ADJECTIVE = depressed, low, sad, unhappy, discouraged, miserable, fed up, dejected
• VERB (*Informal*) = swallow, drink (down), drain, gulp (down), put away (*informal*), toss off
downfall = ruin, fall, destruction, collapse, disgrace, overthrow, undoing, comeuppance (*slang*)
downgrade = demote, degrade, take down a peg (*informal*), lower *or* reduce in rank ≠ promote
downright = complete, absolute, utter, total, plain, outright, unqualified, out-and-out
down-to-earth = sensible, practical, realistic, matter-of-fact, sane, no-nonsense, unsentimental, plain-spoken
downward = descending, declining, heading down, earthward
draft NOUN 1 = outline, plan, sketch, version, rough, abstract 2 = money order, bill (of exchange), cheque, postal order
• VERB = outline, write, plan, produce, create, design, draw, compose
drag VERB = pull, draw, haul, trail, tow, tug, jerk, lug
• NOUN (*Slang*) = nuisance, bore, bother, pest, hassle (*informal*), inconvenience, annoyance
drain VERB 1 = remove, draw, empty, withdraw, tap, pump, bleed 2 = empty 3 = flow out, leak, trickle, ooze, seep, exude, well out, effuse 4 = drink up, swallow, finish, put away (*informal*), quaff, gulp down 5 = exhaust, wear out, strain, weaken, fatigue, debilitate, tire out, enfeeble 6 = consume, exhaust, empty, use up, sap, dissipate
• NOUN 1 = sewer, channel, pipe, sink, ditch, trench, conduit, duct 2 = reduction, strain, drag, exhaustion, sapping, depletion
drama 1 = play, show, stage show, dramatization 2 = theatre, acting, stagecraft, dramaturgy 3 = excitement, crisis, spectacle, turmoil, histrionics
dramatic 1 = exciting, thrilling, tense, sensational, breathtaking, electrifying, melodramatic, climactic 2 = theatrical, Thespian, dramaturgical 3 = expressive 4 = powerful, striking, impressive, vivid, jaw-dropping ≠ ordinary
drape = cover, wrap, fold, swathe
drastic = extreme, strong, radical, desperate, severe, harsh
draught 1 = breeze, current, movement, flow, puff, gust, current of air 2 = drink
draw VERB 1 = sketch, design, outline, trace, portray, paint, depict, mark out 2 = pull, drag, haul, tow, tug 3 = extract, take, remove 4 = deduce, make, take, derive, infer 5 = attract 6 = entice
• NOUN 1 = tie, deadlock, stalemate, impasse, dead heat 2 (*Informal*) = appeal, pull (*informal*), charm, attraction, lure, temptation, fascination, allure
• PHRASES **draw on** *or* **upon something** = make use of, use, employ, rely on, exploit, extract, take from, fall back on
drawback = disadvantage, difficulty, handicap, deficiency, flaw, hitch, snag, downside ≠ advantage
drawing = picture, illustration, representation, cartoon, sketch, portrayal, depiction, study
drawn = tense, worn, stressed, tired, pinched, haggard
dread VERB = fear, shrink from, cringe at the thought of, quail from, shudder to think about, have cold feet about (*informal*), tremble to think about
• NOUN = fear, alarm, horror, terror, dismay, fright, apprehension, trepidation
dreadful 1 = terrible, shocking, awful, appalling, horrible, fearful, hideous, atrocious 2 = serious, terrible, awful, horrendous, monstrous, abysmal 3 = awful, terrible, horrendous, frightful
dream NOUN 1 = vision, illusion, delusion, hallucination 2 = ambition, wish, fantasy, desire, pipe dream 3 = daydream 4 = delight, pleasure, joy, beauty, treasure, gem, marvel, pearler (*Austral. slang*)
• VERB 1 = have dreams, hallucinate 2 = daydream, stargaze, build castles in the air *or* in Spain
• PHRASES **dream of something** *or* **someone** = daydream about, fantasize about
dreamer = idealist, visionary, daydreamer, utopian, escapist, Walter Mitty, fantasist
dreary = dull, boring, tedious, drab, tiresome, monotonous, humdrum, uneventful ≠ exciting
drench = soak, flood, wet, drown, steep, swamp, saturate, inundate
dress NOUN 1 = frock, gown, robe

2 = clothing, clothes, costume, garments, apparel, attire, garb, togs
• VERB 1 = put on clothes, don clothes, slip on *or* into something ≠ undress 2 = clothe 3 = bandage, treat, plaster, bind up 4 = arrange, prepare, get ready

dribble 1 = run, drip, trickle, drop, leak, ooze, seep, fall in drops 2 = drool, drivel, slaver, slobber

drift VERB 1 = float, go (aimlessly), bob, coast, slip, sail, slide, glide 2 = wander, stroll, stray, roam, meander, rove, range 3 = stray, wander, digress, get off the point 4 = pile up, gather, accumulate, amass, bank up
• NOUN 1 = pile, bank, mass, heap, mound, accumulation 2 = meaning, point, gist, direction, import, intention, tendency, significance

drill NOUN 1 = bit, borer, gimlet, boring tool 2 = training, exercise, discipline, instruction, preparation, repetition 3 = practice
• VERB 1 = bore, pierce, penetrate, sink in, puncture, perforate 2 = train, coach, teach, exercise, discipline, practise, instruct, rehearse

drink VERB 1 = swallow, sip, suck, gulp, sup, guzzle, imbibe, quaff 2 = booze (*informal*), tipple, tope, hit the bottle (*informal*)
• NOUN 1 = glass, cup, draught 2 = beverage, refreshment, potion, liquid 3 = alcohol, booze (*informal*), liquor, spirits, the bottle (*informal*), hooch *or* hootch (*informal, chiefly U.S. & Canad.*)

drip VERB = drop, splash, sprinkle, trickle, dribble, exude, plop
• NOUN 1 = drop, bead, trickle, dribble, droplet, globule, pearl 2 (*Informal*) = weakling, wet (*Brit. informal*), weed (*informal*), softie (*informal*), mummy's boy (*informal*), namby-pamby

drive VERB 1 = go (by car), ride (by car), motor, travel by car 2 = operate, manage, direct, guide, handle, steer 3 = push, propel 4 = thrust, push, hammer, ram 5 = herd, urge, impel 6 = force, press, prompt, spur, prod, constrain, coerce, goad
• NOUN 1 = run, ride, trip, journey, spin (*informal*), outing, excursion, jaunt 2 = initiative, energy, enterprise, ambition, motivation, zip (*informal*), vigour, get-up-and-go (*informal*) 3 = campaign, push (*informal*), crusade, action, effort, appeal

drop VERB 1 = fall, decline, diminish 2 *often with* ***away*** = decline, fall, sink 3 = plunge, fall, tumble, descend, plummet 4 = drip, trickle, dribble, fall in drops 5 = sink, fall, descend 6 = quit, give up, axe (*informal*), kick (*informal*), relinquish, discontinue
• NOUN 1 = decrease, fall, cut, lowering, decline, reduction, slump, fall-off 2 = droplet, bead, globule, bubble, pearl, drip 3 = dash, shot (*informal*), spot, trace, sip, tot, trickle, mouthful 4 = fall, plunge, descent
• PHRASES **drop off** 1 = fall asleep, nod (off), doze (off), snooze (*informal*), have forty winks (*informal*) 2 = decrease, lower, decline, shrink, diminish, dwindle, lessen, subside ◆ **drop out** = leave, stop, give up, withdraw, quit, pull out, fall by the wayside ◆ **drop out of something** = discontinue, give up, quit

drought = water shortage, dryness, dry spell, aridity ≠ flood

drove *often plural* = herd, company, crowds, collection, mob, flocks, swarm, horde

drown 1 = go down, go under 2 = drench, flood, soak, steep, swamp, saturate, engulf, submerge 3 = overwhelm, overcome, wipe out, overpower, obliterate, swallow up

drug NOUN 1 = medication, medicine, remedy, physic, medicament 2 = dope (*slang*), narcotic (*slang*), stimulant, opiate, dadah (*Austral. slang*)
• VERB = knock out, dope (*slang*), numb, deaden, stupefy, anaesthetize

drum VERB = pound, beat, tap, rap, thrash, tattoo, throb, pulsate
• PHRASES **drum something into someone** = drive into, hammer into, instil into, din into, harp on about to

drunk ADJECTIVE = intoxicated, plastered (*slang*), drunken, merry (*Brit. informal*), under the influence (*informal*), tipsy, legless (*informal*), inebriated, out to it (*Austral. & N.Z. slang*), babalas (*S. African*)
• NOUN = drunkard, alcoholic, lush (*slang*), boozer (*informal*), wino (*informal*), inebriate, alko *or* alco (*Austral. slang*)

dry ADJECTIVE 1 = dehydrated, dried-up, arid, parched, desiccated ≠ wet 2 = thirsty, parched 3 = sarcastic, cynical, low-key, sly, sardonic, deadpan, droll, ironical 4 = dull, boring, tedious, dreary, tiresome,

monotonous, run-of-the-mill, humdrum ≠ interesting **5** = plain, simple, bare, basic, stark, unembellished
• **VERB 1** = drain, make dry **2** *often with* ***out*** = dehydrate, make dry, desiccate, sear, parch, dehumidify ≠ wet
• **PHRASES dry up** *or* **out** = become dry, harden, wither, shrivel up, wizen

dual = twofold, double, twin, matched, paired, duplicate, binary, duplex

dubious 1 = suspect, suspicious, crooked, dodgy (*Brit., Austral., & N.Z. informal*), questionable, unreliable, fishy (*informal*), disreputable ≠ trustworthy **2** = unsure, uncertain, suspicious, hesitating, doubtful, sceptical, tentative, wavering ≠ sure

duck 1 = bob, drop, lower, bend, bow, dodge, crouch, stoop **2** (*Informal*) = dodge, avoid, escape, evade, elude, sidestep, shirk **3** = dunk, wet, plunge, dip, submerge, immerse, douse, souse

due ADJECTIVE 1 = expected, scheduled **2** = fitting, deserved, appropriate, justified, suitable, merited, proper, rightful **3** = payable, outstanding, owed, owing, unpaid, in arrears
• **ADVERB** = directly, dead, straight, exactly, undeviatingly
• **NOUN** = right(s), privilege, deserts, merits, comeuppance (*informal*)
• **PLURAL NOUN** = membership fee, charges, fee, contribution, levy

duel NOUN 1 = single combat, affair of honour **2** = contest, fight, competition, clash, encounter, engagement, rivalry
• **VERB** = fight, struggle, clash, compete, contest, contend, vie with, lock horns

duff (*Brit., Austral., & N.Z. informal*) = bad, poor, useless, inferior, unsatisfactory, defective, imperfect, substandard, bodger *or* bodgie (*Austral. slang*)

dull ADJECTIVE 1 = boring, tedious, dreary, flat, plain, monotonous, run-of-the-mill, humdrum ≠ exciting **2** = lifeless, indifferent, apathetic, listless, unresponsive, passionless ≠ lively **3** = cloudy, dim, gloomy, dismal, overcast, leaden ≠ bright **4** = blunt, blunted, unsharpened ≠ sharp
• **VERB** = relieve, blunt, lessen, moderate, soften, alleviate, allay, take the edge off

duly 1 = properly, fittingly, correctly, appropriately, accordingly, suitably, deservedly, rightfully **2** = on time, promptly, punctually, at the proper time

dumb 1 = unable to speak, mute ≠ articulate **2** = silent, mute, speechless, tongue-tied, wordless, voiceless, soundless, mum **3** (*Informal*) = stupid, thick, dull, foolish, dense, unintelligent, asinine, dim-witted (*informal*) ≠ clever

dummy NOUN 1 = model, figure, mannequin, form, manikin **2** = imitation, copy, duplicate, sham, counterfeit, replica **3** (*Slang*) = fool, idiot, dunce, oaf, simpleton, nitwit (*informal*), blockhead, dumb-ass (*slang*), dorba *or* dorb (*Austral. slang*), bogan (*Austral. slang*)
• **ADJECTIVE** = imitation, false, fake, artificial, mock, bogus, simulated, sham

dump VERB 1 = drop, deposit, throw down, let fall, fling down **2** = get rid of, tip, dispose of, unload, jettison, empty out, throw away *or* out **3** = scrap, get rid of, abolish, put an end to, discontinue, jettison, put paid to
• **NOUN 1** = rubbish tip, tip, junkyard, rubbish heap, refuse heap **2** (*Informal*) = pigsty, hole (*informal*), slum, hovel

dunny (*Austral. & N.Z. old-fashioned informal*) = toilet, lavatory, bathroom, loo (*Brit. informal*), W.C., bog (*slang*), Gents *or* Ladies, can (*U.S. & Canad. slang*), bogger (*Austral. slang*), brasco (*Austral. slang*)

duplicate VERB 1 = repeat, reproduce, copy, clone, replicate **2** = copy
• **ADJECTIVE** = identical, matched, matching, twin, corresponding, twofold
• **NOUN 1** = copy, facsimile **2** = photocopy, copy, reproduction, replica, carbon copy

durable 1 = hard-wearing, strong, tough, reliable, resistant, sturdy, long-lasting ≠ fragile **2** = enduring, continuing, dependable, unwavering, unfaltering

duration = length, time, period, term, stretch, extent, spell, span

dusk = twilight, evening, evo (*Austral. slang*), nightfall, sunset, dark, sundown, eventide, gloaming (*Scot. poetic*) ≠ dawn

dust NOUN 1 = grime, grit, powder **2** = particles
• **VERB** = sprinkle, cover, powder, spread, spray, scatter, sift, dredge

dusty = dirty, grubby, unclean, unswept

duty NOUN 1 = responsibility, job, task, work, role, function, obligation, assignment **2** = tax, toll, levy, tariff, excise
• **PHRASES on duty** = at work, busy,

engaged, on active service

dwarf VERB 1 = tower above *or* over, dominate, overlook, stand over, loom over, stand head and shoulders above 2 = eclipse, tower above *or* over, put in the shade, diminish
• ADJECTIVE = miniature, small, baby, tiny, diminutive, bonsai, undersized
• NOUN = gnome, midget, Lilliputian, Tom Thumb, pygmy *or* pigmy

dwell (*Formal or literary*) = live, reside, lodge, abide

dwelling (*Formal* or *literary*) = home, house, residence, abode, quarters, lodging, habitation, domicile, whare (*N.Z.*)

dwindle = lessen, decline, fade, shrink, diminish, decrease, wane, subside ≠ increase

dye VERB = colour, stain, tint, tinge, pigment
• NOUN = colouring, colour, pigment, stain, tint, tinge, colorant

dying 1 = near death, moribund, in extremis (*Latin*), at death's door, not long for this world 2 = final, last, parting, departing 3 = failing, declining, foundering, diminishing, decreasing, dwindling, subsiding

dynamic = energetic, powerful, vital, go-ahead, lively, animated, high-powered, forceful ≠ apathetic

dynasty = empire, house, rule, regime, sovereignty

e

each DETERMINER = every, every single
• PRONOUN = every one, all, each one, each and every one, one and all
• ADVERB = apiece, individually, for each, to each, respectively, per person, per head, per capita

eager 1 = anxious, keen, hungry, impatient, itching, thirsty ≠ unenthusiastic 2 = keen, interested, intense, enthusiastic, passionate, avid (*informal*), fervent ≠ uninterested

ear = sensitivity, taste, discrimination, appreciation
RELATED WORD
adjective: aural

early ADVERB 1 = in good time, beforehand, ahead of schedule, in advance, with time to spare ≠ late 2 = too soon, before the usual time, prematurely, ahead of time ≠ late
• ADJECTIVE 1 = first, opening, initial, introductory 2 = premature, forward, advanced, untimely, unseasonable ≠ belated 3 = primitive, first, earliest, young, original, undeveloped, primordial, primeval ≠ developed

earmark 1 = set aside, reserve, label, flag, allocate, designate, mark out 2 = mark out, identify, designate

earn 1 = be paid, make, get, receive, gain, net, collect, bring in 2 = deserve, win, gain, attain, justify, merit, warrant, be entitled to

earnest 1 = serious, grave, intense, dedicated, sincere, thoughtful, solemn, ardent ≠ frivolous 2 = determined, dogged, intent, persistent, persevering, resolute, wholehearted ≠ half-hearted

earnings = income, pay, wages, revenue, proceeds, salary, receipts, remuneration

earth 1 = world, planet, globe, sphere, orb, earthly sphere 2 = ground, land, dry land, terra firma 3 = soil, ground, land, dust, clay, dirt, turf, silt

earthly 1 = worldly, material, secular, mortal, temporal, human ≠ spiritual 2 = sensual, worldly, physical, fleshly, bodily, carnal 3 (*Informal*) = possible, likely, practical, feasible, conceivable, imaginable

ease NOUN 1 = straightforwardness, simplicity, readiness 2 = comfort, luxury, leisure, relaxation, prosperity, affluence, rest, repose ≠ hardship 3 = peace of mind, peace, content, quiet, comfort, happiness, serenity, tranquillity ≠ agitation
• VERB 1 = relieve, calm, soothe, lessen, alleviate, lighten, lower, relax ≠ aggravate 2 = reduce, diminish, lessen, slacken 3 = move carefully, edge, slip, inch, slide, creep, manoeuvre

easily = without difficulty, smoothly, readily, comfortably, effortlessly, with ease, straightforwardly

easy 1 = simple, straightforward, no trouble, not difficult, effortless, painless, uncomplicated, child's play (*informal*) ≠ hard 2 = untroubled, relaxed, peaceful, serene, tranquil, quiet 3 = carefree, comfortable, leisurely, trouble-free, untroubled, cushy (*informal*) ≠ difficult 4 = tolerant, soft, mild, laid-back (*informal*), indulgent, easy-going, lenient, permissive ≠ strict

eat 1 = consume, swallow, chew, scoff (*slang*), devour, munch, tuck into (*informal*), put away 2 = have a meal, lunch, breakfast, dine, snack, feed, graze (*informal*), have lunch

ebb VERB 1 = flow back, go out, withdraw, retreat, wane, recede 2 = decline, flag, diminish, decrease, dwindle, lessen, subside, fall away
• NOUN = flowing back, going out, withdrawal, retreat, wane, low water, low tide, outgoing tide

eccentric ADJECTIVE = odd, strange, peculiar, irregular, quirky, unconventional, idiosyncratic, outlandish ≠ normal
• NOUN = crank (*informal*), character (*informal*), oddball (*informal*), nonconformist, weirdo *or* weirdie (*informal*)

echo NOUN 1 = reverberation, ringing, repetition, answer, resonance, resounding 2 = copy, reflection, clone, reproduction, imitation, duplicate, double, reiteration
• VERB 1 = reverberate, repeat, resound, ring, resonate 2 = recall, reflect, copy, mirror, resemble, imitate, ape

eclipse NOUN = obscuring, covering, blocking, shading, dimming, extinction, darkening, blotting out
• VERB = surpass, exceed, overshadow, excel, transcend, outdo, outclass, outshine

economic 1 = financial, industrial, commercial 2 = profitable, successful, commercial, rewarding, productive, lucrative, worthwhile, viable 3 (*Informal*) = economical, cheap, reasonable, modest, low-priced, inexpensive

economical 1 = thrifty, sparing, careful, prudent, provident, frugal, parsimonious, scrimping ≠ extravagant 2 = efficient, sparing, cost-effective, money-saving, time-saving ≠ wasteful

economy 1 = financial system, financial state 2 = thrift, restraint, prudence, husbandry, frugality, parsimony

ecstasy = rapture, delight, joy, bliss, euphoria, fervour, elation ≠ agony

ecstatic = rapturous, entranced, joyous, elated, overjoyed, blissful, euphoric, enraptured

edge NOUN 1 = border, side, limit, outline, boundary, fringe, verge, brink 2 = verge, point, brink, threshold 3 = advantage, lead, dominance, superiority, upper hand, head start, ascendancy, whip hand 4 = power, force, bite, effectiveness, incisiveness, powerful quality 5 = sharpness, point, bitterness, keenness
• VERB 1 = inch, ease, creep, slink, steal, sidle, move slowly 2 = border, fringe, hem, pipe
• PHRASES **on edge** = tense, nervous, impatient, irritable, apprehensive, edgy, ill at ease, on tenterhooks

edit = revise, improve, correct, polish, adapt, rewrite, condense, redraft

edition = version, copy, issue, programme (*TV, Radio*), printing, volume, impression, publication

educate = teach, school, train, develop, improve, inform, discipline, tutor

educated 1 = cultured, intellectual, learned, sophisticated, refined, cultivated, enlightened, knowledgeable ≠ uncultured 2 = taught, schooled, coached, informed, tutored, instructed, nurtured, well-informed ≠ uneducated

education 1 = teaching, schooling, training, development, discipline, instruction, nurture, tuition 2 = learning, schooling, cultivation, refinement

educational 1 = academic, school, learning, teaching, scholastic, pedagogical, pedagogic 2 = instructive, useful, cultural, illuminating, enlightening, informative, instructional, edifying

eerie = uncanny, strange, frightening, ghostly, weird, mysterious, scary (*informal*), sinister

effect NOUN 1 = result, consequence, conclusion, outcome, event, end result, upshot 2 = impression, feeling, impact, influence 3 = purpose, impression, sense, intent, essence, thread, tenor
• PLURAL NOUN = belongings, goods, things, property, stuff, gear, possessions, paraphernalia
• VERB = bring about, produce, complete,

achieve, perform, fulfil, accomplish, execute

effective 1 = efficient, successful, useful, active, capable, valuable, helpful, adequate ≠ ineffective 2 = powerful, strong, convincing, persuasive, telling, impressive, compelling, forceful ≠ weak 3 = virtual, essential, practical, implied, implicit, tacit, unacknowledged 4 = in operation, official, current, legal, active, in effect, valid, operative ≠ inoperative

efficiency 1 = effectiveness, power, economy, productivity, organization, cost-effectiveness, orderliness 2 = competence, expertise, capability, professionalism, proficiency, adeptness

efficient 1 = effective, successful, structured, productive, systematic, streamlined, cost-effective, methodical ≠ inefficient 2 = competent, professional, capable, organized, productive, proficient, businesslike, well-organized ≠ incompetent

effort 1 = attempt, try, endeavour, shot (*informal*), bid, essay, go (*informal*), stab (*informal*) 2 = exertion, work, trouble, energy, struggle, application, graft, toil

egg NOUN = ovum, gamete, germ cell
• PHRASES **egg someone on** = incite, push, encourage, urge, prompt, spur, provoke, prod

eject 1 = throw out, remove, turn out, expel (*slang*), oust, banish, drive out, evict 2 = bail out, escape, get out

elaborate ADJECTIVE 1 = complicated, detailed, studied, complex, precise, thorough, intricate, painstaking 2 = ornate, involved, complex, fancy, complicated, intricate, baroque, ornamented ≠ plain
• VERB 1 = develop, flesh out 2 = expand (upon), extend, enlarge (on), amplify, embellish, flesh out, add detail (to) ≠ simplify

elastic 1 = flexible, supple, rubbery, pliable, plastic, springy, pliant, tensile ≠ rigid 2 = adaptable, yielding, variable, flexible, accommodating, tolerant, adjustable, supple ≠ inflexible

elbow = joint, angle, curve

elder ADJECTIVE = older, first, senior, first-born
• NOUN = older person, senior

elect 1 = vote for, choose, pick, determine, select, appoint, opt for, settle on 2 = choose, decide, prefer, select, opt

election 1 = vote, poll, ballot, referendum, franchise, plebiscite, show of hands 2 = appointment, picking, choice, selection

electric 1 = electric-powered, powered, cordless, battery-operated, electrically-charged, mains-operated 2 = charged, exciting, stirring, thrilling, stimulating, dynamic, tense, rousing

elegance = style, taste, grace, dignity, sophistication, grandeur, refinement, gracefulness

elegant = stylish, fine, sophisticated, delicate, handsome, refined, chic, exquisite ≠ inelegant

element NOUN 1 = component, part, unit, section, factor, principle, aspect, foundation 2 = group, faction, clique, set, party, circle 3 = trace, suggestion, hint, dash, suspicion, tinge, smattering, soupçon
• PLURAL NOUN = weather conditions, climate, the weather, wind and rain, atmospheric conditions, powers of nature
• PHRASES **be in your element** = be in a situation you enjoy, be in your natural environment, be in familiar surroundings

elementary = simple, clear, easy, plain, straightforward, rudimentary, uncomplicated, undemanding ≠ complicated

elevate 1 = promote, raise, advance, upgrade, exalt, kick upstairs (*informal*), aggrandize, give advancement to 2 = increase, lift, raise, step up, intensify, move up, hoist, raise high 3 = raise, lift, heighten, uplift, hoist, lift up, raise up, hike up

elevated 1 = exalted, important, august, grand, superior, noble, dignified, high-ranking 2 = high-minded, fine, grand, noble, inflated, dignified, sublime, lofty ≠ humble 3 = raised, high, lifted up, upraised

elicit 1 = bring about, cause, derive, bring out, evoke, give rise to, draw out, bring forth 2 = obtain, extract, exact, evoke, wrest, draw out, extort

eligible 1 = entitled, fit, qualified, suitable ≠ ineligible 2 = available, free, single, unmarried, unattached

eliminate = remove, end, stop, withdraw,

get rid of, abolish, cut out, dispose of
elite = aristocracy, best, pick, cream, upper class, nobility, crème de la crème (*French*), flower ≠ rabble
eloquent 1 = silver-tongued, moving, powerful, effective, stirring, articulate, persuasive, forceful ≠ inarticulate 2 = expressive, telling, pointed, significant, vivid, meaningful, indicative, suggestive
elsewhere = in *or* to another place, away, abroad, hence (*archaic*), somewhere else, not here, in other places, in *or* to a different place
elude 1 = evade, escape, lose, avoid, flee, duck (*informal*), dodge, get away from 2 = escape, baffle, frustrate, puzzle, stump, foil, be beyond (someone), thwart
elusive 1 = difficult to catch, tricky, slippery, difficult to find, evasive, shifty 2 = indefinable, fleeting, subtle, indefinite, transient, intangible, indescribable, transitory
emanate = flow, emerge, spring, proceed, arise, stem, derive, originate
embargo NOUN = ban, bar, restriction, boycott, restraint, prohibition, moratorium, stoppage, rahui (*N.Z.*)
• VERB = block, stop, bar, ban, restrict, boycott, prohibit, blacklist
embark VERB = go aboard, climb aboard, board ship, step aboard, go on board, take ship ≠ get off
• PHRASES **embark on something** = begin, start, launch, enter, take up, set out, set about, plunge into
embarrass = shame, distress, show up (*informal*), humiliate, disconcert, fluster, mortify, discomfit
embarrassed = ashamed, shamed, uncomfortable, awkward, abashed, humiliated, uneasy, unsettled
embarrassing = humiliating, upsetting, compromising, delicate, uncomfortable, awkward, sensitive, troublesome, barro (*Austral. slang*)
embarrassment 1 = shame, distress, showing up (*informal*), humiliation, discomfort, unease, self-consciousness, awkwardness 2 = problem, difficulty, nuisance, source of trouble, thorn in your flesh 3 = predicament, problem, difficulty (*informal*), mess, jam (*informal*), plight, scrape (*informal*), pickle (*informal*)
embody 1 = personify, represent, stand for, manifest, exemplify, symbolize, typify, actualize 2 = incorporate, include, contain, combine, collect, take in, encompass
embrace VERB 1 = hug, hold, cuddle, seize, squeeze, clasp, envelop, canoodle (*slang*) 2 = accept, support, welcome, adopt, take up, seize, espouse, take on board 3 = include, involve, cover, contain, take in, incorporate, comprise, encompass
• NOUN = hug, hold, cuddle, squeeze, clinch (*slang*), clasp
embroil = involve, mix up, implicate, entangle, mire, ensnare, enmesh
embryo 1 = foetus, unborn child, fertilized egg 2 = germ, beginning, source, root, seed, nucleus, rudiment
emerge 1 = come out, appear, surface, rise, arise, turn up, spring up, emanate ≠ withdraw 2 = become apparent, come out, become known, come to light, crop up, transpire, become evident, come out in the wash
emergence 1 = coming, development, arrival, surfacing, rise, appearance, arising, turning up 2 = disclosure, publishing, broadcasting, broadcast, publication, declaration, revelation, becoming known
emergency NOUN = crisis, danger, difficulty, accident, disaster, necessity, plight, scrape (*informal*)
• ADJECTIVE 1 = urgent, crisis, immediate 2 = alternative, extra, additional, substitute, replacement, temporary, makeshift, stopgap
emigrate = move abroad, move, relocate, migrate, resettle, leave your country
eminent = prominent, noted, respected, famous, celebrated, distinguished, well-known, esteemed ≠ unknown
emission = giving off *or* out, release, shedding, leak, radiation, discharge, transmission, ejaculation
emit 1 = give off, release, leak, transmit, discharge, send out, radiate, eject ≠ absorb 2 = utter, produce, voice, give out, let out
emotion 1 = feeling, spirit, soul, passion, excitement, sensation, sentiment, fervour 2 = instinct, sentiment, sensibility, intuition, tenderness, gut feeling, soft-heartedness
emotional 1 = psychological, private, personal, hidden, spiritual, inner 2 = moving, touching, affecting, stirring,

sentimental, poignant, emotive, heart-rending **3** = passionate, sentimental, temperamental, excitable, demonstrative, hot-blooded **4** = emotive, sensitive, controversial, delicate, contentious, heated, inflammatory, touchy

emphasis **1** = importance, attention, weight, significance, stress, priority, prominence **2** = stress, accent, force, weight

emphasize **1** = highlight, stress, underline, draw attention to, dwell on, play up, make a point of, give priority to ≠ minimize **2** = stress, accentuate, lay stress on

emphatic **1** = forceful, positive, definite, vigorous, unmistakable, insistent, unequivocal, vehement ≠ hesitant **2** = significant, pronounced, decisive, resounding, conclusive

empire **1** = kingdom, territory, province, federation, commonwealth, realm, domain **2** = organization, company, business, firm, concern, corporation, consortium, syndicate

RELATED WORD

adjective: imperial

empirical *or* **empiric** = first-hand, direct, observed, practical, actual, experimental, pragmatic, factual ≠ hypothetical

employ **1** = hire, commission, appoint, take on, retain, engage, recruit, sign up **2** = use, apply, exercise, exert, make use of, utilize, ply, bring to bear **3** = spend, fill, occupy, involve, engage, take up, make use of, use up

employed **1** = working, in work, having a job, in employment, in a job, earning your living ≠ out of work **2** = busy, active, occupied, engaged, hard at work, in harness, rushed off your feet ≠ idle

employee = worker, labourer, workman, staff member, member of staff, hand, wage-earner, white-collar worker

employer **1** = boss (*informal*), manager, head, leader, director, chief, owner, master, baas (*S. African*) **2** = company, business, firm, organization, establishment, outfit (*informal*)

employment **1** = job, work, position, trade, post, situation, profession, occupation **2** = taking on, commissioning, appointing, hire, hiring, retaining, engaging, appointment **3** = use, application, exertion, exercise, utilization

empower **1** = authorize, allow, commission, qualify, permit, sanction, entitle, delegate **2** = enable, equip, emancipate, give means to, enfranchise

empty ADJECTIVE **1** = bare, clear, abandoned, deserted, vacant, free, void, desolate ≠ full **2** = meaningless, cheap, hollow, vain, idle, futile, insincere **3** = worthless, meaningless, hollow, pointless, futile, senseless, fruitless, inane ≠ meaningful

● VERB **1** = clear, drain, void, unload, pour out, unpack, remove the contents of ≠ fill **2** = exhaust, consume the contents of, void, deplete, use up ≠ replenish **3** = evacuate, clear, vacate

emulate = imitate, follow, copy, mirror, echo, mimic, model yourself on

enable **1** = allow, permit, empower, give someone the opportunity, give someone the means ≠ prevent **2** = authorize, allow, permit, qualify, sanction, entitle, license, warrant ≠ stop

enact **1** = establish, order, command, approve, sanction, proclaim, decree, authorize **2** = perform, play, present, stage, represent, put on, portray, depict

enchant = fascinate, delight, charm, entrance, dazzle, captivate, enthral, beguile

enclose *or* **inclose** **1** = surround, circle, bound, fence, confine, close in, wall in, encircle **2** = send with, include, put in, insert

encompass **1** = include, hold, cover, admit, deal with, contain, take in, embrace **2** = surround, circle, enclose, close in, envelop, encircle, fence in, ring

encounter VERB **1** = experience, meet, face, suffer, have, go through, sustain, endure **2** = meet, confront, come across, bump into (*informal*), run across, come upon, chance upon, meet by chance

● NOUN **1** = meeting, brush, confrontation, rendezvous, chance meeting **2** = battle, conflict, clash, contest, run-in (*informal*), confrontation, head-to-head

encourage **1** = inspire, comfort, cheer, reassure, console, hearten, cheer up, embolden ≠ discourage **2** = urge, persuade, prompt, spur, coax, egg on ≠ dissuade **3** = promote, back, support, increase, foster, advocate, stimulate, endorse ≠ prevent

encouragement 1 = inspiration, support, comfort, comforting, cheer, cheering, reassurance, morale boosting 2 = urging, prompting, stimulus, persuasion, coaxing, egging on, incitement 3 = promotion, backing, support, endorsement, stimulation, furtherance

end NOUN 1 = close, ending, finish, expiry, expiration ≠ beginning 2 = conclusion, ending, climax, completion, finale, culmination, denouement, consummation ≠ start 3 = finish, close, stop, resolution, conclusion, closure, completion, termination 4 = extremity, limit, edge, border, extent, extreme, margin, boundary 5 = tip, point, head, peak, extremity 6 = purpose, point, reason, goal, target, aim, object, mission 7 = outcome, resolution, conclusion 8 = death, dying, ruin, destruction, passing on, doom, demise, extinction 9 = remnant, butt, stub, scrap, fragment, stump, remainder, leftover

• VERB 1 = stop, finish, halt, cease, wind up, terminate, call off, discontinue ≠ start 2 = finish, close, conclude, wind up, culminate, terminate, come to an end, draw to a close ≠ begin

RELATED WORDS

adjectives: final, terminal, ultimate

endanger = put at risk, risk, threaten, compromise, jeopardize, imperil, put in danger, expose to danger ≠ save

endearing = attractive, winning, pleasing, appealing, sweet, engaging, charming, pleasant

endeavour (*Formal*) VERB = try, labour, attempt, aim, struggle, venture, strive, aspire

• NOUN = attempt, try, effort, trial, bid, venture, enterprise, undertaking

ending = finish, end, close, conclusion, summing up, completion, finale, culmination ≠ start

endless = eternal, infinite, continual, unlimited, interminable, incessant, boundless, everlasting ≠ temporary

endorse 1 = approve, back, support, champion, promote, recommend, advocate, uphold 2 = sign, initial, countersign, sign on the back of

endorsement = approval, backing, support, favour, recommendation, acceptance, agreement, upholding

endow 1 = provide, favour, grace, bless, supply, furnish, endue 2 = finance, fund, pay for, award, confer, bestow, bequeath, donate money to 3 = imbue

endowment = provision, funding, award, grant, gift, contribution, subsidy, donation, koha (*N.Z.*)

endurance 1 = staying power, strength, resolution, determination, patience, stamina, fortitude, persistence 2 = permanence, stability, continuity, duration, longevity, durability, continuance

endure 1 = experience, suffer, bear, meet, encounter, cope with, sustain, undergo 2 = last, continue, remain, stay, stand, go on, survive, live on

enemy = foe, rival, opponent, the opposition, competitor, the other side, adversary, antagonist ≠ friend

energetic 1 = forceful, determined, active, aggressive, dynamic, vigorous, hard-hitting, strenuous 2 = lively, active, dynamic, vigorous, animated, tireless, bouncy, indefatigable ≠ lethargic 3 = strenuous, hard, taxing, demanding, tough, exhausting, vigorous, arduous

energy 1 = strength, might, stamina, forcefulness 2 = liveliness, drive, determination, pep, vitality, vigour, verve, resilience 3 = power

enforce 1 = carry out, apply, implement, fulfil, execute, administer, put into effect, put into action 2 = impose, force, insist on

engage 1 *with* ***in*** = participate in, join in, take part in, undertake, embark on, enter into, become involved in, set about 2 = captivate, catch, arrest, fix, capture 3 = occupy, involve, draw, grip, absorb, preoccupy, immerse, engross 4 = employ, appoint, take on, hire, retain, recruit, enlist, enrol ≠ dismiss 5 = set going, apply, trigger, activate, switch on, energize, bring into operation 6 (*Military*) = begin battle with, attack, take on, encounter, fall on, battle with, meet, assail

engaged 1 = occupied, working, employed, busy, tied up 2 = betrothed, promised, pledged, affianced, promised in marriage ≠ unattached 3 = in use, busy, tied up, unavailable ≠ free

engagement 1 = appointment, meeting, interview, date, commitment, arrangement, rendezvous **2** = betrothal, marriage contract, troth (*archaic*), agreement to marry **3** = battle, fight, conflict, action, struggle, clash, encounter, combat **4** = participation, joining, taking part, involvement

engaging = charming, interesting, pleasing, attractive, lovely, entertaining, winning, fetching (*informal*) ≠ unpleasant

engine = machine, motor, mechanism, generator, dynamo

engineer NOUN **1** = designer, producer, architect, developer, deviser, creator, planner, inventor **2** = worker, specialist, operator, practitioner, operative, driver, conductor, technician
• VERB **1** = design, plan, create, construct, devise **2** = bring about, plan, effect, set up (*informal*), scheme, arrange, plot, mastermind

engraving = print, carving, etching, inscription, plate, woodcut, dry point

engulf 1 = immerse, swamp, submerge, overrun, inundate, envelop, swallow up **2** = overwhelm, overcome, crush, swamp

enhance = improve, better, increase, lift, boost, add to, strengthen, reinforce ≠ reduce

enjoy 1 = take pleasure in *or* from, like, love, appreciate, relish, delight in, be pleased with, be fond of ≠ hate **2** = have, use, own, experience, possess, have the benefit of, reap the benefits of, be blessed *or* favoured with

enjoyable = pleasurable, good, great, fine, nice, satisfying, lovely, entertaining ≠ unpleasant

enjoyment 1 = pleasure, liking, fun, delight, entertainment, joy, happiness, relish **2** = benefit, use, advantage, favour, possession, blessing

enlarge VERB **1** = expand, increase, extend, add to, build up, widen, intensify, broaden ≠ reduce **2** = grow, increase, extend, expand, swell, become bigger, puff up, grow larger
• PHRASES **enlarge on something** = expand on, develop, add to, fill out, elaborate on, flesh out, expatiate on, give further details about

enlighten = inform, tell, teach, advise, counsel, educate, instruct, illuminate

enlightened = informed, aware, reasonable, educated, sophisticated, cultivated, open-minded, knowledgeable ≠ ignorant

enlightenment = understanding, learning, education, knowledge, instruction, awareness, wisdom, insight

enlist 1 = join up, join, enter (into), register, volunteer, sign up, enrol **2** = recruit, take on, hire, sign up, call up, muster, mobilize, conscript **3** = obtain, get, gain, secure, engage, procure

enormous = huge, massive, vast, extensive, tremendous, gross, immense, gigantic ≠ tiny

enough DETERMINER = sufficient, adequate, ample, abundant, as much as you need, as much as is necessary
• PRONOUN = sufficiency, plenty, sufficient, abundance, adequacy, right amount, ample supply
• ADVERB = sufficiently, amply, reasonably, adequately, satisfactorily, abundantly, tolerably

enrage = anger, infuriate, incense, madden, inflame, exasperate, antagonize, make you angry ≠ calm

enrich 1 = enhance, develop, improve, boost, supplement, refine, heighten, augment **2** = make rich, make wealthy, make affluent, make prosperous, make well-off

enrol 1 = enlist, register, be accepted, be admitted, join up, put your name down for, sign up *or* on **2** = recruit, take on, enlist

en route = on *or* along the way, travelling, on the road, in transit, on the journey

ensemble 1 = group, company, band, troupe, cast, orchestra, chorus **2** = collection, set, body, whole, total, sum, combination, entity **3** = outfit, suit, get-up (*informal*), costume

ensue = follow, result, develop, proceed, arise, stem, derive, issue ≠ come first

ensure 1 = make certain, guarantee, secure, make sure, confirm, warrant, certify **2** = protect, defend, secure, safeguard, guard, make safe

entail = involve, require, produce, demand, call for, occasion, need, bring about

enter 1 = come *or* go in *or* into, arrive, set foot in somewhere, cross the threshold of somewhere, make an entrance ≠ exit **2** = penetrate, get in, pierce, pass into, perforate **3** = join, start work at, begin work at, enrol in, enlist in ≠ leave **4** = participate in, join (in), be involved in, get involved in, play a part in, partake in, associate yourself with, start to be in **5** = begin, start, take up, move into, commence, set out on, embark upon **6** = compete in, contest, join in, fight, sign up for, go in for **7** = record, note, register, log, list, write down, take down, inscribe

enterprise **1** = firm, company, business, concern, operation, organization, establishment, commercial undertaking **2** = venture, operation, project, adventure, undertaking, programme, pursuit, endeavour **3** = initiative, energy, daring, enthusiasm, imagination, drive, ingenuity, originality

enterprising = resourceful, original, spirited, daring, bold, enthusiastic, imaginative, energetic

entertain **1** = amuse, interest, please, delight, charm, enthral, cheer, regale **2** = show hospitality to, receive, accommodate, treat, put up, lodge, be host to, have company of **3** = consider, imagine, think about, contemplate, conceive of, bear in mind, keep in mind, give thought to

entertainment **1** = enjoyable, fun, pleasure, leisure, relaxation, recreation, enjoyment, amusement **2** = pastime, show, sport, performance, treat, presentation, leisure activity

enthusiasm = keenness, interest, passion, motivation, relish, zeal, zest, fervour

enthusiast = fan, supporter, lover, follower, addict, buff (*informal*), fanatic, devotee

enthusiastic = keen, committed, eager, passionate, vigorous, avid, fervent, zealous ≠ apathetic

entice = lure, attract, invite, persuade, tempt, induce, seduce, lead on

entire = whole, full, complete, total, gross

entirely = completely, totally, absolutely, fully, altogether, thoroughly, wholly, utterly ≠ partly

entitle **1** = give the right to, allow, enable, permit, sanction, license, authorize, empower **2** = call, name, title, term, label, dub, christen, give the title of

entity = thing, being, individual, object, substance, creature, organism

entrance[1] **1** = way in, opening, door, approach, access, entry, gate, passage ≠ exit **2** = appearance, coming in, entry, arrival, introduction ≠ exit **3** = admission, access, entry, entrée, admittance, permission to enter, right of entry

entrance[2] **1** = enchant, delight, charm, fascinate, dazzle, captivate, enthral, beguile ≠ bore **2** = mesmerize, bewitch, hypnotize, put a spell on, cast a spell on, put in a trance

entrant = competitor, player, candidate, entry, participant, applicant, contender, contestant

entrenched *or* **intrenched** = fixed, set, rooted, well-established, ingrained, deep-seated, deep-rooted, unshakeable *or* unshakable

entrepreneur = businessman *or* businesswoman, tycoon, executive, industrialist, speculator, magnate, impresario, business executive

entrust *or* **intrust** **1** = give custody of, deliver, commit, delegate, hand over, turn over, confide **2** = assign

entry **1** = admission, access, entrance, admittance, entrée, permission to enter, right of entry **2** = coming in, entering, appearance, arrival, entrance ≠ exit **3** = introduction, presentation, initiation, inauguration, induction, debut, investiture **4** = record, listing, account, note, statement, item **5** = way in, opening, door, approach, access, gate, passage, entrance

envelope = wrapping, casing, case, covering, cover, jacket, sleeve, wrapper

environment **1** = surroundings, setting, conditions, situation, medium, circumstances, background, atmosphere **2** = habitat, home, surroundings, territory, terrain, locality, natural home

environmental = ecological, green

environmentalist = conservationist, ecologist, green

envisage **1** = imagine, contemplate, conceive (of), visualize, picture, fancy, think up, conceptualize **2** = foresee, see, expect, predict, anticipate, envision

envoy **1** = ambassador, diplomat, emissary **2** = messenger, agent, representative, delegate, courier, intermediary, emissary

envy NOUN = covetousness, resentment, jealousy, bitterness, resentfulness, enviousness (*informal*)

• VERB 1 = be jealous (of), resent, begrudge, be envious (of) 2 = covet, desire, crave, aspire to, yearn for, hanker after
epidemic 1 = outbreak, plague, growth, spread, scourge, contagion 2 = spate, plague, outbreak, wave, rash, eruption, upsurge
episode 1 = event, experience, happening, matter, affair, incident, adventure, occurrence 2 = instalment, part, act, scene, section, chapter, passage 3 = period, attack, spell, phase, bout
equal ADJECTIVE 1 = identical, the same, matching, equivalent, uniform, alike, corresponding ≠ unequal 2 = fair, just, impartial, egalitarian, unbiased, even-handed ≠ unfair 3 = even, balanced, fifty-fifty (*informal*), evenly matched ≠ uneven
• NOUN = match, equivalent, twin, counterpart
• VERB 1 = amount to, make, come to, total, level, parallel, tie with, equate ≠ be unequal to 2 = be equal to, match, reach 3 = be as good as, match, compare with, equate with, measure up to, be as great as
equality 1 = fairness, equal opportunity, equal treatment, egalitarianism, fair treatment, justness ≠ inequality 2 = sameness, balance, identity, similarity, correspondence, parity, likeness, uniformity ≠ disparity
equate 1 = identify, associate, connect, compare, relate, mention in the same breath, think of in connection with 2 = make equal, match, even up 3 = be equal to, parallel, compare with, liken, be commensurate with, correspond with *or* to
equation = equating, comparison, parallel, correspondence
equilibrium = stability, balance, symmetry, steadiness, evenness, equipoise
equip 1 = supply, provide for, stock, arm, array, furnish, fit out, kit out 2 = prepare, qualify, educate, get ready
equipment = apparatus, stock, supplies, stuff, tackle, gear, tools, provisions
equitable = even-handed, just, fair, reasonable, proper, honest, impartial, unbiased
equivalent NOUN = equal, counterpart, twin, parallel, match, opposite number
• ADJECTIVE = equal, same, comparable, parallel, identical, alike, corresponding, tantamount ≠ different
era = age, time, period, date, generation, epoch, day *or* days
eradicate = wipe out, eliminate, remove, destroy, get rid of, erase, extinguish, obliterate
erase 1 = delete, cancel out, wipe out, remove, eradicate, obliterate, blot out, expunge 2 = rub out, remove, wipe out, delete
erect VERB 1 = build, raise, set up, construct, put up, assemble, put together ≠ demolish 2 = found, establish, form, create, set up, institute, organize, put up
• ADJECTIVE = upright, straight, stiff, vertical, elevated, perpendicular, pricked-up ≠ bent
erode 1 = disintegrate, crumble, deteriorate, corrode, break up, grind down, waste away, wear down *or* away 2 = destroy, consume, crumble, eat away, corrode, break up, grind down, abrade 3 = weaken, destroy, undermine, diminish, impair, lessen, wear away
erosion 1 = disintegration, deterioration, wearing down *or* away, grinding down 2 = deterioration, undermining, destruction, weakening, attrition, eating away, abrasion, grinding down
erotic = sexual, sexy (*informal*), crude, explicit, sensual, seductive, vulgar, voluptuous
erratic = unpredictable, variable, unstable, irregular, inconsistent, uneven, unreliable, wayward ≠ regular
error = mistake, slip, blunder, oversight, howler (*informal*), bloomer (*Brit. informal*), miscalculation, solecism
erupt 1 = explode, blow up, emit lava 2 = discharge, expel, emit, eject, spout, throw off, pour forth, spew forth *or* out 3 = gush, burst out, pour forth, belch forth, spew forth *or* out 4 = start, break out, began, explode, flare up, burst out, boil over 5 (*Medical*) = break out, appear, flare up
escalate 1 = grow, increase, extend, intensify, expand, surge, mount, heighten ≠ decrease 2 = increase, develop, extend, intensify, expand, build up, heighten ≠ lessen
escape VERB 1 = get away, flee, take off, fly, bolt, slip away, abscond, make a break

for it **2** = avoid, miss, evade, dodge, shun, elude, duck, steer clear of **3** = leak out, flow out, gush out, emanate, seep out, exude, spill out, pour forth
• NOUN **1** = getaway, break, flight, break-out **2** = avoidance, evasion, circumvention **3** = relaxation, recreation, distraction, diversion, pastime **4** = leak, emission, outpouring, seepage, issue, emanation

escort NOUN **1** = guard, bodyguard, train, convoy, entourage, retinue, cortege **2** = companion, partner, attendant, guide, beau, chaperon
• VERB = accompany, lead, partner, conduct, guide, shepherd, usher, chaperon

especially 1 = notably, mostly, strikingly, conspicuously, outstandingly **2** = very, specially, extremely, remarkably, unusually, exceptionally, markedly, uncommonly

espionage = spying, intelligence, surveillance, counter-intelligence, undercover work

essay NOUN = composition, study, paper, article, piece, assignment, discourse, tract
• VERB (*Formal*) = attempt, try, undertake, endeavour

essence 1 = fundamental nature, nature, being, heart, spirit, soul, core, substance **2** = concentrate, spirits, extract, tincture, distillate

essential ADJECTIVE **1** = vital, important, needed, necessary, critical, crucial, key, indispensable ≠ unimportant **2** = fundamental, main, basic, principal, cardinal, elementary, innate, intrinsic ≠ secondary
• NOUN = prerequisite, fundamental, necessity, must, basic, sine qua non (*Latin*), rudiment

establish 1 = set up, found, create, institute, constitute, inaugurate **2** = prove, confirm, demonstrate, certify, verify, substantiate, corroborate, authenticate **3** = secure, form, ground, settle

establishment NOUN **1** = creation, founding, setting up, foundation, institution, organization, formation, installation **2** = organization, company, business, firm, concern, operation, institution, corporation
• PHRASES **the Establishment** = the authorities, the system, the powers that be, the ruling class

estate 1 = lands, property, area, grounds, domain, manor, holdings **2** = area, centre, park, development, site, zone, plot **3** (*Law*) = property, capital, assets, fortune, goods, effects, wealth, possessions

esteem NOUN = respect, regard, honour, admiration, reverence, estimation, veneration
• VERB = respect, admire, think highly of, love, value, prize, treasure, revere

estimate VERB **1** = calculate roughly, value, guess, judge, reckon, assess, evaluate, gauge **2** = think, believe, consider, rate, judge, hold, rank, reckon
• NOUN **1** = approximate calculation, guess, assessment, judgment, valuation, guesstimate (*informal*), rough calculation, ballpark figure (*informal*) **2** = assessment, opinion, belief, appraisal, evaluation, judgment, estimation

estuary = inlet, mouth, creek, firth, fjord

etch 1 = engrave, cut, impress, stamp, carve, imprint, inscribe **2** = corrode, eat into, burn into

etching = print, impression, carving, engraving, imprint, inscription

eternal 1 = everlasting, lasting, permanent, enduring, endless, perpetual, timeless, unending ≠ transitory **2** = interminable, endless, infinite, continual, immortal, never-ending, everlasting ≠ occasional

eternity 1 (*Theology*) = the afterlife, heaven, paradise, the next world, the hereafter **2** = perpetuity, immortality, infinity, timelessness, endlessness **3** = ages

ethical 1 = moral, behavioural **2** = right, morally acceptable, good, just, fair, responsible, principled ≠ unethical

ethics = moral code, standards, principles, morals, conscience, morality, moral values, moral principles, tikanga (*N.Z.*)

ethnic *or* **ethnical** = cultural, national, traditional, native, folk, racial, genetic, indigenous

euphoria = elation, joy, ecstasy, rapture, exhilaration, jubilation ≠ despondency

evacuate 1 = remove, clear, withdraw, expel, move out, send to a safe place **2** = abandon, leave, clear, desert, quit, withdraw from, pull out of, move out of

evade 1 = avoid, escape, dodge, get away from, elude, steer clear of, sidestep, duck ≠ face **2** = avoid answering, parry, fend off, fudge, hedge, equivocate

evaluate = assess, rate, judge, estimate, reckon, weigh, calculate, gauge
evaporate 1 = disappear, vaporize, dematerialize, vanish, dissolve, dry up, fade away, melt away 2 = dry up, dry, dehydrate, vaporize, desiccate 3 = fade away, disappear, vanish, dissolve, melt away
eve 1 = night before, day before, vigil 2 = brink, point, edge, verge, threshold
even 1 = regular, stable, constant, steady, smooth, uniform, unbroken, uninterrupted ≠ variable 2 = level, straight, flat, smooth, true, steady, uniform, parallel ≠ uneven 3 = equal, like, matching, similar, identical, comparable ≠ unequal 4 = equally matched, level, tied, on a par, neck and neck, fifty-fifty (*informal*), all square ≠ ill-matched 5 = square, quits, on the same level, on an equal footing 6 = calm, composed, cool, well-balanced, placid, unruffled, imperturbable, even-tempered ≠ excitable
evening = dusk (*archaic*), night, sunset, twilight, sundown, gloaming (*Scot. poetic*), close of day, evo (*Austral. slang*)
event 1 = incident, happening, experience, affair, occasion, proceeding, business, circumstance 2 = competition, game, tournament, contest, bout
eventual = final, overall, concluding, ultimate
eventually = in the end, finally, one day, after all, some time, ultimately, at the end of the day, when all is said and done
ever 1 = at any time, at all, in any case, at any point, by any chance, on any occasion, at any period 2 = always, for ever, at all times, evermore 3 = constantly, continually, perpetually
every = each, each and every, every single
everybody = everyone, each one, the whole world, each person, every person, all and sundry, one and all
everyday = ordinary, common, usual, routine, stock, customary, mundane, run-of-the-mill ≠ unusual
everyone = everybody, each one, the whole world, each person, every person, all and sundry, one and all
everything = all, the lot, the whole lot, each thing
everywhere 1 = all over, all around, the world over, high and low, in every nook and cranny, far and wide *or* near, to *or* in every place 2 = all around, all over, in every nook and cranny, ubiquitously, far and wide *or* near, to *or* in every place
evidence NOUN 1 = proof, grounds, demonstration, confirmation, verification, corroboration, authentication, substantiation 2 = sign(s), suggestion, trace, indication 3 = testimony, statement, submission, avowal
• VERB = show, prove, reveal, display, indicate, witness, demonstrate, exhibit
evident = obvious, clear, plain, apparent, visible, manifest, noticeable, unmistakable ≠ hidden
evidently 1 = obviously, clearly, plainly, undoubtedly, manifestly, without question, unmistakably 2 = apparently, seemingly, outwardly, ostensibly, so it seems, to all appearances
evil NOUN 1 = wickedness, bad, vice, sin, wrongdoing, depravity, badness, villainy 2 = harm, suffering, hurt, woe 3 = act of cruelty, crime, ill, horror, outrage, misfortune, mischief, affliction
• ADJECTIVE 1 = wicked, bad, malicious, immoral, sinful, malevolent, depraved, villainous 2 = harmful, disastrous, destructive, dire, catastrophic, pernicious, ruinous 3 = demonic, satanic, diabolical, hellish, devilish, infernal, fiendish 4 = offensive, nasty, foul, unpleasant, vile, noxious, disagreeable, pestilential 5 = unfortunate, unfavourable, ruinous, calamitous
evoke = arouse, cause, induce, awaken, give rise to, stir up, rekindle, summon up ≠ suppress
evolution 1 = rise, development, adaptation, natural selection, Darwinism, survival of the fittest 2 = development, growth, advance, progress, working out, expansion, extension, unfolding
evolve 1 = develop, metamorphose, adapt yourself 2 = grow, develop, advance, progress, mature 3 = work out, develop, progress, expand, unfold
exact ADJECTIVE = accurate, correct, true, right, specific, precise, definite, faultless ≠ approximate
• VERB 1 = demand, claim, force, command, extract, compel, extort 2 = inflict, apply, administer, mete out, deal out
exacting 1 = demanding, hard, taxing,

difficult, tough ≠ easy **2** = strict, severe, harsh, rigorous, stringent
exactly 1 = accurately, correctly, precisely, faithfully, explicitly, scrupulously, truthfully, unerringly **2** = precisely, specifically, bang on (*informal*), to the letter
exaggerate = overstate, enlarge, embroider, amplify, embellish, overestimate, overemphasize, pile it on about (*informal*)
examination 1 = checkup, analysis, going-over (*informal*), exploration, health check, check **2** = exam, test, research, paper, investigation, practical, assessment, quiz
examine 1 = inspect, study, survey, investigate, explore, analyse, scrutinize, peruse **2** = check, analyse, check over **3** = test, question, assess, quiz, evaluate, appraise **4** = question, quiz, interrogate, cross-examine, grill (*informal*), give the third degree to (*informal*)
example 1 = instance, specimen, case, sample, illustration, particular case, particular instance, typical case **2** = illustration, model, ideal, standard, prototype, paradigm, archetype, paragon **3** = warning, lesson, caution, deterrent
exceed 1 = surpass, better, pass, eclipse, beat, cap (*informal*), top, be over **2** = go over the limit of, go beyond, overstep
excel VERB = be superior, eclipse, beat, surpass, transcend, outdo, outshine
• PHRASES **excel in** *or* **at something** = be good at, shine at, be proficient in, show talent in, be skilful at, be talented at
excellence = high quality, merit, distinction, goodness, superiority, greatness, supremacy, eminence
excellent = outstanding, good, great, fine, cool (*informal*), brilliant, very good, superb, booshit (*Austral. slang*), exo (*Austral. slang*), sik (*Austral. slang*) ≠ terrible
except *or* **except for** PREPOSITION = apart from, but for, saving, barring, excepting, other than, excluding, omitting
• VERB = exclude, leave out, omit, disregard, pass over
exception = special case, freak, anomaly, inconsistency, deviation, oddity, peculiarity, irregularity
exceptional 1 = remarkable, special, excellent, extraordinary, outstanding, superior, first-class, marvellous ≠ average **2** = unusual, special, odd, strange, extraordinary, unprecedented, peculiar, abnormal ≠ ordinary
excerpt = extract, part, piece, section, selection, passage, fragment, quotation
excess 1 = surfeit, surplus, overload, glut, superabundance, superfluity ≠ shortage **2** = overindulgence, extravagance, profligacy, debauchery, dissipation, intemperance, indulgence, prodigality ≠ moderation
excessive 1 = immoderate, too much, extreme, exaggerated, unreasonable, disproportionate, undue, uncontrolled **2** = inordinate, unfair, unreasonable, disproportionate, undue, unwarranted, exorbitant, extortionate
exchange VERB = interchange, change, trade, switch, swap, barter, give to each other, give to one another
• NOUN **1** = conversation, talk, word, discussion, chat, dialogue, natter, powwow **2** = interchange, trade, switch, swap, trafficking, swapping, substitution, barter
excite 1 = thrill, inspire, stir, provoke, animate, rouse, exhilarate, inflame **2** = arouse, provoke, rouse, stir up **3** = titillate, thrill, stimulate, turn on (*slang*), arouse, get going (*informal*), electrify
excitement = exhilaration, action, activity, passion, thrill, animation, furore, agitation
exciting 1 = stimulating, dramatic, gripping, stirring, thrilling, sensational, rousing, exhilarating ≠ boring **2** = titillating, stimulating, arousing, erotic
exclaim = cry out, declare, shout, proclaim, yell, utter, call out
exclude 1 = keep out, bar, ban, refuse, forbid, boycott, prohibit, disallow ≠ let in **2** = omit, reject, eliminate, rule out, miss out, leave out ≠ include **3** = eliminate, reject, ignore, rule out, leave out, set aside, omit, pass over
exclusion 1 = ban, bar, veto, boycott, embargo, prohibition, disqualification **2** = elimination, missing out, rejection, leaving out, omission
exclusive 1 = select, fashionable, stylish, restricted, posh (*informal*, *chiefly Brit.*), chic, high-class, up-market ≠ unrestricted **2** = sole, full, whole, complete, total, entire,

absolute, undivided ≠ shared **3** = entire, full, whole, complete, total, absolute, undivided **4** = limited, unique, restricted, confined, peculiar

excursion = trip, tour, journey, outing, expedition, ramble, day trip, jaunt

excuse NOUN = justification, reason, explanation, defence, grounds, plea, apology, vindication ≠ accusation
• VERB **1** = justify, explain, defend, vindicate, mitigate, apologize for, make excuses for ≠ blame **2** = forgive, pardon, overlook, tolerate, acquit, turn a blind eye to, exonerate, make allowances for **3** = free, relieve, exempt, release, spare, discharge, let off, absolve ≠ convict

execute 1 = put to death, kill, shoot, hang, behead, decapitate, guillotine, electrocute **2** = carry out, effect, implement, accomplish, discharge, administer, prosecute, enact **3** = perform, carry out, accomplish

execution 1 = killing, hanging, the death penalty, the rope, capital punishment, beheading, the electric chair, the guillotine **2** = carrying out, performance, operation, administration, prosecution, enforcement, implementation, accomplishment

executive NOUN **1** = administrator, official, director, manager, chairman, managing director, controller, chief executive officer **2** = administration, government, directors, management, leadership, hierarchy, directorate
• ADJECTIVE = administrative, controlling, directing, governing, regulating, decision-making, managerial

exemplify = show, represent, display, demonstrate, illustrate, exhibit, embody, serve as an example of

exempt ADJECTIVE = immune, free, excepted, excused, released, spared, not liable to ≠ liable
• VERB = grant immunity, free, excuse, release, spare, relieve, discharge, let off

exemption = immunity, freedom, relief, exception, discharge, release, dispensation, absolution

exercise VERB **1** = put to use, use, apply, employ, exert, utilize, bring to bear, avail yourself of **2** = train, work out, practise, keep fit, do exercises
• NOUN **1** = use, practice, application, operation, discharge, implementation, fulfilment, utilization **2** = exertion, training, activity, work, labour, effort, movement, toil **3** = manoeuvre, campaign, operation, movement, deployment **4** = task, problem, lesson, assignment, practice

exert VERB = apply, use, exercise, employ, wield, make use of, utilize, bring to bear
• PHRASES **exert yourself** = make an effort, work, labour, struggle, strain, strive, endeavour, toil

exhaust 1 = tire out, fatigue, drain, weaken, weary, sap, wear out, debilitate **2** = use up, spend, consume, waste, go through, run through, deplete, squander

exhausted 1 = worn out, tired out, drained, spent, bushed (*informal*), done in (*informal*), all in (*slang*), fatigued ≠ invigorated **2** = used up, consumed, spent, finished, depleted, dissipated, expended ≠ replenished

exhaustion 1 = tiredness, fatigue, weariness, debilitation **2** = depletion, emptying, consumption, using up

exhibit 1 = show, reveal, display, demonstrate, express, indicate, manifest **2** = display, show, set out, parade, unveil, put on view

exhibition 1 = show, display, representation, presentation, spectacle, showcase, exposition **2** = display, show, performance, demonstration, revelation

exile NOUN **1** = banishment, expulsion, deportation, eviction, expatriation **2** = expatriate, refugee, outcast, émigré, deportee
• VERB = banish, expel, throw out, deport, drive out, eject, expatriate, cast out

exist 1 = live, be present, survive, endure, be in existence, be, have breath **2** = occur, be present **3** = survive, stay alive, make ends meet, subsist, eke out a living, scrape by, scrimp and save, support yourself

existence 1 = reality, being, life, subsistence, actuality **2** = life, situation, way of life, life style

existent = in existence, living, existing, surviving, standing, present, alive, extant

exit NOUN **1** = way out, door, gate, outlet, doorway, gateway, escape route ≠ entry **2** = departure, withdrawal, retreat, farewell, going, goodbye, exodus, decamping
• VERB = depart, leave, go out, withdraw,

retire, quit, retreat, go away ≠ enter
exodus = departure, withdrawal, retreat, leaving, flight, exit, migration, evacuation
exotic 1 = unusual, striking, strange, fascinating, mysterious, colourful, glamorous, unfamiliar ≠ ordinary 2 = foreign, alien, tropical, external, naturalized
expand VERB 1 = get bigger, increase, grow, extend, swell, widen, enlarge, become bigger ≠ contract 2 = make bigger, increase, develop, extend, widen, enlarge, broaden, magnify ≠ reduce 3 = spread (out), stretch (out), unfold, unravel, diffuse, unfurl, unroll
• PHRASES **expand on something** = go into detail about, embellish, elaborate on, develop, flesh out, expound on, enlarge on, expatiate on
expansion 1 = increase, development, growth, spread, magnification, amplification 2 = enlargement, increase, growth, opening out
expatriate NOUN = exile, refugee, emigrant, émigré
• ADJECTIVE = exiled, refugee, banished, emigrant, émigré, expat
expect 1 = think, believe, suppose, assume, trust, imagine, reckon, presume 2 = anticipate, look forward to, predict, envisage, await, hope for, contemplate 3 = require, demand, want, call for, ask for, hope for, insist on
expectation 1 = projection, supposition, assumption, belief, forecast, likelihood, probability, presumption 2 = anticipation, hope, promise, excitement, expectancy, apprehension, suspense
expedition = journey, mission, voyage, tour, quest, trek
expel 1 = throw out, exclude, ban, dismiss, kick out (*informal*), ask to leave, turf out (*informal*), debar ≠ let in 2 = banish, exile, deport, evict, force to leave ≠ take in 3 = drive out, discharge, force out, let out, eject, issue, spew, belch
expenditure 1 = spending, payment, expense, outgoings, cost, outlay 2 = consumption, using, output
expense = cost, charge, expenditure, payment, spending, outlay
expensive = costly, high-priced, lavish, extravagant, dear, stiff, steep (*informal*), pricey ≠ cheap
experience NOUN 1 = knowledge, practice, skill, contact, expertise, involvement, exposure, participation 2 = event, affair, incident, happening, encounter, episode, adventure, occurrence
• VERB = undergo, feel, face, taste, go through, sample, encounter, endure
experienced = knowledgeable, skilled, tried, tested, seasoned, expert, veteran, practised ≠ inexperienced
experiment NOUN 1 = test, trial, investigation, examination, procedure, demonstration, observation, try-out 2 = research, investigation, analysis, observation, research and development, experimentation
• VERB = test, investigate, trial, research, try, examine, pilot, sample
experimental 1 = test, trial, pilot, preliminary, provisional, tentative, speculative, exploratory 2 = innovative, new, original, radical, creative, ingenious, avant-garde, inventive
expert NOUN = specialist, authority, professional, master, genius, guru, pundit, maestro, fundi (*S. African*) ≠ amateur
• ADJECTIVE = skilful, experienced, professional, masterly, qualified, talented, outstanding, practised ≠ unskilled
expertise = skill, knowledge, know-how (*informal*), facility, judgment, mastery, proficiency, adroitness
expire 1 = become invalid, end, finish, conclude, close, stop, run out, cease 2 = die, depart, perish, kick the bucket (*informal*), depart this life, meet your maker, cark it (*Austral. & N.Z. slang*), pass away *or* on
explain 1 = make clear *or* plain, describe, teach, define, resolve, clarify, clear up, simplify 2 = account for, excuse, justify, give a reason for
explanation 1 = reason, answer, account, excuse, motive, justification, vindication 2 = description, report, definition, teaching, interpretation, illustration, clarification, simplification
explicit 1 = clear, obvious, specific, direct, precise, straightforward, definite, overt ≠ vague 2 = frank, specific, graphic, unambiguous, unrestricted, unrestrained, uncensored ≠ indirect
explode 1 = blow up, erupt, burst, go off, shatter 2 = detonate, set off, discharge,

let off **3** = lose your temper, rage, erupt, become angry, hit the roof (*informal*), go crook (*Austral. & N.Z. slang*) **4** = increase, grow, develop, extend, advance, shoot up, soar, boost **5** = disprove, discredit, refute, demolish, repudiate, put paid to, invalidate, debunk

exploit VERB **1** = take advantage of, abuse, use, manipulate, milk, misuse, ill-treat, play on *or* upon **2** = make the best use of, use, make use of, utilize, cash in on (*informal*), capitalize on, use to good advantage, profit by *or* from
• NOUN = feat, act, achievement, enterprise, adventure, stunt, deed, accomplishment

exploitation = misuse, abuse, manipulation, using, ill-treatment

exploration **1** = expedition, tour, trip, survey, travel, journey, reconnaissance **2** = investigation, research, survey, search, inquiry, analysis, examination, inspection

explore **1** = travel around, tour, survey, scout, reconnoitre **2** = investigate, consider, research, survey, search, examine, probe, look into

explosion **1** = blast, crack, burst, bang, discharge, report, blowing up, clap **2** = increase, rise, development, growth, boost, expansion, enlargement, escalation **3** = outburst, fit, storm, attack, surge, flare-up, eruption **4** = outbreak, flare-up, eruption, upsurge

explosive NOUN = bomb, mine, shell, missile, rocket, grenade, charge, torpedo
• ADJECTIVE **1** = unstable, dangerous, volatile, hazardous, unsafe, perilous, combustible, inflammable **2** = sudden, rapid, marked, unexpected, startling, swift, abrupt **3** = fiery, violent, volatile, stormy, touchy, vehement

expose **1** = uncover, show, reveal, display, exhibit, present, unveil, lay bare ≠ hide **2** = make vulnerable, subject, endanger, leave open, jeopardize, put at risk, imperil, lay open

exposure **1** = hypothermia, frostbite, extreme cold, intense cold **2** = uncovering, showing, display, exhibition, revelation, presentation, unveiling

express VERB **1** = state, communicate, convey, articulate, say, word, voice, declare **2** = show, indicate, exhibit, demonstrate, reveal, intimate, convey, signify
• ADJECTIVE **1** = explicit, clear, plain, distinct, definite, unambiguous, categorical **2** = specific, exclusive, particular, sole, special, singular, clear-cut, especial **3** = fast, direct, rapid, priority, prompt, swift, high-speed, speedy

expression **1** = statement, declaration, announcement, communication, utterance, articulation **2** = indication, demonstration, exhibition, display, showing, show, sign, symbol **3** = look, countenance, face, air, appearance, aspect **4** = phrase, saying, word, term, remark, maxim, idiom, adage

expressive = vivid, striking, telling, moving, poignant, eloquent ≠ impassive

expulsion **1** = ejection, exclusion, dismissal, removal, eviction, banishment **2** = discharge, emission, spewing, secretion, excretion, ejection, seepage, suppuration

exquisite **1** = beautiful, elegant, graceful, pleasing, attractive, lovely, charming, comely ≠ unattractive **2** = fine, beautiful, lovely, elegant, precious, delicate, dainty **3** = intense, acute, severe, sharp, keen, extreme

extend **1** = spread out, reach, stretch **2** = stretch, stretch out, spread out, straighten out **3** = last, continue, go on, stretch, carry on **4** = protrude, project, stand out, bulge, stick out, hang, overhang, jut out **5** = widen, increase, expand, add to, enhance, supplement, enlarge, broaden ≠ reduce **6** = make longer, prolong, lengthen, draw out, spin out, drag out ≠ shorten **7** = offer, present, confer, stick out, impart, proffer ≠ withdraw

extension **1** = annexe, addition, supplement, appendix, appendage **2** = lengthening, extra time, continuation, additional period of time **3** = development, expansion, widening, increase, broadening, enlargement, diversification

extensive ADJECTIVE = large, considerable, substantial, spacious, wide, broad, expansive
• ADJECTIVE ≠ confined **2** = comprehensive, complete, wide, pervasive ≠ restricted **3** = great, vast, widespread, large-scale, far-reaching, far-flung, voluminous ≠ limited

extent **1** = magnitude, amount, scale, level, stretch, expanse **2** = size, area, length,

width, breadth
exterior NOUN = outside, face, surface, covering, skin, shell, coating, façade
• ADJECTIVE = outer, outside, external, surface, outward, outermost ≠ inner
external 1 = outer, outside, surface, outward, exterior, outermost ≠ internal **2** = foreign, international, alien, extrinsic ≠ domestic **3** = outside, visiting ≠ inside
extinct = dead, lost, gone, vanished, defunct ≠ living
extinction = dying out, destruction, abolition, oblivion, extermination, annihilation, eradication, obliteration
extra ADJECTIVE 1 = additional, more, added, further, supplementary, auxiliary, ancillary ≠ vital **2** = surplus, excess, spare, redundant, unused, leftover, superfluous
• NOUN = addition, bonus, supplement, accessory ≠ necessity
• ADVERB 1 = in addition, additionally, over and above **2** = exceptionally, very, specially, especially, particularly, extremely, remarkably, unusually
extract VERB 1 = take out, draw, pull, remove, withdraw, pull out, bring out **2** = pull out, remove, take out, draw, uproot, pluck out **3** = elicit, obtain, force, draw, derive, glean, coerce
• NOUN 1 = passage, selection, excerpt, cutting, clipping, quotation, citation **2** = essence, solution, concentrate, juice, distillation
extraordinary 1 = remarkable, outstanding, amazing, fantastic, astonishing, exceptional, phenomenal, extremely good ≠ unremarkable **2** = unusual, strange, remarkable, uncommon ≠ ordinary
extravagant 1 = wasteful, lavish, prodigal, profligate, spendthrift ≠ economical **2** = excessive, outrageous, over the top (*slang*), unreasonable, preposterous ≠ moderate
extreme ADJECTIVE 1 = great, highest, supreme, acute, severe, maximum, intense, ultimate ≠ mild **2** = severe, radical, strict, harsh, rigid, drastic, uncompromising **3** = radical, excessive, fanatical, immoderate ≠ moderate **4** = farthest, furthest, far, remotest, far-off, outermost, most distant ≠ nearest
• NOUN = limit, end, edge, opposite, pole, boundary, antithesis, extremity
extremely = very, particularly, severely, terribly, unusually, exceptionally, extraordinarily, tremendously
extremist NOUN = radical, activist, militant, fanatic, die-hard, bigot, zealot
• ADJECTIVE = extreme, wild, passionate, frenzied, obsessive, fanatical, fervent, zealous
eye NOUN 1 = eyeball, optic (*informal*), organ of vision, organ of sight **2** *often plural* = eyesight, sight, vision, perception, ability to see, power of seeing **3** = appreciation, taste, recognition, judgment, discrimination, perception, discernment **4** = observance, observation, surveillance, vigil, watch, lookout **5** = centre, heart, middle, mid, core, nucleus
• VERB = look at, view, study, watch, survey, observe, contemplate, check out (*informal*)

RELATED WORDS
adjectives: ocular, ophthalmic, optic

f

fable 1 = legend, myth, parable, allegory, story, tale **2** = fiction, fantasy, myth, invention, yarn (*informal*), fabrication, urban myth, tall story (*informal*) ≠ fact
fabric 1 = cloth, material, stuff, textile, web **2** = framework, structure, make-up, organization, frame, foundations, construction, constitution **3** = structure, foundations, construction, framework
fabulous 1 (*Informal*) = wonderful, excellent, brilliant, superb, spectacular, fantastic (*informal*), marvellous, sensational (*informal*) ≠ ordinary **2** = astounding, amazing, extraordinary, remarkable, incredible, astonishing, unbelievable, breathtaking **3** = legendary, imaginary, mythical, fictitious, made-up, fantastic, invented, unreal
façade 1 = front, face, exterior **2** = show,

front, appearance, mask, exterior, guise, pretence, semblance

face NOUN **1** = countenance, features, profile, mug (*slang*), visage **2** = expression, look, air, appearance, aspect, countenance **3** = side, front, outside, surface, exterior, elevation, vertical surface
• VERB **1** = look onto, overlook, be opposite, look out on, front onto **2** = confront, meet, encounter, deal with, oppose, tackle, experience, brave **3** *often with* ***up to*** = accept, deal with, tackle, acknowledge, cope with, confront, come to terms with, meet head-on

facilitate = further, help, forward, promote, speed up, pave the way for, make easy, expedite ≠ hinder

facility 1 *often plural* = amenity, means, aid, opportunity, advantage, resource, equipment, provision **2** = opportunity, possibility, convenience **3** = ability, skill, efficiency, fluency, proficiency, dexterity, adroitness **4** = ease, fluency, effortlessness ≠ difficulty

fact 1 = truth, reality, certainty, verity ≠ fiction **2** = event, happening, act, performance, incident, deed, occurrence, fait accompli (*French*)

faction 1 = group, set, party, gang, bloc, contingent, clique, coterie **2** = dissension, division, conflict, rebellion, disagreement, variance, discord, infighting ≠ agreement

factor = element, part, cause, influence, item, aspect, characteristic, consideration

factory = works, plant, mill, workshop, assembly line, shop floor

factual = true, authentic, real, correct, genuine, exact, precise, dinkum (*Austral. & N.Z. informal*), true-to-life ≠ fictitious

faculty NOUN **1** = ability, power, skill, facility, capacity, propensity, aptitude ≠ failing **2** = department, school **3** = teaching staff, staff, teachers, professors, lecturers (*chiefly U.S.*)
• PLURAL NOUN = powers, reason, senses, intelligence, wits, capabilities, mental abilities, physical abilities

fad = craze, fashion, trend, rage, vogue, whim, mania

fade 1 = become pale, bleach, wash out, discolour, lose colour, decolour **2** = make pale, dim, bleach, wash out, blanch, discolour, decolour **3** = grow dim, fade away, become less loud **4** = dwindle, disappear, vanish, melt away, decline, dissolve, wane, die away

fail VERB **1** = be unsuccessful, founder, fall, break down, flop (*informal*), fizzle out (*informal*), come unstuck, miscarry ≠ succeed **2** = disappoint, abandon, desert, neglect, omit, let down, forsake, be disloyal to **3** = stop working, stop, die, break down, stall, cut out, malfunction, conk out (*informal*) **4** = wither, perish, sag, waste away, shrivel up **5** = go bankrupt, collapse, fold (*informal*), close down, go under, go bust (*informal*), go out of business, be wound up **6** = decline, deteriorate, degenerate **7** = give out, dim, peter out, die away, grow dim
• PHRASES **without fail** = without exception, regularly, constantly, invariably, religiously, unfailingly, conscientiously, like clockwork

failing NOUN = shortcoming, fault, weakness, defect, deficiency, flaw, drawback, blemish ≠ strength
• PREPOSITION = in the absence of, lacking, in default of

failure 1 = lack of success, defeat, collapse, breakdown, overthrow, miscarriage, fiasco, downfall ≠ success **2** = loser, disappointment, flop (*informal*), write-off, no-hoper (*chiefly Austral.*), dud (*informal*), black sheep, washout (*informal*), dead duck (*slang*) **3** = bankruptcy, crash, collapse, ruin, closure, winding up, downfall, going under ≠ prosperity

faint ADJECTIVE **1** = dim, low, soft, faded, distant, vague, unclear, muted ≠ clear **2** = slight, weak, feeble, unenthusiastic, remote, slim, vague, slender **3** = dizzy, giddy, light-headed, weak, exhausted, wobbly, muzzy, woozy (*informal*) ≠ energetic
• VERB = pass out, black out, lose consciousness, keel over (*informal*), go out, collapse, swoon (*literary*), flake out (*informal*)
• NOUN = blackout, collapse, coma, swoon (*literary*), unconsciousness

faintly 1 = slightly, rather, a little, somewhat, dimly **2** = softly, weakly, feebly, in a whisper, indistinctly, unclearly

fair[1] **1** = unbiased, impartial, even-handed, unprejudiced, just, reasonable, proper, legitimate ≠ unfair **2** = respectable, average, reasonable, decent, acceptable, moderate, adequate, satisfactory **3** = light, golden, blonde, blond, yellowish, fair-haired, light-coloured, flaxen-haired **4** = fine, clear, dry, bright, pleasant, sunny, cloudless, unclouded **5** = beautiful, pretty, attractive, lovely, handsome, good-looking, bonny, comely ≠ ugly

fair² = carnival, show, fête, festival, exhibition, mart, bazaar, gala

fairly **1** = equitably, objectively, legitimately, honestly, justly, lawfully, without prejudice, dispassionately **2** = moderately, rather, quite, somewhat, reasonably, adequately, pretty well, tolerably **3** = positively, really, simply, absolutely **4** = deservedly, objectively, honestly, justifiably, justly, impartially, equitably, without fear or favour

fairness = impartiality, justice, equity, legitimacy, decency, disinterestedness, rightfulness, equitableness

fairy = sprite, elf, brownie, pixie, puck, imp, leprechaun, peri

fairy tale *or* **fairy story** **1** = folk tale, romance, traditional story **2** = lie, fiction, invention, fabrication, untruth, urban myth, tall story, urban legend

faith **1** = confidence, trust, credit, conviction, assurance, dependence, reliance, credence ≠ distrust **2** = religion, church, belief, persuasion, creed, communion, denomination, dogma ≠ agnosticism

faithful **1** = loyal, true, committed, constant, devoted, dedicated, reliable, staunch ≠ disloyal **2** = accurate, close, true, strict, exact, precise

fake ADJECTIVE = artificial, false, forged, counterfeit, put-on, pretend (*informal*), mock, imitation ≠ genuine

• NOUN **1** = forgery, copy, fraud, reproduction, dummy, imitation, hoax, counterfeit **2** = charlatan, deceiver, sham, quack

• VERB **1** = forge, copy, reproduce, fabricate, counterfeit, falsify **2** = sham, put on, pretend, simulate, feign, go through the motions of

fall VERB **1** = drop, plunge, tumble, plummet, collapse, sink, go down, come down ≠ rise **2** = decrease, drop, decline, go down, slump, diminish, dwindle, lessen ≠ increase **3** = be overthrown, surrender, succumb, submit, capitulate, be conquered, pass into enemy hands ≠ triumph **4** = be killed, die, perish, meet your end ≠ survive **5** = occur, happen, come about, chance, take place, befall, come to pass

• NOUN **1** = drop, slip, plunge, dive, tumble, descent, plummet, nose dive **2** = decrease, drop, lowering, decline, reduction, slump, dip, lessening **3** = collapse, defeat, downfall, ruin, destruction, overthrow, submission, capitulation

false **1** = incorrect, wrong, mistaken, misleading, faulty, inaccurate, invalid, erroneous ≠ correct **2** = untrue, fraudulent, trumped up, fallacious, untruthful ≠ true **3** = artificial, forged, fake, reproduction, replica, imitation, bogus, simulated ≠ real

falter **1** = hesitate, delay, waver, vacillate ≠ persevere **2** = tumble, totter **3** = stutter, pause, stumble, hesitate, stammer

fame = prominence, glory, celebrity, stardom, reputation, honour, prestige, stature ≠ obscurity

familiar **1** = well-known, recognized, common, ordinary, routine, frequent, accustomed, customary ≠ unfamiliar **2** = friendly, close, dear, intimate, amicable ≠ formal **3** = relaxed, easy, friendly, comfortable, intimate, casual, amicable **4** = disrespectful, forward, bold, intrusive, presumptuous, impudent, overfamiliar

familiarity **1** = acquaintance, experience, understanding, knowledge, awareness, grasp ≠ unfamiliarity **2** = friendliness, intimacy, ease, openness, informality, sociability ≠ formality **3** = disrespect, forwardness, overfamiliarity, cheek, presumption, boldness ≠ respect

family **1** = relations, relatives, household, folk (*informal*), kin, nuclear family, next of kin, kith and kin, ainga (*N.Z.*) **2** = children, kids (*informal*), offspring, little ones, littlies (*Austral. informal*) **3** = ancestors, house, race, tribe, clan, dynasty, line of descent **4** = species, group, class, system, order, network, genre, subdivision

famine = hunger, want, starvation, deprivation, scarcity, dearth

famous = well-known, celebrated, acclaimed, noted, distinguished, prominent, legendary, renowned ≠ unknown

fan¹ NOUN = blower, ventilator, air

conditioner
• VERB = blow, cool, refresh, air-condition, ventilate

fan² = supporter, lover, follower, enthusiast, admirer, buff (*informal*), devotee, aficionado

fanatic = extremist, activist, militant, bigot, zealot

fancy ADJECTIVE = elaborate, decorative, extravagant, intricate, baroque, ornamental, ornate, embellished ≠ plain
• NOUN 1 = whim, thought, idea, desire, urge, notion, humour, impulse 2 = delusion, dream, vision, fantasy, daydream, chimera
• VERB 1 = wish for, want, desire, hope for, long for, crave, yearn for, thirst for 2 (*Informal*) = be attracted to, find attractive, lust after, like, take to, be captivated by, have a thing about (*informal*), have eyes for 3 = suppose, think, believe, imagine, reckon, conjecture, think likely

fantastic 1 (*Informal*) = wonderful, great, excellent, very good, smashing (*informal*), superb, tremendous (*informal*), magnificent, booshit (*Austral. slang*), exo (*Austral. slang*), sik (*Austral. slang*) ≠ ordinary 2 = strange, bizarre, grotesque, fanciful, outlandish 3 = implausible, unlikely, incredible, absurd, preposterous, cock-and-bull (*informal*)

fantasy *or* (*Archaic*) **phantasy** 1 = daydream, dream, wish, reverie, flight of fancy, pipe dream 2 = imagination, fancy, invention, creativity, originality

far ADVERB 1 = a long way, miles, deep, a good way, afar, a great distance 2 = much, greatly, very much, extremely, significantly, considerably, decidedly, markedly
• ADJECTIVE *often with* **off** = remote, distant, far-flung, faraway, out-of-the-way, far-off, outlying, off the beaten track ≠ near

farce 1 = comedy, satire, slapstick, burlesque, buffoonery 2 = mockery, joke, nonsense, parody, shambles, sham, travesty

fare NOUN 1 = charge, price, ticket price, ticket money 2 = food, provisions, board, rations, kai (*N.Z. informal*), nourishment, sustenance, victuals, nutriment
• VERB = get on, do, manage, make out, prosper, get along

farewell INTERJECTION = goodbye, bye (*informal*), so long, see you, take care, good morning, bye-bye (*informal*), good day, haere ra (*N.Z.*)
• NOUN = goodbye, parting, departure, leave-taking, adieu, valediction, sendoff (*informal*)

farm NOUN = smallholding, ranch (*chiefly U.S. & Canad.*), farmstead, station (*Austral. & N.Z.*), vineyard, plantation, croft (*Scot.*), grange, homestead
• VERB = cultivate, work, plant, grow crops on, keep animals on

fascinate = entrance, absorb, intrigue, rivet, captivate, enthral, beguile, transfix ≠ bore

fascinating = captivating, engaging, gripping, compelling, intriguing, very interesting, irresistible, enticing ≠ boring

fascination = attraction, pull, magic, charm, lure, allure, magnetism, enchantment

fashion NOUN 1 = style, look, trend, rage, custom, mode, vogue, craze 2 = method, way, style, manner, mode
• VERB = make, shape, cast, construct, form, create, manufacture, forge

fashionable = popular, in fashion, trendy (*Brit. informal*), in (*informal*), modern, with it (*informal*), stylish, chic ≠ unfashionable

fast¹ ADJECTIVE 1 = quick, flying, rapid, fleet, swift, speedy, brisk, hasty ≠ slow 2 = fixed, firm, sound, stuck, secure, tight, jammed, fastened ≠ unstable 3 = dissipated, wild, exciting, loose, extravagant, reckless, self-indulgent, wanton 4 = close, firm, devoted, faithful, steadfast
• ADVERB 1 = quickly, rapidly, swiftly, hastily, hurriedly, speedily, in haste, at full speed ≠ slowly 2 = securely, firmly, tightly, fixedly 3 = fixedly, firmly, soundly, deeply, securely, tightly

fast² VERB = go hungry, abstain, go without food, deny yourself
• NOUN = fasting, diet, abstinence

fasten 1 = secure, close, do up 2 = tie, bind, tie up 3 = fix, join, link, connect, attach, affix

fat ADJECTIVE 1 = overweight, large, heavy, plump, stout, obese, tubby, portly ≠ thin 2 = fatty, greasy, adipose, oleaginous, oily ≠ lean
• NOUN = fatness, flesh, bulk, obesity, flab, blubber, paunch, fatty tissue

fatal 1 = disastrous, devastating, crippling, catastrophic, ruinous, calamitous, baleful, baneful ≠ minor 2 = lethal, deadly, mortal, causing death, final, killing, terminal, malignant ≠ harmless

fate 1 = destiny, chance, fortune, luck, the stars, providence, nemesis, kismet 2 = fortune, destiny, lot, portion, cup, horoscope

fated = destined, doomed, predestined, preordained, foreordained

father NOUN 1 = daddy (*informal*), dad (*informal*), male parent, pop (*U.S. informal*), old man (*Brit. informal*), pa (*informal*), papa (*old-fashioned informal*), pater 2 = founder, author, maker, architect, creator, inventor, originator, prime mover 3 *usually cap.* = priest, minister, vicar, parson, pastor, cleric, churchman, padre (*informal*) 4 *usually plural* = forefather, predecessor, ancestor, forebear, progenitor, tupuna *or* tipuna (*N.Z.*)
• VERB = sire, parent, conceive, bring to life, beget, procreate, bring into being, give life to

RELATED WORD
adjective: paternal

fatherly = paternal, kindly, protective, supportive, benign, affectionate, patriarchal, benevolent

fatigue NOUN = tiredness, lethargy, weariness, heaviness, languor, listlessness ≠ freshness
• VERB = tire, exhaust, weaken, weary, drain, wear out, take it out of (*informal*), tire out ≠ refresh

fatty = greasy, fat, creamy, oily, adipose, oleaginous, suety, rich

fault NOUN 1 = responsibility, liability, guilt, accountability, culpability 2 = mistake, slip, error, blunder, lapse, oversight, indiscretion, howler (*informal*) 3 = failing, weakness, defect, deficiency, flaw, shortcoming, blemish, imperfection ≠ strength
• VERB = criticize, blame, complain, condemn, moan about, censure, hold (someone) responsible, find fault with
• PHRASES **find fault with something** *or* **someone** = criticize, complain about, whinge about (*informal*), whine about (*informal*), quibble, carp at, take to task, pick holes in ♦ **to a fault** = excessively, unduly, in the extreme, overmuch, immoderately

faulty 1 = defective, damaged, malfunctioning, broken, flawed, impaired, imperfect, out of order 2 = incorrect, flawed, unsound

favour NOUN 1 = approval, goodwill, commendation, approbation ≠ disapproval 2 = favouritism, preferential treatment 3 = support, backing, aid, assistance, patronage, good opinion 4 = good turn, service, benefit, courtesy, kindness, indulgence, boon, good deed ≠ wrong
• VERB 1 = prefer, opt for, like better, incline towards, choose, pick, desire, go for ≠ object to 2 = indulge, reward, side with, smile upon 3 = support, champion, encourage, approve, advocate, subscribe to, commend, stand up for ≠ oppose 4 = help, benefit

favourable 1 = positive, encouraging, approving, praising, reassuring, enthusiastic, sympathetic, commending ≠ disapproving 2 = affirmative, agreeing, confirming, positive, assenting, corroborative 3 = advantageous, promising, encouraging, suitable, helpful, beneficial, auspicious, opportune ≠ disadvantageous

favourite ADJECTIVE = preferred, favoured, best-loved, most-liked, special, choice, dearest, pet
• NOUN = darling, pet, blue-eyed boy (*informal*), beloved, idol, fave (*informal*), teacher's pet, the apple of your eye

fear NOUN 1 = dread, horror, panic, terror, fright, alarm, trepidation, fearfulness 2 = bugbear, bête noire, horror, nightmare, anxiety, terror, dread, spectre
• VERB 1 = be afraid of, dread, shudder at, be fearful of, tremble at, be terrified by, take fright at, shake in your shoes about 2 = regret, feel, suspect, have a feeling, have a hunch, have a sneaking suspicion, have a funny feeling
• PHRASES **fear for something** *or* **someone** = worry about, be anxious about, feel concern for

fearful 1 = scared, afraid, alarmed, frightened, nervous, terrified, petrified ≠ unafraid 2 = timid, afraid, frightened, scared, alarmed, nervous, uneasy, jumpy ≠ brave 3 = frightful, terrible, awful, dreadful, horrific, dire, horrendous,

gruesome
feasible = practicable, possible, reasonable, viable, workable, achievable, attainable, likely ≠ impracticable
feast NOUN 1 = banquet, repast, spread (*informal*), dinner, treat, hakari (*N.Z.*) 2 = festival, holiday, fête, celebration, holy day, red-letter day, religious festival, saint's day
• VERB = eat your fill, wine and dine, overindulge, consume, indulge, gorge, devour, pig out (*slang*)
feat = accomplishment, act, performance, achievement, enterprise, undertaking, exploit, deed
feather NOUN = plume
• PLURAL NOUN = plumage, plumes, down
feature NOUN 1 = aspect, quality, characteristic, property, factor, trait, hallmark, facet 2 = article, report, story, piece, item, column 3 = highlight, attraction, speciality, main item
• PLURAL NOUN = face, countenance, physiognomy, lineaments
• VERB 1 = spotlight, present, emphasize, play up, foreground, give prominence to 2 = star, appear, participate, play a part
federation = union, league, association, alliance, combination, coalition, partnership, consortium
fed up = cheesed off, depressed, bored, tired, discontented, dissatisfied, glum, sick and tired (*informal*), hoha (*N.Z.*)
fee = charge, price, cost, bill, payment, wage, salary, toll
feeble 1 = weak, frail, debilitated, sickly, puny, weedy (*informal*), infirm, effete ≠ strong 2 = inadequate, pathetic, insufficient, lame 3 = unconvincing, poor, thin, tame, pathetic, lame, flimsy, paltry ≠ effective
feed VERB 1 = cater for, provide for, nourish, provide with food, supply, sustain, cook for, wine and dine 2 = graze, eat, browse, pasture 3 = eat, drink milk
• NOUN 1 = food, fodder, provender, pasturage 2 (*Informal*) = meal, spread (*informal*), dinner, lunch, tea, breakfast, feast, supper
feel VERB 1 = experience, bear 2 = touch, handle, manipulate, finger, stroke, paw, caress, fondle 3 = be aware of 4 = perceive, detect, discern, experience, notice, observe 5 = sense, be aware, be convinced, have a feeling, intuit 6 = believe, consider, judge, deem, think, hold
• NOUN 1 = texture, finish, touch, surface, surface quality 2 = impression, feeling, air, sense, quality, atmosphere, mood, aura
feeling 1 = emotion, sentiment 2 = opinion, view, attitude, belief, point of view, instinct, inclination 3 = passion, emotion, intensity, warmth 4 = ardour, love, care, warmth, tenderness, fervour 5 = sympathy, understanding, concern, pity, sensitivity, compassion, sorrow, sensibility 6 = sensation, sense, impression, awareness 7 = sense of touch, perception, sensation 8 = impression, idea, sense, notion, suspicion, hunch, inkling, presentiment 9 = atmosphere, mood, aura, ambience, feel, air, quality
fell 1 = cut down, cut, level, demolish, knock down, hew 2 = knock down
fellow 1 (*Old-fashioned*) = man, person, individual, character, guy (*informal*), bloke (*Brit. informal*), chap (*informal*) 2 = associate, colleague, peer, partner, companion, comrade, crony
fellowship 1 = society, club, league, association, organization, guild, fraternity, brotherhood 2 = camaraderie, brotherhood, companionship, sociability
feminine = womanly, pretty, soft, gentle, tender, delicate, ladylike ≠ masculine
fence NOUN = barrier, wall, defence, railings, hedge, barricade, hedgerow, rampart
• VERB *often with* ***in*** or ***off*** = enclose, surround, bound, protect, pen, confine, encircle
ferocious 1 = fierce, violent, savage, ravening, predatory, rapacious, wild ≠ gentle 2 = cruel, bitter, brutal, vicious, ruthless, bloodthirsty
ferry NOUN = ferry boat, boat, ship, passenger boat, packet boat, packet
• VERB = transport, bring, carry, ship, take, run, shuttle, convey
fertile = productive, rich, lush, prolific, abundant, plentiful, fruitful, teeming ≠ barren
fertility = fruitfulness, abundance, richness, fecundity, luxuriance, productiveness
fertilizer = compost, muck, manure, dung, bone meal, dressing

festival 1 = celebration, fair, carnival, gala, fête, entertainment, jubilee, fiesta 2 = holy day, holiday, feast, commemoration, feast day, red-letter day, saint's day, fiesta

festive = celebratory, happy, merry, jubilant, cheery, joyous, joyful, jovial ≠ mournful

fetch 1 = bring, pick up, collect, go and get, get, carry, deliver, transport 2 = sell for, make, raise, earn, realize, go for, yield, bring in

fetching = attractive, charming, cute, enticing, captivating, alluring, winsome

feud NOUN = hostility, row, conflict, argument, disagreement, rivalry, quarrel, vendetta
• VERB = quarrel, row, clash, dispute, fall out, contend, war, squabble

fever = excitement, frenzy, ferment, agitation, fervour, restlessness, delirium

few = not many, one or two, scarcely any, rare, meagre, negligible, sporadic, sparse

fiasco = flop, failure, disaster, mess (*informal*), catastrophe, debacle, cock-up (*Brit. slang*), washout (*informal*)

fibre = thread, strand, filament, tendril, pile, texture, wisp

fiction 1 = tale, story, novel, legend, myth, romance, narration, creative writing 2 = lie, invention, fabrication, falsehood, untruth, urban myth, tall story, urban legend

fictional = imaginary, made-up, invented, legendary, unreal, nonexistent

fiddle VERB 1 *usually with* ***with*** = fidget, play, finger, tamper, mess about *or* around 2 *usually with* ***with*** = tinker, adjust, interfere, mess about *or* around 3 (*Informal*) = cheat, cook (*informal*), fix, diddle (*informal*), wangle (*informal*)
• NOUN 1 (*Brit. informal*) = fraud, racket, scam (*slang*), fix, swindle 2 = violin

fiddling = trivial, small, petty, trifling, insignificant, unimportant, pettifogging, futile

fidelity 1 = loyalty, devotion, allegiance, constancy, faithfulness, dependability, trustworthiness, staunchness ≠ disloyalty 2 = accuracy, precision, correspondence, closeness, faithfulness, exactness, scrupulousness ≠ inaccuracy

field NOUN 1 = meadow, land, green, lea (*poetic*), pasture 2 = speciality, line, area, department, territory, discipline, province, sphere 3 = line, reach, sweep 4 = competitors, competition, candidates, runners, applicants, entrants, contestants
• VERB 1 (*Informal*) = deal with, answer, handle, respond to, reply to, deflect, turn aside 2 (*Sport*) = retrieve, return, stop, catch, pick up

fierce 1 = ferocious, wild, dangerous, cruel, savage, brutal, aggressive, menacing, aggers (*Austral. slang*), biffo (*Austral. slang*) ≠ gentle 2 = intense, strong, keen, relentless, cut-throat 3 = stormy, strong, powerful, violent, intense, raging, furious, howling ≠ tranquil

fiercely = ferociously, savagely, passionately, furiously, viciously, tooth and nail, tigerishly, with no holds barred

fiery 1 = burning, flaming, blazing, on fire, ablaze, aflame, afire 2 = excitable, fierce, passionate, irritable, impetuous, irascible, hot-headed

fight VERB 1 = oppose, campaign against, dispute, contest, resist, defy, contend, withstand 2 = battle, combat, do battle 3 = engage in, conduct, wage, pursue, carry on
• NOUN 1 = battle, campaign, movement, struggle 2 = conflict, clash, contest, encounter 3 = brawl, scrap (*informal*), confrontation, rumble (*U.S. & N.Z. slang*), duel, skirmish, tussle, biffo (*Austral. slang*) 4 = row, argument, dispute, quarrel, squabble 5 = resistance, spirit, pluck, militancy, belligerence, pluckiness

fighter 1 = boxer, wrestler, pugilist, prize fighter 2 = soldier, warrior, fighting man, man-at-arms

figure NOUN 1 = digit, character, symbol, number, numeral 2 = shape, build, body, frame, proportions, physique 3 = personage, person, individual, character, personality, celebrity, big name, dignitary 4 = diagram, drawing, picture, illustration, representation, sketch 5 = design, shape, pattern 6 = price, cost, value, amount, total, sum
• VERB 1 *usually with* ***in*** = feature, act, appear, contribute to, play a part, be featured 2 = calculate, work out, compute, tot up, total, count, reckon, tally
• PHRASES **figure something** *or* **someone out** = understand, make out, fathom, see, solve, comprehend, make sense of, decipher

figurehead = nominal head, titular head, front man, puppet, mouthpiece

file[1] NOUN **1** = folder, case, portfolio, binder **2** = dossier, record, information, data, documents, case history, report, case **3** = line, row, chain, column, queue, procession
• VERB **1** = arrange, order, classify, put in place, categorize, pigeonhole, put in order **2** = register, record, enter, log, put on record **3** = march, troop, parade, walk in line, walk behind one another

file[2] = smooth, shape, polish, rub, scrape, rasp, abrade

fill 1 = top up, fill up, make full, become full, brim over **2** = swell, expand, become bloated, extend, balloon, fatten **3** = pack, crowd, squeeze, cram, throng **4** = stock, supply, pack, load **5** = plug, close, stop, seal, cork, bung, block up, stop up **6** = saturate, charge, pervade, permeate, imbue, impregnate, suffuse **7** = fulfil, hold, perform, carry out, occupy, execute, discharge **8** *often with* ***up*** = satisfy, stuff, glut

filling NOUN = stuffing, padding, filler, wadding, inside, insides, contents
• ADJECTIVE = satisfying, heavy, square, substantial, ample

film NOUN **1** = movie, picture, flick (*slang*), motion picture **2** = cinema, the movies **3** = layer, covering, cover, skin, coating, dusting, tissue, membrane
• VERB **1** = photograph, record, shoot, video, videotape, take **2** = adapt for the screen, make into a film

filter VERB **1** = purify, treat, strain, refine, riddle, sift, sieve, winnow **2** = trickle, seep, percolate, escape, leak, penetrate, ooze, dribble
• NOUN = sieve, mesh, gauze, strainer, membrane, riddle, sifter

filthy 1 = dirty, foul, polluted, squalid, slimy, unclean, putrid, festy (*Austral. slang*) **2** = grimy, muddy, blackened, grubby, begrimed, festy (*Austral. slang*) **3** = obscene, corrupt, indecent, pornographic, lewd, depraved, impure, smutty

final 1 = last, latest, closing, finishing, concluding, ultimate, terminal ≠ first **2** = irrevocable, absolute, definitive, decided, settled, definite, conclusive, irrefutable

finale = climax, ending, close, conclusion, culmination, denouement, last part, epilogue ≠ opening

finally 1 = eventually, at last, in the end, ultimately, at length, at long last, after a long time **2** = lastly, in the end, ultimately **3** = in conclusion, lastly, in closing, to conclude, to sum up, in summary

finance VERB = fund, back, support, pay for, guarantee, invest in, underwrite, endow
• NOUN = economics, business, money, banking, accounts, investment, commerce
• PLURAL NOUN = resources, money, funds, capital, cash, affairs, budgeting, assets

financial = economic, business, commercial, monetary, fiscal, pecuniary

find VERB **1** = discover, uncover, spot, locate, detect, come across, hit upon, put your finger on ≠ lose **2** = encounter, meet, recognize **3** = observe, learn, note, discover, notice, realize, come up with, perceive
• NOUN = discovery, catch, asset, bargain, acquisition, good buy
• PHRASES **find something out** = learn, discover, realize, observe, perceive, detect, become aware, come to know

fine[1] 1 = excellent, good, striking, masterly, very good, impressive, outstanding, magnificent ≠ poor **2** = satisfactory, good, all right, suitable, acceptable, convenient, fair, O.K. *or* okay (*informal*) **3** = thin, light, narrow, wispy **4** = delicate, light, thin, sheer, flimsy, wispy, gossamer, diaphanous ≠ coarse **5** = stylish, expensive, elegant, refined, tasteful, quality **6** = exquisite, delicate, fragile, dainty **7** = minute, exact, precise, nice **8** = keen, minute, nice, sharp, acute, subtle, precise, hairsplitting **9** = brilliant, quick, keen, alert, clever, penetrating, astute **10** = sunny, clear, fair, dry, bright, pleasant, clement, balmy ≠ cloudy

fine[2] NOUN = penalty, damages, punishment, forfeit, financial penalty
• VERB = penalize, charge, punish

finger = touch, feel, handle, play with, manipulate, paw (*informal*), maul, toy with

finish VERB **1** = stop, close, complete, conclude, cease, wrap up (*informal*), terminate, round off ≠ start **2** = get done, complete, conclude **3** = end, stop, conclude, wind up, terminate

4 = consume, dispose of, devour, polish off, eat, get through **5** = use up, empty, exhaust **6** = coat, polish, stain, texture, wax, varnish, gild, veneer **7** *usually with* ***off*** = destroy, defeat, overcome, bring down, ruin, dispose of, rout, put an end to **8** *usually with* ***off*** = kill, murder, destroy, massacre, butcher, slaughter, slay, exterminate
• NOUN **1** = end, close, conclusion, run-in, completion, finale, culmination, cessation ≠ beginning **2** = surface, polish, shine, texture, glaze, veneer, lacquer, lustre

finished **1** = over, done, through, ended, closed, complete, executed, finalized ≠ begun **2** = ruined, done for (*informal*), doomed, through, lost, defeated, wiped out, undone

fire NOUN **1** = flames, blaze, combustion, inferno, conflagration, holocaust **2** = passion, energy, spirit, enthusiasm, excitement, intensity, sparkle, vitality **3** = bombardment, shooting, firing, shelling, hail, volley, barrage, gunfire
• VERB **1** = let off, shoot, shell, set off, discharge, detonate **2** = shoot, explode, discharge, detonate, pull the trigger **3** (*Informal*) = dismiss, sack (*informal*), get rid of, discharge, lay off, make redundant, cashier, give notice **4** *sometimes with* ***up*** = inspire, excite, stir, stimulate, motivate, awaken, animate, rouse

fireworks **1** = pyrotechnics, illuminations, feux d'artifice **2** (*Informal*) = trouble, row, storm, rage, uproar, hysterics

firm[1] **1** = hard, solid, dense, set, stiff, compacted, rigid, inflexible ≠ soft **2** = secure, fixed, rooted, stable, steady, fast, embedded, immovable ≠ unstable **3** = strong, close, tight, steady **4** = strict, unshakeable, resolute, inflexible, unyielding, unbending **5** = determined, resolved, definite, set on, adamant, resolute, inflexible, unyielding ≠ wavering **6** = definite, hard, clear, confirmed, settled, fixed, hard-and-fast, cut-and-dried (*informal*)

firm[2] = company, business, concern, association, organization, corporation, venture, enterprise

firmly **1** = securely, safely, tightly **2** = immovably, securely, steadily, like a rock, unflinchingly, unshakeably **3** = steadily, securely, tightly, unflinchingly **4** = resolutely, staunchly, steadfastly, definitely, unwaveringly, unchangeably

first ADJECTIVE **1** = earliest, original, primordial **2** = initial, opening, earliest, maiden, introductory **3** = top, best, winning, premier **4** = elementary, key, basic, primary, fundamental, cardinal, rudimentary, elemental **5** = foremost, highest, greatest, leading, head, ruling, chief, prime
• ADVERB = to begin with, firstly, initially, at the beginning, in the first place, beforehand, to start with, at the outset
• NOUN = novelty, innovation, originality, new experience
• PHRASES **from the first** = from the start, from the beginning, from the outset, from the very beginning, from the introduction, from the starting point, from the inception, from the commencement

fish = angle, net, cast, trawl

fit[1] VERB **1** = adapt, shape, arrange, alter, adjust, modify, tweak (*informal*), customize **2** = place, insert **3** = suit, meet, match, belong to, conform to, correspond to, accord with, be appropriate to **4** = equip, provide, arm, prepare, fit out, kit out
• ADJECTIVE **1** = appropriate, suitable, right, becoming, seemly, fitting, skilled, correct ≠ inappropriate **2** = healthy, strong, robust, sturdy, well, trim, strapping, hale ≠ unfit

fit[2] **1** = seizure, attack, bout, spasm, convulsion, paroxysm **2** = bout, burst, outbreak, outburst, spell

fitness **1** = appropriateness, competence, readiness, eligibility, suitability, propriety, aptness **2** = health, strength, good health, vigour, good condition, wellness, robustness

fitting NOUN = accessory, part, piece, unit, component, attachment
• ADJECTIVE = appropriate, suitable, proper, apt, right, becoming, seemly, correct ≠ unsuitable

fix VERB **1** = place, join, stick, attach, set, position, plant, link **2** = decide, set, choose, establish, determine, settle, arrange, arrive at **3** = arrange, organize, sort out, see to, fix up, make arrangements for **4** = repair, mend, service, correct, restore, see to, overhaul, patch up **5** = focus, direct at, fasten on **6** (*Informal*) = rig, set up

(*informal*), influence, manipulate, fiddle (*informal*)
• NOUN (*Informal*) = mess, corner, difficulty, dilemma, embarrassment, plight, pickle (*informal*), uphill (*S. African*)
• PHRASES **fix someone up** = provide, supply, bring about, lay on, arrange for ◆ **fix something up** = arrange, plan, settle, fix, organize, sort out, agree on, make arrangements for

fixed 1 = inflexible, set, steady, resolute, unwavering ≠ wavering 2 = immovable, set, established, secure, rooted, permanent, rigid ≠ mobile 3 = agreed, set, planned, decided, established, settled, arranged, resolved

fizz 1 = bubble, froth, fizzle, effervesce, produce bubbles 2 = sputter, buzz, sparkle, hiss, crackle

flag¹ NOUN = banner, standard, colours, pennant, ensign, streamer, pennon
• VERB = mark, identify, indicate, label, pick out, note
• PHRASES **flag something** *or* **someone down** = hail, stop, signal, wave down

flag² = weaken, fade, weary, falter, wilt, wane, sag, languish

flagging = weakening, declining, waning, fading, deteriorating, wearying, faltering, wilting

flair 1 = ability, feel, talent, gift, genius, faculty, mastery, knack 2 = style, taste, dash, chic, elegance, panache, discernment, stylishness

flake NOUN = chip, scale, layer, peeling, shaving, wafer, sliver
• VERB = chip, peel (off), blister

flamboyant 1 = camp (*informal*), dashing, theatrical, swashbuckling 2 = showy, elaborate, extravagant, ornate, ostentatious 3 = colourful, striking, brilliant, glamorous, stylish, dazzling, glitzy (*slang*), showy

flame NOUN 1 = fire, light, spark, glow, blaze, brightness, inferno 2 (*Informal*) = sweetheart, partner, lover, girlfriend, boyfriend, heart-throb (*Brit.*), beau
• VERB = burn, flash, shine, glow, blaze, flare, glare

flank 1 = side, hip, thigh, loin 2 = wing, side, sector, aspect

flap VERB 1 = flutter, wave, flail 2 = beat, wave, thrash, flutter, wag, vibrate, shake
• NOUN 1 = flutter, beating, waving, shaking, swinging, swish 2 (*Informal*) = panic, state (*informal*), agitation, commotion, sweat (*informal*), dither (*chiefly Brit.*), fluster, tizzy (*informal*)

flare NOUN = flame, burst, flash, blaze, glare, flicker
• VERB 1 = blaze, flame, glare, flicker, burn up 2 = widen, spread, broaden, spread out, dilate, splay

flash NOUN = blaze, burst, spark, beam, streak, flare, dazzle, glare
• VERB 1 = blaze, shine, beam, sparkle, flare, glare, gleam, light up 2 = speed, race, shoot, fly, tear, dash, whistle, streak 3 (*Informal*) = show quickly, display, expose, exhibit, flourish, show off, flaunt
• ADJECTIVE (*Informal*) = ostentatious, smart, trendy, showy

flat¹ ADJECTIVE 1 = even, level, levelled, smooth, horizontal ≠ uneven 2 = punctured, collapsed, burst, blown out, deflated, empty 3 = used up, finished, empty, drained, expired 4 = absolute, firm, positive, explicit, definite, outright, downright, unequivocal 5 = dull, dead, empty, boring, depressing, tedious, lacklustre, tiresome ≠ exciting 6 = without energy, empty, weak, tired, depressed, drained, weary, worn out 7 = monotonous, boring, dull, tedious, tiresome, unchanging
• ADVERB = completely, directly, absolutely, categorically, precisely, exactly, utterly, outright
• PHRASES **flat out** (*Informal*) = at full speed, all out, to the full, hell for leather (*informal*), as hard as possible, at full tilt, for all you are worth

flat² = apartment, rooms, quarters, digs, suite, penthouse, living quarters

flatly = absolutely, completely, positively, categorically, unequivocally, unhesitatingly

flatten 1 = level, squash, compress, trample, iron out, even out, smooth off 2 = destroy, level, ruin, demolish, knock down, pull down, raze

flatter 1 = praise, compliment, pander to, sweet-talk (*informal*), wheedle, soft-soap (*informal*), butter up 2 = suit, become, enhance, set off, embellish, do something for, show to advantage

flattering 1 = becoming, kind, effective, enhancing, well-chosen ≠ unflattering

2 = ingratiating, complimentary, fawning, fulsome, laudatory, adulatory ≠ uncomplimentary

flavour NOUN 1 = taste, seasoning, flavouring, savour, relish, smack, aroma, zest ≠ blandness 2 = quality, feeling, feel, style, character, tone, essence, tinge
• VERB = season, spice, add flavour to, enrich, infuse, imbue, pep up, leaven

flaw = weakness, failing, defect, weak spot, fault, blemish, imperfection, chink in your armour

flawed 1 = damaged, defective, imperfect, blemished, faulty 2 = erroneous, incorrect, invalid, wrong, mistaken, false, faulty, unsound

flee = run away, escape, bolt, fly, take off (*informal*), depart, run off, take flight

fleet = navy, task force, flotilla, armada

fleeting = momentary, passing, brief, temporary, short-lived, transient, ephemeral, transitory ≠ lasting

flesh NOUN 1 = fat, muscle, tissue, brawn 2 = fatness, fat, adipose tissue, corpulence, weight 3 = meat 4 = physical nature, carnality, human nature, flesh and blood, sinful nature
• PHRASES **your own flesh and blood** = family, blood, relations, relatives, kin, kith and kin, blood relations, kinsfolk, ainga (*N.Z.*)

flexibility 1 = elasticity, pliability, springiness, pliancy, give (*informal*) 2 = adaptability, openness, versatility, adjustability 3 = complaisance, accommodation, give and take, amenability

flexible 1 = pliable, plastic, elastic, supple, lithe, springy, pliant, stretchy ≠ rigid 2 = adaptable, open, variable, adjustable, discretionary ≠ inflexible

flick VERB 1 = jerk, pull, tug, lurch, jolt 2 = strike, tap, remove quickly, hit, touch, stroke, flip, whisk
• PHRASES **flick through something** = browse, glance at, skim, leaf through, flip through, thumb through, skip through

flicker VERB 1 = twinkle, flash, sparkle, flare, shimmer, gutter, glimmer 2 = flutter, waver, quiver, vibrate
• NOUN 1 = glimmer, flash, spark, flare, gleam 2 = trace, breath, spark, glimmer, iota

flight[1] 1 = journey, trip, voyage 2 = aviation, flying, aeronautics 3 = flock, group, unit, cloud, formation, squadron, swarm, flying group

flight[2] = escape, fleeing, departure, retreat, exit, running away, exodus, getaway

fling VERB = throw, toss, hurl, launch, cast, propel, sling, catapult
• NOUN = binge, good time, bash, party, spree, night on the town, rave-up (*Brit. slang*)

flip VERB 1 = flick, switch, snap, slick 2 = spin, turn, overturn, turn over, roll over 3 = toss, throw, flick, fling, sling
• NOUN = toss, throw, spin, snap, flick

flirt VERB 1 = chat up, lead on (*informal*), make advances at, make eyes at, philander, make sheep's eyes at 2 *usually with* ***with*** = toy with, consider, entertain, play with, dabble in, trifle with, give a thought to, expose yourself to
• NOUN = tease, philanderer, coquette, heart-breaker

float 1 = glide, sail, drift, move gently, bob, coast, slide, be carried 2 = be buoyant, hang, hover ≠ sink 3 = launch, offer, sell, set up, promote, get going ≠ dissolve

floating 1 = uncommitted, wavering, undecided, indecisive, vacillating, sitting on the fence (*informal*), unaffiliated, independent 2 = free, wandering, variable, fluctuating, unattached, movable

flock NOUN 1 = herd, group, flight, drove, colony, gaggle, skein 2 = crowd, company, group, host, collection, mass, gathering, herd
• VERB 1 = stream, crowd, mass, swarm, throng 2 = gather, crowd, mass, collect, assemble, herd, huddle, converge

flog = beat, whip, lash, thrash, whack, scourge, hit hard, trounce

flood NOUN 1 = deluge, downpour, inundation, tide, overflow, torrent, spate 2 = torrent, flow, rush, stream, tide, abundance, glut, profusion 3 = series, stream, avalanche, barrage, spate, torrent 4 = outpouring, rush, stream, surge, torrent
• VERB 1 = immerse, swamp, submerge, inundate, drown, cover with water 2 = pour over, swamp, run over, overflow, inundate 3 = engulf, sweep into, overwhelm, surge into, swarm into, pour into 4 = saturate, fill, choke, swamp, glut, oversupply, overfill 5 = stream, flow, rush,

pour, surge
floor NOUN 1 = ground 2 = storey, level, stage, tier
• VERB 1 (*Informal*) = disconcert, stump, baffle, confound, throw (*informal*), defeat, puzzle, bewilder 2 = knock down, fell, knock over, prostrate, deck (*slang*)
flop VERB 1 = slump, fall, drop, collapse, sink 2 = hang down, hang, dangle, sag, droop 3 (*Informal*) = fail, fold (*informal*), founder, fall flat, come unstuck, misfire, go belly-up (*slang*) ≠ succeed
• NOUN (*Informal*) = failure, disaster, fiasco, debacle, washout (*informal*), nonstarter ≠ success
floppy = droopy, soft, loose, limp, sagging, baggy, flaccid, pendulous
floral = flowery, flower-patterned
flounder 1 = falter, struggle, stall, slow down, run into trouble, come unstuck (*informal*), be in difficulties, hit a bad patch 2 = dither, struggle, blunder, be confused, falter, be in the dark, be out of your depth 3 = struggle, struggle, toss, thrash, stumble, fumble, grope
flourish VERB 1 = thrive, increase, advance, progress, boom, bloom, blossom, prosper ≠ fail 2 = succeed, move ahead, go places (*informal*) 3 = grow, thrive, flower, succeed, bloom, blossom, prosper 4 = wave, brandish, display, shake, wield, flaunt
• NOUN 1 = wave, sweep, brandish, swish, swing, twirl 2 = show, display, parade, fanfare 3 = curlicue, sweep, decoration, swirl, plume, embellishment, ornamentation
flourishing = thriving, successful, blooming, prospering, rampant, going places, in the pink
flow VERB 1 = run, course, rush, sweep, move, pass, roll, flood 2 = pour, move, sweep, flood, stream 3 = issue, follow, result, emerge, spring, proceed, arise, derive
• NOUN = stream, current, movement, motion, course, flood, drift, tide
flower NOUN 1 = bloom, blossom, efflorescence 2 = elite, best, prime, finest, pick, choice, cream, crème de la crème (*French*) 3 = height, prime, peak
• VERB 1 = bloom, open, mature, flourish, unfold, blossom 2 = blossom, grow, develop, progress, mature, thrive, flourish, bloom
RELATED WORD
adjective: floral
fluctuate 1 = change, swing, vary, alternate, waver, veer, seesaw 2 = shift, oscillate
fluent = effortless, natural, articulate, well-versed, voluble
fluid NOUN = liquid, solution, juice, liquor, sap
• ADJECTIVE = liquid, flowing, watery, molten, melted, runny, liquefied ≠ solid
flurry 1 = commotion, stir, bustle, flutter, excitement, fuss, disturbance, ado 2 = gust, shower, gale, swirl, squall, storm
flush[1] VERB 1 = blush, colour, glow, redden, turn red, go red 2 *often with* ***out*** = cleanse, wash out, rinse out, flood, swill, hose down 3 = expel, drive, dislodge
• NOUN = blush, colour, glow, reddening, redness, rosiness
flush[2] 1 = level, even, true, flat, square 2 (*Informal*) = wealthy, rich, well-off, in the money (*informal*), well-heeled (*informal*), replete, moneyed
flutter VERB 1 = beat, flap, tremble, ripple, waver, quiver, vibrate, palpitate 2 = flit
• NOUN 1 = tremor, tremble, shiver, shudder, palpitation 2 = vibration, twitching, quiver 3 = agitation, state (*informal*), confusion, excitement, flap (*informal*), dither (*chiefly Brit.*), commotion, fluster
fly 1 = take wing, soar, glide, wing, sail, hover, flutter, flit 2 = pilot, control, operate, steer, manoeuvre, navigate 3 = airlift, send by plane, take by plane, take in an aircraft 4 = flutter, wave, float, flap 5 = display, show, flourish, brandish 6 = rush, race, shoot, career, speed, tear, dash, hurry 7 = pass swiftly, pass, glide, slip away, roll on, flit, elapse, run its course 8 = leave, get away, escape, flee, run for it, skedaddle (*informal*), take to your heels
flying = hurried, brief, rushed, fleeting, short-lived, hasty, transitory
foam NOUN = froth, spray, bubbles, lather, suds, spume, head
• VERB = bubble, boil, fizz, froth, lather, effervesce
focus VERB 1 = concentrate, centre, spotlight, direct, aim, pinpoint, zoom in 2 = fix, train, direct, aim

• **NOUN 1** = centre, focal point, central point **2** = focal point, heart, target, hub
foe = enemy, rival, opponent, adversary, antagonist ≠ friend
fog = mist, gloom, haze, smog, murk, miasma, peasouper (*informal*)
foil[1] = thwart, stop, defeat, disappoint, counter, frustrate, hamper, balk
foil[2] = complement, relief, contrast, antithesis
fold VERB 1 = bend, crease, double over **2** (*Informal*) = go bankrupt, fail, crash, collapse, founder, shut down, go under, go bust (*informal*)
• **NOUN** = crease, gather, bend, overlap, wrinkle, pleat, ruffle, furrow
folk 1 = people, persons, individuals, men and women, humanity, inhabitants, mankind, mortals **2** *usually plural* = family, parents, relations, relatives, tribe, clan, kin, kindred, ainga (*N.Z.*)
follow 1 = accompany, attend, escort, go behind, tag along behind, come behind **2** = pursue, track, dog, hunt, chase, shadow, trail, hound ≠ avoid **3** = come after, go after, come next ≠ precede **4** = result, issue, develop, spring, flow, proceed, arise, ensue **5** = obey, observe, adhere to, stick to, heed, conform to, keep to, pay attention to ≠ ignore **6** = succeed, replace, come after, take over from, come next, supersede, supplant, take the place of **7** = understand, realize, appreciate, take in, grasp, catch on (*informal*), comprehend, fathom **8** = keep up with, support, be interested in, cultivate, be a fan of, keep abreast of
follower = supporter, fan, disciple, devotee, apostle, pupil, adherent, groupie (*slang*) ≠ leader
following ADJECTIVE 1 = next, subsequent, successive, ensuing, later, succeeding, consequent **2** = coming, about to be mentioned
• **NOUN** = supporters, backing, train, fans, suite, clientele, entourage, coterie
folly = foolishness, nonsense, madness, stupidity, indiscretion, lunacy, imprudence, rashness ≠ wisdom
fond ADJECTIVE 1 = loving, caring, warm, devoted, tender, adoring, affectionate, indulgent ≠ indifferent **2** = unrealistic, empty, naive, vain, foolish, deluded, overoptimistic, delusive ≠ sensible
• **PHRASES fond of 1** = attached to, in love with, keen on, attracted to, having a soft spot for, enamoured of **2** = keen on, into (*informal*), hooked on, partial to, having a soft spot for, addicted to
fondly 1 = lovingly, tenderly, affectionately, amorously, dearly, possessively, with affection, indulgently **2** = unrealistically, stupidly, vainly, foolishly, naively, credulously
food = nourishment, fare, diet, tucker (*Austral. & N.Z. informal*), rations, nutrition, cuisine, refreshment, nibbles, kai (*N.Z. informal*)
fool NOUN 1 = simpleton, idiot, mug (*Brit. slang*), dummy (*slang*), git (*Brit. slang*), twit (*informal, chiefly Brit.*), dunce, imbecile (*informal*), dorba *or* dorb (*Austral. slang*), bogan (*Austral. slang*) ≠ genius **2** = dupe, mug (*Brit. slang*), sucker (*slang*), stooge (*slang*), laughing stock, pushover (*informal*), fall guy (*informal*) **3** = jester, clown, harlequin, buffoon, court jester
• **VERB** = deceive, mislead, delude, trick, take in, con (*informal*), dupe, beguile
foolish = unwise, silly, absurd, rash, senseless, foolhardy, ill-judged, imprudent ≠ sensible
footing 1 = basis, foundation, base position, groundwork **2** = relationship, position, basis, standing, rank, status, grade
footpath (*Austral. & N.Z.*) = pavement, sidewalk (*U.S. & Canad.*)
footstep = step, tread, footfall
foray = raid, sally, incursion, inroad, attack, assault, invasion, swoop
forbid = prohibit, ban, disallow, exclude, rule out, veto, outlaw, preclude ≠ permit
forbidden = prohibited, banned, vetoed, outlawed, taboo, out of bounds, proscribed
forbidding = threatening, severe, frightening, hostile, menacing, sinister, daunting, ominous ≠ inviting
force VERB 1 = compel, make, drive, press, oblige, constrain, coerce, impel **2** = push, thrust, propel **3** = break open, blast, wrench, prise, wrest
• **NOUN 1** = compulsion, pressure, violence, constraint, oppression, coercion, duress, arm-twisting (*informal*) **2** = power, might,

pressure, energy, strength, momentum, impulse, vigour ≠ weakness **3** = intensity, vigour, vehemence, fierceness, emphasis **4** = army, unit, company, host, troop, squad, patrol, regiment
• PHRASES **in force 1** = valid, working, current, effective, binding, operative, operational, in operation **2** = in great numbers, all together, in full strength

forced 1 = compulsory, enforced, mandatory, obligatory, involuntary, conscripted ≠ voluntary **2** = false, affected, strained, wooden, stiff, artificial, contrived, unnatural ≠ natural

forceful 1 = dynamic, powerful, assertive ≠ weak **2** = powerful, strong, convincing, effective, compelling, persuasive, cogent

forecast NOUN = prediction, prognosis, guess, prophecy, conjecture, forewarning
• VERB = predict, anticipate, foresee, foretell, divine, prophesy, augur, forewarn

forefront = lead, centre, front, fore, spearhead, prominence, vanguard, foreground

foreign = alien, exotic, unknown, strange, imported, remote, external, unfamiliar ≠ native

foreigner = alien, incomer, immigrant, non-native, stranger, settler

foremost = leading, best, highest, chief, prime, primary, supreme, most important

foresee = predict, forecast, anticipate, envisage, prophesy, foretell

forever 1 = evermore, always, ever, for good, for keeps, for all time, in perpetuity, till the cows come home (*informal*) **2** = constantly, always, all the time, continually, endlessly, persistently, eternally, perpetually

forfeit VERB = relinquish, lose, give up, surrender, renounce, be deprived of, say goodbye to, be stripped of
• NOUN = penalty, fine, damages, forfeiture, loss, mulct

forge 1 = form, build, create, establish, set up, fashion, shape, frame **2** = fake, copy, reproduce, imitate, counterfeit, feign, falsify **3** = create, make, work, found, form, model, fashion, shape

forget 1 = neglect, overlook, omit, not remember, be remiss, fail to remember **2** = leave behind, lose, lose sight of, mislay

forgive = excuse, pardon, not hold something against, understand, acquit, condone, let off (*informal*), turn a blind eye to ≠ blame

forgiveness = pardon, mercy, absolution, exoneration, amnesty, acquittal, remission

forgotten = unremembered, lost, past, left behind, omitted, bygone, past recall

fork = branch, part, separate, split, divide, diverge, subdivide, bifurcate

forked = branching, split, branched, divided, angled, pronged, zigzag, Y-shaped

form NOUN **1** = type, sort, kind, variety, class, style **2** = shape, formation, configuration, structure, pattern, appearance **3** = condition, health, shape, nick (*informal*), fitness, trim, fettle **4** = document, paper, sheet, questionnaire, application **5** = procedure, etiquette, use, custom, convention, usage, protocol, wont, kawa (*N.Z.*), tikanga (*N.Z.*) **6** = class, year, set, rank, grade, stream
• VERB **1** = arrange, combine, line up, organize, assemble, draw up **2** = make, produce, fashion, build, create, shape, construct, forge **3** = constitute, make up, compose, comprise **4** = establish, start, launch **5** = take shape, grow, develop, materialize, rise, appear, come into being, crystallize **6** = draw up, devise, formulate, organize **7** = develop, pick up, acquire, cultivate, contract

formal 1 = serious, stiff, detached, official, correct, conventional, remote, precise ≠ informal **2** = official, authorized, endorsed, certified, solemn **3** = ceremonial, traditional, solemn, ritualistic, dressy **4** = conventional, established, traditional

formality 1 = correctness, seriousness, decorum, protocol, etiquette **2** = convention, procedure, custom, ritual, rite

format = arrangement, form, style, make-up, look, plan, design, type

formation 1 = establishment, founding, forming, setting up, starting, production, generation, manufacture **2** = development, shaping, constitution, moulding, genesis **3** = arrangement, grouping, design, structure, pattern, organization, array, configuration

former = previous, one-time, erstwhile, earlier, prior, sometime, foregoing ≠ current

formerly = previously, earlier, in the past, at one time, before, lately, once
formidable 1 = impressive, great, powerful, tremendous, mighty, terrific, awesome, invincible 2 = intimidating, threatening, terrifying, menacing, dismaying, fearful, daunting, frightful ≠ encouraging
formula = method, plan, policy, rule, principle, procedure, recipe, blueprint
formulate 1 = devise, plan, develop, prepare, work out, invent, forge, draw up 2 = express, detail, frame, define, specify, articulate, set down, put into words
fort NOUN = fortress, keep, camp, tower, castle, garrison, stronghold, citadel, fortified pa (*N.Z.*)
• PHRASES **hold the fort** (*Informal*) = take responsibility, cover, stand in, carry on, take over the reins, deputize, keep things on an even keel
forte = speciality, strength, talent, strong point, métier, long suit (*informal*), gift ≠ weak point
forth 1 (*Formal or old-fashioned*) = forward, out, away, ahead, onward, outward 2 = out
forthcoming 1 = approaching, coming, expected, future, imminent, prospective, impending, upcoming 2 = available, ready, accessible, at hand, in evidence, obtainable, on tap (*informal*) 3 = communicative, open, free, informative, expansive, sociable, chatty, talkative
fortify 1 = protect, defend, strengthen, reinforce, support, shore up, augment, buttress 2 = strengthen, add alcohol to ≠ dishearten
fortitude = courage, strength, resolution, grit, bravery, backbone, perseverance, valour
fortress = castle, fort, stronghold, citadel, redoubt, fastness, fortified pa (*N.Z.*)
fortunate 1 = lucky, favoured, jammy (*Brit. slang*), in luck ≠ unfortunate 2 = well-off, rich, successful, wealthy, prosperous, affluent, opulent, well-heeled (*informal*) 3 = providential, fortuitous, felicitous, timely, helpful, convenient, favourable, advantageous
fortunately = luckily, happily, as luck would have it, providentially, by good luck, by a happy chance
fortune NOUN 1 = wealth, means, property, riches, resources, assets, possessions, treasure ≠ poverty 2 = luck, fluke (*informal*), stroke of luck, serendipity, twist of fate, run of luck 3 = chance, fate, destiny, providence, the stars, Lady Luck, kismet
• PLURAL NOUN = destiny, lot, experiences, history, condition, success, means, adventures
forward ADVERB 1 = forth, on, ahead, onwards ≠ backward(s) 2 = on, onward, onwards
• ADJECTIVE 1 = leading, first, head, front, advance, foremost 2 = future, advanced, premature, prospective 3 = presumptuous, familiar, bold, cheeky, brash, pushy (*informal*), brazen, shameless ≠ shy
• VERB 1 = further, advance, promote, assist, hurry, hasten, expedite 2 = send on, send, post, pass on, dispatch, redirect
fossick (*Austral. & N.Z.*) = search, hunt, explore, ferret, check, forage, rummage
foster 1 = bring up, mother, raise, nurse, look after, rear, care for, take care of 2 = develop, support, further, encourage, feed, promote, stimulate, uphold ≠ suppress
foul ADJECTIVE 1 = dirty, unpleasant, stinking, filthy, grubby, repellent, squalid, repulsive, festy (*Austral. slang*), yucko (*Austral. slang*) ≠ clean 2 = obscene, crude, indecent, blue, abusive, coarse, vulgar, lewd 3 = unfair, illegal, crooked, shady (*informal*), fraudulent, dishonest, unscrupulous, underhand 4 = offensive, bad, wrong, evil, corrupt, disgraceful, shameful, immoral ≠ admirable
• VERB = dirty, stain, contaminate, pollute, taint, sully, defile, besmirch ≠ clean
found = establish, start, set up, begin, create, institute, organize, constitute
foundation 1 = basis 2 *often plural* = substructure, underpinning, groundwork, bedrock, base, footing, bottom 3 = setting up, institution, instituting, organization, settlement, establishment, initiating, originating
founder[1] = initiator, father, author, architect, creator, beginner, inventor, originator
founder[2] 1 = fail, collapse, break down, fall through, be unsuccessful, come unstuck,

miscarry, misfire **2** = sink, go down, be lost, submerge, capsize, go to the bottom
fountain **1** = font, spring, reservoir, spout, fount, water feature, well **2** = jet, stream, spray, gush **3** = source, fount, wellspring, cause, origin, derivation, fountainhead
fowl = poultry
foyer = entrance hall, lobby, reception area, vestibule, anteroom, antechamber
fraction = percentage, share, section, slice, portion
fracture NOUN **1** = break, split, crack **2** = cleft, opening, split, crack, rift, rupture, crevice, fissure
• VERB **1** = break, crack **2** = split, separate, divide, rend, fragment, splinter, rupture
fragile **1** = unstable, weak, vulnerable, delicate, uncertain, insecure, precarious, flimsy **2** = fine, weak, delicate, frail, brittle, flimsy, dainty, easily broken ≠ durable **3** = delicate, fine, charming, elegant, neat, exquisite, graceful, petite **4** = unwell, poorly, weak, delicate, crook (*Austral. & N.Z. informal*), shaky, frail, feeble, sickly
fragment NOUN = piece, bit, scrap, particle, portion, shred, speck, sliver
• VERB **1** = break, shatter, crumble, disintegrate, splinter, come apart, break into pieces, come to pieces ≠ fuse **2** = break up, split up
fragrance **1** = scent, smell, perfume, bouquet, aroma, sweet smell, sweet odour, redolence ≠ stink **2** = perfume, scent, cologne, eau de toilette, eau de Cologne, toilet water, Cologne water
fragrant = aromatic, perfumed, balmy, redolent, sweet-smelling, sweet-scented, odorous ≠ stinking
frail **1** = feeble, weak, puny, infirm ≠ strong **2** = flimsy, weak, vulnerable, delicate, fragile, insubstantial
frame NOUN **1** = casing, framework, structure, shell, construction, skeleton, chassis **2** = physique, build, form, body, figure, anatomy, carcass
• VERB **1** = mount, case, enclose **2** = surround, ring, enclose, encompass, envelop, encircle, hem in **3** = devise, draft, compose, sketch, put together, draw up, formulate, map out
• PHRASES **frame of mind** = mood, state, attitude, humour, temper, outlook, disposition, mind-set
framework **1** = system, plan, order, scheme, arrangement, the bare bones **2** = structure, body, frame, foundation, shell, skeleton
frank = candid, open, direct, straightforward, blunt, sincere, outspoken, honest ≠ secretive
frankly **1** = honestly, sincerely, in truth, candidly, to tell you the truth, to be frank, to be frank with someone, to be honest **2** = openly, freely, directly, plainly, bluntly, candidly, without reserve
frantic **1** = frenzied, wild, furious, distracted, distraught, berserk, at the end of your tether, beside yourself, berko (*Austral. slang*) ≠ calm **2** = hectic, desperate, frenzied, fraught (*informal*), frenetic
fraternity **1** = companionship, fellowship, brotherhood, kinship, camaraderie **2** = circle, company, guild **3** = brotherhood, club, union, society, league, association
fraud **1** = deception, deceit, treachery, swindling, trickery, duplicity, double-dealing, chicanery ≠ honesty **2** = scam, deception (*slang*) **3** = hoax, trick, con (*informal*), deception, sham, spoof (*informal*), prank, swindle **4** (*Informal*) = impostor, fake, hoaxer, pretender, charlatan, fraudster, swindler, phoney *or* phony (*informal*)
fraudulent = deceitful, crooked (*informal*), untrue, sham, treacherous, dishonest, swindling, double-dealing ≠ genuine
fray = wear thin, wear, rub, wear out, chafe
freak ADJECTIVE = abnormal, chance, unusual, exceptional, unparalleled
• NOUN **1** (*Informal*) = enthusiast, fan, nut (*slang*), addict, buff (*informal*), fanatic, devotee, fiend (*informal*) **2** = aberration, eccentric, anomaly, oddity, monstrosity, malformation **3** = weirdo *or* weirdie (*informal*), eccentric, character (*informal*), oddball (*informal*), nonconformist
free ADJECTIVE **1** = complimentary, for free (*informal*), for nothing, unpaid, for love, free of charge, on the house, without charge **2** = allowed, permitted, unrestricted, unimpeded, clear, able **3** = at liberty, loose, liberated, at large, on the loose ≠ confined **4** = independent, unfettered, footloose **5** = available, empty, spare, vacant, unused, unoccupied,

untaken **6** = generous, liberal, lavish, unstinting, unsparing ≠ mean
• VERB **1** = clear, disengage, cut loose, release, rescue, extricate **2** = release, liberate, let out, set free, deliver, loose, untie, unchain ≠ confine **3** = disentangle, extricate, disengage, loose, unravel, disconnect, untangle

freedom **1** = independence, democracy, sovereignty, self-determination, emancipation, autarchy, rangatiratanga (*N.Z.*) **2** = liberty, release, discharge, emancipation, deliverance ≠ captivity **3** = licence, latitude, free rein, opportunity, discretion, carte blanche, blank cheque ≠ restriction

freely **1** = abundantly, liberally, lavishly, extravagantly, copiously, unstintingly, amply **2** = openly, frankly, plainly, candidly, unreservedly, straightforwardly, without reserve **3** = willingly, readily, voluntarily, spontaneously, without prompting, of your own free will, of your own accord

freeway (*U.S. & Austral.*) = motorway (*Brit.*), autobahn (*German*), autoroute (*French*), autostrada (*Italian*)

freeze **1** = ice over *or* up, harden, stiffen, solidify, become solid **2** = chill **3** = fix, hold, limit, hold up **4** = suspend, stop, shelve, curb, cut short, discontinue

freezing **1** = icy, biting, bitter, raw, chill, arctic, frosty, glacial **2** = frozen, very cold

freight **1** = transportation, traffic, delivery, carriage, shipment, haulage, conveyance, transport **2** = cargo, goods, load, delivery, burden, shipment, merchandise, consignment

French = Gallic

frenzied = uncontrolled, wild, crazy, furious, frantic, frenetic, feverish, rabid

frenzy = fury, passion, rage, seizure, hysteria, paroxysm, derangement ≠ calm

frequent ADJECTIVE = common, repeated, usual, familiar, everyday, persistent, customary, recurrent ≠ infrequent
• VERB = visit, attend, haunt, be found at, patronize, hang out at (*informal*), visit often, go to regularly ≠ keep away

frequently = often, commonly, repeatedly, many times, habitually, not infrequently, much ≠ infrequently

fresh **1** = additional, more, new, other, added, further, extra, supplementary **2** = natural, unprocessed, unpreserved ≠ preserved **3** = new, original, novel, different, recent, modern, up-to-date, unorthodox ≠ old **4** = invigorating, clean, pure, crisp, bracing, refreshing, brisk, unpolluted ≠ stale **5** = cool, cold, refreshing, brisk, chilly, nippy **6** = lively, keen, alert, refreshed, vigorous, energetic, sprightly, spry ≠ weary **7** = cheeky (*Informal*), impertinent, forward, familiar, audacious, disrespectful, presumptuous, insolent ≠ well-mannered

fret = worry, brood, agonize, obsess, lose sleep, upset yourself, distress yourself

friction **1** = conflict, hostility, resentment, disagreement, animosity, discord, bad blood, dissension **2** = resistance, rubbing, scraping, grating, rasping, chafing, abrasion **3** = rubbing, scraping, grating, rasping, chafing, abrasion

friend **1** = companion, pal, mate (*informal*), buddy (*informal*), best friend, close friend, comrade, chum (*informal*), cobber (*Austral. & N.Z.*), E hoa (*N.Z. old-fashioned informal*) ≠ foe **2** = supporter, ally, associate, sponsor, patron, well-wisher

friendly = amiable, welcoming, warm, neighbourly, pally (*informal*), helpful, sympathetic, affectionate = amicable, warm, familiar, pleasant, intimate, informal, cordial, congenial ≠ unfriendly

friendship **1** = attachment, relationship, bond, link, association, tie **2** = friendliness, affection, harmony, goodwill, intimacy, familiarity, rapport, companionship ≠ unfriendliness

fright **1** = fear, shock, alarm, horror, panic, dread, consternation, trepidation ≠ courage **2** = scare, start, turn, surprise, shock, jolt, the creeps (*informal*), the willies (*slang*)

frighten = scare, shock, alarm, terrify, startle, intimidate, unnerve, petrify ≠ reassure

frightened = afraid, alarmed, scared, terrified, shocked, startled, petrified, flustered

frightening = terrifying, shocking, alarming, startling, horrifying, menacing, scary (*informal*), fearful

fringe NOUN **1** = border, edging, edge, trimming, hem, frill, flounce **2** = edge, limits, border, margin, outskirts, perimeter, periphery, borderline
• ADJECTIVE = unofficial, alternative, radical,

innovative, avant-garde, unconventional, unorthodox

front NOUN **1** = head, start, lead, forefront **2** = exterior, face, façade, frontage **3** = foreground, fore, forefront, nearest part **4** = front line, trenches, vanguard, firing line **5** (*Informal*) = disguise, cover, blind, mask, cover-up, cloak, façade, pretext
• ADJECTIVE **1** = foremost, at the front ≠ back **2** = leading, first, lead, head, foremost, topmost
• VERB = face onto, overlook, look out on, have a view of, look over *or* onto

frontier = border, limit, edge, boundary, verge, perimeter, borderline, dividing line

frost = hoarfrost, freeze, rime

frown VERB = glare, scowl, glower, make a face, look daggers, knit your brows, lour *or* lower
• NOUN = scowl, glare, glower, dirty look

frozen **1** = icy, hard, solid, frosted, arctic, ice-covered, icebound **2** = chilled, cold, iced, refrigerated, ice-cold **3** = ice-cold, freezing, numb, very cold, frigid, frozen stiff

fruit **1** = produce, crop, yield, harvest **2** *often plural* = result, reward, outcome, end result, return, effect, benefit, profit

frustrate = thwart, stop, check, block, defeat, disappoint, counter, spoil, crool *or* cruel (*Austral. slang*) ≠ further

frustrated = disappointed, discouraged, infuriated, exasperated, resentful, embittered, disheartened

frustration **1** = annoyance, disappointment, resentment, irritation, grievance, dissatisfaction, exasperation, vexation **2** = obstruction, blocking, foiling, spoiling, thwarting, circumvention

fudge = misrepresent, hedge, stall, flannel (*Brit. informal*), equivocate

fuel = incitement, ammunition, provocation, incentive

fugitive = runaway, refugee, deserter, escapee

fulfil **1** = carry out, perform, complete, achieve, accomplish ≠ neglect **2** = achieve, realize, satisfy, attain, consummate, bring to fruition **3** = satisfy, please, content, cheer, refresh, gratify, make happy **4** = comply with, meet, fill, satisfy, observe, obey, conform to, answer

fulfilment = achievement, implementation, completion, accomplishment, realization, attainment, consummation

full **1** = filled, stocked, brimming, replete, complete, loaded, saturated ≠ empty **2** = satiated, having had enough, replete **3** = extensive, complete, generous, adequate, ample, abundant, plentiful ≠ incomplete **4** = comprehensive, complete, exhaustive, all-embracing **5** = rounded, strong, rich, powerful, intense, pungent **6** = plump, rounded, voluptuous, shapely, well-rounded, buxom, curvaceous **7** = voluminous, large, loose, baggy, billowing, puffy, capacious, loose-fitting ≠ tight **8** = rich, strong, deep, loud, distinct, resonant, sonorous, clear ≠ thin

full-scale = major, wide-ranging, all-out, sweeping, comprehensive, thorough, in-depth, exhaustive

fully **1** = completely, totally, perfectly, entirely, altogether, thoroughly, wholly, utterly **2** = in all respects, completely, totally, entirely, altogether, thoroughly, wholly

fumble = grope, flounder, scrabble, feel around

fume VERB = rage, seethe, see red (*informal*), storm, rant, smoulder, get hot under the collar (*informal*)
• PLURAL NOUN = smoke, gas, exhaust, pollution, vapour, smog

fun NOUN **1** = amusement, sport, pleasure, entertainment, recreation, enjoyment, merriment, jollity **2** = enjoyment, pleasure, mirth ≠ gloom
• ADJECTIVE = enjoyable, entertaining, pleasant, amusing, lively, diverting, witty, convivial
• PHRASES **make fun of something** *or* **someone** = mock, tease, ridicule, poke fun at, laugh at, mimic, parody, send up (*Brit. informal*)

function NOUN **1** = purpose, business, job, use, role, responsibility, task, duty **2** = reception, party, affair, gathering, bash (*informal*), social occasion, soiree, do (*informal*)
• VERB **1** = work, run, operate, perform, go **2** = act, operate, perform, behave, do duty, have the role of

functional **1** = practical, utilitarian, serviceable, hard-wearing, useful

2 = working, operative, operational, going, prepared, ready, viable, up and running
fund NOUN = reserve, stock, supply, store, collection, pool
• PLURAL NOUN = money, capital, cash, finance, means, savings, resources, assets
• VERB = finance, back, support, pay for, subsidize, provide money for, put up the money for
fundamental 1 = central, key, basic, essential, primary, principal, cardinal ≠ incidental 2 = basic, essential, underlying, profound, elementary, rudimentary
fundamentally 1 = basically, at heart, at bottom 2 = essentially, radically, basically, primarily, profoundly, intrinsically
fundi (*S. African*) = expert
funeral = burial, committal, laying to rest, cremation, interment, obsequies, entombment
funny 1 = humorous, amusing, comical, entertaining, comic, witty, hilarious, riotous ≠ unfunny 2 = comic, comical 3 = peculiar, odd, strange, unusual, bizarre, curious, weird, mysterious 4 = ill, poorly (*informal*), sick, odd, crook (*Austral. & N.Z. informal*), ailing, unhealthy, unwell, off-colour (*informal*)
furious 1 = angry, raging, fuming, infuriated, incensed, enraged, inflamed, very angry, tooshie (*Austral. slang*) ≠ pleased 2 = violent, intense, fierce, savage, turbulent, vehement, unrestrained
furnish 1 = decorate, fit out, stock, equip 2 = supply, give, offer, provide, present, grant, hand out
furniture = household goods, furnishings, fittings, house fittings, goods, things (*informal*), possessions, appliances
furore = commotion, to-do, stir, disturbance, outcry, uproar, hullabaloo
further *or* **farther** ADVERB = in addition, moreover, besides, furthermore, also, to boot, additionally, into the bargain
• ADJECTIVE = additional, more, new, other, extra, fresh, supplementary
• VERB = promote, help, develop, forward, encourage, advance, work for, assist ≠ hinder
furthermore = moreover, further, in addition, besides, too, as well, to boot, additionally
furthest *or* **farthest** = most distant, extreme, ultimate, remotest, furthermost, outmost
fury 1 = anger, passion, rage, madness, frenzy, wrath, impetuosity ≠ calmness 2 = violence, force, intensity, severity, ferocity, savagery, vehemence, fierceness ≠ peace
fuss NOUN 1 = commotion, to-do, bother, stir, excitement, ado, hue and cry, palaver 2 = bother, trouble, struggle, hassle (*informal*), nuisance, inconvenience, hindrance 3 = complaint, row, protest, objection, trouble, argument, squabble, furore
• VERB = worry, flap (*informal*), fret, fidget, take pains, be agitated, get worked up
futile = useless, vain, unsuccessful, pointless, worthless, fruitless, ineffectual, unprofitable ≠ useful
future NOUN 1 = time to come, hereafter, what lies ahead 2 = prospect, expectation, outlook
• ADJECTIVE = forthcoming, coming, later, approaching, to come, succeeding, fated, subsequent ≠ past
fuzzy 1 = frizzy, fluffy, woolly, downy 2 = indistinct, blurred, vague, distorted, unclear, bleary, out of focus, ill-defined ≠ distinct

g

gadget = device, thing, appliance, machine, tool, implement, invention, instrument
gag¹ NOUN = muzzle, tie, restraint
• VERB 1 = suppress, silence, muffle, curb, stifle, muzzle, quieten 2 = retch, heave
gag² (*Informal*) = joke, crack (*slang*), funny (*informal*), quip, pun, jest, wisecrack (*informal*), witticism
gain VERB 1 = acquire, get, receive, pick up, secure, collect, gather, obtain 2 = profit, get, land, secure, collect, gather, capture, acquire ≠ lose 3 = put on, increase in,

gather, build up **4** = attain, get, reach, get to, secure, obtain, acquire, arrive at
• NOUN **1** = rise, increase, growth, advance, improvement, upsurge, upturn, upswing **2** = profit, return, benefit, advantage, yield, dividend ≠ loss
• PLURAL NOUN = profits, earnings, revenue, proceeds, winnings, takings
• PHRASES **gain on something** *or* **someone** = get nearer to, close in on, approach, catch up with, narrow the gap on

gala = festival, fête, celebration, carnival, festivity, pageant, jamboree

gale 1 = storm, hurricane, tornado, cyclone, blast, typhoon, tempest, squall **2** (*Informal*) = outburst, scream, roar, fit, storm, shout, burst, explosion

gall = annoy, provoke, irritate, trouble, disturb, madden, exasperate, vex

gallop 1 = run, race, career, speed, bolt **2** = dash, run, race, career, speed, rush, sprint

gamble NOUN **1** = risk, chance, venture, lottery, speculation, uncertainty, leap in the dark ≠ certainty **2** = bet, flutter (*informal*), punt (*chiefly Brit.*), wager
• VERB **1** = take a chance, speculate, stick your neck out (*informal*) **2** = risk, chance, hazard, wager **3** = bet, play, game, speculate, punt, wager, have a flutter (*informal*)

game NOUN **1** = pastime, sport, activity, entertainment, recreation, distraction, amusement, diversion ≠ job **2** = match, meeting, event, competition, tournament, clash, contest, head-to-head **3** = amusement, joke, entertainment, diversion **4** = wild animals *or* birds, prey, quarry **5** = scheme, plan, design, trick, plot, tactic, manoeuvre, ploy
• ADJECTIVE **1** = willing, prepared, ready, keen, eager, interested, desirous **2** = brave, courageous, spirited, daring, persistent, gritty, intrepid, plucky ≠ cowardly

gang = group, crowd, pack, company, band, bunch, mob

gangster = hoodlum (*chiefly U.S.*), crook (*informal*), bandit, hood (*U.S. slang*), robber, mobster (*U.S. slang*), racketeer, ruffian, tsotsi (*S. African*)

gap 1 = opening, space, hole, break, crack, slot, aperture, cleft **2** = interval, pause, interruption, respite, lull, interlude, breathing space, hiatus **3** = difference, gulf, contrast, disagreement, discrepancy, inconsistency, disparity, divergence

gape 1 = stare, wonder, goggle, gawp (*Brit. slang*), gawk **2** = open, split, crack, yawn

gaping = wide, great, open, broad, vast, yawning, wide open, cavernous

garland NOUN = wreath, band, bays, crown, honours, laurels, festoon, chaplet
• VERB = adorn, crown, deck, festoon, wreathe

garment *often plural* = clothes, dress, clothing, gear (*slang*), uniform, outfit, costume, apparel

garnish NOUN = decoration, embellishment, adornment, ornamentation, trimming
• VERB = decorate, adorn, ornament, embellish, trim ≠ strip

garrison NOUN **1** = troops, group, unit, section, command, armed force, detachment **2** = fort, fortress, camp, base, post, station, stronghold, fortification, fortified pa (*N.Z.*)
• VERB = station, position, post, install, assign, put on duty

gas 1 = fumes, vapour **2** (*U.S., Canad., & N.Z.*) = petrol, gasoline

gasp VERB = pant, blow, puff, choke, gulp, catch your breath
• NOUN = pant, puff, gulp, sharp intake of breath

gate = barrier, opening, door, entrance, exit, gateway, portal

gather 1 = congregate, assemble, collect, meet, mass, come together, muster, converge ≠ scatter **2** = assemble, collect, bring together, muster, call together ≠ disperse **3** = collect, assemble, accumulate, mass, muster, garner, amass, stockpile **4** = pick, harvest, pluck, reap, garner, glean **5** = build up, rise, increase, grow, expand, swell, intensify, heighten **6** = understand, believe, hear, learn, assume, conclude, presume, infer **7** = fold, tuck, pleat

gathering 1 = assembly, group, crowd, meeting, conference, company, congress, mass, hui (*N.Z.*), runanga (*N.Z.*) **2** = collecting, obtaining, attainment

gauge VERB **1** = measure, calculate, evaluate, value, determine, count, weigh, compute **2** = judge, estimate, guess, assess, evaluate, rate, appraise, reckon

• NOUN = meter, dial, measuring instrument
gay ADJECTIVE 1 = homosexual, lesbian, queer (*informal or derogatory*), moffie (*S. African slang*) 2 = cheerful, lively, sparkling, merry, upbeat (*informal*), buoyant, cheery, carefree ≠ sad 3 = colourful, rich, bright, brilliant, vivid, flamboyant, flashy, showy ≠ drab
• NOUN = homosexual, lesbian, auntie *or* aunty (*Austral. slang*), lily (*Austral. slang*) ≠ heterosexual
gaze VERB = stare, look, view, watch, regard, gape
• NOUN = stare, look, fixed look
gazette = newspaper, paper, journal, periodical, news-sheet
gear NOUN 1 = mechanism, works, machinery, cogs, cogwheels, gearwheels 2 = equipment, supplies, tackle, tools, instruments, apparatus, paraphernalia, accoutrements 3 = clothing, wear, dress, clothes, outfit, costume, garments, togs
• VERB *with* ***to*** *or* ***towards*** = equip, fit, adjust, adapt
gem 1 = precious stone, jewel, stone 2 = treasure, prize, jewel, pearl, masterpiece, humdinger (*slang*), taonga (*N.Z.*)
general 1 = widespread, accepted, popular, public, common, broad, extensive, universal ≠ individual 2 = overall, complete, total, global, comprehensive, blanket, inclusive, all-embracing ≠ restricted 3 = universal, overall, widespread, collective, across-the-board ≠ exceptional 4 = vague, loose, blanket, sweeping, unclear, approximate, woolly, indefinite ≠ specific
generally 1 = usually, commonly, typically, normally, on the whole, by and large, ordinarily, as a rule ≠ occasionally 2 = commonly, widely, publicly, universally, extensively, popularly, conventionally, customarily ≠ individually
generate = produce, create, make, cause, give rise to, engender ≠ end
generation 1 = age group, peer group 2 = age, period, era, time, lifetime, span, epoch
generic = collective, general, common, wide, comprehensive, universal, blanket, inclusive ≠ specific
generosity 1 = liberality, charity, bounty, munificence, beneficence, largesse *or* largess 2 = magnanimity, goodness, kindness, selflessness, charity, unselfishness, high-mindedness, nobleness
generous 1 = liberal, lavish, charitable, hospitable, bountiful, open-handed, unstinting, beneficent ≠ mean 2 = magnanimous, kind, noble, good, high-minded, unselfish, big-hearted 3 = plentiful, lavish, ample, abundant, full, rich, liberal, copious ≠ meagre
genesis = beginning, origin, start, birth, creation, formation, inception ≠ end
genius 1 = brilliance, ability, talent, capacity, gift, bent, excellence, flair 2 = master, expert, mastermind, maestro, virtuoso, whiz (*informal*), hotshot (*informal*), brainbox, fundi (*S. African*) ≠ dunce
genre = type, group, order, sort, kind, class, style, species
gentle 1 = kind, kindly, tender, mild, humane, compassionate, meek, placid ≠ unkind 2 = slow, easy, slight, moderate, gradual, imperceptible 3 = moderate, light, soft, slight, mild, soothing ≠ violent
gentlemanly = chivalrous, refined, polite, civil, courteous, gallant, genteel, well-mannered
genuine 1 = authentic, real, actual, true, valid, legitimate, veritable, bona fide, dinkum (*Austral. & N.Z. informal*) ≠ counterfeit 2 = heartfelt, sincere, honest, earnest, real, true, frank, unaffected ≠ affected 3 = sincere, honest, frank, candid, dinkum (*Austral. & N.Z. informal*), guileless ≠ hypocritical
germ 1 = microbe, virus, bug (*informal*), bacterium, bacillus, microorganism 2 = beginning, root, seed, origin, spark, embryo, rudiment
gesture NOUN = sign, action, signal, motion, indication, gesticulation
• VERB = signal, sign, wave, indicate, motion, beckon, gesticulate
get VERB 1 = become, grow, turn, come to be 2 = persuade, convince, induce, influence, entice, incite, impel, prevail upon 3 (*Informal*) = annoy, upset, anger, disturb, trouble, bug (*informal*), irritate, gall 4 = obtain, receive, gain, acquire, win, land, net, pick up 5 = fetch, bring, collect 6 = understand, follow, catch, see, realize,

take in, perceive, grasp **7** = catch, develop, contract, succumb to, fall victim to, go down with, come down with **8** = arrest, catch, grab, capture, seize, take, nab (*informal*), apprehend
• PHRASES **get at someone** = criticize, attack, blame, put down, knock (*informal*), nag, pick on, disparage ♦ **get at something 1** = reach, touch, grasp, get (a) hold of, stretch to **2** = find out, learn, reach, reveal, discover, acquire, detect, uncover **3** = imply, mean, suggest, hint, intimate, lead up to, insinuate ♦ **get by** = manage, survive, cope, fare, exist, get along, make do, muddle through ♦ **get something across** = communicate, pass on, transmit, convey, impart, bring home, make known, put over

ghastly = horrible, shocking, terrible, awful, dreadful, horrendous, hideous, frightful ≠ lovely

ghost 1 = spirit, soul, phantom, spectre, spook (*informal*), apparition, wraith, atua (*N.Z.*), kehua (*N.Z.*), wairua (*N.Z.*) **2** = trace, shadow, suggestion, hint, suspicion, glimmer, semblance
RELATED WORD
adjective: spectral

ghostly = unearthly, phantom, eerie, supernatural, spooky (*informal*), spectral

giant ADJECTIVE = huge, vast, enormous, tremendous, immense, titanic, gigantic, monumental ≠ tiny
• NOUN = ogre, monster, titan, colossus

gidday *or* **g'day** (*Austral. & N.Z.*) = hello, hi (*informal*), greetings, how do you do?, good morning, good evening, good afternoon, welcome, kia ora (*N.Z.*)

gift 1 = donation, offering, present, contribution, grant, legacy, hand-out, endowment, bonsela (*S. African*), koha (*N.Z.*) **2** = talent, ability, capacity, genius, power, capability, flair, knack

gifted = talented, able, skilled, expert, masterly, brilliant, capable, clever ≠ talentless

gigantic = huge, large, giant, massive, enormous, tremendous, immense, titanic ≠ tiny

giggle VERB = laugh, chuckle, snigger, chortle, titter, twitter
• NOUN = laugh, chuckle, snigger, chortle, titter, twitter

girl = female child, lass, lassie (*informal*), miss, maiden (*archaic*), maid (*archaic*)

give VERB **1** = perform, do, carry out, execute **2** = communicate, announce, transmit, pronounce, utter, issue **3** = produce, make, cause, occasion, engender **4** = present, contribute, donate, provide, supply, award, grant, deliver ≠ take **5** = concede, allow, grant **6** = surrender, yield, devote, hand over, relinquish, part with
• PHRASES **give in** = admit defeat, yield, concede, collapse, quit, submit, surrender, succumb ♦ **give something away** = reveal, expose, leak, disclose, betray, uncover, let out, divulge ♦ **give something off** *or* **out** = emit, produce, release, discharge, send out, throw out, exude ♦ **give something up** = abandon, stop, quit, cease, renounce, leave off, desist

glad 1 = happy, pleased, delighted, contented, gratified, joyful, overjoyed ≠ unhappy **2** (*Archaic*) = pleasing, happy, cheering, pleasant, cheerful, gratifying

gladly 1 = happily, cheerfully, gleefully **2** = willingly, freely, happily, readily, cheerfully, with pleasure ≠ reluctantly

glamorous 1 = attractive, elegant, dazzling ≠ unglamorous **2** = exciting, glittering, prestigious, glossy ≠ unglamorous

glamour 1 = charm, appeal, beauty, attraction, fascination, allure, enchantment **2** = excitement, magic, thrill, romance, prestige, glitz (*slang*)

glance VERB = peek, look, view, glimpse, peep ≠ scrutinize
• NOUN = peek, look, glimpse, peep, dekko (*slang*) ≠ good look

glare VERB **1** = scowl, frown, glower, look daggers, lour *or* lower **2** = dazzle, blaze, flare, flame
• NOUN **1** = scowl, frown, glower, dirty look, black look, lour *or* lower **2** = dazzle, glow, blaze, flame, brilliance

glaring 1 = obvious, gross, outrageous, manifest, blatant, conspicuous, flagrant, unconcealed ≠ inconspicuous **2** = dazzling, strong, bright, glowing, blazing ≠ subdued

glaze NOUN = coat, finish, polish, shine, gloss, varnish, enamel, lacquer
• VERB = coat, polish, gloss, varnish, enamel, lacquer

gleam VERB = shine, flash, glow, sparkle, glitter, shimmer, glint, glimmer
• NOUN 1 = glimmer, flash, beam, glow, sparkle 2 = trace, suggestion, hint, flicker, glimmer, inkling

glide = slip, sail, slide

glimpse NOUN = look, sighting, sight, glance, peep, peek
• VERB = catch sight of, spot, sight, view, spy, espy

glitter VERB = shine, flash, sparkle, glare, gleam, shimmer, twinkle, glint
• NOUN 1 = glamour, show, display, splendour, tinsel, pageantry, gaudiness, showiness 2 = sparkle, flash, shine, glare, gleam, sheen, shimmer, brightness

global 1 = worldwide, world, international, universal 2 = comprehensive, general, total, unlimited, exhaustive, all-inclusive ≠ limited

globe = planet, world, earth, sphere, orb

gloom 1 = darkness, dark, shadow, shade, twilight, dusk, obscurity, blackness ≠ light 2 = depression, sorrow, woe, melancholy, unhappiness, despondency, dejection, low spirits ≠ happiness

gloomy 1 = dark, dull, dim, dismal, black, grey, murky, dreary ≠ light 2 = miserable, sad, pessimistic, melancholy, glum, dejected, dispirited, downcast ≠ happy 3 = depressing, bad, dreary, sombre, dispiriting, disheartening, cheerless

glorious 1 = splendid, beautiful, brilliant, shining, superb, gorgeous, dazzling ≠ dull 2 = delightful, fine, wonderful, excellent, marvellous, gorgeous 3 = illustrious, famous, celebrated, distinguished, honoured, magnificent, renowned, eminent ≠ ordinary

glory NOUN 1 = honour, praise, fame, distinction, acclaim, prestige, eminence, renown ≠ shame 2 = splendour, majesty, greatness, grandeur, nobility, pomp, magnificence, pageantry
• VERB = triumph, boast, relish, revel, exult, take delight, pride yourself

gloss[1] = shine, gleam, sheen, polish, brightness, veneer, lustre, patina

gloss[2] NOUN = interpretation, comment, note, explanation, commentary, translation, footnote, elucidation
• VERB = interpret, explain, comment, translate, annotate, elucidate

glossy = shiny, polished, shining, glazed, bright, silky, glassy, lustrous ≠ dull

glow NOUN = light, gleam, splendour, glimmer, brilliance, brightness, radiance, luminosity ≠ dullness
• VERB 1 = shine, burn, gleam, brighten, glimmer, smoulder 2 = be pink

glowing 1 = complimentary, enthusiastic, rave (*informal*), ecstatic, rhapsodic, laudatory, adulatory ≠ scathing 2 = aglow, bright, radiant ≠ pale

glue NOUN = adhesive, cement, gum, paste
• VERB = stick, fix, seal, cement, gum, paste, affix

go VERB 1 = move, travel, advance, journey, proceed, pass, set off ≠ stay 2 = leave, withdraw, depart, move out, slope off, make tracks 3 = elapse, pass, flow, fly by, expire, lapse, slip away 4 = be given, be spent, be awarded, be allotted 5 = function, work, run, move, operate, perform ≠ fail 6 = match, blend, correspond, fit, suit, chime, harmonize 7 = serve, help, tend
• NOUN 1 = attempt, try, effort, bid, shot (*informal*), crack (*informal*) 2 = turn, shot (*informal*), stint 3 (*Informal*) = energy, life, drive, spirit, vitality, vigour, verve, force
• PHRASES **go off** 1 = depart, leave, quit, go away, move out, decamp, slope off 2 = explode, fire, blow up, detonate, come about 3 (*Informal*) = go bad, turn, spoil, rot, go stale ◆ **go out** 1 = see someone, court, date (*informal, chiefly U.S.*), woo, go steady (*informal*), be romantically involved with 2 = be extinguished, die out, fade out ◆ **go through something** 1 = suffer, experience, bear, endure, brave, undergo, tolerate, withstand 2 = search, look through, rummage through, rifle through, hunt through, fossick through (*Austral. & N.Z.*), ferret about in 3 = examine, check, search, explore, look through

goal = aim, end, target, purpose, object, intention, objective, ambition

god = deity, immortal, divinity, divine being, supreme being, atua (*N.Z.*)

godly = devout, religious, holy, righteous, pious, good, saintly, god-fearing

gogga (*S. African*) = insect, bug, creepy-crawly (*Brit. informal*)

golden 1 = yellow, blonde, blond, flaxen ≠ dark 2 = successful, glorious, prosperous, rich, flourishing, halcyon ≠ worst

3 = promising, excellent, favourable, opportune ≠ unfavourable
gone 1 = missing, lost, away, vanished, absent, astray 2 = past, over, ended, finished, elapsed
good ADJECTIVE 1 = excellent, great, fine, pleasing, acceptable, first-class, splendid, satisfactory, booshit (*Austral. slang*), exo (*Austral. slang*), sik (*Austral. slang*) ≠ bad 2 = proficient, able, skilled, expert, talented, clever, accomplished, first-class ≠ bad 3 = beneficial, useful, helpful, favourable, wholesome, advantageous ≠ harmful 4 = honourable, moral, worthy, ethical, upright, admirable, honest, righteous ≠ bad 5 = well-behaved, polite, orderly, obedient, dutiful, well-mannered ≠ naughty 6 = kind, kindly, friendly, obliging, charitable, humane, benevolent, merciful ≠ unkind 7 = true, real, genuine, proper, dinkum (*Austral. & N.Z. informal*) 8 = full, complete, extensive ≠ scant 9 = considerable, large, substantial, sufficient, adequate, ample 10 = valid, convincing, compelling, legitimate, authentic, persuasive, bona fide ≠ invalid 11 = convenient, timely, fitting, appropriate, suitable ≠ inconvenient
• NOUN 1 = benefit, interest, gain, advantage, use, profit, welfare, usefulness ≠ disadvantage 2 = virtue, goodness, righteousness, worth, merit, excellence, morality, rectitude ≠ evil
• PHRASES **for good** = permanently, finally, for ever, once and for all, irrevocably
goodbye NOUN = farewell, parting, leave-taking
• INTERJECTION = farewell, see you, see you later, ciao (*Italian*), cheerio, adieu, ta-ta, au revoir (*French*), haere ra (*N.Z.*)
goodness 1 = virtue, honour, merit, integrity, morality, honesty, righteousness, probity ≠ badness 2 = excellence, value, quality, worth, merit, superiority 3 = nutrition, benefit, advantage, wholesomeness, salubriousness 4 = kindness, charity, humanity, goodwill, mercy, compassion, generosity, friendliness
goods 1 = merchandise, stock, products, stuff, commodities, wares 2 = property, things, effects, gear, possessions, belongings, trappings, paraphernalia
goodwill = friendliness, friendship, benevolence, amity, kindliness
gore[1] = blood, slaughter, bloodshed, carnage, butchery
gore[2] = pierce, wound, transfix, impale
gorge NOUN = ravine, canyon, pass, chasm, cleft, fissure, defile, gulch
• VERB 1 = overeat, devour, gobble, wolf, gulp, guzzle 2 *usually reflexive* = stuff, feed, cram, glut
gorgeous 1 = magnificent, beautiful, superb, spectacular, splendid, dazzling, sumptuous ≠ shabby 2 = delightful, good, great, wonderful, excellent, lovely, fantastic, pleasant ≠ awful 3 (*Informal*) = beautiful, lovely, stunning (*informal*), elegant, handsome, exquisite, ravishing ≠ ugly
gospel 1 = doctrine, news, teachings, message, revelation, creed, credo, tidings 2 = truth, fact, certainty, the last word
gossip NOUN 1 = idle talk, scandal, hearsay, tittle-tattle, small talk, chitchat, blether, chinwag (*Brit. informal*) 2 = busybody, chatterbox (*informal*), chatterer, scandalmonger, gossipmonger
• VERB = chat, chatter, jaw (*slang*), blether
gourmet = connoisseur, foodie (*informal*), bon vivant (*French*), epicure, gastronome
govern 1 = rule, lead, control, command, manage, direct, guide, handle 2 = restrain, control, check, master, discipline, regulate, curb, tame
government 1 = administration, executive, ministry, regime, powers-that-be 2 = rule, authority, administration, sovereignty, governance, statecraft
governor = leader, administrator, ruler, head, director, manager, chief, executive, baas (*S. African*)
gown = dress, costume, garment, robe, frock, garb, habit
grab = snatch, catch, seize, capture, grip, grasp, clutch, snap up
grace NOUN 1 = elegance, poise, ease, polish, refinement, fluency, suppleness, gracefulness ≠ ungainliness 2 = manners, decency, etiquette, consideration, propriety, tact, decorum ≠ bad manners 3 = indulgence, mercy, pardon, reprieve 4 = benevolence, favour, goodness, goodwill, generosity, kindness, kindliness ≠ ill will 5 = prayer, thanks, blessing, thanksgiving, benediction 6 = favour,

regard, respect, approval, approbation, good opinion ≠ disfavour
• VERB 1 = adorn, enhance, decorate, enrich, set off, ornament, embellish 2 = honour, favour, dignify ≠ insult

graceful 1 = elegant, easy, pleasing, beautiful ≠ inelegant 2 = polite, mannerly, charming, gracious, civil, courteous, well-mannered

gracious = courteous, polite, civil, accommodating, kind, friendly, cordial, well-mannered ≠ ungracious

grade VERB = classify, rate, order, class, group, sort, range, rank
• NOUN 1 = class 2 degree 3 = level, rank, group, class, stage, category, echelon

gradual = steady, slow, regular, gentle, progressive, piecemeal, unhurried ≠ sudden

gradually = steadily, slowly, progressively, gently, step by step, little by little, by degrees, unhurriedly

graduate 1 = mark off, grade, proportion, regulate, gauge, calibrate, measure out 2 = classify, rank, grade, group, order, sort, arrange

graft NOUN 1 = shoot, bud, implant, sprout, splice, scion 2 (*Informal*) = labour, work, effort, struggle, sweat, toil, slog, exertion
• VERB 1 = join, insert, transplant, implant, splice, affix 2 = work, labour, struggle, sweat (*informal*), slave, strive, toil

grain 1 = seed, kernel, grist 2 = cereal, corn 3 = bit, piece, trace, scrap, particle, fragment, speck, morsel 4 = texture, pattern, surface, fibre, weave, nap

grand 1 = impressive, great, large, magnificent, imposing, splendid, regal, stately ≠ unimposing 2 = ambitious, great, grandiose 3 = superior, great, dignified, stately 4 = excellent, great (*informal*), fine, wonderful, outstanding, smashing (*informal*), first-class, splendid ≠ bad

grandeur = splendour, glory, majesty, nobility, pomp, magnificence, sumptuousness, sublimity

grant NOUN = award, allowance, donation, endowment, gift, subsidy, hand-out
• VERB 1 = give, allow, present, award, permit, assign, allocate, hand out 2 = accept, allow, admit, acknowledge, concede

graphic 1 = vivid, clear, detailed, striking, explicit, expressive ≠ vague 2 = pictorial, visual, diagrammatic ≠ impressionistic

grapple 1 = deal, tackle, struggle, take on, confront, get to grips, address yourself to 2 = struggle, fight, combat, wrestle, battle, clash, tussle, scuffle

grasp VERB 1 = grip, hold, catch, grab, seize, snatch, clutch, clinch 2 = understand, realize, take in, get, see, catch on, comprehend, catch *or* get the drift of
• NOUN 1 = grip, hold, possession, embrace, clutches, clasp 2 = understanding, knowledge, grip, awareness, mastery, comprehension 3 = reach, power, control, scope

grasping = greedy, acquisitive, rapacious, avaricious, covetous, snoep (*S. African informal*) ≠ generous

grate 1 = shred, mince, pulverize 2 = scrape, grind, rub, scratch, creak, rasp

grateful = thankful, obliged, in (someone's) debt, indebted, appreciative, beholden

grating[1] = grille, grid, grate, lattice, trellis, gridiron

grating[2] = irritating, harsh, annoying, jarring, unpleasant, raucous, strident, discordant ≠ pleasing

gratitude = thankfulness, thanks, recognition, obligation, appreciation, indebtedness, gratefulness ≠ ingratitude

grave[1] = tomb, vault, crypt, mausoleum, sepulchre, pit, burying place

grave[2] 1 = serious, important, critical, pressing, threatening, dangerous, acute, severe ≠ trifling 2 = solemn, sober, sombre, dour, unsmiling ≠ carefree

graveyard = cemetery, churchyard, burial ground, charnel house, necropolis

gravity 1 = seriousness, importance, significance, urgency, severity, acuteness, weightiness, momentousness ≠ triviality 2 = solemnity, seriousness, gravitas ≠ frivolity

graze[1] = feed, crop, browse, pasture

graze[2] VERB 1 = scratch, skin, scrape, chafe, abrade 2 = touch, brush, rub, scrape, shave, skim, glance off
• NOUN = scratch, scrape, abrasion

greasy = fatty, slippery, oily, slimy, oleaginous

great 1 = large, big, huge, vast, enormous, immense, gigantic, prodigious ≠ small 2 = important, serious, significant, critical, crucial, momentous ≠ unimportant

3 = famous, outstanding, remarkable, prominent, renowned, eminent, illustrious, noteworthy 4 (*Informal*) = excellent, fine, wonderful, superb, fantastic (*informal*), tremendous (*informal*), marvellous (*informal*), terrific (*informal*), booshit (*Austral. slang*), exo (*Austral. slang*), sik (*Austral. slang*) ≠ poor 5 = very, really, extremely, exceedingly

greatly = very much, hugely, vastly, considerably, remarkably, enormously, immensely, tremendously

greatness 1 = grandeur, glory, majesty, splendour, pomp, magnificence 2 = fame, glory, celebrity, distinction, eminence, note, renown, illustriousness

greed *or* **greediness** 1 = gluttony, voracity 2 = avarice, longing, desire, hunger, craving, selfishness, acquisitiveness, covetousness ≠ generosity

greedy 1 = gluttonous, insatiable, voracious, ravenous, piggish 2 = avaricious, grasping, selfish, insatiable, acquisitive, rapacious, materialistic, desirous ≠ generous

green ADJECTIVE 1 = verdant, leafy, grassy 2 = ecological, conservationist, environment-friendly, ozone-friendly, non-polluting 3 = inexperienced, new, raw, naive, immature, gullible, untrained, wet behind the ears (*informal*) 4 = jealous, grudging, resentful, envious, covetous
• NOUN = lawn, common, turf, sward

greet 1 = salute, hail, say hello to, address, accost 2 = welcome, meet, receive, karanga (*N.Z.*), mihi (*N.Z.*) 3 = receive, take, respond to, react to

greeting = welcome, reception, salute, address, salutation, hongi (*N.Z.*), kia ora (*N.Z.*)

grey 1 = dull, dark, dim, gloomy, drab 2 = boring, dull, anonymous, faceless, colourless, nondescript, characterless 3 = pale, wan, pallid, ashen 4 = ambiguous, uncertain, neutral, unclear, debatable

grief = sadness, suffering, regret, distress, misery, sorrow, woe, anguish ≠ joy

grievance = complaint, gripe (*informal*), axe to grind

grieve 1 = mourn, suffer, weep, lament 2 = sadden, hurt, injure, distress, wound, pain, afflict, upset ≠ gladden

grim = terrible, severe, harsh, forbidding, formidable, sinister

grind VERB 1 = crush, mill, powder, grate, pulverize, pound, abrade, granulate 2 = press, push, crush, jam, mash, force down 3 = grate, scrape, gnash 4 = sharpen, polish, sand, smooth, whet
• NOUN = hard work (*Informal*), labour, sweat (*informal*), chore, toil, drudgery

grip VERB 1 = grasp, hold, catch, seize, clutch, clasp, take hold of 2 = engross, fascinate, absorb, entrance, hold, compel, rivet, enthral
• NOUN 1 = clasp, hold, grasp 2 = control, rule, influence, command, power, possession, domination, mastery 3 = hold, purchase, friction, traction 4 = understanding, sense, command, awareness, grasp, appreciation, mastery, comprehension

gripping = fascinating, exciting, thrilling, entrancing, compelling, riveting, enthralling, engrossing

grit NOUN 1 = gravel, sand, dust, pebbles 2 = courage, spirit, resolution, determination, guts (*informal*), backbone, fortitude, tenacity
• VERB = clench, grind, grate, gnash

gritty 1 = rough, sandy, dusty, rasping, gravelly, granular 2 = courageous, dogged, determined, spirited, brave, resolute, tenacious, plucky

groan VERB 1 = moan, cry, sigh 2 (*Informal*) = complain, object, moan, grumble, gripe (*informal*), carp, lament, whine
• NOUN 1 = moan, cry, sigh, whine 2 (*Informal*) = complaint, protest, objection, grumble, grouse, gripe (*informal*)

groom NOUN 1 = stableman, stableboy, hostler *or* ostler (*archaic*) 2 = newly-wed, husband, bridegroom, marriage partner
• VERB 1 = brush, clean, tend, rub down, curry 2 = smarten up, clean, tidy, preen, spruce up, primp 3 = train, prime, prepare, coach, ready, educate, drill, nurture

groove = indentation, cut, hollow, channel, trench, flute, trough, furrow

grope = feel, search, fumble, flounder, fish, scrabble, cast about, fossick (*Austral. & N.Z.*)

gross ADJECTIVE 1 = flagrant, blatant, rank, sheer, utter, grievous, heinous, unmitigated ≠ qualified 2 = vulgar, offensive, crude, obscene, coarse,

indelicate ≠ decent **3** = fat, obese, overweight, hulking, corpulent ≠ slim **4** = total, whole, entire, aggregate, before tax, before deductions ≠ net
• **VERB** = earn, make, take, bring in, rake in (*informal*)

grotesque **1** = unnatural, bizarre, strange, fantastic, distorted, deformed, outlandish, freakish ≠ natural **2** = absurd, preposterous ≠ natural

ground **NOUN** **1** = earth, land, dry land, terra firma **2** = arena, pitch, stadium, park (*informal*), field, enclosure
• **PLURAL NOUN** **1** = estate, land, fields, gardens, territory **2** = reason, cause, basis, occasion, foundation, excuse, motive, justification **3** = dregs, lees, deposit, sediment
• **VERB** **1** = base, found, establish, set, settle, fix **2** = instruct, train, teach, initiate, tutor, acquaint with, familiarize with

group **NOUN** = crowd, party, band, pack, gang, bunch
• **VERB** = arrange, order, sort, class, classify, marshal, bracket

grove = wood, plantation, covert, thicket, copse, coppice, spinney

grow **1** = develop, get bigger ≠ shrink **2** = get bigger, spread, swell, stretch, expand, enlarge, multiply **3** = cultivate, produce, raise, farm, breed, nurture, propagate **4** = become, get, turn, come to be **5** = originate, spring, arise, stem, issue **6** = improve, advance, progress, succeed, thrive, flourish, prosper

grown-up **NOUN** = adult, man, woman
• **ADJECTIVE** = mature, adult, of age, fully-grown

growth **1** = increase, development, expansion, proliferation, enlargement, multiplication ≠ decline **2** = progress, success, improvement, expansion, advance, prosperity ≠ failure **3** (*Medical*) = tumour, cancer, swelling, lump, carcinoma (*Pathology*), sarcoma (*Medical*)

grudge **NOUN** = resentment, bitterness, grievance, dislike, animosity, antipathy, enmity, rancour ≠ goodwill
• **VERB** = resent, mind, envy, covet, begrudge ≠ welcome

gruelling = exhausting, demanding, tiring, taxing, severe, punishing, strenuous, arduous ≠ easy

gruesome = horrific, shocking, terrible, horrible, grim, ghastly, grisly, macabre ≠ pleasant

grumble **VERB** **1** = complain, moan, gripe (*informal*), whinge (*informal*), carp, whine, grouse, bleat **2** = rumble, growl, gurgle
• **NOUN** **1** = complaint, protest, objection, moan, grievance, grouse, gripe (*informal*), grouch (*informal*) **2** = rumble, growl, gurgle

guarantee **VERB** **1** = ensure, secure, assure, warrant, make certain **2** = promise, pledge, undertake
• **NOUN** **1** = promise, pledge, assurance, certainty, word of honour **2** = warranty, contract, bond

guard **VERB** = protect, defend, secure, mind, preserve, shield, safeguard, watch over
• **NOUN** **1** = sentry, warder, warden, custodian, watch, lookout, watchman, sentinel **2** = shield, security, defence, screen, protection, safeguard, buffer

guarded = cautious, reserved, careful, suspicious, wary, prudent, reticent, circumspect

guardian = keeper, champion, defender, guard, warden, curator, protector, custodian

guerrilla = freedom fighter, partisan, underground fighter

guess **VERB** **1** = estimate, predict, work out, speculate, conjecture, postulate, hypothesize ≠ know **2** = suppose, think, believe, suspect, judge, imagine, reckon, fancy
• **NOUN** **1** = estimate, speculation, judgment, hypothesis, conjecture, shot in the dark ≠ certainty **2** = supposition, idea, theory, hypothesis

guest = visitor, company, caller, manu(w)hiri (*N.Z.*)

guidance = advice, direction, leadership, instruction, help, management, teaching, counselling

guide **NOUN** **1** = handbook, manual, guidebook, instructions, catalogue **2** = directory, street map **3** = escort, leader, usher **4** = pointer, sign, landmark, marker, beacon, signpost, guiding light, lodestar **5** = model, example, standard, ideal, inspiration, paradigm
• **VERB** **1** = lead, direct, escort, conduct, accompany, shepherd, usher, show the way **2** = steer, control, manage,

direct, handle, command, manoeuvre **3** = supervise, train, teach, influence, advise, counsel, instruct, oversee

guild = society, union, league, association, company, club, order, organization

guilt **1** = shame, regret, remorse, contrition, guilty conscience, self-reproach ≠ pride **2** = culpability, blame, responsibility, misconduct, wickedness, sinfulness, guiltiness ≠ innocence

guilty **1** = ashamed, sorry, rueful, sheepish, contrite, remorseful, regretful, shamefaced ≠ proud **2** = culpable, responsible, to blame, offending, erring, at fault, reprehensible, blameworthy ≠ innocent

guise **1** = form, appearance, shape, aspect, mode, semblance **2** = pretence, disguise, aspect, semblance

gulf **1** = bay, bight, sea inlet **2** = chasm, opening, split, gap, separation, void, rift, abyss

gum NOUN = glue, adhesive, resin, cement, paste
• VERB = stick, glue, affix, cement, paste

gun = firearm, shooter (*slang*), piece (*slang*), handgun

gunman = armed man, gunslinger (*U.S. slang*)

guru **1** = authority, expert, leader, master, pundit, Svengali, fundi (*S. African*) **2** = teacher, mentor, sage, master, tutor

gush VERB **1** = flow, run, rush, flood, pour, stream, cascade, spurt **2** = enthuse, rave, spout, overstate, effuse
• NOUN = stream, flow, rush, flood, jet, cascade, torrent, spurt

gut NOUN = paunch (*Informal*), belly, spare tyre (*Brit. slang*), potbelly, puku (*N.Z.*)
• PLURAL NOUN **1** = intestines, insides (*informal*), stomach, belly, bowels, innards (*informal*), entrails **2** (*Informal*) = courage, spirit, nerve, daring, pluck, backbone, bottle (*slang*), audacity
• VERB **1** = disembowel, clean **2** = ravage, empty, clean out, despoil
• ADJECTIVE = instinctive, natural, basic, spontaneous, intuitive, involuntary, heartfelt, unthinking

gutter = drain, channel, ditch, trench, trough, conduit, sluice

guy (*Informal*) = man, person, fellow, lad, bloke (*Brit. informal*), chap

Gypsy *or* **Gipsy** = traveller, roamer, wanderer, Bohemian, rover, rambler, nomad, Romany

h

habit **1** = mannerism, custom, way, practice, characteristic, tendency, quirk, propensity **2** = addiction, dependence, compulsion

hack[1] = cut, chop, slash, mutilate, mangle, mangulate (*Austral. slang*), hew, lacerate

hack[2] = reporter, writer, correspondent, journalist, scribbler, contributor, literary hack

hail[1] VERB **1** = acclaim, honour, acknowledge, cheer, applaud ≠ condemn **2** = salute, greet, address, welcome, say hello to, halloo ≠ snub **3** = flag down, summon, signal to, wave down
• PHRASES **hail from somewhere** = come from, be born in, originate in, be a native of, have your roots in

hail[2] NOUN **1** = hailstones, sleet, hailstorm, frozen rain **2** = shower, rain, storm, battery, volley, barrage, bombardment, downpour
• VERB **1** = rain, shower, pelt **2** = batter, rain, bombard, pelt, rain down on, beat down upon

hair = locks, mane, tresses, shock, mop, head of hair

hairdresser = stylist, barber, coiffeur *or* coiffeuse

hairy **1** = shaggy, woolly, furry, stubbly, bushy, unshaven, hirsute **2** (*Slang*) = dangerous, risky, unpredictable, hazardous, perilous

hale (*Old-fashioned*) = healthy, well, strong, sound, fit, flourishing, robust, vigorous

half NOUN = fifty per cent, equal part
• ADJECTIVE = partial, limited, moderate, halved
• ADVERB = partially, partly, in part

RELATED WORDS
prefixes: bi-, demi-, hemi-, semi-

halfway ADVERB = midway, to *or* in the middle
• ADJECTIVE = midway, middle, mid, central, intermediate, equidistant

hall **1** = passage, lobby, corridor, hallway,

foyer, entry, passageway, entrance hall **2** = meeting place, chamber, auditorium, concert hall, assembly room

hallmark 1 = trademark, sure sign, telltale sign **2** (*Brit.*) = mark, sign, device, stamp, seal, symbol

halt VERB **1** = stop, break off, stand still, wait, rest ≠ continue **2** = come to an end, stop, cease **3** = hold back, end, check, block, curb, terminate, cut short, bring to an end ≠ aid
• NOUN = stop, end, close, pause, standstill, stoppage ≠ continuation

halting = faltering, stumbling, awkward, hesitant, laboured, stammering, stuttering

halve 1 = cut in half, reduce by fifty per cent, decrease by fifty per cent, lessen by fifty per cent **2** = split in two, cut in half, bisect, divide in two, share equally, divide equally

hammer 1 = hit, drive, knock, beat, strike, tap, bang **2** (*Informal*) = defeat, beat, thrash, trounce, run rings around (*informal*), wipe the floor with (*informal*), drub

hamper = hinder, handicap, prevent, restrict, frustrate, hamstring, interfere with, obstruct ≠ help

hand NOUN **1** = palm, fist, paw (*informal*), mitt (*slang*) **2** = worker, employee, labourer, workman, operative, craftsman, artisan, hired man **3** = round of applause, clap, ovation, big hand **4** = writing, script, handwriting, calligraphy
• VERB = give, pass, hand over, present to, deliver

handbook = guidebook, guide, manual, instruction book

handcuff VERB = shackle, secure, restrain, fetter, manacle
• PLURAL NOUN = shackles, cuffs (*informal*), fetters, manacles

handful = few, sprinkling, small amount, smattering, small number ≠ a lot

handicap NOUN **1** = disability, defect, impairment, physical abnormality **2** = disadvantage, barrier, restriction, obstacle, limitation, drawback, stumbling block, impediment ≠ advantage **3** = advantage, head start
• VERB = hinder, limit, restrict, burden, hamstring, hamper, hold back, impede ≠ help

handle NOUN = grip, hilt, haft, stock
• VERB **1** = manage, deal with, tackle, cope with **2** = deal with, manage **3** = control, manage, direct, guide, manipulate, manoeuvre **4** = hold, feel, touch, pick up, finger, grasp

handsome 1 = good-looking, attractive, gorgeous, elegant, personable, dishy (*informal, chiefly Brit.*), comely ≠ ugly **2** = generous, large, princely, liberal, considerable, lavish, ample, abundant ≠ mean

handy 1 = useful, practical, helpful, neat, convenient, easy to use, manageable, user-friendly ≠ useless **2** = convenient, close, available, nearby, accessible, on hand, at hand, within reach ≠ inconvenient **3** = skilful, skilled, expert, adept, deft, proficient, adroit, dexterous ≠ unskilled

hang VERB **1** = dangle, swing, suspend **2** = lower, suspend, dangle **3** = lean **4** = execute, lynch, string up (*informal*)
• PHRASES **get the hang of something** = grasp, understand, learn, master, comprehend, catch on to, acquire the technique of ♦ **hang back** = be reluctant, hesitate, hold back, recoil, demur

hangover = aftereffects, morning after (*informal*)

hang-up (*Informal*) = preoccupation, thing (*informal*), problem, block, difficulty, obsession, mania, inhibition

hank = coil, roll, length, bunch, piece, loop, clump, skein

happen 1 = occur, take place, come about, result, develop, transpire (*informal*), come to pass **2** = chance, turn out (*informal*)

happening = event, incident, experience, affair, proceeding, episode, occurrence

happily 1 = luckily, fortunately, providentially, opportunely **2** = joyfully, cheerfully, gleefully, blithely, merrily, gaily, joyously **3** = willingly, freely, gladly, with pleasure

happiness = pleasure, delight, joy, satisfaction, ecstasy, bliss, contentment, elation ≠ unhappiness

happy 1 = pleased, delighted, content, thrilled, glad, cheerful, merry, ecstatic **2** = contented, joyful, blissful ≠ sad **3** = fortunate, lucky, timely, favourable, auspicious, propitious, advantageous ≠ unfortunate

harass = annoy, trouble, bother, harry, plague, hound, hassle (*informal*), persecute
harassed = hassled, worried, troubled, strained, under pressure, tormented, distraught (*informal*), vexed
harassment = hassle, trouble, bother, irritation, persecution (*informal*), nuisance, annoyance, pestering
harbour NOUN = port, haven, dock, mooring, marina, pier, wharf, anchorage
• VERB 1 = hold, bear, maintain, nurse, retain, foster, entertain, nurture 2 = shelter, protect, hide, shield, provide refuge, give asylum to
hard ADJECTIVE 1 = tough, strong, firm, solid, stiff, rigid, resistant, compressed ≠ soft 2 = difficult, involved, complicated, puzzling, intricate, perplexing, impenetrable, thorny ≠ easy 3 = exhausting, tough, exacting, rigorous, gruelling, strenuous, arduous, laborious ≠ easy 4 = harsh, cold, cruel, stern, callous, unkind, unsympathetic, pitiless ≠ kind 5 = grim, painful, distressing, harsh, unpleasant, intolerable, grievous, disagreeable
• ADVERB 1 = strenuously, steadily, persistently, doggedly, diligently, energetically, industriously, untiringly 2 = intently, closely, carefully, sharply, keenly 3 = forcefully, strongly, heavily, sharply, severely, fiercely, vigorously, intensely ≠ softly
harden 1 = solidify, set, freeze, cake, bake, clot, thicken, stiffen 2 = accustom, season, toughen, train, inure, habituate
hardened 1 = habitual, chronic, shameless, inveterate, incorrigible ≠ occasional 2 = seasoned, experienced, accustomed, toughened, inured, habituated ≠ naive
hardly 1 = barely, only just, scarcely, just, with difficulty, with effort ≠ completely 2 = only just, just, barely, scarcely
hardship = suffering, need, difficulty, misfortune, adversity, tribulation, privation ≠ ease
hardy = strong, tough, robust, sound, rugged, sturdy, stout ≠ frail
harm VERB 1 = injure, hurt, wound, abuse, ill-treat, maltreat ≠ heal 2 = damage, hurt, ruin, spoil
• NOUN 1 = injury, suffering, damage, ill, hurt, distress 2 = damage, loss, ill, hurt, misfortune, mischief ≠ good
harmful = damaging, dangerous, negative, destructive, hazardous, unhealthy, detrimental, hurtful ≠ harmless
harmless 1 = safe, benign, wholesome, innocuous, nontoxic ≠ dangerous 2 = inoffensive, innocent, innocuous, gentle, tame, unobjectionable
harmony 1 = accord, peace, agreement, friendship, sympathy, cooperation, rapport, compatibility ≠ conflict 2 = tune, melody, unison, tunefulness, euphony ≠ discord
harness VERB = exploit, control, channel, employ, utilize, mobilize
• NOUN = equipment, tackle, gear, tack
harrowing = distressing, disturbing, painful, terrifying, traumatic, tormenting, agonizing, nerve-racking
harry = pester, bother, plague, harass, hassle (*informal*), badger, chivvy
harsh 1 = severe, hard, tough, stark, austere, inhospitable 2 = bleak, freezing, severe, icy 3 = cruel, savage, ruthless, barbarous, pitiless 4 = hard, severe, cruel, stern, pitiless ≠ kind 5 = drastic, punitive, Draconian 6 = raucous, rough, grating, strident, rasping, discordant, guttural, dissonant ≠ soft
harshly = severely, roughly, cruelly, strictly, sternly, brutally
harvest NOUN 1 = harvesting, picking, gathering, collecting, reaping, harvest-time 2 = crop, yield, year's growth, produce
• VERB = gather, pick, collect, bring in, pluck, reap
hassle (*Informal*) NOUN = trouble, problem, difficulty, bother, grief (*informal*), uphill (*S. African*), inconvenience
• VERB = bother, bug (*informal*), annoy, hound, harass, badger, pester
hasten = rush, race, fly, speed, dash, hurry (up), scurry, make haste ≠ dawdle
hastily 1 = quickly, rapidly, promptly, speedily 2 = hurriedly, rashly, precipitately, impetuously
hatch 1 = incubate, breed, sit on, brood, bring forth 2 = devise, design, invent, put together, conceive, brew, formulate, contrive
hate VERB 1 = detest, loathe, despise, dislike, abhor, recoil from, not be able to

bear ≠ love **2** = dislike, detest, shrink from, recoil from, not be able to bear ≠ like **3** = be unwilling, regret, be reluctant, hesitate, be sorry, be loath, feel disinclined ● **NOUN** = dislike, hostility, hatred, loathing, animosity, aversion, antipathy, enmity ≠ love

hatred = hate, dislike, animosity, aversion, revulsion, antipathy, enmity, repugnance ≠ love

haul VERB = drag, draw, pull, heave ● **NOUN** = yield, gain, spoils, catch, harvest, loot, takings, booty

haunt VERB = plague, trouble, obsess, torment, possess, stay with, recur, prey on ● **NOUN** = meeting place, hangout (*informal*), rendezvous, stamping ground

haunted 1 = possessed, ghostly, cursed, eerie, spooky (*informal*), jinxed **2** = preoccupied, worried, troubled, plagued, obsessed, tormented

haunting = evocative, poignant, unforgettable

have VERB 1 = own, keep, possess, hold, retain, boast, be the owner of **2** = get, obtain, take, receive, accept, gain, secure, acquire **3** = suffer, experience, undergo, sustain, endure, be suffering from **4** = give birth to, bear, deliver, bring forth, beget **5** = experience, go through, undergo, meet with, come across, run into, be faced with ● **PHRASES have someone on** = tease, kid (*informal*), wind up (*Brit. slang*), trick, deceive, take the mickey, pull someone's leg ◆ **have something on** = wear, be wearing, be dressed in, be clothed in, be attired in ◆ **have to 1** = must, should, be forced, ought, be obliged, be bound, have got to, be compelled **2** = have got to, must

haven = sanctuary, shelter, retreat, asylum, refuge, oasis, sanctum

havoc 1 = devastation, damage, destruction, ruin **2** (*Informal*) = disorder, confusion, chaos, disruption, mayhem, shambles

hazard NOUN = danger, risk, threat, problem, menace, peril, jeopardy, pitfall ● **VERB** = jeopardize, risk, endanger, threaten, expose, imperil, put in jeopardy ● **PHRASES hazard a guess** = guess, conjecture, presume, take a guess

hazardous = dangerous, risky, difficult, insecure, unsafe, precarious, perilous, dicey (*informal, chiefly Brit.*) ≠ safe

haze = mist, cloud, fog, obscurity, vapour

head NOUN 1 = skull, crown, pate, nut (*slang*), loaf (*slang*) **2** = mind, reasoning, understanding, thought, sense, brain, brains (*informal*), intelligence **3** = top, crown, summit, peak, crest, pinnacle **4** (*Informal*) = head teacher, principal **5** = leader, president, director, manager, chief, boss (*informal*), captain, master ● **ADJECTIVE** = chief, main, leading, first, prime, premier, supreme, principal ● **VERB 1** = lead, precede, be the leader of, be *or* go first, be *or* go at the front of, lead the way **2** = top, lead, crown, cap **3** = be in charge of, run, manage, lead, control, direct, guide, command ● **PHRASES go to your head 1** = intoxicate **2** = make someone conceited, puff someone up, make someone full of themselves ◆ **head over heels** = completely, thoroughly, utterly, intensely, wholeheartedly, uncontrollably

headache 1 = migraine, head (*informal*), neuralgia **2** = problem (*Informal*), worry, trouble, bother, nuisance, inconvenience, bane, vexation

heading = title, name, caption, headline, rubric

heady 1 = exciting, thrilling, stimulating, exhilarating, intoxicating **2** = intoxicating, strong, potent, inebriating

heal 1 *sometimes with* ***up*** = mend, get better, get well, cure, regenerate, show improvement **2** = cure, restore, mend, make better, remedy, make good, make well ≠ injure

health 1 = condition, state, shape, constitution, fettle **2** = wellbeing, strength, fitness, vigour, good condition, soundness, robustness, healthiness ≠ illness **3** = state, condition, shape

healthy 1 = well, fit, strong, active, robust, in good shape (*informal*), in the pink, in fine fettle ≠ ill **2** = wholesome, beneficial, nourishing, nutritious, salutary, hygienic, salubrious ≠ unwholesome **3** = invigorating, beneficial, salutary, salubrious

heap NOUN 1 = pile, lot, collection, mass, stack, mound, accumulation, hoard **2** *often plural* (*Informal*) = a lot, lots (*informal*), plenty, masses, load(s) (*informal*), great

deal, tons, stack(s)
• VERB *sometimes with* ***up*** = pile, collect, gather, stack, accumulate, amass, hoard
• PHRASES **heap something on someone** = load with, confer on, assign to, bestow on, shower upon

hear 1 = overhear, catch, detect 2 = listen to 3 (*Law*) = try, judge, examine, investigate 4 = learn, discover, find out, pick up, gather, ascertain, get wind of (*informal*)

hearing = inquiry, trial, investigation, industrial tribunal

heart NOUN 1 = emotions, feelings, love, affection 2 = nature, character, soul, constitution, essence, temperament, disposition 3 = root, core, centre, nucleus, hub, gist, nitty-gritty (*informal*), nub 4 = courage, will, spirit, purpose, bottle (*Brit. informal*), resolution, resolve, stomach
• PHRASES **by heart** = from *or* by memory, verbatim, word for word, pat, word-perfect, by rote, off by heart, off pat
RELATED WORD
adjective: cardiac

heat VERB *sometimes with* ***up*** = warm (up), cook, boil, roast, reheat, make hot ≠ chill
• NOUN 1 = warmth, hotness, temperature ≠ cold 2 = hot weather, warmth, closeness, high temperature, heatwave, warm weather, hot climate, mugginess 3 = passion, excitement, intensity, fury, fervour, vehemence ≠ calmness
RELATED WORD
adjective: thermal

heated 1 = impassioned, intense, spirited, excited, angry, furious, fierce, lively ≠ calm 2 = wound up, worked up, keyed up, het up (*informal*)

heaven NOUN 1 = paradise, next world, hereafter, nirvana (*Buddhism, Hinduism*), bliss, Zion (*Christianity*), life everlasting, Elysium *or* Elysian fields (*Greek myth*) 2 (*Informal*) = happiness, paradise, ecstasy, bliss, utopia, rapture, seventh heaven
• PHRASES **the heavens** (*Old-fashioned*) = sky, ether, firmament

heavenly 1 = celestial, holy, divine, blessed, immortal, angelic ≠ earthly 2 (*Informal*) = wonderful, lovely, delightful, beautiful, divine (*informal*), exquisite, sublime, blissful ≠ awful

heavily 1 = excessively, to excess, very much, a great deal, considerably, copiously, without restraint, immoderately 2 = densely, closely, thickly, compactly 3 = hard, clumsily, awkwardly, weightily

heavy 1 = weighty, large, massive, hefty, bulky, ponderous ≠ light 2 = intensive, severe, serious, concentrated, fierce, excessive, relentless 3 = considerable, large, huge, substantial, abundant, copious, profuse ≠ slight

hectic = frantic, chaotic, heated, animated, turbulent, frenetic, feverish ≠ peaceful

hedge VERB = prevaricate, evade, sidestep, duck, dodge, flannel (*Brit. informal*), equivocate, temporize
• PHRASES **hedge against something** = protect against, insure against, guard against, safeguard against, shield against, cover against

heed (*Formal*) VERB = pay attention to, listen to, take notice of, follow, consider, note, observe, obey ≠ ignore
• NOUN = thought, care, mind, attention, regard, respect, notice ≠ disregard

heel (*Slang*) = swine, cad (*Brit. informal*), bounder (*Brit. old-fashioned slang*), rotter (*slang, chiefly Brit.*)

hefty (*Informal*) = big, strong, massive, strapping, robust, muscular, burly, hulking ≠ small

height 1 = tallness, stature, highness, loftiness ≠ shortness 2 = altitude, measurement, highness, elevation, tallness ≠ depth 3 = peak, top, crown, summit, crest, pinnacle, apex ≠ valley 4 = culmination, climax, zenith, limit, maximum, ultimate ≠ low point

heighten = intensify, increase, add to, improve, strengthen, enhance, sharpen, magnify

heir = successor, beneficiary, inheritor, heiress (*fem.*), next in line

hell 1 = the underworld, the abyss, Hades (*Greek myth*), hellfire, the inferno, fire and brimstone, the nether world, the bad fire (*informal*) 2 (*Informal*) = torment, suffering, agony, nightmare, misery, ordeal, anguish, wretchedness

hello = hi (*informal*), greetings, how do you do?, good morning, good evening, good afternoon, welcome, kia ora (*N.Z.*), gidday *or* g'day (*Austral. & N.Z.*)

helm (*Nautical*) = tiller, wheel, rudder

help VERB 1 *sometimes with* ***out*** = aid,

support, assist, cooperate with, abet, lend a hand, succour ≠ hinder **2** = improve, ease, relieve, facilitate, alleviate, mitigate, ameliorate ≠ make worse **3** = assist, aid, support **4** = resist, refrain from, avoid, prevent, keep from
• NOUN = assistance, aid, support, advice, guidance, cooperation, helping hand ≠ hindrance

helper = assistant, ally, supporter, mate, second, aide, attendant, collaborator

helpful **1** = cooperative, accommodating, kind, friendly, neighbourly, sympathetic, supportive, considerate **2** = useful, practical, profitable, constructive **3** = beneficial, advantageous

helping = portion, serving, ration, piece, dollop (*informal*), plateful

helpless = powerless, weak, disabled, incapable, paralysed, impotent, infirm ≠ powerful

hem NOUN = edge, border, margin, trimming, fringe
• PHRASES **hem something** *or* **someone in** **1** = surround, confine, enclose, shut in **2** = restrict, confine, beset, circumscribe

hence = therefore, thus, consequently, for this reason, in consequence, ergo, on that account

herald VERB = indicate, promise, usher in, presage, portend, foretoken
• NOUN **1** (*Often literary*) = forerunner, sign, signal, indication, token, omen, precursor, harbinger **2** = messenger, courier, proclaimer, announcer, crier, town crier

herd = flock, crowd, collection, mass, drove, mob, swarm, horde

hereditary **1** = genetic, inborn, inbred, transmissible, inheritable **2** (*Law*) = inherited, passed down, traditional, ancestral

heritage = inheritance, legacy, birthright, tradition, endowment, bequest

hero **1** = protagonist, leading man **2** = star, champion, victor, superstar, conqueror **3** = idol, favourite, pin-up (*slang*), fave (*informal*)

heroic = courageous, brave, daring, fearless, gallant, intrepid, valiant, lion-hearted ≠ cowardly

heroine **1** = protagonist, leading lady, diva, prima donna **2** = idol, favourite, pin-up (*slang*), fave (*informal*)

hesitate **1** = waver, delay, pause, wait, doubt, falter, dither (*chiefly Brit.*), vacillate ≠ be decisive **2** = be reluctant, be unwilling, shrink from, think twice, scruple, demur, hang back, be disinclined ≠ be determined

hesitation = reluctance, reservation(s), misgiving(s), ambivalence, qualm(s), unwillingness, scruple(s), compunction

hidden **1** = secret, veiled, latent **2** = concealed, secret, covert, unseen, clandestine, secreted, under wraps

hide[1] **1** = conceal, stash (*informal*), secrete, put out of sight ≠ display **2** = go into hiding, take cover, keep out of sight, hole up, lie low, go underground, go to ground, go to earth **3** = keep secret, suppress, withhold, keep quiet about, hush up, draw a veil over, keep dark, keep under your hat ≠ disclose **4** = obscure, cover, mask, disguise, conceal, veil, cloak, shroud ≠ reveal

hide[2] = skin, leather, pelt

hideous = ugly, revolting, ghastly, monstrous, grotesque, gruesome, grisly, unsightly ≠ beautiful

hiding (*Informal*) = beating, whipping, thrashing, licking (*informal*), spanking, walloping (*informal*), drubbing

hierarchy = grading, ranking, social order, pecking order, class system, social stratum

high ADJECTIVE **1** = tall, towering, soaring, steep, elevated, lofty ≠ short **2** = extreme, great, acute, severe, extraordinary, excessive ≠ low **3** = strong, violent, extreme, blustery, squally, sharp **4** = important, chief, powerful, superior, eminent, exalted ≠ lowly **5** = high-pitched, piercing, shrill, penetrating, strident, sharp, acute, piping ≠ deep **6** (*Informal*) = intoxicated, stoned (*slang*), tripping (*informal*)
• ADVERB = way up, aloft, far up, to a great height

high-flown = extravagant, elaborate, pretentious, exaggerated, inflated, lofty, grandiose, overblown ≠ straightforward

highlight VERB = emphasize, stress, accent, show up, underline, spotlight, accentuate, call attention to ≠ play down
• NOUN = high point, peak, climax, feature, focus, focal point, high spot ≠ low point

highly = extremely, very, greatly, vastly, exceptionally, immensely, tremendously

hijack = seize, take over, commandeer, expropriate
hike NOUN = walk, march, trek, ramble, tramp, traipse
• VERB = walk, march, trek, ramble, tramp, back-pack
hilarious 1 = funny, entertaining, amusing, hysterical, humorous, comical, side-splitting 2 = merry, uproarious, rollicking ≠ serious
hill = mount, fell, height, mound, hilltop, tor, knoll, hillock, kopje *or* koppie (*S. African*)
hinder = obstruct, stop, check, block, delay, frustrate, handicap, interrupt ≠ help
hint NOUN 1 = clue, suggestion, implication, indication, pointer, allusion, innuendo, intimation 2 *often plural* = advice, help, tip(s), suggestion(s), pointer(s) 3 = trace, touch, suggestion, dash, suspicion, tinge, undertone
• VERB *sometimes with* ***at*** = suggest, indicate, imply, intimate, insinuate
hire VERB 1 = employ, commission, take on, engage, appoint, sign up, enlist 2 = rent, charter, lease, let, engage
• NOUN 1 = rental, hiring, rent, lease 2 = charge, rental, price, cost, fee
hiss VERB 1 = whistle, wheeze, whiz, whirr, sibilate 2 = jeer, mock, deride
• NOUN = fizz, buzz, hissing, fizzing, sibilation
historic = significant, notable, momentous, famous, extraordinary, outstanding, remarkable, ground-breaking ≠ unimportant
historical = factual, real, documented, actual, authentic, attested ≠ contemporary
history 1 = the past, antiquity, yesterday, yesteryear, olden days 2 = chronicle, record, story, account, narrative, recital, annals
hit VERB 1 = strike, beat, knock, bang, slap, smack, thump, clout (*informal*) 2 = collide with, run into, bump into, clash with, smash into, crash against, bang into 3 = affect, damage, harm, ruin, devastate, overwhelm, touch, impact on 4 = reach, gain, achieve, arrive at, accomplish, attain
• NOUN 1 = shot, blow 2 = blow, knock, stroke, belt (*informal*), rap, slap, smack, clout (*informal*) 3 = success, winner, triumph, smash (*informal*), sensation
• PHRASES **hit it off** (*Informal*) = get on (well) with, click (*slang*), be on good terms, get on like a house on fire (*informal*)
◆ **hit on** *or* **upon something** = think up, discover, arrive at, invent, stumble on, light upon, strike upon
hitch NOUN = problem, catch, difficulty, hold-up, obstacle, drawback, snag, uphill (*S. African*), impediment
• VERB 1 (*Informal*) = hitchhike, thumb a lift 2 = fasten, join, attach, couple, tie, connect, harness, tether
• PHRASES **hitch something up** = pull up, tug, jerk, yank
hitherto (*Formal*) = previously, so far, until now, thus far, heretofore
hobby = pastime, relaxation, leisure pursuit, diversion, avocation, (leisure) activity
hoist VERB = raise, lift, erect, elevate, heave
• NOUN = lift, crane, elevator, winch
hold VERB 1 = embrace, grasp, clutch, hug, squeeze, cradle, clasp, enfold 2 = restrain ≠ release 3 = accommodate, take, contain, seat, have a capacity for 4 = consider, think, believe, judge, regard, assume, reckon, deem ≠ deny 5 = occupy, have, fill, maintain, retain, possess, hold down (*informal*) 6 = conduct, convene, call, run, preside over ≠ cancel 7 = detain, confine, imprison, impound ≠ release
• NOUN 1 = grip, grasp, clasp 2 = foothold, footing 3 = control, influence, mastery, mana (*N.Z.*)
holder 1 = owner, bearer, possessor, keeper, proprietor 2 = case, cover, container
hold-up 1 = robbery, theft, mugging (*informal*), stick-up (*slang, chiefly U.S.*) 2 = delay, wait, hitch, setback, snag, traffic jam, stoppage, bottleneck
hole 1 = cavity, pit, hollow, chamber, cave, cavern 2 = opening, crack, tear, gap, breach, vent, puncture, aperture 3 = burrow, den, earth, shelter, lair 4 (*Informal*) = hovel, dump (*informal*), dive (*slang*), slum 5 (*Informal*) = predicament, spot (*informal*), fix (*informal*), mess, jam (*informal*), dilemma, scrape (*informal*), hot water (*informal*)
holiday 1 = vacation, leave, break, time off, recess 2 = festival, fête, celebration, feast, gala
hollow ADJECTIVE 1 = empty, vacant, void,

unfilled ≠ solid **2** = worthless, useless, vain, meaningless, pointless, futile, fruitless ≠ meaningful **3** = dull, low, deep, muted, toneless, reverberant ≠ vibrant
• NOUN **1** = cavity, hole, bowl, depression, pit, basin, crater, trough ≠ mound **2** = valley, dale, glen, dell, dingle ≠ hill
• VERB *often followed by* ***out*** = scoop out, dig out, excavate, gouge out

holocaust 1 = devastation, destruction, genocide, annihilation, conflagration **2** = genocide, massacre, annihilation

holy 1 = sacred, blessed, hallowed, venerable, consecrated, sacrosanct, sanctified ≠ unsanctified **2** = devout, godly, religious, pure, righteous, pious, virtuous, saintly ≠ sinful

homage = respect, honour, worship, devotion, reverence, deference, adulation, adoration ≠ contempt

home NOUN **1** = dwelling, house, residence, abode, habitation, pad (*slang*), domicile **2** = birthplace, homeland, home town, native land
• ADJECTIVE **1** = domestic, local, internal, native
• PHRASES **at home 1** = in, present, available **2** = at ease, relaxed, comfortable, content, at peace ♦ **bring something home to someone** = make clear, emphasize, drive home, press home, impress upon

homeland = native land, birthplace, motherland, fatherland, country of origin, mother country

homeless = destitute, displaced, dispossessed, down-and-out

homely 1 = comfortable, welcoming, friendly, cosy, homespun **2** = plain, simple, ordinary, modest ≠ elaborate

homicide = murder, killing, manslaughter, slaying, bloodshed

hone 1 = improve, better, enhance, upgrade, refine, sharpen, help **2** = sharpen, point, grind, edge, file, polish, whet

honest 1 = trustworthy, upright, ethical, honourable, reputable, truthful, virtuous, law-abiding ≠ dishonest **2** = open, direct, frank, plain, sincere, candid, forthright, upfront (*informal*) ≠ secretive

honestly 1 = ethically, legally, lawfully, honourably, by fair means **2** = frankly, plainly, candidly, straight (out), truthfully, to your face, in all sincerity

honesty 1 = integrity, honour, virtue, morality, probity, rectitude, truthfulness, trustworthiness **2** = frankness, openness, sincerity, candour, bluntness, outspokenness, straightforwardness

honorary = nominal, unofficial, titular, in name *or* title only

honour NOUN **1** = integrity, morality, honesty, goodness, fairness, decency, probity, rectitude ≠ dishonour **2** = prestige, credit, reputation, glory, fame, distinction, dignity, renown ≠ disgrace **3** = reputation, standing, prestige, image, status, stature, good name, cachet **4** = acclaim, praise, recognition, compliments, homage, accolades, commendation ≠ contempt **5** = privilege, credit, pleasure, compliment
• VERB **1** = acclaim, praise, decorate, commemorate, commend **2** = respect, value, esteem, prize, appreciate, adore ≠ scorn **3** = fulfil, keep, carry out, observe, discharge, live up to, be true to **4** = pay, take, accept, pass, acknowledge ≠ refuse

honourable 1 = principled, moral, ethical, fair, upright, honest, virtuous, trustworthy **2** = proper, respectable, virtuous, creditable

hook NOUN = fastener, catch, link, peg, clasp
• VERB **1** = fasten, fix, secure, clasp **2** = catch, land, trap, entrap

hooked 1 = bent, curved, aquiline, hook-shaped **2** (*Informal*) = obsessed, addicted, taken, devoted, turned on (*slang*), enamoured **3** (*Informal*) = addicted, dependent, using (*informal*), having a habit

hooligan = delinquent, vandal, hoon (*Austral. & N.Z.*), ruffian, lager lout, yob *or* yobbo (*Brit. slang*), cougan (*Austral. slang*), scozza (*Austral. slang*), bogan (*Austral. slang*)

hoop = ring, band, loop, wheel, round, girdle, circlet

hop VERB = jump, spring, bound, leap, skip, vault, caper
• NOUN = jump, step, spring, bound, leap, bounce, skip, vault

hope VERB = believe, look forward to, cross your fingers
• NOUN = belief, confidence, expectation, longing, dream, desire, ambition, assumption ≠ despair

hopeful 1 = optimistic, confident, looking forward to, buoyant, sanguine, expectant ≠ despairing 2 = promising, encouraging, bright, reassuring, rosy, heartening, auspicious ≠ unpromising
hopefully = optimistically, confidently, expectantly, with anticipation
hopeless = impossible, pointless, futile, useless, vain, no-win, unattainable
horde = crowd, mob, swarm, host, band, pack, drove, gang
horizon = skyline, view, vista
horizontal = level, flat, parallel
horrible 1 (*Informal*) = dreadful, terrible, awful, nasty, cruel, mean, unpleasant, horrid ≠ wonderful 2 = terrible, appalling, terrifying, shocking, grim, dreadful, revolting, ghastly
horrific = horrifying, shocking, appalling, awful, terrifying, dreadful, horrendous, ghastly
horrify 1 = terrify, alarm, frighten, scare, intimidate, petrify, make your hair stand on end ≠ comfort 2 = shock, appal, dismay, sicken, outrage ≠ delight
horror 1 = terror, fear, alarm, panic, dread, fright, consternation, trepidation 2 = hatred, disgust, loathing, aversion, revulsion, repugnance, odium, detestation ≠ love
horse = nag, mount, mare, colt, filly, stallion, steed (*archaic or literary*), moke (*Austral. slang*), yarraman *or* yarramin (*Austral.*), gee-gee (*slang*)

RELATED WORDS
adjectives: equestrian, equine
male: stallion
female: mare
young: foal, colt, filly

hospitality = welcome, warmth, kindness, friendliness, sociability, conviviality, neighbourliness, cordiality
host[1] *or* **hostess** NOUN 1 = master of ceremonies, proprietor, innkeeper, landlord *or* landlady 2 = presenter, compere (*Brit.*), anchorman *or* anchorwoman
• VERB = present, introduce, compere (*Brit.*), front (*informal*)
host[2] 1 = multitude, lot, load (*informal*), wealth, array, myriad, great quantity, large number 2 = crowd, army, pack, drove, mob, herd, legion, swarm
hostage = captive, prisoner, pawn
hostile 1 = antagonistic, opposed, contrary, ill-disposed 2 = unfriendly, belligerent, antagonistic, rancorous, ill-disposed ≠ friendly 3 = inhospitable, adverse, uncongenial, unsympathetic, unwelcoming ≠ hospitable
hostility NOUN 1 = unfriendliness, hatred, animosity, spite, bitterness, malice, venom, enmity ≠ friendliness 2 = opposition, resentment, antipathy, aversion, antagonism, ill feeling, ill-will, animus ≠ approval
• PLURAL NOUN = warfare, war, fighting, conflict, combat, armed conflict ≠ peace
hot 1 = heated, boiling, steaming, roasting, searing, scorching, scalding 2 = warm, close, stifling, humid, torrid, sultry, sweltering, balmy ≠ cold 3 = spicy, pungent, peppery, piquant, biting, sharp ≠ mild 4 = intense, passionate, heated, spirited, fierce, lively, animated, ardent 5 = new, latest, fresh, recent, up to date, just out, up to the minute, bang up to date (*informal*) ≠ old 6 = popular, hip, fashionable, cool, in demand, sought-after, must-see, in vogue ≠ unpopular 7 = fierce, intense, strong, keen, competitive, cut-throat 8 = fiery, violent, raging, passionate, stormy ≠ calm
hound = harass, harry, bother, provoke, annoy, torment, hassle (*informal*), badger

RELATED WORD
collective noun: pack

house NOUN 1 = home, residence, dwelling, pad (*slang*), homestead, abode, habitation, domicile, whare (*N.Z.*) 2 = household, family 3 = firm, company, business, organization, outfit (*informal*) 4 = assembly, parliament, Commons, legislative body 5 = dynasty, tribe, clan
• VERB 1 = accommodate, quarter, take in, put up, lodge, harbour, billet 2 = contain, keep, hold, cover, store, protect, shelter 3 = take, accommodate, sleep, provide shelter for, give a bed to
• PHRASES **on the house** = free, for free (*informal*), for nothing, free of charge, gratis
household = family, home, house, family circle, ainga (*N.Z.*)
housing 1 = accommodation, homes, houses, dwellings, domiciles 2 = case, casing, covering, cover, shell, jacket, holder, container

hover 1 = float, fly, hang, drift, flutter 2 = linger, loiter, hang about *or* around (*informal*) 3 = waver, fluctuate, dither (*chiefly Brit.*), oscillate, vacillate

however = but, nevertheless, still, though, yet, nonetheless, notwithstanding, anyhow

howl VERB 1 = bay, cry 2 = cry, scream, roar, weep, yell, wail, shriek, bellow
• NOUN 1 = baying, cry, bay, bark, barking, yelping 2 = cry, scream, roar, bay, wail, shriek, clamour, bawl

hub = centre, heart, focus, core, middle, focal point, nerve centre

huddle VERB 1 = curl up, crouch, hunch up 2 = crowd, press, gather, collect, squeeze, cluster, flock, herd
• NOUN (*Informal*) = discussion, conference, meeting, hui (*N.Z.*), powwow, confab (*informal*), korero (*N.Z.*)

hue = colour, tone, shade, dye, tint, tinge

hug VERB = embrace, cuddle, squeeze, clasp, enfold, hold close, take in your arms
• NOUN = embrace, squeeze, bear hug, clinch (*slang*), clasp

huge = enormous, large, massive, vast, tremendous, immense, gigantic, monumental ≠ tiny

hui (*N.Z.*) = meeting, gathering, assembly, conference, congress, rally, convention, get-together (*informal*)

hull = framework, casing, body, covering, frame

hum 1 = drone, buzz, murmur, throb, vibrate, purr, thrum, whir 2 (*Informal*) = be busy, buzz, bustle, stir, pulse, pulsate

human ADJECTIVE = mortal, manlike ≠ nonhuman
• NOUN = human being, person, individual, creature, mortal, man *or* woman ≠ nonhuman

humane = kind, compassionate, understanding, forgiving, tender, sympathetic, benign, merciful ≠ cruel

humanitarian ADJECTIVE 1 = compassionate, charitable, humane, benevolent, altruistic 2 = charitable, philanthropic, public-spirited
• NOUN = philanthropist, benefactor, Good Samaritan, altruist

humanity 1 = the human race, man, mankind, people, mortals, humankind, Homo sapiens 2 = human nature, mortality 3 = kindness, charity, compassion, sympathy, mercy, philanthropy, fellow feeling, kind-heartedness

humble ADJECTIVE 1 = modest, meek, unassuming, unpretentious, self-effacing, unostentatious ≠ proud 2 = lowly, poor, mean, simple, ordinary, modest, obscure, undistinguished ≠ distinguished
• VERB = humiliate, disgrace, crush, subdue, chasten, put (someone) in their place, take down a peg (*informal*) ≠ exalt

humidity = damp, moisture, dampness, wetness, moistness, dankness, clamminess, mugginess

humiliate = embarrass, shame, humble, crush, put down, degrade, chasten, mortify ≠ honour

humiliating = embarrassing, shaming, humbling, mortifying, crushing, degrading, ignominious, barro (*Austral. slang*)

humiliation = embarrassment, shame, disgrace, humbling, put-down, degradation, indignity, ignominy

humorous = funny, comic, amusing, entertaining, witty, comical, droll, jocular ≠ serious

humour NOUN 1 = comedy, funniness, fun, amusement, funny side, jocularity, facetiousness, ludicrousness ≠ seriousness 2 = mood, spirits, temper, disposition, frame of mind 3 = joking, comedy, wit, farce, jesting, wisecracks (*informal*), witticisms
• VERB = indulge, accommodate, go along with, flatter, gratify, pander to, mollify ≠ oppose

hunch NOUN = feeling, idea, impression, suspicion, intuition, premonition, inkling, presentiment
• VERB = crouch, bend, curve, arch, draw in

hunger NOUN 1 = appetite, emptiness, hungriness, ravenousness 2 = starvation, famine, malnutrition, undernourishment 3 = desire, appetite, craving, ache, lust, yearning, itch, thirst
• PHRASES **hunger for** *or* **after something** = want, desire, crave, long for, wish for, yearn for, hanker after, ache for

hungry 1 = starving, ravenous, famished, starved, empty, voracious, peckish (*informal*, *chiefly Brit.*) 2 = eager, keen, craving, yearning, greedy, avid, desirous, covetous

hunk = lump, piece, chunk, block, mass, wedge, slab, nugget

hunt VERB = stalk, track, chase, pursue, trail, hound

• NOUN = search, hunting, investigation, chase, pursuit, quest

• PHRASES **hunt for something** *or* **someone** = search for, look for, seek for, forage for, scour for, fossick for (*Austral. & N.Z.*), ferret about for

hurdle 1 = obstacle, difficulty, barrier, handicap, hazard, uphill (*S. African*), obstruction, stumbling block 2 = fence, barrier, barricade

hurl = throw, fling, launch, cast, pitch, toss, propel, sling

hurricane = storm, gale, tornado, cyclone, typhoon, tempest, twister (*U.S. informal*), willy-willy (*Austral.*)

hurried 1 = hasty, quick, brief, rushed, short, swift, speedy 2 = rushed, perfunctory, speedy, hasty, cursory

hurry VERB 1 = rush, fly, dash, scurry, scoot ≠ dawdle 2 = make haste, rush, get a move on (*informal*), step on it (*informal*)

• NOUN = rush, haste, speed, urgency, flurry, quickness ≠ slowness

hurt VERB 1 = injure, damage, wound, cut, disable, bruise, scrape, impair ≠ heal 2 = ache, be sore, be painful, burn, smart, sting, throb, be tender 3 = harm, injure, ill-treat, maltreat 4 = upset, distress, pain, wound, annoy, grieve, sadden

• NOUN = distress, suffering, pain, grief, misery, sorrow, heartache, wretchedness ≠ happiness

• ADJECTIVE 1 = injured, wounded, damaged, harmed, cut, bruised, scarred ≠ healed 2 = upset, wounded, crushed, offended, aggrieved, tooshie (*Austral. slang*) ≠ calmed

hurtle = rush, charge, race, shoot, fly, speed, tear, crash

husband NOUN = partner, spouse, mate, better half (*humorous*)

• VERB = conserve, budget, save, store, hoard, economize on, use economically ≠ squander

hush VERB = quieten, silence, mute, muzzle, shush

• NOUN = quiet, silence, calm, peace, tranquillity, stillness

hut 1 = cabin, shack, shanty, hovel, whare (*N.Z.*) 2 = shed, outhouse, lean-to, lockup

hybrid 1 = crossbreed, cross, mixture, compound, composite, amalgam, mongrel, half-breed 2 = mixture, compound, composite, amalgam

hygiene = cleanliness, sanitation, disinfection, sterility

hymn 1 = religious song, song of praise, carol, chant, anthem, psalm, paean 2 = song of praise, anthem, paean

hype (*Slang*) = publicity, promotion, plugging (*informal*), razzmatazz (*slang*), brouhaha, ballyhoo (*informal*)

hypocrisy = insincerity, pretence, deception, cant, duplicity, deceitfulness ≠ sincerity

hypothesis = theory, premise, proposition, assumption, thesis, postulate, supposition

hysteria = frenzy, panic, madness, agitation, delirium, hysterics

hysterical 1 = frenzied, frantic, raving, distracted, distraught, crazed, overwrought, berko (*Austral. slang*) ≠ calm 2 (*Informal*) = hilarious, uproarious, side-splitting, comical ≠ serious

I

icy 1 = cold, freezing, bitter, biting, raw, chill, chilly, frosty ≠ hot 2 = slippery, glassy, slippy (*informal* or *dialect*), like a sheet of glass 3 = unfriendly, cold, distant, aloof, frosty, frigid, unwelcoming ≠ friendly

idea 1 = notion, thought, view, teaching, opinion, belief, conclusion, hypothesis 2 = understanding, thought, view, opinion, concept, impression, perception 3 = intention, aim, purpose, object, plan, objective

ideal NOUN 1 = epitome, standard, dream, pattern, perfection, last word, paragon 2 = model, prototype, paradigm

• ADJECTIVE = perfect, best, model, classic, supreme, ultimate, archetypal, exemplary

≠ imperfect
ideally = in a perfect world, all things being equal, if you had your way
identical = alike, matching, twin, duplicate, indistinguishable, interchangeable ≠ different
identification 1 = discovery, recognition, determining, establishment, diagnosis, confirmation, divination 2 = recognition, naming, distinguishing, confirmation, pinpointing 3 = connection, relationship, association 4 = understanding, relationship, involvement, unity, sympathy, empathy, rapport, fellow feeling
identify VERB 1 = recognize, place, name, remember, spot, diagnose, make out, pinpoint 2 = establish, spot, confirm, demonstrate, pick out, certify, verify, mark out
• PHRASES **identify something** *or* **someone with something** *or* **someone** = equate with, associate with ◆ **identify with someone** = relate to, respond to, feel for, empathize with
identity = individuality, self, character, personality, existence, originality, separateness
idiot = fool, moron, twit (*informal*, *chiefly Brit.*), chump, imbecile, cretin, simpleton, halfwit, galah (*Austral. & N.Z. informal*), dorba *or* dorb (*Austral. slang*), bogan (*Austral. slang*)
idle ADJECTIVE 1 = unoccupied, unemployed, redundant, inactive ≠ occupied 2 = unused, inactive, out of order, out of service 3 = lazy, slow, slack, sluggish, lax, negligent, inactive, inert ≠ busy 4 = useless, vain, pointless, unsuccessful, ineffective, worthless, futile, fruitless ≠ useful
• VERB *often with* ***away*** = fritter, lounge, potter, loaf, dally, loiter, dawdle, laze
idol 1 = hero, pin-up, favourite, pet, darling, beloved (*slang*), fave (*informal*) 2 = graven image, god, deity
if 1 = provided, assuming, given that, providing, supposing, presuming, on condition that, as long as 2 = when, whenever, every time, any time
ignite 1 = catch fire, burn, burst into flames, inflame, flare up, take fire 2 = set fire to, light, set alight, torch, kindle
ignorance 1 = lack of education, stupidity, foolishness ≠ knowledge 2 *with* ***of*** = unawareness of, inexperience of, unfamiliarity with, innocence of, unconsciousness of
ignorant 1 = uneducated, illiterate ≠ educated 2 = insensitive, rude, crass 3 *with* ***of*** = uninformed of, unaware of, oblivious to, innocent of, unconscious of, inexperienced of, uninitiated about, unenlightened about ≠ informed
ignore 1 = pay no attention to, neglect, disregard, slight, overlook, scorn, spurn, rebuff ≠ pay attention to 2 = overlook, discount, disregard, reject, neglect, shrug off, pass over, brush aside 3 = snub, slight, rebuff
ill ADJECTIVE 1 = unwell, sick, poorly (*informal*), diseased, weak, crook (*Austral. & N.Z. slang*), ailing, frail ≠ healthy 2 = harmful, bad, damaging, evil, foul, unfortunate, destructive, detrimental ≠ favourable
• NOUN = problem, trouble, suffering, worry, injury, hurt, strain, harm ≠ good
• ADVERB 1 = badly, unfortunately, unfavourably, inauspiciously 2 = hardly, barely, scarcely, just, only just, by no means, at a push ≠ well
illegal = unlawful, banned, forbidden, prohibited, criminal, outlawed, illicit, unlicensed ≠ legal
illicit 1 = illegal, criminal, prohibited, unlawful, illegitimate, unlicensed, unauthorized, felonious ≠ legal 2 = forbidden, improper, immoral, guilty, clandestine, furtive
illness = sickness, disease, infection, disorder, bug (*informal*), ailment, affliction, malady
illuminate 1 = light up, brighten ≠ darken 2 = explain, interpret, make clear, clarify, clear up, enlighten, shed light on, elucidate ≠ obscure
illuminating = informative, revealing, enlightening, helpful, explanatory, instructive ≠ confusing
illusion 1 = delusion, misconception, misapprehension, fancy, fallacy, false impression, false belief 2 = false impression, appearance, impression, deception, fallacy ≠ reality 3 = fantasy, vision, hallucination, trick, spectre, mirage, daydream, apparition
illustrate 1 = demonstrate, emphasize 2 = explain, sum up, summarize, bring

home, point up, elucidate
illustrated = pictured, decorated, pictorial
illustration 1 = example, case, instance, sample, specimen, exemplar 2 = picture, drawing, painting, image, print, plate, figure, portrait
image 1 = thought, idea, vision, concept, impression, perception, mental picture, conceptualization 2 = figure of speech 3 = reflection, likeness, mirror image 4 = figure, idol, icon, fetish, talisman 5 = replica, copy, reproduction, counterpart, clone, facsimile, spitting image (*informal*), Doppelgänger 6 = picture, photo, photograph, representation, reproduction, snapshot
imaginary = fictional, made-up, invented, imagined, unreal, hypothetical, fictitious, illusory ≠ real
imagination 1 = creativity, vision, invention, ingenuity, enterprise, originality, inventiveness, resourcefulness 2 = mind's eye, fancy
imaginative = creative, original, inspired, enterprising, clever, ingenious, inventive ≠ unimaginative
imagine 1 = envisage, see, picture, plan, think of, conjure up, envision, visualize 2 = believe, think, suppose, assume, suspect, guess (*informal*, *chiefly U.S. & Canad.*), take it, reckon
imitate 1 = copy, follow, repeat, echo, emulate, ape, simulate, mirror 2 = do an impression of, mimic, copy
imitation NOUN 1 = replica, fake, reproduction, sham, forgery, counterfeiting, likeness, duplication 2 = copying, resemblance, mimicry 3 = impression, impersonation
• ADJECTIVE = artificial, mock, reproduction, dummy, synthetic, man-made, simulated, sham ≠ real
immaculate 1 = clean, spotless, neat, spruce, squeaky-clean, spick-and-span ≠ dirty 2 = pure, perfect, impeccable, flawless, faultless, above reproach ≠ corrupt 3 = perfect, flawless, impeccable, faultless, unblemished, untarnished, unexceptionable ≠ tainted
immediate 1 = instant, prompt, instantaneous, quick, on-the-spot, split-second ≠ later 2 = nearest, next, direct, close, near ≠ far
immediately = at once, now, instantly, straight away, directly, promptly, right away, without delay
immense = huge, great, massive, vast, enormous, extensive, tremendous, very big ≠ tiny
immerse 1 = engross, involve, absorb, busy, occupy, engage 2 = plunge, dip, submerge, sink, duck, bathe, douse, dunk
immigrant = settler, incomer, alien, stranger, outsider, newcomer, migrant, emigrant
imminent = near, coming, close, approaching, gathering, forthcoming, looming, impending ≠ remote
immoral = wicked, bad, wrong, corrupt, indecent, sinful, unethical, depraved ≠ moral
immortal ADJECTIVE 1 = timeless, eternal, everlasting, lasting, traditional, classic, enduring, perennial ≠ ephemeral 2 = undying, eternal, imperishable, deathless ≠ mortal
• NOUN 1 = hero, genius, great 2 = god, goddess, deity, divine being, immortal being, atua (*N.Z.*)
immune
• PHRASES **immune from** = exempt from, free from ◆ **immune to** 1 = resistant to, free from, protected from, safe from, not open to, spared from, secure against, invulnerable to 2 = unaffected by, invulnerable to
immunity 1 = exemption, amnesty, indemnity, release, freedom, invulnerability 2 *with* ***to*** = resistance to, protection from, resilience to, inoculation against, immunization from ≠ susceptibility to
impact NOUN 1 = effect, influence, consequences, impression, repercussions, ramifications 2 = collision, contact, crash, knock, stroke, smash, bump, thump
• VERB = hit, strike, crash, clash, crush, ram, smack, collide
impair = worsen, reduce, damage, injure, harm, undermine, weaken, diminish ≠ improve
impaired = damaged, flawed, faulty, defective, imperfect, unsound
impasse = deadlock, stalemate, standstill, dead end, standoff
impatient 1 = cross, annoyed, irritated, prickly, touchy, bad-tempered, intolerant,

ill-tempered ≠ easy-going **2** = eager, longing, keen, anxious, hungry, enthusiastic, restless, avid ≠ calm

impeccable = faultless, perfect, immaculate, flawless, squeaky-clean, unblemished, unimpeachable, irreproachable ≠ flawed

impending = looming, coming, approaching, near, forthcoming, imminent, upcoming, in the pipeline

imperative = urgent, essential, pressing, vital, crucial ≠ unnecessary

imperial = royal, regal, kingly, queenly, princely, sovereign, majestic, monarchial

impetus 1 = incentive, push, spur, motivation, impulse, stimulus, catalyst, goad **2** = force, power, energy, momentum

implant 1 = insert, fix, graft **2** = instil, infuse, inculcate

implement VERB = carry out, effect, carry through, complete, apply, perform, realize, fulfil ≠ hinder

• NOUN = tool, machine, device, instrument, appliance, apparatus, gadget, utensil

implicate VERB = incriminate, involve, embroil, entangle, inculpate ≠ dissociate

• PHRASES **implicate something** *or* **someone in something** = involve in, associate with

implication NOUN = suggestion, hint, inference, meaning, significance, presumption, overtone, innuendo

• PLURAL NOUN = consequences, result, developments, upshot

implicit 1 = implied, understood, suggested, hinted at, taken for granted, unspoken, inferred, tacit ≠ explicit **2** = inherent, underlying, intrinsic, latent, ingrained, inbuilt **3** = absolute, full, complete, firm, fixed, constant, utter, outright

implied = suggested, indirect, hinted at, implicit, unspoken, tacit, undeclared, unstated

imply 1 = suggest, hint, insinuate, indicate, intimate, signify **2** = involve, mean, entail, require, indicate, point to, signify, presuppose

import VERB = bring in, buy in, ship in, introduce

• NOUN **1** (*Formal*) = significance, concern, value, weight, consequence, substance, moment, magnitude **2** = meaning, implication, significance, sense, intention, substance, drift, thrust

importance 1 = significance, interest, concern, moment, value, weight, import, consequence **2** = prestige, standing, status, rule, authority, influence, distinction, esteem, mana (*N.Z.*)

important 1 = significant, critical, substantial, urgent, serious, far-reaching, momentous, seminal ≠ unimportant **2** = powerful, prominent, commanding, dominant, influential, eminent, high-ranking, authoritative

impose

• PHRASES **impose something on** *or* **upon someone 1** = levy, introduce, charge, establish, fix, institute, decree, ordain **2** = inflict, force, enforce, visit, press, apply, thrust, saddle (someone) with

imposing = impressive, striking, grand, powerful, commanding, awesome, majestic, dignified ≠ unimposing

imposition 1 = application, introduction, levying **2** = intrusion, liberty, presumption

impossible 1 = not possible, out of the question, impracticable, unfeasible **2** = unachievable, out of the question, vain, unthinkable, inconceivable, far-fetched, unworkable, implausible ≠ possible **3** = absurd, crazy (*informal*), ridiculous, outrageous, ludicrous, unreasonable, preposterous, farcical

impotence = powerlessness, inability, helplessness, weakness, incompetence, paralysis, frailty, incapacity ≠ powerfulness

impoverish 1 = bankrupt, ruin, beggar, break **2** = deplete, drain, exhaust, diminish, use up, sap, wear out, reduce

impoverished = poor, needy, destitute, bankrupt, poverty-stricken, impecunious, penurious ≠ rich

impress VERB = excite, move, strike, touch, affect, inspire, amaze, overcome

• PHRASES **impress something on** *or* **upon someone** = stress, bring home to, instil in, drum into, knock into, emphasize to, fix in, inculcate in

impression 1 = idea, feeling, thought, sense, view, assessment, judgment, reaction **2** = effect, influence, impact **3** = imitation, parody, impersonation, send-up (*Brit. informal*), takeoff (*informal*) **4** = mark, imprint, stamp, outline, hollow, dent, indentation

impressive = grand, striking, splendid, good, great (*informal*), fine, powerful, exciting ≠ unimpressive
imprint NOUN = mark, impression, stamp, indentation
• VERB = engrave, print, stamp, impress, etch, emboss
imprison = jail, confine, detain, lock up, put away, intern, incarcerate, send down (*informal*) ≠ free
imprisoned = jailed, confined, locked up, inside (*slang*), in jail, captive, behind bars, incarcerated
imprisonment = confinement, custody, detention, captivity, incarceration
improbable 1 = doubtful, unlikely, dubious, questionable, fanciful, far-fetched, implausible ≠ probable 2 = unconvincing, weak, unbelievable, preposterous ≠ convincing
improper 1 = inappropriate, unfit, unsuitable, out of place, unwarranted, uncalled-for ≠ appropriate 2 = indecent, vulgar, suggestive, unseemly, untoward, risqué, smutty, unbecoming ≠ decent
improve 1 = enhance, better, add to, upgrade, touch up, ameliorate ≠ worsen 2 = get better, pick up, develop, advance
improvement 1 = enhancement, advancement, betterment 2 = advance, development, progress, recovery, upswing
improvise 1 = devise, contrive, concoct, throw together 2 = ad-lib, invent, busk, wing it (*informal*), play it by ear (*informal*), extemporize, speak off the cuff (*informal*)
impulse = urge, longing, wish, notion, yearning, inclination, itch, whim
inaccurate = incorrect, wrong, mistaken, faulty, unreliable, defective, erroneous, unsound ≠ accurate
inadequacy 1 = shortage, poverty, dearth, paucity, insufficiency, meagreness, scantiness 2 = incompetence, inability, deficiency, incapacity, ineffectiveness 3 = shortcoming, failing, weakness, defect, imperfection
inadequate 1 = insufficient, meagre, poor, lacking, scant, sparse, sketchy ≠ adequate 2 = incapable, incompetent, faulty, deficient, unqualified, not up to scratch (*informal*) ≠ capable
inadvertently = unintentionally, accidentally, by accident, mistakenly, unwittingly, by mistake, involuntarily ≠ deliberately
inaugural = first, opening, initial, maiden, introductory
incarnation = embodiment, manifestation, epitome, type, personification
incense = anger, infuriate, enrage, irritate, madden, inflame, rile (*informal*), make your blood boil (*informal*)
incensed = angry, furious, fuming, infuriated, enraged, maddened, indignant, irate, tooshie (*Austral. slang*), off the air (*Austral. slang*)
incentive = inducement, encouragement, spur, lure, bait, motivation, carrot (*informal*), stimulus ≠ disincentive
incident 1 = disturbance, scene, clash, disorder, confrontation, brawl, fracas, commotion 2 = adventure, drama, excitement, crisis, spectacle 3 = happening, event, affair, business, fact, matter, occasion, episode
incidentally = by the way, in passing, en passant, parenthetically, by the bye
inclination 1 = desire, longing, aspiration, craving, hankering 2 = tendency, liking, disposition, penchant, propensity, predisposition, predilection, proclivity ≠ aversion
incline VERB = predispose, influence, persuade, prejudice, sway, dispose
• NOUN = slope, rise, dip, grade, descent, ascent, gradient
inclined 1 = disposed, given, prone, likely, liable, apt, predisposed 2 = willing, minded, disposed
include 1 = contain, involve, incorporate, cover, consist of, take in, embrace, comprise ≠ exclude 2 = count 3 = add, enter, put in, insert
inclusion = addition, incorporation, introduction, insertion ≠ exclusion
inclusive = comprehensive, general, global, sweeping, blanket, umbrella, across-the-board, all-embracing ≠ limited
income = revenue, earnings, pay, returns, profits, wages, yield, proceeds
incoming 1 = arriving, landing, approaching, entering, returning, homeward ≠ departing 2 = new
incompatible = inconsistent, conflicting, contradictory, incongruous, unsuited, mismatched ≠ compatible
incompetence = ineptitude, inability,

inadequacy, incapacity, ineffectiveness, uselessness, unfitness, incapability
incompetent = inept, useless, incapable, floundering, bungling, unfit, ineffectual, inexpert ≠ competent
incomplete = unfinished, partial, wanting, deficient, imperfect, fragmentary, half-pie (*N.Z. informal*) ≠ complete
inconsistency 1 = unreliability, instability, unpredictability, fickleness, unsteadiness 2 = incompatibility, discrepancy, disparity, disagreement, variance, divergence, incongruity
inconsistent 1 = changeable, variable, unpredictable, unstable, erratic, fickle, capricious, unsteady ≠ consistent 2 = incompatible, conflicting, at odds, contradictory, incongruous, discordant, out of step, irreconcilable ≠ compatible
inconvenience NOUN = trouble, difficulty, bother, fuss, disadvantage, disturbance, disruption, nuisance, uphill (*S. African*) • VERB = trouble, bother, disturb, upset, disrupt, put out, discommode
incorporate 1 = include, contain, take in, embrace, integrate, encompass, assimilate, comprise of 2 = integrate, include, absorb, merge, fuse, assimilate, subsume 3 = blend, combine, compound, mingle
incorrect = false, wrong, mistaken, flawed, faulty, inaccurate, untrue, erroneous ≠ correct
increase VERB 1 = raise, extend, boost, expand, develop, advance, strengthen, widen ≠ decrease 2 = grow, develop, spread, expand, swell, enlarge, escalate, multiply ≠ shrink • NOUN = growth, rise, development, gain, expansion, extension, proliferation, enlargement
increasingly = progressively, more and more
incredible 1 (*Informal*) = amazing, wonderful, stunning, extraordinary, overwhelming, astonishing, staggering, sensational (*informal*) 2 = unbelievable, unthinkable, improbable, inconceivable, preposterous, unconvincing, unimaginable, far-fetched
incumbent NOUN = holder, keeper, bearer • ADJECTIVE (*Formal*) = obligatory, required, necessary, essential, binding, compulsory, mandatory, imperative
incur = sustain, experience, suffer, gain, earn, collect, meet with, provoke
indecent 1 = obscene, lewd, dirty, inappropriate, rude, crude, filthy, improper ≠ decent 2 = unbecoming, unsuitable, vulgar, unseemly, undignified, indecorous ≠ proper
indeed 1 = certainly, yes, definitely, surely, truly, undoubtedly, without doubt, indisputably 2 = really, actually, in fact, certainly, genuinely, in truth, in actuality
indefinitely = endlessly, continually, for ever, ad infinitum
independence = freedom, liberty, autonomy, sovereignty, self-rule, self-sufficiency, self-reliance, rangatiratanga (*N.Z.*) ≠ subjugation
independent 1 = separate, unattached, uncontrolled, unconstrained ≠ controlled 2 = self-sufficient, free, liberated, self-contained, self-reliant, self-supporting 3 = self-governing, free, autonomous, liberated, sovereign, self-determining, nonaligned ≠ subject
independently = separately, alone, solo, on your own, by yourself, unaided, individually, autonomously
indicate 1 = show, suggest, reveal, display, demonstrate, point to, imply, manifest 2 = imply, suggest, hint, intimate, signify, insinuate 3 = point to, point out, specify, gesture towards, designate 4 = register, show, record, read, express, display, demonstrate
indication = sign, mark, evidence, suggestion, symptom, hint, clue, manifestation
indicator = sign, mark, measure, guide, signal, symbol, meter, gauge
indict = charge, accuse, prosecute, summon, impeach, arraign
indictment = charge, allegation, prosecution, accusation, impeachment, summons, arraignment
indifference = disregard, apathy, negligence, detachment, coolness, coldness, nonchalance, aloofness ≠ concern
indifferent 1 = unconcerned, detached, cold, cool, callous, aloof, unmoved, unsympathetic ≠ concerned 2 = mediocre, ordinary, moderate, so-so (*informal*), passable, undistinguished, no great shakes (*informal*), half-pie (*N.Z. informal*) ≠ excellent

indignation = resentment, anger, rage, exasperation, pique, umbrage
indirect 1 = related, secondary, subsidiary, incidental, unintended 2 = circuitous, roundabout, curving, wandering, rambling, deviant, meandering, tortuous ≠ direct
indispensable = essential, necessary, needed, key, vital, crucial, imperative, requisite ≠ dispensable
individual ADJECTIVE 1 = separate, independent, isolated, lone, solitary ≠ collective 2 = unique, special, fresh, novel, exclusive, singular, idiosyncratic, unorthodox ≠ conventional
• NOUN = person, being, human, unit, character, soul, creature
individually = separately, independently, singly, one by one, one at a time
induce 1 = cause, produce, create, effect, lead to, occasion, generate, bring about ≠ prevent 2 = persuade, encourage, influence, convince, urge, prompt, sway, entice ≠ dissuade
indulge VERB 1 = gratify, satisfy, feed, give way to, yield to, pander to, gladden 2 = spoil, pamper, cosset, humour, give in to, coddle, mollycoddle, overindulge
• PHRASES **indulge yourself** = treat yourself, splash out, spoil yourself, luxuriate in something, overindulge yourself
indulgence 1 = luxury, treat, extravagance, favour, privilege 2 = gratification, satisfaction, fulfilment, appeasement, satiation
industrialist = capitalist, tycoon, magnate, manufacturer, captain of industry, big businessman
industry 1 = business, production, manufacturing, trade, commerce 2 = trade, world, business, service, line, field, profession, occupation 3 = diligence, effort, labour, hard work, trouble, activity, application, endeavour
ineffective 1 = unproductive, useless, futile, vain, unsuccessful, pointless, fruitless, ineffectual ≠ effective 2 = inefficient, useless, poor, powerless, unfit, worthless, inept, impotent
inefficient 1 = wasteful, uneconomical, profligate 2 = incompetent, inept, weak, bungling, ineffectual, disorganized ≠ efficient
inequality = disparity, prejudice, difference, bias, diversity, irregularity, unevenness, disproportion
inevitable = unavoidable, inescapable, inexorable, sure, certain, fixed, assured, fated ≠ avoidable
inevitably = unavoidably, naturally, necessarily, surely, certainly, as a result, automatically, consequently
inexpensive = cheap, reasonable, budget, bargain, modest, economical ≠ expensive
inexperienced = new, green, raw, callow, immature, untried, unpractised, unversed ≠ experienced
infamous = notorious, ignominious, disreputable, ill-famed ≠ esteemed
infancy = beginnings, start, birth, roots, seeds, origins, dawn, outset ≠ end
infant = baby, child, babe, toddler, tot, bairn (*Scot.*), littlie (*Austral. informal*), ankle-biter (*Austral. slang*), tacker (*Austral. slang*)
infect 1 = contaminate 2 = pollute, poison, corrupt, contaminate, taint, defile 3 = affect, move, upset, overcome, stir, disturb
infection = disease, condition, complaint, illness, virus, disorder, corruption, poison
infectious = catching, spreading, contagious, communicable, virulent, transmittable
inferior ADJECTIVE = lower, minor, secondary, subsidiary, lesser, humble, subordinate, lowly ≠ superior
• NOUN = underling, junior, subordinate, lesser, menial, minion
infertility = sterility, barrenness, unproductiveness, infecundity
infiltrate = penetrate, pervade, permeate, percolate, filter through to, make inroads into, sneak into (*informal*), insinuate yourself
infinite 1 = vast, enormous, immense, countless, measureless 2 = limitless, endless, unlimited, eternal, never-ending, boundless, everlasting, inexhaustible ≠ finite
inflame = enrage, stimulate, provoke, excite, anger, arouse, rouse, infuriate ≠ calm
inflamed = swollen, sore, red, hot, infected, fevered
inflate 1 = blow up, pump up, swell, dilate,

distend, bloat, puff up *or* out ≠ deflate **2** = increase, expand, enlarge ≠ diminish **3** = exaggerate, embroider, embellish, enlarge, amplify, overstate, overestimate, overemphasize

inflated = exaggerated, swollen, overblown

inflation = increase, expansion, extension, swelling, escalation, enlargement

inflict = impose, administer, visit, apply, deliver, levy, wreak, mete *or* deal out

influence NOUN **1** = control, power, authority, direction, command, domination, supremacy, mastery, mana (*N.Z.*) **2** = power, authority, pull (*informal*), importance, prestige, clout (*informal*), leverage **3** = spell, hold, power, weight, magic, sway, allure, magnetism
• VERB **1** = affect, have an effect on, have an impact on, control, concern, direct, guide, bear upon **2** = persuade, prompt, urge, induce, entice, coax, incite, instigate

influential **1** = important, powerful, telling, leading, inspiring, potent, authoritative, weighty ≠ unimportant **2** = instrumental, important, significant, crucial

influx = arrival, rush, invasion, incursion, inundation, inrush

inform VERB = tell, advise, notify, instruct, enlighten, communicate to, tip someone off
• PHRASES **inform on someone** = betray, denounce, shop (*slang, chiefly Brit.*), give someone away, incriminate, blow the whistle on (*informal*), grass on (*Brit. slang*), double-cross (*informal*), dob someone in (*Austral. & N.Z. slang*)

informal **1** = natural, relaxed, casual, familiar, unofficial, laid-back, easy-going, colloquial **2** = relaxed, easy, comfortable, simple, natural, casual, cosy, laid-back (*informal*) ≠ formal **3** = casual, comfortable, leisure, everyday, simple **4** = unofficial, irregular ≠ official

information = facts, news, report, message, notice, knowledge, data, intelligence, drum (*Austral. informal*)

informative = instructive, revealing, educational, forthcoming, illuminating, enlightening, chatty, communicative

informed = knowledgeable, up to date, enlightened, learned, expert, familiar, versed, in the picture

infuriate = enrage, anger, provoke, irritate, incense, madden, exasperate, rile ≠ soothe

infuriating = annoying, irritating, provoking, galling, maddening, exasperating, vexatious

ingenious = creative, original, brilliant, clever, bright, shrewd, inventive, crafty ≠ unimaginative

ingredient = component, part, element, feature, piece, unit, item, aspect

inhabit = live in, occupy, populate, reside in, dwell in, abide in

inhabitant = occupant, resident, citizen, local, native, tenant, inmate, dweller

inhabited = populated, peopled, occupied, developed, settled, tenanted, colonized

inhale = breathe in, gasp, draw in, suck in, respire ≠ exhale

inherent = intrinsic, natural, essential, native, fundamental, hereditary, instinctive, innate ≠ extraneous

inherit = be left, come into, be willed, succeed to, fall heir to

inheritance = legacy, heritage, bequest, birthright, patrimony

inhibit **1** = hinder, check, frustrate, curb, restrain, constrain, obstruct, impede ≠ further **2** = prevent, stop, frustrate ≠ allow

inhibited = shy, reserved, guarded, subdued, repressed, constrained, self-conscious, reticent ≠ uninhibited

initial = opening, first, earliest, beginning, primary, maiden, introductory, embryonic ≠ final

initially = at first, first, firstly, originally, primarily, in the beginning, at *or* in the beginning

initiate VERB **1** = begin, start, open, launch, kick off (*informal*), embark on, originate, set about **2** = introduce, admit, enlist, enrol, launch, establish, invest, recruit
• NOUN = novice, member, pupil, convert, amateur, newcomer, beginner, trainee
• PHRASES **initiate someone into something** = instruct in, train in, coach in, acquaint with, drill in, make aware of, teach about, tutor in

initiative **1** = advantage, start, lead, upper hand **2** = enterprise, drive, energy, leadership, ambition, daring, enthusiasm, dynamism

inject **1** = vaccinate, administer, inoculate **2** = introduce, bring in, insert, instil, infuse, breathe

injection **1** = vaccination, shot (*informal*), jab (*informal*), dose, booster, immunization, inoculation **2** = introduction, investment, insertion, advancement, dose, infusion

injunction = order, ruling, command, instruction, mandate, precept, exhortation

injure **1** = hurt, wound, harm, damage, smash, crush, mar, shatter, mangulate (*Austral. slang*) **2** = damage, harm, ruin, wreck, spoil, impair, crool *or* cruel (*Austral. slang*) **3** = undermine, damage

injured = hurt, damaged, wounded, broken, cut, crushed, disabled, weakened, crook (*Austral. & N.Z. slang*)

injury **1** = wound, cut, damage, trauma (*Pathology*), gash, lesion, laceration **2** = harm, suffering, damage, ill, hurt, disability, misfortune, affliction **3** = wrong, offence, insult, detriment, disservice

injustice **1** = unfairness, discrimination, prejudice, bias, inequality, oppression, intolerance, bigotry ≠ justice **2** = wrong, injury, crime, error, offence, sin, misdeed, transgression

inland = interior, internal, upcountry

inner **1** = inside, internal, interior, inward ≠ outer **2** = central, middle, internal, interior **3** = hidden, deep, secret, underlying, obscure, repressed, unrevealed ≠ obvious

innocence **1** = naiveté, simplicity, inexperience, credulity, gullibility, ingenuousness, artlessness, unworldliness ≠ worldliness **2** = blamelessness, clean hands, uprightness, irreproachability, guiltlessness ≠ guilt **3** = chastity, virtue, purity, modesty, celibacy, continence, maidenhood

innocent **1** = not guilty, in the clear, blameless, clean, honest, uninvolved, irreproachable, guiltless ≠ guilty **2** = naive, open, trusting, simple, childlike, gullible, unsophisticated, unworldly ≠ worldly **3** = harmless, innocuous, inoffensive, well-meant, unobjectionable, well-intentioned

innovation **1** = change, revolution, departure, introduction, variation, transformation, upheaval, alteration **2** = newness, novelty, originality, freshness, modernization, uniqueness

inquest = inquiry, investigation, probe, inquisition

inquire *or* **enquire** VERB = ask, question, query, quiz
• PHRASES **inquire into something** = investigate, study, examine, research, explore, look into, probe into, make inquiries into

inquiry *or* **enquiry** **1** = question, query, investigation **2** = investigation, study, review, survey, examination, probe, inspection, exploration **3** = research, investigation, analysis, inspection, exploration, interrogation

insane **1** = mad, crazy, mentally ill, crazed, demented, deranged, out of your mind, off the air (*Austral. slang*), porangi (*N.Z.*) ≠ sane **2** = stupid, foolish, daft (*informal*), irresponsible, irrational, senseless, preposterous, impractical ≠ reasonable

insect = bug, creepy-crawly (*Brit. informal*), gogga (*S. African informal*)

insecure **1** = unconfident, worried, anxious, afraid, shy, uncertain, unsure, timid ≠ confident **2** = unsafe, exposed, vulnerable, wide-open, unprotected, defenceless, unguarded ≠ safe

insecurity = anxiety, fear, worry, uncertainty ≠ confidence

insert = put, place, position, slip, slide, slot, thrust, stick in

inside NOUN = interior, contents, core, nucleus
• PLURAL NOUN (*Informal*) = stomach, guts, belly, bowels, innards (*informal*), entrails, viscera, vitals
• ADJECTIVE **1** = inner, internal, interior, inward ≠ outside **2** = confidential, private, secret, internal, exclusive, restricted, privileged, classified
• ADVERB = indoors, in, within, under cover

insight **1** = understanding, perception, sense, knowledge, vision, judgment, awareness, grasp **2** *with* ***into*** = understanding of, perception of, awareness of, experience of, description of, introduction to, observation of, judgment of

insignificant = unimportant, minor, irrelevant, petty, trivial, meaningless, trifling, paltry ≠ important

insist **1** lay down the law, put your foot down (*informal*) **2** = demand, order, require, command, dictate, entreat

3 = assert, state, maintain, claim, declare, repeat, vow, swear

insistence 1 = demand, command, dictate, entreaty, importunity 2 = assertion, claim, statement, declaration, persistence, pronouncement

inspect 1 = examine, check, look at, view, survey, look over, scrutinize, go over *or* through 2 = check, examine, investigate, look at, survey, vet, look over, go over *or* through

inspection 1 = examination, investigation, scrutiny, once-over (*informal*) 2 = check, search, investigation, review, survey, examination, scrutiny, once-over (*informal*)

inspector = examiner, investigator, supervisor, monitor, superintendent, auditor, censor, surveyor

inspiration 1 = imagination, creativity, ingenuity, insight, originality, inventiveness, cleverness 2 = motivation, example, model, boost, spur, incentive, revelation, stimulus ≠ deterrent 3 = influence, spur, stimulus, muse

inspire 1 = motivate, stimulate, encourage, influence, spur, animate, enliven, galvanize ≠ discourage 2 = give rise to, produce, result in, engender

inspired 1 = brilliant, wonderful, impressive, outstanding, thrilling, memorable, dazzling, superlative 2 = stimulated, uplifted, exhilarated, enthused, elated

inspiring = uplifting, exciting, moving, stirring, stimulating, rousing, exhilarating, heartening ≠ uninspiring

instability 1 = uncertainty, insecurity, vulnerability, volatility, unpredictability, fluctuation, impermanence, unsteadiness ≠ stability 2 = imbalance, variability, unpredictability, unsteadiness, changeableness

install 1 = set up, put in, place, position, station, establish, lay, fix 2 = institute, establish, introduce, invest, ordain, inaugurate, induct 3 = settle, position, plant, establish, lodge, ensconce

installation 1 = setting up, fitting, instalment, placing, positioning, establishment 2 = appointment, ordination, inauguration, induction, investiture

instalment 1 = payment, repayment, part payment 2 = part, section, chapter, episode, portion, division

instance NOUN = example, case, occurrence, occasion, sample, illustration
• VERB = name, mention, identify, point out, advance, quote, refer to, point to

instant NOUN 1 = moment, second, flash, split second, jiffy (*informal*), trice, twinkling of an eye (*informal*) 2 = time, point, hour, moment, stage, occasion, phase, juncture
• ADJECTIVE 1 = immediate, prompt, instantaneous, direct, quick, on-the-spot, split-second 2 = ready-made, fast, convenience, ready-mixed, ready-cooked, precooked

instantly = immediately, at once, straight away, now, directly, right away, instantaneously, this minute

instead ADVERB = rather, alternatively, preferably, in preference, in lieu, on second thoughts
• PHRASES **instead of** = in place of, rather than, in preference to, in lieu of, in contrast with

instinct 1 = natural inclination, talent, tendency, faculty, inclination, knack, predisposition, proclivity 2 = talent, skill, gift, capacity, bent, genius, faculty, knack 3 = intuition, impulse

instinctive = natural, inborn, automatic, unconscious, inherent, spontaneous, reflex, innate ≠ acquired

instinctively = intuitively, naturally, automatically, without thinking, involuntarily, by instinct

institute NOUN = establishment, body, centre, school, university, society, association, college
• VERB = establish, start, found, launch, set up, introduce, fix, organize ≠ end

institution 1 = establishment, body, centre, school, university, society, association, college 2 = custom, practice, tradition, law, rule, procedure, convention, ritual

institutional = conventional, accepted, established, formal, routine, orthodox, procedural

instruct 1 = order, tell, direct, charge, bid, command, mandate, enjoin 2 = teach, school, train, coach, educate, drill, tutor

instruction NOUN 1 = order, ruling, command, rule, demand, regulation,

dictate, decree **2** = teaching, schooling, training, grounding, education, coaching, lesson(s), guidance
• PLURAL NOUN = information, rules, advice, directions, recommendations, guidance, specifications

instructor = teacher, coach, guide, adviser, trainer, demonstrator, tutor, mentor

instrument 1 = tool, device, implement, mechanism, appliance, apparatus, gadget, contraption (*informal*) **2** = agent, means, medium, agency, vehicle, mechanism, organ

instrumental = active, involved, influential, useful, helpful, contributory

insufficient = inadequate, scant, meagre, short, sparse, deficient, lacking ≠ ample

insulate = isolate, protect, screen, defend, shelter, shield, cut off, cushion

insult VERB = offend, abuse, wound, slight, put down, snub, malign, affront ≠ praise
• NOUN **1** = jibe, slight, put-down, abuse, snub, barb, affront, abusive remark **2** = offence, slight, snub, slur, affront, slap in the face (*informal*), kick in the teeth (*informal*), insolence

insulting = offensive, rude, abusive, degrading, contemptuous, disparaging, scurrilous, insolent ≠ complimentary

insurance 1 = assurance, cover, security, protection, safeguard, indemnity **2** = protection, security, guarantee, shelter, safeguard, warranty

insure 1 = assure, cover, protect, guarantee, warrant, underwrite, indemnify **2** = protect, cover, safeguard

intact = undamaged, whole, complete, sound, perfect, entire, unscathed, unbroken ≠ damaged

integral = essential, basic, fundamental, necessary, component, constituent, indispensable, intrinsic ≠ inessential

integrate = join, unite, combine, blend, incorporate, merge, fuse, assimilate ≠ separate

integrity 1 = honesty, principle, honour, virtue, goodness, morality, purity, probity ≠ dishonesty **2** = unity, unification, cohesion, coherence, wholeness, soundness, completeness

intellect = intelligence, mind, reason, understanding, sense, brains (*informal*), judgment

intellectual ADJECTIVE = scholarly, learned, academic, lettered, intelligent, cerebral, erudite, scholastic ≠ stupid
• NOUN = academic, expert, genius, thinker, master, mastermind, maestro, highbrow, fundi (*S. African*), acca (*Austral. slang*) ≠ idiot

intelligence 1 = intellect, understanding, brains (*informal*), sense, knowledge, judgment, wit, perception ≠ stupidity **2** = information, news, facts, report, findings, knowledge, data, notification ≠ misinformation

intelligent = clever, bright, smart, sharp, enlightened, knowledgeable, well-informed, brainy (*informal*) ≠ stupid

intend = plan, mean, aim, propose, purpose, have in mind *or* view

intense 1 = extreme, great, severe, fierce, deep, powerful, supreme, acute ≠ mild **2** = fierce, tough **3** = passionate, emotional, fierce, heightened, ardent, fanatical, fervent, heartfelt ≠ indifferent

intensify 1 = increase, raise, add to, strengthen, reinforce, widen, heighten, sharpen ≠ decrease **2** = escalate, increase, widen, deepen

intensity 1 = force, strength, fierceness **2** = passion, emotion, fervour, force, strength, fanaticism, ardour, vehemence

intensive = concentrated, thorough, exhaustive, full, demanding, detailed, complete, serious

intent ADJECTIVE = absorbed, intense, fascinated, preoccupied, enthralled, attentive, watchful, engrossed ≠ indifferent
• NOUN = intention, aim, purpose, meaning, end, plan, goal, design ≠ chance

intention = aim, plan, idea, goal, end, design, target, wish

inter = bury, lay to rest, entomb, consign to the grave

intercept = catch, stop, block, seize, cut off, interrupt, head off, obstruct

intercourse 1 = sexual intercourse, sex (*informal*), copulation, coitus, carnal knowledge **2** = contact, communication, commerce, dealings

interest NOUN **1** *often plural* = hobby, activity, pursuit, entertainment, recreation, amusement, preoccupation, diversion **2** *often plural* = advantage, good, benefit, profit **3** = stake, investment

• VERB = arouse your curiosity, fascinate, attract, grip, entertain, intrigue, divert, captivate ≠ bore
interested 1 = curious, attracted, excited, drawn, keen, gripped, fascinated, captivated ≠ uninterested 2 = involved, concerned, affected, implicated
interesting = intriguing, absorbing, appealing, attractive, engaging, gripping, entrancing, stimulating ≠ uninteresting
interface = connection, link, boundary, border, frontier
interfere VERB = meddle, intervene, intrude, butt in, tamper, pry, encroach, stick your oar in (*informal*)
• PHRASES **interfere with something** *or* **someone** = conflict with, check, clash, handicap, hamper, disrupt, inhibit, thwart
interference = intrusion, intervention, meddling, opposition, conflict, obstruction, prying
interim = temporary, provisional, makeshift, acting, caretaker, improvised, stopgap
interior NOUN = inside, centre, heart, middle, depths, core, nucleus
• ADJECTIVE 1 = inside, internal, inner ≠ exterior 2 = mental, emotional, psychological, private, personal, secret, hidden, spiritual
intermediary = mediator, agent, middleman, broker, go-between
intermediate = middle, mid, halfway, in-between (*informal*), midway, intervening, transitional, median
internal 1 = domestic, home, national, local, civic, in-house, intramural 2 = inner, inside, interior ≠ external
international = global, world, worldwide, universal, cosmopolitan, intercontinental
Internet
• PHRASES **the Internet** = the information superhighway, the net (*informal*), the web (*informal*), the World Wide Web, cyberspace
interpret 1 = take, understand, explain, construe 2 = translate, transliterate 3 = explain, make sense of, decode, decipher, elucidate 4 = understand, read, crack, solve, figure out (*informal*), comprehend, decode, deduce 5 = portray, present, perform, render, depict, enact, act out
interpretation 1 = explanation, analysis, exposition, elucidation 2 = performance, portrayal, presentation, reading, rendition 3 = reading, study, review, version, analysis, explanation, examination, evaluation
interpreter = translator
interrogation = questioning, inquiry, examination, grilling (*informal*), cross-examination, inquisition, third degree (*informal*)
interrupt 1 = intrude, disturb, intervene, interfere (with), break in, heckle, butt in, barge in (*informal*) 2 = suspend, stop, end, delay, cease, postpone, shelve, put off
interruption 1 = disruption, break, disturbance, hitch, intrusion 2 = stoppage, pause, suspension
interval 1 = period, spell, space, stretch, pause, span 2 = break, interlude, intermission, rest, gap, pause, respite, lull 3 = delay, gap, hold-up, stoppage 4 = stretch, space
intervene 1 = step in (*informal*), interfere, mediate, intrude, intercede, arbitrate, take a hand (*informal*) 2 = interrupt, involve yourself 3 = happen, occur, take place, follow, arise, ensue, befall, materialize
intervention = mediation, interference, intrusion, arbitration, conciliation, agency
interview NOUN 1 = meeting 2 = audience, talk, conference, exchange, dialogue, consultation, press conference
• VERB 1 = examine, talk to 2 = question, interrogate, examine, investigate, pump, grill (*informal*), quiz, cross-examine
interviewer = questioner, reporter, investigator, examiner, interrogator
intimacy = familiarity, closeness, confidentiality ≠ aloofness
intimate[1] ADJECTIVE 1 = close, dear, loving, near, familiar, thick (*informal*), devoted, confidential ≠ distant 2 = private, personal, confidential, special, individual, secret, exclusive ≠ public 3 = detailed, minute, full, deep, particular, immediate, comprehensive, profound 4 = cosy, relaxed, friendly, informal, harmonious, snug, comfy (*informal*), warm
• NOUN = friend, close friend, crony, cobber (*Austral. & N.Z. old-fashioned informal*), confidant *or* confidante, (constant) companion, E hoa (*N.Z.*) ≠ stranger
intimate[2] 1 = suggest, indicate, hint, imply, insinuate 2 = announce, state,

declare, communicate, make known
intimately 1 = closely, personally, warmly, familiarly, tenderly, affectionately, confidentially, confidingly 2 = fully, very well, thoroughly, in detail, inside out
intimidate = frighten, pressure, threaten, scare, bully, plague, hound, daunt
intimidation = bullying, pressure, threat(s), menaces, coercion, arm-twisting (*informal*), browbeating, terrorization
intricate = complicated, involved, complex, fancy, elaborate, tangled, tortuous, convoluted ≠ simple
intrigue NOUN 1 = plot, scheme, conspiracy, manoeuvre, collusion, stratagem, chicanery, wile 2 = affair, romance, intimacy, liaison, amour
• VERB 1 = interest, fascinate, attract, rivet, titillate 2 = plot, scheme, manoeuvre, conspire, connive, machinate
intriguing = interesting, fascinating, absorbing, exciting, engaging, gripping, stimulating, compelling
introduce 1 = bring in, establish, set up, start, found, launch, institute, pioneer 2 = present, acquaint, make known, familiarize 3 = suggest, air, advance, submit, bring up, put forward, broach, moot 4 = add, insert, inject, throw in (*informal*), infuse
introduction 1 = launch, institution, pioneering, inauguration ≠ elimination 2 = opening, prelude, preface, lead-in, preamble, foreword, prologue, intro (*informal*) ≠ conclusion
introductory 1 = preliminary, first, initial, inaugural, preparatory ≠ concluding 2 = starting, opening, initial
intruder = trespasser, invader, prowler, interloper, infiltrator, gate-crasher (*informal*)
intrusion 1 = interruption, interference, infringement, trespass, encroachment 2 = invasion, breach, infringement, encroachment, infraction, usurpation
intuition 1 = instinct, perception, insight, sixth sense 2 = feeling, idea, impression, suspicion, premonition, inkling, presentiment
invade 1 = attack, storm, assault, capture, occupy, seize, raid, overwhelm 2 = infest, swarm, overrun, ravage, beset, pervade, permeate
invader = attacker, raider, plunderer, aggressor, trespasser
invalid[1] NOUN = patient, sufferer, convalescent, valetudinarian
• ADJECTIVE = disabled, ill, sick, ailing, frail, infirm, bedridden
invalid[2] 1 = null and void, void, worthless, inoperative ≠ valid 2 = unfounded, false, illogical, irrational, unsound, fallacious ≠ sound
invaluable = precious, valuable, priceless, inestimable, worth your *or* its weight in gold ≠ worthless
invariably = always, regularly, constantly, repeatedly, consistently, continually, eternally, habitually
invasion 1 = attack, assault, capture, takeover, raid, offensive, occupation, conquering 2 = intrusion, breach, violation, disturbance, disruption, infringement, encroachment, infraction
invent 1 = create, make, produce, design, discover, manufacture, devise, conceive 2 = make up, devise, concoct, forge, fake, fabricate, feign, falsify
invention 1 = creation, machine, device, design, instrument, discovery, innovation, gadget 2 = development, design, production, setting up, foundation, construction, creation, discovery 3 = fiction, fantasy, lie, yarn, fabrication, falsehood, untruth 4 = creativity, imagination, initiative, enterprise, genius, ingenuity, originality, inventiveness
inventive = creative, original, innovative, imaginative, inspired, fertile, ingenious, resourceful ≠ uninspired
inventor = creator, maker, author, designer, architect, coiner, originator
inventory = list, record, catalogue, listing, account, roll, file, register
invest VERB 1 = spend, expend, advance, venture, put in, devote, lay out, sink in 2 = empower, provide, charge, sanction, license, authorize, vest
• PHRASES **invest in something** = buy, get, purchase, pay for, obtain, acquire, procure
investigate = examine, study, research, go into, explore, look into, inspect, probe into
investigation = examination, study, inquiry, review, search, survey, probe, inspection
investigator = examiner, researcher,

monitor, detective, analyser, explorer, scrutinizer, inquirer

investment 1 = investing, backing, funding, financing, contribution, speculation, transaction, expenditure **2** = stake, interest, share, concern, portion, ante (*informal*) **3** = buy, asset, acquisition, venture, risk, gamble

invisible = unseen, imperceptible, indiscernible, unseeable ≠ visible

invitation = request, call, invite (*informal*), summons

invite 1 = ask **2** = request, look for, bid for, appeal for **3** = encourage, attract, cause, court, ask for (*informal*), generate, foster, tempt

inviting = tempting, appealing, attractive, welcoming, enticing, seductive, alluring, mouthwatering ≠ uninviting

invoke 1 = apply, use, implement, initiate, resort to, put into effect **2** = call upon, appeal to, pray to, petition, beseech, entreat, supplicate

involve 1 = entail, mean, require, occasion, imply, give rise to, necessitate **2** = concern, draw in, bear on

involved = complicated, complex, intricate, hard, confused, confusing, elaborate, tangled ≠ straightforward

involvement = connection, interest, association, commitment, attachment

inward 1 = incoming, entering, inbound, ingoing **2** = internal, inner, private, personal, inside, secret, hidden, interior ≠ outward

Ireland = Hibernia (*Latin*)

iron ADJECTIVE **1** = ferrous, ferric **2** = inflexible, hard, strong, tough, rigid, adamant, unconditional, steely ≠ weak

• PHRASES **iron something out** = settle, resolve, sort out, get rid of, reconcile, clear up, put right, straighten out

RELATED WORDS

adjectives: ferric, ferrous

ironic *or* **ironical** 1 = sarcastic, dry, acid, bitter, mocking, wry, satirical, tongue-in-cheek **2** = paradoxical, contradictory, puzzling, baffling, confounding, enigmatic, incongruous

irony 1 = sarcasm, mockery, ridicule, satire, cynicism, derision **2** = paradox, incongruity

irrational = illogical, crazy, absurd, unreasonable, preposterous, nonsensical ≠ rational

irregular 1 = variable, erratic, occasional, random, casual, shaky, sporadic, haphazard ≠ steady **2** = uneven, rough, ragged, crooked, jagged, bumpy, contorted, lopsided ≠ even **3** = inappropriate, unconventional, unethical, unusual, extraordinary, exceptional, peculiar, unofficial **4** = unofficial, underground, guerrilla, resistance, partisan, rogue, paramilitary, mercenary

irrelevant = unconnected, unrelated, unimportant, inappropriate, peripheral, immaterial, extraneous, beside the point ≠ relevant

irresistible = overwhelming, compelling, overpowering, urgent, compulsive

irresponsible = thoughtless, reckless, careless, unreliable, untrustworthy, shiftless, scatterbrained ≠ responsible

irritate 1 = annoy, anger, bother, needle (*informal*), infuriate, exasperate, nettle, irk ≠ placate **2** = inflame, pain, rub, scratch, scrape, chafe

irritated = annoyed, cross, angry, bothered, put out, exasperated, nettled, vexed, tooshie (*Austral. slang*), hoha (*N.Z.*)

irritating = annoying, trying, infuriating, disturbing, nagging, troublesome, maddening, irksome ≠ pleasing

irritation 1 = annoyance, anger, fury, resentment, gall, indignation, displeasure, exasperation ≠ pleasure **2** = nuisance, irritant, drag (*informal*), pain in the neck (*informal*), thorn in your flesh

island = isle, atoll, islet, ait *or* eyot (*dialect*), cay *or* key

RELATED WORD

adjective: insular

isolate 1 = separate, break up, cut off, detach, split up, insulate, segregate, disconnect **2** = quarantine

isolated = remote, far, distant, lonely, out-of-the-way, hidden, secluded, inaccessible

isolation = separation, segregation, detachment, solitude, seclusion, remoteness

issue NOUN **1** = topic, point, matter, problem, question, subject, theme **2** = point, question, bone of contention **3** = edition, printing, copy, publication, number, version **4** = children, offspring, babies, kids (*informal*), heirs, descendants,

progeny ≠ parent
• VERB = give out, release, publish, announce, deliver, spread, broadcast, distribute
• PHRASES **take issue with something** *or* **someone** = disagree with, question, challenge, oppose, dispute, object to, argue with, take exception to
itch VERB **1** = prickle, tickle, tingle **2** = long, ache, crave, pine, hunger, lust, yearn, hanker
• NOUN **1** = irritation, tingling, prickling, itchiness **2** = desire, longing, craving, passion, yen (*informal*), hunger, lust, yearning
item 1 = article, thing, object, piece, unit, component **2** = matter, point, issue, case, question, concern, detail, subject **3** = report, story, piece, account, note, feature, notice, article
itinerary = schedule, programme, route, timetable

J

jab VERB = poke, dig, punch, thrust, tap, stab, nudge, prod
• NOUN = poke, dig, punch, thrust, tap, stab, nudge, prod
jacket = covering, casing, case, cover, skin, shell, coat, wrapping
jackpot = prize, winnings, award, reward, bonanza
jail NOUN = prison, penitentiary (*U.S.*), confinement, dungeon, nick (*Brit. slang*), slammer (*slang*), reformatory, boob (*Austral. slang*)
• VERB = imprison, confine, detain, lock up, put away, intern, incarcerate, send down
jam NOUN = predicament, tight spot, situation, trouble, hole (*slang*), fix (*informal*), mess, pinch
• VERB **1** = pack, force, press, stuff, squeeze, ram, wedge, cram **2** = crowd, throng, crush, mass, surge, flock, swarm, congregate **3** = congest, block, clog, stick, stall, obstruct
jar[1] = pot, container, drum, vase, jug, pitcher, urn, crock
jar[2] 1 *usually with* ***on*** = irritate, annoy, offend, nettle, irk, grate on, get on your nerves (*informal*) **2** = jolt, rock, shake, bump, rattle, vibrate, convulse
jargon = parlance, idiom, usage, argot
jaw PLURAL NOUN = opening, entrance, mouth
• VERB (*Informal*) = talk, chat, gossip, chatter, spout, natter
jealous 1 = suspicious, protective, wary, doubtful, sceptical, vigilant, watchful, possessive ≠ trusting **2** = envious, grudging, resentful, green, green with envy, desirous, covetous ≠ satisfied
jealousy = suspicion, mistrust, possessiveness, doubt, spite, resentment, wariness, dubiety
jeer VERB = mock, deride, heckle, barrack, ridicule, taunt, scoff, gibe ≠ cheer
• NOUN = mockery, abuse, ridicule, taunt, boo, derision, gibe, catcall ≠ applause
jeopardy = danger, risk, peril, vulnerability, insecurity
jerk VERB = jolt, bang, bump, lurch
• NOUN = lurch, movement, thrust, twitch, jolt
jet NOUN = stream, current, spring, flow, rush, flood, burst, spray
• VERB = fly, wing, cruise, soar, zoom
jewel 1 = gemstone, gem, ornament, sparkler (*informal*), rock (*slang*) **2** = treasure, wonder, darling, pearl, gem, paragon, pride and joy, taonga (*N.Z.*)
jewellery = jewels, treasure, gems, trinkets, ornaments, finery, regalia
job 1 = position, work, calling, business, field, career, employment, profession **2** = task, duty, work, venture, enterprise, undertaking, assignment, chore
jobless = unemployed, redundant, out of work, inactive, unoccupied, idle
jog 1 = run, trot, canter, lope **2** = nudge, push, shake, prod **3** = stimulate, stir, prod
join 1 = enrol in, enter, sign up for, enlist in **2** = connect, unite, couple, link, combine, attach, fasten, add ≠ detach
joint ADJECTIVE = shared, mutual, collective, communal, united, joined, allied, combined
• NOUN = junction, connection, brace,

bracket, hinge, intersection, node, nexus
jointly = collectively, together, in conjunction, as one, in common, mutually, in partnership, in league ≠ separately
joke NOUN **1** = jest, gag (*informal*), wisecrack (*informal*), witticism, crack (*informal*), quip, pun, one-liner (*informal*) **2** = laugh, jest, jape **3** = prank, trick, practical joke, lark (*informal*), escapade, jape **4** = laughing stock, clown, buffoon
• VERB = jest, kid (*informal*), mock, tease, taunt, quip, banter, play the fool
joker = comedian, comic, wit, clown, wag, jester, prankster, buffoon
jolly = happy, cheerful, merry, upbeat (*informal*), playful, cheery, genial, chirpy (*informal*) ≠ miserable
jolt VERB **1** = jerk, push, shake, knock, jar, shove, jog, jostle **2** = surprise, stun, disturb, stagger, startle, perturb, discompose
• NOUN **1** = jerk, start, jump, shake, bump, jar, jog, lurch **2** = surprise, blow, shock, setback, bombshell, bolt from the blue
journal 1 = magazine, publication, gazette, periodical **2** = newspaper, paper, daily, weekly, monthly **3** = diary, record, history, log, notebook, chronicle, annals, yearbook
journalist = reporter, writer, correspondent, newsman *or* newswoman, commentator, broadcaster, hack (*derogatory*), columnist
journey NOUN **1** = trip, drive, tour, flight, excursion, trek, expedition, voyage **2** = progress, voyage, pilgrimage, odyssey
• VERB = travel, go, move, tour, progress, proceed, wander, trek, go walkabout (*Austral.*)
joy = delight, pleasure, satisfaction, ecstasy, enjoyment, bliss, glee, rapture ≠ sorrow
jubilee = celebration, holiday, festival, festivity
judge NOUN **1** = magistrate, justice, beak (*Brit. slang*), His, Her *or* Your Honour **2** = referee, expert, specialist, umpire, mediator, examiner, connoisseur, assessor **3** = critic, assessor, arbiter
• VERB **1** = adjudicate, referee, umpire, mediate, officiate, arbitrate **2** = evaluate, rate, consider, view, value, esteem **3** = estimate, guess, assess, calculate, evaluate, gauge

RELATED WORD

adjective: judicial

judgment 1 = opinion, view, estimate, belief, assessment, diagnosis, valuation, appraisal **2** = verdict, finding, ruling, decision, sentence, decree, arbitration, adjudication **3** = sense, good sense, understanding, discrimination, perception, wisdom, wit, prudence
judicial = legal, official
jug = container, pitcher, urn, carafe, creamer (*U.S. & Canad.*), vessel, jar, crock
juggle = manipulate, change, alter, modify, manoeuvre
juice 1 = liquid, extract, fluid, liquor, sap, nectar **2** = secretion
juicy 1 = moist, lush, succulent **2** (*Informal*) = interesting, colourful, sensational, vivid, provocative, spicy (*informal*), suggestive, racy
jumble NOUN = muddle, mixture, mess, disorder, confusion, clutter, disarray, mishmash
• VERB = mix, mistake, confuse, disorder, shuffle, muddle, disorganize
jumbo = giant, large, huge, immense, gigantic, oversized ≠ tiny
jump VERB **1** = leap, spring, bound, bounce, hop, skip **2** = vault, hurdle, go over, sail over, hop over **3** = spring, bound, bounce **4** = recoil, start, jolt, flinch, shake, jerk, quake, shudder **5** = increase, rise, climb, escalate, advance, soar, surge, spiral **6** = miss, avoid, skip, omit, evade
• NOUN **1** = leap, spring, skip, bound, hop, vault **2** = rise, increase, upswing, advance, upsurge, upturn, increment
jumped-up = conceited, arrogant, pompous, overbearing, presumptuous, insolent
jumper = sweater, top, jersey, cardigan, woolly, pullover
junior 1 = minor, lower, secondary, lesser, subordinate, inferior **2** = younger ≠ senior
junk = rubbish, refuse, waste, scrap, litter, debris, garbage (*chiefly U.S.*), trash
jurisdiction 1 = authority, power, control, rule, influence, command, mana (*N.Z.*) **2** = range, area, field, bounds, province, scope, sphere, compass
just ADVERB **1** = recently, lately, only now **2** = merely, only, simply, solely **3** = barely, hardly, by a whisker, by the skin of your

teeth **4** = exactly, really, quite, completely, totally, perfectly, entirely, truly
• ADJECTIVE **1** = fair, good, legitimate, upright, honest, equitable, conscientious, virtuous ≠ unfair **2** = fitting, due, correct, deserved, appropriate, justified, decent, merited ≠ inappropriate

justice **1** = fairness, equity, integrity, honesty, decency, rightfulness, right ≠ injustice **2** = justness, fairness, legitimacy, right, integrity, honesty, legality, rightfulness **3** = judge, magistrate, beak (*Brit. slang*), His, Her *or* Your Honour

justification = reason, grounds, defence, basis, excuse, warrant, rationale, vindication

justify = explain, support, warrant, defend, excuse, uphold, vindicate, exonerate

juvenile NOUN = child, youth, minor, girl, boy, teenager, infant, adolescent ≠ adult
• ADJECTIVE **1** = young, junior, adolescent, youthful, immature ≠ adult **2** = immature, childish, infantile, puerile, young, youthful, inexperienced, callow

k

kai (*N.Z. informal*) = food, grub (*slang*), provisions, fare, tucker (*Austral. & N.Z. informal*), refreshment, foodstuffs

kak (*S. African taboo*) **1** = faeces, excrement, manure, dung, droppings, waste matter **2** = rubbish, nonsense, garbage (*informal*), rot, drivel, tripe (*informal*), bizzo (*Austral. slang*), bull's wool (*Austral. & N.Z. slang*)

keen **1** = eager, intense, enthusiastic, passionate, ardent, avid, fervent, impassioned ≠ unenthusiastic **2** = earnest, fierce, intense, vehement, passionate, heightened, ardent, fanatical **3** = sharp, incisive, cutting, edged, razor-like ≠ dull **4** = perceptive, quick, sharp, acute, smart, wise, clever, shrewd ≠ obtuse **5** = intense, strong, fierce, relentless, cut-throat

keep[1] VERB **1** *usually with* ***from*** = prevent, restrain, hinder, keep back **2** = hold on to, maintain, retain, save, preserve, nurture, cherish, conserve ≠ lose **3** = store, put, place, house, hold, deposit, stack, stow **4** = carry, stock, sell, supply, handle **5** = support, maintain, sustain, provide for, mind, fund, finance, feed **6** = raise, own, maintain, tend, farm, breed, look after, rear **7** = manage, run, administer, be in charge (of), direct, handle, supervise **8** = delay, detain, hinder, impede, obstruct, set back ≠ release
• NOUN = board, food, maintenance, living, kai (*N.Z. informal*)
• PHRASES **keep something up** **1** = continue, make, maintain, carry on, persist in, persevere with **2** = maintain, sustain, perpetuate, retain, preserve, prolong ◆ **keep up** = keep pace

keep[2] = tower, castle

keeper = curator, guardian, steward, attendant, caretaker, preserver

keeping NOUN = care, charge, protection, possession, custody, guardianship, safekeeping
• PHRASES **in keeping with** = in agreement with, in harmony with, in accord with, in compliance with, in conformity with, in balance with, in correspondence with, in proportion with

key NOUN **1** = opener, door key, latchkey **2** = answer
• ADJECTIVE = essential, leading, major, main, important, necessary, vital, crucial ≠ minor

kia ora (*N.Z.*) = hello, hi (*informal*), greetings, gidday *or* g'day (*Austral. & N.Z.*), how do you do?, good morning, good evening, good afternoon

kick VERB **1** = boot, knock, punt **2** (*Informal*) = give up, break, stop, abandon, quit, cease, eschew, leave off
• NOUN (*Informal*) = thrill, buzz (*slang*), tingle, high (*slang*)
• PHRASES **kick off** (*Informal*) = begin, start, open, commence, initiate, get on the road ◆ **kick someone out** (*Informal*) = dismiss, remove, get rid of, expel, eject, evict, sack (*informal*)

kid[1] (*Informal*) = child, baby, teenager, youngster, infant, adolescent, juvenile, toddler, littlie (*Austral. informal*), ankle-

biter (*Austral. slang*), tacker (*Austral. slang*)
kid² = tease, joke, trick, fool, pretend, wind up (*Brit. slang*), hoax, delude
kidnap = abduct, capture, seize, snatch (*slang*), hijack, hold to ransom
kill 1 = slay, murder, execute, slaughter, destroy, massacre, butcher, cut down 2 (*Informal*) = destroy, crush, scotch, stop, halt, wreck, shatter, suppress
killer = murderer, slayer, hit man (*slang*), butcher, gunman, assassin, terminator, executioner
killing NOUN = murder, massacre, slaughter, dispatch, manslaughter, elimination, slaying, homicide
• ADJECTIVE (*Informal*) = tiring, taxing, exhausting, punishing, fatiguing, gruelling, sapping, debilitating
• PHRASES **make a killing** (*Informal*) = profit, gain, clean up (*informal*), be lucky, be successful, make a fortune, strike it rich (*informal*), make a bomb (*slang*)
kind¹ 1 = class, sort, type, variety, brand, category, genre 2 = sort, set, type, family, species, breed
kind² = considerate, kindly, concerned, friendly, generous, obliging, charitable, benign ≠ unkind
kindly ADJECTIVE = benevolent, kind, caring, warm, helpful, pleasant, sympathetic, benign ≠ cruel
• ADVERB = benevolently, politely, generously, thoughtfully, tenderly, lovingly, cordially, affectionately ≠ unkindly
kindness = goodwill, understanding, charity, humanity, compassion, generosity, philanthropy, benevolence ≠ malice
king = ruler, monarch, sovereign, leader, lord, Crown, emperor, head of state
kingdom = country, state, nation, territory, realm
kiss VERB 1 = peck (*informal*), osculate, neck (*informal*) 2 = brush, touch, shave, scrape, graze, glance off, stroke
• NOUN = peck (*informal*), snog (*Brit. slang*), smacker (*slang*), French kiss, osculation
kit NOUN 1 = equipment, materials, tackle, tools, apparatus, paraphernalia 2 = gear, things, stuff, equipment, uniform
• PHRASES **kit something** *or* **someone out** *or* **up** = equip, fit, supply, provide with, arm, stock, costume, furnish
knack = skill, art, ability, facility, talent, gift, capacity, trick ≠ ineptitude
kneel = genuflect, stoop
knickers = underwear, smalls, briefs, drawers, panties, bloomers
knife NOUN = blade, carver, cutter
• VERB = cut, wound, stab, slash, thrust, pierce, spear, jab
knit 1 = join, unite, link, tie, bond, combine, bind, weave 2 = heal, unite, join, link, bind, fasten, intertwine 3 = furrow, tighten, knot, wrinkle, crease, screw up, pucker, scrunch up
knob = ball, stud, knot, lump, bump, projection, hump, protrusion
knock VERB 1 = bang, strike, tap, rap, thump, pummel 2 = hit, strike, punch, belt (*informal*), smack, thump, cuff 3 (*Informal*) = criticize, condemn, put down, run down, abuse, slate (*informal*), censure, denigrate
• NOUN 1 = knocking, pounding, beating, tap, bang, banging, rap, thump 2 = bang, blow, impact, jar, collision, jolt, smash 3 = blow, hit, punch, crack, clip, slap, bash, smack 4 (*Informal*) = setback, check, defeat, blow, reverse, disappointment, hold-up, hitch
• PHRASES **knock about** *or* **around** = wander, travel, roam, rove, range, drift, stray, ramble, go walkabout (*Austral.*)
◆ **knock about** *or* **around with someone** = mix with, associate with, mingle with, consort with, hobnob with, socialize with, accompany ◆ **knock off** (*Informal*) = stop work, get out, call it a day (*informal*), finish work, clock off, clock out ◆ **knock someone about** *or* **around** = hit, attack, beat, strike, abuse, injure, assault, batter ◆ **knock someone down** = run over, hit, run down, knock over, mow down ◆ **knock something down** = demolish, destroy, flatten, tear down, level, fell, dismantle, bulldoze
◆ **knock something off** (*Slang*) = steal, take, nick (*slang, chiefly Brit.*), thieve, rob, pinch
knockout 1 = killer blow, coup de grâce (*French*), KO *or* K.O. (*slang*) 2 (*Informal*) = success, hit, winner, triumph, smash, sensation, smash hit ≠ failure
knot NOUN = connection, tie, bond, joint, loop, ligature
• VERB = tie, secure, bind, loop, tether
know 1 = have knowledge of, see,

understand, recognize, perceive, be aware of, be conscious of **2** = be acquainted with, recognize, be familiar with, be friends with, be friendly with, have knowledge of, have dealings with, socialize with ≠ be unfamiliar with **3** *sometimes with* ***about*** *or* ***of*** = be familiar with, understand, comprehend, have knowledge of, be acquainted with, feel certain of, have dealings in, be versed in ≠ be ignorant of

know-how (*Informal*) = expertise, ability, skill, knowledge, facility, talent, command, capability

knowing = meaningful, significant, expressive, enigmatic, suggestive

knowledge **1** = understanding, sense, judgment, perception, awareness, insight, grasp, appreciation **2** = learning, education, intelligence, instruction, wisdom, scholarship, enlightenment, erudition ≠ ignorance **3** = acquaintance, intimacy, familiarity ≠ unfamiliarity

knowledgeable **1** = well-informed, conversant, au fait (*French*), experienced, aware, familiar, in the know (*informal*), cognizant **2** = intelligent, learned, educated, scholarly, erudite

known = famous, well-known, celebrated, noted, acknowledged, recognized, avowed ≠ unknown

kopje *or* **koppie** (*S. African*) = hill, down (*archaic*), fell, mount, hilltop, knoll, hillock, brae (*Scot.*)

l

label NOUN = tag, ticket, tab, marker, sticker • VERB = tag, mark, stamp, ticket, tab

labour NOUN **1** = workers, employees, workforce, labourers, hands **2** = work, effort, employment, toil, industry **3** = childbirth, birth, delivery, parturition • VERB **1** = work, toil, strive, work hard, sweat (*informal*), slave, endeavour, slog away (*informal*) ≠ rest **2** = struggle, work, strain, work hard, strive, grapple, toil, make an effort **3** = overemphasize, stress, elaborate, exaggerate, strain, dwell on, overdo, go on about **4** *usually with* ***under*** = be disadvantaged by, suffer from, be a victim of, be burdened by

Labour = left-wing, Democrat (*U.S.*)

laboured = difficult, forced, strained, heavy, awkward

labourer = worker, manual worker, hand, blue-collar worker, drudge, navvy (*Brit. informal*)

lace NOUN **1** = netting, net, filigree, meshwork, openwork **2** = cord, tie, string, lacing, shoelace, bootlace • VERB **1** = fasten, tie, tie up, do up, secure, bind, thread **2** = mix, drug, doctor, add to, spike, contaminate, fortify, adulterate **3** = intertwine, interweave, entwine, twine, interlink

lack NOUN = shortage, want, absence, deficiency, need, inadequacy, scarcity, dearth ≠ abundance • VERB = miss, want, need, require, not have, be without, be short of, be in need of ≠ have

lad = boy, kid (*informal*), guy (*informal*), youth, fellow, youngster, juvenile, nipper (*informal*)

laden = loaded, burdened, full, charged, weighed down, encumbered

lady **1** = gentlewoman, duchess, noble, dame, baroness, countess, aristocrat, viscountess **2** = woman, female, girl, damsel, charlie (*Austral. slang*), chook (*Austral. slang*), wahine (*N.Z.*)

lag = hang back, delay, trail, linger, loiter, straggle, dawdle, tarry

laid-back = relaxed, calm, casual, easy-going, unflappable (*informal*), unhurried, free and easy ≠ tense

lake = pond, pool, reservoir, loch (*Scot.*), lagoon, mere, lough (*Irish*), tarn

lame **1** = disabled, handicapped, crippled, limping, hobbling, game **2** = unconvincing, poor, pathetic, inadequate, thin, weak, feeble, unsatisfactory

lament VERB = bemoan, grieve, mourn, weep over, complain about, regret, wail

about, deplore
• **NOUN 1** = complaint, moan, wailing, lamentation **2** = dirge, requiem, elegy, threnody

land NOUN 1 = ground, earth, dry land, terra firma **2** = soil, ground, earth, clay, dirt, sod, loam **3** = countryside, farmland **4** (*Law*) = property, grounds, estate, real estate, realty, acreage **5** = country, nation, region, state, district, territory, province, kingdom
• **VERB 1** = arrive, dock, put down, moor, alight, touch down, disembark, come to rest **2** (*Informal*) = gain, get, win, secure, acquire
• **PHRASES land up** = end up, turn up, wind up, finish up, fetch up (*informal*)
RELATED WORD
adjective: terrestrial

landlord 1 = owner, landowner, proprietor, freeholder, lessor, landholder **2** = innkeeper, host, hotelier

landmark 1 = feature, spectacle, monument **2** = milestone, turning point, watershed, critical point

landscape = scenery, country, view, land, scene, prospect, countryside, outlook

landslide = landslip, avalanche, rockfall

lane = road, street, track, path, way, passage, trail, pathway

language 1 = tongue, dialect, vernacular, patois **2** = speech, communication, expression, speaking, talk, talking, discourse, parlance

languish 1 = decline, fade away, wither away, flag, weaken, wilt ≠ flourish **2** (*Literary*) = waste away, suffer, rot, be abandoned, be neglected ≠ thrive **3** *often with* ***for*** = pine, long, desire, hunger, yearn, hanker

lap¹ = circuit, tour, leg, stretch, circle, orbit, loop

lap² VERB 1 = ripple, wash, splash, swish, gurgle, slosh, purl, plash **2** = drink, sip, lick, swallow, gulp, sup
• **PHRASES lap something up** = relish, like, enjoy, delight in, savour, revel in, wallow in, accept eagerly

lapse NOUN 1 = decline, fall, drop, deterioration **2** = mistake, failing, fault, failure, error, slip, negligence, omission **3** = interval, break, gap, pause, interruption, lull, breathing space, intermission
• **VERB 1** = slip, fall, decline, sink, drop, slide, deteriorate, degenerate **2** = end, stop, run out, expire, terminate

lapsed = expired, ended, finished, run out, invalid, out of date, discontinued

large ADJECTIVE 1 = big, great, huge, heavy, massive, vast, enormous, tall ≠ small **2** = massive, great, big, huge, vast, enormous, considerable, substantial ≠ small
• **PHRASES at large 1** = in general, generally, chiefly, mainly, as a whole, in the main **2** = free, on the run, fugitive, at liberty, on the loose, unchained, unconfined ◆ **by and large** = on the whole, generally, mostly, in general, all things considered, predominantly, in the main, all in all

largely = mainly, generally, chiefly, mostly, principally, primarily, predominantly, by and large

large-scale = wide-ranging, global, sweeping, broad, wide, vast, extensive, wholesale

lash¹ VERB 1 = pound, beat, strike, hammer, drum, smack (*dialect*) **2** = censure, attack, blast, put down, criticize, slate (*informal*, *chiefly Brit.*), scold, tear into (*informal*) **3** = whip, beat, thrash, birch, flog, scourge
• **NOUN** = blow, hit, strike, stroke, stripe, swipe (*informal*)

lash² = fasten, tie, secure, bind, strap, make fast

last¹ ADJECTIVE 1 = most recent, latest, previous **2** = hindmost, final, at the end, remotest, furthest behind, most distant, rearmost ≠ foremost **3** = final, closing, concluding, ultimate ≠ first
• **ADVERB** = in *or* at the end, after, behind, in the rear, bringing up the rear
• **PHRASES the last word 1** = final decision, final say, final statement, conclusive comment **2** = leading, finest, cream, supreme, elite, foremost, pre-eminent, unsurpassed

last² = continue, remain, survive, carry on, endure, persist, keep on, abide ≠ end

lasting = continuing, long-term, permanent, enduring, remaining, abiding, long-standing, perennial ≠ passing

latch NOUN = fastening, catch, bar, lock, hook, bolt, hasp
• VERB = fasten, bar, secure, bolt, make fast

late ADJECTIVE **1** = overdue, delayed, last-minute, belated, tardy, behind time, behindhand ≠ early **2** = dead, deceased, departed, passed on, former, defunct ≠ alive **3** = recent, new, advanced, fresh ≠ old
• ADVERB = behind time, belatedly, tardily, behindhand, dilatorily ≠ early

lately = recently, of late, just now, in recent times, not long ago, latterly

later ADVERB = afterwards, after, eventually, in time, subsequently, later on, thereafter, in a while
• ADJECTIVE = subsequent, next, following, ensuing

latest = up-to-date, current, fresh, newest, modern, most recent, up-to-the-minute

latitude = scope, liberty, freedom, play, space, licence, leeway, laxity

latter PRONOUN = second, last, last-mentioned, second-mentioned
• ADJECTIVE = last, ending, closing, final, concluding ≠ earlier

laugh VERB = chuckle, giggle, snigger, cackle, chortle, guffaw, titter, be in stitches
• NOUN **1** = chortle, giggle, chuckle, snigger, guffaw, titter **2** (*Informal*) = joke, scream (*informal*), hoot (*informal*), lark, prank **3** (*Informal*) = clown, character (*informal*), scream (*informal*), entertainer, card (*informal*), joker, hoot (*informal*)
• PHRASES **laugh something off** = disregard, ignore, dismiss, overlook, shrug off, minimize, brush aside, make light of

laughter = amusement, entertainment, humour, glee, fun, mirth, hilarity, merriment

launch VERB **1** = propel, fire, dispatch, discharge, project, send off, set in motion, send into orbit **2** = begin, start, open, initiate, introduce, found, set up, originate
• PHRASES **launch into something** = start enthusiastically, begin, initiate, embark on, instigate, inaugurate, embark upon

laurel
• PHRASES **rest on your laurels** = sit back, relax, take it easy, relax your efforts

lavatory = toilet, bathroom, loo (*Brit. informal*), privy, cloakroom (*Brit.*), urinal, latrine, washroom, dunny (*Austral. & N.Z. old-fashioned informal*), bogger (*Austral. slang*), brasco (*Austral. slang*)

lavish ADJECTIVE **1** = grand, magnificent, splendid, abundant, copious, profuse ≠ stingy **2** = extravagant, wild, excessive, exaggerated, wasteful, prodigal, unrestrained, immoderate ≠ thrifty **3** = generous, free, liberal, bountiful, open-handed, unstinting, munificent ≠ stingy
• VERB = shower, pour, heap, deluge, dissipate ≠ stint

law **1** = constitution, code, legislation, charter **2** = statute, act, bill, rule, order, command, regulation, resolution **3** = principle, code, canon, precept, axiom, kaupapa (*N.Z.*) **4** = the legal profession, the bar, barristers

RELATED WORDS
adjectives: legal, judicial

lawsuit = case, action, trial, suit, proceedings, dispute, prosecution, legal action

lawyer = legal adviser, attorney, solicitor, counsel, advocate, barrister, counsellor, legal representative

lay[1] VERB **1** = place, put, set, spread, plant, leave, deposit, put down **2** = devise, plan, design, prepare, work out, plot, hatch, contrive **3** = produce, bear, deposit **4** = arrange, prepare, make, organize, position, set out, devise, put together **5** = attribute, assign, allocate, allot, ascribe, impute **6** = put forward, offer, present, advance, lodge, submit, bring forward **7** = bet, stake, venture, gamble, chance, risk, hazard, wager
• PHRASES **lay someone off** = dismiss, fire (*informal*), release, sack (*informal*), pay off, discharge, let go, make redundant ◆ **lay someone out** (*Informal*) = knock out, fell, floor, knock unconscious, knock for six ◆ **lay something out** **1** = arrange, order, design, display, exhibit, put out, spread out **2** (*Informal*) = spend, pay, invest, fork out (*slang*), expend, shell out (*informal*), disburse

lay[2] **1** = nonclerical, secular, non-ordained **2** = nonspecialist, amateur, unqualified, untrained, inexpert, nonprofessional

layer = tier, level, seam, stratum

layout = arrangement, design, outline, format, plan, formation

lazy 1 = idle, inactive, indolent, slack, negligent, inert, workshy, slothful ≠ industrious 2 = lethargic, languorous, slow-moving, languid, sleepy, sluggish, drowsy, somnolent ≠ quick

leach = extract, strain, drain, filter, seep, percolate

lead VERB 1 = go in front (of), head, be in front, be at the head (of), walk in front (of) 2 = guide, conduct, steer, escort, precede, usher, pilot, show the way 3 = connect to, link, open onto 4 = be ahead (of), be first, exceed, be winning, excel, surpass, come first, transcend 5 = command, rule, govern, preside over, head, control, manage, direct 6 = live, have, spend, experience, pass, undergo 7 = result in, cause, produce, contribute, generate, bring about, bring on, give rise to 8 = cause, prompt, persuade, move, draw, influence, motivate, prevail
• NOUN 1 = first place, winning position, primary position, vanguard 2 = advantage, start, edge, margin, winning margin 3 = example, direction, leadership, guidance, model, pattern 4 = clue, suggestion, hint, indication, pointer, tip-off 5 = leading role, principal, protagonist, title role, principal part 6 = leash, line, cord, rein, tether
• ADJECTIVE = main, prime, top, leading, first, head, chief, premier
• PHRASES **lead someone on** = entice, tempt, lure, mislead, draw on, seduce, deceive, beguile ◆ **lead up to something** = introduce, prepare for, pave the way for

leader = principal, president, head, chief, boss (*informal*), director, manager, chairman, baas (*S. African*) ≠ follower

leadership 1 = authority, control, influence, command, premiership, captaincy, governance, headship 2 = guidance, government, authority, management, direction, supervision, domination, superintendency

leading = principal, top, major, main, first, highest, greatest, chief ≠ minor

leaf NOUN 1 = frond, blade, cotyledon 2 = page, sheet, folio
• PHRASES **leaf through something** (with *book, magazine* etc. as object) = skim, glance, scan, browse, look through, dip into, flick through, flip through

leaflet = booklet, notice, brochure, circular, flyer, tract, pamphlet, handout

leafy = green, shaded, shady, verdant

league 1 = association, union, alliance, coalition, group, corporation, partnership, federation 2 (*Informal*) = class, group, level, category

leak VERB 1 = escape, pass, spill, release, drip, trickle, ooze, seep 2 = disclose, tell, reveal, pass on, give away, make public, divulge, let slip
• NOUN 1 = leakage, discharge, drip, seepage, percolation 2 = hole, opening, crack, puncture, aperture, chink, crevice, fissure 3 = disclosure, exposé, exposure, admission, revelation, uncovering, betrayal, unearthing

lean[1] VERB 1 = bend, tip, slope, incline, tilt, heel, slant 2 = rest, prop, be supported, recline, repose 3 = tend, prefer, favour, incline, be prone to, be disposed to
• PHRASES **lean on someone** = depend on, trust, rely on, cling to, count on, have faith in

lean[2] = thin, slim, slender, skinny, angular, trim, spare, gaunt ≠ fat

leaning = tendency, bias, inclination, bent, disposition, penchant, propensity, predilection

leap VERB = jump, spring, bound, bounce, hop, skip
• NOUN 1 = jump, spring, bound, vault 2 = rise, change, increase, soaring, surge, escalation, upsurge, upswing
• PHRASES **leap at something** = accept eagerly, seize on, jump at

learn 1 = master, grasp, pick up, take in, familiarize yourself with 2 = discover, hear, understand, find out about, become aware, discern, ascertain, come to know 3 = memorize, commit to memory, learn by heart, learn by rote, learn parrot-fashion, get off pat

learned = scholarly, academic, intellectual, versed, well-informed, erudite, highbrow, well-read ≠ uneducated

learner = student, novice, beginner, apprentice, neophyte, tyro ≠ expert

learning = knowledge, study, education, scholarship, enlightenment

lease = hire, rent, let, loan, charter, rent out, hire out

least = smallest, meanest, fewest, lowest,

tiniest, minimum, slightest, minimal

leave VERB 1 = depart from, withdraw from, go from, escape from, quit, flee, exit, pull out of ≠ arrive 2 = quit, give up, get out of, resign from, drop out of 3 = give up, abandon, dump (*informal*), drop, surrender, ditch (*informal*), chuck (*informal*), discard ≠ stay with 4 = entrust, commit, delegate, refer, hand over, assign, consign, allot 5 = bequeath, will, transfer, endow, confer, hand down 6 = forget, leave behind, mislay 7 = cause, produce, result in, generate, deposit

• NOUN 1 = holiday, break, vacation, time off, sabbatical, leave of absence, furlough 2 = permission, freedom, sanction, liberty, concession, consent, allowance, warrant ≠ refusal 3 = departure, parting, withdrawal, goodbye, farewell, retirement, leave-taking, adieu ≠ arrival

• PHRASES **leave something** *or* **someone out** = omit, exclude, miss out, forget, reject, ignore, overlook, neglect

lecture NOUN 1 = talk, address, speech, lesson, instruction, presentation, discourse, sermon 2 = telling-off (*informal*), rebuke, reprimand, talking-to (*informal*), scolding, dressing-down (*informal*), reproof

• VERB 1 = talk, speak, teach, address, discourse, spout, expound, hold forth 2 = tell off (*informal*), berate, scold, reprimand, censure, castigate, admonish, reprove

lees = sediment, grounds, deposit, dregs

left 1 = left-hand, port, larboard (*Nautical*) 2 (*of politics*) = socialist, radical, left-wing, leftist

left-wing = socialist, communist, red (*informal*), radical, revolutionary, militant, Bolshevik, Leninist

leg NOUN 1 = limb, member, shank, lower limb, pin (*informal*), stump (*informal*) 2 = support, prop, brace, upright 3 = stage, part, section, stretch, lap, segment, portion

• PHRASES **pull someone's leg** (*Informal*) = tease, trick, fool, kid (*informal*), wind up (*Brit. slang*), hoax, make fun of, lead up the garden path

legacy = bequest, inheritance, gift, estate, heirloom

legal 1 = judicial, judiciary, forensic, juridical, jurisdictive 2 = lawful, allowed, sanctioned, constitutional, valid, legitimate, authorized, permissible

legend 1 = myth, story, tale, fiction, saga, fable, folk tale, folk story 2 = celebrity, star, phenomenon, genius, prodigy, luminary, megastar (*informal*) 3 = inscription, title, caption, device, motto, rubric

legendary 1 = famous, celebrated, well-known, acclaimed, renowned, famed, immortal, illustrious ≠ unknown 2 = mythical, fabled, traditional, romantic, fabulous, fictitious, storybook, apocryphal ≠ factual

legion 1 = army, company, force, division, troop, brigade 2 = multitude, host, mass, drove, number, horde, myriad, throng

legislation 1 = law, act, ruling, rule, bill, measure, regulation, charter 2 = lawmaking, regulation, prescription, enactment

legislative = law-making, judicial, law-giving

legislator = lawmaker, lawgiver

legislature = parliament, congress, senate, assembly, chamber

legitimate ADJECTIVE 1 = lawful, legal, genuine, authentic, authorized, rightful, kosher (*informal*), dinkum (*Austral. & N.Z. informal*), licit ≠ unlawful 2 = reasonable, correct, sensible, valid, warranted, logical, justifiable, well-founded ≠ unreasonable

• VERB = legitimize, allow, permit, sanction, authorize, legalize, pronounce lawful

leisure = spare, free, rest, ease, relaxation, recreation ≠ work

lekker (*S. African slang*) = delicious, tasty, luscious, palatable, delectable, mouthwatering, scrumptious (*informal*), appetizing, yummo (*Austral. slang*)

lemon

RELATED WORDS

adjectives: citric, citrous

lend VERB 1 = loan, advance, sub (*Brit. informal*) 2 = give, provide, add, supply, grant, confer, bestow, impart

• PHRASES **lend itself to something** = be appropriate for, suit, be suitable for, be appropriate to, be serviceable for

length NOUN 1 = distance, reach, measure, extent, span, longitude 2 = duration, term, period, space, stretch, span, expanse 3 = piece, measure, section, segment, portion

• PHRASES **at length** 1 = at last, finally, eventually, in time, in the end, at long last **2** = for a long time, completely, fully, thoroughly, for hours, in detail, for ages, in depth

lengthen **1** = extend, continue, increase, stretch, expand, elongate ≠ shorten **2** = protract, extend, prolong, draw out, spin out, make longer ≠ cut down

lengthy **1** = protracted, long, prolonged, tedious, drawn-out, interminable, long-winded, long-drawn-out **2** = very long, rambling, interminable, long-winded, wordy, discursive, extended ≠ brief

lesbian = homosexual, gay, les (*slang*), sapphic, lesbo (*slang*)

less DETERMINER = smaller, shorter, not so much
• PREPOSITION = minus, without, lacking, excepting, subtracting

lessen **1** = reduce, lower, diminish, decrease, ease, narrow, minimize ≠ increase **2** = grow less, diminish, decrease, contract, ease, shrink

lesser = lower, secondary, subsidiary, inferior, less important ≠ greater

lesson **1** = class, schooling, period, teaching, coaching, session, instruction, lecture **2** = example, warning, message, moral, deterrent **3** = Bible reading, reading, text, Bible passage, Scripture passage

let VERB **1** = allow, permit, authorize, give the go-ahead, give permission **2** = lease, hire, rent, rent out, hire out, sublease
• PHRASES **let on** (*Informal*) **1** = reveal, disclose, say, tell, admit, give away, divulge, let slip ♦ **let someone down** = disappoint, fail, abandon, desert, disillusion, fall short, leave stranded, leave in the lurch ♦ **let someone off** = excuse, release, discharge, pardon, spare, forgive, exempt, exonerate ♦ **let something** *or* **someone in** = admit, include, receive, welcome, greet, take in, incorporate, give access to ♦ **let something down** = deflate, empty, exhaust, flatten, puncture ♦ **let something off** **1** = fire, explode, set off, discharge, detonate **2** = emit, release, leak, exude, give off ♦ **let something out** **1** = release, discharge **2** = emit, make, produce, give vent to ♦ **let up** = stop, diminish, decrease, subside, relax, ease (up), moderate, lessen

lethal = deadly, terminal, fatal, dangerous, devastating, destructive, mortal, murderous ≠ harmless

letter **1** = message, line, note, communication, dispatch, missive, epistle **2** = character, mark, sign, symbol

level NOUN = position, standard, degree, grade, standing, stage, rank, status
• ADJECTIVE **1** = equal, balanced, at the same height **2** = horizontal, even, flat, smooth, uniform ≠ slanted **3** = even, tied, equal, drawn, neck and neck, all square, level pegging
• VERB **1** = equalize, balance, even up **2** = destroy, devastate, demolish, flatten, knock down, pull down, tear down, bulldoze ≠ build **3** = direct, point, turn, train, aim, focus **4** = flatten, plane, smooth, even off *or* out
• PHRASES **on the level** (*Informal*) = honest, genuine, straight, fair, square, dinkum (*Austral. & N.Z. informal*), above board

lever NOUN = handle, bar
• VERB = prise, force

leverage **1** = influence, authority, pull (*informal*), weight, clout (*informal*) **2** = force, hold, pull, strength, grip, grasp

levy NOUN = tax, fee, toll, tariff, duty, excise, exaction
• VERB = impose, charge, collect, demand, exact

liability **1** = disadvantage, burden, drawback, inconvenience, handicap, nuisance, hindrance, millstone **2** = responsibility, accountability, culpability, answerability

liable **1** = likely, tending, inclined, disposed, prone, apt **2** = vulnerable, subject, exposed, prone, susceptible, open, at risk of **3** = responsible, accountable, answerable, obligated

liaison **1** = contact, communication, connection, interchange **2** = intermediary, contact, hook-up **3** = affair, romance, intrigue, fling, love affair, amour, entanglement

liar = falsifier, perjurer, fibber, fabricator

libel NOUN = defamation, misrepresentation, denigration, smear, calumny, aspersion
• VERB = defame, smear, slur, blacken, malign, denigrate, revile, vilify

liberal **1** = tolerant, open-minded, permissive, indulgent, easy-going, broad-minded ≠ intolerant **2** = progressive, radical, reformist, libertarian, forward-looking, free-thinking ≠ conservative **3** = abundant, generous, handsome, lavish, ample, rich, plentiful, copious ≠ limited **4** = generous, kind, charitable, extravagant, open-hearted, bountiful, magnanimous, open-handed ≠ stingy

liberate = free, release, rescue, save, deliver, let out, set free, let loose ≠ imprison

liberty NOUN = independence, sovereignty, liberation, autonomy, immunity, self-determination, emancipation, self-government ≠ restraint

• PHRASES **at liberty 1** = free, escaped, unlimited, at large, not confined, untied, on the loose, unchained **2** = able, free, allowed, permitted, entitled, authorized

◆ **take liberties** *or* **a liberty** = not show enough respect, show disrespect, act presumptuously, behave too familiarly, behave impertinently

licence NOUN **1** = certificate, document, permit, charter, warrant **2** = permission, the right, authority, leave, sanction, liberty, immunity, entitlement ≠ denial **3** = freedom, creativity, latitude, independence, liberty, deviation, leeway, free rein ≠ restraint **4** = laxity, excess, indulgence, irresponsibility, licentiousness, immoderation ≠ moderation

• PHRASES **under licence** = with permission, under a charter, under warrant, under a permit, with authorization, under a patent

license = permit, sanction, allow, warrant, authorize, empower, certify, accredit ≠ forbid

lick VERB **1** = taste, lap, tongue **2** (*Informal*) = beat, defeat, overcome, rout, outstrip, outdo, trounce, vanquish **3** (*of flames*) = flicker, touch, flick, dart, ripple, play over

• NOUN **1** = dab, bit, touch, stroke **2** (*Informal*) = pace, rate, speed, clip (*informal*)

lie¹ NOUN = falsehood, deceit, fabrication, fib, fiction, invention, deception, untruth

• VERB = fib, fabricate, falsify, prevaricate, not tell the truth, equivocate, dissimulate, tell untruths

• PHRASES **give the lie to something** = disprove, expose, discredit, contradict, refute, negate, invalidate, rebut

lie² 1 = recline, rest, lounge, sprawl, stretch out, loll, repose **2** = be placed, be, rest, exist, be situated **3** = be situated, sit, be located, be positioned **4** = be buried, remain, rest, be, be entombed

life 1 = being, existence, vitality, sentience **2** = existence, being, lifetime, time, days, span **3** = way of life, situation, conduct, behaviour, life style **4** = liveliness, energy, spirit, vitality, animation, vigour, verve, zest **5** = biography, story, history, profile, confessions, autobiography, memoirs, life story

RELATED WORDS

adjectives: animate, vital

lifelong = long-lasting, enduring, lasting, persistent, long-standing, perennial

lifetime = existence, time, day(s), span

lift VERB **1** = raise, pick up, hoist, draw up, elevate, uplift, heave up, upraise ≠ lower **2** = revoke, end, remove, withdraw, stop, cancel, terminate, rescind ≠ impose **3** = disappear, clear, vanish, disperse, dissipate, rise, be dispelled

• NOUN **1** = boost, encouragement, stimulus, pick-me-up, fillip, shot in the arm (*informal*), gee-up ≠ blow **2** = elevator (*chiefly U.S.*), hoist, paternoster **3** = ride, run, drive, hitch (*informal*)

• PHRASES **lift off** = take off, be launched, blast off, take to the air

light¹ NOUN **1** = brightness, illumination, luminosity, shining, glow, glare, gleam, brilliance ≠ dark **2** = lamp, torch, candle, flare, beacon, lantern, taper **3** = match, spark, flame, lighter **4** = aspect, context, angle, point of view, interpretation, viewpoint, slant, standpoint

• ADJECTIVE **1** = bright, brilliant, shining, illuminated, luminous, well-lit, lustrous, well-illuminated ≠ dark **2** = pale, fair, faded, blonde, blond, bleached, pastel, light-coloured ≠ dark

• VERB **1** = illuminate, light up, brighten ≠ darken **2** = ignite, inflame, kindle, touch off, set alight ≠ put out

• PHRASES **light up 1** = cheer, shine, blaze, sparkle, animate, brighten, lighten, irradiate **2** = shine, flash, beam, blaze, sparkle, flare, glare, gleam

light² ADJECTIVE **1** = insubstantial, thin, slight, portable, buoyant, airy, flimsy, underweight ≠ heavy **2** = weak, soft, gentle, moderate, slight, mild, faint,

indistinct ≠ strong **3** = digestible, modest, frugal ≠ substantial **4** = insignificant, small, slight, petty, trivial, trifling, inconsequential, inconsiderable ≠ serious **5** = light-hearted, funny, entertaining, amusing, witty, humorous, frivolous, unserious ≠ serious **6** = nimble, graceful, deft, agile, sprightly, lithe, limber, lissom ≠ clumsy
• PHRASES **light on** *or* **upon something** **1** = settle, land, perch, alight **2** = come across, find, discover, encounter, stumble on, hit upon, happen upon

lighten[1] = brighten, illuminate, light up, irradiate, become light

lighten[2] **1** = ease, relieve, alleviate, allay, reduce, lessen, mitigate, assuage ≠ intensify **2** = cheer, lift, revive, brighten, perk up, buoy up ≠ depress

lightly **1** = moderately, thinly, slightly, sparsely, sparingly ≠ heavily **2** = gently, softly, slightly, faintly, delicately ≠ forcefully **3** = carelessly, breezily, thoughtlessly, flippantly, frivolously, heedlessly ≠ seriously **4** = easily, simply, readily, effortlessly, unthinkingly, without thought, flippantly, heedlessly ≠ with difficulty

lightweight **1** = thin, fine, delicate, sheer, flimsy, gossamer, diaphanous, filmy **2** = unimportant, shallow, trivial, insignificant, slight, petty, worthless, trifling ≠ significant

like[1] = similar to, same as, equivalent to, parallel to, identical to, alike, corresponding to, comparable to ≠ different

like[2] **1** = enjoy, love, delight in, go for, relish, savour, revel in, be fond of ≠ dislike **2** = admire, approve of, appreciate, prize, take to, esteem, cherish, hold dear ≠ dislike **3** = wish, want, choose, prefer, desire, fancy, care, feel inclined

likelihood = probability, chance, possibility, prospect

likely **1** = inclined, disposed, prone, liable, tending, apt **2** = probable, expected, anticipated, odds-on, on the cards, to be expected **3** = plausible, possible, reasonable, credible, feasible, believable

liken = compare, match, relate, parallel, equate, set beside

likewise = similarly, the same, in the same way, in similar fashion, in like manner

liking = fondness, love, taste, weakness, preference, affection, inclination, penchant ≠ dislike

limb **1** = part, member, arm, leg, wing, extremity, appendage **2** = branch, spur, projection, offshoot, bough

limelight = publicity, recognition, fame, the spotlight, attention, prominence, stardom, public eye

limit NOUN **1** = end, ultimate, deadline, breaking point, extremity **2** = boundary, edge, border, frontier, perimeter
• VERB = restrict, control, check, bound, confine, curb, restrain, ration

limitation **1** = restriction, control, check, curb, restraint, constraint **2** = weakness, failing, qualification, reservation, defect, flaw, shortcoming, imperfection

limited = restricted, controlled, checked, bounded, confined, curbed, constrained, finite ≠ unlimited

limp[1] VERB = hobble, stagger, stumble, shuffle, hop, falter, shamble, totter
• NOUN = lameness, hobble

limp[2] = floppy, soft, slack, drooping, flabby, pliable, flaccid ≠ stiff

line NOUN **1** = stroke, mark, score, band, scratch, slash, streak, stripe **2** = wrinkle, mark, crease, furrow, crow's foot **3** = row, queue, rank, file, column, convoy, procession **4** = string, cable, wire, rope, thread, cord **5** = trajectory, way, course, track, channel, direction, route, path **6** = boundary, limit, edge, border, frontier, partition, borderline **7** = occupation, work, calling, business, job, area, trade, field
• VERB **1** = border, edge, bound, fringe **2** = mark, crease, furrow, rule, score
• PHRASES **in line for** = due for, shortlisted for, in the running for

lined **1** = wrinkled, worn, furrowed, wizened **2** = ruled, feint

line-up = arrangement, team, row, selection, array

linger = stay, remain, stop, wait, delay, hang around, idle, dally

link NOUN **1** = connection, relationship, association, tie-up, affinity **2** = relationship, association, bond, connection, attachment, affinity **3** = component, part, piece, element, constituent
• VERB **1** = associate, relate, identify, connect, bracket **2** = connect, join, unite,

couple, tie, bind, attach, fasten ≠ separate
lip **1** = edge, rim, brim, margin, brink **2** (*Slang*) = impudence, insolence, impertinence, cheek (*informal*), effrontery, backchat (*informal*), brass neck (*informal*)
liquid **NOUN** = fluid, solution, juice, sap • **ADJECTIVE** **1** = fluid, running, flowing, melted, watery, molten, runny, aqueous **2** (*of assets*) = convertible, disposable, negotiable, realizable
liquor **1** = alcohol, drink, spirits, booze (*informal*), hard stuff (*informal*), strong drink **2** = juice, stock, liquid, extract, broth
list[1] **NOUN** = inventory, record, series, roll, index, register, catalogue, directory • **VERB** = itemize, record, enter, register, catalogue, enumerate, note down, tabulate
list[2] **VERB** = lean, tip, incline, tilt, heel over, careen • **NOUN** = tilt, leaning, slant, cant
listen **1** = hear, attend, pay attention, lend an ear, prick up your ears **2** = pay attention, observe, obey, mind, heed, take notice, take note of, take heed of
literacy = education, learning, knowledge
literal **1** = exact, close, strict, accurate, faithful, verbatim, word for word **2** = actual, real, true, simple, plain, genuine, bona fide, unvarnished
literally = exactly, really, closely, actually, truly, precisely, strictly, faithfully
literary = well-read, learned, formal, intellectual, scholarly, erudite, bookish
literate = educated, informed, knowledgeable
literature = writings, letters, compositions, lore, creative writing
litigation = lawsuit, case, action, prosecution
litter **NOUN** **1** = rubbish, refuse, waste, junk, debris, garbage (*chiefly U.S.*), trash, muck **2** = brood, young, offspring, progeny • **VERB** **1** = clutter, mess up, clutter up, be scattered about, disorder, disarrange, derange **2** = scatter, spread, shower, strew
little **ADJECTIVE** **1** = small, minute, short, tiny, wee, compact, miniature, diminutive ≠ big **2** = young, small, junior, infant, immature, undeveloped, babyish • **ADVERB** **1** = hardly, barely, scarcely ≠ much **2** = rarely, seldom, scarcely, not often, infrequently, hardly ever ≠ always • **NOUN** = bit, touch, spot, trace, hint, particle, fragment, speck ≠ lot • **PHRASES** **a little** = to a small extent, slightly, to some extent, to a certain extent, to a small degree
live[1] **1** = dwell, board, settle, lodge, occupy, abide, inhabit, reside **2** = exist, last, prevail, be, have being, breathe, persist, be alive **3** = survive, get along, make a living, make ends meet, subsist, eke out a living, support yourself, maintain yourself **4** = thrive, flourish, prosper, have fun, enjoy yourself, live life to the full
live[2] **1** = living, alive, breathing, animate **2** = active, unexploded **3** = topical, important, pressing, current, hot, burning, controversial, prevalent
livelihood = occupation, work, employment, living, job, bread and butter (*informal*)
lively **1** = animated, spirited, quick, keen, active, alert, dynamic, vigorous ≠ dull **2** = vivid, strong, striking, bright, exciting, stimulating, bold, colourful ≠ dull **3** = enthusiastic, strong, keen, stimulating, eager, formidable, vigorous, animated
living **NOUN** = lifestyle, ways, situation, conduct, behaviour, customs, lifestyle, way of life • **ADJECTIVE** **1** = alive, existing, moving, active, breathing, animate ≠ dead **2** = current, present, active, contemporary, in use, extant ≠ obsolete
load **VERB** **1** = fill, stuff, pack, pile, stack, heap, cram, freight **2** = make ready, charge, prime • **NOUN** **1** = cargo, delivery, haul, shipment, batch, freight, consignment **2** = oppression, charge, worry, trouble, weight, responsibility, burden, onus • **PHRASES** **load someone down** = burden, worry, oppress, weigh down, saddle with, encumber, snow under
loaded **1** = tricky, charged, sensitive, delicate, manipulative, emotive, insidious, artful **2** = biased, weighted, rigged, distorted **3** (*Slang*) = rich, wealthy, affluent, well off, flush (*informal*), well-heeled (*informal*), well-to-do, moneyed
loaf[1] **1** = lump, block, cake, cube, slab **2** (*Slang*) = head, mind, sense, common sense, nous (*Brit. slang*), gumption (*Brit. informal*)
loaf[2] = idle, hang around, take it easy, lie around, loiter, laze, lounge around

loan NOUN = advance, credit, overdraft
• VERB = lend, advance, let out
loathe = hate, dislike, despise, detest, abhor, abominate
loathing = hatred, hate, disgust, aversion, revulsion, antipathy, repulsion, abhorrence
lobby VERB = campaign, press, pressure, push, influence, promote, urge, persuade
• NOUN 1 = pressure group, group, camp, faction, lobbyists, interest group, special-interest group, ginger group 2 = corridor, passage, entrance, porch, hallway, foyer, entrance hall, vestibule
lobola (*S. African*) = dowry, portion, marriage settlement, dot (*archaic*)
local ADJECTIVE 1 = community, regional 2 = confined, limited, restricted
• NOUN = resident, native, inhabitant
locate 1 = find, discover, detect, come across, track down, pinpoint, unearth, pin down 2 = place, put, set, position, seat, site, establish, settle
location = place, point, setting, position, situation, spot, venue, locale
lock¹ VERB 1 = fasten, close, secure, shut, bar, seal, bolt 2 = unite, join, link, engage, clench, entangle, interlock, entwine 3 = embrace, press, grasp, clutch, hug, enclose, clasp, encircle
• NOUN = fastening, catch, bolt, clasp, padlock
• PHRASES **lock someone up** = imprison, jail, confine, cage, detain, shut up, incarcerate, send down (*informal*)
lock² = strand, curl, tuft, tress, ringlet
lodge NOUN 1 = cabin, shelter, cottage, hut, chalet, gatehouse 2 = society, group, club, section, wing, chapter, branch
• VERB 1 = register, enter, file, submit, put on record 2 = stay, room, board, reside 3 = stick, remain, implant, come to rest, imbed
lodging *often plural* = accommodation, rooms, apartments, quarters, digs (*Brit. informal*), shelter, residence, abode
lofty 1 = noble, grand, distinguished, renowned, elevated, dignified, illustrious, exalted ≠ humble 2 = high, raised, towering, soaring, elevated ≠ low 3 = haughty, proud, arrogant, patronizing, condescending, disdainful, supercilious ≠ modest
log NOUN 1 = stump, block, branch, chunk, trunk 2 = record, account, register, journal, diary, logbook
• VERB = record, enter, note, register, chart, put down, set down
logic = reason, reasoning, sense, good sense
logical 1 = rational, clear, reasoned, sound, consistent, valid, coherent, well-organized ≠ illogical 2 = reasonable, sensible, natural, wise, plausible ≠ unlikely
lone = solitary, single, one, only, sole, unaccompanied
loneliness = solitude, isolation, desolation, seclusion
lonely 1 = solitary, alone, isolated, abandoned, lone, withdrawn, single, forsaken ≠ accompanied 2 = desolate, deserted, remote, isolated, out-of-the-way, secluded, uninhabited, godforsaken ≠ crowded
lonesome (*Chiefly U.S. & Canad.*) = lonely, gloomy, dreary, desolate, forlorn, friendless, companionless
long¹ 1 = elongated, extended, stretched, expanded, extensive, lengthy, far-reaching, spread out ≠ short 2 = prolonged, sustained, lengthy, lingering, protracted, interminable, spun out, long-drawn-out ≠ brief
long² = desire, want, wish, burn, pine, lust, crave, yearn
longing = desire, hope, wish, burning, urge, ambition, hunger, yen (*informal*) ≠ indifference
long-standing = established, fixed, enduring, abiding, long-lasting, long-established, time-honoured
look VERB 1 = see, view, consider, watch, eye, study, survey, examine 2 = search, seek, hunt, forage, fossick (*Austral. & N.Z.*) 3 = consider, contemplate 4 = face, overlook 5 = hope, expect, await, anticipate, reckon on 6 = seem, appear, look like, strike you as
• NOUN 1 = glimpse, view, glance, observation, sight, examination, gaze, inspection 2 = appearance, bearing, air, style, aspect, manner, expression, impression
• PHRASES **look after something** *or* **someone** = take care of, mind, protect, tend, guard, nurse, care for, supervise
◆ **look down on** *or* **upon someone** = disdain, despise, scorn, sneer at, spurn,

contemn (*formal*) ◆ **look forward to something** = anticipate, expect, look for, wait for, await, hope for, long for ◆ **look out for something** = be careful of, beware, watch out for, pay attention to, be wary of, keep an eye out for ◆ **look someone up** = visit, call on, drop in on (*informal*), look in on ◆ **look something up** = research, find, search for, hunt for, track down, seek out ◆ **look up** = improve, develop, advance, pick up, progress, get better, shape up (*informal*), perk up ◆ **look up to someone** = respect, honour, admire, esteem, revere, defer to, think highly of

lookout **1** = watchman, guard, sentry, sentinel **2** = watch, guard, vigil **3** = watchtower, post, observatory, observation post **4** (*Informal*) = concern, business, worry

loom = appear, emerge, hover, take shape, threaten, bulk, menace, come into view

loop NOUN = curve, ring, circle, twist, curl, spiral, coil, twirl
• VERB = twist, turn, roll, knot, curl, spiral, coil, wind round

loophole = let-out, escape, excuse

loose ADJECTIVE **1** = free, detached, insecure, unfettered, unrestricted, untied, unattached, unfastened **2** = slack, easy, relaxed, sloppy, loose-fitting ≠ tight **3** (*Old-fashioned*) = promiscuous, fast, abandoned, immoral, dissipated, profligate, debauched, dissolute ≠ chaste **4** = vague, random, inaccurate, rambling, imprecise, ill-defined, indistinct, inexact ≠ precise
• VERB = free, release, liberate, detach, unleash, disconnect, set free, untie ≠ fasten

loosen VERB = untie, undo, release, separate, detach, unloose
• PHRASES **loosen up** = relax, chill (*slang*), soften, unwind, go easy (*informal*), hang loose, outspan (*S. African*), ease up *or* off

loot VERB = plunder, rob, raid, sack, rifle, ravage, ransack, pillage
• NOUN = plunder, goods, prize, haul, spoils, booty, swag (*slang*)

lord NOUN **1** = peer, nobleman, count, duke, gentleman, earl, noble, baron **2** = ruler, leader, chief, master, governor, commander, superior, liege
• PHRASES **lord it over someone** = boss around *or* about (*informal*), order around, threaten, bully, menace, intimidate, hector, bluster ◆ **the Lord** *or* **Our Lord** = Jesus Christ, God, Christ, Messiah, Jehovah, the Almighty

lose **1** = be defeated, be beaten, lose out, come to grief **2** = mislay, drop, forget, be deprived of, lose track of, misplace **3** = forfeit, miss, yield, be deprived of, pass up (*informal*)

loser = failure, flop (*informal*), also-ran, no-hoper (*Austral. slang*), dud (*informal*), non-achiever

loss NOUN **1** = losing, waste, squandering, forfeiture ≠ gain **2** *sometimes plural* = deficit, debt, deficiency, debit, depletion ≠ gain **3** = damage, cost, injury, hurt, harm ≠ advantage
• PHRASES **at a loss** = confused, puzzled, baffled, bewildered, helpless, stumped, perplexed, mystified

lost = missing, disappeared, vanished, wayward, misplaced, mislaid

lot NOUN **1** = bunch (*informal*), group, crowd, crew, set, band, quantity, assortment **2** = destiny, situation, circumstances, fortune, chance, accident, fate, doom
• PHRASES **a lot** *or* **lots** **1** = plenty, scores, masses (*informal*), load(s) (*informal*), wealth, piles (*informal*), a great deal, stack(s) **2** = often, regularly, a great deal, frequently, a good deal

lotion = cream, solution, balm, salve, liniment, embrocation

lottery **1** = raffle, draw, lotto (*Brit., N.Z., & S. African*), sweepstake **2** = gamble, chance, risk, hazard, toss-up (*informal*)

loud **1** = noisy, booming, roaring, thundering, forte (*Music*), resounding, deafening, thunderous ≠ quiet **2** = garish, bold, glaring, flamboyant, brash, flashy, lurid, gaudy ≠ sombre

loudly = noisily, vigorously, vehemently, vociferously, uproariously, lustily, shrilly, fortissimo (*Music*)

lounge VERB = relax, loaf, sprawl, lie about, take it easy, loiter, loll, laze, outspan (*S. African*)
• NOUN = sitting room, living room, parlour, drawing room, front room, reception room, television room

love VERB **1** = adore, care for, treasure, cherish, prize, worship, be devoted to,

dote on ≠ hate **2** = enjoy, like, appreciate, relish, delight in, savour, take pleasure in, have a soft spot for ≠ dislike
• NOUN **1** = passion, affection, warmth, attachment, intimacy, devotion, tenderness, adoration, aroha (*N.Z.*) ≠ hatred **2** = liking, taste, bent for, weakness for, relish for, enjoyment, devotion to, penchant for **3** = beloved, dear, dearest, lover, darling, honey, sweetheart, truelove ≠ enemy **4** = sympathy, understanding, pity, humanity, warmth, mercy, sorrow, kindness, aroha (*N.Z.*)
• PHRASES **make love** = have sexual intercourse, have sex, go to bed, sleep together, do it (*informal*), mate, have sexual relations, have it off (*slang*)

love affair = romance, relationship, affair, intrigue, liaison, amour

lovely 1 = beautiful, appealing, attractive, charming, pretty, handsome, good-looking, exquisite ≠ ugly **2** = wonderful, pleasing, nice, pleasant, engaging, marvellous, delightful, enjoyable ≠ horrible

lover = sweetheart, beloved, loved one, flame (*informal*), mistress, admirer, suitor, woman friend

loving 1 = affectionate, dear, devoted, tender, fond, doting, amorous, warm-hearted ≠ cruel **2** = tender, kind, caring, warm, gentle, sympathetic, considerate

low 1 = small, little, short, stunted, squat ≠ tall **2** = inferior, bad, poor, inadequate, unsatisfactory, deficient, second-rate, shoddy, half-pie (*N.Z. informal*), bodger *or* bodgie (*Austral. slang*) **3** = quiet, soft, gentle, whispered, muted, subdued, hushed, muffled ≠ loud **4** = dejected, depressed, miserable, fed up, moody, gloomy, glum, despondent ≠ happy **5** = coarse, common, rough, crude, rude, vulgar, undignified, disreputable **6** = ill, weak, frail, stricken, debilitated ≠ strong

lower ADJECTIVE **1** = subordinate, under, smaller, junior, minor, secondary, lesser, inferior **2** = reduced, cut, diminished, decreased, lessened, curtailed ≠ increased
• VERB **1** = drop, sink, depress, let down, submerge, take down, let fall ≠ raise **2** = lessen, cut, reduce, diminish, slash, decrease, prune, minimize ≠ increase

low-key = subdued, quiet, restrained, muted, understated, toned down

loyal = faithful, true, devoted, dependable, constant, staunch, trustworthy, trusty ≠ disloyal

loyalty = faithfulness, commitment, devotion, allegiance, fidelity, homage, obedience, constancy

luck NOUN **1** = good fortune, success, advantage, prosperity, blessing, windfall, godsend, serendipity **2** = fortune, lot, stars, chance, accident, fate, destiny, twist of fate
• PHRASES **in luck** = fortunate, successful, favoured, well-off, jammy (*Brit. slang*)
◆ **out of luck** = unfortunate, cursed, unlucky, unsuccessful

luckily = fortunately, happily, opportunely

lucky = fortunate, successful, favoured, charmed, blessed, jammy (*Brit. slang*), serendipitous ≠ unlucky

lucrative = profitable, rewarding, productive, fruitful, well-paid, advantageous, remunerative

ludicrous = ridiculous, crazy, absurd, preposterous, silly, laughable, farcical, outlandish ≠ sensible

luggage = baggage, things, cases, bags, gear, suitcases, paraphernalia, impedimenta

lull NOUN = respite, pause, quiet, silence, calm, hush, let-up (*informal*)
• VERB = calm, soothe, subdue, quell, allay, pacify, tranquillize

lumber[1] VERB (*Brit. informal*) = burden, land, load, saddle, encumber
• NOUN (*Brit.*) = junk, refuse, rubbish, trash, clutter, jumble

lumber[2] = plod, shuffle, shamble, trudge, stump, waddle, trundle

lumbering = awkward, heavy, hulking, ponderous, ungainly

lump NOUN **1** = piece, ball, block, mass, chunk, hunk, nugget **2** = swelling, growth, bump, tumour, bulge, hump, protrusion
• VERB = group, throw, mass, combine, collect, pool, consolidate, conglomerate

lunatic NOUN = madman, maniac, psychopath, nutcase (*slang*)
• ADJECTIVE = mad, crazy, insane, irrational, daft, deranged, crackpot (*informal*), crackbrained, off the air (*Austral. slang*)

lunge VERB = pounce, charge, dive, leap, plunge, thrust
• NOUN = thrust, charge, pounce, spring, swing, jab

lurch 1 = tilt, roll, pitch, list, rock, lean, heel 2 = stagger, reel, stumble, weave, sway, totter

lure VERB = tempt, draw, attract, invite, trick, seduce, entice, allure
• NOUN = temptation, attraction, incentive, bait, carrot (*informal*), inducement, enticement, allurement

lurk = hide, sneak, prowl, lie in wait, slink, skulk, conceal yourself

lush 1 = abundant, green, flourishing, dense, rank, verdant 2 = luxurious, grand, elaborate, lavish, extravagant, sumptuous, plush (*informal*), ornate

lust NOUN 1 = lechery, sensuality, lewdness, lasciviousness 2 = desire, longing, passion, appetite, craving, greed, thirst
• PHRASES **lust for** *or* **after someone** = desire, want, crave, yearn for, covet, hunger for *or* after ♦ **lust for** *or* **after something** = desire, crave, yearn for, covet

luxurious = sumptuous, expensive, comfortable, magnificent, splendid, lavish, plush (*informal*), opulent

luxury 1 = opulence, splendour, richness, extravagance, affluence, hedonism, a bed of roses, the life of Riley ≠ poverty 2 = extravagance, treat, extra, indulgence, frill ≠ necessity

lying NOUN = dishonesty, perjury, deceit, misrepresentation, mendacity, untruthfulness
• ADJECTIVE = deceitful, false, deceiving, treacherous, dishonest, two-faced, mendacious, perfidious ≠ truthful

lyrical = enthusiastic, inspired, poetic, impassioned, effusive, rhapsodic

m

machine 1 = appliance, device, apparatus, engine, tool, instrument, mechanism, gadget 2 = system, structure, organization, machinery, setup (*informal*)

machinery = equipment, gear, instruments, apparatus, technology, tackle, tools, gadgetry

macho = manly, masculine, chauvinist, virile

mad 1 = insane, crazy (*informal*), nuts (*slang*), raving, unstable, psychotic, demented, deranged, off the air (*Austral. slang*) ≠ sane 2 = foolish, absurd, wild, stupid, daft (*informal*), irrational, senseless, preposterous ≠ sensible 3 (*Informal*) = angry, furious, incensed, enraged, livid (*informal*), berserk, berko (*Austral. slang*), tooshie (*Austral. slang*), off the air (*Austral. slang*) ≠ calm 4 = enthusiastic, wild, crazy (*informal*), ardent, fanatical, avid, impassioned, infatuated ≠ nonchalant 5 = frenzied, wild, excited, frenetic, uncontrolled, unrestrained

madden = infuriate, irritate, incense, enrage, upset, annoy, inflame, drive you crazy ≠ calm

madly 1 (*Informal*) = passionately, wildly, desperately, intensely, to distraction, devotedly 2 = foolishly, wildly, absurdly, ludicrously, irrationally, senselessly 3 = energetically, wildly, furiously, excitedly, recklessly, speedily, like mad (*informal*) 4 = insanely, frantically, hysterically, crazily, deliriously, distractedly, frenziedly

madness 1 = insanity, mental illness, delusion, mania, dementia, distraction, aberration, psychosis 2 = foolishness, nonsense, folly, absurdity, idiocy, wildness, daftness (*informal*), foolhardiness

magazine = journal, publication, supplement, rag (*informal*), issue, glossy (*informal*), pamphlet, periodical

magic NOUN 1 = sorcery, wizardry, witchcraft, enchantment, black art, necromancy 2 = conjuring, illusion, trickery, sleight of hand, legerdemain, prestidigitation 3 = charm, power, glamour, fascination, magnetism, enchantment, allurement
• ADJECTIVE = miraculous, entrancing, charming, fascinating, marvellous, magical, enchanting, bewitching

magician 1 = conjuror, illusionist, prestidigitator 2 = sorcerer, witch, wizard, illusionist, warlock, necromancer, enchanter *or* enchantress

magistrate = judge, justice, justice of the

peace, J.P.
magnetic = attractive, irresistible, seductive, captivating, charming, fascinating, charismatic, hypnotic ≠ repulsive
magnificent **1** = splendid, impressive, imposing, glorious, gorgeous, majestic, regal, sublime ≠ ordinary **2** = brilliant, fine, excellent, outstanding, superb, splendid
magnify **1** = enlarge, increase, boost, expand, intensify, blow up (*informal*), heighten, amplify ≠ reduce **2** = make worse, exaggerate, intensify, worsen, exacerbate, increase, inflame **3** = exaggerate, overstate, inflate, overplay, overemphasize ≠ understate
magnitude **1** = importance, consequence, significance, moment, note, weight, greatness ≠ unimportance **2** = immensity, size, extent, enormity, volume, vastness ≠ smallness **3** = intensity, amplitude
maid **1** = servant, chambermaid, housemaid, menial, maidservant, female servant, domestic (*archaic*), parlourmaid **2** (*Literary*) = girl, maiden, lass, damsel, lassie (*informal*), wench
maiden NOUN (*Literary*) = girl, maid, lass, damsel, virgin, lassie (*informal*), wench
• ADJECTIVE **1** = first, initial, inaugural, introductory **2** = unmarried, unwed
mail NOUN = letters, post, correspondence
• VERB = post, send, forward, e-mail, dispatch
main ADJECTIVE = chief, leading, head, central, essential, primary, principal, foremost ≠ minor
• PLURAL NOUN **1** = pipeline, channel, pipe, conduit, duct **2** = cable, line, electricity supply, mains supply
• PHRASES **in the main** = on the whole, generally, mainly, mostly, in general, for the most part
mainly = chiefly, mostly, largely, principally, primarily, on the whole, predominantly, in the main
mainstream = conventional, general, established, received, accepted, current, prevailing, orthodox ≠ unconventional
maintain **1** = continue, retain, preserve, sustain, carry on, keep up, prolong, perpetuate ≠ end **2** = assert, state, claim, insist, declare, contend, profess, avow ≠ disavow **3** = look after, care for, take care of, conserve, keep in good condition
maintenance **1** = upkeep, keeping, care, repairs, conservation, nurture, preservation **2** = allowance, support, keep, alimony **3** = continuation, carrying-on, perpetuation, prolongation
majestic = grand, magnificent, impressive, superb, splendid, regal, stately, monumental ≠ modest
majesty = grandeur, glory, splendour, magnificence, nobility ≠ triviality
major **1** = important, critical, significant, great, serious, crucial, outstanding, notable **2** = main, higher, greater, bigger, leading, chief, senior, supreme ≠ minor
majority **1** = most, mass, bulk, best part, better part, lion's share, preponderance, greater number **2** = adulthood, maturity, age of consent, seniority, manhood *or* womanhood
make VERB **1** = produce, cause, create, effect, lead to, generate, bring about, give rise to **2** = perform, do, effect, carry out, execute **3** = force, cause, compel, drive, require, oblige, induce, constrain **4** = create, build, produce, manufacture, form, fashion, construct, assemble **5** = earn, get, gain, net, win, clear, obtain, bring in **6** = amount to, total, constitute, add up to, count as, tot up to (*informal*)
• NOUN = brand, sort, style, model, kind, type, variety, marque
• PHRASES **make for something** = head for, aim for, head towards, be bound for ◆ **make it** (*Informal*) = succeed, prosper, arrive (*informal*), get on, crack it (*informal*) ◆ **make off** = flee, clear out (*informal*), bolt, take to your heels, run away *or* off ◆ **make something up** = invent, create, construct, compose, frame, coin, devise, originate ◆ **make up** = settle your differences, bury the hatchet, call it quits, declare a truce, be friends again ◆ **make up for something** = compensate for, make amends for, atone for, balance out, offset, make recompense for ◆ **make up something** **1** = form, account for, constitute, compose, comprise **2** = complete, supply, fill, round off
maker = manufacturer, producer, builder, constructor
makeshift = temporary, provisional, substitute, expedient, stopgap
make-up **1** = cosmetics, paint (*informal*),

powder, face (*informal*), greasepaint (*Theatre*) **2** = nature, character, constitution, temperament, disposition **3** = structure, organization, arrangement, construction, assembly, constitution, format, composition

making NOUN = creation, production, manufacture, construction, assembly, composition, fabrication
• PLURAL NOUN = beginnings, potential, capacity, ingredients

male = masculine, manly, macho, virile ≠ female

malicious = spiteful, malevolent, resentful, vengeful, rancorous, ill-disposed, ill-natured ≠ benevolent

mammoth = colossal, huge, giant, massive, enormous, immense, gigantic, monumental ≠ tiny

man NOUN **1** = male, guy (*informal*), fellow (*informal*), gentleman, bloke (*Brit. informal*), chap (*Brit. informal*), dude (*U.S. informal*), geezer (*informal*) **2** = human, human being, person, individual, soul **3** = mankind, humanity, people, human race, humankind, Homo sapiens
• VERB = staff, people, crew, occupy, garrison

mana (*N.Z.*) = authority, influence, power, might, standing, status, importance, eminence

manage **1** = be in charge of, run, handle, direct, conduct, command, administer, supervise **2** = organize, use, handle, regulate **3** = cope, survive, succeed, carry on, make do, get by (*informal*), muddle through **4** = perform, do, achieve, carry out, undertake, cope with, accomplish, contrive **5** = control, handle, manipulate

management **1** = administration, control, running, operation, handling, direction, command, supervision **2** = directors, board, executive(s), administration, employers

manager = supervisor, head, director, executive, boss (*informal*), governor, administrator, organizer, baas (*S. African*)

mandate = command, order, commission, instruction, decree, directive, edict

mandatory = compulsory, required, binding, obligatory, requisite ≠ optional

manhood = manliness, masculinity, virility

manifest ADJECTIVE = obvious, apparent, patent, evident, clear, glaring, noticeable, blatant ≠ concealed
• VERB = display, show, reveal, express, demonstrate, expose, exhibit ≠ conceal

manifestation **1** = sign, symptom, indication, mark, example, evidence, proof, testimony **2** = display, show, exhibition, expression, demonstration

manipulate **1** = influence, control, direct, negotiate, exploit, manoeuvre **2** = work, use, operate, handle

mankind = people, man, humanity, human race, humankind, Homo sapiens

manly = virile, masculine, strong, brave, bold, strapping, vigorous, courageous ≠ effeminate

man-made = artificial, manufactured, mock, synthetic, ersatz

manner NOUN **1** = style, way, fashion, method, custom, mode **2** = behaviour, air, bearing, conduct, aspect, demeanour **3** = type, form, sort, kind, variety, brand, category
• PLURAL NOUN **1** = conduct, behaviour, demeanour **2** = politeness, courtesy, etiquette, refinement, decorum, p's and q's **3** = protocol, customs, social graces

mannered = affected, artificial, pretentious, stilted, arty-farty (*informal*) ≠ natural

manoeuvre VERB **1** = scheme, wangle (*informal*), machinate **2** = manipulate, arrange, organize, set up, engineer, fix, orchestrate, contrive
• NOUN **1** = stratagem, scheme, trick, tactic, intrigue, dodge, ploy, ruse **2** *often plural* = movement, operation, exercise, war game

mansion = residence, manor, hall, villa, seat

mantle **1** = covering, screen, curtain, blanket, veil, shroud, canopy, pall **2** = cloak, wrap, cape, hood, shawl

manual ADJECTIVE **1** = physical, human **2** = hand-operated, hand, non-automatic
• NOUN = handbook, guide, instructions, bible

manufacture VERB **1** = make, build, produce, construct, create, turn out, assemble, put together **2** = concoct, make up, invent, devise, fabricate, think up, cook up (*informal*), trump up
• NOUN = making, production, construction, assembly, creation

manufacturer = maker, producer,

builder, creator, industrialist, constructor
many DETERMINER = numerous, various, countless, abundant, myriad, innumerable, manifold, umpteen (*informal*)
• PRONOUN = a lot, lots (*informal*), plenty, scores, heaps (*informal*)
mar 1 = harm, damage, hurt, spoil, stain, taint, tarnish 2 = ruin, spoil, scar, flaw, impair, detract from, deform, blemish ≠ improve
march VERB 1 = parade, walk, file, pace, stride, swagger 2 = walk, strut, storm, sweep, stride, flounce
• NOUN 1 = walk, trek, slog, yomp (*Brit. informal*), routemarch 2 = progress, development, advance, evolution, progression
margin = edge, side, border, boundary, verge, brink, rim, perimeter
marginal 1 = insignificant, small, minor, slight, minimal, negligible 2 = borderline, bordering, on the edge, peripheral
marijuana = cannabis, pot (*slang*), dope (*slang*), grass (*slang*), hemp, dagga (*S. African*)
marine = nautical, maritime, naval, seafaring, seagoing
mariner = sailor, seaman, sea dog, seafarer, salt
marital = matrimonial, nuptial, conjugal, connubial
maritime 1 = nautical, marine, naval, oceanic, seafaring 2 = coastal, seaside, littoral
mark NOUN 1 = spot, stain, streak, smudge, line, scratch, scar, blot 2 = characteristic, feature, standard, quality, measure, stamp, attribute, criterion 3 = indication, sign, symbol, token 4 = brand, impression, label, device, flag, symbol, token, emblem 5 = target, goal, aim, purpose, object, objective
• VERB 1 = scar, scratch, stain, streak, blot, smudge, blemish 2 = label, identify, brand, flag, stamp, characterize 3 = grade, correct, assess, evaluate, appraise 4 = distinguish, show, illustrate, exemplify, denote 5 = observe, mind, note, notice, attend to, pay attention to, pay heed to
marked = noticeable, clear, decided, striking, obvious, prominent, patent, distinct ≠ imperceptible
markedly = noticeably, clearly, obviously, considerably, distinctly, decidedly, strikingly, conspicuously
market NOUN = fair, mart, bazaar, souk (*Arabic*)
• VERB = sell, promote, retail, peddle, vend
maroon = abandon, leave, desert, strand, leave high and dry (*informal*)
marriage = wedding, match, nuptials, wedlock, matrimony
RELATED WORDS
adjectives: conjugal, marital, nuptial
marry 1 = tie the knot (*informal*), wed, get hitched (*slang*) 2 = unite, join, link, bond, ally, merge, knit, unify
marsh = swamp, bog, slough, fen, quagmire, morass
marshal 1 = conduct, take, lead, guide, steer, escort, shepherd, usher 2 = arrange, group, order, line up, organize, deploy, array, draw up
martial = military, belligerent, warlike, bellicose
marvel VERB = be amazed, wonder, gape, be awed
• NOUN 1 = wonder, phenomenon, miracle, portent 2 = genius, prodigy
marvellous = excellent, great (*informal*), wonderful, brilliant, amazing, extraordinary, superb, spectacular, booshit (*Austral. slang*), exo (*Austral. slang*), sik (*Austral. slang*) ≠ terrible
masculine = male, manly, mannish, manlike, virile
mask NOUN = façade, disguise, front, cover, screen, veil, guise, camouflage
• VERB = disguise, hide, conceal, obscure, cover (up), screen, blanket, veil
mass NOUN 1 = lot, collection, load, pile, quantity, bunch, stack, heap 2 = piece, block, lump, chunk, hunk 3 = size, matter, weight, extent, bulk, magnitude, greatness
• ADJECTIVE = large-scale, general, widespread, extensive, universal, wholesale, indiscriminate
• VERB = gather, assemble, accumulate, collect, rally, swarm, throng, congregate
massacre NOUN = slaughter, murder, holocaust, carnage, extermination, annihilation, butchery, blood bath
• VERB = slaughter, kill, murder, butcher, wipe out, exterminate, mow down, cut to pieces
massage NOUN = rub-down, manipulation
• VERB 1 = rub down, manipulate, knead 2 = manipulate, alter, distort, doctor,

cook (*informal*), fix (*informal*), rig, fiddle (*informal*)

massive = huge, big, enormous, immense, hefty, gigantic, monumental, mammoth ≠ tiny

master NOUN **1** = lord, ruler, commander, chief, director, manager, boss (*informal*), head, baas (*S. African*) ≠ servant **2** = expert, maestro, ace (*informal*), genius, wizard, virtuoso, doyen, past master, fundi (*S. African*) ≠ amateur **3** = teacher, tutor, instructor ≠ student
• ADJECTIVE = main, principal, chief, prime, foremost, predominant ≠ lesser
• VERB **1** = learn, understand, pick up, grasp, get the hang of (*informal*), know inside out, know backwards **2** = overcome, defeat, conquer, tame, triumph over, vanquish ≠ give in to

masterly = skilful, expert, crack (*informal*), supreme, world-class, consummate, first-rate, masterful

mastermind VERB = plan, manage, direct, organize, devise, conceive
• NOUN = organizer, director, manager, engineer, brain(s) (*informal*), architect, planner

masterpiece = classic, tour de force (*French*), pièce de résistance (*French*), magnum opus, jewel

mastery **1** = understanding, skill, know-how, expertise, prowess, finesse, proficiency, virtuosity **2** = control, command, domination, superiority, supremacy, upper hand, ascendancy, mana (*N.Z.*), whip hand

match NOUN **1** = game, test, competition, trial, tie, contest, fixture, bout **2** = marriage, pairing, alliance, partnership **3** = equal, rival, peer, counterpart
• VERB **1** = correspond with, go with, fit with, harmonize with **2** = correspond, agree, accord, square, coincide, tally, conform, match up **3** = rival, equal, compete with, compare with, emulate, measure up to

matching = identical, like, twin, equivalent, corresponding, coordinating ≠ different

mate NOUN **1** (*Informal*) = friend, pal (*informal*), companion, buddy (*informal*), comrade, chum (*informal*), mucker (*Brit. informal*), crony, cobber (*Austral. & N.Z. old-fashioned informal*), E hoa (*N.Z.*) **2** = partner, lover, companion, spouse, consort, helpmeet, husband *or* wife **3** = assistant, subordinate, apprentice, helper, accomplice, sidekick (*informal*) **4** = colleague, associate, companion
• VERB = pair, couple, breed

material NOUN **1** = substance, matter, stuff **2** = cloth, fabric, textile **3** = information, details, facts, notes, evidence, particulars, data, info (*informal*)
• ADJECTIVE **1** = physical, solid, substantial, concrete, bodily, tangible, palpable, corporeal **2** = relevant, important, significant, essential, vital, serious, meaningful, applicable

materially = significantly, much, greatly, essentially, seriously, gravely, substantially ≠ insignificantly

maternal = motherly, protective, nurturing, maternalistic

maternity = motherhood, parenthood, motherliness

matted = tangled, knotted, unkempt, knotty, tousled, ratty, uncombed

matter NOUN **1** = situation, concern, business, question, event, subject, affair, incident **2** = substance, material, body, stuff
• VERB = be important, make a difference, count, be relevant, make any difference, carry weight, cut any ice (*informal*), be of account

matter-of-fact = unsentimental, plain, sober, down-to-earth, mundane, prosaic, deadpan, unimaginative

mature VERB = develop, grow up, bloom, blossom, come of age, age
• ADJECTIVE **1** = matured, seasoned, ripe, mellow **2** = grown-up, adult, of age, fully fledged, full-grown ≠ immature

maturity **1** = adulthood, puberty, coming of age, pubescence, manhood *or* womanhood ≠ immaturity **2** = ripeness

maul **1** = mangle, claw, lacerate, tear, mangulate (*Austral. slang*) **2** = ill-treat, abuse, batter, molest, manhandle

maverick NOUN = rebel, radical, dissenter, individualist, protester, eccentric, heretic, nonconformist ≠ traditionalist
• ADJECTIVE = rebel, radical, dissenting, individualistic, eccentric, heretical, iconoclastic, nonconformist

maximum ADJECTIVE = greatest, highest, supreme, paramount, utmost, most,

topmost ≠ minimal
• NOUN = top, peak, ceiling, utmost, upper limit ≠ minimum
maybe = perhaps, possibly, perchance (*archaic*)
mayhem = chaos, trouble, violence, disorder, destruction, confusion, havoc, fracas
maze = web, confusion, tangle, labyrinth, imbroglio, complex network
meadow = field, pasture, grassland, lea (*poetic*)
mean[1] 1 = signify, indicate, represent, express, stand for, convey, spell out, symbolize 2 = imply, suggest, intend, hint at, insinuate 3 = intend, want, plan, expect, design, aim, wish, think
mean[2] 1 = miserly, stingy, parsimonious, niggardly, mercenary, penny-pinching, ungenerous, tight-fisted, snoep (*S. African informal*) ≠ generous 2 = dishonourable, petty, shameful, shabby, vile, callous, sordid, despicable, scungy (*Austral. & N.Z.*) ≠ honourable
mean[3] NOUN = average, middle, balance, norm, midpoint
• ADJECTIVE = average, middle, standard
meaning 1 = significance, message, substance, drift, connotation, gist 2 = definition, sense
meaningful = significant, important, material, useful, relevant, valid, worthwhile, purposeful ≠ trivial
meaningless = nonsensical, senseless, inconsequential, inane ≠ worthwhile
means PLURAL NOUN 1 = method, way, process, medium, agency, instrument, mode 2 = money, funds, capital, income, resources, fortune, wealth, affluence
• PHRASES **by all means** = certainly, surely, of course, definitely, doubtlessly ◆ **by no means** = in no way, definitely not, not in the least, on no account
meantime *or* **meanwhile** = at the same time, simultaneously, concurrently
meanwhile *or* **meantime** = for now, in the interim
measure VERB = quantify, determine, assess, weigh, calculate, evaluate, compute, gauge
• NOUN 1 = quantity, share, amount, allowance, portion, quota, ration, allotment 2 = action, act, step, procedure, means, control, initiative, manoeuvre 3 = gauge, rule, scale, metre, ruler, yardstick 4 = law, act, bill, legislation, resolution, statute
measured 1 = steady, even, slow, regular, dignified, stately, solemn, leisurely 2 = considered, reasoned, studied, calculated, deliberate, sober, well-thought-out
measurement = calculation, assessment, evaluation, valuation, computation, calibration, mensuration
meat = food, flesh, kai (*N.Z. informal*)
mechanical 1 = automatic, automated, mechanized, power-driven, motor-driven ≠ manual 2 = unthinking, routine, automatic, instinctive, involuntary, impersonal, cursory, perfunctory ≠ conscious
mechanism 1 = process, way, means, system, operation, agency, method, technique 2 = machine, device, tool, instrument, appliance, apparatus, contrivance
mediate = intervene, step in (*informal*), intercede, referee, umpire, reconcile, arbitrate, conciliate
mediation = arbitration, intervention, reconciliation, conciliation, intercession
mediator = negotiator, arbitrator, referee, umpire, intermediary, middleman, arbiter, peacemaker
medicine = remedy, drug, cure, prescription, medication, nostrum, medicament
mediocre = second-rate, average, ordinary, indifferent, middling, pedestrian, inferior, so-so (*informal*), half-pie (*N.Z. informal*) ≠ excellent
meditation = reflection, thought, study, musing, pondering, contemplation, rumination, cogitation
medium ADJECTIVE = average, mean, middle, middling, fair, intermediate, midway, mediocre ≠ extraordinary
• NOUN 1 = spiritualist, seer, clairvoyant, fortune teller, channeller 2 = middle, mean, centre, average, compromise, midpoint
meet 1 = encounter, come across, run into, happen on, find, contact, confront, bump into (*informal*) ≠ avoid 2 = gather, collect, assemble, get together, come together, muster, convene, congregate ≠ disperse 3 = fulfil, match (up to), answer, satisfy,

discharge, comply with, come up to, conform to ≠ fall short of **4** = experience, face, suffer, bear, go through, encounter, endure, undergo **5** = converge, join, cross, touch, connect, come together, link up, intersect ≠ diverge

meeting **1** = conference, gathering, assembly, congress, session, convention, get-together (*informal*), reunion, hui (*N.Z.*) **2** = encounter, introduction, confrontation, engagement, rendezvous, tryst, assignation

melancholy ADJECTIVE = sad, depressed, miserable, gloomy, glum, mournful, despondent, dispirited ≠ happy
• NOUN = sadness, depression, misery, gloom, sorrow, unhappiness, despondency, dejection ≠ happiness

mellow ADJECTIVE **1** = full-flavoured, rich, sweet, delicate **2** = ripe, mature, ripened ≠ unripe
• VERB **1** = relax, improve, settle, calm, mature, soften, sweeten **2** = season, develop, improve, ripen

melody **1** = tune, song, theme, air, music, strain **2** = tunefulness, harmony, musicality, euphony, melodiousness

melt **1** = dissolve, run, soften, fuse, thaw, defrost, liquefy, unfreeze **2** *often with* ***away*** = disappear, fade, vanish, dissolve, disperse, evaporate, evanesce **3** = soften, relax, disarm, mollify

member = representative, associate, supporter, fellow, subscriber, comrade, disciple

membership **1** = participation, belonging, fellowship, enrolment **2** = members, body, associates, fellows

memoir = account, life, record, journal, essay, biography, narrative, monograph

memoirs = autobiography, diary, life story, experiences, memories, journals, recollections, reminiscences

memorable = noteworthy, celebrated, historic, striking, famous, significant, remarkable, notable ≠ forgettable

memorandum = note, minute, message, communication, reminder, memo, jotting

memorial NOUN = monument, shrine, plaque, cenotaph
• ADJECTIVE = commemorative, remembrance, monumental

memory **1** = recall, mind, retention, ability to remember, powers of recall, powers of retention **2** = recollection, reminder, reminiscence, impression, echo, remembrance **3** = commemoration, respect, honour, recognition, tribute, remembrance, observance

menace NOUN **1** (*Informal*) = nuisance, plague, pest, annoyance, troublemaker **2** = threat, warning, intimidation, ill-omen, ominousness
• VERB = bully, threaten, intimidate, terrorize, frighten, scare

menacing = threatening, frightening, forbidding, looming, intimidating, ominous, louring *or* lowering ≠ encouraging

mend VERB **1** = repair, fix, restore, renew, patch up, renovate, refit, retouch **2** = darn, repair, patch, stitch, sew **3** = heal, improve, recover, get better, be all right, be cured, recuperate, pull through **4** = improve, reform, correct, revise, amend, rectify, ameliorate, emend
• PHRASES **on the mend** = convalescent, improving, recovering, getting better, recuperating

mental **1** = intellectual, rational, theoretical, cognitive, brain, conceptual, cerebral **2** (*Informal*) = insane, mad, disturbed, unstable, mentally ill, psychotic, unbalanced, deranged

mentality = attitude, character, personality, psychology, make-up, outlook, disposition, cast of mind

mentally = psychologically, intellectually, inwardly

mention VERB = refer to, point out, bring up, state, reveal, declare, disclose, intimate
• NOUN **1** *often with* ***of*** = reference to, observation, indication, remark on, allusion to **2** = acknowledgment, recognition, tribute, citation, honourable mention

mentor = guide, teacher, coach, adviser, tutor, instructor, counsellor, guru

menu = bill of fare, tariff (*chiefly Brit.*), set menu, table d'hôte, carte du jour (*French*)

merchandise = goods, produce, stock, products, commodities, wares

merchant = tradesman, dealer, trader, broker, retailer, supplier, seller, salesman

mercy **1** = compassion, pity, forgiveness, grace, kindness, clemency, leniency, forbearance ≠ cruelty **2** = blessing, boon, godsend

mere **1** = simple, nothing more than, common, plain, pure **2** = bare, slender, trifling, meagre, just, only, basic, no more than

merge **1** = combine, blend, fuse, amalgamate, unite, join, mix, mingle ≠ separate **2** = join, unite, combine, fuse ≠ separate **3** = melt, blend, mingle

merger = union, fusion, consolidation, amalgamation, combination, coalition, incorporation

merit NOUN = advantage, value, quality, worth, strength, asset, virtue, strong point
• VERB = deserve, warrant, be entitled to, earn, have a right to, be worthy of

merry **1** = cheerful, happy, carefree, jolly, festive, joyous, convivial, blithe ≠ gloomy **2** (*Brit. informal*) = tipsy, happy, mellow, tiddly (*slang, chiefly Brit.*), squiffy (*Brit. informal*)

mesh NOUN = net, netting, network, web, tracery
• VERB = engage, combine, connect, knit, coordinate, interlock, dovetail, harmonize

mess NOUN **1** = untidiness, disorder, confusion, chaos, litter, clutter, disarray, jumble **2** = shambles **3** = difficulty, dilemma, plight, hole (*informal*), fix (*informal*), jam (*informal*), muddle, pickle (*informal*), uphill (*S. African*)
• PHRASES **mess about** *or* **around** = potter about, dabble, amuse yourself, fool about *or* around, muck about *or* around (*informal*), play about *or* around, trifle ◆ **mess something up** **1** = botch, muck something up (*Brit. slang*), muddle something up **2** = dirty, pollute, clutter, disarrange, dishevel ◆ **mess with something** *or* **someone** = interfere, play, fiddle (*informal*), tamper, tinker, meddle

message **1** = communication, note, bulletin, word, letter, dispatch, memorandum, communiqué **2** = point, meaning, idea, moral, theme, import, purport

messenger = courier, runner, carrier, herald, envoy, go-between, emissary, delivery boy

messy **1** = disorganized, sloppy (*informal*), untidy **2** = dirty **3** = untidy, disordered, chaotic, muddled, cluttered, shambolic, disorganized ≠ tidy **4** = dishevelled, ruffled, untidy, rumpled, bedraggled, tousled, uncombed **5** = confusing, difficult, complex, confused, tangled, chaotic, tortuous

metaphor = figure of speech, image, symbol, analogy, conceit (*literary*), allegory, trope, figurative expression

method **1** = manner, process, approach, technique, way, system, style, procedure **2** = orderliness, planning, order, system, purpose, pattern, organization, regularity

midday = noon, twelve o'clock, noonday

middle NOUN = centre, heart, midst, halfway point, midpoint, midsection
• ADJECTIVE **1** = central, medium, mid, intervening, halfway, intermediate, median **2** = intermediate, intervening

middle-class = bourgeois, traditional, conventional

middling **1** = mediocre, all right, indifferent, so-so (*informal*), unremarkable, tolerable, run-of-the-mill, passable, half-pie (*N.Z. informal*) **2** = moderate, medium, average, fair, ordinary, modest, adequate

midnight = twelve o'clock, middle of the night, dead of night, the witching hour

midst
PHRASES **in the midst of** = among, during, in the middle of, surrounded by, amidst, in the thick of

midway ADJECTIVE *or* ADVERB = halfway, in the middle of, part-way, equidistant, at the midpoint, betwixt and between

might NOUN = power, force, energy, strength, vigour
• PHRASES **with all your might** = forcefully, vigorously, mightily, manfully, lustily

mighty = powerful, strong, strapping, robust, vigorous, sturdy, forceful, lusty ≠ weak

migrant NOUN = wanderer, immigrant, traveller, rover, nomad, emigrant, itinerant, drifter
• ADJECTIVE = itinerant, wandering, drifting, roving, travelling, shifting, immigrant, transient

migrate = move, travel, journey, wander, trek, voyage, roam, emigrate

migration = wandering, journey, voyage, travel, movement, trek, emigration, roving

mild **1** = gentle, calm, easy-going, meek, placid, docile, peaceable, equable ≠ harsh **2** = temperate, warm, calm, moderate,

tranquil, balmy ≠ cold **3** = bland, thin, smooth, tasteless, insipid, flavourless
militant = aggressive, active, vigorous, assertive, combative ≠ peaceful
military ADJECTIVE = warlike, armed, soldierly, martial
• NOUN = armed forces, forces, services, army
milk = exploit, pump, take advantage of
RELATED WORD
adjective: lactic
mill NOUN **1** = grinder, crusher, quern **2** = factory, works, plant, workshop, foundry
• VERB = grind, pound, crush, powder, grate
• PHRASES **mill about** *or* **around** = swarm, crowd, stream, surge, throng
mimic VERB = imitate, do (*informal*), take off (*informal*), ape, parody, caricature, impersonate
• NOUN = imitator, impressionist, copycat (*informal*), impersonator, caricaturist
mince **1** = cut, grind, crumble, dice, hash, chop up **2** = tone down, spare, moderate, weaken, soften
mincing = affected, camp (*informal*), precious, pretentious, dainty, sissy, effeminate, foppish
mind NOUN **1** = memory, recollection, remembrance, powers of recollection **2** = intelligence, reason, reasoning, understanding, sense, brain(s) (*informal*), wits, intellect **3** = intention, wish, desire, urge, fancy, leaning, notion, inclination **4** = sanity, reason, senses, judgment, wits, marbles (*informal*), rationality, mental balance
• VERB **1** = take offence at, dislike, care about, object to, resent, disapprove of, be bothered by, be affronted by **2** = be careful, watch, take care, be wary, be cautious, be on your guard **3** = look after, watch, protect, tend, guard, take care of, attend to, keep an eye on **4** = pay attention to, mark, note, listen to, observe, obey, heed, take heed of
RELATED WORD
adjective: mental
mine NOUN **1** = pit, deposit, shaft, colliery, excavation **2** = source, store, fund, stock, supply, reserve, treasury, wealth
• VERB = dig up, extract, quarry, unearth, excavate, hew, dig for
miner = coalminer, pitman (*Brit.*), collier (*Brit.*)
mingle **1** = mix, combine, blend, merge, unite, join, interweave, intermingle ≠ separate **2** = associate, consort, socialize, rub shoulders (*informal*), hobnob, fraternize, hang about *or* around ≠ dissociate
miniature = small, little, minute, tiny, toy, scaled-down, diminutive, minuscule ≠ giant
minimal = minimum, smallest, least, slightest, token, nominal, negligible, least possible
minimize **1** = reduce, decrease, shrink, diminish, prune, curtail, miniaturize ≠ increase **2** = play down, discount, belittle, disparage, decry, underrate, deprecate, make light *or* little of ≠ praise
minimum ADJECTIVE = lowest, smallest, least, slightest, minimal, least possible ≠ maximum
• NOUN = lowest, least, lowest level, nadir
minister NOUN = clergyman, priest, vicar, parson, preacher, pastor, cleric, rector
• VERB *often with* ***to*** = attend, serve, tend, take care of, cater to, pander to, administer to
ministry **1** = department, office, bureau, government department **2** = administration, council **3** = the priesthood, the church, the cloth, holy orders
minor = small, lesser, slight, petty, trivial, insignificant, unimportant, inconsequential ≠ major
mint = make, produce, strike, cast, stamp, punch, coin
minute[1] NOUN = moment, second, bit, flash, instant, tick (*Brit. informal*), sec (*informal*), short time
• PLURAL NOUN = record, notes, proceedings, transactions, transcript, memorandum
minute[2] **1** = small, little, tiny, miniature, microscopic, diminutive, minuscule, infinitesimal ≠ huge **2** = precise, close, detailed, critical, exact, meticulous, exhaustive, painstaking ≠ imprecise
miracle = wonder, phenomenon, sensation, marvel, amazing achievement, astonishing feat
miraculous = wonderful, amazing, extraordinary, incredible, astonishing,

unbelievable, phenomenal, astounding ≠ ordinary

mirror NOUN = looking-glass, glass (*Brit.*), reflector
• VERB = reflect, follow, copy, echo, emulate

miscarriage = failure, error, breakdown, mishap, perversion

misconduct = immorality, wrongdoing, mismanagement, malpractice, impropriety

miserable 1 = sad, depressed, gloomy, forlorn, dejected, despondent, sorrowful, wretched ≠ happy 2 = pathetic, sorry, shameful, despicable, deplorable, lamentable ≠ respectable

misery 1 = unhappiness, distress, despair, grief, suffering, depression, gloom, torment ≠ happiness 2 (*Brit. informal*) = moaner, pessimist, killjoy, spoilsport, prophet of doom, wet blanket (*informal*), sourpuss (*informal*), wowser (*Austral. & N.Z. slang*)

misfortune 1 *often plural* = bad luck, adversity, hard luck, ill luck, infelicity 2 = mishap, trouble, disaster, reverse, tragedy, setback, calamity, affliction ≠ good luck

misguided = unwise, mistaken, misplaced, deluded, ill-advised, imprudent, injudicious

mislead = deceive, fool, delude, take someone in (*informal*), misdirect, misinform, hoodwink, misguide

misleading = confusing, false, ambiguous, deceptive, evasive, disingenuous ≠ straightforward

miss VERB 1 = fail to notice, overlook, pass over 2 = long for, yearn for, pine for, long to see, ache for, feel the loss of, regret the absence of 3 = not go to, skip, cut, omit, be absent from, fail to attend, skive off (*informal*), play truant from, bludge (*Austral. & N.Z. informal*) 4 = avoid, beat, escape, skirt, duck, cheat, bypass, dodge
• NOUN = mistake, failure, error, blunder, omission, oversight

missile = projectile, weapon, shell, rocket

missing = lost, misplaced, not present, astray, unaccounted for, mislaid

mission = task, job, commission, duty, undertaking, quest, assignment, vocation

missionary = evangelist, preacher, apostle

mist = fog, cloud, steam, spray, film, haze, vapour, smog

mistake NOUN 1 = error, blunder, oversight, slip, gaffe (*informal*), miscalculation, faux pas 2 = oversight, error, slip, fault, howler (*informal*), erratum
• VERB 1 = confuse with, take for, mix up with 2 = misunderstand, misinterpret, misjudge, misread, misconstrue, misapprehend

mistaken 1 = wrong, incorrect, misguided, wide of the mark ≠ correct 2 = inaccurate, false, faulty, erroneous, unsound ≠ accurate

mistress = lover, girlfriend, concubine, kept woman, paramour

misunderstand 1 = misinterpret, misread, mistake, misjudge, misconstrue, misapprehend, be at cross-purposes with 2 = miss the point, get the wrong end of the stick

misunderstanding = mistake, error, mix-up, misconception, misinterpretation, misjudgment

misuse NOUN 1 = waste, squandering 2 = abuse 3 = misapplication, abuse, illegal use, wrong use 4 = perversion, desecration 5 = misapplication
• VERB 1 = abuse, misapply, prostitute 2 = waste, squander, embezzle, misappropriate

mix VERB 1 = combine, blend, merge, join, cross, fuse, mingle, jumble 2 = socialize, associate, hang out (*informal*), mingle, circulate, consort, hobnob, fraternize 3 *often with* ***up*** = combine, marry, blend, integrate, amalgamate, coalesce, meld
• NOUN = mixture, combination, blend, fusion, compound, assortment, alloy, medley
• PHRASES **mix something up** 1 = confuse, scramble, muddle, confound 2 = blend, beat, mix, stir, fold

mixed 1 = varied, diverse, different, differing, cosmopolitan, assorted, jumbled, disparate ≠ homogeneous 2 = combined, blended, united, compound, composite, mingled, amalgamated ≠ pure

mixed-up = confused, disturbed, puzzled, bewildered, at sea, upset, distraught, muddled

mixture 1 = blend, mix, variety, fusion, assortment, brew, jumble, medley 2 = composite, compound 3 = cross,

combination, blend **4** = concoction, compound, blend, brew, amalgam
mix-up = confusion, mistake, misunderstanding, mess, tangle, muddle
moan VERB **1** = groan, sigh, sob, whine, lament **2** (*Informal*) = grumble, complain, groan, whine, carp, grouse, whinge (*informal*), bleat
• NOUN **1** = groan, sigh, sob, lament, wail, grunt, whine **2** (*Informal*) = complaint, protest, grumble, whine, grouse, gripe (*informal*), grouch (*informal*)
mob NOUN **1** = crowd, pack, mass, host, drove, flock, swarm, horde **2** (*Slang*) = gang, group, set, lot, crew (*informal*)
• VERB = surround, besiege, jostle, fall on, set upon, crowd around, swarm around
mobile = movable, moving, travelling, wandering, portable, itinerant, peripatetic
mobilize **1** = rally, organize, stimulate, excite, prompt, marshal, activate, awaken **2** = deploy, prepare, ready, rally, assemble, call up, marshal, muster
mock VERB = laugh at, tease, ridicule, taunt, scorn, sneer, scoff, deride ≠ respect
• ADJECTIVE = imitation, pretended, artificial, fake, false, dummy, sham, feigned ≠ genuine
mocking = scornful, scoffing, satirical, contemptuous, sarcastic, sardonic, disrespectful, disdainful
mode **1** = method, way, system, form, process, style, technique, manner **2** = fashion, style, trend, rage, vogue, look, craze
model NOUN **1** = representation, image, copy, miniature, dummy, replica, imitation, duplicate **2** = pattern, example, standard, original, ideal, prototype, paradigm, archetype **3** = sitter, subject, poser
• VERB **1** = show off (*informal*), wear, display, sport **2** = shape, form, design, fashion, carve, mould, sculpt
moderate ADJECTIVE **1** = mild, reasonable, controlled, limited, steady, modest, restrained, middle-of-the-road ≠ extreme **2** = average, middling, fair, ordinary, indifferent, mediocre, so-so (*informal*), passable, half-pie (*N.Z. informal*)
• VERB **1** = soften, control, temper, regulate, curb, restrain, subdue, lessen **2** = lessen, ease ≠ intensify
modern **1** = current, contemporary, recent, present-day, latter-day **2** = up-to-date, fresh, new, novel, newfangled ≠ old-fashioned
modest **1** = moderate, small, limited, fair, ordinary, middling, meagre, frugal **2** = unpretentious, reserved, retiring, shy, coy, reticent, self-effacing, demure
modesty = reserve, humility, shyness, reticence, timidity, diffidence, coyness, bashfulness ≠ conceit
modification = change, variation, qualification, adjustment, revision, alteration, refinement
modify **1** = change, reform, convert, alter, adjust, adapt, revise, remodel **2** = tone down, lower, qualify, ease, moderate, temper, soften, restrain
mogul = tycoon, baron, magnate, big shot (*informal*), big noise (*informal*), big hitter (*informal*), heavy hitter (*informal*), V.I.P.
moist = damp, wet, soggy, humid, clammy, dewy
moisture = damp, water, liquid, dew, wetness
molecule = particle, jot, speck
moment **1** = instant, second, flash, twinkling, split second, jiffy (*informal*), trice **2** = time, point, stage, juncture
momentous = significant, important, vital, critical, crucial, historic, pivotal, fateful ≠ unimportant
momentum = impetus, force, power, drive, push, energy, strength, thrust
monarch = ruler, king *or* queen, sovereign, tsar, potentate, emperor *or* empress, prince *or* princess
monarchy **1** = sovereignty, autocracy, kingship, royalism, monocracy **2** = kingdom, empire, realm, principality
monastery = abbey, convent, priory, cloister, nunnery, friary
monetary = financial, money, economic, capital, cash, fiscal, budgetary, pecuniary
money = cash, capital, currency, hard cash, readies (*informal*), riches, silver, coin
monitor VERB = check, follow, watch, survey, observe, keep an eye on, keep track of, keep tabs on
• NOUN **1** = guide, observer, supervisor, invigilator **2** = prefect (*Brit.*), head girl, head boy, senior boy, senior girl
monk (*Loosely*) = friar, brother

RELATED WORD
adjective: monastic

monkey **1** = simian, ape, primate

2 = rascal, horror, devil, rogue, imp, tyke, scallywag, scamp, nointer (*Austral. slang*)
RELATED WORD
adjective: simian

monster NOUN 1 = giant, mammoth, titan, colossus, monstrosity 2 = brute, devil, beast, demon, villain, fiend
• ADJECTIVE = huge, massive, enormous, tremendous, immense, gigantic, mammoth, colossal

monstrous 1 = outrageous, shocking, foul, intolerable, disgraceful, scandalous, inhuman, diabolical ≠ decent 2 = huge, massive, enormous, tremendous, immense, mammoth, colossal, prodigious ≠ tiny 3 = unnatural, horrible, hideous, grotesque, gruesome, frightful, freakish, fiendish ≠ normal

monument = memorial, cairn, marker, shrine, tombstone, mausoleum, commemoration, headstone

monumental 1 = important, significant, enormous, historic, memorable, awesome, majestic, unforgettable ≠ unimportant 2 (*Informal*) = immense, great, massive, staggering, colossal ≠ tiny

mood = state of mind, spirit, humour, temper, disposition, frame of mind

moody 1 = changeable, volatile, unpredictable, erratic, fickle, temperamental, impulsive, mercurial ≠ stable 2 = sulky, irritable, temperamental, touchy, ill-tempered, tooshie (*Austral. slang*) ≠ cheerful 3 = gloomy, sad, sullen, glum, morose ≠ cheerful 4 = sad, gloomy, melancholy, sombre

moon NOUN = satellite
• VERB = idle, drift, loaf, languish, waste time, daydream, mope
RELATED WORD
adjective: lunar

moor[1] = moorland, fell (*Brit.*), heath

moor[2] = tie up, secure, anchor, dock, lash, berth, make fast

mop NOUN 1 = squeegee, sponge, swab 2 = mane, shock, mass, tangle, mat, thatch
• VERB = clean, wash, wipe, sponge, swab

moral ADJECTIVE = good, just, right, principled, decent, noble, ethical, honourable ≠ immoral
• NOUN = lesson, meaning, point, message, teaching, import, significance, precept
• PLURAL NOUN = morality, standards, conduct, principles, behaviour, manners, habits, ethics

morale = confidence, heart, spirit, self-esteem, team spirit, esprit de corps

morality 1 = virtue, justice, morals, honour, integrity, goodness, honesty, decency 2 = ethics, conduct, principles, morals, manners, philosophy, mores 3 = rights and wrongs, ethics

moratorium = postponement, freeze, halt, suspension, standstill

more ADJECTIVE = extra, additional, new, other, added, further, new-found, supplementary
• ADVERB 1 = to a greater extent, longer, better, further, some more 2 = moreover, also, in addition, besides, furthermore, what's more, on top of that, to boot

moreover = furthermore, also, further, in addition, too, as well, besides, additionally

morning 1 = before noon, forenoon, morn (*poetic*), a.m. 2 = dawn, sunrise, first light, daybreak, break of day

mortal ADJECTIVE 1 = human, worldly, passing, fleshly, temporal, transient, ephemeral, perishable 2 = fatal, killing, terminal, deadly, destructive, lethal, murderous, death-dealing
• NOUN = human being, being, man, woman, person, human, individual, earthling

mortality 1 = humanity, transience, impermanence, corporeality, impermanency 2 = death, dying, fatality

mostly 1 = mainly, largely, chiefly, principally, primarily, on the whole, predominantly 2 = generally, usually, on the whole, as a rule

mother NOUN = female parent, mum (*Brit. informal*), ma (*informal*), mater, dam, mummy (*Brit. informal*), foster mother, biological mother
• VERB = nurture, raise, protect, tend, nurse, rear, care for, cherish
• ADJECTIVE = native, natural, innate, inborn
RELATED WORD
adjective: maternal

motherly = maternal, loving, caring, comforting, sheltering, protective, affectionate

motif 1 = design, shape, decoration, ornament 2 = theme, idea, subject, concept, leitmotif

motion NOUN 1 = movement,

mobility, travel, progress, flow, locomotion **2** = proposal, suggestion, recommendation, proposition, submission • **VERB** = gesture, direct, wave, signal, nod, beckon, gesticulate

motivate **1** = inspire, drive, stimulate, move, cause, prompt, stir, induce **2** = stimulate, drive, inspire, stir, arouse, galvanize, incentivize

motivation = incentive, inspiration, motive, stimulus, reason, spur, inducement, incitement

motive = reason, ground(s), purpose, object, incentive, inspiration, stimulus, rationale

motto = saying, slogan, maxim, rule, adage, proverb, dictum, precept

mould[1] **NOUN 1** = cast, shape, pattern **2** = design, style, fashion, build, form, kind, shape, pattern **3** = nature, character, sort, kind, quality, type, stamp, calibre • **VERB 1** = shape, make, work, form, create, model, fashion, construct **2** = influence, make, form, control, direct, affect, shape

mould[2] = fungus, blight, mildew

mound **1** = heap, pile, drift, stack, rick **2** = hill, bank, rise, dune, embankment, knoll, hillock, kopje *or* koppie (*S. African*)

mount **VERB 1** = increase, build, grow, swell, intensify, escalate, multiply ≠ decrease **2** = accumulate, increase, collect, gather, build up, pile up, amass **3** = ascend, scale, climb (up), go up, clamber up ≠ descend **4** = get (up) on, jump on, straddle, climb onto, hop on to, bestride, get on the back of ≠ get off **5** = display, present, prepare, put on, organize, put on display • **NOUN 1** = horse, steed (*literary*) **2** = backing, setting, support, stand, base, frame

mountain **1** = peak, mount, horn, ridge, fell (*Brit.*), berg (*S. African*), alp, pinnacle **2** = heap, mass, masses, pile, a great deal, ton, stack, abundance

mourn **1** *often with* ***for*** = grieve for, lament, weep for, wail for **2** = bemoan, rue, deplore, bewail

mourning **1** = grieving, grief, bereavement, weeping, woe, lamentation **2** = black, sackcloth and ashes, widow's weeds

mouth **1** = lips, jaws, gob (*slang, esp. Brit.*), maw, cakehole (*Brit. slang*) **2** = entrance, opening, gateway, door, aperture, orifice **3** = opening **4** = inlet, outlet, estuary, firth, outfall, debouchment

RELATED WORD
adjective: oral

move **VERB 1** = transfer, change, switch, shift, transpose **2** = go, advance, progress, shift, proceed, stir, budge, make a move **3** = relocate, leave, remove, quit, migrate, emigrate, decamp, up sticks (*Brit. informal*) **4** = drive, cause, influence, persuade, shift, inspire, prompt, induce ≠ discourage **5** = touch, affect, excite, impress, stir, disquiet **6** = propose, suggest, urge, recommend, request, advocate, submit, put forward • **NOUN 1** = action, step, manoeuvre **2** = ploy, action, measure, step, initiative, stroke, tactic, manoeuvre **3** = transfer, posting, shift, removal, relocation **4** = turn, go, play, chance, shot (*informal*), opportunity

movement **1** = group, party, organization, grouping, front, faction **2** = campaign, drive, push, crusade **3** = move, action, motion, manoeuvre **4** = activity, moving, stirring, bustle **5** = advance, progress, flow **6** = transfer, transportation, displacement **7** = development, change, variation, fluctuation **8** = progression, progress **9** (*Music*) = section, part, division, passage

movie = film, picture, feature, flick (*slang*)

moving **1** = emotional, touching, affecting, inspiring, stirring, poignant ≠ unemotional **2** = mobile, running, active, going, operational, in motion, driving, kinetic ≠ stationary

mow **VERB** = cut, crop, trim, shear, scythe • **PHRASES** **mow something** *or* **someone down** = massacre, butcher, slaughter, cut down, shoot down, cut to pieces

much **ADVERB 1** = greatly, a lot, considerably, decidedly, exceedingly, appreciably ≠ hardly **2** = often, a lot, routinely, a great deal, many times, habitually, on many occasions, customarily • **DETERMINER** = great, a lot of, plenty of, considerable, substantial, piles of (*informal*), ample, abundant ≠ little • **PRONOUN** = a lot, plenty, a great deal, lots (*informal*), masses (*informal*), loads (*informal*), tons (*informal*), heaps (*informal*) ≠ little

muck 1 = dirt, mud, filth, ooze, sludge, mire, slime, gunge (*informal*), kak (*S. African informal*) 2 = manure, dung, ordure
mud = dirt, clay, ooze, silt, sludge, mire, slime
muddle NOUN = confusion, mess, disorder, chaos, tangle, mix-up, disarray, predicament
• VERB 1 = jumble, disorder, scramble, tangle, mix up 2 = confuse, bewilder, daze, confound, perplex, disorient, stupefy, befuddle
muddy 1 = boggy, swampy, marshy, quaggy 2 = dirty, soiled, grimy, mucky, mud-caked, bespattered
mug¹ = cup, pot, beaker, tankard
mug² (*Informal*) 1 = face, features, countenance, visage 2 = fool, sucker (*slang*), chump (*informal*), simpleton, easy *or* soft touch (*slang*), dorba *or* dorb (*Austral. slang*), bogan (*Austral. slang*)
mug³ VERB = attack, assault, beat up, rob, set about *or* upon
• PHRASES **mug up (on) something** = study, cram (*informal*), bone up on (*informal*), swot up on (*Brit. informal*)
multiple = many, several, various, numerous, sundry, manifold, multitudinous
multiply 1 = increase, extend, expand, spread, build up, proliferate ≠ decrease 2 = reproduce, breed, propagate
multitude 1 = great number, host, army, mass, horde, myriad 2 = crowd, host, mass, mob, swarm, horde, throng
mundane 1 = ordinary, routine, commonplace, banal, everyday, day-to-day, prosaic, humdrum ≠ extraordinary 2 = earthly, worldly, secular, mortal, terrestrial, temporal ≠ spiritual
municipal = civic, public, local, council, district, urban, metropolitan
murder NOUN = killing, homicide, massacre, assassination, slaying, bloodshed, carnage, butchery
• VERB = kill, massacre, slaughter, assassinate, eliminate (*slang*), butcher, slay, bump off (*slang*)
murderer = killer, assassin, slayer, butcher, slaughterer, cut-throat, hit man (*slang*)
murderous = deadly, savage, brutal, cruel, lethal, ferocious, cut-throat, bloodthirsty
murky 1 = dark, gloomy, grey, dull, dim, cloudy, misty, overcast ≠ bright 2 = dark, cloudy
murmur VERB = mumble, whisper, mutter
• NOUN = whisper, drone, purr
muscle NOUN 1 = tendon, sinew 2 = strength, might, power, weight, stamina, brawn
• PHRASES **muscle in** (*Informal*) = impose yourself, encroach, butt in, force your way in
muscular = strong, powerful, athletic, strapping, robust, vigorous, sturdy, sinewy
muse = ponder, consider, reflect, contemplate, deliberate, brood, meditate, mull over
musical = melodious, lyrical, harmonious, melodic, tuneful, dulcet, sweet-sounding, euphonious ≠ discordant
must = necessity, essential, requirement, fundamental, imperative, requisite, prerequisite, sine qua non (*Latin*)
muster VERB 1 = summon up, marshal 2 = rally, gather, assemble, marshal, mobilize, call together 3 = assemble, convene
• NOUN = assembly, meeting, collection, gathering, rally, convention, congregation, roundup, hui (*N.Z.*), runanga (*N.Z.*)
mutation 1 = anomaly, variation, deviant, freak of nature 2 = change, variation, evolution, transformation, modification, alteration, metamorphosis, transfiguration
mute 1 = close-mouthed, silent 2 = silent, dumb, unspoken, tacit, wordless, voiceless, unvoiced 3 = dumb, speechless, voiceless
mutter = grumble, complain, murmur, rumble, whine, mumble, grouse, bleat
mutual = shared, common, joint, returned, reciprocal, interchangeable, requited
myriad NOUN = multitude, host, army, swarm, horde
• ADJECTIVE = innumerable, countless, untold, incalculable, immeasurable, multitudinous
mysterious 1 = strange, puzzling, secret, weird, perplexing, uncanny, mystifying, arcane ≠ clear 2 = secretive, enigmatic, evasive, discreet, covert, reticent, furtive, inscrutable
mystery = puzzle, problem, question, secret, riddle, enigma, conundrum, teaser
mystic *or* **mystical** = supernatural, mysterious, transcendental, occult, metaphysical, paranormal, inscrutable,

otherworldly
myth **1** = legend, story, fiction, saga, fable, allegory, fairy story, folk tale **2** = illusion, story, fancy, fantasy, imagination, invention, delusion, superstition
mythology = legend, folklore, tradition, lore

n

nab = catch, arrest, apprehend, seize, grab, capture, collar (*informal*), snatch
nag[1] VERB = scold, harass, badger, pester, worry, plague, hassle (*informal*), upbraid
• NOUN = scold, complainer, grumbler, virago, shrew, tartar, moaner, harpy
nag[2] = horse (*U.S.*), hack
nagging **1** = continuous, persistent, continual, niggling, repeated, constant, endless, perpetual **2** = scolding, shrewish
nail NOUN **1** = tack, spike, rivet, hobnail, brad (*technical*) **2** = fingernail, toenail, talon, thumbnail, claw
• VERB **1** = fasten, fix, secure, attach, pin, hammer, tack **2** (*informal*) = catch, arrest, capture, apprehend, trap, snare, ensnare, entrap
naive *or* **naïve** = gullible, trusting, credulous, unsuspicious, green, simple, innocent, callow ≠ worldly
naked = nude, stripped, exposed, bare, undressed, starkers (*informal*), stark-naked, unclothed ≠ dressed
name NOUN = title, nickname, designation, term, handle (*slang*), epithet, sobriquet, moniker *or* monicker (*slang*)
• VERB **1** = call, christen, baptize, dub, term, style, label, entitle **2** = nominate, choose, select, appoint, specify, designate
namely = specifically, to wit, viz.
nap[1] NOUN = sleep, rest, kip (*Brit. slang*), siesta, catnap, forty winks (*informal*)
• VERB = sleep, rest, drop off (*informal*), doze, kip (*Brit. slang*), snooze (*informal*), nod off (*informal*), catnap
nap[2] = pile, down, fibre, weave, grain
napkin = serviette, cloth
narcotic NOUN = drug, anaesthetic, painkiller, sedative, opiate, tranquillizer, anodyne, analgesic
• ADJECTIVE = sedative, calming, hypnotic, analgesic, soporific, painkilling
narrative = story, report, history, account, statement, tale, chronicle
narrator = storyteller, writer, author, reporter, commentator, chronicler
narrow ADJECTIVE **1** = thin, fine, slim, slender, tapering, attenuated ≠ broad **2** = limited, restricted, confined, tight, close, meagre, constricted ≠ wide **3** = insular, prejudiced, partial, dogmatic, intolerant, narrow-minded, small-minded, illiberal ≠ broad-minded
• VERB **1** = restrict, limit, reduce, constrict **2** = get narrower, taper, shrink, tighten, constrict
narrowly = just, barely, only just, scarcely, by the skin of your teeth
nasty **1** = unpleasant, ugly, disagreeable ≠ pleasant **2** = spiteful, mean, offensive, vicious, unpleasant, vile, malicious, despicable ≠ pleasant **3** = disgusting, unpleasant, offensive, vile, distasteful, obnoxious, objectionable, disagreeable, festy (*Austral. slang*), yucko (*Austral. slang*) **4** = serious, bad, dangerous, critical, severe, painful
nation **1** = country, state, realm **2** = public, people, society
national ADJECTIVE = nationwide, public, widespread, countrywide
• NOUN = citizen, subject, resident, native, inhabitant
nationalism = patriotism, loyalty to your country, chauvinism, jingoism, allegiance
nationality **1** = citizenship, birth **2** = race, nation
nationwide = national, general, widespread, countrywide
native ADJECTIVE = mother, indigenous, vernacular
• NOUN = inhabitant, national, resident, citizen, countryman, aborigine (*often offensive*), dweller
natural **1** = logical, valid, legitimate **2** = normal, common, regular, usual, ordinary, typical, everyday ≠ abnormal **3** = innate, native, characteristic, inherent, instinctive, intuitive, inborn,

essential **4** = unaffected, open, genuine, spontaneous, unpretentious, unsophisticated, dinkum (*Austral. & N.Z. informal*), ingenuous, real ≠ affected **5** = pure, plain, organic, whole, unrefined ≠ processed

naturally **1** = of course, certainly **2** = typically, simply, normally, spontaneously

nature **1** = creation, world, earth, environment, universe, cosmos, natural world **2** = quality, character, make-up, constitution, essence, complexion **3** = temperament, character, personality, disposition, outlook, mood, humour, temper **4** = kind, sort, style, type, variety, species, category, description

naughty **1** = disobedient, bad, mischievous, badly behaved, wayward, wicked, impish, refractory ≠ good **2** = obscene, vulgar, improper, lewd, risqué, smutty, ribald ≠ clean

nausea = sickness, vomiting, retching, squeamishness, queasiness, biliousness

naval = nautical, marine, maritime

navigation = sailing, voyaging, seamanship, helmsmanship

navy = fleet, flotilla, armada

near **1** = close, neighbouring, nearby, adjacent, adjoining ≠ far **2** = imminent, forthcoming, approaching, looming, impending, upcoming, nigh, in the offing ≠ far-off

nearby = neighbouring, adjacent, adjoining

nearly **1** = practically, almost, virtually, just about, as good as, well-nigh **2** = almost, approaching, roughly, just about, approximately

neat **1** = tidy, trim, orderly, spruce, shipshape, spick-and-span ≠ untidy **2** = methodical, tidy, systematic, fastidious ≠ disorganized **3** = smart, trim, tidy, spruce, dapper, natty (*informal*), well-groomed, well-turned out **4** = graceful, elegant, adept, nimble, adroit, efficient ≠ clumsy **5** = clever, efficient, handy, apt, well-judged ≠ inefficient **6** = cool, great (*informal*), excellent, brilliant, superb, fantastic (*informal*), tremendous, fabulous (*informal*), booshit (*Austral. slang*), exo (*Austral. slang*), sik (*Austral. slang*) ≠ terrible **7** (*of alcoholic drinks*) = undiluted, straight, pure, unmixed

neatly **1** = tidily, smartly, systematically, methodically, fastidiously **2** = smartly, elegantly, tidily, nattily **3** = gracefully, expertly, efficiently, adeptly, skilfully, nimbly, adroitly, dexterously **4** = cleverly, efficiently

necessarily **1** = automatically, naturally, definitely, undoubtedly, certainly **2** = inevitably, of necessity, unavoidably, incontrovertibly, nolens volens (*Latin*)

necessary **1** = needed, required, essential, vital, compulsory, mandatory, imperative, indispensable ≠ unnecessary **2** = inevitable, certain, unavoidable, inescapable ≠ avoidable

necessity NOUN **1** = essential, need, requirement, fundamental, requisite, prerequisite, sine qua non (*Latin*), desideratum **2** = inevitability, certainty
● PLURAL NOUN = essentials, needs, requirements, fundamentals

need VERB **1** = want, miss, require, lack, have to have, demand **2** = require, want, demand, call for, entail, necessitate **3** = have to, be obliged to
● NOUN **1** = requirement, demand, essential, necessity, requisite, desideratum **2** = necessity, call, demand, obligation **3** = emergency, want, necessity, urgency, exigency **4** = poverty, deprivation, destitution, penury

needed = necessary, wanted, required, lacked, called for, desired

needle = irritate, provoke, annoy, harass, taunt, nag, goad, rile

needless = unnecessary, pointless, gratuitous, useless, unwanted, redundant, superfluous, groundless ≠ essential

needy = poor, deprived, disadvantaged, impoverished, penniless, destitute, poverty-stricken, underprivileged ≠ wealthy

negative ADJECTIVE **1** = pessimistic, cynical, unwilling, gloomy, jaundiced, uncooperative ≠ optimistic **2** = dissenting, contradictory, refusing, denying, rejecting, opposing, resisting, contrary ≠ assenting
● NOUN = denial, no, refusal, rejection, contradiction

neglect VERB **1** = disregard, ignore, fail to look after ≠ look after **2** = shirk, forget, overlook, omit, evade, pass over, skimp, be remiss in *or* about **3** = fail, forget, omit
● NOUN **1** = negligence, inattention

≠ care **2** = shirking, failure, oversight, carelessness, dereliction, slackness, laxity
neglected **1** = uncared-for, abandoned, underestimated, disregarded, undervalued, unappreciated **2** = run down, derelict, overgrown, uncared-for
negligence = carelessness, neglect, disregard, dereliction, slackness, inattention, laxity, thoughtlessness
negotiate **1** = bargain, deal, discuss, debate, mediate, hold talks, cut a deal, conciliate **2** = arrange, work out, bring about, transact **3** = get round, clear, pass, cross, get over, get past, surmount
negotiation **1** = bargaining, debate, discussion, transaction, dialogue, mediation, arbitration, wheeling and dealing (*informal*) **2** = arrangement, working out, transaction, bringing about
negotiator = mediator, ambassador, diplomat, delegate, intermediary, moderator, honest broker
neighbourhood **1** = district, community, quarter, region, locality, locale **2** = vicinity, environs
neighbouring = nearby, next, near, bordering, surrounding, connecting, adjacent, adjoining ≠ remote
neighbourly = helpful, kind, friendly, obliging, harmonious, considerate, sociable, hospitable
nerve NOUN **1** = bravery, courage, bottle (*Brit. slang*), resolution, daring, guts (*informal*), pluck, grit **2** (*Informal*) = impudence, cheek (*informal*), audacity, boldness, temerity, insolence, impertinence, brazenness
• PLURAL NOUN = tension, stress, strain, anxiety, butterflies (in your stomach) (*informal*), nervousness, cold feet (*informal*), worry
• PHRASES **nerve yourself** = brace yourself, prepare yourself, steel yourself, fortify yourself, gear yourself up, gee yourself up
nervous = apprehensive, anxious, uneasy, edgy, worried, tense, fearful, uptight (*informal*), toey (*Austral. slang*) ≠ calm
nest = refuge, retreat, haunt, den, hideaway
nestle = snuggle, cuddle, huddle, curl up, nuzzle
nestling = chick, fledgling, baby bird
net[1] NOUN = mesh, netting, network, web, lattice, openwork
• VERB = catch, bag, capture, trap, entangle, ensnare, enmesh
net[2] *or* **nett** ADJECTIVE = after taxes, final, clear, take-home
• VERB = earn, make, clear, gain, realize, bring in, accumulate, reap
network **1** = web, system, arrangement, grid, lattice **2** = maze, warren, labyrinth
neurotic = unstable, nervous, disturbed, abnormal, obsessive, compulsive, manic, unhealthy ≠ rational
neutral **1** = unbiased, impartial, disinterested, even-handed, uninvolved, nonpartisan, unprejudiced, nonaligned ≠ biased **2** = expressionless, dull **3** = uncontroversial *or* noncontroversial, inoffensive **4** = colourless
never **1** = at no time, not once, not ever ≠ always **2** = under no circumstances, not at all, on no account, not ever
nevertheless = even so, still, however, yet, regardless, nonetheless, notwithstanding, in spite of that
new **1** = modern, recent, contemporary, up-to-date, latest, current, original, fresh ≠ old-fashioned **2** = brand new **3** = extra, more, added, new-found, supplementary **4** = unfamiliar, strange **5** = renewed, changed, improved, restored, altered, revitalized
newcomer **1** = new arrival, stranger **2** = beginner, novice, new arrival, parvenu, Johnny-come-lately (*informal*)
news = information, latest (*informal*), report, story, exposé, intelligence, rumour, revelation
next ADJECTIVE **1** = following, later, succeeding, subsequent **2** = adjacent, closest, nearest, neighbouring, adjoining
• ADVERB = afterwards, then, later, following, subsequently, thereafter
nice **1** = pleasant, delightful, agreeable, good, attractive, charming, pleasurable, enjoyable ≠ unpleasant **2** = kind, helpful, obliging, considerate ≠ unkind **3** = likable *or* likeable, friendly, engaging, charming, pleasant, agreeable **4** = polite, courteous, well-mannered ≠ vulgar **5** = precise, fine, careful, strict, subtle, delicate, meticulous, fastidious ≠ vague
nicely **1** = pleasantly, well, delightfully, attractively, charmingly, agreeably, acceptably, pleasurably ≠ unpleasantly

2 = kindly, politely, thoughtfully, amiably, courteously

niche 1 = recess, opening, corner, hollow, nook, alcove 2 = position, calling, place, slot (*informal*), vocation, pigeonhole (*informal*)

nick VERB 1 (*Slang*) = steal, pinch (*informal*), swipe (*slang*), pilfer 2 = cut, mark, score, chip, scratch, scar, notch, dent
• NOUN = cut, mark, scratch, chip, scar, notch, dent

nickname = pet name, label, diminutive, epithet, sobriquet, moniker *or* monicker (*slang*)

night = darkness, dark, night-time
RELATED WORD
adjective: nocturnal

nightly ADJECTIVE = nocturnal, night-time
• ADVERB = every night, nights (*informal*), each night, night after night

nightmare 1 = bad dream, hallucination 2 = ordeal, trial, hell, horror, torture, torment, tribulation, purgatory

nil 1 = nothing, love, zero 2 = zero, nothing, none, naught

nip[1] VERB 1 = pop, go, run, rush, dash 2 = bite 3 = pinch, squeeze, tweak
• PHRASES **nip something in the bud** = thwart, check, frustrate

nip[2] = dram, shot (*informal*), drop, sip, draught, mouthful, snifter (*informal*)

nirvana = paradise, peace, joy, bliss, serenity, tranquillity

no INTERJECTION = not at all, certainly not, of course not, absolutely not, never, no way, nay ≠ yes
• NOUN = refusal, rejection, denial, negation ≠ consent

noble ADJECTIVE 1 = worthy, generous, upright, honourable, virtuous, magnanimous ≠ despicable 2 = dignified, great, imposing, impressive, distinguished, splendid, stately ≠ lowly 3 = aristocratic, lordly, titled, patrician, blue-blooded, highborn ≠ humble
• NOUN = lord, peer, aristocrat, nobleman ≠ commoner

nobody PRONOUN = no-one
• NOUN = nonentity, lightweight (*informal*), zero, cipher ≠ celebrity

nod VERB 1 = incline, bow 2 = signal, indicate, motion, gesture 3 = salute, acknowledge
• NOUN 1 = signal, sign, motion, gesture, indication 2 = salute, greeting, acknowledgment

noise = sound, row, racket, clamour, din, uproar, commotion, hubbub ≠ silence, calm

noisy 1 = rowdy, strident, boisterous, vociferous, uproarious, clamorous ≠ quiet 2 = loud, piercing, deafening, tumultuous, ear-splitting, cacophonous, clamorous ≠ quiet

nominal 1 = titular, formal, purported, in name only, supposed, so-called, theoretical, professed 2 = token, small, symbolic, minimal, trivial, trifling, insignificant, inconsiderable

nominate 1 = propose, suggest, recommend, put forward 2 = appoint, name, choose, select, elect, assign, designate

nomination 1 = proposal, suggestion, recommendation 2 = appointment, election, selection, designation, choice

nominee = candidate, applicant, entrant, contestant, aspirant, runner

none 1 = not any, nothing, zero, not one, nil 2 = no-one, nobody, not one

nonetheless = nevertheless, however, yet, even so, despite that, in spite of that

non-existent *or* **nonexistent** = imaginary, fictional, mythical, unreal, hypothetical, illusory ≠ real

nonsense 1 = rubbish, hot air (*informal*), twaddle, drivel, tripe (*informal*), gibberish, claptrap (*informal*), double Dutch (*Brit. informal*), bizzo (*Austral. slang*), bull's wool (*Austral. & N.Z. slang*) ≠ sense 2 = idiocy, stupidity

non-stop *or* **nonstop** ADJECTIVE = continuous, constant, relentless, uninterrupted, endless, unbroken, interminable, incessant ≠ occasional
• ADVERB = continuously, constantly, endlessly, relentlessly, perpetually, incessantly, ceaselessly, interminably

noon NOUN = midday, high noon, noonday, twelve noon, noontide
• ADJECTIVE = midday, noonday, noontide

norm = standard, rule, pattern, average, par, criterion, benchmark, yardstick

normal 1 = usual, common, standard, average, natural, regular, ordinary, typical ≠ unusual 2 = sane, reasonable, rational, well-adjusted, compos mentis (*Latin*), in your right mind, mentally sound

normally 1 = usually, generally, commonly, regularly, typically, ordinarily, as a rule, habitually 2 = as usual, naturally, properly, conventionally, in the usual way

north ADJECTIVE = northern, polar, arctic, boreal, northerly
• ADVERB = northward(s), in a northerly direction

nose NOUN = snout, bill, beak, hooter (*slang*), proboscis
• VERB = ease forward, push, edge, shove, nudge
RELATED WORD
adjective: nasal

nostalgia = reminiscence, longing, pining, yearning, remembrance, homesickness, wistfulness

nostalgic = sentimental, longing, emotional, homesick, wistful, maudlin, regretful

notable ADJECTIVE 1 = remarkable, striking, unusual, extraordinary, outstanding, memorable, uncommon, conspicuous ≠ imperceptible 2 = prominent, famous ≠ unknown
• NOUN = celebrity, big name, dignitary, luminary, personage, V.I.P.

notably = remarkably, unusually, extraordinarily, noticeably, strikingly, singularly, outstandingly, uncommonly

notch NOUN 1 = level (*Informal*), step, degree, grade 2 = cut, nick, incision, indentation, mark, score, cleft
• VERB = cut, mark, score, nick, scratch, indent

note NOUN 1 = message, letter, communication, memo, memorandum, epistle 2 = record, reminder, memo, memorandum, jotting, minute 3 = annotation, comment, remark 4 = document, form, record, certificate 5 = symbol, mark, sign, indication, token 6 = tone, touch, trace, hint, sound
• VERB 1 = notice, see, observe, perceive 2 = bear in mind, be aware, take into account 3 = mention, record, mark, indicate, register, remark 4 = write down, record, scribble, set down, jot down

notebook = notepad, exercise book, journal, diary

noted = famous, celebrated, distinguished, well-known, prominent, acclaimed, notable, renowned ≠ unknown

nothing 1 = nought, zero, nil, not a thing, zilch (*slang*) 2 = a trifle 3 = nobody, cipher, nonentity 4 = void, emptiness, nothingness, nullity

notice VERB = observe, see, note, spot, distinguish, perceive, detect, discern ≠ overlook
• NOUN 1 = notification, warning, advice, intimation, news, communication, announcement, instruction 2 = attention, interest, note, regard, consideration, observation, scrutiny, heed ≠ oversight 3 = the sack (*informal*), dismissal, the boot (*slang*), the push (*slang*), marching orders (*informal*)

noticeable = obvious, clear, striking, plain, evident, manifest, conspicuous, perceptible

notify = inform, tell, advise, alert to, announce, warn, make known to

notion 1 = idea, view, opinion, belief, concept, impression, sentiment, inkling 2 = whim, wish, desire, fancy, impulse, inclination, caprice

notorious = infamous, disreputable, opprobrious

notoriously = infamously, disreputably

notwithstanding = despite, in spite of, regardless of

nought *or* (*Archaic or literary*) **naught** = zero, nothing, nil

nourish 1 = feed, supply, sustain, nurture 2 = encourage, support, maintain, promote, sustain, foster

nourishing = nutritious, beneficial, wholesome, nutritive

novel[1] = story, tale, fiction, romance, narrative

novel[2] = new, different, original, fresh, unusual, innovative, uncommon ≠ ordinary

novelty 1 = newness, originality, freshness, innovation, surprise, uniqueness, strangeness, unfamiliarity 2 = curiosity, rarity, oddity, wonder 3 = trinket, souvenir, memento, bauble, trifle, knick-knack

novice = beginner, pupil, amateur, newcomer, trainee, apprentice, learner, probationer ≠ expert

now ADVERB 1 = nowadays, at the moment 2 = immediately, promptly, instantly, at once, straightaway
• PHRASES **now and then** *or* **again** = occasionally, sometimes, from time

to time, on and off, intermittently, infrequently, sporadically
nowadays = now, today, at the moment, in this day and age
nucleus = centre, heart, focus, basis, core, pivot, kernel, nub
nude = naked, stripped, bare, undressed, stark-naked, disrobed, unclothed, unclad ≠ dressed
nudge VERB **1** = push, touch, dig, jog, prod, elbow, shove, poke **2** = prompt, influence, persuade, spur, prod, coax
• NOUN **1** = push, touch, dig, elbow, bump, shove, poke, jog **2** = prompting, push, encouragement, prod
nuisance = trouble, problem, trial, drag (*informal*), bother, pest, irritation, hassle (*informal*) ≠ benefit
numb ADJECTIVE **1** = unfeeling, dead, frozen, paralysed, insensitive, deadened, immobilized, torpid ≠ sensitive **2** = stupefied, deadened, unfeeling
• VERB **1** = stun, knock out, paralyse, daze **2** = deaden, freeze, dull, paralyse, immobilize, benumb
number NOUN **1** = numeral, figure, character, digit, integer **2** = amount, quantity, collection, aggregate ≠ shortage **3** = crowd, horde, multitude, throng **4** = group, set, band, crowd, gang **5** = issue, copy, edition, imprint, printing
• VERB **1** = amount to, come to, total, add up to **2** = calculate, account, reckon, compute, enumerate ≠ guess **3** = include, count
numerous = many, several, countless, lots, abundant, plentiful, innumerable, copious ≠ few
nurse 1 = look after, treat, tend, care for, take care of, minister to **2** = harbour, have, maintain, preserve, entertain, cherish **3** = breast-feed, feed, nurture, nourish, suckle, wet-nurse
nursery = crèche, kindergarten, playgroup
nurture VERB = bring up, raise, look after, rear, care for, develop ≠ neglect
• NOUN = upbringing, training, education, instruction, rearing, development
nut 1 (*Slang*) = madman, psycho (*slang*), crank (*informal*), lunatic, maniac, nutcase (*slang*) **2** (*Slang*) = head, skull
nutrition = food, nourishment, sustenance, nutriment

O

oath 1 = promise, bond, pledge, vow, word, affirmation, avowal **2** = swear word, curse, obscenity, blasphemy, expletive, four-letter word, profanity
obedience = compliance, respect, reverence, observance, subservience, submissiveness, docility ≠ disobedience
obey 1 = submit to, surrender (to), give way to, bow to, give in to, yield to, do what you are told by ≠ disobey **2** = carry out, follow, implement, act upon, carry through ≠ disregard **3** = abide by, keep, follow, comply with, observe, heed, conform to, keep to
object[1] **1** = thing, article, body, item, entity **2** = purpose, aim, end, point, plan, idea, goal, design **3** = target, victim, focus, recipient
object[2] **1** *with* ***to*** = protest against, oppose, argue against, draw the line at, take exception to, cry out against, complain against, expostulate against ≠ accept **2** = disagree, demur, remonstrate, express disapproval ≠ agree
objection = protest, opposition, complaint, doubt, dissent, outcry, protestation, scruple ≠ agreement
objective NOUN = purpose, aim, goal, end, plan, hope, idea, target
• ADJECTIVE **1** = factual, real **2** = unbiased, detached, fair, open-minded, impartial, impersonal, disinterested, even-handed ≠ subjective
objectively = impartially, neutrally, fairly, justly, without prejudice, dispassionately, with an open mind, equitably
obligation 1 = duty, compulsion **2** = task, job, duty, work, charge, role, function, mission **3** = responsibility, duty, liability, accountability, answerability
oblige 1 = compel, make, force, require, bind, constrain, necessitate, impel **2** = help, assist, benefit, please, humour, accommodate, indulge, gratify ≠ bother
obliged 1 = forced, required, bound,

compelled, duty-bound **2** = grateful, in (someone's) debt, thankful, indebted, appreciative, beholden

obliging = accommodating, kind, helpful, willing, polite, cooperative, agreeable, considerate ≠ unhelpful

obscene **1** = indecent, dirty, offensive, filthy, improper, immoral, pornographic, lewd ≠ decent **2** = offensive, shocking, evil, disgusting, outrageous, revolting, sickening, vile

obscure ADJECTIVE **1** = unknown, little-known, humble, unfamiliar, out-of-the-way, lowly, unheard-of, undistinguished ≠ famous **2** = abstruse, complex, confusing, mysterious, vague, unclear, ambiguous, enigmatic ≠ straightforward **3** = unclear, uncertain, confused, mysterious, doubtful, indeterminate ≠ well-known **4** = indistinct, vague, blurred, dark, faint, dim, gloomy, murky ≠ clear

• VERB **1** = obstruct, hinder **2** = hide, screen, mask, disguise, conceal, veil, cloak, camouflage ≠ expose

observation **1** = watching, study, survey, review, investigation, monitoring, examination, inspection **2** = comment, thought, note, statement, opinion, remark, explanation, reflection **3** = remark, comment, statement, reflection, utterance **4** = observance of, compliance with, honouring of, fulfilment of, carrying out of

observe **1** = watch, study, view, look at, check, survey, monitor, keep an eye on (*informal*) **2** = notice, see, note, discover, spot, regard, witness, distinguish **3** = remark, say, comment, state, note, reflect, mention, opine **4** = comply with, keep, follow, respect, carry out, honour, discharge, obey ≠ disregard

observer **1** = witness, viewer, spectator, looker-on, watcher, onlooker, eyewitness, bystander **2** = commentator, reporter, special correspondent **3** = monitor, watchdog, supervisor, scrutineer

obsessed = absorbed, dominated, gripped, haunted, distracted, hung up (*slang*), preoccupied ≠ indifferent

obsession = preoccupation, thing (*informal*), complex, hang-up (*informal*), mania, phobia, fetish, fixation

obsessive = compulsive, gripping, consuming, haunting, irresistible, neurotic, besetting, uncontrollable

obsolete = outdated, old, passé, old-fashioned, discarded, extinct, out of date, archaic ≠ up-to-date

obstacle **1** = obstruction, block, barrier, hurdle, snag, impediment, blockage, hindrance **2** = hindrance, bar, difficulty, barrier, handicap, hurdle, hitch, drawback, uphill (*S. African*) ≠ help

obstruct **1** = block, close, bar, plug, barricade, stop up, bung up (*informal*) **2** = hold up, stop, check, block, restrict, slow down, hamper, hinder **3** = impede, hamper, hold back, thwart, hinder ≠ help **4** = obscure, screen, cover

obtain **1** = get, gain, acquire, land, net, pick up, secure, procure ≠ lose **2** = achieve, get, gain, accomplish, attain **3** (*Formal*) = prevail, hold, exist, be the case, abound, predominate, be in force, be current

obvious = clear, plain, apparent, evident, distinct, manifest, noticeable, conspicuous ≠ unclear

obviously **1** = clearly, of course, without doubt, assuredly **2** = plainly, patently, undoubtedly, evidently, manifestly, markedly, without doubt, unquestionably

occasion NOUN **1** = time, moment, point, stage, instance, juncture **2** = function, event, affair, do (*informal*), happening, experience, gathering, celebration **3** = opportunity, chance, time, opening, window **4** = reason, cause, call, ground(s), excuse, incentive, motive, justification

• VERB (*Formal*) = cause, produce, lead to, inspire, result in, generate, prompt, provoke

occasional = infrequent, odd, rare, irregular, sporadic, intermittent, few and far between, periodic ≠ constant

occasionally = sometimes, at times, from time to time, now and then, irregularly, now and again, periodically, once in a while ≠ constantly

occult NOUN = magic, witchcraft, sorcery, wizardry, enchantment, black art, necromancy

• ADJECTIVE = supernatural, magical, mysterious, psychic, mystical, unearthly, esoteric, uncanny

occupant = occupier, resident, tenant, inmate, inhabitant, incumbent, dweller, lessee

occupation **1** = job, calling, business,

line (of work), trade, career, employment, profession 2 = hobby, pastime, diversion, relaxation, leisure pursuit, (leisure) activity 3 = invasion, seizure, conquest, incursion, subjugation 4 = occupancy, residence, holding, control, possession, tenure, tenancy

occupied 1 = in use, taken, full, engaged, unavailable 2 = inhabited, peopled, lived-in, settled, tenanted ≠ uninhabited 3 = busy, engaged, employed, working, active, hard at work, rushed off your feet

occupy 1 = inhabit, own, live in, dwell in, reside in, abide in ≠ vacate 2 = invade, take over, capture, seize, conquer, overrun, annex, colonize ≠ withdraw 3 = hold, control, dominate, possess 4 = take up, consume, tie up, use up, monopolize 5 *often passive* = engage, involve, employ, divert, preoccupy, engross 6 = fill, take up, cover, fill up, pervade, permeate, extend over

occur VERB 1 = happen, take place, come about, turn up (*informal*), crop up (*informal*), transpire (*informal*), befall 2 = exist, appear, be found, develop, turn up, be present, manifest itself, present itself

• PHRASES **occur to someone** = come to mind, strike someone, dawn on someone, spring to mind, cross someone's mind, enter someone's head, suggest itself to someone

occurrence 1 = incident, happening, event, fact, matter, affair, circumstance, episode 2 = existence, instance, appearance, manifestation, materialization

odd 1 = peculiar, strange, unusual, extraordinary, bizarre, offbeat, freakish 2 = unusual, strange, rare, extraordinary, remarkable, bizarre, peculiar, irregular ≠ normal 3 = occasional, various, random, casual, irregular, periodic, sundry, incidental ≠ regular 4 = spare, remaining, extra, surplus, solitary, leftover, unmatched, unpaired ≠ matched

odds PLURAL NOUN 1 = probability, chances, likelihood

• PHRASES **at odds** 1 = in conflict, arguing, quarrelling, at loggerheads, at daggers drawn 2 = at variance, conflicting, contrary to, at odds, out of line, out of step, at sixes and sevens (*informal*)

◆ **odds and ends** = scraps, bits, remains, fragments, debris, remnants, bits and pieces, bric-a-brac

odour = smell, scent, perfume, fragrance, stink, bouquet, aroma, stench

odyssey = journey, tour, trip, quest, trek, expedition, voyage, crusade

off ADVERB = away, out, apart, elsewhere, aside, hence, from here

• ADJECTIVE 1 = absent, gone, unavailable 2 = cancelled, abandoned, postponed, shelved 3 = bad, rotten, rancid, mouldy, turned, spoiled, sour, decayed

offence 1 = crime, sin, fault, violation, wrongdoing, trespass, felony, misdemeanour 2 = outrage, shock, anger, trouble, bother, resentment, irritation, hassle (*informal*) 3 = insult, slight, hurt, outrage, injustice, snub, affront, indignity

offend 1 = distress, upset, outrage, wound, slight, insult, annoy, snub ≠ please 2 = break the law, sin, err, do wrong, fall, go astray

offended = upset, hurt, bothered, disturbed, distressed, outraged, stung, put out (*informal*), tooshie (*Austral. slang*)

offender = criminal, convict, crook, villain, culprit, sinner, delinquent, felon

offensive ADJECTIVE 1 = insulting, rude, abusive, degrading, contemptuous, disparaging, objectionable, disrespectful ≠ respectful 2 = disgusting, gross, foul, unpleasant, revolting, vile, repellent, obnoxious, festy (*Austral. slang*), yucko (*Austral. slang*) ≠ pleasant 3 = attacking, threatening, aggressive, striking, hostile, invading, combative ≠ defensive

• NOUN = attack, charge, campaign, strike, push (*informal*), assault, raid, drive

offer VERB 1 = provide, present, furnish, afford ≠ withhold 2 = volunteer, come forward, offer your services 3 = propose, suggest, advance, submit 4 = give, show, bring, provide, render, impart 5 = put up for sale, sell 6 = bid, submit, propose, tender, proffer

• NOUN 1 = proposal, suggestion, proposition, submission 2 = bid, tender, bidding price

offering 1 = contribution, gift, donation, present, subscription, hand-out 2 = sacrifice, tribute, libation, burnt offering

office 1 = place of work, workplace, base,

workroom, place of business **2** = branch, department, division, section, wing, subdivision, subsection **3** = post, place, role, situation, responsibility, function, occupation

officer **1** = official, executive, agent, representative, appointee, functionary, office-holder, office bearer **2** = police officer, detective, PC, police constable, police man, police woman

official ADJECTIVE **1** = authorized, formal, sanctioned, licensed, proper, legitimate, authentic, certified ≠ unofficial **2** = formal, bureaucratic, ceremonial, solemn, ritualistic
• NOUN = officer, executive, agent, representative, bureaucrat, appointee, functionary, office-holder

offset = cancel out, balance, set off, make up for, compensate for, counteract, neutralize, counterbalance

offspring **1** = child, baby, kid (*informal*), youngster, infant, successor, babe, toddler, littlie (*Austral. informal*), ankle-biter (*Austral. slang*), tacker (*Austral. slang*) ≠ parent **2** = children, young, family, issue, stock, heirs, descendants, brood

often = frequently, generally, commonly, repeatedly, time and again, habitually, not infrequently ≠ never

oil VERB = lubricate, grease
• NOUN **1** = lubricant, grease, lubrication, fuel oil **2** = lotion, cream, balm, salve, liniment, embrocation, solution

oily = greasy, slimy, fatty, slippery, oleaginous

OK *or* **okay** ADJECTIVE (*Informal*) **1** = all right, fine, fitting, in order, permitted, suitable, acceptable, allowable ≠ unacceptable **2** = fine, good, average, fair, all right, acceptable, adequate, satisfactory ≠ unsatisfactory **3** = well, all right, safe, sound, healthy, unharmed, uninjured
• INTERJECTION = all right, right, yes, agreed, very good, roger, very well, ya (*S. African*), righto (*Brit. informal*), yebo (*S. African informal*)
• VERB = approve, allow, agree to, permit, sanction, endorse, authorize, rubber-stamp (*informal*)
• NOUN = authorization, agreement, sanction, approval, go-ahead (*informal*), blessing, permission, consent

old **1** = aged, elderly, ancient, mature, venerable, antiquated, senile, decrepit ≠ young **2** = former, earlier, past, previous, prior, one-time, erstwhile **3** = long-standing, established, fixed, enduring, abiding, long-lasting, long-established, time-honoured **4** = stale, worn-out, banal, threadbare, trite, overused, timeworn

old-fashioned **1** = out of date, dated, outdated, unfashionable, outmoded, passé, old hat, behind the times ≠ up-to-date **2** = oldfangled, square (*informal*), outdated, unfashionable, obsolescent

ominous = threatening, sinister, grim, fateful, foreboding, unpromising, portentous, inauspicious ≠ promising

omission **1** = exclusion, removal, elimination, deletion, excision ≠ inclusion **2** = gap, space, exclusion, lacuna **3** = failure, neglect, negligence, oversight, carelessness, dereliction, slackness, laxity

omit **1** = leave out, drop, exclude, eliminate, skip ≠ include **2** = forget, overlook, neglect, pass over, lose sight of

once ADVERB **1** = on one occasion, one time, one single time **2** = at one time, previously, formerly, long ago, once upon a time
• CONJUNCTION = as soon as, when, after, the moment, immediately, the instant
• PHRASES **at once** **1** = immediately, now, straight away, directly, promptly, instantly, right away, forthwith **2** = simultaneously, together, at the same time, concurrently

one-sided **1** = unequal, unfair, uneven, unjust, unbalanced, lopsided, ill-matched ≠ equal **2** = biased, prejudiced, weighted, unfair, partial, distorted, partisan, slanted ≠ unbiased

ongoing = in progress, developing, progressing, evolving, unfolding, unfinished

onlooker = spectator, witness, observer, viewer, looker-on, watcher, eyewitness, bystander

only ADJECTIVE = sole, one, single, individual, exclusive, unique, lone, solitary
• ADVERB **1** = just, simply, purely, merely **2** = hardly, just, barely, only just, scarcely, at a push

onset = beginning, start, birth, outbreak, inception, commencement ≠ end

onslaught = attack, charge, campaign, strike, assault, raid, invasion, offensive

≠ retreat
onward *or* **onwards** = forward, on, forwards, ahead, beyond, in front, forth
ooze[1] **1** = seep, well, escape, leak, drain, filter, drip, trickle **2** = emit, release, leak, drip, dribble, give off, pour forth **3** = exude, emit
ooze[2] = mud, clay, dirt, silt, sludge, mire, slime, alluvium
open VERB **1** = unfasten, unlock ≠ close **2** = unwrap, uncover, undo, unravel, untie ≠ wrap **3** = uncork **4** = unfold, spread (out), expand, unfurl, unroll ≠ fold **5** = clear, unblock ≠ block **6** = undo, unbutton, unfasten ≠ fasten **7** = begin business **8** = start, begin, launch, trigger, kick off (*informal*), initiate, commence, get going ≠ end **9** = begin, start, commence ≠ end
• ADJECTIVE **1** = unclosed, unlocked, ajar, unfastened, yawning ≠ closed **2** = unsealed, unstoppered ≠ unopened **3** = extended, unfolded, stretched out, unfurled, straightened out, unrolled ≠ shut **4** = frank, direct, straightforward, sincere, transparent, honest, candid, truthful ≠ sly **5** = receptive, sympathetic, responsive, amenable **6** = unresolved, unsettled, undecided, debatable, moot, arguable **7** = clear, passable, unhindered, unimpeded, navigable, unobstructed ≠ obstructed **8** = available, to hand, accessible, handy, at your disposal **9** = general, public, free, universal, blanket, across-the-board, unrestricted, overarching ≠ restricted **10** = vacant, free, available, empty, unoccupied, unfilled
open-air = outdoor, outside, out-of-door(s), alfresco
opening ADJECTIVE = first, earliest, beginning, premier, primary, initial, maiden, inaugural
• NOUN **1** = beginning, start, launch, dawn, outset, initiation, inception, commencement ≠ ending **2** = hole, space, tear, crack, gap, slot, puncture, aperture ≠ blockage **3** = opportunity, chance, time, moment, occasion, look-in (*informal*) **4** = job, position, post, situation, opportunity, vacancy
openly = frankly, plainly, honestly, overtly, candidly, unreservedly, unhesitatingly, forthrightly ≠ privately
open-minded = unprejudiced, liberal, balanced, objective, reasonable, tolerant, impartial, receptive ≠ narrow-minded
operate 1 = manage, run, direct, handle, supervise, be in charge of **2** = function, work, act **3** = run, work, use, control, manoeuvre **4** = work, go, run, perform, function ≠ break down
operation = performance, action, movement, motion
operational = working, going, running, ready, functioning, operative, viable, functional ≠ inoperative
operative ADJECTIVE = in force, effective, functioning, active, in effect, operational, in operation ≠ inoperative
• NOUN **1** = worker, employee, labourer, workman, artisan **2** (*U.S. & Canad.*) = spy, undercover agent, mole, nark (*Brit., Austral., & N.Z. slang*)
operator = worker, driver, mechanic, operative, conductor, technician, handler
opinion 1 = belief, feeling, view, idea, theory, conviction, point of view, sentiment **2** = estimation, view, impression, assessment, judgment, appraisal, considered opinion
opponent 1 = adversary, rival, enemy, competitor, challenger, foe, contestant, antagonist ≠ ally **2** = opposer, dissident, objector ≠ supporter
opportunity = chance, opening, time, turn, moment, possibility, occasion, slot
oppose = be against, fight (against), block, take on, counter, contest, resist, combat ≠ support
opposed 1 *with* ***to*** = against, hostile, adverse, in opposition, averse, antagonistic, (dead) set against **2** = contrary, conflicting, clashing, counter, adverse, contradictory, dissentient
opposing 1 = conflicting, different, contrasting, opposite, differing, contrary, contradictory, incompatible **2** = rival, conflicting, competing, enemy, opposite, hostile
opposite PREPOSITION = facing, face to face with, across from, eyeball to eyeball (*informal*)
• ADJECTIVE **1** = facing, other, opposing **2** = different, conflicting, contrasted, contrasting, unlike, contrary, dissimilar, divergent ≠ alike **3** = rival, conflicting, opposing, competing
• NOUN = reverse, contrary, converse,

antithesis, contradiction, inverse, obverse
opposition 1 = hostility, resistance, resentment, disapproval, obstruction, animosity, antagonism, antipathy ≠ support 2 = opponent(s), competition, rival(s), enemy, competitor(s), other side, challenger(s), foe
oppress 1 = subjugate, abuse, suppress, wrong, master, overcome, subdue, persecute ≠ liberate 2 = depress, burden, discourage, torment, harass, afflict, sadden, vex
oppression = persecution, control, abuse, injury, injustice, cruelty, domination, repression ≠ justice
oppressive 1 = tyrannical, severe, harsh, cruel, brutal, authoritarian, unjust, repressive ≠ merciful 2 = stifling, close, sticky, stuffy, humid, sultry, airless, muggy
opt VERB = choose, decide, prefer, select, elect ≠ reject
• PHRASES **opt for something** *or* **someone** = choose, pick, select, adopt, go for, designate, decide on, plump for
optimistic 1 = hopeful, positive, confident, encouraged, cheerful, rosy, buoyant, sanguine ≠ pessimistic 2 = encouraging, promising, bright, good, reassuring, rosy, heartening, auspicious ≠ discouraging
optimum *or* **optimal** = ideal, best, highest, finest, perfect, supreme, peak, outstanding ≠ worst
option = choice, alternative, selection, preference, freedom of choice, power to choose
optional = voluntary, open, discretionary, possible, extra, elective ≠ compulsory
opus = work, piece, production, creation, composition, work of art, brainchild, oeuvre (*French*)
oral = spoken, vocal, verbal, unwritten
orbit NOUN 1 = path, course, cycle, circle, revolution, rotation, trajectory, sweep 2 = sphere of influence, reach, range, influence, province, scope, domain, compass
• VERB = circle, ring, go round, revolve around, encircle, circumscribe, circumnavigate
orchestrate 1 = organize, plan, run, set up, arrange, put together, marshal, coordinate 2 = score, set, arrange, adapt
ordain 1 = appoint, name, commission, select, invest, nominate, anoint, consecrate 2 (*Formal*) = order, will, rule, demand, require, direct, command, dictate
ordeal = hardship, trial, difficulty, test, suffering, nightmare, torture, agony ≠ pleasure
order VERB 1 = command, instruct, direct, charge, demand, require, bid, compel ≠ forbid 2 = decree, rule, demand, prescribe, pronounce, ordain ≠ ban 3 = request, ask (for), book, seek, reserve, apply for, solicit, send away for 4 = arrange, group, sort, position, line up, organize, catalogue, sort out ≠ disarrange
• NOUN 1 = instruction, ruling, demand, direction, command, dictate, decree, mandate 2 = request, booking, demand, commission, application, reservation, requisition 3 = sequence, grouping, series, structure, chain, arrangement, line-up, array 4 = organization, system, method, pattern, symmetry, regularity, neatness, tidiness ≠ chaos 5 = peace, control, law, quiet, calm, discipline, law and order, tranquillity 6 = society, company, group, club, community, association, institute, organization 7 = class, set, rank, grade, caste 8 = kind, group, class, family, sort, type, variety, category
orderly 1 = well-behaved, controlled, disciplined, quiet, restrained, law-abiding, peaceable ≠ disorderly 2 = well-organized, regular, in order, organized, precise, neat, tidy, systematic ≠ disorganized
ordinary 1 = usual, standard, normal, common, regular, typical, conventional, routine 2 = commonplace, plain, modest, humble, mundane, banal, unremarkable, run-of-the-mill ≠ extraordinary
organ 1 = body part, part of the body, element, biological structure 2 = newspaper, medium, voice, vehicle, gazette, mouthpiece
organic 1 = natural, biological, living, live, animate 2 = systematic, ordered, structured, organized, integrated, orderly, methodical
organism = creature, being, thing, body, animal, structure, beast, entity
organization 1 = group, company, party, body, association, band, institution, corporation 2 = management, running, planning, control, operation, handling, structuring, administration 3 = structure,

form, pattern, make-up, arrangement, construction, format, formation

organize 1 = arrange, run, plan, prepare, set up, devise, put together, take care of, jack up (*N.Z. informal*) ≠ disrupt 2 = put in order, arrange, group, list, file, index, classify, inventory ≠ muddle

orient *or* **orientate** 1 = adjust, adapt, alter, accustom, align, familiarize, acclimatize 2 = get your bearings, establish your location

orientation 1 = inclination, tendency, disposition, predisposition, predilection, proclivity, partiality 2 = induction, introduction, adjustment, settling in, adaptation, assimilation, familiarization, acclimatization 3 = position, situation, location, bearings, direction, arrangement, whereabouts

origin 1 = beginning, start, birth, launch, foundation, creation, emergence, onset ≠ end 2 = root, source, basis, base, seed, foundation, nucleus, derivation

original ADJECTIVE 1 = first, earliest, initial 2 = initial, first, starting, opening, primary, introductory ≠ final 3 = new, fresh, novel, unusual, unprecedented, innovative, unfamiliar, seminal ≠ unoriginal 4 = creative, inspired, imaginative, artistic, fertile, ingenious, visionary, inventive • NOUN = prototype, master, pattern ≠ copy

originally = initially, first, firstly, at first, primarily, to begin with, in the beginning

originate 1 = begin, start, emerge, come, happen, rise, appear, spring ≠ end 2 = invent, create, design, launch, introduce, institute, generate, pioneer

ornament NOUN 1 = decoration, trimming, accessory, festoon, trinket, bauble, knick-knack 2 = embellishment, decoration, embroidery, elaboration, adornment, ornamentation • VERB = decorate, adorn, array, do up (*informal*), embellish, festoon, beautify, prettify

orthodox 1 = established, official, accepted, received, common, traditional, normal, usual ≠ unorthodox 2 = conformist, conservative, traditional, strict, devout, observant ≠ nonconformist

orthodoxy 1 = doctrine, teaching, opinion, principle, belief, convention, creed, dogma 2 = conformity, received wisdom, traditionalism, conventionality ≠ nonconformity

other 1 = additional, more, further, new, added, extra, fresh, spare 2 = different, alternative, contrasting, distinct, diverse, dissimilar, separate, alternative

otherwise 1 = or else, or, if not, or then 2 = apart from that, in other ways, in (all) other respects 3 = differently, any other way, contrarily

ounce = shred, bit, drop, trace, scrap, grain, fragment, atom

oust = expel, turn out, dismiss, exclude, exile, throw out, displace, topple

out ADJECTIVE 1 = not in, away, elsewhere, outside, gone, abroad, from home, absent 2 = extinguished, ended, finished, dead, exhausted, expired, used up, at an end ≠ alight 3 = in bloom, opening, open, flowering, blooming, in flower, in full bloom 4 = available, on sale, in the shops, to be had, purchasable 5 = revealed, exposed, common knowledge, public knowledge, (out) in the open ≠ kept secret • VERB = expose

outbreak 1 = eruption, burst, explosion, epidemic, rash, outburst, flare-up, upsurge 2 = onset, beginning, outset, opening, dawn, commencement

outburst = explosion, fit, surge, outbreak, flare-up, eruption, spasm, outpouring

outcome = result, end, consequence, conclusion, payoff (*informal*), upshot

outcry = protest, complaint, objection, dissent, outburst, clamour, uproar, commotion

outdated = old-fashioned, dated, obsolete, out of date, passé, archaic, unfashionable, antiquated ≠ modern

outdoor = open-air, outside, out-of-door(s), alfresco ≠ indoor

outer 1 = external, outside, outward, exterior, exposed, outermost ≠ inner 2 = surface 3 = outlying, distant, provincial, out-of-the-way, peripheral, far-flung ≠ central

outfit 1 = costume, dress, clothes, clothing, suit, get-up (*informal*), kit, ensemble 2 (*Informal*) = group, company, team, party, unit, crowd, squad, organization

outgoing 1 = leaving, former, previous, retiring, withdrawing, prior, departing, erstwhile ≠ incoming 2 = sociable, open, social, warm, friendly, expansive, affable, extrovert ≠ reserved

outgoings = expenses, costs, payments, expenditure, overheads, outlay

outing = journey, run, trip, tour, expedition, excursion, spin (*informal*), jaunt

outlaw VERB **1** = ban, bar, veto, forbid, exclude, prohibit, disallow, proscribe ≠ legalise **2** = banish, put a price on (someone's) head
• NOUN (*History*) = bandit, criminal, thief, robber, fugitive, outcast, felon, highwayman

outlet **1** = shop, store, supermarket, market, boutique, emporium, hypermarket **2** = channel, release, medium, avenue, vent, conduit **3** = pipe, opening, channel, exit, duct

outline VERB **1** = summarize, draft, plan, trace, sketch (in), sum up, encapsulate, delineate **2** = silhouette, etch
• NOUN **1** = summary, review, résumé, rundown, synopsis, précis, thumbnail sketch, recapitulation **2** = shape, lines, form, figure, profile, silhouette, configuration, contour(s)

outlook **1** = attitude, opinion, position, approach, mood, perspective, point of view, stance **2** = prospect(s), future, expectations, forecast, prediction, probability, prognosis

out of date **1** = old-fashioned, dated, outdated, obsolete, démodé (*French*), antiquated, outmoded, passé ≠ modern **2** = invalid, expired, lapsed, void, null and void

output = production, manufacture, manufacturing, yield, productivity

outrage VERB = offend, shock, upset, wound, insult, infuriate, incense, madden
• NOUN = indignation, shock, anger, rage, fury, hurt, resentment, scorn

outrageous **1** = atrocious, shocking, terrible, offensive, appalling, cruel, savage, horrifying ≠ mild **2** = unreasonable, unfair, steep (*informal*), shocking, extravagant, scandalous, preposterous, unwarranted ≠ reasonable

outright ADJECTIVE **1** = absolute, complete, total, perfect, sheer, thorough, unconditional, unqualified **2** = definite, clear, certain, flat, absolute, black-and-white, straightforward, unequivocal
• ADVERB **1** = openly, frankly, plainly, overtly, candidly, unreservedly, unhesitatingly, forthrightly **2** = absolutely, completely, totally, fully, entirely, thoroughly, wholly, utterly

outset = beginning, start, opening, onset, inauguration, inception, commencement, kickoff (*informal*) ≠ finish

outside NOUN = exterior, face, front, covering, skin, surface, shell, coating
• ADJECTIVE **1** = external, outer, exterior, outward, extraneous ≠ inner **2** = remote, small, unlikely, slight, slim, distant, faint, marginal
• ADVERB = outdoors, out of the house, out-of-doors

outsider = stranger, incomer, visitor, newcomer, intruder, interloper, odd one out

outskirts = edge, boundary, suburbs, fringe, perimeter, periphery, suburbia, environs

outspan (*S. African*) = relax, chill out (*slang, chiefly U.S.*), take it easy, loosen up, put your feet up

outspoken = forthright, open, frank, straightforward, blunt, explicit, upfront (*informal*), unequivocal ≠ reserved

outstanding **1** = excellent, good, great, important, special, fine, brilliant, impressive, booshit (*Austral. slang*), exo (*Austral. slang*), sik (*Austral. slang*) ≠ mediocre **2** = unpaid, remaining, due, pending, payable, unsettled, uncollected **3** = undone, left, omitted, unfinished, unfulfilled, unperformed

outward = apparent, seeming, surface, ostensible ≠ inward

outwardly = apparently, externally, seemingly, it seems that, on the surface, it appears that, ostensibly, on the face of it

outweigh = override, cancel (out), eclipse, offset, compensate for, supersede, neutralize, counterbalance

oval = elliptical, egg-shaped, ovoid

ovation = applause, hand, cheers, praise, tribute, acclaim, clapping, accolade ≠ derision

over PREPOSITION **1** = above, on top of **2** = on top of, on, across, upon **3** = across, (looking) onto **4** = more than, above, exceeding, in excess of, upwards of **5** = about, regarding, relating to, concerning, apropos of
• ADVERB **1** = above, overhead, in the sky, on high, aloft, up above **2** = extra, more,

further, beyond, additional, in addition, surplus, in excess
• ADJECTIVE = finished, done (with), through, ended, closed, past, completed, complete
RELATED WORDS
prefixes: hyper-, super-

overall ADJECTIVE = total, full, whole, general, complete, entire, global, comprehensive
• ADVERB = in general, generally, mostly, all things considered, on average, on the whole, predominantly, in the main

overcome VERB 1 = defeat, beat, conquer, master, overwhelm, subdue, rout, overpower 2 = conquer, beat, master, subdue, triumph over, vanquish
• ADJECTIVE = overwhelmed, moved, affected, emotional, choked, speechless, bowled over (*informal*), at a loss for words

overdue 1 = delayed, belated, late, behind schedule, tardy, unpunctual, behindhand ≠ early 2 = unpaid, owing

overflow VERB = spill over, well over, run over, pour over, bubble over, brim over
• NOUN 1 = flood, spilling over 2 = surplus, extra, excess, overspill, overabundance, additional people *or* things

overhaul VERB 1 = check, service, maintain, examine, restore, tune (up), repair, go over 2 = overtake, pass, leave behind, catch up with, get past, outstrip, get ahead of, outdistance
• NOUN = check, service, examination, going-over (*informal*), inspection, once-over (*informal*), checkup, reconditioning

overhead ADJECTIVE = raised, suspended, elevated, aerial, overhanging
• ADVERB = above, in the sky, on high, aloft, up above ≠ underneath

overheads = running costs, expenses, outgoings, operating costs

overlook 1 = look over *or* out on, have a view of 2 = miss, forget, neglect, omit, disregard, pass over ≠ notice 3 = ignore, excuse, forgive, pardon, disregard, condone, turn a blind eye to, wink at

overpower 1 = overcome, master, overwhelm, overthrow, subdue, quell, subjugate, prevail over 2 defeat, crush, triumph over, vanquish 3 = overwhelm, overcome, bowl over (*informal*), stagger

override 1 = outweigh, eclipse, supersede, take precedence over, prevail over 2 = overrule, cancel, overturn, repeal, rescind, annul, nullify, countermand 3 = ignore, reject, discount, overlook, disregard, pass over, take no notice of

overrun 1 = overwhelm, attack, assault, occupy, raid, invade, penetrate, rout 2 = spread over, overwhelm, choke, swamp, infest, inundate, permeate, swarm over 3 = exceed, go beyond, surpass, overshoot, run over *or* on

overshadow 1 = spoil, ruin, mar, wreck, blight, crool *or* cruel (*Austral. slang*), mess up, put a damper on 2 = outshine, eclipse, surpass, dwarf, tower above, leave *or* put in the shade

overt = open, obvious, plain, public, manifest, blatant, observable, undisguised ≠ hidden

overtake 1 = pass, leave behind, overhaul, catch up with, get past, outdistance, go by *or* past 2 = outdo, top, exceed, eclipse, surpass, outstrip, get the better of, outclass 3 = befall, hit, happen to, catch off guard, catch unawares 4 = engulf, overwhelm, hit, strike, swamp, envelop, swallow up

overthrow VERB = defeat, overcome, conquer, bring down, oust, topple, rout, overpower ≠ uphold
• NOUN = downfall, fall, defeat, collapse, destruction, ousting, undoing, unseating ≠ preservation

overturn 1 = tip over, topple, upturn, capsize, upend, keel over, overbalance 2 = knock over *or* down, upturn, tip over, upend 3 = reverse, change, cancel, abolish, overthrow, set aside, repeal, quash 4 = overthrow, defeat, destroy, overcome, bring down, oust, topple, depose

overweight = fat, heavy, stout, hefty, plump, bulky, chunky, chubby ≠ underweight

overwhelm 1 = overcome, devastate, stagger, bowl over (*informal*), knock (someone) for six (*informal*), sweep (someone) off his *or* her feet, take (someone's) breath away 2 = destroy, defeat, overcome, crush, massacre, conquer, wipe out, overthrow

overwhelming 1 = overpowering, strong, powerful, towering, stunning, crushing, devastating, shattering ≠ negligible 2 = vast, huge, massive, enormous, tremendous, immense, very large

≠ insignificant
owe = be in debt (to), be in arrears (to), be overdrawn (by), be obligated *or* indebted (to)
owing to = because of, thanks to, as a result of, on account of, by reason of
own ADJECTIVE = personal, special, private, individual, particular, exclusive
• VERB = possess, have, keep, hold, enjoy, retain, be in possession of, have to your name
owner = possessor, holder, proprietor, titleholder, landlord *or* landlady
ownership = possession, occupation, tenure, dominion

p

pace NOUN **1** = speed, rate, tempo, velocity **2** = step, walk, stride, tread, gait **3** = footstep, step, stride
• VERB = stride, walk, pound, patrol, march up and down
pack VERB **1** = package, load, store, bundle, stow **2** = cram, crowd, press, fill, stuff, jam, ram, compress
• NOUN **1** = packet, box, package, carton **2** = bundle, parcel, load, burden, rucksack, knapsack, back pack, kitbag **3** = group, crowd, company, band, troop, gang, bunch, mob
• PHRASES **pack someone off** = send away, dismiss, send packing (*informal*) ◆ **pack something in 1** (*Brit. informal*) = resign from, leave, give up, quit (*informal*), chuck (*informal*), jack in (*informal*) **2** = stop, give up, kick (*informal*), cease, chuck (*informal*)
package NOUN **1** = parcel, box, container, packet, carton **2** = collection, lot, unit, combination, compilation
• VERB = pack, box, parcel (up)
packet 1 = container, box, package, carton **2** = package, parcel **3** (*Slang*) = a fortune, a bomb (*Brit. slang*), a pile (*informal*), a small fortune, a tidy sum (*informal*), a king's ransom (*informal*)
pact = agreement, alliance, treaty, deal, understanding, bargain, covenant
pad[1] NOUN **1** = wad, dressing, pack, padding, compress, wadding **2** = cushion, filling, stuffing, pillow, bolster, upholstery **3** = notepad, block, notebook, jotter, writing pad **4** (*Slang*) = home, flat, apartment, place **5** = paw, foot, sole
• VERB = pack, fill, protect, stuff, cushion
pad[2] = sneak, creep, steal, go barefoot
padding 1 = filling, stuffing, packing, wadding **2** = waffle (*informal, chiefly Brit.*), hot air (*informal*), verbiage, wordiness, verbosity
paddle[1] NOUN = oar, scull
• VERB = row, pull, scull
paddle[2] = wade, splash (about), slop
pagan ADJECTIVE = heathen, infidel, polytheistic, idolatrous
• NOUN = heathen, infidel, polytheist, idolater
page[1] = folio, side, leaf, sheet
page[2] VERB = call, summon, send for
• NOUN **1** = attendant, pageboy **2** = servant, attendant, squire, pageboy
pain NOUN **1** = suffering, discomfort, hurt, irritation, tenderness, soreness **2** = ache, stinging, aching, cramp, throb, throbbing, pang, twinge **3** = sorrow, suffering, torture, distress, despair, misery, agony, sadness
• PLURAL NOUN = trouble, effort, care, bother, diligence
• VERB **1** = distress, hurt, torture, grieve, torment, sadden, agonize, cut to the quick **2** = hurt
painful 1 = sore, smarting, aching, tender ≠ painless **2** = distressing, unpleasant, grievous, distasteful, agonizing, disagreeable ≠ pleasant **3** = difficult, arduous, trying, hard, troublesome, laborious ≠ easy
painfully = distressingly, clearly, sadly, unfortunately, dreadfully
paint NOUN = colouring, colour, stain, dye, tint, pigment, emulsion
• VERB **1** = colour, cover, coat, stain, whitewash, daub, distemper, apply paint to **2** = depict, draw, portray, picture, represent, sketch
pair NOUN **1** = set **2** = couple, brace, duo
• VERB = team, match (up), join, couple, twin, bracket
pal (*Informal*) = friend, companion, mate (*informal*), buddy (*informal*), comrade,

chum (*informal*), crony, cobber (*Austral. & N.Z. old-fashioned informal*), E hoa (*N.Z.*)
pale ADJECTIVE 1 = light, soft, faded, subtle, muted, bleached, pastel, light-coloured 2 = dim, weak, faint, feeble, thin, wan, watery 3 = white, pasty, bleached, wan, colourless, pallid, ashen ≠ rosy-cheeked
• VERB = become pale, blanch, whiten, go white, lose colour
pamper = spoil, indulge, pet, cosset, coddle, mollycoddle
pamphlet = booklet, leaflet, brochure, circular, tract
pan[1] NOUN = pot, container, saucepan
• VERB 1 (*Informal*) = criticize, knock, slam (*slang*), censure, tear into (*informal*) 2 = sift out, look for, search for
pan[2] = move along *or* across, follow, track, sweep
panic NOUN = fear, alarm, terror, anxiety, hysteria, fright, trepidation, a flap (*informal*)
• VERB 1 = go to pieces, become hysterical, lose your nerve 2 = alarm, scare, unnerve
panorama 1 = view, prospect, vista 2 = survey, perspective, overview, overall picture
pant = puff, blow, breathe, gasp, wheeze, heave
pants 1 (*Brit.*) = underpants, briefs, drawers, knickers, panties, boxer shorts, broekies (*S. African*), underdaks (*Austral. slang*) 2 (*U.S.*) = trousers, slacks
paper NOUN 1 = newspaper, daily, journal, gazette 2 = essay, article, treatise, dissertation 3 = examination, test, exam 4 = report
• PLURAL NOUN 1 = letters, records, documents, file, diaries, archive, paperwork, dossier 2 = documents, records, certificates, identification, deeds, identity papers, I.D. (*informal*)
• VERB = wallpaper, hang
parade NOUN 1 = procession, march, pageant, cavalcade 2 = show, display, spectacle
• VERB 1 = march, process, promenade 2 = flaunt, display, exhibit, show off (*informal*) 3 = strut, show off (*informal*), swagger, swank
paradigm = model, example, pattern, ideal
paradise 1 = heaven, Promised Land, Happy Valley (*Islam*), Elysian fields 2 = bliss, delight, heaven, felicity, utopia
paradox = contradiction, puzzle, anomaly, enigma, oddity
paragraph = section, part, item, passage, clause, subdivision
parallel NOUN 1 = equivalent, counterpart, match, equal, twin, analogue ≠ opposite 2 = similarity, comparison, analogy, resemblance, likeness ≠ difference
• ADJECTIVE 1 = matching, corresponding, like, similar, resembling, analogous ≠ different 2 = equidistant, alongside, side by side ≠ divergent
paralyse 1 = disable, cripple, lame, incapacitate 2 = freeze, stun, numb, petrify, halt, immobilize 3 = immobilize, freeze, halt, disable, cripple, incapacitate, bring to a standstill
paralysis 1 = immobility, palsy 2 = standstill, breakdown, stoppage, halt
parameter (*Informal*) *usually plural* = limit, restriction, framework, limitation, specification
paramount = principal, prime, first, chief, main, primary, supreme, cardinal ≠ secondary
paranoid 1 (*Informal*) = suspicious, worried, nervous, fearful, antsy (*informal*) 2 = obsessive, disturbed, manic, neurotic, mentally ill, psychotic, deluded, paranoiac
parasite = sponger (*informal*), leech, hanger-on, scrounger (*informal*), bloodsucker (*informal*), quandong (*Austral. slang*)
parcel NOUN = package, case, box, pack, bundle
• VERB *often with* ***up*** = wrap, pack, package, tie up, do up, gift-wrap, box up, fasten together
pardon VERB 1 = forgive, excuse ≠ condemn 2 = acquit, let off (*informal*), exonerate, absolve ≠ punish
• NOUN 1 = forgiveness, absolution ≠ condemnation 2 = acquittal, amnesty, exoneration ≠ punishment
parent = father *or* mother, sire, progenitor, procreator, old (*Austral. & N.Z. informal*), patriarch
parish 1 = district, community 2 = community, flock, church, congregation
park 1 = recreation ground, garden, playground, pleasure garden, playpark, domain (*N.Z.*), forest park (*N.Z.*)

2 = parkland, grounds, estate, lawns, woodland, grassland 3 = field, pitch, playing field

parliament 1 = assembly, council, congress, senate, convention, legislature 2 = sitting

parliamentary = governmental, legislative, law-making

parlour *or* (*U.S.*) **parlor** 1 (*Old-fashioned*) = sitting room, lounge, living room, drawing room, front room 2 = establishment, shop, store, salon

parody NOUN = takeoff (*informal*), satire, caricature, send-up (*Brit. informal*), spoof (*informal*), skit, burlesque
• VERB = take off (*informal*), caricature, send up (*Brit. informal*), burlesque, satirize, do a takeoff of (*informal*)

parrot = repeat, echo, imitate, copy, mimic

parry 1 = evade, avoid, dodge, sidestep 2 = ward off, block, deflect, repel, rebuff, repulse

parson = clergyman, minister, priest, vicar, preacher, pastor, cleric, churchman

part NOUN 1 = piece, share, proportion, percentage, bit, section, scrap, portion ≠ entirety 2 *often plural* = region, area, district, neighbourhood, quarter, vicinity 3 = component, bit, unit, constituent 4 = branch, division, office, section, wing, subdivision, subsection 5 = organ, member, limb 6 (*Theatre*) = role, representation, persona, portrayal, depiction, character part 7 (*Theatre*) = lines, words, script, dialogue 8 = side, behalf
• VERB 1 = divide, separate, break, tear, split, rend, detach, sever ≠ join 2 = part company, separate, split up ≠ meet
• PHRASES **in good part** = good-naturedly, well, cheerfully, without offence

partial 1 = incomplete, unfinished, imperfect, uncompleted ≠ complete 2 = biased, prejudiced, discriminatory, partisan, unfair, one-sided, unjust ≠ unbiased

partially = partly, somewhat, in part, not wholly, fractionally, incompletely

participant = participator, member, player, contributor, stakeholder

participate = take part, be involved, perform, join, partake ≠ refrain from

participation = taking part, contribution, involvement, sharing in, joining in, partaking

particle = bit, piece, scrap, grain, shred, mite, jot, speck

particular ADJECTIVE 1 = specific, special, exact, precise, distinct, peculiar ≠ general 2 = special, exceptional, notable, uncommon, marked, unusual, remarkable, singular 3 = fussy, demanding, fastidious, choosy (*informal*), picky (*informal*), finicky, pernickety (*informal*) ≠ indiscriminate
• NOUN *usually plural* = detail, fact, feature, item, circumstance, specification

particularly 1 = specifically, expressly, explicitly, especially, in particular, distinctly 2 = especially, notably, unusually, exceptionally, singularly, uncommonly

parting 1 = farewell, goodbye 2 = division, breaking, split, separation, rift, rupture

partisan ADJECTIVE = prejudiced, one-sided, biased, partial, sectarian ≠ unbiased
• NOUN 1 = supporter, devotee, adherent, upholder ≠ opponent 2 = underground fighter, guerrilla, freedom fighter, resistance fighter

partition NOUN 1 = screen, wall, barrier 2 = division, separation, segregation
• VERB = separate, screen, divide

partly = partially, somewhat, slightly ≠ completely

partner 1 = spouse, consort, significant other (*U.S. informal*), mate, husband *or* wife 2 = companion, ally, colleague, associate, mate, comrade 3 = associate, colleague, collaborator

partnership 1 = cooperation, alliance, sharing, union, connection, participation, copartnership 2 = company, firm, house, interest, society, cooperative

party 1 = faction, set, side, league, camp, clique, coterie 2 = get-together (*informal*), celebration, do (*informal*), gathering, function, reception, festivity, social gathering 3 = group, team, band, company, unit, squad, crew, gang

pass VERB 1 = go by *or* past, overtake, drive past, lap, leave behind, pull ahead of ≠ stop 2 = go, move, travel, progress, flow, proceed 3 = run, move, stroke 4 = give, hand, send, transfer, deliver, convey 5 = be left, come, be bequeathed, be inherited by 6 = kick, hit, loft, head, lob 7 = elapse, progress, go by, lapse, wear on, go past, tick by 8 = end, go, cease, blow over 9 = spend, fill, occupy, while away

10 = exceed, beat, overtake, go beyond, surpass, outstrip, outdo **11** = be successful in, qualify (in), succeed (in), graduate (in), get through, do, gain a pass in ≠ fail **12** = approve, accept, decree, enact, ratify, ordain, legislate (for) ≠ ban
• NOUN **1** = licence, ticket, permit, passport, warrant, authorization **2** = gap, route, canyon, gorge, ravine
• PHRASES **pass away** *or* **on** (*Euphemistic*) = die, pass on, expire, pass over, snuff it (*informal*), kick the bucket (*slang*), shuffle off this mortal coil, cark it (*Austral. & N.Z. informal*) ◆ **pass out** (*Informal*) = faint, black out (*informal*), lose consciousness, become unconscious ◆ **pass something over** = disregard, ignore, not dwell on ◆ **pass something up** (*Informal*) = miss, let slip, decline, neglect, forgo, abstain from, give (something) a miss (*informal*)

passage **1** = corridor, hall, lobby, vestibule **2** = alley, way, close (*Brit.*), course, road, channel, route, path **3** = extract, reading, piece, section, text, excerpt, quotation **4** = journey, crossing, trip, trek, voyage **5** = safe-conduct, right to travel, freedom to travel, permission to travel

passenger = traveller, rider, fare, commuter, fare payer

passer-by = bystander, witness, observer, viewer, spectator, looker-on, watcher, onlooker

passing **1** = momentary, fleeting, short-lived, transient, ephemeral, brief, temporary, transitory **2** = superficial, short, quick, glancing, casual, summary, cursory, perfunctory

passion **1** = love, desire, lust, infatuation, ardour **2** = emotion, feeling, fire, heat, excitement, intensity, warmth, zeal ≠ indifference **3** = mania, enthusiasm, obsession, bug (*informal*), craving, fascination, craze **4** = rage, fit, storm, anger, fury, outburst, frenzy, paroxysm

passionate **1** = emotional, eager, strong, intense, fierce, ardent, fervent, heartfelt ≠ unemotional **2** = loving, erotic, hot, ardent, amorous, lustful ≠ cold

passive **1** = submissive, compliant, receptive, docile, quiescent ≠ spirited **2** = inactive, uninvolved ≠ active

past NOUN **1** = former times, long ago, days gone by, the olden days ≠ future **2** = background, life, history, past life, life story, career to date
• ADJECTIVE **1** = former, early, previous, ancient, bygone, olden ≠ future **2** = previous, former, one-time, ex- **3** = last, previous **4** = over, done, ended, finished, gone
• PREPOSITION **1** = after, beyond, later than **2** = by, across, in front of
• ADVERB = on, by, along

paste NOUN **1** = adhesive, glue, cement, gum **2** = purée, pâté, spread
• VERB = stick, glue, cement, gum

pastel = pale, light, soft, delicate, muted ≠ bright

pastime = activity, game, entertainment, hobby, recreation, amusement, diversion

pastor = clergyman, minister, priest, vicar, parson, rector, curate, churchman

pastoral **1** = ecclesiastical, priestly, ministerial, clerical **2** = rustic, country, rural, bucolic

pasture = grassland, grass, meadow, grazing

pat VERB = stroke, touch, tap, pet, caress, fondle
• NOUN = tap, stroke, clap

patch NOUN **1** = spot, bit, scrap, shred, small piece **2** = plot, area, ground, land, tract **3** = reinforcement, piece of fabric, piece of cloth, piece of material, piece sewn on
• VERB *often with* ***up*** = mend, cover, repair, reinforce, stitch (up), sew (up)

patent NOUN = copyright, licence, franchise, registered trademark
• ADJECTIVE = obvious, apparent, evident, clear, glaring, manifest

path **1** = way, road, walk, track, trail, avenue, footpath, berm (*N.Z.*) **2** = route, way, course, direction **3** = course, way, road, route

pathetic = sad, moving, touching, affecting, distressing, tender, poignant, plaintive ≠ funny

patience **1** = forbearance, tolerance, serenity, restraint, calmness, sufferance ≠ impatience **2** = endurance, resignation, submission, fortitude, long-suffering, perseverance, stoicism, constancy

patient NOUN = sick person, case, sufferer, invalid
• ADJECTIVE **1** = forbearing, understanding, forgiving, mild, tolerant, indulgent, lenient,

even-tempered ≠ impatient **2** = long-suffering, resigned, calm, enduring, philosophical, persevering, stoical, submissive
patriot = nationalist, loyalist, chauvinist
patriotic = nationalistic, loyal, chauvinistic, jingoistic
patriotism = nationalism, jingoism
patrol VERB = police, guard, keep watch (on), inspect, safeguard, keep guard (on)
• NOUN = guard, watch, watchman, sentinel, patrolman
patron **1** = supporter, friend, champion, sponsor, backer, helper, benefactor, philanthropist **2** = customer, client, buyer, frequenter, shopper, habitué
patronage = support, promotion, sponsorship, backing, help, aid, assistance
pattern **1** = order, plan, system, method, sequence **2** = design, arrangement, motif, figure, device, decoration **3** = plan, design, original, guide, diagram, stencil, template
pause VERB = stop briefly, delay, break, wait, rest, halt, cease, interrupt ≠ continue
• NOUN = stop, break, interval, rest, gap, halt, respite, lull ≠ continuance
pave = cover, floor, surface, concrete, tile
paw (*Informal*) = manhandle, grab, maul, molest, handle roughly
pay VERB **1** = reward, compensate, reimburse, recompense, requite, remunerate **2** = spend, give, fork out (*informal*), remit, shell out (*informal*) **3** = settle **4** = bring in, earn, return, net, yield **5** = be profitable, make money, make a return **6** = benefit, repay, be worthwhile **7** = give, extend, present with, grant, hand out, bestow
• NOUN = wages, income, payment, earnings, fee, reward, salary, allowance
• PHRASES **pay off** = succeed, work, be effective ◆ **pay something off** = settle, clear, square, discharge, pay in full
payable = due, outstanding, owed, owing
payment **1** = remittance, advance, deposit, premium, instalment **2** = settlement, paying, discharge, remittance **3** = wages, fee, reward, hire, remuneration
peace **1** = truce, ceasefire, treaty, armistice ≠ war **2** = stillness, rest, quiet, silence, calm, hush, tranquillity, seclusion **3** = serenity, calm, composure, contentment, repose, equanimity, peacefulness, harmoniousness **4** = harmony, accord, agreement, concord
peaceful **1** = at peace, friendly, harmonious, amicable, nonviolent ≠ hostile **2** = peace-loving, conciliatory, peaceable, unwarlike ≠ belligerent **3** = calm, still, quiet, tranquil, restful ≠ agitated **4** = serene, placid, undisturbed
peak NOUN **1** = high point, crown, climax, culmination, zenith, acme **2** = point, top, tip, summit, brow, crest, pinnacle, apex
• VERB = culminate, climax, come to a head
peasant = rustic, countryman
peck VERB **1** = pick, hit, strike, tap, poke, jab, prick **2** = kiss, plant a kiss, give someone a smacker, give someone a peck *or* kiss
• NOUN = kiss, smacker, osculation (*rare*)
peculiar **1** = odd, strange, unusual, bizarre, funny, extraordinary, curious, weird ≠ ordinary **2** = special, particular, unique, characteristic ≠ common
peddle = sell, trade, push (*informal*), market, hawk, flog (*slang*)
pedestrian NOUN = walker, foot-traveller ≠ driver
• ADJECTIVE = dull, ordinary, boring, commonplace, mundane, mediocre, banal, prosaic, half-pie (*N.Z. informal*) ≠ exciting
pedigree ADJECTIVE = purebred, thoroughbred, full-blooded
• NOUN = lineage, family, line, race, stock, blood, breed, descent
peel NOUN = rind, skin, peeling
• VERB = skin, scale, strip, pare, shuck, flake off, take the skin *or* rind off
peep VERB = peek, look, eyeball (*slang*), sneak a look, steal a look
• NOUN = look, glimpse, peek, look-see (*slang*)
peer[1] = squint, look, spy, gaze, scan, inspect, peep, peek
peer[2] **1** = noble, lord, aristocrat, nobleman **2** = equal, like, fellow, contemporary, compeer
peg NOUN = pin, spike, rivet, skewer, dowel, spigot
• VERB = fasten, join, fix, secure, attach
pen[1] = write (down), draft, compose, pencil, draw up, scribble, take down, inscribe
pen[2] NOUN = enclosure, pound, fold, cage, coop, hutch, sty
• VERB = enclose, confine, cage, fence in,

coop up, hedge in, shut up *or* in
penalty = punishment, price, fine, handicap, forfeit
pending ADJECTIVE **1** = undecided, unsettled, in the balance, undetermined **2** = forthcoming, imminent, prospective, impending, in the wind
• PREPOSITION = awaiting, until, waiting for, till
penetrate 1 = pierce, enter, go through, bore, stab, prick **2** = grasp, work out, figure out (*informal*), comprehend, fathom, decipher, suss (out) (*slang*), get to the bottom of
penetrating 1 = sharp, harsh, piercing, carrying, piping, loud, strident, shrill ≠ sweet **2** = pungent **3** = piercing **4** = intelligent, quick, sharp, keen, acute, shrewd, astute, perceptive ≠ dull **5** = perceptive, sharp, keen ≠ unperceptive
penetration 1 = piercing, entry, entrance, puncturing, incision **2** = entry, entrance
pension = allowance, benefit, welfare, annuity, superannuation
pensioner = senior citizen, retired person, retiree (*U.S.*), old-age pensioner, O.A.P.
people PLURAL NOUN **1** = persons, individuals, folk (*informal*), men and women, humanity, mankind, mortals, the human race **2** = nation, public, community, subjects, population, residents, citizens, folk **3** = race, tribe **4** = family, parents, relations, relatives, folk, folks (*informal*), clan, kin
• VERB = inhabit, occupy, settle, populate, colonize
pepper NOUN = seasoning, flavour, spice
• VERB **1** = pelt, hit, shower, blitz, rake, bombard, assail, strafe **2** = sprinkle, spot, scatter, dot, fleck, intersperse, speck, spatter
perceive 1 = see, notice, note, identify, discover, spot, observe, recognize **2** = understand, gather, see, learn, realize, grasp, comprehend, suss (out) (*slang*) **3** = consider, believe, judge, suppose, rate, deem, adjudge
perception 1 = awareness, understanding, sense, impression, feeling, idea, notion, consciousness **2** = understanding, intelligence, observation, discrimination, insight, sharpness, cleverness, keenness
perch VERB **1** = sit, rest, balance, settle **2** = place, put, rest, balance **3** = land, alight, roost
• NOUN = resting place, post, branch, pole
perennial = continual, lasting, constant, enduring, persistent, abiding, recurrent, incessant
perfect ADJECTIVE **1** = faultless, correct, pure, impeccable, exemplary, flawless, foolproof ≠ deficient **2** = excellent, ideal, supreme, superb, splendid, sublime, superlative **3** = immaculate, impeccable, flawless, spotless, unblemished ≠ flawed **4** = complete, absolute, sheer, utter, consummate, unmitigated ≠ partial **5** = exact, true, accurate, precise, correct, faithful, unerring
• VERB = improve, develop, polish, refine ≠ mar
perfection = excellence, integrity, superiority, purity, wholeness, sublimity, exquisiteness, faultlessness
perfectly 1 = completely, totally, absolutely, quite, fully, altogether, thoroughly, wholly ≠ partially **2** = flawlessly, ideally, wonderfully, superbly, supremely, impeccably, faultlessly ≠ badly
perform 1 = do, achieve, carry out, complete, fulfil, accomplish, execute, pull off **2** = fulfil, carry out, execute, discharge **3** = present, act (out), stage, play, produce, represent, put on, enact **4** = appear on stage, act **5** = function, go, work, run, operate, handle, respond, behave
performance 1 = presentation, playing, acting (out), staging, production, exhibition, rendering, portrayal **2** = show, appearance, concert, gig (*informal*), recital **3** = work, acts, conduct, exploits, feats **4** = carrying out, practice, achievement, execution, completion, accomplishment, fulfilment
performer = artiste, player, Thespian, trouper, actor *or* actress
perfume 1 = fragrance, scent **2** = scent, smell, fragrance, bouquet, aroma, odour
perhaps = maybe, possibly, it may be, it is possible (that), conceivably, perchance (*archaic*), feasibly, happen (*Northern English dialect*)
peril 1 = danger, risk, threat, hazard,

menace, jeopardy, perilousness **2** *often plural* = pitfall, problem, risk, hazard ≠ safety

perimeter = boundary, edge, border, bounds, limit, margin, confines, periphery ≠ centre

period = time, term, season, space, run, stretch, spell, phase

periodic = recurrent, regular, repeated, occasional, cyclical, sporadic, intermittent

peripheral **1** = secondary, minor, marginal, irrelevant, unimportant, incidental, inessential **2** = outermost, outside, external, outer, exterior

perish **1** = die, be killed, expire, pass away, lose your life, cark it (*Austral. & N.Z. slang*) **2** = be destroyed, fall, decline, collapse, disappear, vanish **3** = rot, waste away, decay, disintegrate, decompose, moulder

perk (*Brit. informal*) = bonus, benefit, extra, plus, fringe benefit, perquisite

permanent **1** = lasting, constant, enduring, persistent, eternal, abiding, perpetual, everlasting ≠ temporary **2** = long-term, established, secure, stable, steady ≠ temporary

permission = authorization, sanction, licence, approval, leave, go-ahead (*informal*), liberty, consent ≠ prohibition

permit VERB **1** = allow, grant, sanction, let, entitle, license, authorize, consent to ≠ forbid **2** = enable, let, allow, cause
• NOUN = licence, pass, document, certificate, passport, visa, warrant, authorization ≠ prohibition

perpetual **1** = everlasting, permanent, endless, eternal, lasting, perennial, infinite, never-ending ≠ temporary **2** = continual, repeated, constant, endless, continuous, persistent, recurrent, never-ending ≠ brief

perpetuate = maintain, preserve, keep going, immortalize ≠ end

persecute **1** = victimize, torture, torment, oppress, pick on, ill-treat, maltreat ≠ mollycoddle **2** = harass, bother, annoy, tease, hassle (*informal*), badger, pester ≠ leave alone

persist **1** = continue, last, remain, carry on, keep up, linger **2** = persevere, continue, go on, carry on, keep on, keep going, press on, not give up

persistence = determination, resolution, grit, endurance, tenacity, perseverance, doggedness, pertinacity

persistent **1** = continuous, constant, repeated, endless, perpetual, continual, never-ending, incessant ≠ occasional **2** = determined, dogged, steady, stubborn, persevering, tireless, tenacious, steadfast ≠ irresolute

person NOUN = individual, being, body, human, soul, creature, mortal, man *or* woman
• PHRASES **in person** **1** = personally, yourself **2** = in the flesh, actually, physically, bodily

personal **1** = own, special, private, individual, particular, peculiar **2** = individual, special, particular, exclusive **3** = private **4** = offensive, nasty, insulting, disparaging, derogatory

personality **1** = nature, character, make-up, identity, temperament, disposition, individuality **2** = character, charm, attraction, charisma, magnetism **3** = celebrity, star, notable, household name, famous name, personage, megastar (*informal*)

personally **1** = in your opinion, in your book, for your part, from your own viewpoint, in your own view **2** = by yourself, alone, independently, solely, on your own **3** = individually, specially, subjectively, individualistically **4** = privately, in private, off the record

personnel = employees, people, staff, workers, workforce, human resources, helpers

perspective **1** = outlook, attitude, context, angle, frame of reference **2** = objectivity, proportion, relation, relativity, relative importance

persuade **1** = talk (someone) into, urge, influence, win (someone) over, induce, sway, entice, coax ≠ dissuade **2** = cause, lead, move, influence, motivate, induce, incline, dispose **3** = convince, satisfy, assure, cause to believe

persuasion **1** = urging, inducement, wheedling, enticement, cajolery **2** = belief, views, opinion, party, school, side, camp, faith

persuasive = convincing, telling, effective, sound, compelling, influential, valid, credible ≠ unconvincing

pervasive = widespread, general, common, extensive, universal, prevalent, ubiquitous, rife

perverse 1 = stubborn, contrary, dogged, troublesome, rebellious, wayward, intractable, wilful ≠ cooperative 2 = ill-natured, cross, surly, fractious, churlish, ill-tempered, stroppy (*Brit. slang*), peevish ≠ good-natured 3 = abnormal, unhealthy, improper, deviant

pervert VERB 1 = distort, abuse, twist, misuse, warp, misrepresent, falsify 2 = corrupt, degrade, deprave, debase, debauch, lead astray
• NOUN = deviant, degenerate, sicko (*informal*), weirdo *or* weirdie (*informal*)

pessimistic = gloomy, dark, despairing, bleak, depressed, cynical, hopeless, glum ≠ optimistic

pest 1 = infection, bug, insect, plague, epidemic, blight, scourge, pestilence, gogga (*S. African informal*) 2 = nuisance, trial, pain (*informal*), drag (*informal*), bother, irritation, annoyance, bane

pet ADJECTIVE = favourite, favoured, dearest, cherished, fave (*informal*), dear to your heart
• NOUN = favourite, treasure, darling, jewel, idol
• VERB 1 = fondle, pat, stroke, caress 2 = pamper, spoil, indulge, cosset, baby, dote on, coddle, mollycoddle 3 (*Informal*) = cuddle, kiss, snog (*Brit. slang*), smooch (*informal*), neck (*informal*), canoodle (*slang*)

petition NOUN 1 = appeal, round robin, list of signatures 2 = entreaty, appeal, suit, application, request, prayer, plea, solicitation
• VERB = appeal, plead, ask, pray, beg, solicit, beseech, entreat

petty 1 = trivial, insignificant, little, small, slight, trifling, negligible, unimportant ≠ important 2 = small-minded, mean, shabby, spiteful, ungenerous, mean-minded ≠ broad-minded

phantom = spectre, ghost, spirit, shade (*literary*), spook (*informal*), apparition, wraith, phantasm

phase NOUN = stage, time, point, position, step, development, period, chapter
• PHRASES **phase something in** = introduce, incorporate, ease in, start ♦ **phase something out** = eliminate, close, remove, withdraw, pull out, wind up, run down, terminate

phenomenal = extraordinary, outstanding, remarkable, fantastic, unusual, marvellous, exceptional, miraculous ≠ unremarkable

phenomenon 1 = occurrence, happening, fact, event, incident, circumstance, episode 2 = wonder, sensation, exception, miracle, marvel, prodigy, rarity

philosopher = thinker, theorist, sage, wise man, logician, metaphysician

philosophical *or* **philosophic** 1 = theoretical, abstract, wise, rational, logical, thoughtful, sagacious ≠ practical 2 = stoical, calm, composed, cool, collected, serene, tranquil, unruffled ≠ emotional

philosophy 1 = thought, knowledge, thinking, reasoning, wisdom, logic, metaphysics 2 = outlook, values, principles, convictions, thinking, beliefs, doctrine, ideology

phone NOUN 1 = telephone, blower (*informal*) 2 = call, ring (*informal, chiefly Brit.*), tinkle (*Brit. informal*)
• VERB = call, telephone, ring (up) (*informal, chiefly Brit.*), give someone a call, give someone a ring (*informal, chiefly Brit.*), make a call, give someone a tinkle (*Brit. informal*), get on the blower (*informal*)

photograph NOUN = picture, photo (*informal*), shot, print, snap (*informal*), snapshot, transparency
• VERB = take a picture of, record, film, shoot, snap (*informal*), take (someone's) picture

photographic 1 = pictorial, visual, graphic, cinematic, filmic 2 = accurate, exact, precise, faithful, retentive

phrase NOUN = expression, saying, remark, construction, quotation, maxim, idiom, adage
• VERB = express, say, word, put, voice, communicate, convey, put into words

physical 1 = corporal, fleshly, bodily, corporeal 2 = earthly, fleshly, mortal, incarnate 3 = material, real, substantial, natural, solid, tangible, palpable

physician = doctor, doc (*informal*), medic (*informal*), general practitioner, medical practitioner, doctor of medicine, G.P., M.D.

pick VERB 1 = select, choose, identify, elect, nominate, specify, opt for, single out ≠ reject 2 = gather, pull, collect, take in,

harvest, pluck, garner **3** = provoke, start, cause, stir up, incite, instigate **4** = open, force, crack (*informal*), break into, break open
• **NOUN 1** = choice, decision, option, selection, preference **2** = best, prime, finest, elect, elite, cream, jewel in the crown, crème de la crème (*French*)
• **PHRASES pick on someone** **1** = torment, bully, bait, tease, get at (*informal*), badger, persecute, hector **2** = choose, select, prefer, elect, single out, fix on, settle upon ◆ **pick something** *or* **someone out** = identify, recognize, distinguish, perceive, discriminate, make someone *or* something out, tell someone *or* something apart ◆ **pick something** *or* **someone up** **1** = lift, raise, gather, take up, grasp, uplift **2** = collect, get, call for ◆ **pick something up** **1** = learn, master, acquire, get the hang of (*informal*), become proficient in **2** = obtain, get, find, buy, discover, purchase, acquire, locate ◆ **pick up** **1** = improve, recover, rally, get better, bounce back, make progress, perk up, turn the corner **2** = recover, improve, rally, get better, mend, turn the corner, be on the mend, take a turn for the better

picket **VERB** = blockade, boycott, demonstrate outside
• **NOUN 1** = demonstration, strike, blockade **2** = protester, demonstrator, picketer **3** = lookout, watch, guard, patrol, sentry, sentinel **4** = stake, post, pale, paling, upright, stanchion

pickle **VERB** = preserve, marinade, steep
• **NOUN 1** = chutney, relish, piccalilli **2** (*Informal*) = predicament, fix (*informal*), difficulty, bind (*informal*), jam (*informal*), dilemma, scrape (*informal*), hot water (*informal*), uphill (*S. African*)

pick-up = improvement, recovery, rise, rally, strengthening, revival, upturn, change for the better

picnic = excursion, barbecue, barbie (*informal*), cookout (*U.S. & Canad.*), alfresco meal, clambake (*U.S. & Canad.*), outdoor meal, outing

picture **NOUN 1** = representation, drawing, painting, portrait, image, print, illustration, sketch **2** = photograph, photo, still, shot, image, print, frame, slide **3** = film, movie (*U.S. informal*), flick (*slang*), feature film, motion picture **4** = idea, vision, concept, impression, notion, visualization, mental picture, mental image **5** = description, impression, explanation, report, account, image, sketch, depiction **6** = personification, embodiment, essence, epitome
• **VERB 1** = imagine, see, envision, visualize, conceive of, fantasize about, conjure up an image of **2** = represent, show, draw, paint, illustrate, sketch, depict **3** = show, photograph, capture on film

picturesque **1** = interesting, pretty, beautiful, attractive, charming, scenic, quaint ≠ unattractive **2** = vivid, striking, graphic, colourful, memorable ≠ dull

piece **1** = bit, slice, part, block, quantity, segment, portion, fragment **2** = component, part, section, bit, unit, segment, constituent, module **3** = item, report, story, study, review, article **4** = composition, work, production, opus **5** = work of art, work, creation **6** = share, cut (*informal*), slice, percentage, quantity, portion, quota, fraction

pier **1** = jetty, wharf, quay, promenade, landing place **2** = pillar, support, post, column, pile, upright, buttress

pierce = penetrate, stab, spike, enter, bore, drill, puncture, prick

piercing **1** (*of sound*) = penetrating, sharp, loud, shrill, high-pitched, ear-splitting ≠ low **2** = perceptive, sharp, keen, alert, penetrating, shrewd, perspicacious, quick-witted ≠ unperceptive **3** = sharp, acute, severe, intense, painful, stabbing, excruciating, agonizing **4** (*of weather*) = cold, biting, freezing, bitter, arctic, wintry, nippy

pig **1** = hog, sow, boar, swine, porker **2** (*Informal*) = slob, glutton **3** (*Informal*) = brute, monster, scoundrel, rogue, swine, rotter, boor

pigment = colour, colouring, paint, stain, dye, tint, tincture

pile¹ **NOUN 1** = heap, collection, mountain, mass, stack, mound, accumulation, hoard **2** (*Informal*) *often plural* = lot(s), mountain(s), load(s) (*informal*), oceans, wealth, great deal, stack(s), abundance **3** = mansion, building, residence, manor, country house, seat, big house, stately home
• **VERB 1** = load, stuff, pack, stack, charge, heap, cram, lade **2** = crowd, pack, rush,

climb, flood, stream, crush, squeeze
• PHRASES **pile up** = accumulate, collect, gather (up), build up, amass
pile² = foundation, support, post, column, beam, upright, pillar
pile³ = nap, fibre, down, hair, fur, plush
pile-up (*Informal*) = collision, crash, accident, smash, smash-up (*informal*), multiple collision
pilgrim = traveller, wanderer, devotee, wayfarer
pilgrimage = journey, tour, trip, mission, expedition, excursion
pill = tablet, capsule, pellet
pillar 1 = support, post, column, prop, shaft, upright, pier, stanchion 2 = supporter, leader, mainstay, leading light (*informal*), upholder
pilot NOUN 1 = airman, flyer, aviator, aeronaut 2 = helmsman, navigator, steersman
• VERB 1 = fly, operate, be at the controls of 2 = navigate, drive, direct, guide, handle, conduct, steer 3 = direct, conduct, steer
• ADJECTIVE = trial, test, model, sample, experimental
pin NOUN 1 = tack, nail, needle, safety pin 2 = peg, rod, brace, bolt
• VERB 1 = fasten, stick, attach, join, fix, secure, nail, clip 2 = hold fast, hold down, constrain, immobilize, pinion
• PHRASES **pin someone down** = force, pressure, compel, put pressure on, pressurize, nail someone down, make someone commit themselves ♦ **pin something down** = determine, identify, locate, name, specify, pinpoint
pinch VERB 1 = nip, press, squeeze, grasp, compress 2 = hurt, crush, squeeze, pain, cramp 3 (*Brit. informal*) = steal, lift (*informal*), nick (*slang, chiefly Brit.*), swipe (*slang*), knock off (*slang*), pilfer, purloin, filch
• NOUN 1 = nip, squeeze 2 = dash, bit, mite, jot, speck, soupçon (*French*) 3 = emergency, crisis, difficulty, plight, scrape (*informal*), strait, uphill (*S. African*), predicament
pine VERB = waste, decline, sicken, fade, languish
• PHRASES **pine for something** *or* **someone** 1 = long, ache, crave, yearn, eat your heart out over 2 = hanker after, crave, wish for, yearn for, thirst for, hunger for
pink NOUN *or* ADJECTIVE = rosy, rose, salmon, flushed, reddish, roseate
pinnacle 1 = summit, top, height, peak 2 = height, top, crown, crest, zenith, apex, vertex
pinpoint 1 = identify, discover, define, distinguish, put your finger on 2 = locate, find, identify, zero in on
pioneer NOUN 1 = founder, leader, developer, innovator, trailblazer 2 = settler, explorer, colonist
• VERB = develop, create, establish, start, discover, institute, invent, initiate
pipe NOUN = tube, drain, canal, pipeline, line, main, passage, cylinder
• VERB = convey, channel, conduct
• PHRASES **pipe down** (*Informal*) = be quiet, shut up (*informal*), hush, stop talking, quieten down, shush, shut your mouth, hold your tongue
pipeline = tube, passage, pipe, conduit, duct
pirate NOUN = buccaneer, raider, marauder, corsair, freebooter
• VERB = copy, steal, reproduce, bootleg, appropriate, poach, crib (*informal*), plagiarize
pit NOUN 1 = coal mine, mine, shaft, colliery, mine shaft 2 = hole, depression, hollow, crater, trough, cavity, abyss, chasm
• VERB = scar, mark, dent, indent, pockmark
pitch NOUN 1 = sports field, ground, stadium, arena, park, field of play 2 = tone, sound, key, frequency, timbre, modulation 3 = level, point, degree, summit, extent, height, intensity, high point 4 = talk, patter, spiel (*informal*)
• VERB 1 = throw, cast, toss, hurl, fling, chuck (*informal*), sling, lob (*informal*) 2 = fall, drop, plunge, dive, tumble, topple, plummet, fall headlong 3 = set up, raise, settle, put up, erect 4 = toss (about), roll, plunge, lurch
• PHRASES **pitch in** = help, contribute, participate, join in, cooperate, chip in (*informal*), get stuck in (*Brit. informal*), lend a hand
pitfall *usually plural* = danger, difficulty, peril, catch, trap, hazard, drawback, snag, uphill (*S. African*)
pity NOUN 1 = compassion, charity, sympathy, kindness, fellow feeling ≠ mercilessness 2 = shame, sin (*informal*), misfortune, bummer (*slang*), crying

shame **3** = mercy, kindness, clemency, forbearance
• **VERB** = feel sorry for, feel for, sympathize with, grieve for, weep for, bleed for, have compassion for

pivotal = crucial, central, vital, critical, decisive

place **NOUN 1** = spot, point, position, site, area, location, venue, whereabouts **2** = region, quarter, district, neighbourhood, vicinity, locality, locale, dorp (*S. African*) **3** = position, point, spot, location **4** = space, position, seat, chair **5** = rank, standing, position, footing, station, status, grade, niche **6** = situation, position, circumstances, shoes (*informal*) **7** = job, position, post, situation, office, employment, appointment **8** = home, house, room, property, accommodation, pad (*slang*), residence, dwelling **9** (In this context, the construction is always negative) = duty, right, job, charge, concern, role, affair, responsibility
• **VERB 1** = lay (down), put (down), set (down), stand, position, rest, station, stick (*informal*) **2** = put, lay, set, invest, pin **3** = classify, class, group, put, order, sort, rank, arrange **4** = entrust to, give to, assign to, appoint to, allocate to, find a home for **5** = identify, remember, recognize, pin someone down, put your finger on, put a name to
• **PHRASES** **take place** = happen, occur, go on, go down (*U.S. & Canad.*), arise, come about, crop up, transpire (*informal*)

plague **NOUN 1** = disease, infection, epidemic, pestilence **2** = infestation, invasion, epidemic, influx, host, swarm, multitude
• **VERB 1** = torment, trouble, torture **2** = pester, trouble, bother, annoy, tease, harry, harass, hassle

plain **ADJECTIVE 1** = unadorned, simple, basic, severe, bare, stark, austere, spartan ≠ ornate **2** = clear, obvious, patent, evident, visible, distinct, understandable, manifest ≠ hidden **3** = straightforward, open, direct, frank, blunt, outspoken, honest, downright ≠ roundabout **4** = ugly, unattractive, homely (*U.S. & Canad.*), unlovely, unprepossessing, not beautiful, no oil painting (*informal*), ill-favoured ≠ attractive **5** = ordinary, common, simple, everyday, commonplace, unaffected, unpretentious ≠ sophisticated
• **NOUN** = flatland, plateau, prairie, grassland, steppe, veld

plan **NOUN 1** = scheme, system, design, programme, proposal, strategy, method, suggestion **2** = diagram, map, drawing, chart, representation, sketch, blueprint, layout
• **VERB 1** = devise, arrange, scheme, plot, draft, organize, outline, formulate **2** = intend, aim, mean, propose, purpose **3** = design, outline, draw up a plan of

plane **NOUN 1** = aeroplane, aircraft, jet, airliner, jumbo jet **2** = flat surface, the flat, horizontal, level surface **3** = level, position, stage, condition, standard, degree, rung, echelon
• **ADJECTIVE** = level, even, flat, regular, smooth, horizontal
• **VERB** = skim, sail, skate, glide

plant[1] **NOUN** = flower, bush, vegetable, herb, weed, shrub
• **VERB 1** = sow, scatter, transplant, implant, put in the ground **2** = seed, sow, implant **3** = place, put, set, fix **4** = hide, put, place, conceal **5** = place, put, establish, found, fix, insert

plant[2] **1** = factory, works, shop, yard, mill, foundry **2** = machinery, equipment, gear, apparatus

plaster **NOUN 1** = mortar, stucco, gypsum, plaster of Paris **2** = bandage, dressing, sticking plaster, Elastoplast®, adhesive plaster
• **VERB** = cover, spread, coat, smear, overlay, daub

plastic = pliant, soft, flexible, supple, pliable, ductile, mouldable ≠ rigid

plate **NOUN 1** = platter, dish, dinner plate, salver, trencher (*archaic*) **2** = helping, course, serving, dish, portion, platter, plateful **3** = layer, panel, sheet, slab **4** = illustration, picture, photograph, print, engraving, lithograph
• **VERB** = coat, gild, laminate, cover, overlay

plateau **1** = upland, table, highland, tableland **2** = levelling off, level, stage, stability

platform **1** = stage, stand, podium, rostrum, dais, soapbox **2** = policy, programme, principle, objective(s), manifesto, party line

plausible **1** = believable, possible, likely, reasonable, credible, probable, persuasive, conceivable ≠ unbelievable **2** = glib, smooth, specious, smooth-talking, smooth-tongued

play VERB **1** = amuse yourself, have fun, sport, fool, romp, revel, trifle, entertain yourself **2** = take part in, be involved in, engage in, participate in, compete in **3** = compete against, challenge, take on, oppose, contend against **4** = perform, carry out **5** = act, portray, represent, perform, act the part of **6** = perform on, strum, make music on

• NOUN **1** = amusement, pleasure, leisure, games, sport, fun, entertainment, relaxation **2** = drama, show, piece, comedy, tragedy, farce, soapie (*Austral. slang*), pantomime

• PHRASES **play on** *or* **upon something** = take advantage of, abuse, exploit, impose on, trade on, capitalize on ◆ **play something down** = minimize, make light of, gloss over, talk down, underrate, underplay, pooh-pooh (*informal*), soft-pedal (*informal*) ◆ **play something up** = emphasize, highlight, underline, stress, accentuate ◆ **play up 1** (*Brit. informal*) = hurt, be painful, bother you, trouble you, be sore, pain you **2** (*Brit. informal*) = malfunction, not work properly, be on the blink (*slang*) **3** (*Brit. informal*) = be awkward, misbehave, give trouble, be disobedient, be stroppy (*Brit. slang*)

playboy = womanizer, philanderer, rake, lady-killer (*informal*), roué, ladies' man

player 1 = sportsman *or* sportswoman, competitor, participant, contestant **2** = musician, artist, performer, virtuoso, instrumentalist **3** = performer, entertainer, Thespian, trouper, actor *or* actress

plea 1 = appeal, request, suit, prayer, petition, entreaty, intercession, supplication **2** = excuse, defence, explanation, justification

plead = appeal, ask, request, beg, petition, implore, beseech, entreat

pleasant 1 = pleasing, nice, fine, lovely, amusing, delightful, enjoyable, agreeable, lekker (*S. African slang*) ≠ horrible **2** = friendly, nice, agreeable, likable *or* likeable, engaging, charming, amiable, genial ≠ disagreeable

please = delight, entertain, humour, amuse, suit, satisfy, indulge, gratify ≠ annoy

pleased = happy, delighted, contented, satisfied, thrilled, glad, gratified, over the moon (*informal*)

pleasing 1 = enjoyable, satisfying, charming, delightful, gratifying, agreeable, pleasurable ≠ unpleasant **2** = likable *or* likeable, engaging, charming, delightful, agreeable ≠ disagreeable

pleasure 1 = happiness, delight, satisfaction, enjoyment, bliss, gratification, gladness, delectation ≠ displeasure **2** = amusement, joy ≠ duty

pledge NOUN **1** = promise, vow, assurance, word, undertaking, warrant, oath, covenant **2** = guarantee, security, deposit, bail, collateral, pawn, surety

• VERB = promise, vow, swear, contract, engage, give your word, give your oath

plentiful = abundant, liberal, generous, lavish, ample, overflowing, copious, bountiful ≠ scarce

plenty 1 = abundance, wealth, prosperity, fertility, profusion, affluence, plenitude, fruitfulness **2** *usually with* ***of*** = lots of (*informal*), enough, a great deal of, masses of, piles of (*informal*), stacks of, heaps of (*informal*), an abundance of

plight = difficulty, condition, state, situation, trouble, predicament

plot¹ NOUN **1** = plan, scheme, intrigue, conspiracy, cabal, stratagem, machination **2** = story, action, subject, theme, outline, scenario, narrative, story line

• VERB **1** = plan, scheme, conspire, intrigue, manoeuvre, contrive, collude, machinate **2** = devise, design, lay, conceive, hatch, contrive, concoct, cook up (*informal*) **3** = chart, mark, map, locate, calculate, outline

plot² = patch, lot, area, ground, parcel, tract, allotment

plough VERB = turn over, dig, till, cultivate

• PHRASES **plough through something** = forge, cut, drive, press, push, plunge, wade

ploy = tactic, move, trick, device, scheme, manoeuvre, dodge, ruse

pluck VERB **1** = pull out *or* off, pick, draw, collect, gather, harvest **2** = tug, catch, snatch, clutch, jerk, yank, tweak, pull at **3** = strum, pick, finger, twang

• NOUN = courage, nerve, bottle (*Brit. slang*), guts (*informal*), grit, bravery, backbone, boldness

plug NOUN **1** = stopper, cork, bung, spigot **2** (*Informal*) = mention, advertisement, advert (*Brit. informal*), push, publicity, hype
• VERB **1** = seal, close, stop, fill, block, stuff, pack, cork **2** (*Informal*) = mention, push, promote, publicize, advertise, build up, hype
• PHRASES **plug away** (*Informal*) = slog away, labour, toil away, grind away (*informal*), peg away, plod away

plum = choice, prize, first-class

plumb VERB = delve into, explore, probe, go into, penetrate, gauge, unravel, fathom
• ADVERB = exactly, precisely, bang, slap, spot-on (*Brit. informal*)

plummet 1 = drop, fall, crash, nose-dive, descend rapidly **2** = plunge, fall, drop, crash, tumble, nose-dive, descend rapidly

plump = chubby, fat, stout, round, tubby, dumpy, roly-poly, rotund ≠ scrawny

plunder VERB **1** = loot, strip, sack, rob, raid, rifle, ransack, pillage **2** = steal, rob, take, nick (*informal*), pinch (*informal*), embezzle, pilfer, thieve
• NOUN **1** = pillage **2** = loot, spoils, booty, swag (*slang*), ill-gotten gains

plunge VERB **1** = descend, fall, drop, crash, pitch, sink, dive, tumble **2** = hurtle, charge, career, jump, tear, rush, dive, dash **3** = submerge, dip **4** = throw, cast, pitch, propel **5** = fall steeply, drop, crash (*informal*), slump, plummet, take a nosedive (*informal*)
• NOUN **1** = dive, jump, duck, descent **2** = fall, crash (*informal*), slump, drop, tumble

plus PREPOSITION = and, with, added to, coupled with
• NOUN (*Informal*) = advantage, benefit, asset, gain, extra, bonus, good point
• ADJECTIVE = additional, added, extra, supplementary, add-on

plush = luxurious, luxury, lavish, rich, sumptuous, opulent, de luxe

ply = work at, follow, exercise, pursue, carry on, practise

pocket NOUN = pouch, bag, sack, compartment, receptacle
• ADJECTIVE = small, compact, miniature, portable, little
• VERB = steal, take, lift (*informal*), appropriate, pilfer, purloin, filch

pod = shell, case, hull, husk, shuck

podium = platform, stand, stage, rostrum, dais

poem = verse, song, lyric, rhyme, sonnet, ode, verse composition

poet = bard, rhymer, lyricist, lyric poet, versifier, elegist

poetic 1 = figurative, creative, lyric, symbolic, lyrical **2** = lyrical, lyric, elegiac, metrical

poetry = verse, poems, rhyme, rhyming, verse composition

poignant = moving, touching, sad, bitter, intense, painful, distressing, pathetic

point NOUN **1** = essence, meaning, subject, question, heart, import, drift, thrust **2** = purpose, aim, object, end, reason, goal, intention, objective **3** = aspect, detail, feature, quality, particular, respect, item, characteristic **4** = place, area, position, site, spot, location, locality, locale **5** = moment, time, stage, period, phase, instant, juncture, moment in time **6** = stage, level, position, condition, degree, pitch, circumstance, extent **7** = end, tip, sharp end, top, spur, spike, apex, prong **8** = score, tally, mark **9** = pinpoint, mark, spot, dot, fleck
• VERB **1** = aim, level, train, direct **2** = indicate, show, signal, point to, gesture towards **3** = face, look, direct
• PHRASES **point at** *or* **to something** *or* **someone** = indicate, point out, specify, designate, gesture towards

pointed 1 = sharp, edged, acute, barbed **2** = cutting, telling, biting, sharp, keen, acute, penetrating, pertinent

pointer 1 = hint, tip, suggestion, recommendation, caution, piece of information, piece of advice **2** = indicator, hand, guide, needle, arrow

pointless = senseless, meaningless, futile, fruitless, stupid, silly, useless, absurd ≠ worthwhile

poised 1 = ready, waiting, prepared, standing by, all set **2** = composed, calm, together (*informal*), collected, dignified, self-confident, self-possessed ≠ agitated

poison NOUN = toxin, venom, bane (*archaic*)
• VERB **1** = murder, kill, give someone poison, administer poison to **2** = contaminate, foul, infect, spoil, pollute, blight, taint, befoul **3** = corrupt, colour, undermine, bias, sour, pervert, warp, taint

poisonous 1 = toxic, fatal, deadly, lethal,

mortal, virulent, noxious, venomous **2** = evil, malicious, corrupting, pernicious, baleful

poke VERB **1** = jab, push, stick, dig, stab, thrust, shove, nudge **2** = protrude, stick, thrust, jut
• NOUN = jab, dig, thrust, nudge, prod

pole = rod, post, support, staff, bar, stick, stake, paling

police NOUN = the law (*informal*), police force, constabulary, fuzz (*slang*), boys in blue (*informal*), the Old Bill (*slang*), rozzers (*slang*)
• VERB = control, patrol, guard, watch, protect, regulate

policy **1** = procedure, plan, action, practice, scheme, code, custom **2** = line, rules, approach

polish NOUN **1** = varnish, wax, glaze, lacquer, japan **2** = sheen, finish, glaze, gloss, brightness, lustre **3** = style, class (*informal*), finish, breeding, grace, elegance, refinement, finesse
• VERB **1** = shine, wax, smooth, rub, buff, brighten, burnish **2** *often with* ***up*** = perfect, improve, enhance, refine, finish, brush up, touch up

polished **1** = elegant, sophisticated, refined, polite, cultivated, suave, well-bred ≠ unsophisticated **2** = accomplished, professional, masterly, fine, expert, skilful, adept, superlative ≠ amateurish **3** = shining, bright, smooth, gleaming, glossy, burnished ≠ dull

polite **1** = mannerly, civil, courteous, gracious, respectful, well-behaved, complaisant, well-mannered ≠ rude **2** = refined, cultured, civilized, polished, sophisticated, elegant, genteel, well-bred ≠ uncultured

politic = wise, diplomatic, sensible, prudent, advisable, expedient, judicious

political = governmental, government, state, parliamentary, constitutional, administrative, legislative, ministerial

politician = statesman *or* stateswoman, representative, senator (*U.S.*), congressman (*U.S.*), Member of Parliament, legislator, public servant, congresswoman (*U.S.*)

politics **1** = affairs of state, government, public affairs, civics **2** = political beliefs, party politics, political allegiances, political leanings, political sympathies **3** = political science, statesmanship, civics, statecraft

poll NOUN **1** = survey, figures, count, sampling, returns, ballot, tally, census **2** = election, vote, voting, referendum, ballot, plebiscite
• VERB **1** = question, interview, survey, sample, ballot, canvass **2** = gain, return, record, register, tally

pollute **1** = contaminate, dirty, poison, soil, foul, infect, spoil, stain ≠ decontaminate **2** = defile, corrupt, sully, deprave, debase, profane, desecrate, dishonour ≠ honour

pollution **1** = contamination, dirtying, corruption, taint, foulness, defilement, uncleanness **2** = waste, poisons, dirt, impurities

pond = pool, tarn, small lake, fish pond, duck pond, millpond

ponder = think about, consider, reflect on, contemplate, deliberate about, muse on, brood on, meditate on

pool[1] **1** = swimming pool, lido, swimming bath(s) (*Brit.*), bathing pool (*archaic*) **2** = pond, lake, mere, tarn **3** = puddle, drop, patch

pool[2] NOUN **1** = supply, reserve, fall-back **2** = kitty, bank, fund, stock, store, pot, jackpot, stockpile
• VERB = combine, share, merge, put together, amalgamate, lump together, join forces on

poor **1** = impoverished, broke (*informal*), hard up (*informal*), short, needy, penniless, destitute, poverty-stricken ≠ rich **2** = unfortunate, unlucky, hapless, pitiful, luckless, wretched, ill-starred, pitiable ≠ fortunate **3** = inferior, unsatisfactory, mediocre, second-rate, rotten (*informal*), low-grade, below par, substandard, half-pie (*N.Z. informal*), bodger *or* bodgie (*Austral. slang*) ≠ excellent **4** = meagre, inadequate, insufficient, lacking, incomplete, scant, deficient, skimpy ≠ ample

poorly ADVERB = badly, incompetently, inadequately, unsuccessfully, insufficiently, unsatisfactorily, inexpertly ≠ well
• ADJECTIVE (*Informal*) = ill, sick, unwell, crook (*Austral. & N.Z. informal*), seedy (*informal*), below par, off colour, under the weather (*informal*), feeling rotten (*informal*) ≠ healthy

pop NOUN = bang, report, crack, noise, burst, explosion
• VERB **1** = burst, crack, snap, bang, explode, go off (with a bang) **2** = put, insert, push, stick, slip, thrust, tuck, shove

pope = Holy Father, pontiff, His Holiness, Bishop of Rome, Vicar of Christ

popular 1 = well-liked, liked, in, accepted, favourite, approved, in favour, fashionable ≠ unpopular **2** = common, general, prevailing, current, conventional, universal, prevalent ≠ rare

popularity 1 = favour, esteem, acclaim, regard, approval, vogue **2** = currency, acceptance, circulation, vogue, prevalence

populate 1 = inhabit, people, live in, occupy, reside in, dwell in (*formal*) **2** = settle, occupy, pioneer, colonize

population = inhabitants, people, community, society, residents, natives, folk, occupants

pore = opening, hole, outlet, orifice

pornography = obscenity, porn (*informal*), dirt, filth, indecency, smut

port = harbour, haven, anchorage, seaport

portable = light, compact, convenient, handy, manageable, movable, easily carried

porter[1] (*Chiefly Brit.*) = doorman, caretaker, janitor, concierge, gatekeeper

porter[2] = baggage attendant, carrier, bearer, baggage-carrier

portion 1 = part, bit, piece, section, scrap, segment, fragment, chunk **2** = helping, serving, piece, plateful **3** = share, allowance, lot, measure, quantity, quota, ration, allocation

portrait 1 = picture, painting, image, photograph, representation, likeness **2** = description, profile, portrayal, depiction, characterization, thumbnail sketch

portray 1 = play, take the role of, act the part of, represent, personate (*rare*) **2** = describe, present, depict, evoke, delineate, put in words **3** = represent, draw, paint, illustrate, sketch, figure, picture, depict **4** = characterize, represent, depict

portrayal 1 = performance, interpretation, characterization **2** = depiction, picture, representation, sketch, rendering **3** = description, account, representation **4** = characterization, representation, depiction

pose VERB **1** = position yourself, sit, model, arrange yourself **2** = put on airs, posture, show off (*informal*)
• NOUN **1** = posture, position, bearing, attitude, stance **2** = act, façade, air, front, posturing, pretence, mannerism, affectation
• PHRASES **pose as something** *or* **someone** = impersonate, pretend to be, profess to be, masquerade as, pass yourself off as

posh (*Informal, chiefly Brit.*) **1** = smart, grand, stylish, luxurious, classy (*slang*), swish (*informal, chiefly Brit.*), up-market, swanky (*informal*) **2** = upper-class, high-class

position NOUN **1** = location, place, point, area, post, situation, station, spot **2** = posture, attitude, arrangement, pose, stance **3** = status, place, standing, footing, station, rank, reputation, importance **4** = job, place, post, opening, office, role, situation, duty **5** = place, standing, rank, status **6** = attitude, view, perspective, point of view, opinion, belief, stance, outlook
• VERB = place, put, set, stand, arrange, locate, lay out

positive 1 = beneficial, useful, practical, helpful, progressive, productive, worthwhile, constructive ≠ harmful **2** = certain, sure, convinced, confident, satisfied, assured, free from doubt ≠ uncertain **3** = definite, real, clear, firm, certain, express, absolute, decisive ≠ inconclusive **4** (*Informal*) = absolute, complete, perfect, right (*Brit. informal*), real, total, sheer, utter

positively 1 = definitely, surely, firmly, certainly, absolutely, emphatically, unquestionably, categorically **2** = really, completely, simply, plain (*informal*), absolutely, thoroughly, utterly, downright

possess 1 = own, have, hold, be in possession of, be the owner of, have in your possession **2** = be endowed with, have, enjoy, benefit from, be possessed of, be gifted with **3** = seize, hold, control, dominate, occupy, take someone over, have power over, have mastery over

possession NOUN = ownership, control, custody, hold, hands, tenure

• **PLURAL NOUN** = property, things, effects, estate, assets, belongings, chattels

possibility 1 = feasibility, likelihood, potentiality, practicability, workableness 2 = likelihood, chance, risk, odds, prospect, liability, probability 3 *often plural* = potential, promise, prospects, talent, capabilities, potentiality

possible 1 = feasible, viable, workable, achievable, practicable, attainable, doable, realizable ≠ unfeasible 2 = likely, potential, anticipated, probable, odds-on, on the cards ≠ improbable 3 = conceivable, likely, credible, plausible, hypothetical, imaginable, believable, thinkable ≠ inconceivable 4 = aspiring, would-be, promising, hopeful, prospective, wannabe (*informal*)

possibly = perhaps, maybe, perchance (*archaic*)

post[1] **NOUN** 1 = mail, collection, delivery, postal service, snail mail (*informal*) 2 = correspondence, letters, cards, mail
• **VERB** = send (off), forward, mail, get off, transmit, dispatch, consign
• **PHRASES** **keep someone posted** = notify, brief, advise, inform, report to, keep someone informed, keep someone up to date, apprise

post[2] **NOUN** 1 = job, place, office, position, situation, employment, appointment, assignment 2 = position, place, base, beat, station
• **VERB** = station, assign, put, place, position, situate, put on duty

post[3] **NOUN** = support, stake, pole, column, shaft, upright, pillar, picket
• **VERB** = put something up, display, affix, pin something up

poster = notice, bill, announcement, advertisement, sticker, placard, public notice

postpone = put off, delay, suspend, adjourn, shelve, defer, put back, put on the back burner (*informal*) ≠ go ahead with

posture **NOUN** = bearing, set, attitude, stance, carriage, disposition
• **VERB** = show off (*informal*), pose, affect, put on airs

pot = container, bowl, pan, vessel, basin, cauldron, skillet

potent 1 = powerful, commanding, dynamic, dominant, influential, authoritative 2 = strong, powerful, mighty, vigorous, forceful ≠ weak

potential **ADJECTIVE** 1 = possible, future, likely, promising, probable 2 = hidden, possible, inherent, dormant, latent
• **NOUN** = ability, possibilities, capacity, capability, aptitude, wherewithal, potentiality

potter *usually with* ***around*** or ***about*** = mess about, tinker, dabble, footle (*informal*)

pottery = ceramics, terracotta, crockery, earthenware, stoneware

pounce = attack, strike, jump, leap, swoop

pound[1] = enclosure, yard, pen, compound, kennels

pound[2] 1 *sometimes with* ***on*** = beat, strike, hammer, batter, thrash, thump, clobber (*slang*), pummel 2 = crush, powder, pulverize 3 = pulsate, beat, pulse, throb, palpitate 4 = stomp, tramp, march, thunder (*informal*)

pour 1 = let flow, spill, splash, dribble, drizzle, slop (*informal*), slosh (*informal*), decant 2 = flow, stream, run, course, rush, emit, cascade, gush 3 = rain, pelt (down), teem, bucket down (*informal*) 4 = stream, crowd, flood, swarm, gush, throng, teem

pout **VERB** = sulk, glower, look petulant, pull a long face
• **NOUN** = sullen look, glower, long face

poverty 1 = pennilessness, want, need, hardship, insolvency, privation, penury, destitution ≠ wealth 2 = scarcity, lack, absence, want, deficit, shortage, deficiency, inadequacy ≠ abundance

powder **NOUN** = dust, talc, fine grains, loose particles
• **VERB** = dust, cover, scatter, sprinkle, strew, dredge

power 1 = control, authority, influence, command, dominance, domination, mastery, dominion, mana (*N.Z.*) 2 = ability, capacity, faculty, property, potential, capability, competence, competency ≠ inability 3 = authority, right, licence, privilege, warrant, prerogative, authorization 4 = strength, might, energy, muscle, vigour, potency, brawn ≠ weakness 5 = forcefulness, force, strength, punch (*informal*), intensity, potency, eloquence, persuasiveness

powerful 1 = influential, dominant,

controlling, commanding, prevailing, authoritative ≠ powerless **2** = strong, strapping, mighty, vigorous, potent, energetic, sturdy ≠ weak **3** = persuasive, convincing, telling, moving, striking, storming, dramatic, impressive

powerless 1 = defenceless, vulnerable, dependent, subject, tied, ineffective, unarmed **2** = weak, disabled, helpless, incapable, frail, feeble, debilitated, impotent ≠ strong

practical 1 = functional, realistic, pragmatic ≠ impractical **2** = empirical, real, applied, actual, hands-on, in the field, experimental, factual ≠ theoretical **3** = sensible, ordinary, realistic, down-to-earth, matter-of-fact, businesslike, hard-headed ≠ impractical **4** = feasible, possible, viable, workable, practicable, doable ≠ impractical **5** = useful, ordinary, appropriate, sensible, everyday, functional, utilitarian, serviceable **6** = skilled, experienced, efficient, accomplished, proficient ≠ inexperienced

practically 1 = almost, nearly, essentially, virtually, basically, fundamentally, all but, just about **2** = sensibly, reasonably, matter-of-factly, realistically, rationally, pragmatically

practice 1 = custom, way, system, rule, method, tradition, habit, routine, tikanga (*N.Z.*) **2** = training, study, exercise, preparation, drill, rehearsal, repetition **3** = profession, work, business, career, occupation, pursuit, vocation **4** = business, company, office, firm, enterprise, partnership, outfit (*informal*) **5** = use, experience, action, operation, application, enactment

practise 1 = rehearse, study, prepare, perfect, repeat, go through, go over, refine **2** = do, train, exercise, drill **3** = carry out, follow, apply, perform, observe, engage in **4** = work at, pursue, carry on

practised = skilled, trained, experienced, seasoned, able, expert, accomplished, proficient ≠ inexperienced

pragmatic = practical, sensible, realistic, down-to-earth, utilitarian, businesslike, hard-headed ≠ idealistic

praise VERB **1** = acclaim, approve of, honour, cheer, admire, applaud, compliment, congratulate ≠ criticize **2** = give thanks to, bless, worship, adore, glorify, exalt
• NOUN **1** = approval, acclaim, tribute, compliment, congratulations, eulogy, commendation, approbation ≠ criticism **2** = thanks, glory, worship, homage, adoration

pray 1 = say your prayers, offer a prayer, recite the rosary **2** = beg, ask, plead, petition, request, solicit, implore, beseech

prayer 1 = supplication, devotion **2** = orison, litany, invocation, intercession **3** = plea, appeal, request, petition, entreaty, supplication

preach 1 *often with* ***to*** = deliver a sermon, address, evangelize, preach a sermon **2** = urge, teach, champion, recommend, advise, counsel, advocate, exhort

preacher = clergyman, minister, parson, missionary, evangelist

precarious 1 = insecure, dangerous, tricky, risky, dodgy (*Brit., Austral., & N.Z. informal*), unsure, hazardous, shaky ≠ secure **2** = dangerous, shaky, insecure, unsafe, unreliable ≠ stable

precaution 1 = safeguard, insurance, protection, provision, safety measure **2** = forethought, care, caution, prudence, providence, wariness

precede 1 = go before, antedate **2** = go ahead of, lead, head, go before **3** = preface, introduce, go before

precedent = instance, example, standard, model, pattern, prototype, paradigm, antecedent

precinct = area, quarter, section, sector, district, zone

precious 1 = valuable, expensive, fine, prized, dear, costly, invaluable, priceless ≠ worthless **2** = loved, prized, dear, treasured, darling, beloved, adored, cherished **3** = affected, artificial, twee (*Brit. informal*), overrefined, overnice

precipitate VERB **1** = quicken, trigger, accelerate, advance, hurry, speed up, bring on, hasten **2** = throw, launch, cast, hurl, fling, let fly
• ADJECTIVE **1** = hasty, rash, reckless, impulsive, precipitous, impetuous, heedless **2** = sudden, quick, brief, rushing, rapid, unexpected, swift, abrupt

precise 1 = exact, specific, particular, express, correct, absolute, accurate, explicit ≠ vague **2** = strict, particular, exact, formal, careful, stiff, rigid, meticulous ≠ inexact

precisely 1 = exactly, squarely, correctly, absolutely, strictly, accurately, plumb (*informal*), square on 2 = just so, yes, absolutely, exactly, quite so, you bet (*informal*), without a doubt, indubitably 3 = just, entirely, absolutely, altogether, exactly, in all respects 4 = word for word, literally, exactly, to the letter

precision = exactness, care, accuracy, particularity, meticulousness, preciseness

predecessor 1 = previous job holder, precursor, forerunner, antecedent 2 = ancestor, forebear, antecedent, forefather, tupuna *or* tipuna (*N.Z.*)

predicament = fix (*informal*), situation, spot (*informal*), hole (*slang*), mess, jam (*informal*), dilemma, pinch

predict = foretell, forecast, divine, prophesy, augur, portend

predictable = likely, expected, sure, certain, anticipated, reliable, foreseeable ≠ unpredictable

prediction = prophecy, forecast, prognosis, divination, prognostication, augury

predominantly = mainly, largely, chiefly, mostly, generally, principally, primarily, for the most part

prefer 1 = like better, favour, go for, pick, fancy, opt for, incline towards, be partial to 2 = choose, opt for, pick, desire, would rather, would sooner, incline towards

preferable = better, best, chosen, preferred, recommended, favoured, superior, more suitable ≠ undesirable

preferably = ideally, if possible, rather, sooner, by choice, in *or* for preference

preference 1 = liking, wish, taste, desire, leaning, bent, bias, inclination 2 = first choice, choice, favourite, pick, option, selection 3 = priority, first place, precedence, favouritism, favoured treatment

pregnant 1 = expectant, expecting (*informal*), with child, in the club (*Brit. slang*), big *or* heavy with child 2 = meaningful, pointed, charged, significant, telling, loaded, expressive, eloquent

prejudice NOUN 1 = discrimination, injustice, intolerance, bigotry, unfairness, chauvinism, narrow-mindedness 2 = bias, preconception, partiality, preconceived notion, prejudgment
• VERB 1 = bias, influence, colour, poison, distort, slant, predispose 2 = harm, damage, hurt, injure, mar, undermine, spoil, impair, crool *or* cruel (*Austral. slang*)

prejudiced = biased, influenced, unfair, one-sided, bigoted, intolerant, opinionated, narrow-minded ≠ unbiased

preliminary ADJECTIVE 1 = first, opening, trial, initial, test, pilot, prior, introductory 2 = qualifying, eliminating
• NOUN = introduction, opening, beginning, start, prelude, preface, overture, preamble

prelude 1 = introduction, beginning, start 2 = overture, opening, introduction, introductory movement

premature 1 = early, untimely, before time, unseasonable 2 = hasty, rash, too soon, untimely, ill-timed, overhasty

premier NOUN = head of government, prime minister, chancellor, chief minister, P.M.
• ADJECTIVE = chief, leading, first, highest, head, main, prime, primary

premiere = first night, opening, debut

premise = assumption, proposition, argument, hypothesis, assertion, supposition, presupposition, postulation

premises = building(s), place, office, property, site, establishment

premium NOUN 1 = fee, charge, payment, instalment 2 = surcharge, extra charge, additional fee *or* charge 3 = bonus, reward, prize, perk (*Brit. informal*), bounty, perquisite
• PHRASES **at a premium** = in great demand, rare, scarce, in short supply, hard to come by

preoccupation 1 = obsession, fixation, bee in your bonnet 2 = absorption, abstraction, daydreaming, immersion, reverie, absent-mindedness, engrossment, woolgathering

preoccupied 1 = absorbed, lost, wrapped up, immersed, engrossed, rapt 2 = lost in thought, distracted, oblivious, absent-minded

preparation 1 = groundwork, preparing, getting ready 2 *usually plural* = arrangement, plan, measure, provision 3 = mixture, medicine, compound, concoction

prepare 1 = make *or* get ready, arrange, jack up (*N.Z. informal*) 2 = train, guide, prime, direct, brief, discipline, put someone in the picture 3 = make, cook, put together, get, produce, assemble, muster, concoct 4 = get ready 5 = practise, get ready, train, exercise, warm up, get into shape

prepared 1 = willing, inclined, disposed 2 = ready, set 3 = fit, primed, in order, arranged, in readiness

prescribe 1 = specify, order, direct, stipulate, write a prescription for 2 = ordain, set, order, rule, recommend, dictate, lay down, decree

prescription 1 = instruction, direction, formula, script (*informal*), recipe 2 = medicine, drug, treatment, preparation, cure, mixture, dose, remedy

presence NOUN 1 = being, existence, residence, attendance, showing up, occupancy, inhabitance 2 = personality, bearing, appearance, aspect, air, carriage, aura, poise
• PHRASES **presence of mind** = level-headedness, assurance, composure, poise, cool (*slang*), wits, countenance, coolness

present[1] ADJECTIVE 1 = current, existing, immediate, contemporary, present-day, existent 2 = here, there, near, ready, nearby, at hand ≠ absent 3 = in existence, existing, existent, extant
• PHRASES **the present** = now, today, the time being, here and now, the present moment

present[2] NOUN = gift, offering, grant, donation, hand-out, endowment, boon, gratuity, bonsela (*S. African*), koha (*N.Z.*)
• VERB 1 = give, award, hand over, grant, hand out, confer, bestow 2 = put on, stage, perform, give, show, render 3 = launch, display, parade, exhibit, unveil 4 = introduce, make known, acquaint someone with

presentation 1 = giving, award, offering, donation, bestowal, conferral 2 = appearance, look, display, packaging, arrangement, layout 3 = performance, production, show

presently 1 = at present, currently, now, today, these days, nowadays, at the present time, in this day and age 2 = soon, shortly, directly, before long, momentarily (*U.S. & Canad.*), by and by, in a jiffy (*informal*)

preservation 1 = upholding, support, maintenance 2 = protection, safety, maintenance, conservation, salvation, safeguarding, safekeeping

preserve VERB 1 = maintain, keep, continue, sustain, keep up, prolong, uphold, conserve ≠ end 2 = protect, keep, save, maintain, defend, shelter, shield, care for ≠ attack
• NOUN = area, department, field, territory, province, arena, sphere

preside = officiate, chair, moderate, be chairperson

press 1 = push (down), depress, lean on, press down, force down 2 = push, squeeze, jam, thrust, ram, wedge, shove 3 = hug, squeeze, embrace, clasp, crush, hold close, fold in your arms 4 = urge, beg, petition, exhort, implore, pressurize, entreat 5 = plead, present, lodge, submit, tender, advance insistently 6 = steam, iron, smooth, flatten 7 = compress, grind, reduce, mill, crush, pound, squeeze, tread 8 = crowd, push, gather, surge, flock, herd, swarm, seethe

pressing = urgent, serious, vital, crucial, imperative, important, high-priority, importunate ≠ unimportant

pressure 1 = force, crushing, squeezing, compressing, weight, compression 2 = power, influence, force, constraint, sway, compulsion, coercion 3 = stress, demands, strain, heat, load, burden, urgency, hassle (*informal*), uphill (*S. African*)

prestige = status, standing, credit, reputation, honour, importance, fame, distinction, mana (*N.Z.*)

prestigious = celebrated, respected, prominent, great, important, esteemed, notable, renowned ≠ unknown

presumably = it would seem, probably, apparently, seemingly, on the face of it, in all probability, in all likelihood

presume 1 = believe, think, suppose, assume, guess (*informal, chiefly U.S. & Canad.*), take for granted, infer, conjecture 2 = dare, venture, go so far as, take the liberty, make so bold as

pretend 1 = feign, affect, assume, allege, fake, simulate, profess, sham 2 = make believe, suppose, imagine, act, make up

pretty ADJECTIVE = attractive, beautiful,

lovely, charming, fair, good-looking, bonny, comely ≠ plain
• ADVERB (*Informal*) = fairly, rather, quite, kind of (*informal*), somewhat, moderately, reasonably
prevail 1 = win, succeed, triumph, overcome, overrule, be victorious 2 = be widespread, abound, predominate, be current, be prevalent, exist generally
prevailing 1 = widespread, general, established, popular, common, current, usual, ordinary 2 = predominating, ruling, main, existing, principal
prevalent = common, established, popular, general, current, usual, widespread, universal ≠ rare
prevent = stop, avoid, frustrate, hamper, foil, inhibit, avert, thwart ≠ help
prevention = elimination, safeguard, precaution, thwarting, avoidance, deterrence
preview = sample, sneak preview, trailer, taster, foretaste, advance showing
previous 1 = earlier, former, past, prior, preceding, erstwhile ≠ later 2 = preceding, past, prior, foregoing
previously = before, earlier, once, in the past, formerly, hitherto, beforehand
prey 1 = quarry, game, kill 2 = victim, target, mug (*Brit. slang*), dupe, fall guy (*informal*)
price NOUN 1 = cost, value, rate, charge, figure, worth, damage (*informal*), amount 2 = consequences, penalty, cost, result, toll, forfeit
• VERB = evaluate, value, estimate, rate, cost, assess
priceless = valuable, expensive, precious, invaluable, dear, costly ≠ worthless
prick VERB = pierce, stab, puncture, punch, lance, jab, perforate
• NOUN = puncture, hole, wound, perforation, pinhole
prickly 1 = spiny, barbed, thorny, bristly 2 = itchy, sharp, smarting, stinging, crawling, tingling, scratchy
pride 1 = satisfaction, achievement, fulfilment, delight, content, pleasure, joy, gratification 2 = self-respect, honour, ego, dignity, self-esteem, self-image, self-worth 3 = conceit, vanity, arrogance, pretension, hubris, self-importance, egotism, self-love ≠ humility
priest = clergyman, minister, father, divine, vicar, pastor, cleric, curate
primarily 1 = chiefly, largely, generally, mainly, essentially, mostly, principally, fundamentally 2 = at first, originally, initially, in the first place, in the beginning, first and foremost, at *or* from the start
primary = chief, main, first, highest, greatest, prime, principal, cardinal ≠ subordinate
prime ADJECTIVE 1 = main, leading, chief, central, major, key, primary, supreme 2 = best, top, select, highest, quality, choice, excellent, first-class
• NOUN = peak, flower, bloom, height, heyday, zenith
• VERB 1 = inform, tell, train, coach, brief, fill in (*informal*), notify, clue in (*informal*) 2 = prepare, set up, load, equip, get ready, make ready
primitive 1 = early, first, earliest, original, primary, elementary, primordial, primeval ≠ modern 2 = crude, simple, rough, rudimentary, unrefined ≠ elaborate
prince = ruler, lord, monarch, sovereign, crown prince, liege, prince regent, crowned head
princely 1 = substantial, considerable, large, huge, massive, enormous, sizable *or* sizeable 2 = regal, royal, imperial, noble, sovereign, majestic
princess = ruler, lady, monarch, sovereign, liege, crowned head, crowned princess, dynast
principal ADJECTIVE = main, leading, chief, prime, first, key, essential, primary ≠ minor
• NOUN 1 = headmaster *or* headmistress, head (*informal*), dean, head teacher, rector, master *or* mistress 2 = star, lead, leader, prima ballerina, leading man *or* lady, coryphée 3 = capital, money, assets, working capital
principally = mainly, largely, chiefly, especially, mostly, primarily, above all, predominantly
principle NOUN 1 = morals, standards, ideals, honour, virtue, ethics, integrity, conscience, kaupapa (*N.Z.*) 2 = rule, law, truth, precept
• PHRASES **in principle** 1 = in general 2 = in theory, ideally, on paper, theoretically, in an ideal world, en principe (*French*)
print VERB 1 = run off, publish, copy, reproduce, issue, engrave 2 = publish,

release, circulate, issue, disseminate **3** = mark, impress, stamp, imprint • NOUN **1** = photograph, photo, snap **2** = picture, plate, etching, engraving, lithograph, woodcut, linocut **3** = copy, photo (*informal*), picture, reproduction, replica

prior ADJECTIVE = earlier, previous, former, preceding, foregoing, pre-existing, pre-existent
• PHRASES **prior to** = before, preceding, earlier than, in advance of, previous to

priority 1 = prime concern **2** = precedence, preference, primacy, predominance **3** = supremacy, rank, precedence, seniority, right of way, pre-eminence

prison = jail, confinement, nick (*Brit. slang*), cooler (*slang*), jug (*slang*), dungeon, clink (*slang*), gaol, boob (*Austral. slang*)

prisoner 1 = convict, con (*slang*), lag (*slang*), jailbird **2** = captive, hostage, detainee, internee

privacy = seclusion, isolation, solitude, retirement, retreat

private 1 = exclusive, individual, privately owned, own, special, reserved ≠ public **2** = secret, confidential, covert, unofficial, clandestine, off the record, hush-hush (*informal*) ≠ public **3** = personal, individual, secret, intimate, undisclosed, unspoken, innermost, unvoiced **4** = secluded, secret, separate, isolated, sequestered ≠ busy **5** = solitary, reserved, retiring, withdrawn, discreet, secretive, self-contained, reclusive ≠ sociable

privilege = right, due, advantage, claim, freedom, liberty, concession, entitlement

privileged = special, advantaged, favoured, honoured, entitled, elite

prize[1] NOUN **1** = reward, cup, award, honour, medal, trophy, accolade **2** = winnings, haul, jackpot, stakes, purse
• ADJECTIVE = champion, best, winning, top, outstanding, award-winning, first-rate

prize[2] = value, treasure, esteem, cherish, hold dear

prize[3] *or* **prise 1** = force, pull, lever **2** = drag, force, draw, wring, extort

probability 1 = likelihood, prospect, chance, odds, expectation, liability, likeliness **2** = chance, odds, possibility, likelihood

probable = likely, possible, apparent, reasonable to think, credible, plausible, feasible, presumable ≠ unlikely

probably = likely, perhaps, maybe, possibly, presumably, most likely, doubtless, perchance (*archaic*)

probation = trial period, trial, apprenticeship

probe VERB **1** *often with* ***into*** = examine, go into, investigate, explore, search, look into, analyze, dissect **2** = explore, examine, poke, prod, feel around
• NOUN = investigation, study, inquiry, analysis, examination, exploration, scrutiny, scrutinization

problem 1 = difficulty, trouble, dispute, plight, obstacle, dilemma, headache (*informal*), complication **2** = puzzle, question, riddle, enigma, conundrum, poser

problematic = tricky, puzzling, doubtful, dubious, debatable, problematical ≠ clear

procedure = method, policy, process, course, system, action, practice, strategy

proceed 1 = begin, go ahead **2** = continue, go on, progress, carry on, go ahead, press on ≠ discontinue **3** = go on, continue, progress, carry on, go ahead, move on, move forward, press on ≠ stop **4** = arise, come, issue, result, spring, flow, stem, derive

proceeding = action, process, procedure, move, act, step, measure, deed

proceeds = income, profit, revenue, returns, products, gain, earnings, yield

process NOUN **1** = procedure, means, course, system, action, performance, operation, measure **2** = development, growth, progress, movement, advance, evolution, progression **3** = method, system, practice, technique, procedure
• VERB = handle, manage, action, deal with, fulfil

procession = parade, train, march, file, cavalcade, cortege

proclaim 1 = announce, declare, advertise, publish, indicate, herald, circulate, profess ≠ keep secret **2** = pronounce, announce, declare

prod VERB **1** = poke, push, dig, shove, nudge, jab **2** = prompt, move, urge, motivate, spur, stimulate, rouse, incite
• NOUN **1** = poke, push, dig, shove, nudge, jab **2** = prompt, signal, cue, reminder, stimulus

prodigy = genius, talent, wizard, mastermind, whizz (*informal*)

produce VERB **1** = cause, effect, generate, bring about, give rise to **2** = make, create, develop, manufacture, construct, invent, fabricate **3** = create, develop, write, turn out, compose, originate, churn out (*informal*) **4** = yield, provide, grow, bear, give, supply, afford, render **5** = bring forth, bear, deliver, breed, give birth to, beget, bring into the world **6** = show, provide, present, advance, demonstrate, offer, come up with, exhibit **7** = display, show, present, proffer **8** = present, stage, direct, put on, do, show, mount, exhibit
• NOUN = fruit and vegetables, goods, food, products, crops, yield, harvest, greengrocery (*Brit.*)

producer **1** = director, promoter, impresario **2** = maker, manufacturer, builder, creator, fabricator **3** = grower, farmer

product **1** = goods, produce, creation, commodity, invention, merchandise, artefact **2** = result, consequence, effect, outcome, upshot

production **1** = producing, making, manufacture, manufacturing, construction, formation, fabrication **2** = creation, development, fashioning, composition, origination **3** = management, administration, direction **4** = presentation, staging, mounting

productive **1** = fertile, rich, prolific, plentiful, fruitful, fecund ≠ barren **2** = creative, inventive **3** = useful, rewarding, valuable, profitable, effective, worthwhile, beneficial, constructive ≠ useless

productivity = output, production, capacity, yield, efficiency, work rate

profess **1** = claim, allege, pretend, fake, make out, purport, feign **2** = state, admit, announce, declare, confess, assert, proclaim, affirm

professed **1** = supposed, would-be, alleged, so-called, pretended, purported, self-styled, ostensible **2** = declared, confirmed, confessed, proclaimed, self-confessed, avowed, self-acknowledged

profession = occupation, calling, business, career, employment, office, position, sphere

professional ADJECTIVE **1** = qualified, trained, skilled, white-collar **2** = expert, experienced, skilled, masterly, efficient, competent, adept, proficient ≠ amateurish
• NOUN = expert, master, pro (*informal*), specialist, guru, adept, maestro, virtuoso, fundi (*S. African*)

professor = don (*Brit.*), fellow (*Brit.*), prof (*informal*)

profile **1** = outline, lines, form, figure, silhouette, contour, side view **2** = biography, sketch, vignette, characterization, thumbnail sketch

profit NOUN **1** *often plural* = earnings, return, revenue, gain, yield, proceeds, receipts, takings ≠ loss **2** = benefit, good, use, value, gain, advantage, advancement ≠ disadvantage
• VERB **1** = make money, gain, earn **2** = benefit, help, serve, gain, promote, be of advantage to

profitable **1** = money-making, lucrative, paying, commercial, worthwhile, cost-effective, fruitful, remunerative **2** = beneficial, useful, rewarding, valuable, productive, worthwhile, fruitful, advantageous ≠ useless

profound **1** = sincere, acute, intense, great, keen, extreme, heartfelt, deeply felt ≠ insincere **2** = wise, learned, deep, penetrating, philosophical, sage, abstruse, sagacious ≠ uninformed

programme **1** = schedule, plan, agenda, timetable, listing, list, line-up, calendar **2** = course, curriculum, syllabus **3** = show, performance, production, broadcast, episode, presentation, transmission, telecast

progress NOUN **1** = development, growth, advance, gain, improvement, breakthrough, headway ≠ regression **2** = movement forward, passage, advancement, course, advance, headway ≠ movement backward
• VERB **1** = move on, continue, travel, advance, proceed, go forward, make headway ≠ move back **2** = develop, improve, advance, grow, gain ≠ get behind
• PHRASES **in progress** = going on, happening, continuing, being done, occurring, taking place, proceeding, under way

progression **1** = progress, advance,

advancement, gain, headway, furtherance, movement forward **2** = sequence, course, series, chain, cycle, string, succession

progressive **1** = enlightened, liberal, modern, advanced, radical, revolutionary, avant-garde, reformist **2** = growing, continuing, increasing, developing, advancing, ongoing

prohibit **1** = forbid, ban, veto, outlaw, disallow, proscribe, debar ≠ permit **2** = prevent, restrict, stop, hamper, hinder, impede ≠ allow

prohibition = ban, boycott, embargo, bar, veto, prevention, exclusion, injunction

project NOUN **1** = scheme, plan, job, idea, campaign, operation, activity, venture **2** = assignment, task, homework, piece of research
• VERB **1** = forecast, expect, estimate, predict, reckon, calculate, gauge, extrapolate **2** = stick out, extend, stand out, bulge, protrude, overhang, jut

projection = forecast, estimate, reckoning, calculation, estimation, computation, extrapolation

proliferation = multiplication, increase, spread, expansion

prolific **1** = productive, creative, fertile, inventive, copious **2** = fruitful, fertile, abundant, luxuriant, profuse, fecund ≠ unproductive

prolong = lengthen, continue, perpetuate, draw out, extend, delay, stretch out, spin out ≠ shorten

prominence **1** = fame, name, reputation, importance, celebrity, distinction, prestige, eminence **2** = conspicuousness, markedness

prominent **1** = famous, leading, top, important, main, distinguished, well-known, notable ≠ unknown **2** = noticeable, obvious, outstanding, pronounced, conspicuous, eye-catching, obtrusive ≠ inconspicuous

promise VERB **1** = guarantee, pledge, vow, swear, contract, assure, undertake, warrant **2** = seem likely, look like, show signs of, augur, betoken
• NOUN **1** = guarantee, word, bond, vow, commitment, pledge, undertaking, assurance **2** = potential, ability, talent, capacity, capability, aptitude

promising **1** = encouraging, likely, bright, reassuring, hopeful, favourable, rosy, auspicious ≠ unpromising **2** = talented, able, gifted, rising

promote **1** = help, back, support, aid, forward, encourage, advance, boost ≠ impede **2** = advertise, sell, hype, publicize, push, plug (*informal*) **3** = raise, upgrade, elevate, exalt ≠ demote

promotion **1** = rise, upgrading, move up, advancement, elevation, exaltation, preferment **2** = publicity, advertising, plugging (*informal*) **3** = encouragement, support, boosting, advancement, furtherance

prompt VERB **1** = cause, occasion, provoke, give rise to, elicit **2** = remind, assist, cue, help out
• ADJECTIVE = immediate, quick, rapid, instant, timely, early, swift, speedy ≠ slow
• ADVERB (*Informal*) = exactly, sharp, promptly, on the dot, punctually

promptly **1** = immediately, swiftly, directly, quickly, at once, speedily **2** = punctually, on time, spot on (*informal*), bang on (*informal*), on the dot, on the button (*U.S.*), on the nail

prone **1** = liable, given, subject, inclined, tending, bent, disposed, susceptible ≠ disinclined **2** = face down, flat, horizontal, prostrate, recumbent ≠ face up

pronounce **1** = say, speak, sound, articulate, enunciate **2** = declare, announce, deliver, proclaim, decree, affirm

pronounced = noticeable, decided, marked, striking, obvious, evident, distinct, definite ≠ imperceptible

proof NOUN = evidence, demonstration, testimony, confirmation, verification, corroboration, authentication, substantiation
• ADJECTIVE = impervious, strong, resistant, impenetrable, repellent

prop VERB **1** = lean, place, set, stand, position, rest, lay, balance **2** *often with* **up** = support, sustain, hold up, brace, uphold, bolster, buttress
• NOUN **1** = support, stay, brace, mainstay, buttress, stanchion **2** = mainstay, support, sustainer, anchor, backbone, cornerstone, upholder

propaganda = information, advertising, promotion, publicity, hype, disinformation

propel **1** = drive, launch, force, send, shoot, push, thrust, shove ≠ stop **2** = impel, drive, push, prompt, spur, motivate ≠ hold back

proper 1 = real, actual, genuine, true, bona fide, dinkum (*Austral. & N.Z. informal*) 2 = correct, accepted, established, appropriate, right, formal, conventional, precise ≠ improper 3 = polite, right, becoming, seemly, fitting, fit, mannerly, suitable ≠ unseemly
properly 1 = correctly, rightly, fittingly, appropriately, accurately, suitably, aptly ≠ incorrectly 2 = politely, decently, respectably ≠ badly
property 1 = possessions, goods, effects, holdings, capital, riches, estate, assets 2 = land, holding, estate, real estate, freehold 3 = quality, feature, characteristic, attribute, trait, hallmark
prophecy 1 = prediction, forecast, prognostication, augury 2 = second sight, divination, augury, telling the future, soothsaying
prophet *or* **prophetess** = soothsayer, forecaster, diviner, oracle, seer, sibyl, prophesier
proportion NOUN 1 = part, share, amount, division, percentage, segment, quota, fraction 2 = relative amount, relationship, ratio 3 = balance, harmony, correspondence, symmetry, concord, congruity
• PLURAL NOUN = dimensions, size, volume, capacity, extent, expanse
proportional *or* **proportionate** = correspondent, corresponding, even, balanced, consistent, compatible, equitable, in proportion ≠ disproportionate
proposal = suggestion, plan, programme, scheme, offer, project, bid, recommendation
propose 1 = put forward, present, suggest, advance, submit 2 = intend, mean, plan, aim, design, scheme, have in mind 3 = nominate, name, present, recommend 4 = offer marriage, pop the question (*informal*), ask for someone's hand (in marriage)
proposition NOUN 1 = task, problem, activity, job, affair, venture, undertaking 2 = theory, idea, argument, concept, thesis, hypothesis, theorem, premiss 3 = proposal, plan, suggestion, scheme, bid, recommendation 4 = advance, pass (*informal*), proposal, overture, improper suggestion, come-on (*informal*)
• VERB = make a pass at, solicit, accost, make an improper suggestion to
proprietor *or* **proprietress** = owner, titleholder, landlord *or* landlady
prosecute (*Law*) = take someone to court, try, sue, indict, arraign, put someone on trial, litigate, bring someone to trial
prospect NOUN 1 = likelihood, chance, possibility, hope, promise, odds, expectation, probability 2 = idea, outlook 3 = view, landscape, scene, sight, outlook, spectacle, vista
• PLURAL NOUN = possibilities, chances, future, potential, expectations, outlook, scope
• VERB = look, search, seek, dowse
prospective 1 = potential, possible 2 = expected, coming, future, likely, intended, anticipated, forthcoming, imminent
prospectus = catalogue, list, programme, outline, syllabus, synopsis
prosper = succeed, advance, progress, thrive, get on, do well, flourish
prosperity = success, riches, plenty, fortune, wealth, luxury, good fortune, affluence ≠ poverty
prosperous 1 = wealthy, rich, affluent, well-off, well-heeled (*informal*), well-to-do, moneyed ≠ poor 2 = successful, booming, thriving, flourishing, doing well ≠ unsuccessful
prostitute NOUN = whore, hooker (*U.S. slang*), pro (*slang*), tart (*informal*), call girl, harlot, streetwalker, loose woman
• VERB = cheapen, sell out, pervert, degrade, devalue, squander, demean, debase
protagonist 1 = supporter, champion, advocate, exponent 2 = leading character, principal, central character, hero *or* heroine
protect = keep someone safe, defend, support, save, guard, preserve, look after, shelter ≠ endanger
protection 1 = safety, care, defence, protecting, security, custody, safeguard, aegis 2 = safeguard, cover, guard, shelter, screen, barrier, shield, buffer 3 = armour, cover, screen, barrier, shelter, shield
protective 1 = protecting 2 = caring, defensive, motherly, fatherly, maternal, vigilant, watchful, paternal
protector 1 = defender, champion, guard,

guardian, patron, bodyguard **2** = guard, screen, protection, shield, pad, cushion, buffer

protest VERB **1** = object, demonstrate, oppose, complain, disagree, cry out, disapprove, demur **2** = assert, insist, maintain, declare, affirm, profess, attest, avow

• NOUN **1** = demonstration, march, rally, sit-in, demo (*informal*), hikoi (*N.Z.*) **2** = objection, complaint, dissent, outcry, protestation, remonstrance

protocol = code of behaviour, manners, conventions, customs, etiquette, propriety, decorum

prototype = original, model, first, example, standard

protracted = extended, prolonged, drawn-out, spun out, dragged out, long-drawn-out

proud **1** = satisfied, pleased, content, thrilled, glad, gratified, joyful, well-pleased ≠ dissatisfied **2** = conceited, arrogant, lordly, imperious, overbearing, haughty, snobbish, self-satisfied ≠ humble

prove **1** = turn out, come out, end up **2** = verify, establish, determine, show, confirm, demonstrate, justify, substantiate ≠ disprove

proven = established, proved, confirmed, tested, reliable, definite, verified, attested

provide VERB **1** = supply, give, distribute, outfit, equip, donate, furnish, dispense ≠ withhold **2** = give, bring, add, produce, present, serve, afford, yield

• PHRASES **provide for someone** = support, care for, keep, maintain, sustain, take care of, fend for ◆ **provide for something** = take precautions against, plan for, prepare for, anticipate, plan ahead for, forearm for

provided *often with* ***that*** = if, given, on condition, as long as

provider **1** = supplier, giver, source, donor **2** = breadwinner, supporter, earner, wage earner

providing *often with* ***that*** = on condition that, given that, as long as

province **1** = region, section, district, zone, patch, colony, domain **2** = area, business, concern, responsibility, line, role, department, field

provincial ADJECTIVE **1** = regional, state, local, county, district, territorial, parochial **2** = rural, country, local, rustic, homespun, hick (*informal, chiefly U.S. & Canad.*), backwoods ≠ urban **3** = parochial, insular, narrow-minded, unsophisticated, limited, narrow, small-town (*chiefly U.S.*), inward-looking ≠ cosmopolitan

provision NOUN **1** = supplying, giving, providing, supply, delivery, distribution, catering, presentation **2** = condition, term, requirement, demand, rider, restriction, qualification, clause

• PLURAL NOUN = food, supplies, stores, fare, rations, foodstuff, kai (*N.Z. informal*), victuals, edibles

provisional **1** = temporary, interim ≠ permanent **2** = conditional, limited, qualified, contingent, tentative ≠ definite

provocation **1** = cause, reason, grounds, motivation, stimulus, incitement **2** = offence, challenge, insult, taunt, injury, dare, grievance, annoyance

provocative = offensive, provoking, insulting, stimulating, annoying, galling, goading

provoke **1** = anger, annoy, irritate, infuriate, hassle (*informal*), aggravate (*informal*), incense, enrage ≠ pacify **2** = rouse, cause, produce, promote, occasion, prompt, stir, induce ≠ curb

prowess **1** = skill, ability, talent, expertise, genius, excellence, accomplishment, mastery ≠ inability **2** = bravery, daring, courage, heroism, mettle, valour, fearlessness, valiance ≠ cowardice

proximity = nearness, closeness

proxy = representative, agent, deputy, substitute, factor, delegate

prudent **1** = cautious, careful, wary, discreet, vigilant ≠ careless **2** = wise, politic, sensible, shrewd, discerning, judicious ≠ unwise **3** = thrifty, economical, sparing, careful, canny, provident, frugal, far-sighted ≠ extravagant

prune **1** = cut, trim, clip, dock, shape, shorten, snip **2** = reduce, cut, cut back, trim, cut down, pare down, make reductions in

psyche = soul, mind, self, spirit, personality, individuality, anima, wairua (*N.Z.*)

psychiatrist = psychotherapist, analyst, therapist, psychologist, shrink (*slang*), psychoanalyst, headshrinker (*slang*)

psychic ADJECTIVE **1** = supernatural,

mystic, occult **2** = mystical, spiritual, magical, other-worldly, paranormal, preternatural **3** = psychological, emotional, mental, spiritual, inner, psychiatric, cognitive
• **NOUN** = clairvoyant, fortune teller

psychological **1** = mental, emotional, intellectual, inner, cognitive, cerebral **2** = imaginary, psychosomatic, irrational, unreal, all in the mind

psychology **1** = behaviourism, study of personality, science of mind **2** (*Informal*) = way of thinking, attitude, behaviour, temperament, mentality, thought processes, mental processes, what makes you tick

pub *or* **public house** = tavern, bar, inn, saloon

public **NOUN** = people, society, community, nation, everyone, citizens, electorate, populace
• **ADJECTIVE** **1** = civic, government, state, national, local, official, community, social **2** = general, popular, national, shared, common, widespread, universal, collective **3** = open, accessible, communal, unrestricted ≠ private **4** = well-known, leading, important, respected, famous, celebrated, recognized, distinguished **5** = known, open, obvious, acknowledged, plain, patent, overt ≠ secret

publication **1** = pamphlet, newspaper, magazine, issue, title, leaflet, brochure, periodical **2** = announcement, publishing, broadcasting, reporting, declaration, disclosure, proclamation, notification

publicity **1** = advertising, press, promotion, hype, boost, plug (*informal*) **2** = attention, exposure, fame, celebrity, fuss, public interest, limelight, notoriety

publish **1** = put out, issue, produce, print **2** = announce, reveal, spread, advertise, broadcast, disclose, proclaim, circulate

pudding = dessert, afters (*Brit. informal*), sweet, pud (*informal*)

puff **VERB** **1** = smoke, draw, drag (*slang*), suck, inhale, pull at *or* on **2** = breathe heavily, pant, exhale, blow, gasp, gulp, wheeze, fight for breath
• **NOUN** **1** = drag, pull (*slang*), moke **2** = blast, breath, whiff, draught, gust

pull **VERB** **1** = draw, haul, drag, trail, tow, tug, jerk, yank ≠ push **2** = extract, pick, remove, gather, take out, pluck, uproot, draw out ≠ insert **3** (*Informal*) = attract, draw, bring in, tempt, lure, interest, entice, pull in ≠ repel **4** = strain, tear, stretch, rip, wrench, dislocate, sprain
• **NOUN** **1** = tug, jerk, yank, twitch, heave ≠ shove **2** = puff, drag (*slang*), inhalation **3** (*Informal*) = influence, power, weight, muscle, clout (*informal*), kai (*N.Z. informal*)
• **PHRASES** **pull out (of)** **1** = withdraw, quit **2** = leave, abandon, get out, quit, retreat from, depart, evacuate ♦ **pull someone up** = reprimand, rebuke, admonish, read the riot act to, tell someone off (*informal*), reprove, bawl someone out (*informal*), tear someone off a strip (*Brit. informal*) ♦ **pull something off** (*Informal*) = succeed in, manage, carry out, accomplish ♦ **pull something out** = produce, draw, bring out, draw out ♦ **pull up** = stop, halt, brake

pulp **NOUN** **1** = paste, mash, mush **2** = flesh, meat, soft part
• **ADJECTIVE** = cheap, lurid, trashy, rubbishy
• **VERB** = crush, squash, mash, pulverize

pulse **NOUN** = beat, rhythm, vibration, beating, throb, throbbing, pulsation
• **VERB** = beat, throb, vibrate, pulsate

pump **1** = supply, send, pour, inject **2** = interrogate, probe, quiz, cross-examine

punch[1] **VERB** = hit, strike, box, smash, belt (*informal*), sock (*slang*), swipe (*informal*), bop (*informal*)
• **NOUN** **1** = blow, hit, sock (*slang*), jab, swipe (*informal*), bop (*informal*), wallop (*informal*) **2** (*Informal*) = effectiveness, bite, impact, drive, vigour, verve, forcefulness

punch[2] = pierce, cut, bore, drill, stamp, puncture, prick, perforate

punctuate = interrupt, break, pepper, sprinkle, intersperse

puncture **NOUN** **1** = flat tyre, flat, flattie (*N.Z.*) **2** = hole, opening, break, cut, nick, leak, slit
• **VERB** = pierce, cut, nick, penetrate, prick, rupture, perforate, bore a hole

punish = discipline, correct, castigate, chastise, sentence, chasten, penalize

punishing = hard, taxing, wearing, tiring, exhausting, gruelling, strenuous, arduous ≠ easy

punishment **1** = penalizing, discipline, correction, retribution, chastening,

chastisement **2** = penalty, penance
punitive = retaliatory, in reprisal, retaliative
punt VERB = bet, back, stake, gamble, lay, wager
• NOUN = bet, stake, gamble, wager
punter **1** = gambler, better, backer **2** (*Informal*) = person, man in the street
pupil **1** = student, schoolboy *or* schoolgirl, schoolchild ≠ teacher **2** = learner, novice, beginner, disciple ≠ instructor
puppet **1** = marionette, doll, glove puppet, finger puppet **2** = pawn, tool, instrument, mouthpiece, stooge, cat's-paw
purchase VERB = buy, pay for, obtain, get, score (*slang*), gain, pick up, acquire ≠ sell
• NOUN **1** = acquisition, buy, investment, property, gain, asset, possession **2** = grip, hold, support, leverage, foothold
pure **1** = unmixed, real, simple, natural, straight, genuine, neat, authentic ≠ adulterated **2** = clean, wholesome, sanitary, spotless, sterilized, squeaky-clean, untainted, uncontaminated ≠ contaminated **3** = complete, total, perfect, absolute, sheer, patent, utter, outright ≠ qualified **4** = innocent, modest, good, moral, impeccable, righteous, virtuous, squeaky-clean ≠ corrupt
purely = absolutely, just, only, completely, simply, entirely, exclusively, merely
purge VERB **1** = rid, clear, cleanse, strip, empty, void **2** = get rid of, remove, expel, wipe out, eradicate, do away with, exterminate
• NOUN = removal, elimination, expulsion, eradication, ejection
purity **1** = cleanness, cleanliness, wholesomeness, pureness, faultlessness, immaculateness ≠ impurity **2** = innocence, virtue, integrity, honesty, decency, virginity, chastity, chasteness ≠ immorality
purport = claim, allege, assert, profess
purpose NOUN **1** = reason, point, idea, aim, object, intention **2** = aim, end, plan, hope, goal, wish, desire, object **3** = determination, resolve, will, resolution, ambition, persistence, tenacity, firmness
• PHRASES **on purpose** = deliberately, purposely, intentionally, knowingly, designedly
purposely = deliberately, expressly, consciously, intentionally, knowingly, with intent, on purpose ≠ accidentally
purse NOUN **1** = pouch, wallet, money-bag **2** (*U.S.*) = handbag, bag, shoulder bag, pocket book, clutch bag **3** = funds, means, money, resources, treasury, wealth, exchequer
• VERB = pucker, contract, tighten, pout, press together
pursue **1** = engage in, perform, conduct, carry on, practise **2** = try for, seek, desire, search for, aim for, work towards, strive for **3** = continue, maintain, carry on, keep on, persist in, proceed in, persevere in **4** = follow, track, hunt, chase, dog, shadow, tail (*informal*), hound ≠ flee
pursuit **1** = quest, seeking, search, aim of, aspiration for, striving towards **2** = pursuing, seeking, search, hunt, chase, trailing **3** = occupation, activity, interest, line, pleasure, hobby, pastime
push VERB **1** = shove, force, press, thrust, drive, knock, sweep, plunge ≠ pull **2** = press, operate, depress, squeeze, activate, hold down **3** = make *or* force your way, move, shoulder, inch, squeeze, thrust, elbow, shove **4** = urge, encourage, persuade, spur, press, incite, impel ≠ discourage
• NOUN **1** = shove, thrust, butt, elbow, nudge ≠ pull **2** (*Informal*) = drive, go (*informal*), energy, initiative, enterprise, ambition, vitality, vigour
• PHRASES **the push** (*Informal, chiefly Brit.*) = dismissal, the sack (*informal*), discharge, the boot (*slang*), your cards (*informal*)
put VERB **1** = place, leave, set, position, rest, park (*informal*), plant, lay **2** = express, state, word, phrase, utter
• PHRASES **put someone off** **1** = discourage, intimidate, deter, daunt, dissuade, demoralize, scare off, dishearten **2** = disconcert, confuse, unsettle, throw (*informal*), dismay, perturb, faze, discomfit ◆ **put someone up** **1** = accommodate, house, board, lodge, quarter, take someone in, billet **2** = nominate, put forward, offer, present, propose, recommend, submit ◆ **put something across** *or* **over** = communicate, explain, convey, make clear, get across, make yourself understood ◆ **put something off** = postpone, delay, defer, adjourn, hold over, put on the back burner (*informal*),

take a rain check on (*U.S. & Canad. informal*) ◆ **put something up**
1 = build, raise, set up, construct, erect, fabricate 2 = offer, present, mount, put forward

puzzle VERB = perplex, confuse, baffle, stump, bewilder, confound, mystify, faze
• NOUN 1 = problem, riddle, question, conundrum, poser 2 = mystery, problem, paradox, enigma, conundrum

puzzling = perplexing, baffling, bewildering, involved, enigmatic, incomprehensible, mystifying, abstruse ≠ simple

q

quake = shake, tremble, quiver, move, rock, shiver, shudder, vibrate

qualification 1 = eligibility, quality, ability, skill, fitness, attribute, capability, aptitude 2 = condition, proviso, requirement, rider, reservation, limitation, modification, caveat

qualified 1 = capable, trained, experienced, seasoned, able, fit, expert, chartered ≠ untrained 2 = restricted, limited, provisional, conditional, reserved, bounded, adjusted, moderated ≠ unconditional

qualify 1 = certify, equip, empower, train, prepare, fit, ready, permit ≠ disqualify
2 = restrict, limit, reduce, ease, moderate, regulate, diminish, temper

quality 1 = standard, standing, class, condition, rank, grade, merit, classification
2 = excellence, status, merit, position, value, worth, distinction, virtue
3 = characteristic, feature, attribute, point, side, mark, property, aspect 4 = nature, character, make, sort, kind

quantity 1 = amount, lot, total, sum, part, number 2 = size, measure, mass, volume, length, capacity, extent, bulk

quarrel NOUN = disagreement, fight, row, argument, dispute, controversy, breach, contention, biffo (*Austral. slang*) ≠ accord
• VERB = disagree, fight, argue, row, clash, dispute, differ, fall out (*informal*) ≠ get on *or* along (with)

quarry = prey, victim, game, goal, aim, prize, objective

quarter NOUN 1 = district, region, neighbourhood, place, part, side, area, zone 2 = mercy, pity, compassion, charity, sympathy, tolerance, kindness, forgiveness
• PLURAL NOUN = lodgings, rooms, chambers, residence, dwelling, barracks, abode, habitation
• VERB = accommodate, house, lodge, place, board, post, station, billet

quash 1 = annul, overturn, reverse, cancel, overthrow, revoke, overrule, rescind 2 = suppress, crush, put down, beat, overthrow, squash, subdue, repress

queen 1 = sovereign, ruler, monarch, leader, Crown, princess, majesty, head of state 2 = leading light, star, favourite, celebrity, darling, mistress, big name

queer 1 = strange, odd, funny, unusual, extraordinary, curious, weird, peculiar ≠ normal 2 = faint, dizzy, giddy, queasy, light-headed

query NOUN 1 = question, inquiry, problem
2 = doubt, suspicion, objection
• VERB 1 = question, challenge, doubt, suspect, dispute, object to, distrust, mistrust
2 = ask, inquire *or* enquire, question

quest 1 = search, hunt, mission, enterprise, crusade 2 = expedition, journey, adventure

question NOUN 1 = inquiry, enquiry, query, investigation, examination, interrogation ≠ answer 2 = difficulty, problem, doubt, argument, dispute, controversy, query, contention 3 = issue, point, matter, subject, problem, debate, proposal, theme
• VERB 1 = interrogate, cross-examine, interview, examine, probe, quiz, ask questions 2 = dispute, challenge, doubt, suspect, oppose, query, mistrust, disbelieve ≠ accept
• PHRASES **out of the question** = impossible, unthinkable, inconceivable, not on (*informal*), hopeless, unimaginable, unworkable, unattainable

questionable = dubious, suspect, doubtful, controversial, suspicious, dodgy (*Brit., Austral., & N.Z. informal*), debatable, moot ≠ indisputable

queue = line, row, file, train, series, chain, string, column

quick 1 = fast, swift, speedy, express, cracking (*Brit. informal*), smart, rapid, fleet ≠ slow 2 = brief, passing, hurried, flying, fleeting, summary, lightning, short-lived ≠ long 3 = immediate, instant, prompt, sudden, abrupt, instantaneous 4 = excitable, passionate, irritable, touchy, irascible, testy ≠ calm 5 = intelligent, bright (*informal*), alert, sharp, acute, smart, clever, shrewd ≠ stupid

quicken 1 = speed up, hurry, accelerate, hasten, gee up (*informal*) 2 = stimulate, inspire, arouse, excite, revive, incite, energize, invigorate

quickly 1 = swiftly, rapidly, hurriedly, fast, hastily, briskly, apace ≠ slowly 2 = soon, speedily, as soon as possible, momentarily (*U.S.*), instantaneously, pronto (*informal*), a.s.a.p. (*informal*) 3 = immediately, at once, directly, promptly, abruptly, without delay

quiet ADJECTIVE 1 = soft, low, muted, lowered, whispered, faint, suppressed, stifled ≠ loud 2 = peaceful, silent, hushed, soundless, noiseless ≠ noisy 3 = calm, peaceful, tranquil, mild, serene, placid, restful ≠ exciting 4 = still, calm, peaceful, tranquil ≠ troubled 5 = undisturbed, isolated, secluded, private, sequestered, unfrequented ≠ crowded 6 = silent 7 = reserved, retiring, shy, gentle, mild, sedate, meek ≠ excitable
• NOUN = peace, rest, tranquillity, ease, silence, solitude, serenity, stillness ≠ noise

quietly 1 = noiselessly, silently 2 = softly, inaudibly, in an undertone, under your breath 3 = calmly, serenely, placidly, patiently, mildly 4 = silently, mutely

quilt = bedspread, duvet, coverlet, eiderdown, counterpane, doona (*Austral.*), continental quilt

quip = joke, sally, jest, riposte, wisecrack (*informal*), retort, pleasantry, gibe

quirky = odd, unusual, eccentric, idiosyncratic, peculiar, offbeat

quit 1 = resign (from), leave, retire (from), pull out (of), step down (from) (*informal*), abdicate 2 = stop, give up, cease, end, drop, abandon, halt, discontinue ≠ continue 3 = leave, depart from, go out of, go away from, pull out from

quite 1 = somewhat, rather, fairly, reasonably, relatively, moderately 2 = absolutely, perfectly, completely, totally, fully, entirely, wholly

quiz NOUN = examination, questioning, interrogation, interview, investigation, grilling (*informal*), cross-examination, cross-questioning
• VERB = question, ask, interrogate, examine, investigate

quota = share, allowance, ration, part, limit, slice, quantity, portion

quotation 1 = passage, quote (*informal*), excerpt, reference, extract, citation 2 (*Commerce*) = estimate, price, tender, rate, cost, charge, figure, quote (*informal*)

quote 1 = repeat, recite, recall 2 = refer to, cite, give, name, detail, relate, mention, instance

r

race[1] NOUN 1 = competition, contest, chase, dash, pursuit 2 = contest, competition, rivalry
• VERB 1 = compete against, run against 2 = compete, run, contend, take part in a race 3 = run, fly, career, speed, tear, dash, hurry, dart

race[2] = people, nation, blood, stock, type, folk, tribe

racial = ethnic, ethnological, national, folk, genetic, tribal, genealogical

rack NOUN = frame, stand, structure, framework
• VERB = torture, torment, afflict, oppress, harrow, crucify, agonize, pain

racket 1 = noise, row, fuss, disturbance, outcry, clamour, din, pandemonium 2 = fraud, scheme

radiate 1 = emit, spread, send out, pour, shed, scatter 2 = shine, be diffused 3 = show, display, demonstrate, exhibit, emanate, give off *or* out 4 = spread out, diverge, branch out

radical ADJECTIVE 1 = extreme, complete, entire, sweeping, severe, thorough, drastic 2 = revolutionary, extremist, fanatical 3 = fundamental, natural, basic, profound, innate, deep-seated ≠ superficial
• NOUN = extremist, revolutionary, militant,

fanatic ≠ conservative
rage NOUN 1 = fury, temper, frenzy, rampage, tantrum, foulie (*Austral. slang*) ≠ calmness 2 = anger, passion, madness, wrath, ire 3 = craze, fashion, enthusiasm, vogue, fad (*informal*), latest thing
• VERB = be furious, blow up (*informal*), fume, lose it (*informal*), seethe, lose the plot (*informal*), go ballistic (*slang, chiefly U.S.*), lose your temper ≠ stay calm
ragged 1 = tatty, worn, torn, run-down, shabby, seedy, scruffy, in tatters ≠ smart 2 = rough, rugged, unfinished, uneven, jagged, serrated
raid VERB 1 = steal from, plunder, pillage, sack 2 = attack, invade, assault 3 = make a search of, search, bust (*informal*), make a raid on, make a swoop on
• NOUN 1 = attack, invasion, foray, sortie, incursion, sally, inroad 2 = bust (*informal*), swoop 3 = robbery, sacking
raider = attacker, thief, robber, plunderer, invader, marauder
railing = fence, rails, barrier, paling, balustrade
rain NOUN = rainfall, fall, showers, deluge, drizzle, downpour, raindrops, cloudburst
• VERB 1 = pour, pelt (down), teem, bucket down (*informal*), drizzle, come down in buckets (*informal*) 2 = fall, shower, be dropped, sprinkle, be deposited
rainy = wet, damp, drizzly, showery ≠ dry
raise 1 = lift, elevate, uplift, heave 2 = set upright, lift, elevate 3 = increase, intensify, heighten, advance, boost, strengthen, enhance, enlarge ≠ reduce 4 = make louder, heighten, amplify, louden 5 = collect, gather, obtain 6 = cause, start, produce, create, occasion, provoke, originate, engender 7 = put forward, suggest, introduce, advance, broach, moot 8 = bring up, develop, rear, nurture 9 = build, construct, put up, erect ≠ demolish
rake[1] 1 = gather, collect, remove 2 = search, comb, scour, scrutinize, fossick (*Austral. & N.Z.*)
rake[2] = libertine, playboy, swinger (*slang*), lecher, roué, debauchee ≠ puritan
rally NOUN 1 = gathering, convention, meeting, congress, assembly, hui (*N.Z.*) 2 = recovery, improvement, revival, recuperation ≠ relapse
• VERB 1 = gather together, unite, regroup, reorganize, reassemble 2 = recover, improve, revive, get better, recuperate ≠ get worse
ram 1 = hit, force, drive into, crash, impact, smash, dash, butt 2 = cram, force, stuff, jam, thrust
ramble NOUN = walk, tour, stroll, hike, roaming, roving, saunter
• VERB 1 = walk, range, wander, stroll, stray, roam, rove, saunter, go walkabout (*Austral.*) 2 *often with* **on** = babble, rabbit (on) (*Brit. informal*), waffle (*informal, chiefly Brit.*), witter on (*informal*)
ramp = slope, incline, gradient, rise
rampage VERB = go berserk, storm, rage, run riot, run amok
• PHRASES **on the rampage** = berserk, wild, violent, raging, out of control, amok, riotous, berko (*Austral. slang*)
rampant 1 = widespread, prevalent, rife, uncontrolled, unchecked, unrestrained, profuse, spreading like wildfire 2 (*Heraldry*) = upright, standing, rearing, erect
random ADJECTIVE 1 = chance, casual, accidental, incidental, haphazard, fortuitous, hit or miss, adventitious ≠ planned 2 = casual
• PHRASES **at random** = haphazardly, randomly, arbitrarily, by chance, willy-nilly, unsystematically
randy (*Informal*) = lustful, hot, turned-on (*slang*), aroused, horny (*slang*), amorous, lascivious
range NOUN 1 = series, variety, selection, assortment, lot, collection, gamut 2 = limits, reach 3 = scope, area, bounds, province, orbit, radius
• VERB 1 = vary, run, reach, extend, stretch 2 = roam, wander, rove, ramble, traverse
rank[1] NOUN 1 = status, level, position, grade, order, sort, type, division 2 = class, caste 3 = row, line, file, column, group, range, series, tier
• VERB 1 = order, dispose 2 = arrange, sort, line up, array, align
rank[2] 1 = absolute, complete, total, gross, sheer, utter, thorough, blatant 2 = foul, bad, offensive, disgusting, revolting, stinking, noxious, rancid, festy (*Austral. slang*) 3 = abundant, lush, luxuriant, dense, profuse
ransom = payment, money, price, payoff
rant = shout, roar, yell, rave, cry, declaim

rap VERB = hit, strike, knock, crack, tap
• NOUN 1 = blow, knock, crack, tap, clout (*informal*) 2 (*Slang*) = rebuke, blame, responsibility, punishment

rape VERB = sexually assault, violate, abuse, ravish, force, outrage
• NOUN = sexual assault, violation, ravishment, outrage

rapid 1 = sudden, prompt, speedy, express, swift ≠ gradual 2 = quick, fast, hurried, swift, brisk, hasty ≠ slow

rapidly = quickly, fast, swiftly, briskly, promptly, hastily, hurriedly, speedily

rare 1 = uncommon, unusual, few, strange, scarce, singular, sparse, infrequent ≠ common 2 = superb, great, fine, excellent, superlative, choice, peerless

rarely = seldom, hardly, hardly ever, infrequently ≠ often

raring (in construction *raring to do something*) = eager, impatient, longing, ready, keen, desperate, enthusiastic

rarity 1 = curio, find, treasure, gem, collector's item 2 = uncommonness, scarcity, infrequency, unusualness, shortage, strangeness, sparseness

rash¹ = reckless, hasty, impulsive, imprudent, careless, ill-advised, foolhardy, impetuous ≠ cautious

rash² 1 = outbreak of spots, (skin) eruption 2 = spate, series, wave, flood, plague, outbreak

rate NOUN 1 = speed, pace, tempo, velocity, frequency 2 = degree, standard, scale, proportion, ratio 3 = charge, price, cost, fee, figure
• VERB 1 = evaluate, consider, rank, reckon, value, measure, estimate, count 2 = deserve, merit, be entitled to, be worthy of
• PHRASES **at any rate** = in any case, anyway, anyhow, at all events

rather 1 = preferably, sooner, more readily, more willingly 2 = to some extent, quite, a little, fairly, relatively, somewhat, moderately, to some degree

ratify = approve, establish, confirm, sanction, endorse, uphold, authorize, affirm ≠ annul

rating = position, placing, rate, order, class, degree, rank, status

ratio = proportion, rate, relation, percentage, fraction

ration NOUN = allowance, quota, allotment, helping, part, share, measure, portion
• VERB = limit, control, restrict, budget

rational = sensible, sound, wise, reasonable, intelligent, realistic, logical, sane ≠ insane

rationale = reason, grounds, theory, principle, philosophy, logic, motivation, raison d'être (*French*)

rattle 1 = clatter, bang, jangle 2 = shake, jolt, vibrate, bounce, jar 3 (*Informal*) = fluster, shake, upset, disturb, disconcert, perturb, faze

ravage VERB = destroy, ruin, devastate, spoil, demolish, ransack, lay waste, despoil
• PLURAL NOUN = damage, destruction, devastation, ruin, havoc, ruination, spoliation

rave 1 = rant, rage, roar, go mad (*informal*), babble, be delirious 2 (*Informal*) = enthuse, praise, gush, be mad about (*informal*), be wild about (*informal*)

raving = mad, wild, crazy, hysterical, insane, irrational, crazed, delirious, berko (*Austral. slang*), off the air (*Austral. slang*)

raw 1 = unrefined, natural, crude, unprocessed, basic, rough, coarse, unfinished ≠ refined 2 = uncooked, natural, fresh ≠ cooked 3 = inexperienced, new, green, immature, callow ≠ experienced 4 = chilly, biting, cold, freezing, bitter, piercing, parky (*Brit. informal*)

ray = beam, bar, flash, shaft, gleam

re = concerning, about, regarding, with regard to, with reference to, apropos

reach VERB 1 = arrive at, get to, make, attain 2 = attain, get to 3 = touch, grasp, extend to, stretch to, contact 4 = contact, get in touch with, get through to, communicate with, get hold of
• NOUN 1 = grasp, range, distance, stretch, capacity, extent, extension, scope 2 = jurisdiction, power, influence

react = respond, act, proceed, behave

reaction 1 = response, answer, reply 2 = counteraction, backlash, recoil 3 = conservatism, the right

reactionary ADJECTIVE = conservative,

right-wing
• NOUN = conservative, die-hard, right-winger ≠ radical
read 1 = scan, study, look at, pore over, peruse 2 = understand, interpret, comprehend, construe, decipher, see, discover 3 = register, show, record, display, indicate
readily 1 = willingly, freely, quickly, gladly, eagerly ≠ reluctantly 2 = promptly, quickly, easily, smoothly, effortlessly, speedily, unhesitatingly ≠ with difficulty
readiness 1 = willingness, eagerness, keenness 2 = promptness, facility, ease, dexterity, adroitness
reading 1 = perusal, study, examination, inspection, scrutiny 2 = learning, education, knowledge, scholarship, erudition 3 = recital, performance, lesson, sermon 4 = interpretation, version, impression, grasp
ready 1 = prepared, set, primed, organized ≠ unprepared 2 = completed, arranged 3 = mature, ripe, mellow, ripened, seasoned 4 = willing, happy, glad, disposed, keen, eager, inclined, prone ≠ reluctant 5 = prompt, smart, quick, bright, sharp, keen, alert, clever ≠ slow 6 = available, handy, present, near, accessible, convenient ≠ unavailable
real 1 = true, genuine, sincere, factual, dinkum (*Austral. & N.Z. informal*), unfeigned 2 = genuine, authentic, dinkum (*Austral. & N.Z. informal*) ≠ fake 3 = proper, true, valid 4 = true, actual 5 = typical, true, genuine, sincere, dinkum (*Austral. & N.Z. informal*), unfeigned 6 = complete, total, perfect, utter, thorough
realistic 1 = practical, real, sensible, common-sense, down-to-earth, matter-of-fact, level-headed ≠ impractical 2 = attainable, sensible 3 = lifelike, true to life, authentic, true, natural, genuine, faithful
reality 1 = fact, truth, realism, validity, verity, actuality 2 = truth, fact, actuality
realization 1 = awareness, understanding, recognition, perception, grasp, conception, comprehension, cognizance 2 = achievement, accomplishment, fulfilment
realize 1 = become aware of, understand, take in, grasp, comprehend, get the message 2 = fulfil, achieve, accomplish, make real 3 = achieve, do, effect, complete, perform, fulfil, accomplish, carry out *or* through
really 1 = certainly, genuinely, positively, surely 2 = truly, actually, in fact, indeed, in actuality
realm 1 = field, world, area, province, sphere, department, branch, territory 2 = kingdom, country, empire, land, domain, dominion
reap 1 = get, gain, obtain, acquire, derive 2 = collect, gather, bring in, harvest, garner, cut
rear[1] NOUN 1 = back part, back ≠ front 2 = back, end, tail, rearguard, tail end
• ADJECTIVE = back, hind, last, following ≠ front
rear[2] 1 = bring up, raise, educate, train, foster, nurture 2 = breed, keep 3 = rise, tower, soar, loom
reason NOUN 1 = cause, grounds, purpose, motive, goal, aim, object, intention 2 = sense, mind, understanding, judgment, logic, intellect, sanity, rationality ≠ emotion
• VERB = deduce, conclude, work out, make out, infer, think
• PHRASES **reason with someone** = persuade, bring round, urge, win over, prevail upon (*informal*), talk into *or* out of
reasonable 1 = sensible, sound, practical, wise, logical, sober, plausible, sane ≠ irrational 2 = fair, just, right, moderate, equitable, tenable ≠ unfair 3 = within reason, fit, proper ≠ impossible 4 = low, cheap, competitive, moderate, modest, inexpensive 5 = average, fair, moderate, modest, O.K. *or* okay (*informal*)
reassure = encourage, comfort, hearten, gee up, restore confidence to, put *or* set your mind at rest
rebate = refund, discount, reduction, bonus, allowance, deduction
rebel NOUN 1 = revolutionary, insurgent, secessionist, revolutionist 2 = nonconformist, dissenter, heretic, apostate, schismatic
• VERB 1 = revolt, resist, rise up, mutiny 2 = defy, dissent, disobey
• ADJECTIVE = rebellious, revolutionary, insurgent, insurrectionary
rebellion 1 = resistance, rising, revolution, revolt, uprising, mutiny 2 = nonconformity, defiance, heresy, schism

rebellious 1 = defiant, difficult, resistant, unmanageable, refractory ≠ obedient 2 = revolutionary, rebel, disorderly, unruly, insurgent, disloyal, seditious, mutinous ≠ obedient
rebound 1 = bounce, ricochet, recoil 2 = misfire, backfire, recoil, boomerang
rebuff VERB = reject, refuse, turn down, cut, slight, snub, spurn, knock back (*slang*) ≠ encourage
• NOUN = rejection, snub, knock-back, slight, refusal, repulse, cold shoulder, slap in the face (*informal*) ≠ encouragement
rebuke VERB = scold, censure, reprimand, castigate, chide, dress down (*informal*), admonish, tell off (*informal*) ≠ praise
• NOUN = scolding, censure, reprimand, row, dressing down (*informal*), telling-off (*informal*), admonition ≠ praise
recall VERB 1 = recollect, remember, evoke, call to mind 2 = call back 3 = annul, withdraw, cancel, repeal, revoke, retract, countermand
• NOUN 1 = recollection, memory, remembrance 2 = annulment, withdrawal, repeal, cancellation, retraction, rescindment
recede = fall back, withdraw, retreat, return, retire, regress
receipt 1 = sales slip, proof of purchase, counterfoil 2 = receiving, delivery, reception, acceptance
receive 1 = get, accept, be given, pick up, collect, obtain, acquire, take 2 = experience, suffer, bear, encounter, sustain, undergo 3 = greet, meet, admit, welcome, entertain, accommodate
recent = new, modern, up-to-date, late, current, fresh, novel, present-day ≠ old
recently = not long ago, newly, lately, currently, freshly, of late, latterly
reception 1 = party, gathering, get-together, social gathering, function, celebration, festivity, soirée 2 = response, reaction, acknowledgment, treatment, welcome, greeting
recess 1 = break, rest, holiday, interval, vacation, respite, intermission 2 = alcove, corner, bay, hollow, niche, nook
recession = depression, drop, decline, slump ≠ boom
recipe = directions, instructions, ingredients
recital 1 = performance, rendering, rehearsal, reading 2 = account, telling, statement, relation, narrative 3 = recitation
recite = perform, deliver, repeat, declaim
reckless = careless, wild, rash, precipitate, hasty, mindless, headlong, thoughtless ≠ cautious
reckon 1 (*Informal*) = think, believe, suppose, imagine, assume, guess (*informal, chiefly U.S. & Canad.*) 2 = consider, rate, account, judge, regard, count, esteem, deem 3 = count, figure, total, calculate, compute, add up, tally, number
reckoning = count, estimate, calculation, addition
reclaim 1 = retrieve, regain 2 = regain, salvage, recapture
recognition 1 = identification, recollection, discovery, remembrance 2 = acceptance, admission, allowance, confession
recognize 1 = identify, know, place, remember, spot, notice, recall, recollect 2 = acknowledge, allow, accept, admit, grant, concede ≠ ignore 3 = appreciate, respect, notice
recollection = memory, recall, impression, remembrance, reminiscence
recommend 1 = advocate, suggest, propose, approve, endorse, commend ≠ disapprove of 2 = put forward, approve, endorse, commend, praise 3 = advise, suggest, advance, propose, counsel, advocate, prescribe, put forward
recommendation 1 = advice, proposal, suggestion, counsel 2 = commendation, reference, praise, sanction, approval, endorsement, advocacy, testimonial
reconcile 1 = resolve, settle, square, adjust, compose, rectify, put to rights 2 = reunite, bring back together, conciliate 3 = make peace between, reunite, propitiate
reconciliation = reunion, conciliation, pacification, reconcilement ≠ separation
reconsider = rethink, review, revise, think again, reassess
reconstruct 1 = rebuild, restore, recreate, remake, renovate, remodel, regenerate 2 = build up a picture of, build up, piece together, deduce
record NOUN 1 = document, file, register, log, report, account, entry, journal

2 = evidence, trace, documentation, testimony, witness **3** = disc, single, album, LP, vinyl **4** = background, history, performance, career
• **VERB 1** = set down, minute, note, enter, document, register, log, chronicle **2** = make a recording of, video, tape, video-tape, tape-record **3** = register, show, indicate, give evidence of

recorder = chronicler, archivist, historian, clerk, scribe, diarist

recording = record, video, tape, disc

recount = tell, report, describe, relate, repeat, depict, recite, narrate

recover 1 = get better, improve, get well, recuperate, heal, revive, mend, convalesce ≠ relapse **2** = rally **3** = save, rescue, retrieve, salvage, reclaim ≠ abandon **4** = recoup, restore, get back, regain, retrieve, reclaim, redeem, recapture ≠ lose

recovery 1 = improvement, healing, revival, mending, recuperation, convalescence **2** = retrieval, repossession, reclamation, restoration

recreation = leisure, play, sport, fun, entertainment, relaxation, enjoyment, amusement

recruit VERB 1 = gather, obtain, engage, procure **2** = assemble, raise, levy, muster, mobilize **3** = enlist, draft, enrol ≠ dismiss
• **NOUN** = beginner, trainee, apprentice, novice, convert, initiate, helper, learner

recur = happen again, return, repeat, persist, revert, reappear, come again

recycle = reprocess, reuse, salvage, reclaim, save

red NOUN *or* **ADJECTIVE 1** = crimson, scarlet, ruby, vermilion, cherry, coral, carmine **2** = flushed, embarrassed, blushing, florid, shamefaced **3** (*of hair*) = chestnut, reddish, flame-coloured, sandy, Titian, carroty
• **PHRASES in the red** (*Informal*) = in debt, insolvent, in arrears, overdrawn ◆ **see red** (*Informal*) = lose your temper, lose it (*informal*), go mad (*informal*), crack up (*informal*), lose the plot (*informal*), go ballistic (*slang, chiefly U.S.*), fly off the handle (*informal*), blow your top

redeem 1 = reinstate, absolve, restore to favour **2** = make up for, compensate for, atone for, make amends for **3** = buy back, recover, regain, retrieve, reclaim, repurchase **4** = save, free, deliver, liberate, ransom, emancipate

redemption 1 = compensation, amends, reparation, atonement **2** = salvation, release, rescue, liberation, emancipation, deliverance

redress VERB 1 = make amends for, make up for, compensate for **2** = put right, balance, correct, adjust, regulate, rectify, even up
• **NOUN** = amends, payment, compensation, reparation, atonement, recompense

reduce 1 = lessen, cut, lower, moderate, weaken, diminish, decrease, cut down ≠ increase **2** = degrade, downgrade, break, humble, bring low ≠ promote

redundancy 1 = layoff, sacking, dismissal **2** = unemployment, the sack (*informal*), the axe (*informal*), joblessness

redundant = superfluous, extra, surplus, unnecessary, unwanted, inessential, supernumerary ≠ essential

reel 1 = stagger, rock, roll, pitch, sway, lurch **2** = whirl, spin, revolve, swirl

refer VERB = direct, point, send, guide
• **PHRASES refer to something** *or* **someone 1** = allude to, mention, cite, speak of, bring up **2** = relate to, concern, apply to, pertain to, be relevant to **3** = consult, go, apply, turn to, look up

referee NOUN = umpire, judge, ref (*informal*), arbiter, arbitrator, adjudicator
• **VERB** = umpire, judge, mediate, adjudicate, arbitrate

reference 1 = allusion, note, mention, quotation **2** = citation **3** = testimonial, recommendation, credentials, endorsement, character reference

referendum = public vote, popular vote, plebiscite

refine 1 = purify, process, filter, cleanse, clarify, distil **2** = improve, perfect, polish, hone

refined 1 = purified, processed, pure, filtered, clean, clarified, distilled ≠ unrefined **2** = cultured, polished, elegant, polite, cultivated, civilized, well-bred ≠ coarse **3** = discerning, fine, sensitive, delicate, precise, discriminating, fastidious

reflect 1 = show, reveal, display, indicate, demonstrate, manifest **2** = throw back, return, mirror, echo, reproduce **3** = consider, think, muse, ponder,

meditate, ruminate, cogitate, wonder
reflection 1 = image, echo, mirror image 2 = consideration, thinking, thought, idea, opinion, observation, musing, meditation
reflective = thoughtful, contemplative, meditative, pensive
reform NOUN = improvement, amendment, rehabilitation, betterment
• VERB 1 = improve, correct, restore, amend, mend, rectify 2 = mend your ways, go straight (*informal*), shape up (*informal*), turn over a new leaf, clean up your act (*informal*), pull your socks up (*Brit. informal*)
refrain¹ = stop, avoid, cease, renounce, abstain, leave off, desist, forbear
refrain² = chorus, tune, melody
refresh 1 = revive, freshen, revitalize, stimulate, brace, enliven, invigorate 2 = stimulate, prompt, renew, jog
refreshing 1 = new, original, novel 2 = stimulating, fresh, bracing, invigorating ≠ tiring
refreshment = food and drink, drinks, snacks, titbits, kai (*N.Z. informal*)
refuge 1 = protection, shelter, asylum 2 = haven, retreat, sanctuary, hide-out
refugee = exile, émigré, displaced person, escapee
refund NOUN = repayment, reimbursement, return
• VERB = repay, return, restore, pay back, reimburse
refurbish = renovate, restore, repair, clean up, overhaul, revamp, mend, do up (*informal*)
refusal = rejection, denial, rebuff, knock-back (*slang*)
refuse¹ 1 = decline, reject, turn down, say no to 2 = deny, decline, withhold ≠ allow
refuse² = rubbish, waste, junk (*informal*), litter, garbage, trash
regain 1 = recover, get back, retrieve, recapture, win back, take back, recoup 2 = get back to, return to, reach again
regal = royal, majestic, kingly *or* queenly, noble, princely, magnificent
regard VERB 1 = consider, see, rate, view, judge, think of, esteem, deem 2 = look at, view, eye, watch, observe, clock (*Brit. slang*), check out (*informal*), gaze at
• NOUN 1 = respect, esteem, thought, concern, care, consideration 2 = look, gaze, scrutiny, stare, glance
• PLURAL NOUN = good wishes, respects, greetings, compliments, best wishes
• PHRASES **as regards** = concerning, regarding, relating to, pertaining to
regarding = concerning, about, on the subject of, re, respecting, as regards, with reference to, in *or* with regard to
regardless 1 = in spite of everything, anyway, nevertheless, in any case 2 *with* ***of*** = irrespective of, heedless of, unmindful of
regime 1 = government, rule, management, leadership, reign 2 = plan, course, system, policy, programme, scheme, regimen
region = area, place, part, quarter, section, sector, district, territory
regional = local, district, provincial, parochial, zonal
register NOUN = list, record, roll, file, diary, catalogue, log, archives
• VERB 1 = enrol, enlist, list, note, enter 2 = record, catalogue, chronicle 3 = indicate, show 4 = show, mark, indicate, manifest 5 = express, show, reveal, display, exhibit
regret VERB 1 = be *or* feel sorry about, rue, deplore, bemoan, repent (of), bewail ≠ be satisfied with 2 = mourn, miss, grieve for *or* over
• NOUN 1 = remorse, compunction, bitterness, repentance, contrition, penitence 2 = sorrow ≠ satisfaction
regular 1 = frequent 2 = normal, common, usual, ordinary, typical, routine, customary, habitual ≠ infrequent 3 = steady, consistent 4 = even, level, balanced, straight, flat, fixed, smooth, uniform ≠ uneven
regulate 1 = control, run, rule, manage, direct, guide, handle, govern 2 = moderate, control, modulate, fit, tune, adjust
regulation 1 = rule, order, law, dictate, decree, statute, edict, precept 2 = control, government, management, direction, supervision
rehearsal = practice, rehearsing, run-through, preparation, drill
rehearse = practise, prepare, run through, go over, train, repeat, drill, recite
reign VERB 1 = be supreme, prevail, predominate, hold sway 2 = rule, govern, be in power, influence, command

• NOUN = rule, power, control, command, monarchy, dominion
rein = control, harness, bridle, hold, check, brake, curb, restraint
reincarnation = rebirth, transmigration of souls
reinforce 1 = support, strengthen, fortify, toughen, stress, prop, supplement, emphasize 2 = increase, extend, add to, strengthen, supplement
reinforcement NOUN 1 = strengthening, increase, fortification, augmentation 2 = support, stay, prop, brace, buttress
• PLURAL NOUN = reserves, support, auxiliaries, additional *or* fresh troops
reinstate = restore, recall, re-establish, return
reiterate (*Formal*) = repeat, restate, say again, do again
reject VERB 1 = rebuff, jilt, turn down, spurn, refuse, say no to, repulse ≠ accept 2 = deny, exclude, veto, relinquish, renounce, disallow, forsake, disown ≠ approve 3 = discard, decline, eliminate, scrap, jettison, throw away *or* out ≠ accept
• NOUN 1 = castoff, second, discard ≠ treasure 2 = failure, loser, flop
rejection 1 = denial, veto, dismissal, exclusion, disowning, thumbs down, renunciation, repudiation ≠ approval 2 = rebuff, refusal, knock-back (*slang*), kick in the teeth (*slang*), brushoff (*slang*) ≠ acceptance
rejoice = be glad, celebrate, be happy, glory, be overjoyed, exult ≠ lament
rejoin = reply, answer, respond, retort, riposte
relate VERB = tell, recount, report, detail, describe, recite, narrate
• PHRASES **relate to something** *or* **someone** 1 = concern, refer to, apply to, have to do with, pertain to, be relevant to 2 = connect with, associate with, link with, couple with, join with, correlate to
related 1 = associated, linked, joint, connected, affiliated, akin, interconnected ≠ unconnected 2 = akin, kindred ≠ unrelated
relation NOUN 1 = similarity, link, bearing, bond, comparison, correlation, connection 2 = relative, kin, kinsman *or* kinswoman
• PLURAL NOUN 1 = dealings, relationship, affairs, contact, connections, interaction, intercourse 2 = family, relatives, tribe, clan, kin, kindred, kinsmen, kinsfolk, ainga (*N.Z.*)
relationship 1 = association, bond, connection, affinity, rapport, kinship 2 = affair, romance, liaison, amour, intrigue 3 = connection, link, parallel, similarity, tie-up, correlation
relative NOUN = relation, kinsman *or* kinswoman, member of your *or* the family
• ADJECTIVE 1 = comparative 2 = corresponding 3 *with* ***to*** = in proportion to, proportionate to
relatively = comparatively, rather, somewhat
relax 1 = be *or* feel at ease, chill out (*slang, chiefly U.S.*), take it easy, lighten up (*slang*), outspan (*S. African*) ≠ be alarmed 2 = calm down, calm, unwind 3 = make less tense, rest 4 = lessen, reduce, ease, relieve, weaken, loosen, let up, slacken ≠ tighten 5 = moderate, ease, relieve, weaken, slacken ≠ tighten up
relaxation = leisure, rest, fun, pleasure, recreation, enjoyment
relay = broadcast, carry, spread, communicate, transmit, send out
release VERB 1 = set free, free, discharge, liberate, drop, loose, undo, extricate ≠ imprison 2 = acquit, let go, let off, exonerate, absolve 3 = issue, publish, make public, make known, launch, distribute, put out, circulate ≠ withhold
• NOUN 1 = liberation, freedom, liberty, discharge, emancipation, deliverance ≠ imprisonment 2 = acquittal, exemption, absolution, exoneration 3 = issue, publication, proclamation
relegate = demote, degrade, downgrade
relentless 1 = merciless, fierce, cruel, ruthless, unrelenting, implacable, remorseless, pitiless ≠ merciful 2 = unremitting, persistent, unrelenting, incessant, nonstop, unrelieved
relevant = significant, appropriate, related, fitting, to the point, apt, pertinent, apposite ≠ irrelevant
reliable 1 = dependable, trustworthy, sure, sound, true, faithful, staunch ≠ unreliable 2 = safe, dependable 3 = definitive, sound, dependable, trustworthy
reliance 1 = dependency, dependence 2 = trust, confidence, belief, faith
relic = remnant, vestige, memento, trace, fragment, souvenir, keepsake

relief 1 = ease, release, comfort, cure, remedy, solace, deliverance, mitigation 2 = rest, respite, relaxation, break, breather (*informal*) 3 = aid, help, support, assistance, succour

relieve 1 = ease, soothe, alleviate, relax, comfort, calm, cure, soften ≠ intensify 2 = help, support, aid, sustain, assist, succour

religion = belief, faith, theology, creed

religious 1 = spiritual, holy, sacred, devotional 2 = conscientious, faithful, rigid, meticulous, scrupulous, punctilious

relinquish (*Formal*) = give up, leave, drop, abandon, surrender, let go, renounce, forsake

relish VERB 1 = enjoy, like, savour, revel in ≠ dislike 2 = look forward to, fancy, delight in
• NOUN 1 = enjoyment, liking, love, taste, fancy, penchant, fondness, gusto ≠ distaste 2 = condiment, seasoning, sauce

reluctance = unwillingness, dislike, loathing, distaste, aversion, disinclination, repugnance

reluctant = unwilling, hesitant, loath, disinclined, unenthusiastic ≠ willing

rely on 1 = depend on, lean on 2 = be confident of, bank on, trust, count on, bet on

remain 1 = stay, continue, go on, stand, dwell 2 = stay behind, wait, delay ≠ go 3 = continue, be left, linger

remainder = rest, remains, balance, excess, surplus, remnant, residue, leavings

remains 1 = remnants, leftovers, rest, debris, residue, dregs, leavings 2 = corpse, body, carcass, cadaver 3 = relics

remark VERB 1 = comment, say, state, reflect, mention, declare, observe, pass comment 2 = notice, note, observe, perceive, see, mark, make out, espy
• NOUN = comment, observation, reflection, statement, utterance

remarkable = extraordinary, striking, outstanding, wonderful, rare, unusual, surprising, notable ≠ ordinary

remedy NOUN = cure, treatment, medicine, nostrum
• VERB = put right, rectify, fix, correct, set to rights

remember 1 = recall, think back to, recollect, reminisce about, call to mind ≠ forget 2 = bear in mind, keep in mind 3 = look back (on), commemorate

remembrance 1 = commemoration, memorial 2 = souvenir, token, reminder, monument, memento, keepsake 3 = memory, recollection, thought, recall, reminiscence

remind = jog your memory, prompt, make you remember

reminiscent = suggestive, evocative, similar

remnant = remainder, remains, trace, fragment, end, rest, residue, leftovers

remorse = regret, shame, guilt, grief, sorrow, anguish, repentance, contrition

remote 1 = distant, far, isolated, out-of-the-way, secluded, inaccessible, in the middle of nowhere ≠ nearby 2 = far, distant 3 = slight, small, outside, unlikely, slim, faint, doubtful, dubious ≠ strong 4 = aloof, cold, reserved, withdrawn, distant, abstracted, detached, uncommunicative ≠ outgoing

removal 1 = extraction, withdrawal, uprooting, eradication, dislodgment, taking away *or* off *or* out 2 = dismissal, expulsion, elimination, ejection 3 = move, transfer, departure, relocation, flitting (*Scot. & Northern English dialect*)

remove 1 = take out, withdraw, extract ≠ insert 2 = take off ≠ put on 3 = erase, eliminate, take out 4 = dismiss, eliminate, get rid of, discharge, abolish, expel, throw out, oust ≠ appoint 5 = get rid of, erase, eradicate, expunge 6 = take away, detach, displace ≠ put back 7 = delete, get rid of, erase, excise 8 = move, depart, relocate, flit (*Scot. & Northern English dialect*)

renaissance *or* **renascence** = rebirth, revival, restoration, renewal, resurgence, reappearance, reawakening

rend (*Literary*) = tear, rip, separate, wrench, rupture

render 1 = make, cause to become, leave 2 = provide, give, pay, present, supply, submit, tender, hand out 3 = represent, portray, depict, do, give, play, act, perform

renew 1 = recommence, continue, extend, repeat, resume, reopen, recreate, reaffirm 2 = reaffirm, resume, recommence 3 = replace, refresh, replenish, restock 4 = restore, repair, overhaul, mend, refurbish, renovate, refit, modernize

renounce 1 = disown, quit, forsake,

recant, forswear, abjure **2** = disclaim, deny, give up, relinquish, waive, abjure ≠ assert

renovate = restore, repair, refurbish, do up (*informal*), renew, overhaul, refit, modernize

renowned = famous, noted, celebrated, well-known, distinguished, esteemed, notable, eminent ≠ unknown

rent[1] **VERB 1** = hire, lease **2** = let, lease
• **NOUN** = hire, rental, lease, fee, payment

rent[2] **1** = tear, split, rip, slash, slit, gash, hole **2** = opening, hole

repair VERB 1 = mend, fix, restore, heal, patch, renovate, patch up ≠ damage **2** = put right, make up for, compensate for, rectify, redress
• **NOUN 1** = mend, restoration, overhaul **2** = darn, mend, patch **3** = condition, state, form, shape (*informal*)

repay = pay back, refund, settle up, return, square, compensate, reimburse, recompense

repeal VERB = abolish, reverse, revoke, annul, recall, cancel, invalidate, nullify ≠ pass
• **NOUN** = abolition, cancellation, annulment, invalidation, rescindment ≠ passing

repeat VERB 1 = reiterate, restate **2** = retell, echo, replay, reproduce, rerun, reshow
• **NOUN 1** = repetition, echo, reiteration **2** = rerun, replay, reshowing

repeatedly = over and over, often, frequently, many times

repel 1 = drive off, fight, resist, parry, hold off, rebuff, ward off, repulse ≠ submit to **2** = disgust, offend, revolt, sicken, nauseate, gross out (*U.S. slang*) ≠ delight

repertoire = range, list, stock, supply, store, collection, repertory

repetition 1 = recurrence, repeating, echo **2** = repeating, replication, restatement, reiteration, tautology

replace 1 = take the place of, follow, succeed, oust, take over from, supersede, supplant **2** = substitute, change, exchange, switch, swap **3** = put back, restore

replacement 1 = replacing **2** = successor, double, substitute, stand-in, proxy, surrogate, understudy

replica 1 = reproduction, model, copy, imitation, facsimile, carbon copy ≠ original **2** = duplicate, copy, carbon copy

replicate = copy, reproduce, recreate, mimic, duplicate, reduplicate

reply VERB = answer, respond, retort, counter, rejoin, retaliate, reciprocate
• **NOUN** = answer, response, reaction, counter, retort, retaliation, counterattack, rejoinder

report VERB 1 = inform of, communicate, recount **2** *often with* ***on*** = communicate, tell, state, detail, describe, relate, broadcast, pass on **3** = present yourself, come, appear, arrive, turn up
• **NOUN 1** = article, story, piece, write-up **2** = account, record, statement, communication, description, narrative **3** *often plural* = news, word **4** = bang, sound, crack, noise, blast, boom, explosion, discharge **5** = rumour, talk, buzz, gossip, hearsay

reporter = journalist, writer, correspondent, hack (*derogatory*), pressman, journo (*slang*)

represent 1 = act for, speak for **2** = stand for, serve as **3** = express, correspond to, symbolize, mean **4** = exemplify, embody, symbolize, typify, personify, epitomize **5** = depict, show, describe, picture, illustrate, outline, portray, denote

representation 1 = picture, model, image, portrait, illustration, likeness **2** = portrayal, depiction, account, description

representative NOUN 1 = delegate, member, agent, deputy, proxy, spokesman *or* spokeswoman **2** = agent, salesman, rep, commercial traveller
• **ADJECTIVE 1** = typical, characteristic, archetypal, exemplary ≠ uncharacteristic **2** = symbolic

repress 1 = control, suppress, hold back, bottle up, check, curb, restrain, inhibit ≠ release **2** = hold back, suppress, stifle **3** = subdue, abuse, wrong, persecute, quell, subjugate, maltreat ≠ liberate

repression 1 = subjugation, control, constraint, domination, tyranny, despotism **2** = suppression, crushing, quashing **3** = inhibition, control, restraint, bottling up

reprieve VERB = grant a stay of execution to, pardon, let off the hook (*slang*)
• **NOUN** = stay of execution, amnesty, pardon, remission, deferment, postponement of punishment

reproduce 1 = copy, recreate, replicate, duplicate, match, mirror, echo, imitate 2 = print, copy 3 (*Biology*) = breed, procreate, multiply, spawn, propagate

reproduction 1 = copy, picture, print, replica, imitation, duplicate, facsimile ≠ original 2 (*Biology*) = breeding, increase, generation, multiplication

Republican ADJECTIVE = right-wing, Conservative
• NOUN = right-winger, Conservative

reputation = name, standing, character, esteem, stature, renown, repute

request VERB 1 = ask for, appeal for, put in for, demand, desire 2 = invite, entreat 3 = seek, ask (for), solicit
• NOUN 1 = appeal, call, demand, plea, desire, entreaty, suit 2 = asking, plea

require 1 = need, crave, want, miss, lack, wish, desire 2 = order, demand, command, compel, exact, oblige, call upon, insist upon 3 = ask

requirement = necessity, demand, stipulation, want, need, must, essential, prerequisite

rescue VERB 1 = save, get out, release, deliver, recover, liberate ≠ desert 2 = salvage, deliver, redeem
• NOUN = saving, salvage, deliverance, release, recovery, liberation, salvation, redemption

research NOUN = investigation, study, analysis, examination, probe, exploration
• VERB = investigate, study, examine, explore, probe, analyse

resemblance = similarity, correspondence, parallel, likeness, kinship, sameness, similitude ≠ dissimilarity

resemble = be like, look like, mirror, parallel, be similar to, bear a resemblance to

resent = be bitter about, object to, grudge, begrudge, take exception to, take offence at ≠ be content with

resentment = bitterness, indignation, ill feeling, ill will, grudge, animosity, pique, rancour

reservation 1 *often plural* = doubt, scruples, hesitancy 2 = reserve, territory, preserve, sanctuary

reserve VERB 1 = book, prearrange, engage 2 = put by, secure 3 = keep, hold, save, store, retain, set aside, stockpile, hoard
• NOUN 1 = store, fund, savings, stock, supply, reservoir, hoard, cache 2 = park, reservation, preserve, sanctuary, tract, forest park (*N.Z.*) 3 = shyness, silence, restraint, constraint, reticence, secretiveness, taciturnity 4 = reservation, doubt, delay, uncertainty, indecision, hesitancy, vacillation, irresolution
• ADJECTIVE = substitute, extra, spare, secondary, fall-back, auxiliary

reserved 1 = uncommunicative, retiring, silent, shy, restrained, secretive, reticent, taciturn ≠ uninhibited 2 = set aside, taken, kept, held, booked, retained, engaged, restricted

reservoir 1 = lake, pond, basin 2 = store, stock, source, supply, reserves, pool

reside (*Formal*) = live, lodge, dwell, stay, abide ≠ visit

residence = home, house, dwelling, place, flat, lodging, abode, habitation

resident 1 = inhabitant, citizen, local ≠ nonresident 2 = tenant, occupant, lodger 3 = guest, lodger

residue = remainder, remains, remnant, leftovers, rest, extra, excess, surplus

resign VERB 1 = quit, leave, step down (*informal*), vacate, abdicate, give *or* hand in your notice 2 = give up, abandon, yield, surrender, relinquish, renounce, forsake, forgo
• PHRASES **resign yourself to something** = accept, succumb to, submit to, give in to, yield to, acquiesce to

resignation 1 = leaving, departure, abandonment, abdication 2 = acceptance, patience, submission, compliance, endurance, passivity, acquiescence, sufferance ≠ resistance

resigned = stoical, patient, subdued, long-suffering, compliant, unresisting

resist 1 = oppose, battle against, combat, defy, stand up to, hinder ≠ accept 2 = refrain from, avoid, keep from, forgo, abstain from, forbear ≠ indulge in 3 = withstand, be proof against

resistance 1 = opposition, hostility, aversion 2 = fighting, fight, battle, struggle, defiance, obstruction, impediment, hindrance

resistant 1 = opposed, hostile, unwilling, intractable, antagonistic, intransigent 2 = impervious, hard, strong, tough, unaffected

resolution 1 = declaration 2 = decision, resolve, intention, aim, purpose, determination, intent 3 = determination, purpose, resolve, tenacity, perseverance, willpower, firmness, steadfastness
resolve VERB 1 = work out, answer, clear up, crack, fathom 2 = decide, determine, agree, purpose, intend, fix, conclude
• NOUN 1 = determination, resolution, willpower, firmness, steadfastness, resoluteness ≠ indecision 2 = decision, resolution, objective, purpose, intention
resort 1 = holiday centre, spot, retreat, haunt, tourist centre 2 = recourse to, reference to
resound 1 = echo, resonate, reverberate, re-echo 2 = ring
resounding = echoing, full, ringing, powerful, booming, reverberating, resonant, sonorous
resource NOUN 1 = facility 2 = means, course, resort, device, expedient
• PLURAL NOUN 1 = funds, holdings, money, capital, riches, assets, wealth 2 = reserves, supplies, stocks
respect VERB 1 = think highly of, value, honour, admire, esteem, look up to, defer to, have a good *or* high opinion of 2 = show consideration for, honour, observe, heed 3 = abide by, follow, observe, comply with, obey, heed, keep to, adhere to ≠ disregard
• NOUN 1 = regard, honour, recognition, esteem, admiration, estimation ≠ contempt 2 = consideration, kindness, deference, tact, thoughtfulness, considerateness 3 = particular, way, point, matter, sense, detail, feature, aspect
respectable 1 = honourable, good, decent, worthy, upright, honest, reputable, estimable ≠ disreputable 2 = decent, neat, spruce 3 = reasonable, considerable, substantial, fair, ample, appreciable, sizable *or* sizeable ≠ small
respective = specific, own, individual, particular, relevant
respite = pause, break, rest, relief, halt, interval, recess, lull
respond 1 = answer, return, reply, counter, retort, rejoin ≠ remain silent 2 *often with to* = reply to, answer 3 = react, retaliate, reciprocate
response = answer, return, reply, reaction, feedback, retort, counterattack, rejoinder
responsibility 1 = duty, business, job, role, task, accountability, answerability 2 = fault, blame, liability, guilt, culpability 3 = obligation, duty, liability, charge, care 4 = authority, power, importance, mana (*N.Z.*) 5 = job, task, function, role 6 = level-headedness, rationality, dependability, trustworthiness, conscientiousness, sensibleness
responsible 1 = to blame, guilty, at fault, culpable 2 = in charge, in control, in authority 3 = accountable, liable, answerable ≠ unaccountable 4 = sensible, reliable, rational, dependable, trustworthy, level-headed ≠ unreliable
responsive = sensitive, open, alive, susceptible, receptive, reactive, impressionable ≠ unresponsive
rest[1] VERB 1 = relax, take it easy, sit down, be at ease, put your feet up, outspan (*S. African*) ≠ work 2 = stop, have a break, break off, take a breather (*informal*), halt, cease ≠ keep going 3 = place, repose, sit, lean, prop 4 = be placed, sit, lie, be supported, recline
• NOUN 1 = relaxation, repose, leisure ≠ work 2 = pause, break, stop, halt, interval, respite, lull, interlude 3 = refreshment, release, relief, ease, comfort, cure, remedy, solace 4 = inactivity 5 = support, stand, base, holder, prop 6 = calm, tranquillity, stillness
rest[2] = remainder, remains, excess, remnants, others, balance, surplus, residue
restaurant = café, diner (*chiefly U.S. & Canad.*), bistro, cafeteria, tearoom, eatery *or* eaterie
restless 1 = unsettled, nervous, edgy, fidgeting, on edge, restive, jumpy, fidgety ≠ relaxed 2 = moving, wandering, unsettled, unstable, roving, transient, nomadic ≠ settled
restoration 1 = reinstatement, return, revival, restitution, re-establishment, replacement ≠ abolition 2 = repair, reconstruction, renewal, renovation, revitalization ≠ demolition
restore 1 = reinstate, re-establish, reintroduce ≠ abolish 2 = revive, build up, strengthen, refresh, revitalize ≠ make worse 3 = re-establish, replace, reinstate, give back 4 = repair, refurbish, renovate, reconstruct, fix (up), renew, rebuild, mend ≠ demolish 5 = return, replace, recover,

bring back, send back, hand back
restrain 1 = hold back, control, check, contain, restrict, curb, hamper, hinder ≠ encourage 2 = control, inhibit
restrained 1 = controlled, moderate, self-controlled, calm, mild, undemonstrative ≠ hot-headed 2 = unobtrusive, discreet, subdued, tasteful, quiet ≠ garish
restraint 1 = limitation, limit, check, ban, embargo, curb, rein, interdict ≠ freedom 2 = self-control, self-discipline, self-restraint, self-possession ≠ self-indulgence 3 = constraint, limitation, inhibition, control, restriction
restrict 1 = limit, regulate, curb, ration ≠ widen 2 = hamper, handicap, restrain, inhibit
restriction 1 = control, rule, regulation, curb, restraint, confinement 2 = limitation, handicap, inhibition
result NOUN 1 = consequence, effect, outcome, end result, product, sequel, upshot ≠ cause 2 = outcome, end
• VERB = arise, follow, issue, happen, appear, develop, spring, derive
resume = begin again, continue, go on with, proceed with, carry on, reopen, restart ≠ discontinue
résumé = summary, synopsis, précis, rundown, recapitulation
resumption = continuation, carrying on, reopening, renewal, restart, resurgence, re-establishment
resurgence = revival, return, renaissance, resurrection, resumption, rebirth, re-emergence
resurrect 1 = revive, renew, bring back, reintroduce 2 = restore to life, raise from the dead
resurrection 1 = revival, restoration, renewal, resurgence, return, renaissance, rebirth, reappearance ≠ killing off 2 *usually caps* = raising *or* rising from the dead, return from the dead ≠ demise
retain 1 = maintain, reserve, preserve, keep up, continue to have 2 = keep, save ≠ let go
retaliate = pay someone back, hit back, strike back, reciprocate, take revenge, get even with (*informal*), get your own back (*informal*) ≠ turn the other cheek
retaliation = revenge, repayment, vengeance, reprisal, an eye for an eye, reciprocation, requital, counterblow
retard = slow down, check, arrest, delay, handicap, hinder, impede, set back ≠ speed up
retire 1 = stop working, give up work 2 = withdraw, leave, exit, go away, depart 3 = go to bed, turn in (*informal*), hit the sack (*slang*), hit the hay (*slang*)
retirement = withdrawal, retreat, privacy, solitude, seclusion
retiring = shy, reserved, quiet, timid, unassuming, self-effacing, bashful, unassertive ≠ outgoing
retort VERB = reply, return, answer, respond, counter, come back with, riposte
• NOUN = reply, answer, response, comeback, riposte, rejoinder
retreat VERB = withdraw, back off, draw back, leave, go back, depart, fall back, pull back ≠ advance
• NOUN 1 = flight, retirement, departure, withdrawal, evacuation ≠ advance 2 = refuge, haven, shelter, sanctuary, hideaway, seclusion
retrieve 1 = get back, regain, recover, restore, recapture 2 = redeem, save, win back, recoup
retrospect = hindsight, review, re-examination ≠ foresight
return VERB 1 = come back, go back, retreat, turn back, revert, reappear ≠ depart 2 = put back, replace, restore, reinstate ≠ keep 3 = give back, repay, refund, pay back, reimburse, recompense ≠ keep 4 = recur, repeat, persist, revert, happen again, reappear, come again 5 = elect, choose, vote in
• NOUN 1 = reappearance ≠ departure 2 = restoration, reinstatement, re-establishment ≠ removal 3 = recurrence, repetition, reappearance, reversion, persistence 4 = profit, interest, gain, income, revenue, yield, proceeds, takings 5 = statement, report, form, list, account, summary
revamp = renovate, restore, overhaul, refurbish, do up (*informal*), recondition
reveal 1 = make known, disclose, give away, make public, tell, announce, proclaim, let out ≠ keep secret 2 = show, display, exhibit, unveil, uncover, manifest, unearth, unmask ≠ hide
revel VERB = celebrate, carouse, live it up (*informal*), make merry
• NOUN *often plural* = merrymaking, party,

celebration, spree, festivity, carousal
revelation 1 = disclosure, news, announcement, publication, leak, confession, divulgence 2 = exhibition, publication, exposure, unveiling, uncovering, unearthing, proclamation
revenge NOUN = retaliation, vengeance, reprisal, retribution, an eye for an eye
• VERB = avenge, repay, take revenge for, get your own back for (*informal*)
revenue = income, returns, profits, gain, yield, proceeds, receipts, takings ≠ expenditure
revere = be in awe of, respect, honour, worship, reverence, exalt, look up to, venerate ≠ despise
reverse VERB 1 (*Law*) = change, cancel, overturn, overthrow, undo, repeal, quash, revoke ≠ implement 2 = turn round, turn over, turn upside down, upend 3 = transpose, change, move, exchange, transfer, switch, shift, alter 4 = go backwards, retreat, back up, turn back, move backwards, back ≠ go forward
• NOUN 1 = opposite, contrary, converse, inverse 2 = misfortune, blow, failure, disappointment, setback, hardship, reversal, adversity 3 = back, rear, other side, wrong side, underside ≠ front
• ADJECTIVE = opposite, contrary, converse
revert 1 = go back, return, come back, resume 2 = return
review NOUN 1 = survey, study, analysis, examination, scrutiny 2 = critique, commentary, evaluation, notice, criticism, judgment 3 = inspection, parade, march past 4 = magazine, journal, periodical, zine (*informal*)
• VERB 1 = reconsider, revise, rethink, reassess, re-examine, re-evaluate, think over 2 = assess, study, judge, evaluate, criticize 3 = inspect, check, survey, examine, vet 4 = look back on, remember, recall, reflect on, recollect
reviewer = critic, judge, commentator
revise 1 = change, review 2 = edit, correct, alter, update, amend, rework, redo, emend 3 = study, go over, run through, cram (*informal*), swot up on (*Brit. informal*)
revision 1 = emendation, updating, correction 2 = change, amendment 3 = studying, cramming (*informal*), swotting (*Brit. informal*), homework
revival 1 = resurgence ≠ decline 2 = reawakening, renaissance, renewal, resurrection, rebirth, revitalization
revive 1 = revitalize, restore, renew, rekindle, invigorate, reanimate 2 = bring round, awaken 3 = come round, recover 4 = refresh ≠ exhaust
revolt NOUN = uprising, rising, revolution, rebellion, mutiny, insurrection, insurgency
• VERB 1 = rebel, rise up, resist, mutiny 2 = disgust, sicken, repel, repulse, nauseate, gross out (*U.S. slang*), turn your stomach, make your flesh creep
revolting = disgusting, foul, horrible, sickening, horrid, repellent, repulsive, nauseating, yucko (*Austral. slang*) ≠ delightful
revolution 1 = revolt, rising, coup, rebellion, uprising, mutiny, insurgency 2 = transformation, shift, innovation, upheaval, reformation, sea change 3 = rotation, turn, cycle, circle, spin, lap, circuit, orbit
revolutionary ADJECTIVE 1 = rebel, radical, extremist, subversive, insurgent ≠ reactionary 2 = innovative, new, different, novel, radical, progressive, drastic, ground-breaking ≠ conventional
• NOUN = rebel, insurgent, revolutionist ≠ reactionary
revolve 1 = go round, circle, orbit 2 = rotate, turn, wheel, spin, twist, whirl
reward NOUN 1 = punishment, retribution, comeuppance (*slang*), just deserts 2 = payment, return, prize, wages, compensation, bonus, premium, repayment ≠ penalty
• VERB = compensate, pay, repay, recompense, remunerate ≠ penalize
rewarding = satisfying, fulfilling, valuable, profitable, productive, worthwhile, beneficial, enriching ≠ unrewarding
rhetoric 1 = hyperbole, bombast, wordiness, verbosity, grandiloquence, magniloquence 2 = oratory, eloquence, public speaking, speech-making, elocution, declamation, grandiloquence, whaikorero (*N.Z.*)
rhetorical = high-flown, bombastic, verbose, oratorical, grandiloquent, declamatory, arty-farty (*informal*), magniloquent
rhyme = poem, song, verse, ode
rhythm 1 = beat, swing, accent, pulse, tempo, cadence, lilt 2 = metre, time

rich 1 = wealthy, affluent, well-off, loaded (*slang*), prosperous, well-heeled (*informal*), well-to-do, moneyed ≠ poor 2 = well-stocked, full, productive, ample, abundant, plentiful, copious, well-supplied ≠ scarce 3 = full-bodied, sweet, fatty, tasty, creamy, luscious, succulent ≠ bland 4 = fruitful, productive, fertile, prolific ≠ barren 5 = abounding, luxurious, lush, abundant

riches 1 = wealth, assets, plenty, fortune, substance, treasure, affluence ≠ poverty 2 = resources, treasures

richly 1 = elaborately, lavishly, elegantly, splendidly, exquisitely, expensively, luxuriously, gorgeously 2 = fully, well, thoroughly, amply, appropriately, properly, suitably

rid VERB = free, clear, deliver, relieve, purge, unburden, make free, disencumber
• PHRASES **get rid of something** *or* **someone** = dispose of, throw away *or* out, dump, remove, eliminate, expel, eject

riddle[1] 1 = puzzle, problem, conundrum, poser 2 = enigma, question, secret, mystery, puzzle, conundrum, teaser, problem

riddle[2] 1 = pierce, pepper, puncture, perforate, honeycomb 2 = pervade, fill, spread through

riddled = filled, spoilt, pervaded, infested, permeated

ride VERB 1 = control, handle, manage 2 = travel, be carried, go, move
• NOUN = journey, drive, trip, lift, outing, jaunt

ridicule VERB = laugh at, mock, make fun of, sneer at, jeer at, deride, poke fun at, chaff
• NOUN = mockery, scorn, derision, laughter, jeer, chaff, gibe, raillery

ridiculous = laughable, stupid, silly, absurd, ludicrous, farcical, comical, risible ≠ sensible

rife = widespread, rampant, general, common, universal, frequent, prevalent, ubiquitous

rifle = ransack, rob, burgle, loot, strip, sack, plunder, pillage

rift 1 = breach, division, split, separation, falling out (*informal*), disagreement, quarrel 2 = split, opening, crack, gap, break, fault, flaw, cleft

rig VERB 1 = fix, engineer (*informal*), arrange, manipulate, tamper with, gerrymander 2 (*Nautical*) = equip, fit out, kit out, outfit, supply, furnish
• PHRASES **rig something up** = set up, build, construct, put up, arrange, assemble, put together, erect

right ADJECTIVE 1 = correct, true, genuine, accurate, exact, precise, valid, factual, dinkum (*Austral. & N.Z. informal*) ≠ wrong 2 = proper, done, becoming, seemly, fitting, fit, appropriate, suitable ≠ inappropriate 3 = just, good, fair, moral, proper, ethical, honest, equitable ≠ unfair
• ADVERB 1 = correctly, truly, precisely, exactly, genuinely, accurately ≠ wrongly 2 = suitably, fittingly, appropriately, properly, aptly ≠ improperly 3 = exactly, squarely, precisely 4 = directly, straight, precisely, exactly, unswervingly, without deviation, by the shortest route, in a beeline 5 = straight, directly, quickly, promptly, straightaway ≠ indirectly
• NOUN 1 = prerogative, business, power, claim, authority, due, freedom, licence 2 = justice, truth, fairness, legality, righteousness, lawfulness ≠ injustice
• VERB = rectify, settle, fix, correct, sort out, straighten, redress, put right

right away = immediately, now, directly, instantly, at once, straightaway, forthwith, pronto (*informal*)

righteous = virtuous, good, just, fair, moral, pure, ethical, upright ≠ wicked

rigid 1 = strict, set, fixed, exact, rigorous, stringent ≠ flexible 2 = inflexible, uncompromising, unbending 3 = stiff, inflexible, inelastic ≠ pliable

rigorous = strict, hard, demanding, tough, severe, exacting, harsh, stern ≠ soft

rim 1 = edge, lip, brim 2 = border, edge, trim 3 = margin, border, verge, brink

ring[1] VERB 1 = phone, call, telephone, buzz (*informal, chiefly Brit.*) 2 = chime, sound, toll, reverberate, clang, peal 3 = reverberate
• NOUN 1 = call, phone call, buzz (*informal, chiefly Brit.*) 2 = chime, knell, peal

ring[2] NOUN 1 = circle, round, band, circuit, loop, hoop, halo 2 = arena, enclosure, circus, rink 3 = gang, group, association, band, circle, mob, syndicate, cartel
• VERB = encircle, surround, enclose, girdle, gird

rinse VERB = wash, clean, dip, splash, cleanse, bathe

• NOUN = wash, dip, splash, bath

riot NOUN **1** = disturbance, disorder, confusion, turmoil, upheaval, strife, turbulence, lawlessness **2** = display, show, splash, extravaganza, profusion **3** = laugh, joke, scream (*informal*), hoot (*informal*), lark
• VERB = rampage, run riot, go on the rampage
• PHRASES **run riot 1** = rampage, go wild, be out of control **2** = grow profusely, spread like wildfire

rip VERB **1** = tear, cut, split, burst, rend, slash, claw, slit **2** = be torn, tear, split, burst
• NOUN = tear, cut, hole, split, rent, slash, slit, gash
• PHRASES **rip someone off** (*Slang*) = cheat, rob, con (*informal*), skin (*slang*), fleece, defraud, swindle

ripe 1 = ripened, seasoned, ready, mature, mellow ≠ unripe **2** = right, suitable **3** = mature **4** = suitable, timely, ideal, favourable, auspicious, opportune ≠ unsuitable

rip-off *or* **ripoff** (*Slang*) = cheat, con (*informal*), scam (*slang*), con trick (*informal*), fraud, theft, swindle

rise VERB **1** = get up, stand up, get to your feet **2** = arise **3** = go up, climb, ascend ≠ descend **4** = loom, tower **5** = get steeper, ascend, go uphill, slope upwards ≠ drop **6** = increase, mount ≠ decrease **7** = grow, go up, intensify **8** = rebel, revolt, mutiny **9** = advance, progress, get on, prosper
• NOUN **1** = upward slope, incline, elevation, ascent, kopje *or* koppie (*S. African*) **2** = increase, upturn, upswing, upsurge ≠ decrease **3** = pay increase, raise (*U.S.*), increment **4** = advancement, progress, climb, promotion
• PHRASES **give rise to something** = cause, produce, effect, result in, bring about

risk NOUN **1** = danger, chance, possibility, hazard **2** = gamble, chance, speculation, leap in the dark **3** = peril, jeopardy
• VERB **1** = stand a chance of **2** = dare, endanger, jeopardize, imperil, venture, gamble, hazard

risky = dangerous, hazardous, unsafe, perilous, uncertain, dodgy (*Brit., Austral., & N.Z. informal*), dicey (*informal, chiefly Brit.*), chancy (*informal*) ≠ safe

rite = ceremony, custom, ritual, practice, procedure, observance

ritual NOUN **1** = ceremony, rite, observance **2** = custom, tradition, routine, convention, practice, procedure, habit, protocol, tikanga (*N.Z.*)
• ADJECTIVE = ceremonial, conventional, routine, customary, habitual

rival NOUN = opponent, competitor, contender, contestant, adversary ≠ supporter
• VERB = compete with, match, equal, compare with, come up to, be a match for
• ADJECTIVE = competing, conflicting, opposing

rivalry = competition, opposition, conflict, contest, contention

river 1 = stream, brook, creek, waterway, tributary, burn (*Scot.*) **2** = flow, rush, flood, spate, torrent

riveting = enthralling, gripping, fascinating, absorbing, captivating, hypnotic, engrossing, spellbinding

road 1 = roadway, highway, motorway, track, route, path, lane, pathway **2** = way, path

roam = wander, walk, range, travel, stray, ramble, prowl, rove

roar VERB **1** = thunder **2** = guffaw, laugh heartily, hoot, split your sides (*informal*) **3** = cry, shout, yell, howl, bellow, bawl, bay
• NOUN **1** = guffaw, hoot **2** = cry, shout, yell, howl, outcry, bellow

rob 1 = steal from, hold up, mug (*informal*) **2** = raid, hold up, loot, plunder, burgle, pillage **3** = dispossess, con (*informal*), cheat, defraud **4** = deprive, do out of (*informal*)

robber = thief, raider, burglar, looter, fraud, cheat, bandit, plunderer

robbery 1 = burglary, raid, hold-up, rip-off (*slang*), stick-up (*slang, chiefly U.S.*) **2** = theft, stealing, mugging (*informal*), plunder, swindle, pillage, larceny

robe = gown, costume, habit

robot = machine, automaton, android, mechanical man

robust = strong, tough, powerful, fit, healthy, strapping, hardy, vigorous ≠ weak

rock¹ = stone, boulder

rock² 1 = sway, pitch, swing, reel, toss, lurch, roll **2** = shock, surprise, shake, stun, astonish, stagger, astound

rocky¹ = rough, rugged, stony, craggy

rocky² = unstable, shaky, wobbly, rickety, unsteady
rod 1 = stick, bar, pole, shaft, cane 2 = staff, baton, wand
rogue 1 = scoundrel, crook (*informal*), villain, fraud, blackguard, skelm (*S. African*), rorter (*Austral. slang*) 2 = scamp, rascal, scally (*Northwest English dialect*), nointer (*Austral. slang*)
role 1 = job, part, position, post, task, duty, function, capacity 2 = part, character, representation, portrayal
roll VERB 1 = turn, wheel, spin, go round, revolve, rotate, whirl, swivel 2 = trundle, go, move 3 = flow, run, course 4 *often with* ***up*** = wind, bind, wrap, swathe, envelop, furl, enfold 5 = level, even, press, smooth, flatten 6 = toss, rock, lurch, reel, tumble, sway
• NOUN 1 = rumble, boom, roar, thunder, reverberation 2 = register, record, list, index, census 3 = turn, spin, rotation, cycle, wheel, revolution, reel, whirl
romance 1 = love affair, relationship, affair, attachment, liaison, amour 2 = excitement, colour, charm, mystery, glamour, fascination 3 = story, tale, fantasy, legend, fairy tale, love story, melodrama
romantic ADJECTIVE 1 = loving, tender, passionate, fond, sentimental, amorous, icky (*informal*) ≠ unromantic 2 = idealistic, unrealistic, impractical, dreamy, starry-eyed ≠ realistic 3 = exciting, fascinating, mysterious, colourful, glamorous ≠ unexciting
• NOUN = idealist, dreamer, sentimentalist
romp VERB = frolic, sport, have fun, caper, cavort, frisk, gambol
• NOUN = frolic, lark (*informal*), caper
room 1 = chamber, office, apartment 2 = space, area, capacity, extent, expanse 3 = opportunity, scope, leeway, chance, range, occasion, margin
root¹ NOUN 1 = stem, tuber, rhizome 2 = source, cause, heart, bottom, base, seat, seed, foundation
• PLURAL NOUN = sense of belonging, origins, heritage, birthplace, home, family, cradle
• PHRASES **root something** *or* **someone out** = get rid of, remove, eliminate, abolish, eradicate, do away with, weed out, exterminate
root² = dig, burrow, ferret
rope NOUN = cord, line, cable, strand, hawser
• PHRASES **know the ropes** = be experienced, be knowledgeable, be an old hand ♦ **rope someone in** *or* **into something** (*Brit.*) = persuade, involve, engage, enlist, talk into, inveigle
rosy ADJECTIVE 1 = glowing, blooming, radiant, ruddy, healthy-looking ≠ pale 2 = promising, encouraging, bright, optimistic, hopeful, cheerful, favourable, auspicious ≠ gloomy
• NOUN = pink, red
rot VERB 1 = decay, spoil, deteriorate, perish, decompose, moulder, go bad, putrefy 2 = crumble 3 = deteriorate, decline, waste away
• NOUN 1 = decay, decomposition, corruption, mould, blight, canker, putrefaction 2 (*Informal*) = nonsense, rubbish, drivel, twaddle, garbage (*chiefly U.S.*), trash, tripe (*informal*), claptrap (*informal*), bizzo (*Austral. slang*), bull's wool (*Austral. & N.Z. slang*)
RELATED WORD
adjective: putrid
rotate 1 = revolve, turn, wheel, spin, reel, go round, swivel, pivot 2 = follow in sequence, switch, alternate, take turns
rotation 1 = revolution, turning, turn, wheel, spin, spinning, reel, orbit 2 = sequence, switching, cycle, succession, alternation
rotten 1 = decaying, bad, rank, corrupt, sour, stinking, perished, festering, festy (*Austral. slang*) ≠ fresh 2 = crumbling, perished 3 (*Informal*) = despicable, mean, base, dirty, nasty, contemptible 4 (*Informal*) = inferior, poor, inadequate, duff (*Brit. informal*), unsatisfactory, lousy (*slang*), substandard, crummy (*slang*), bodger *or* bodgie (*Austral. slang*) 5 = corrupt, immoral, crooked (*informal*), dishonest, dishonourable, perfidious ≠ honourable
rough ADJECTIVE 1 = uneven, broken, rocky, irregular, jagged, bumpy, stony, craggy ≠ even 2 = boisterous, hard, tough, arduous 3 = ungracious, blunt, rude, coarse, brusque, uncouth, impolite, uncivil ≠ refined 4 = unpleasant, hard, difficult, tough, uncomfortable ≠ easy 5 = approximate, estimated ≠ exact 6 = vague, general, sketchy, imprecise,

inexact **7** = basic, crude, unfinished, incomplete, imperfect, rudimentary, sketchy, unrefined ≠ complete **8** = stormy, wild, turbulent, choppy, squally ≠ calm **9** = harsh, tough, nasty, cruel, unfeeling ≠ gentle
• NOUN = outline, draft, mock-up, preliminary sketch
• PHRASES **rough and ready** **1** = makeshift, crude, provisional, improvised, sketchy, stopgap **2** = unrefined, shabby, untidy, unkempt, unpolished, ill-groomed ◆ **rough something out** = outline, plan, draft, sketch

round NOUN **1** = series, session, cycle, sequence, succession **2** = stage, turn, level, period, division, session, lap **3** = sphere, ball, band, ring, circle, disc, globe, orb **4** = course, tour, circuit, beat, series, schedule, routine
• ADJECTIVE **1** = spherical, rounded, curved, circular, cylindrical, rotund, globular **2** = plump, full, ample, fleshy, rotund, full-fleshed
• VERB = go round, circle, skirt, flank, bypass, encircle, turn
• PHRASES **round something** *or* **someone up** = gather, muster, group, drive, collect, rally, herd, marshal

roundabout **1** = indirect, devious, tortuous, circuitous, evasive, discursive ≠ direct **2** = oblique, implied, indirect, circuitous

roundup = muster, collection, rally, assembly, herding

rouse **1** = wake up, call, wake, awaken **2** = excite, move, stir, provoke, anger, animate, agitate, inflame **3** = stimulate, provoke, incite

rousing = lively, moving, spirited, exciting, inspiring, stirring, stimulating ≠ dull

rout VERB = defeat, beat, overthrow, thrash, destroy, crush, conquer, wipe the floor with (*informal*)
• NOUN = defeat, beating, overthrow, thrashing, pasting (*slang*), debacle, drubbing

route **1** = way, course, road, direction, path, journey, itinerary **2** = beat, circuit

routine NOUN = procedure, programme, order, practice, method, pattern, custom
• ADJECTIVE **1** = usual, standard, normal, customary, ordinary, typical, everyday, habitual ≠ unusual **2** = boring, dull, predictable, tedious, tiresome, humdrum

row[1] NOUN = line, bank, range, series, file, string, column
• PHRASES **in a row** = consecutively, running, in turn, one after the other, successively, in sequence

row[2] NOUN (*Informal*) **1** = quarrel, dispute, argument, squabble, tiff, trouble, brawl **2** = disturbance, noise, racket, uproar, commotion, rumpus, tumult
• VERB = quarrel, fight, argue, dispute, squabble, wrangle

royal **1** = regal, kingly, queenly, princely, imperial, sovereign **2** = splendid, grand, impressive, magnificent, majestic, stately

rub VERB **1** = stroke, massage, caress **2** = polish, clean, shine, wipe, scour **3** = chafe, scrape, grate, abrade
• NOUN **1** = massage, caress, kneading **2** = polish, stroke, shine, wipe
• PHRASES **rub something out** = erase, remove, cancel, wipe out, delete, obliterate, efface

rubbish **1** = waste, refuse, scrap, junk (*informal*), litter, garbage (*chiefly U.S.*), trash, lumber **2** = nonsense, garbage (*chiefly U.S.*), twaddle, rot, trash, hot air (*informal*), tripe (*informal*), claptrap (*informal*), bizzo (*Austral. slang*), bull's wool (*Austral. & N.Z. slang*)

rude **1** = impolite, insulting, cheeky, abusive, disrespectful, impertinent, insolent, impudent ≠ polite **2** = uncivilized, rough, coarse, brutish, boorish, uncouth, loutish, graceless **3** = vulgar ≠ refined **4** = unpleasant, sharp, sudden, harsh, startling, abrupt **5** = roughly-made, simple, rough, raw, crude, primitive, makeshift, artless ≠ well-made

rue (*Literary*) = regret, mourn, lament, repent, be sorry for, kick yourself for

ruffle **1** = disarrange, disorder, mess up, rumple, tousle, dishevel **2** = annoy, upset, irritate, agitate, nettle, fluster, peeve (*informal*) ≠ calm

rugged **1** = rocky, broken, rough, craggy, difficult, ragged, irregular, uneven ≠ even **2** = strong-featured, rough-hewn, weather-beaten ≠ delicate **3** = well-built, strong, tough, robust, sturdy **4** = tough, strong, robust, muscular, sturdy, burly, husky (*informal*), brawny ≠ delicate

ruin VERB **1** = destroy, devastate, wreck, defeat, smash, crush, demolish, lay waste ≠ create **2** = bankrupt, break, impoverish, beggar, pauperize **3** = spoil, damage, mess up, blow (*slang*), screw up (*informal*), botch, make a mess of, crool *or* cruel (*Austral. slang*) ≠ improve
• NOUN **1** = bankruptcy, insolvency, destitution **2** = disrepair, decay, disintegration, ruination, wreckage **3** = destruction, fall, breakdown, defeat, collapse, wreck, undoing, downfall ≠ preservation

rule NOUN **1** = regulation, law, direction, guideline, decree **2** = precept, principle, canon, maxim, tenet, axiom **3** = custom, procedure, practice, routine, tradition, habit, convention **4** = government, power, control, authority, command, regime, reign, jurisdiction, mana (*N.Z.*)
• VERB **1** = govern, control, direct, have power over, command over, have charge of **2** = reign, govern, be in power, be in authority **3** = decree, decide, judge, settle, pronounce **4** = be prevalent, prevail, predominate, be customary, preponderate
• PHRASES **as a rule** = usually, generally, mainly, normally, on the whole, ordinarily ♦ **rule someone out** = exclude, eliminate, disqualify, ban, reject, dismiss, prohibit, leave out ♦ **rule something out** = reject, exclude, eliminate

ruler 1 = governor, leader, lord, commander, controller, monarch, sovereign, head of state **2** = measure, rule, yardstick

ruling ADJECTIVE **1** = governing, reigning, controlling, commanding **2** = predominant, dominant, prevailing, preponderant, chief, main, principal, pre-eminent ≠ minor
• NOUN = decision, verdict, judgment, decree, adjudication, pronouncement

rumour = story, news, report, talk, word, whisper, buzz, gossip

run VERB **1** = race, rush, dash, hurry, sprint, bolt, gallop, hare (*Brit. informal*) ≠ dawdle **2** = flee, escape, take off (*informal*), bolt, beat it (*slang*), leg it (*informal*), take flight, do a runner (*slang*) ≠ stay **3** = take part, compete **4** = continue, go, stretch, reach, extend, proceed ≠ stop **5** (*Chiefly U.S. & Canad.*) = compete, stand, contend, be a candidate, put yourself up for, take part **6** = manage, lead, direct, be in charge of, head, control, operate, handle **7** = go, work, operate, perform, function **8** = perform, carry out **9** = work, go, operate, function **10** = pass, go, move, roll, glide, skim **11** = flow, pour, stream, go, leak, spill, discharge, gush **12** = publish, feature, display, print **13** = melt, dissolve, liquefy, go soft **14** = smuggle, traffic in, bootleg
• NOUN **1** = race, rush, dash, sprint, gallop, jog, spurt **2** = ride, drive, trip, spin (*informal*), outing, excursion, jaunt **3** = sequence, period, stretch, spell, course, season, series, string **4** = enclosure, pen, coop
• PHRASES **run away** = flee, escape, bolt, abscond, do a runner (*slang*), make a run for it, scram (*informal*), fly the coop (*U.S. & Canad. informal*) ♦ **run into someone** = meet, encounter, bump into, run across, come across *or* upon ♦ **run into something 1** = be beset by, encounter, come across *or* upon, face, experience **2** = collide with, hit, strike ♦ **run out 1** = be used up, dry up, give out, fail, finish, be exhausted **2** = expire, end, terminate ♦ **run over something 1** = exceed, overstep, go over the top of, go over the limit of **2** = review, check, go through, go over, run through, rehearse ♦ **run over something** *or* **someone** = knock down, hit, run down, knock over ♦ **run something** *or* **someone down 1** = criticize, denigrate, belittle, knock (*informal*), rubbish (*informal*), slag (off) (*slang*), disparage, decry **2** = downsize, cut, reduce, trim, decrease, cut back, curtail **3** = knock down, hit, run into, run over, knock over

run-down *or* **rundown 1** = exhausted, weak, drained, weary, unhealthy, worn-out, debilitated, below par ≠ fit **2** = dilapidated, broken-down, shabby, worn-out, seedy, ramshackle, decrepit

runner 1 = athlete, sprinter, jogger **2** = messenger, courier, errand boy, dispatch bearer

running NOUN **1** = management, control, administration, direction, leadership, organization, supervision **2** = working, performance, operation, functioning, maintenance
• ADJECTIVE **1** = continuous, constant, perpetual, uninterrupted, incessant **2** = in succession, unbroken **3** = flowing, moving,

streaming, coursing
rupture NOUN = break, tear, split, crack, rent, burst, breach, fissure
• VERB = break, separate, tear, split, crack, burst, sever
rural 1 = agricultural, country 2 = rustic, country, pastoral, sylvan ≠ urban
rush VERB 1 = hurry, run, race, shoot, fly, career, speed, tear ≠ dawdle 2 = push, hurry, press, hustle 3 = attack, storm, charge at
• NOUN 1 = dash, charge, race, scramble, stampede 2 = hurry, haste, hustle 3 = surge, flow, gush 4 = attack, charge, assault, onslaught
• ADJECTIVE = hasty, fast, quick, hurried, rapid, urgent, swift ≠ leisurely
rust NOUN 1 = corrosion, oxidation 2 = mildew, must, mould, rot, blight
• VERB = corrode, oxidize
rusty 1 = corroded, rusted, oxidized, rust-covered 2 = out of practice, weak, stale, unpractised 3 = reddish-brown, chestnut, reddish, russet, coppery, rust-coloured
ruthless = merciless, harsh, cruel, brutal, relentless, callous, heartless, remorseless ≠ merciful

S

sabotage VERB = damage, destroy, wreck, disable, disrupt, subvert, incapacitate, vandalize
• NOUN = damage, destruction, wrecking
sack[1] NOUN 1 = bag, pocket, sac, pouch, receptacle 2 = dismissal, discharge, the boot (*slang*), the axe (*informal*), the push (*slang*)
• VERB (*Informal*) = dismiss, fire (*informal*), axe (*informal*), discharge, kiss off (*slang, chiefly U.S. & Canad.*), give (someone) the push (*informal*)
sack[2] VERB = plunder, loot, pillage, strip, rob, raid, ruin
• NOUN = plundering, looting, pillage
sacred 1 = holy, hallowed, blessed, divine, revered, sanctified ≠ secular 2 = religious, holy, ecclesiastical, hallowed ≠ unconsecrated 3 = inviolable, protected, sacrosanct, hallowed, inalienable, unalterable
sacrifice VERB 1 = offer, offer up, immolate 2 = give up, abandon, relinquish, lose, surrender, let go, do without, renounce
• NOUN 1 = offering, oblation 2 = surrender, loss, giving up, rejection, abdication, renunciation, repudiation, forswearing
sad 1 = unhappy, down, low, blue, depressed, melancholy, mournful, dejected ≠ happy 2 = tragic, moving, upsetting, depressing, dismal, pathetic, poignant, harrowing 3 = deplorable, bad, sorry, terrible, unfortunate, regrettable, lamentable, wretched ≠ good
sadden = upset, depress, distress, grieve, make sad, deject
saddle = burden, load, lumber (*Brit. informal*), encumber
sadness = unhappiness, sorrow, grief, depression, the blues, misery, melancholy, poignancy ≠ happiness
safe ADJECTIVE 1 = protected, secure, impregnable, out of danger, safe and sound, in safe hands, out of harm's way ≠ endangered 2 = all right, intact, unscathed, unhurt, unharmed, undamaged, O.K. *or* okay (*informal*) 3 = risk-free, sound, secure, certain, impregnable
• NOUN = strongbox, vault, coffer, repository, deposit box, safe-deposit box
safeguard VERB = protect, guard, defend, save, preserve, look after, keep safe
• NOUN = protection, security, defence, guard
safely = in safety, with impunity, without risk, safe and sound
safety 1 = security, protection, safeguards, precautions, safety measures, impregnability ≠ risk 2 = shelter, haven, protection, cover, retreat, asylum, refuge, sanctuary
sag 1 = sink, bag, droop, fall, slump, dip, give way, hang loosely 2 = drop, sink, slump, flop, droop, loll 3 = decline, tire, flag, weaken, wilt, wane, droop
saga 1 = carry-on (*informal, chiefly Brit.*), performance (*informal*), pantomime (*informal*) 2 = epic, story, tale, narrative, yarn

sage NOUN = wise man, philosopher, guru, master, elder, tohunga (*N.Z.*)
• ADJECTIVE = wise, sensible, judicious, sagacious, sapient

sail NOUN = sheet, canvas
• VERB 1 = go by water, cruise, voyage, ride the waves, go by sea 2 = set sail, embark, get under way, put to sea, put off, leave port, hoist sail, cast *or* weigh anchor 3 = pilot, steer 4 = glide, sweep, float, fly, wing, soar, drift, skim

sailor = mariner, marine, seaman, sea dog, seafarer

sake NOUN = purpose, interest, reason, end, aim, objective, motive
• PHRASES **for someone's sake** = in someone's interests, to someone's advantage, on someone's account, for the benefit of, for the good of, for the welfare of, out of respect for, out of consideration for

salary = pay, income, wage, fee, payment, wages, earnings, allowance

sale 1 = selling, marketing, dealing, transaction, disposal 2 = auction, fair, mart, bazaar

salt NOUN = seasoning
• ADJECTIVE = salty, saline, brackish, briny

salute VERB 1 = greet, welcome, acknowledge, address, hail, mihi (*N.Z.*) 2 = honour, acknowledge, recognize, pay tribute *or* homage to
• NOUN = greeting, recognition, salutation, address

salvage = save, recover, rescue, get back, retrieve, redeem

salvation = saving, rescue, recovery, salvage, redemption, deliverance ≠ ruin

same 1 = identical, similar, alike, equal, twin, corresponding, duplicate ≠ different 2 = the very same, one and the same, selfsame 3 = aforementioned, aforesaid 4 = unchanged, consistent, constant, unaltered, invariable, unvarying, changeless ≠ altered

sample NOUN 1 = specimen, example, model, pattern, instance 2 = cross section
• VERB = test, try, experience, taste, inspect
• ADJECTIVE = test, trial, specimen, representative

sanction VERB = permit, allow, approve, endorse, authorize ≠ forbid
• NOUN 1 *often plural* = ban, boycott, embargo, exclusion, penalty, coercive measures ≠ permission 2 = permission, backing, authority, approval, authorization, O.K. *or* okay (*informal*), stamp *or* seal of approval ≠ ban

sanctuary 1 = protection, shelter, refuge, haven, retreat, asylum 2 = reserve, park, preserve, reservation, national park, tract, nature reserve, conservation area

sane 1 = rational, all there (*informal*), of sound mind, compos mentis (*Latin*), in your right mind, mentally sound ≠ insane 2 = sensible, sound, reasonable, balanced, judicious, level-headed ≠ foolish

sap[1] 1 = juice, essence, vital fluid, lifeblood 2 (*Slang*) = fool, jerk (*slang, chiefly U.S. & Canad.*), idiot, wally (*slang*), twit (*informal*), simpleton, ninny, dorba *or* dorb (*Austral. slang*), bogan (*Austral. slang*)

sap[2] = weaken, drain, undermine, exhaust, deplete

satanic = evil, demonic, hellish, black, wicked, devilish, infernal, fiendish ≠ godly

satire 1 = mockery, irony, ridicule 2 = parody, mockery, caricature, lampoon, burlesque

satisfaction 1 = fulfilment, pleasure, achievement, relish, gratification, pride ≠ dissatisfaction 2 = contentment, content, comfort, pleasure, happiness, enjoyment, satiety, repletion ≠ discontent

satisfactory = adequate, acceptable, good enough, average, fair, all right, sufficient, passable ≠ unsatisfactory

satisfy 1 = content, please, indulge, gratify, pander to, assuage, pacify, quench ≠ dissatisfy 2 = convince, persuade, assure, reassure ≠ dissuade 3 = comply with, meet, fulfil, answer, serve, fill, observe, obey ≠ fail to meet

saturate 1 = flood, overwhelm, swamp, overrun 2 = soak, steep, drench, imbue, suffuse, wet through, waterlog, souse

saturated = soaked, soaking (wet), drenched, sodden, dripping, waterlogged, sopping (wet), wet through

sauce = dressing, dip, relish, condiment

savage ADJECTIVE 1 = cruel, brutal, vicious, fierce, harsh, ruthless, ferocious, sadistic ≠ gentle 2 = wild, fierce, ferocious, unbroken, feral, untamed, undomesticated ≠ tame 3 = primitive, undeveloped, uncultivated, uncivilized 4 = uncultivated, rugged, unspoilt, uninhabited, rough, uncivilized

≠ cultivated
• NOUN = lout, yob (*Brit. slang*), barbarian, yahoo, hoon (*Austral. & N.Z.*), boor, cougan (*Austral. slang*), scozza (*Austral. slang*), bogan (*Austral. slang*)
• VERB = maul, tear, claw, attack, mangle, lacerate, mangulate (*Austral. slang*)

save 1 = rescue, free, release, deliver, recover, get out, liberate, salvage ≠ endanger 2 = keep, reserve, set aside, store, collect, gather, hold, hoard ≠ spend 3 = protect, keep, guard, preserve, look after, safeguard, salvage, conserve 4 = put aside, keep, reserve, collect, retain, set aside, put by

saving NOUN = economy, discount, reduction, bargain
• PLURAL NOUN = nest egg, fund, store, reserves, resources

saviour = rescuer, deliverer, defender, protector, liberator, redeemer, preserver

Saviour = Christ, Jesus, the Messiah, the Redeemer

savour VERB 1 = relish, delight in, revel in, luxuriate in 2 = enjoy, appreciate, relish, delight in, revel in, luxuriate in
• NOUN = flavour, taste, smell, relish, smack, tang, piquancy

say VERB 1 = state, declare, remark, announce, maintain, mention, assert, affirm 2 = speak, utter, voice, express, pronounce 3 = suggest, express, imply, communicate, disclose, give away, convey, divulge 4 = suppose, supposing, imagine, assume, presume 5 = estimate, suppose, guess, conjecture, surmise
• NOUN 1 = influence, power, control, authority, weight, clout (*informal*), mana (*N.Z.*) 2 = chance to speak, vote, voice

saying = proverb, maxim, adage, dictum, axiom, aphorism

scale[1] = flake, plate, layer, lamina

scale[2] NOUN 1 = degree, size, range, extent, dimensions, scope, magnitude, breadth 2 = system of measurement, measuring system 3 = ranking, ladder, hierarchy, series, sequence, progression 4 = ratio, proportion
• VERB = climb up, mount, ascend, surmount, clamber up, escalade

scan 1 = glance over, skim, look over, eye, check, examine, check out (*informal*), run over 2 = survey, search, investigate, sweep, scour, scrutinize

scandal 1 = disgrace, crime, offence, sin, embarrassment, wrongdoing, dishonourable behaviour, discreditable behaviour 2 = gossip, talk, rumours, dirt, slander, tattle, aspersion 3 = shame, disgrace, stigma, infamy, opprobrium 4 = outrage, shame, insult, disgrace, injustice, crying shame

scant = inadequate, meagre, sparse, little, minimal, barely sufficient ≠ adequate

scapegoat = fall guy, whipping boy

scar NOUN 1 = mark, injury, wound, blemish 2 = trauma, suffering, pain, torture, anguish
• VERB = mark, disfigure, damage, mar, mutilate, blemish, deface

scarce 1 = in short supply, insufficient ≠ plentiful 2 = rare, few, uncommon, few and far between, infrequent ≠ common

scarcely 1 = hardly, barely 2 (*Often used ironically*) = by no means, hardly, definitely not

scare VERB = frighten, alarm, terrify, panic, shock, startle, intimidate, dismay
• NOUN 1 = fright, shock, start 2 = panic, hysteria 3 = alert, warning, alarm

scared = afraid, alarmed, frightened, terrified, shaken, startled, fearful, petrified

scary (*Informal*) = frightening, alarming, terrifying, chilling, horrifying, spooky (*informal*), creepy (*informal*), spine-chilling

scatter 1 = throw about, spread, sprinkle, strew, shower, fling, diffuse, disseminate ≠ gather 2 = disperse, dispel, disband, dissipate ≠ assemble

scenario 1 = situation 2 = story line, résumé, outline, summary, synopsis

scene 1 = act, part, division, episode 2 = setting, set, background, location, backdrop 3 = site, place, setting, area, position, spot, locality 4 (*Informal*) = world, business, environment, arena 5 = view, prospect, panorama, vista, landscape, outlook 6 = fuss, to-do, row, performance, exhibition, carry-on (*informal, chiefly Brit.*), tantrum, commotion

scenery 1 = landscape, view, surroundings, terrain, vista 2 (*Theatre*) = set, setting, backdrop, flats, stage set

scenic = picturesque, beautiful, spectacular, striking, panoramic

scent NOUN **1** = fragrance, smell, perfume, bouquet, aroma, odour **2** = trail, track, spoor
• VERB = smell, sense, detect, sniff, discern, nose out

scented = fragrant, perfumed, aromatic, sweet-smelling, odoriferous

sceptic 1 = doubter, cynic, disbeliever **2** = agnostic, doubter, unbeliever, doubting Thomas

sceptical = doubtful, cynical, dubious, unconvinced, disbelieving, incredulous, mistrustful ≠ convinced

scepticism = doubt, suspicion, disbelief, cynicism, incredulity

schedule NOUN = plan, programme, agenda, calendar, timetable
• VERB = plan, set up, book, programme, arrange, organize

scheme NOUN **1** = plan, programme, strategy, system, project, proposal, tactics **2** = plot, ploy, ruse, intrigue, conspiracy, manoeuvre, subterfuge, stratagem
• VERB = plot, plan, intrigue, manoeuvre, conspire, contrive, collude, machinate

scheming = calculating, cunning, sly, tricky, wily, artful, conniving, underhand ≠ straightforward

scholar 1 = intellectual, academic, savant, acca (*Austral. slang*) **2** = student, pupil, learner, schoolboy *or* schoolgirl

scholarly = learned, academic, intellectual, lettered, erudite, scholastic, bookish ≠ uneducated

scholarship 1 = grant, award, payment, endowment, fellowship, bursary **2** = learning, education, knowledge, erudition, book-learning

school NOUN **1** = academy, college, institution, institute, seminary **2** = group, set, circle, faction, followers, disciples, devotees, denomination
• VERB = train, coach, discipline, educate, drill, tutor, instruct

science = discipline, body of knowledge, branch of knowledge

scientific = systematic, accurate, exact, precise, controlled, mathematical

scientist = researcher, inventor, boffin (*informal*), technophile

scoff[1] = scorn, mock, laugh at, ridicule, knock (*informal*), despise, sneer, jeer

scoff[2] = gobble (up), wolf, devour, bolt, guzzle, gulp down, gorge yourself on

scoop VERB = win, get, land, gain, achieve, earn, secure, obtain
• NOUN **1** = ladle, spoon, dipper **2** = exclusive, exposé, revelation, sensation
• PHRASES **scoop something** *or* **someone up** = gather up, lift, pick up, take up, sweep up *or* away ◆ **scoop something out 1** = take out, empty, spoon out, bail *or* bale out **2** = dig, shovel, excavate, gouge, hollow out

scope 1 = opportunity, room, freedom, space, liberty, latitude **2** = range, capacity, reach, area, outlook, orbit, span, sphere

scorch = burn, sear, roast, wither, shrivel, parch, singe

scorching = burning, boiling, baking, flaming, roasting, searing, fiery, red-hot

score VERB **1** = gain, win, achieve, make, get, attain, notch up (*informal*), chalk up (*informal*) **2** (*Music*) = arrange, set, orchestrate, adapt **3** = cut, scratch, mark, slash, scrape, graze, gouge, deface
• NOUN **1** = rating, mark, grade, percentage **2** = points, result, total, outcome **3** = composition, soundtrack, arrangement, orchestration **4** = grievance, wrong, injury, injustice, grudge
• PLURAL NOUN = lots, loads, many, millions, hundreds, masses, swarms, multitudes
• PHRASES **score something out** *or* **through** = cross out, delete, strike out, cancel, obliterate

scorn NOUN = contempt, disdain, mockery, derision, sarcasm, disparagement ≠ respect
• VERB = despise, reject, disdain, slight, be above, spurn, deride, flout ≠ respect

scour[1] = scrub, clean, polish, rub, buff, abrade

scour[2] = search, hunt, comb, ransack

scout NOUN = vanguard, lookout, precursor, outrider, reconnoitrer, advance guard
• VERB = reconnoitre, investigate, watch, survey, observe, spy, probe, recce (*slang*)

scramble VERB **1** = struggle, climb, crawl, swarm, scrabble **2** = strive, rush, contend, vie, run, push, jostle **3** = jumble, mix up, muddle, shuffle
• NOUN **1** = clamber, ascent **2** = race, competition, struggle, rush, confusion, commotion, melee *or* mêlée

scrap¹ NOUN **1** = piece, fragment, bit, grain, particle, portion, part, crumb **2** = waste, junk, off cuts
• PLURAL NOUN = leftovers, remains, bits, leavings
• VERB = get rid of, drop, abandon, ditch (*slang*), discard, write off, jettison, throw away *or* out ≠ bring back

scrap² (*Informal*) NOUN = fight, battle, row, argument, dispute, disagreement, quarrel, squabble, biffo (*Austral. slang*)
• VERB = fight, argue, row, squabble, wrangle

scrape VERB **1** = rake, sweep, drag, brush **2** = grate, grind, scratch, squeak, rasp **3** = graze, skin, scratch, bark, scuff, rub **4** = clean, remove, scour
• NOUN (*Informal*) = predicament, difficulty, fix (*informal*), mess, dilemma, plight, tight spot, awkward situation

scratch VERB **1** = rub, scrape, claw at **2** = mark, cut, score, damage, grate, graze, etch, lacerate
• NOUN = mark, scrape, graze, blemish, gash, laceration, claw mark
• PHRASES **up to scratch** (*Informal*) = adequate, acceptable, satisfactory, sufficient, up to standard

scream VERB = cry, yell, shriek, screech, bawl, howl
• NOUN = cry, yell, howl, shriek, screech, yelp

screen NOUN = cover, guard, shade, shelter, shield, partition, cloak, canopy
• VERB **1** = broadcast, show, put on, present, air, cable, beam, transmit **2** = cover, hide, conceal, shade, mask, veil, cloak **3** = investigate, test, check, examine, scan **4** = process, sort, examine, filter, scan, evaluate, gauge, sift **5** = protect, guard, shield, defend, shelter

screw NOUN = nail, pin, tack, rivet, fastener, spike
• VERB **1** = fasten, fix, attach, bolt, clamp, rivet **2** = turn, twist, tighten **3** (*Informal*) = cheat, do (*slang*), rip (someone) off (*slang*), skin (*slang*), trick, con, sting (*informal*), fleece **4** (*Informal*) *often with* ***out of*** = squeeze, wring, extract, wrest
• PHRASES **screw something up 1** = contort, wrinkle, distort, pucker **2** (*Informal*) = bungle, botch, mess up, spoil, mishandle, make a mess of (*slang*), make a hash of (*informal*), crool *or* cruel (*Austral. slang*)

scribble = scrawl, write, jot, dash off

script NOUN **1** = text, lines, words, book, copy, dialogue, libretto **2** = handwriting, writing, calligraphy, penmanship
• VERB = write, draft

scripture = The Bible, The Gospels, The Scriptures, The Good Book, Holy Scripture, Holy Writ, Holy Bible

scrub 1 = scour, clean, polish, rub, wash, cleanse, buff **2** (*Informal*) = cancel, drop, give up, abolish, forget about, call off, delete

scrutiny = examination, study, investigation, search, analysis, inspection, exploration, perusal

sculpture NOUN = statue, figure, model, bust, effigy, figurine, statuette
• VERB = carve, form, model, fashion, shape, mould, sculpt, chisel

sea NOUN **1** = ocean, the deep, the waves, main **2** = mass, army, host, crowd, mob, abundance, swarm, horde
• PHRASES **at sea** = bewildered, lost, confused, puzzled, baffled, perplexed, mystified, flummoxed

RELATED WORDS
adjectives: marine, maritime

seal VERB = settle, clinch, conclude, consummate, finalize
• NOUN **1** = sealant, sealer, adhesive **2** = authentication, stamp, confirmation, ratification, insignia, imprimatur

seam 1 = joint, closure **2** = layer, vein, stratum, lode

sear = wither, burn, scorch, sizzle

search VERB = examine, investigate, explore, inspect, comb, scour, ransack, scrutinize, fossick (*Austral. & N.Z.*)
• NOUN = hunt, look, investigation, examination, pursuit, quest, inspection, exploration
• PHRASES **search for something** *or* **someone** = look for, hunt for, pursue

searching = keen, sharp, probing, close, intent, piercing, penetrating, quizzical ≠ superficial

searing 1 = acute, intense, shooting, severe, painful, stabbing, piercing, gut-wrenching **2** = cutting, biting, bitter, harsh, barbed, hurtful, caustic

season NOUN = period, time, term, spell
• VERB = flavour, salt, spice, enliven, pep up

seasoned = experienced, veteran, practised, hardened, time-served ≠ inexperienced
seasoning = flavouring, spice, salt and pepper, condiment
seat NOUN **1** = chair, bench, stall, stool, pew, settle **2** = membership, place, constituency, chair, incumbency **3** = centre, place, site, heart, capital, situation, source, hub **4** = mansion, house, residence, abode, ancestral hall
• VERB **1** = sit, place, settle, set, fix, locate, install **2** = hold, take, accommodate, sit, contain, cater for
second[1] ADJECTIVE **1** = next, following, succeeding, subsequent **2** = additional, other, further, extra, alternative **3** = inferior, secondary, subordinate, lower, lesser
• NOUN = supporter, assistant, aide, colleague, backer, helper, right-hand man
• VERB = support, back, endorse, approve, go along with
second[2] = moment, minute, instant, flash, sec (*informal*), jiffy (*informal*), trice
secondary **1** = subordinate, minor, lesser, lower, inferior, unimportant ≠ main **2** = resultant, contingent, derived, indirect ≠ original
second-hand = used, old, hand-me-down (*informal*), nearly new
secondly = next, second, moreover, furthermore, also, in the second place
secrecy **1** = mystery, stealth, concealment, furtiveness, secretiveness, clandestineness, covertness **2** = confidentiality, privacy **3** = privacy, silence, seclusion
secret ADJECTIVE **1** = undisclosed, unknown, confidential, underground, undercover, unrevealed **2** = concealed, hidden, disguised ≠ unconcealed **3** = undercover, furtive ≠ open **4** = secretive, reserved, close ≠ frank **5** = mysterious, cryptic, abstruse, occult, clandestine, arcane ≠ straightforward
• NOUN = private affair
• PHRASES **in secret** = secretly, surreptitiously, slyly
secretive = reticent, reserved, close, deep, uncommunicative, tight-lipped ≠ open
secretly = in secret, privately, surreptitiously, quietly, covertly, furtively, stealthily, clandestinely
sect = group, division, faction, party, camp, denomination, schism
section **1** = part, piece, portion, division, slice, passage, segment, fraction **2** = district, area, region, sector, zone
sector **1** = part, division **2** = area, part, region, district, zone, quarter
secular = worldly, lay, earthly, civil, temporal, nonspiritual ≠ religious
secure VERB **1** = obtain, get, acquire, score (*slang*), gain, procure ≠ lose **2** = attach, stick, fix, bind, fasten ≠ detach
• ADJECTIVE **1** = safe, protected, immune, unassailable ≠ unprotected **2** = fast, firm, fixed, stable, steady, fastened, immovable ≠ insecure **3** = confident, sure, easy, certain, assured, reassured ≠ uneasy
security **1** = precautions, defence, safeguards, protection, safety measures **2** = assurance, confidence, conviction, certainty, reliance, sureness, positiveness ≠ insecurity **3** = pledge, insurance, guarantee, hostage, collateral, pawn, gage, surety **4** = protection, safety, custody, refuge, sanctuary, safekeeping ≠ vulnerability
sediment = dregs, grounds, residue, lees, deposit
seduce **1** = tempt, lure, entice, mislead, deceive, beguile, lead astray, inveigle **2** = corrupt, deprave, dishonour, debauch, deflower
seductive = tempting, inviting, attractive, enticing, provocative, alluring, bewitching
see VERB **1** = perceive, spot, notice, sight, witness, observe, distinguish, glimpse **2** = understand, get, follow, realize, appreciate, grasp, comprehend, fathom **3** = find out, learn, discover, determine, verify, ascertain **4** = consider, decide, reflect, deliberate, think over **5** = make sure, ensure, guarantee, make certain, see to it **6** = accompany, show, escort, lead, walk, usher **7** = speak to, receive, interview, consult, confer with **8** = meet, come across, happen on, bump into, run across, chance on **9** = go out with, court, date (*informal, chiefly U.S.*), go steady with (*informal*)
• PHRASES **seeing as** = since, as, in view of the fact that, inasmuch as
seed NOUN **1** = grain, pip, germ, kernel, egg, embryo, spore, ovum **2** = beginning, start, germ **3** = origin, source, nucleus **4** (*Chiefly Bible*) = offspring, children,

descendants, issue, progeny
• PHRASES **go** *or* **run to seed** = decline, deteriorate, degenerate, decay, go downhill (*informal*), let yourself go, go to pot
seek 1 = look for, pursue, search for, be after, hunt 2 = try, attempt, aim, strive, endeavour, essay, aspire to
seem = appear, give the impression of being, look
seep = ooze, well, leak, soak, trickle, exude, permeate
seethe 1 = be furious, rage, fume, simmer, see red (*informal*), be livid, go ballistic (*slang, chiefly U.S.*) 2 = boil, bubble, foam, fizz, froth
segment = section, part, piece, division, slice, portion, wedge
segregate = set apart, divide, separate, isolate, discriminate against, dissociate ≠ unite
segregation = separation, discrimination, apartheid, isolation
seize 1 = grab, grip, grasp, take, snatch, clutch, snap up, pluck ≠ let go 2 = take by storm, take over, acquire, occupy, conquer 3 = capture, catch, arrest, apprehend, take captive ≠ release
seizure 1 = attack, fit, spasm, convulsion, paroxysm 2 = taking, grabbing, annexation, confiscation, commandeering 3 = capture, arrest, apprehension
seldom = rarely, not often, infrequently, hardly ever ≠ often
select VERB = choose, take, pick, opt for, decide on, single out, adopt, settle upon ≠ reject
• ADJECTIVE 1 = choice, special, excellent, superior, first-class, hand-picked, top-notch (*informal*) ≠ ordinary 2 = exclusive, elite, privileged, cliquish ≠ indiscriminate
selection 1 = choice, choosing, pick, option, preference 2 = anthology, collection, medley, choice
selective = particular, discriminating, careful, discerning, tasteful, fastidious ≠ indiscriminate
selfish = self-centred, self-interested, greedy, ungenerous, egoistic *or* egoistical, egotistic *or* egoistical ≠ unselfish
sell VERB 1 = trade, exchange, barter ≠ buy 2 = deal in, market, trade in, stock, handle, retail, peddle, traffic in ≠ buy
• PHRASES **sell out of something** = run out of, be out of stock of
seller = dealer, merchant, vendor, agent, retailer, supplier, purveyor, salesman *or* saleswoman
send VERB 1 = dispatch, forward, direct, convey, remit 2 = propel, hurl, fling, shoot, fire, cast, let fly
• PHRASES **send something** *or* **someone up** (*Brit. informal*) = mock, mimic, parody, spoof (*informal*), imitate, take off (*informal*), make fun of, lampoon
send-off = farewell, departure, leave-taking, valediction
senior 1 = higher ranking, superior ≠ subordinate 2 = the elder, major (*Brit.*) ≠ junior
sensation 1 = feeling, sense, impression, perception, awareness, consciousness 2 = excitement, thrill, stir, furore, commotion
sensational 1 = amazing, dramatic, thrilling, astounding ≠ dull 2 = shocking, exciting, melodramatic, shock-horror (*facetious*) ≠ unexciting 3 (*Informal*) = excellent, superb, mean (*slang*), impressive, smashing (*informal*), fabulous (*informal*), marvellous, out of this world (*informal*), booshit (*Austral. slang*), exo (*Austral. slang*), sik (*Austral. slang*) ≠ ordinary
sense NOUN 1 = faculty 2 = feeling, impression, perception, awareness, consciousness, atmosphere, aura 3 = understanding, awareness 4 *sometimes plural* = intelligence, reason, understanding, brains (*informal*), judgment, wisdom, wit(s), common sense ≠ foolishness 5 = meaning, significance, import, implication, drift, gist
• VERB = perceive, feel, understand, pick up, realize, be aware of, discern, get the impression ≠ be unaware of
sensibility *often plural* = feelings, emotions, sentiments, susceptibilities, moral sense
sensible 1 = wise, practical, prudent, shrewd, judicious ≠ foolish 2 = intelligent, practical, rational, sound, realistic, sage, shrewd, down-to-earth ≠ senseless
sensitive 1 = thoughtful, kindly, concerned, patient, attentive, tactful, unselfish 2 = delicate, tender 3 = susceptible to, responsive to, easily affected by 4 = touchy, oversensitive,

easily upset, easily offended, easily hurt ≠ insensitive **5** = precise, fine, acute, keen, responsive ≠ imprecise

sensitivity 1 = susceptibility, responsiveness, receptiveness, sensitiveness **2** = consideration, patience, thoughtfulness **3** = touchiness, oversensitivity **4** = responsiveness, precision, keenness, acuteness

sensual 1 = sexual, erotic, raunchy (*slang*), lewd, lascivious, lustful, lecherous **2** = physical, bodily, voluptuous, animal, luxurious, fleshly, carnal

sentence NOUN **1** = punishment, condemnation **2** = verdict, order, ruling, decision, judgment, decree
• VERB **1** = condemn, doom **2** = convict, condemn, penalize

sentiment 1 = feeling, idea, view, opinion, attitude, belief, judgment **2** = sentimentality, emotion, tenderness, romanticism, sensibility, emotionalism, mawkishness

sentimental = romantic, touching, emotional, nostalgic, maudlin, weepy (*informal*), slushy (*informal*), schmaltzy (*slang*) ≠ unsentimental

separate ADJECTIVE **1** = unconnected, individual, particular, divided, divorced, isolated, detached, disconnected ≠ connected **2** = individual, independent, apart, distinct ≠ joined
• VERB **1** = divide, detach, disconnect, disjoin ≠ combine **2** = come apart, split, come away ≠ connect **3** = sever, break apart, split in two, divide in two ≠ join **4** = split up, part, divorce, break up, part company, get divorced, be estranged **5** = distinguish, mark, single out, set apart ≠ link

separated 1 = estranged, parted, separate, apart, disunited **2** = disconnected, parted, divided, separate, disassociated, disunited, sundered

separately 1 = alone, apart, not together, severally ≠ together **2** = individually, singly

separation 1 = division, break, dissociation, disconnection, disunion **2** = split-up, parting, split, divorce, break-up, rift

sequel 1 = follow-up, continuation, development **2** = consequence, result, outcome, conclusion, end, upshot

sequence = succession, course, series, order, chain, cycle, arrangement, progression

series 1 = sequence, course, chain, succession, run, set, order, train **2** = drama, serial, soap (*informal*), sitcom (*informal*), soap opera, soapie (*Austral. slang*), situation comedy

serious 1 = grave, bad, critical, dangerous, acute, severe **2** = important, crucial, urgent, pressing, worrying, significant, grim, momentous ≠ unimportant **3** = thoughtful, detailed, careful, deep, profound, in-depth **4** = deep, sophisticated **5** = solemn, earnest, grave, sober, staid, humourless, unsmiling ≠ light-hearted **6** = sincere, earnest, genuine, honest, in earnest ≠ insincere

seriously 1 = truly, in earnest, all joking aside **2** = badly, severely, gravely, critically, acutely, dangerously

seriousness 1 = importance, gravity, urgency, significance **2** = solemnity, gravity, earnestness, gravitas

sermon = homily, address

servant = attendant, domestic, slave, maid, help, retainer, skivvy (*chiefly Brit.*)

serve 1 = work for, help, aid, assist, be in the service of **2** = perform, do, complete, fulfil, discharge **3** = be adequate, do, suffice, suit, satisfy, be acceptable, answer the purpose **4** = present, provide, supply, deliver, set out, dish up

service NOUN **1** = facility, system, resource, utility, amenity **2** = ceremony, worship, rite, observance **3** = work, labour, employment, business, office, duty **4** = check, maintenance check
• VERB = overhaul, check, maintain, tune (up), go over, fine tune

session = meeting, hearing, sitting, period, conference, congress, discussion, assembly

set[1] VERB **1** = put, place, lay, position, rest, plant, station, stick **2** = arrange, decide (upon), settle, establish, determine, fix, schedule, appoint **3** = assign, give, allot, prescribe **4** = harden, stiffen, solidify, cake, thicken, crystallize, congeal **5** = go down, sink, dip, decline, disappear, vanish, subside **6** = prepare, lay, spread, arrange, make ready
• ADJECTIVE **1** = established, planned,

decided, agreed, arranged, rigid, definite, inflexible **2** = strict, rigid, stubborn, inflexible ≠ flexible **3** = conventional, traditional, stereotyped, unspontaneous
• NOUN **1** = scenery, setting, scene, stage set **2** = position, bearing, attitude, carriage, posture
• PHRASES **be set on** *or* **upon something** = be determined to, be intent on, be bent on, be resolute about ◆ **set something up 1** = arrange, organize, prepare, prearrange **2** = establish, begin, found, institute, initiate **3** = build, raise, construct, put up, assemble, put together, erect **4** = assemble, put up

set² **1** = series, collection, assortment, batch, compendium, ensemble **2** = group, company, crowd, circle, band, gang, faction, clique

setback = hold-up, check, defeat, blow, reverse, disappointment, hitch, misfortune

setting = surroundings, site, location, set, scene, background, context, backdrop

settle 1 = resolve, work out, put an end to, straighten out **2** = pay, clear, square (up), discharge **3** = move to, take up residence in, live in, dwell in, inhabit, reside in, set up home in, put down roots in **4** = colonize, populate, people, pioneer **5** = land, alight, descend, light, come to rest **6** = calm, quiet, relax, relieve, reassure, soothe, lull, quell ≠ disturb

settlement 1 = agreement, arrangement, working out, conclusion, establishment, confirmation **2** = payment, clearing, discharge **3** = colony, community, outpost, encampment, kainga *or* kaika (*N.Z.*)

settler = colonist, immigrant, pioneer, frontiersman

set-up (*Informal*) = arrangement, system, structure, organization, conditions, regime

sever 1 = cut, separate, split, part, divide, detach, disconnect, cut in two ≠ join **2** = discontinue, terminate, break off, put an end to, dissociate ≠ continue

several ADJECTIVE = some, a few, a number of, a handful of
• PRONOUN = various, different, diverse, sundry

severe 1 = serious, critical, terrible, desperate, extreme, awful, drastic, catastrophic **2** = acute, intense, violent, piercing, harrowing, unbearable, agonizing, insufferable **3** = strict, hard, harsh, cruel, rigid, drastic, oppressive, austere ≠ lenient **4** = grim, serious, grave, forbidding, stern, unsmiling, tight-lipped ≠ genial **5** = plain, simple, austere, classic, restrained, Spartan, unadorned, unfussy ≠ fancy

severely 1 = seriously, badly, extremely, gravely, acutely **2** = strictly, harshly, sternly, sharply

severity = strictness, harshness, toughness, hardness, sternness, severeness

sew = stitch, tack, seam, hem

sex 1 = gender **2** (*Informal*) = lovemaking, sexual relations, copulation, fornication, coitus, coition

sexual 1 = carnal, erotic, intimate **2** = sexy, erotic, sensual, arousing, naughty, provocative, seductive, sensuous

sexuality = desire, lust, eroticism, sensuality, sexiness (*informal*), carnality

sexy = erotic, sensual, seductive, arousing, naughty, provocative, sensuous, suggestive

shabby 1 = tatty, worn, ragged, scruffy, tattered, threadbare ≠ smart **2** = run-down, seedy, mean, dilapidated **3** = mean, low, rotten (*informal*), cheap, dirty, despicable, contemptible, scurvy ≠ fair

shack = hut, cabin, shanty, whare (*N.Z.*)

shade NOUN **1** = hue, tone, colour, tint **2** = shadow **3** = dash, trace, hint, suggestion **4** = nuance, difference, degree **5** = screen, covering, cover, blind, curtain, shield, veil, canopy **6** (*Literary*) = ghost, spirit, phantom, spectre, apparition, kehua (*N.Z.*)
• VERB **1** = darken, shadow, cloud, dim **2** = cover, protect, screen, hide, shield, conceal, obscure, veil

shadow NOUN **1** = silhouette, shape, outline, profile **2** = shade, dimness, darkness, gloom, cover, dusk
• VERB **1** = shade, screen, shield, darken, overhang **2** = follow, tail (*informal*), trail, stalk

shady 1 = shaded, cool, dim ≠ sunny **2** (*Informal*) = crooked, dodgy (*Brit., Austral., & N.Z. informal*), unethical, suspect, suspicious, dubious, questionable, shifty ≠ honest

shaft 1 = tunnel, hole, passage, burrow, passageway, channel **2** = handle, staff, pole, rod, stem, baton, shank **3** = ray, beam, gleam

shake VERB **1** = jiggle, agitate **2** = tremble, shiver, quake, quiver **3** = rock, totter **4** = wave, wield, flourish, brandish **5** = upset, shock, frighten, disturb, distress, rattle (*informal*), unnerve, traumatize • NOUN = vibration, trembling, quaking, jerk, shiver, shudder, jolt, tremor

shaky 1 = unstable, weak, precarious, rickety ≠ stable **2** = unsteady, faint, trembling, faltering, quivery **3** = uncertain, suspect, dubious, questionable, iffy (*informal*) ≠ reliable

shallow = superficial, surface, empty, slight, foolish, trivial, meaningless, frivolous ≠ deep

sham NOUN = fraud, imitation, hoax, pretence, forgery, counterfeit, humbug, impostor ≠ the real thing • ADJECTIVE = false, artificial, bogus, pretended, mock, imitation, simulated, counterfeit ≠ real

shambles 1 = chaos, mess, disorder, confusion, muddle, havoc, disarray, madhouse **2** = mess, jumble, untidiness

shame NOUN **1** = embarrassment, humiliation, ignominy, mortification, abashment ≠ shamelessness **2** = disgrace, scandal, discredit, smear, disrepute, reproach, dishonour, infamy ≠ honour • VERB **1** = embarrass, disgrace, humiliate, humble, mortify, abash ≠ make proud **2** = dishonour, degrade, stain, smear, blot, debase, defile ≠ honour

shameful = disgraceful, outrageous, scandalous, mean, low, base, wicked, dishonourable ≠ admirable

shape NOUN **1** = appearance, form, aspect, guise, likeness, semblance **2** = form, profile, outline, lines, build, figure, silhouette, configuration **3** = pattern, model, frame, mould **4** = condition, state, health, trim, fettle • VERB **1** = form, make, produce, create, model, fashion, mould **2** = mould, form, make, fashion, model, frame

share NOUN = part, portion, quota, ration, lot, due, contribution, allowance • VERB **1** = divide, split, distribute, assign **2** = go halves on, go fifty-fifty on (*informal*)

sharp ADJECTIVE **1** = keen, jagged, serrated ≠ blunt **2** = quick-witted, clever, astute, knowing, quick, bright, alert, penetrating ≠ dim **3** = cutting, biting, bitter, harsh, barbed, hurtful, caustic ≠ gentle **4** = sudden, marked, abrupt, extreme, distinct ≠ gradual **5** = clear, distinct, well-defined, crisp ≠ indistinct **6** = sour, tart, pungent, hot, acid, acrid, piquant ≠ bland **7** = acute, severe, intense, painful, shooting, stabbing, piercing, gut-wrenching • ADVERB = promptly, precisely, exactly, on time, on the dot, punctually ≠ approximately

sharpen = make sharp, hone, whet, grind, edge

shatter 1 = smash, break, burst, crack, crush, pulverize **2** = destroy, ruin, wreck, demolish, torpedo

shattered 1 = devastated, crushed, gutted (*slang*) **2** (*Informal*) = exhausted, drained, worn out, done in (*informal*), all in (*slang*), knackered (*slang*), tired out, ready to drop

shave 1 = trim, crop **2** = scrape, trim, shear, pare

shed[1] = hut, shack, outhouse, whare (*N.Z.*)

shed[2] **1** = drop, spill, scatter **2** = cast off, discard, moult, slough off **3** = give out, cast, emit, give, radiate

sheen = shine, gleam, gloss, polish, brightness, lustre

sheer 1 = total, complete, absolute, utter, pure, downright, out-and-out, unmitigated ≠ moderate **2** = steep, abrupt, precipitous ≠ gradual **3** = fine, thin, transparent, see-through, gossamer, diaphanous, gauzy ≠ thick

sheet 1 = page, leaf, folio, piece of paper **2** = plate, piece, panel, slab **3** = coat, film, layer, surface, stratum, veneer, overlay, lamina **4** = expanse, area, stretch, sweep, covering, blanket

shell NOUN **1** = husk, case, pod **2** = carapace **3** = frame, structure, hull, framework, chassis • VERB = bomb, bombard, attack, blitz, strafe • PHRASES **shell something out** (with money or a specified sum of money as object) = pay out, fork out (*slang*), give, hand over

shelter NOUN **1** = cover, screen **2** = protection, safety, refuge, cover **3** = refuge, haven, sanctuary, retreat, asylum

• VERB 1 = take shelter, hide, seek refuge, take cover 2 = protect, shield, harbour, safeguard, cover, hide, guard, defend ≠ endanger

sheltered 1 = screened, covered, protected, shielded, secluded ≠ exposed 2 = protected, screened, shielded, quiet, isolated, secluded, cloistered

shelve = postpone, defer, freeze, suspend, put aside, put on ice, put on the back burner (*informal*), take a rain check on (*U.S. & Canad. informal*)

shepherd NOUN = drover, stockman, herdsman, grazier

• VERB = guide, conduct, steer, herd, usher

RELATED WORD

adjective: pastoral

shield NOUN = protection, cover, defence, screen, guard, shelter, safeguard

• VERB = protect, cover, screen, guard, defend, shelter, safeguard

shift VERB 1 = move, move around, budge 2 = remove, move, displace, relocate, rearrange, reposition

• NOUN 1 = change, shifting, displacement 2 = move, rearrangement

shimmer VERB = gleam, twinkle, glisten, scintillate

• NOUN = gleam, iridescence

shine VERB 1 = gleam, flash, beam, glow, sparkle, glitter, glare, radiate 2 = polish, buff, burnish, brush 3 = be outstanding, stand out, excel, be conspicuous

• NOUN 1 = polish, gloss, sheen, lustre 2 = brightness, light, sparkle, radiance

shining = bright, brilliant, gleaming, beaming, sparkling, shimmering, radiant, luminous

shiny = bright, gleaming, glossy, glistening, polished, lustrous

ship = vessel, boat, craft

shiver VERB = shudder, shake, tremble, quake, quiver

• NOUN = tremble, shudder, quiver, trembling, flutter, tremor

shock NOUN 1 = upset, blow, trauma, bombshell, turn (*informal*), distress, disturbance 2 = impact, blow, clash, collision 3 = start, scare, fright, turn, jolt

• VERB 1 = shake, stun, stagger, jolt, stupefy 2 = horrify, appal, disgust, revolt, sicken, nauseate, scandalize

shocking 1 (*Informal*) = terrible, appalling, dreadful, bad, horrendous, ghastly, deplorable, abysmal 2 = appalling, outrageous, disgraceful, disgusting, dreadful, horrifying, revolting, sickening ≠ wonderful

shoot VERB 1 = open fire on, blast (*slang*), hit, kill, plug (*slang*), bring down 2 = fire, launch, discharge, project, hurl, fling, propel, emit 3 = speed, race, rush, charge, fly, tear, dash, barrel (along) (*informal, chiefly U.S. & Canad.*)

• NOUN = sprout, branch, bud, sprig, offshoot

shop = store, supermarket, boutique, emporium, hypermarket, dairy (*N.Z.*)

shore = beach, coast, sands, strand (*poetic*), seashore

short ADJECTIVE 1 = brief, fleeting, momentary ≠ long 2 = concise, brief, succinct, summary, compressed, terse, laconic, pithy ≠ lengthy 3 = small, little, squat, diminutive, petite, dumpy ≠ tall 4 = abrupt, sharp, terse, curt, brusque, impolite, discourteous, uncivil ≠ polite 5 = scarce, wanting, low, limited, lacking, scant, deficient ≠ plentiful

• ADVERB = abruptly, suddenly, without warning ≠ gradually

shortage = deficiency, want, lack, scarcity, dearth, paucity, insufficiency ≠ abundance

shortcoming = failing, fault, weakness, defect, flaw, imperfection

shorten 1 = cut, reduce, decrease, diminish, lessen, curtail, abbreviate, abridge ≠ increase 2 = turn up

shortly = soon, presently, before long, in a little while

shot 1 = discharge, gunfire, crack, blast, explosion, bang 2 = ammunition, bullet, slug, pellet, projectile, lead, ball 3 = marksman, shooter, markswoman 4 (*Informal*) = strike, throw, lob 5 = attempt, go (*informal*), try, turn, effort, stab (*informal*), endeavour

shoulder 1 = bear, carry, take on, accept, assume, be responsible for 2 = push, elbow, shove, jostle, press

shout VERB = cry (out), call (out), yell, scream, roar, bellow, bawl, holler (*informal*)

• NOUN = cry, call, yell, scream, roar, bellow

• PHRASES **shout someone down** = drown out, overwhelm, drown, silence

shove VERB = push, thrust, elbow, drive, press, propel, jostle, impel

• NOUN = push, knock, thrust, elbow, bump, nudge, jostle
• PHRASES **shove off** (*Informal*) = go away, leave, clear off (*informal*), depart, push off (*informal*), scram (*informal*)

shovel **1** = move, scoop, dredge, load, heap **2** = stuff, ladle

show VERB **1** = indicate, demonstrate, prove, reveal, display, point out, manifest, testify to ≠ disprove **2** = display, exhibit **3** = guide, lead, conduct, accompany, direct, escort **4** = demonstrate, describe, explain, teach, illustrate, instruct **5** = be visible ≠ be invisible **6** = express, display, reveal, indicate, register, demonstrate, manifest ≠ hide **7** = turn up, appear, attend **8** = broadcast, transmit, air, beam, relay, televise, put on the air
• NOUN **1** = display, sight, spectacle, array **2** = exhibition, fair, display, parade, pageant **3** = appearance, display, pose, parade **4** = pretence, appearance, illusion, affectation **5** = programme, broadcast, presentation, production **6** = entertainment, production, presentation
• PHRASES **show off** (*Informal*) = boast, brag, blow your own trumpet, swagger ♦ **show someone up** (*Informal*) = embarrass, let down, mortify, put to shame ♦ **show something off** = exhibit, display, parade, demonstrate, flaunt ♦ **show something up** = reveal, expose, highlight, lay bare

showdown (*Informal*) = confrontation, clash, face-off (*slang*)

shower NOUN = deluge
• VERB **1** = cover, dust, spray, sprinkle **2** = inundate, heap, lavish, pour, deluge

show-off (*Informal*) = exhibitionist, boaster, poseur, braggart

shred **1** = strip, bit, piece, scrap, fragment, sliver, tatter **2** = particle, trace, scrap, grain, atom, jot, iota

shrewd = astute, clever, sharp, keen, smart, calculating, intelligent, cunning ≠ naive

shriek VERB = scream, cry, yell, screech, squeal
• NOUN = scream, cry, yell, screech, squeal

shrink = decrease, dwindle, lessen, grow *or* get smaller, contract, narrow, diminish, shorten ≠ grow

shroud NOUN **1** = winding sheet, grave clothes **2** = covering, veil, mantle, screen, pall
• VERB = conceal, cover, screen, hide, blanket, veil, cloak, envelop

shudder VERB = shiver, shake, tremble, quake, quiver, convulse
• NOUN = shiver, tremor, quiver, spasm

shuffle **1** = shamble, stagger, stumble, dodder **2** = scuffle, drag, scrape **3** = rearrange, jumble, mix, disorder, disarrange

shun = avoid, steer clear of, keep away from

shut VERB = close, secure, fasten, seal, slam ≠ open
• ADJECTIVE = closed, fastened, sealed, locked ≠ open
• PHRASES **shut down** = stop work, halt work, close down

shuttle = go back and forth, commute, go to and fro, alternate

shy ADJECTIVE **1** = timid, self-conscious, bashful, retiring, shrinking, coy, self-effacing, diffident ≠ confident **2** = cautious, wary, hesitant, suspicious, distrustful, chary ≠ reckless
• VERB *sometimes with* ***off*** *or* ***away*** = recoil, flinch, draw back, start, balk

sick **1** = unwell, ill, poorly (*informal*), diseased, crook (*Austral. & N.Z. informal*), ailing, under the weather, indisposed ≠ well **2** = nauseous, ill, queasy, nauseated **3** = tired, bored, fed up, weary, jaded **4** (*Informal*) = morbid, sadistic, black, macabre, ghoulish

sicken **1** = disgust, revolt, nauseate, repel, gross out (*U.S. slang*), turn your stomach **2** = fall ill, take sick, ail

sickening = disgusting, revolting, offensive, foul, distasteful, repulsive, nauseating, loathsome, yucko (*Austral. slang*) ≠ delightful

sickness **1** = illness, disorder, ailment, disease, complaint, bug (*informal*), affliction, malady **2** = nausea, queasiness **3** = vomiting

side NOUN **1** = border, margin, boundary, verge, flank, rim, perimeter, edge ≠ middle **2** = face, surface, facet **3** = party, camp, faction, cause **4** = point of view, viewpoint, position, opinion, angle, slant, standpoint **5** = team, squad, line-up **6** = aspect, feature, angle, facet
• ADJECTIVE = subordinate, minor,

secondary, subsidiary, lesser, marginal, incidental, ancillary ≠ main
• PHRASES **side with someone** = support, agree with, stand up for, favour, go along with, take the part of, ally yourself with
sidewalk (*U.S. & Canad.*) = pavement, footpath (*Austral. & N.Z.*)
sideways ADVERB **1** = indirectly, obliquely **2** = to the side, laterally
• ADJECTIVE = sidelong, oblique
sift 1 = part, filter, strain, separate, sieve **2** = examine, investigate, go through, research, analyse, work over, scrutinize
sight NOUN **1** = vision, eyes, eyesight, seeing, eye **2** = spectacle, show, scene, display, exhibition, vista, pageant **3** = view, range of vision, visibility **4** (*Informal*) = eyesore, mess, monstrosity
• VERB = spot, see, observe, distinguish, perceive, make out, discern, behold
RELATED WORDS
adjectives: optical, visual
sign NOUN **1** = symbol, mark, device, logo, badge, emblem **2** = figure **3** = notice, board, warning, placard **4** = indication, evidence, mark, signal, symptom, hint, proof, gesture **5** = omen, warning, portent, foreboding, augury, auspice
• VERB **1** = gesture, indicate, signal, beckon, gesticulate **2** = autograph, initial, inscribe
signal NOUN **1** = flare, beam, beacon **2** = cue, sign, prompting, reminder **3** = sign, gesture, indication, mark, note, expression, token
• VERB = gesture, sign, wave, indicate, motion, beckon, gesticulate
significance = importance, consequence, moment, weight
significant 1 = important, serious, material, vital, critical, momentous, weighty, noteworthy ≠ insignificant **2** = meaningful, expressive, eloquent, indicative, suggestive ≠ meaningless
signify = indicate, mean, suggest, imply, intimate, be a sign of, denote, connote
silence NOUN **1** = quiet, peace, calm, hush, lull, stillness ≠ noise **2** = reticence, dumbness, taciturnity, muteness ≠ speech
• VERB = quieten, still, quiet, cut off, stifle, cut short, muffle, deaden ≠ make louder
silent 1 = mute, dumb, speechless, wordless, voiceless ≠ noisy **2** = uncommunicative, quiet, taciturn **3** = quiet, still, hushed, soundless, noiseless, muted ≠ loud
silently 1 = quietly, in silence, soundlessly, noiselessly, inaudibly, without a sound **2** = mutely, in silence, wordlessly
silhouette NOUN = outline, form, shape, profile
• VERB = outline, etch
silly 1 = stupid, ridiculous, absurd, daft, inane, senseless, idiotic, fatuous ≠ clever **2** = foolish, stupid, unwise, rash, irresponsible, thoughtless, imprudent ≠ sensible
similar 1 = alike, resembling, comparable ≠ different **2** *with* ***to*** = like, comparable to, analogous to, close to
similarity = resemblance, likeness, sameness, agreement, correspondence, analogy, affinity, closeness ≠ difference
simmer VERB **1** = bubble, boil gently, seethe **2** = fume, seethe, smoulder, rage, be angry
• PHRASES **simmer down** (*Informal*) = calm down, control yourself, cool off *or* down
simple 1 = uncomplicated, clear, plain, understandable, lucid, recognizable, comprehensible, intelligible ≠ complicated **2** = easy, straightforward, not difficult, effortless, painless, uncomplicated, undemanding **3** = plain, natural, classic, unfussy, unembellished ≠ elaborate **4** = pure, mere, sheer, unalloyed **5** = artless, innocent, naive, natural, sincere, unaffected, childlike, unsophisticated ≠ sophisticated **6** = unpretentious, modest, humble, homely, unfussy, unembellished ≠ fancy
simplicity 1 = straightforwardness, ease, clarity, clearness ≠ complexity **2** = plainness, restraint, purity, lack of adornment ≠ elaborateness
simplify = make simpler, streamline, disentangle, dumb down, reduce to essentials
simply 1 = just, only, merely, purely, solely **2** = totally, really, completely, absolutely, wholly, utterly **3** = clearly, straightforwardly, directly, plainly, intelligibly **4** = plainly, naturally, modestly, unpretentiously **5** = without doubt, surely, certainly, definitely, beyond question
simulate = pretend, act, feign, affect, put

on, sham
simultaneous = coinciding, concurrent, contemporaneous, coincident, synchronous, happening at the same time
simultaneously = at the same time, together, concurrently
sin NOUN **1** = wickedness, evil, crime, error, transgression, iniquity **2** = crime, offence, error, wrongdoing, misdeed, transgression, act of evil, guilt
• VERB = transgress, offend, lapse, err, go astray, do wrong
sincere = honest, genuine, real, true, serious, earnest, frank, candid, dinkum (*Austral. & N.Z. informal*) ≠ false
sincerely = honestly, truly, genuinely, seriously, earnestly, wholeheartedly, in earnest
sincerity = honesty, truth, candour, frankness, seriousness, genuineness
sing **1** = croon, carol, chant, warble, yodel, pipe **2** = trill, chirp, warble
singer = vocalist, crooner, minstrel, soloist, chorister, balladeer
single ADJECTIVE **1** = one, sole, lone, solitary, only, only one **2** = individual, separate, distinct **3** = unmarried, free, unattached, unwed **4** = separate, individual, exclusive, undivided, unshared **5** = simple, unmixed, unblended
• PHRASES **single something** *or* **someone out** = pick, choose, select, separate, distinguish, fix on, set apart, pick on *or* out
singly = one by one, individually, one at a time, separately
singular **1** = single, individual **2** = remarkable, outstanding, exceptional, notable, eminent, noteworthy ≠ ordinary **3** = unusual, odd, strange, extraordinary, curious, peculiar, eccentric, queer ≠ conventional
sinister = threatening, evil, menacing, dire, ominous, malign, disquieting ≠ reassuring
sink **1** = go down, founder, go under, submerge, capsize **2** = slump, drop **3** = fall, drop, slip, plunge, subside, abate **4** = drop, fall **5** = stoop, be reduced to, lower yourself **6** = decline, fade, fail, flag, weaken, diminish, decrease, deteriorate ≠ improve **7** = dig, bore, drill, drive, excavate
sip VERB = drink, taste, sample, sup
• NOUN = swallow, drop, taste, thimbleful
sit **1** = take a seat, perch, settle down **2** = place, set, put, position, rest, lay, settle, deposit **3** = be a member of, serve on, have a seat on, preside on **4** = convene, meet, assemble, officiate
site NOUN **1** = area, plot **2** = location, place, setting, point, position, situation, spot
• VERB = locate, put, place, set, position, establish, install, situate
situation **1** = position, state, case, condition, circumstances, equation, plight, state of affairs **2** = scenario, state of affairs **3** = location, place, setting, position, site, spot
size NOUN = dimensions, extent, range, amount, mass, volume, proportions, bulk
• PHRASES **size something** *or* **someone up** (*Informal*) = assess, evaluate, appraise, take stock of
sizeable *or* **sizable** = large, considerable, substantial, goodly, decent, respectable, largish
sizzle = hiss, spit, crackle, fry, frizzle
skeleton = bones, bare bones
sketch NOUN = drawing, design, draft, delineation
• VERB = draw, outline, represent, draft, depict, delineate, rough out
skilful = expert, skilled, masterly, able, professional, clever, practised, competent ≠ clumsy
skill = expertise, ability, proficiency, art, technique, facility, talent, craft ≠ clumsiness
skilled = expert, professional, able, masterly, skilful, proficient ≠ unskilled
skim **1** = remove, separate, cream **2** = glide, fly, coast, sail, float **3** *usually with* ***over*** *or* ***through*** = scan, glance, run your eye over
skin NOUN **1** = hide, pelt, fell **2** = peel, rind, husk, casing, outside, crust **3** = film, coating
• VERB **1** = peel **2** = scrape, flay
skinny = thin, lean, scrawny, emaciated, undernourished ≠ fat
skip **1** = hop, dance, bob, trip, bounce, caper, prance, frisk **2** = miss out, omit, leave out, overlook, pass over, eschew, give (something) a miss
skirt **1** = border, edge, flank **2** *often with* ***around*** *or* ***round*** = go round, circumvent

3 *often with* ***around*** *or* ***round*** = avoid, evade, steer clear of, circumvent
sky = heavens, firmament, rangi (*N.Z.*)
RELATED WORD
adjective: celestial
slab = piece, slice, lump, chunk, wedge, portion
slack ADJECTIVE **1** = limp, relaxed, loose, lax **2** = loose, baggy ≠ taut **3** = slow, quiet, inactive, dull, sluggish, slow-moving ≠ busy **4** = negligent, lazy, lax, idle, inactive, slapdash, neglectful, slipshod ≠ strict
• VERB = shirk, idle, dodge, skive (*Brit. slang*), bludge (*Austral. & N.Z. informal*)
• NOUN **1** = surplus, excess, glut, surfeit, superabundance, superfluity **2** = room, excess, leeway, give (*informal*)
slam **1** = bang, crash, smash **2** = throw, dash, hurl, fling
slant VERB **1** = slope, incline, tilt, list, bend, lean, heel, cant **2** = bias, colour, twist, angle, distort
• NOUN **1** = slope, incline, tilt, gradient, camber **2** = bias, emphasis, prejudice, angle, point of view, one-sidedness
slanting = sloping, angled, inclined, tilted, tilting, bent, diagonal, oblique
slap VERB = smack, beat, clap, cuff, swipe, spank, clobber (*slang*), wallop (*informal*)
• NOUN = smack, blow, cuff, swipe, spank
slash VERB **1** = cut, slit, gash, lacerate, score, rend, rip, hack **2** = reduce, cut, decrease, drop, lower, moderate, diminish, cut down
• NOUN = cut, slit, gash, rent, rip, incision, laceration
slate (*Informal, chiefly Brit.*) = criticize, censure, rebuke, scold, tear into (*informal*)
slaughter VERB **1** = kill, murder, massacre, destroy, execute, assassinate **2** = butcher, kill, slay, massacre
• NOUN = slaying, killing, murder, massacre, bloodshed, carnage, butchery
slave NOUN **1** = servant, serf, vassal **2** = drudge, skivvy (*chiefly Brit.*)
• VERB = toil, drudge, slog
slavery = enslavement, servitude, subjugation, captivity, bondage ≠ freedom
slay **1** (*Archaic or literary*) = kill, slaughter, massacre, butcher **2** = murder, kill, massacre, slaughter, mow down
sleaze (*Informal*) = corruption, fraud, dishonesty, bribery, extortion, venality, unscrupulousness
sleek = glossy, shiny, lustrous, smooth ≠ shaggy
sleep NOUN = slumber(s), nap, doze, snooze (*informal*), hibernation, siesta, forty winks (*informal*), zizz (*Brit. informal*)
• VERB = slumber, doze, snooze (*informal*), hibernate, take a nap, catnap, drowse
sleepy = drowsy, sluggish, lethargic, heavy, dull, inactive ≠ wide-awake
slender **1** = slim, narrow, slight, lean, willowy ≠ chubby **2** = faint, slight, remote, slim, thin, tenuous ≠ strong **3** = meagre, little, small, scant, scanty ≠ large
slice NOUN = piece, segment, portion, wedge, sliver, helping, share, cut
• VERB = cut, divide, carve, sever, dissect, bisect
slick ADJECTIVE **1** = skilful, deft, adroit, dexterous, professional, polished ≠ clumsy **2** = glib, smooth, plausible, polished, specious
• VERB = smooth, sleek, plaster down
slide = slip, slither, glide, skim, coast
slight ADJECTIVE **1** = small, minor, insignificant, trivial, feeble, trifling, meagre, unimportant ≠ large **2** = slim, small, delicate, spare, fragile, lightly-built ≠ sturdy
• VERB = snub, insult, ignore, affront, scorn, disdain ≠ compliment
• NOUN = insult, snub, affront, rebuff, slap in the face (*informal*), (the) cold shoulder ≠ compliment
slightly = a little, a bit, somewhat
slim ADJECTIVE **1** = slender, slight, trim, thin, narrow, lean, svelte, willowy ≠ chubby **2** = slight, remote, faint, slender ≠ strong
• VERB = lose weight, diet ≠ put on weight
sling **1** (*Informal*) = throw, cast, toss, hurl, fling, chuck (*informal*), lob (*informal*), heave **2** = hang, suspend
slip VERB **1** = fall, skid **2** = slide, slither **3** = sneak, creep, steal
• NOUN = mistake, failure, error, blunder, lapse, omission, oversight
• PHRASES **give someone the slip** = escape from, get away from, evade, elude, lose (someone), flee, dodge
◆ **slip up** = make a mistake, blunder, err, miscalculate
slippery **1** = smooth, icy, greasy, glassy, slippy (*informal, dialect*), unsafe

2 = untrustworthy, tricky, cunning, dishonest, devious, crafty, evasive, shifty

slit VERB = cut (open), rip, slash, knife, pierce, lance, gash
• NOUN 1 = cut, gash, incision, tear, rent 2 = opening, split

slogan = catch phrase, motto, tag-line, catchword

slope NOUN = inclination, rise, incline, tilt, slant, ramp, gradient
• VERB = slant, incline, drop away, fall, rise, lean, tilt
• PHRASES **slope off** (*Informal*) = slink away, slip away, creep away

sloping = slanting, leaning, inclined, oblique

sloppy 1 (*Informal*) = careless, slovenly, slipshod, messy, untidy 2 (*Informal*) = sentimental, soppy (*Brit. informal*), slushy (*informal*), gushing, mawkish, icky (*informal*)

slot NOUN 1 = opening, hole, groove, vent, slit, aperture 2 (*Informal*) = place, time, space, opening, position, vacancy
• VERB = fit, insert

slow ADJECTIVE 1 = unhurried, sluggish, leisurely, lazy, ponderous, dawdling, laggard, lackadaisical ≠ quick 2 = prolonged, protracted, long-drawn-out, lingering, gradual 3 = late, behind, tardy 4 = stupid, dim, dense, thick, retarded, dozy (*Brit. informal*), obtuse, braindead (*informal*) ≠ bright
• VERB 1 *often with **down*** = decelerate, brake 2 *often with **down*** = delay, hold up, handicap, retard ≠ speed up

slowly = gradually, unhurriedly ≠ quickly

sluggish = inactive, slow, lethargic, heavy, dull, inert, indolent, torpid ≠ energetic

slum = hovel, ghetto, shanty

slump VERB 1 = fall, sink, plunge, crash, collapse, slip ≠ increase 2 = sag, hunch, droop, slouch, loll
• NOUN 1 = fall, drop, decline, crash, collapse, reverse, downturn, trough ≠ increase 2 = recession, depression, stagnation, inactivity, hard *or* bad times

slur = insult, stain, smear, affront, innuendo, calumny, insinuation, aspersion

sly ADJECTIVE 1 = roguish, knowing, arch, mischievous, impish 2 = cunning, scheming, devious, secret, clever, subtle, wily, crafty ≠ open
• PHRASES **on the sly** = secretly, privately, covertly, surreptitiously, on the quiet

smack VERB 1 = slap, hit, strike, clap, cuff, swipe, spank 2 = drive, hit, strike
• NOUN = slap, blow, cuff, swipe, spank
• ADVERB (*Informal*) = directly, right, straight, squarely, precisely, exactly, slap (*informal*)

small 1 = little, minute, tiny, mini, miniature, minuscule, diminutive, petite ≠ big 2 = young, little, junior, wee, juvenile, youthful, immature 3 = unimportant, minor, trivial, insignificant, little, petty, trifling, negligible ≠ important 4 = modest, humble, unpretentious ≠ grand

smart ADJECTIVE 1 = chic, trim, neat, stylish, elegant, spruce, snappy, natty (*informal*) ≠ scruffy 2 = clever, bright, intelligent, quick, sharp, keen, acute, shrewd ≠ stupid 3 = brisk, quick, lively, vigorous
• VERB = sting, burn, hurt

smash VERB 1 = break, crush, shatter, crack, demolish, pulverize 2 = shatter, break, disintegrate, crack, splinter 3 = collide, crash, meet head-on, clash, come into collision 4 = destroy, ruin, wreck, trash (*slang*), lay waste
• NOUN = collision, crash, accident

smashing (*Informal, chiefly Brit.*) = excellent, mean (*slang*), great (*informal*), wonderful, brilliant (*informal*), cracking (*Brit. informal*), superb, fantastic (*informal*), booshit (*Austral. slang*), exo (*Austral. slang*), sik (*Austral. slang*) ≠ awful

smear VERB 1 = spread over, daub, rub on, cover, coat, bedaub 2 = slander, malign, blacken, besmirch 3 = smudge, soil, dirty, stain, sully
• NOUN 1 = smudge, daub, streak, blot, blotch, splotch 2 = slander, libel, defamation, calumny

smell NOUN 1 = odour, scent, fragrance, perfume, bouquet, aroma 2 = stink, stench, pong (*Brit. informal*), fetor
• VERB 1 = stink, reek, pong (*Brit. informal*) 2 = sniff, scent

smile VERB = grin, beam, smirk, twinkle, grin from ear to ear
• NOUN = grin, beam, smirk

smooth ADJECTIVE 1 = even, level, flat, plane, flush, horizontal ≠ uneven 2 = sleek, polished, shiny, glossy, silky, velvety ≠ rough 3 = mellow, pleasant, mild, agreeable 4 = flowing, steady, regular,

uniform, rhythmic **5** = easy, effortless, well-ordered **6** = suave, slick, persuasive, urbane, glib, facile, unctuous, smarmy (*Brit. informal*)
• VERB **1** = flatten, level, press, plane, iron **2** = ease, facilitate ≠ hinder

smother **1** = extinguish, put out, stifle, snuff **2** = suffocate, choke, strangle, stifle **3** = suppress, stifle, repress, hide, conceal, muffle

smug = self-satisfied, superior, complacent, conceited

snack = light meal, bite, refreshment(s)

snag NOUN = difficulty, hitch, problem, obstacle, catch, disadvantage, complication, drawback
• VERB = catch, tear, rip

snake = serpent
RELATED WORD
adjective: serpentine

snap VERB **1** = break, crack, separate **2** = pop, click, crackle **3** = speak sharply, bark, lash out at, jump down (someone's) throat (*informal*) **4** = bite at, bite, nip
• ADJECTIVE = instant, immediate, sudden, spur-of-the-moment
• PHRASES **snap something up** = grab, seize, take advantage of, pounce upon

snare NOUN = trap, net, wire, gin, noose
• VERB = trap, catch, net, wire, seize, entrap

snatch VERB **1** = grab, grip, grasp, clutch **2** = steal, take, nick (*slang, chiefly Brit.*), pinch (*informal*), lift (*informal*), pilfer, filch, thieve **3** = win **4** = save, recover, get out, salvage
• NOUN = bit, part, fragment, piece, snippet

sneak VERB **1** = slink, slip, steal, pad, skulk **2** = slip, smuggle, spirit
• NOUN = informer, betrayer, telltale, Judas, accuser, stool pigeon, nark (*Brit., Austral., & N.Z. slang*), fizgig (*Austral. slang*)

sneaking **1** = nagging, worrying, persistent, uncomfortable **2** = secret, private, hidden, unexpressed, unvoiced, undivulged

sneer VERB **1** = scorn, mock, ridicule, laugh, jeer, disdain, deride **2** = say contemptuously, snigger
• NOUN = scorn, ridicule, mockery, derision, jeer, gibe

sniff **1** = breathe in, inhale **2** = smell, scent **3** = inhale, breathe in, suck in, draw in

snub VERB = insult, slight, put down, humiliate, cut (*informal*), rebuff, cold-shoulder
• NOUN = insult, put-down, affront, slap in the face

so = therefore, thus, hence, consequently, then, as a result, accordingly, thence

soak VERB **1** = steep **2** = wet, damp, saturate, drench, moisten, suffuse, wet through, waterlog **3** = penetrate, permeate, seep
• PHRASES **soak something up** = absorb, suck up, assimilate

soaking = soaked, dripping, saturated, drenched, sodden, streaming, sopping, wet through

soar **1** = rise, increase, grow, mount, climb, go up, rocket, escalate **2** = fly, wing, climb, ascend ≠ plunge **3** = tower, climb, go up

sob VERB = cry, weep, howl, shed tears
• NOUN = cry, whimper, howl

sober **1** = abstinent, temperate, abstemious, moderate ≠ drunk **2** = serious, cool, grave, reasonable, steady, composed, rational, solemn ≠ frivolous **3** = plain, dark, sombre, quiet, subdued, drab ≠ bright

so-called = alleged, supposed, professed, pretended, self-styled

social ADJECTIVE **1** = communal, community, collective, group, public, general, common **2** = organized, gregarious
• NOUN = get-together (*informal*), party, gathering, function, reception, social gathering

society **1** = the community, people, the public, humanity, civilization, mankind **2** = culture, community, population **3** = organization, group, club, union, league, association, institute, circle **4** = upper classes, gentry, elite, high society, beau monde **5** (*Old-fashioned*) = companionship, company, fellowship, friendship

sofa = couch, settee, divan, chaise longue

soft **1** = velvety, smooth, silky, feathery, downy, fleecy ≠ rough **2** = yielding, elastic ≠ hard **3** = soggy, swampy, marshy, boggy **4** = squashy, sloppy, mushy, spongy, gelatinous, pulpy **5** = pliable, flexible, supple, malleable, plastic, elastic, bendable, mouldable **6** = quiet, gentle, murmured, muted, dulcet, soft-toned ≠ loud **7** = lenient, easy-going, lax, indulgent, permissive, spineless, overindulgent ≠ harsh **8** = kind, tender, sentimental, compassionate, sensitive, gentle, tenderhearted, touchy-feely (*informal*) **9** (*Informal*) = easy, comfortable, undemanding, cushy (*informal*) **10** = pale, light, subdued, pastel, bland, mellow ≠ bright **11** = dim, faint, dimmed ≠ bright **12** = mild, temperate, balmy

soften **1** = melt, tenderize **2** = lessen, moderate, temper, ease, cushion, subdue, allay, mitigate

soil[1] **1** = earth, ground, clay, dust, dirt **2** = territory, country, land

soil[2] = dirty, foul, stain, pollute, tarnish, sully, defile, besmirch ≠ clean

soldier = fighter, serviceman, trooper, warrior, man-at-arms, squaddie *or* squaddy (*Brit. slang*)

sole = only, one, single, individual, alone, exclusive, solitary

solely = only, completely, entirely, exclusively, alone, merely

solemn **1** = serious, earnest, grave, sober, sedate, staid ≠ cheerful **2** = formal, grand, grave, dignified, ceremonial, stately, momentous ≠ informal

solid **1** = firm, hard, compact, dense, concrete ≠ unsubstantial **2** = strong, stable, sturdy, substantial, unshakable ≠ unstable **3** = reliable, dependable, upstanding, worthy, upright, trusty ≠ unreliable **4** = sound, real, reliable, good, genuine, dinkum (*Austral. & N.Z. informal*) ≠ unsound

solidarity = unity, unification, accord, cohesion, team spirit, unanimity, concordance, like-mindedness, kotahitanga (*N.Z.*)

solitary **1** = unsociable, reclusive, unsocial, isolated, lonely, cloistered, lonesome, friendless ≠ sociable **2** = lone, alone **3** = isolated, remote, out-of-the-way, hidden, unfrequented ≠ busy

solution **1** = answer, key, result, explanation **2** (*Chemistry*) = mixture, mix, compound, blend, solvent

solve = answer, work out, resolve, crack, clear up, unravel, decipher, suss (out) (*slang*)

sombre **1** = gloomy, sad, sober, grave, dismal, mournful, lugubrious, joyless ≠ cheerful **2** = dark, dull, gloomy, sober, drab ≠ bright

somebody = celebrity, name, star, notable, household name, dignitary, luminary, personage ≠ nobody

somehow = one way or another, come what may, come hell or high water (*informal*), by fair means or foul, by hook or (by) crook, by some means or other

sometimes = occasionally, at times, now and then ≠ always

song = ballad, air, tune, carol, chant, chorus, anthem, number, waiata (*N.Z.*)

soon = before long, shortly, in the near future

soothe **1** = calm, still, quiet, hush, appease, lull, pacify, mollify ≠ upset **2** = relieve, ease, alleviate, assuage ≠ irritate

soothing **1** = calming, relaxing, peaceful, quiet, calm, restful **2** = emollient, palliative

sophisticated **1** = complex, advanced, complicated, subtle, delicate, elaborate, refined, intricate ≠ simple **2** = cultured, refined, cultivated, worldly, cosmopolitan, urbane ≠ unsophisticated

sophistication = poise, worldliness, savoir-faire, urbanity, finesse, worldly wisdom

sore **1** = painful, smarting, raw, tender, burning, angry, sensitive, irritated **2** = annoyed, cross, angry, pained, hurt, upset, stung, irritated, tooshie (*Austral. slang*), hoha (*N.Z.*) **3** = annoying, troublesome **4** (*Literary*) = urgent, desperate, extreme, dire, pressing, critical, acute

sorrow NOUN **1** = grief, sadness, woe, regret, distress, misery, mourning, anguish ≠ joy **2** = hardship, trial, tribulation, affliction, trouble, woe, misfortune ≠ good fortune

• VERB = grieve, mourn, lament, be sad, bemoan, agonize, bewail ≠ rejoice

sorry **1** = regretful, apologetic, contrite, repentant, remorseful, penitent, shamefaced, conscience-stricken ≠ unapologetic **2** = sympathetic, moved, full of pity, compassionate, commiserative ≠ unsympathetic **3** = wretched, miserable, pathetic, mean, poor, sad, pitiful, deplorable

sort NOUN = kind, type, class, make, order, style, quality, nature

• VERB = arrange, group, order, rank, divide, grade, classify, categorize

soul **1** = spirit, essence, life, vital force,

wairua (*N.Z.*) **2** = embodiment, essence, epitome, personification, quintessence, type **3** = person, being, individual, body, creature, man *or* woman

sound[1] NOUN **1** = noise, din, report, tone, reverberation **2** = idea, impression, drift **3** = cry, noise, peep, squeak **4** = tone, music, note
• VERB **1** = toll, set off **2** = resound, echo, go off, toll, set off, chime, reverberate, clang **3** = seem, seem to be, appear to be
RELATED WORDS
adjectives: sonic, acoustic

sound[2] **1** = fit, healthy, perfect, intact, unhurt, uninjured, unimpaired ≠ frail **2** = sturdy, strong, solid, stable **3** = sensible, wise, reasonable, right, correct, proper, valid, rational ≠ irresponsible **4** = deep, unbroken, undisturbed, untroubled ≠ troubled

sour **1** = sharp, acid, tart, bitter, pungent, acetic ≠ sweet **2** = rancid, turned, gone off, curdled, gone bad, off ≠ fresh **3** = bitter, tart, acrimonious, embittered, disagreeable, ill-tempered, waspish, ungenerous ≠ good-natured

source **1** = cause, origin, derivation, beginning, author **2** = informant, authority **3** = origin, fount

souvenir = keepsake, reminder, memento

sovereign ADJECTIVE **1** = supreme, ruling, absolute, royal, principal, imperial, kingly *or* queenly **2** = excellent, efficient, effectual
• NOUN = monarch, ruler, king *or* queen, chief, potentate, emperor *or* empress, prince *or* princess

sovereignty = supreme power, domination, supremacy, primacy, kingship, rangatiratanga (*N.Z.*)

sow = scatter, plant, seed, implant

space **1** = room, capacity, extent, margin, scope, play, expanse, leeway **2** = period, interval, time, while, span, duration **3** = outer space, the universe, the galaxy, the solar system, the cosmos **4** = blank, gap, interval

spacious = roomy, large, huge, broad, extensive, ample, expansive, capacious ≠ limited

span NOUN **1** = period, term, duration, spell **2** = extent, reach, spread, length, distance, stretch
• VERB = extend across, cross, bridge, cover, link, traverse

spar = argue, row, squabble, scrap (*informal*), wrangle, bicker

spare ADJECTIVE **1** = back-up, reserve, second, extra, additional, auxiliary **2** = extra, surplus, leftover, over, free, odd, unwanted, unused ≠ necessary **3** = free, leisure, unoccupied **4** = thin, lean, meagre, gaunt, wiry ≠ plump
• VERB **1** = afford, give, grant, do without, part with, manage without, let someone have **2** = have mercy on, pardon, leave, let off (*informal*), go easy on (*informal*), save (from harm) ≠ show no mercy to

sparing = economical, frugal, thrifty, saving, careful, prudent ≠ lavish

spark NOUN **1** = flicker, flash, gleam, glint, flare **2** = trace, hint, scrap, atom, jot, vestige
• VERB *often with* ***off*** = start, stimulate, provoke, inspire, trigger (off), set off, precipitate

sparkle VERB = glitter, flash, shine, gleam, shimmer, twinkle, dance, glint
• NOUN **1** = glitter, flash, gleam, flicker, brilliance, twinkle, glint **2** = vivacity, life, spirit, dash, vitality, élan, liveliness

spate = flood, flow, torrent, rush, deluge, outpouring

speak **1** = talk, say something **2** = articulate, say, pronounce, utter, tell, state, talk, express **3** = converse, talk, chat, discourse, confer, commune, exchange views, korero (*N.Z.*) **4** = lecture, address an audience

speaker = orator, public speaker, lecturer, spokesperson, spokesman *or* spokeswoman

spearhead = lead, head, pioneer, launch, set off, initiate, set in motion

special **1** = exceptional, important, significant, particular, unique, unusual, extraordinary, memorable ≠ ordinary **2** = specific, particular, distinctive, individual, appropriate, precise ≠ general

specialist = expert, authority, professional, master, consultant, guru, buff (*informal*), connoisseur, fundi (*S. African*)

speciality = forte, métier, specialty, bag (*slang*), pièce de résistance (*French*)

species = kind, sort, type, group, class, variety, breed, category

specific **1** = particular, special, characteristic, distinguishing ≠ general

2 = precise, exact, explicit, definite, express, clear-cut, unequivocal ≠ vague 3 = peculiar, appropriate, individual, particular, unique

specification = requirement, detail, particular, stipulation, condition, qualification

specify = state, designate, stipulate, name, detail, mention, indicate, define

specimen 1 = sample, example, model, type, pattern, instance, representative, exemplification 2 = example, model, type

spectacle 1 = show, display, exhibition, event, performance, extravaganza, pageant 2 = sight, wonder, scene, phenomenon, curiosity, marvel

spectacular ADJECTIVE = impressive, striking, dramatic, stunning (*informal*), grand, magnificent, splendid, dazzling ≠ unimpressive

• NOUN = show, display, spectacle

spectator = onlooker, observer, viewer, looker-on, watcher, bystander ≠ participant

spectre = ghost, spirit, phantom, vision, apparition, wraith, kehua (*N.Z.*)

speculate 1 = conjecture, consider, wonder, guess, surmise, theorize, hypothesize 2 = gamble, risk, venture, hazard

speculation 1 = theory, opinion, hypothesis, conjecture, guess, surmise, guesswork, supposition 2 = gamble, risk, hazard

speculative = hypothetical, academic, theoretical, notional, conjectural, suppositional

speech 1 = communication, talk, conversation, discussion, dialogue 2 = diction, pronunciation, articulation, delivery, fluency, inflection, intonation, elocution 3 = language, tongue, jargon, dialect, idiom, parlance, articulation, diction 4 = talk, address, lecture, discourse, homily, oration, spiel (*informal*), whaikorero (*N.Z.*)

speed NOUN 1 = rate, pace 2 = swiftness, rush, hurry, haste, rapidity, quickness ≠ slowness

• VERB 1 = race, rush, hurry, zoom, career, tear, barrel (along) (*informal, chiefly U.S. & Canad.*), gallop ≠ crawl 2 = help, advance, aid, boost, assist, facilitate, expedite ≠ hinder

speedy = quick, fast, rapid, swift, express, immediate, prompt, hurried ≠ slow

spell[1] = indicate, mean, signify, point to, imply, augur, portend

spell[2] 1 = incantation, charm, makutu (*N.Z.*) 2 = enchantment, magic, fascination, glamour, allure, bewitchment

spell[3] = period, time, term, stretch, course, season, interval, bout

spend 1 = pay out, fork out (*slang*), expend, disburse ≠ save 2 = pass, fill, occupy, while away 3 = use up, waste, squander, empty, drain, exhaust, consume, run through ≠ save

sphere 1 = ball, globe, orb, globule, circle 2 = field, department, function, territory, capacity, province, patch, scope

spice 1 = seasoning 2 = excitement, zest, colour, pep, zing (*informal*), piquancy

spicy 1 = hot, seasoned, aromatic, savoury, piquant 2 (*Informal*) = risqué, racy, ribald, hot (*informal*), suggestive, titillating, indelicate

RELATED WORD

fear of: arachnophobia

spike NOUN = point, stake, spine, barb, prong

• VERB = impale, spit, spear, stick

spill 1 = tip over, overturn, capsize, knock over 2 = shed, discharge, disgorge 3 = slop, flow, pour, run, overflow

spin VERB 1 = revolve, turn, rotate, reel, whirl, twirl, gyrate, pirouette 2 = reel, swim, whirl

• NOUN 1 (*Informal*) = drive, ride, joy ride (*informal*) 2 = revolution, roll, whirl, gyration

• PHRASES **spin something out** = prolong, extend, lengthen, draw out, drag out, delay, amplify

spine 1 = backbone, vertebrae, spinal column, vertebral column 2 = barb, spur, needle, spike, ray, quill

spiral ADJECTIVE = coiled, winding, whorled, helical

• NOUN = coil, helix, corkscrew, whorl

spirit NOUN 1 = soul, life 2 = life force, vital spark, mauri (*N.Z.*) 3 = ghost, phantom, spectre, apparition, atua (*N.Z.*), kehua (*N.Z.*) 4 = courage, guts (*informal*), grit, backbone, spunk (*informal*), gameness 5 = liveliness, energy, vigour, life, force, fire, enthusiasm, animation 6 = attitude, character, temper, outlook, temperament,

disposition **7** = heart, sense, nature, soul, core, substance, essence, quintessence **8** = intention, meaning, purpose, purport, gist **9** = feeling, atmosphere, character, tone, mood, tenor, ambience
• PLURAL NOUN = mood, feelings, morale, temper, disposition, state of mind, frame of mind

spirited = lively, energetic, animated, active, feisty (*informal, chiefly U.S. & Canad.*), vivacious, mettlesome ≠ lifeless

spiritual 1 = nonmaterial, immaterial, incorporeal ≠ material **2** = sacred, religious, holy, divine, devotional

spit VERB **1** = expectorate **2** = eject, throw out
• NOUN = saliva, dribble, spittle, drool, slaver

spite NOUN = malice, malevolence, ill will, hatred, animosity, venom, spleen, spitefulness ≠ kindness
• VERB = annoy, hurt, injure, harm, vex ≠ benefit
• PHRASES **in spite of** = despite, regardless of, notwithstanding, (even) though

splash VERB **1** = paddle, plunge, bathe, dabble, wade, wallow **2** = scatter, shower, spray, sprinkle, wet, spatter, slop **3** = spatter, mark, stain, speck, speckle
• NOUN **1** = dash, touch, spattering **2** = spot, burst, patch, spurt **3** = blob, spot, smudge, stain, smear, fleck, speck

splendid 1 = excellent, wonderful, marvellous, great (*informal*), cracking (*Brit. informal*), fantastic (*informal*), first-class, glorious, booshit (*Austral. slang*), exo (*Austral. slang*), sik (*Austral. slang*) ≠ poor **2** = magnificent, grand, impressive, rich, superb, costly, gorgeous, lavish ≠ squalid

splendour = magnificence, grandeur, show, display, spectacle, richness, nobility, pomp ≠ squalor

splinter NOUN = sliver, fragment, chip, flake
• VERB = shatter, split, fracture, disintegrate

split VERB **1** = break, crack, burst, open, give way, come apart, come undone **2** = cut, break, crack, snap, chop **3** = divide, separate, disunite, disband, cleave **4** = diverge, separate, branch, fork, part **5** = tear, rend, rip **6** = share out, divide, distribute, halve, allocate, partition, allot, apportion
• NOUN **1** = division, breach, rift, rupture, discord, schism, estrangement, dissension **2** = separation, break-up, split-up **3** = crack, tear, rip, gap, rent, breach, slit, fissure
• ADJECTIVE **1** = divided **2** = broken, cracked, fractured, ruptured, cleft

spoil VERB **1** = ruin, destroy, wreck, damage, injure, harm, mar, trash (*slang*), crool *or* cruel (*Austral. slang*) ≠ improve **2** = overindulge, indulge, pamper, cosset, coddle, mollycoddle ≠ deprive **3** = indulge, pamper, satisfy, gratify, pander to **4** = go bad, turn, go off (*Brit. informal*), rot, decay, decompose, curdle, addle
• PLURAL NOUN = booty, loot, plunder, prey, swag (*slang*)

spoken = verbal, voiced, expressed, uttered, oral, said, told, unwritten

spokesperson = speaker, official, spokesman *or* spokeswoman, voice, spin doctor (*informal*), mouthpiece

sponsor VERB = back, fund, finance, promote, subsidize, patronize
• NOUN = backer, patron, promoter

spontaneous = unplanned, impromptu, unprompted, willing, natural, voluntary, instinctive, impulsive ≠ planned

sport NOUN **1** = game, exercise, recreation, play, amusement, diversion, pastime **2** = fun, joking, teasing, banter, jest, badinage
• VERB (*Informal*) = wear, display, flaunt, exhibit, flourish, show off, vaunt

sporting = fair, sportsmanlike, game (*informal*) ≠ unfair

sporty = athletic, outdoor, energetic

spot NOUN **1** = mark, stain, speck, scar, blot, smudge, blemish, speckle **2** = pimple, pustule, zit (*slang*) **3** = place, site, point, position, scene, location **4** (*Informal*) = predicament, trouble, difficulty, mess, plight, hot water (*informal*), quandary, tight spot
• VERB **1** = see, observe, catch sight of, sight, recognize, detect, make out, discern **2** = mark, stain, soil, dirty, fleck, spatter, speckle, splodge

spotlight NOUN = attention, limelight, public eye, fame
• VERB = highlight, draw attention to, accentuate

spotted = speckled, dotted, flecked,

mottled, dappled

spouse = partner, mate, husband *or* wife, consort, significant other (*U.S. informal*)

sprawl = loll, slump, lounge, flop, slouch

spray[1] NOUN 1 = droplets, fine mist, drizzle 2 = aerosol, sprinkler, atomizer
• VERB = scatter, shower, sprinkle, diffuse

spray[2] = sprig, floral arrangement, branch, corsage

spread VERB 1 = open (out), extend, stretch, unfold, sprawl, unroll 2 = extend, open, stretch 3 = grow, increase, expand, widen, escalate, proliferate, multiply, broaden 4 = circulate, broadcast, propagate, disseminate, make known ≠ suppress 5 = diffuse, cast, shed, radiate
• NOUN 1 = increase, development, advance, expansion, proliferation, dissemination, dispersal 2 = extent, span, stretch, sweep

spree = fling, binge (*informal*), orgy

spring NOUN = flexibility, bounce, resilience, elasticity, buoyancy
• VERB 1 = jump, bound, leap, bounce, vault 2 *often with* ***from*** = originate, come, derive, start, issue, proceed, arise, stem

RELATED WORD
adjective: vernal

sprinkle = scatter, dust, strew, pepper, shower, spray, powder, dredge

sprinkling = scattering, dusting, few, dash, handful, sprinkle

sprint = run, race, shoot, tear, dash, dart, hare (*Brit. informal*)

sprout 1 = germinate, bud, shoot, spring 2 = grow, develop, ripen

spur VERB = incite, drive, prompt, urge, stimulate, animate, prod, prick
• NOUN = stimulus, incentive, impetus, motive, impulse, inducement, incitement
• PHRASES **on the spur of the moment** = on impulse, impulsively, on the spot, impromptu, without planning

spurn = reject, slight, scorn, rebuff, snub, despise, disdain, repulse ≠ accept

spy NOUN = undercover agent, mole, nark (*Brit., Austral., & N.Z. slang*)
• VERB = catch sight of, spot, notice, observe, glimpse, espy

squabble VERB = quarrel, fight, argue, row, dispute, wrangle, bicker
• NOUN = quarrel, fight, row, argument, dispute, disagreement, tiff

squad = team, group, band, company, force, troop, crew, gang

squander = waste, spend, fritter away, blow (*slang*), misuse, expend, misspend ≠ save

square ADJECTIVE = fair, straight, genuine, ethical, honest, on the level (*informal*), kosher (*informal*), dinkum (*Austral. & N.Z. informal*), above board
• VERB *often with* ***with*** = agree, match, fit, correspond, tally, reconcile

squash 1 = crush, press, flatten, mash, smash, distort, pulp, compress 2 = suppress, quell, silence, crush, annihilate 3 = embarrass, put down, shame, degrade, mortify

squeeze VERB 1 = press, crush, squash, pinch 2 = clutch, press, grip, crush, pinch, squash, compress, wring 3 = cram, press, crowd, force, stuff, pack, jam, ram 4 = hug, embrace, cuddle, clasp, enfold
• NOUN 1 = press, grip, clasp, crush, pinch, squash, wring 2 = crush, jam, squash, press, crowd, congestion 3 = hug, embrace, clasp

stab VERB = pierce, stick, wound, knife, thrust, spear, jab, transfix
• NOUN 1 (*Informal*) = attempt, go, try, endeavour 2 = twinge, prick, pang, ache

stability = firmness, strength, soundness, solidity, steadiness ≠ instability

stable 1 = secure, lasting, strong, sound, fast, sure, established, permanent ≠ insecure 2 = well-balanced, balanced, sensible, reasonable, rational 3 = solid, firm, fixed, substantial, durable, well-made, well-built, immovable ≠ unstable

stack NOUN 1 = pile, heap, mountain, mass, load, mound 2 = lot, mass, load (*informal*), ton (*informal*), heap (*informal*), great amount
• VERB = pile, heap up, load, assemble, accumulate, amass

staff 1 = workers, employees, personnel, workforce, team 2 = stick, pole, rod, crook, cane, stave, wand, sceptre

stage = step, leg, phase, point, level, period, division, lap

stagger 1 = totter, reel, sway, lurch, wobble 2 = astound, amaze, stun, shock, shake, overwhelm, astonish, confound

stain NOUN 1 = mark, spot, blot, blemish, discoloration, smirch 2 = stigma, shame, disgrace, slur, dishonour 3 = dye, colour, tint

• VERB 1 = mark, soil, discolour, dirty, tinge, spot, blot, blemish 2 = dye, colour, tint
stake[1] = pole, post, stick, pale, paling, picket, palisade
stake[2] NOUN = bet, ante, wager
• VERB 1 = bet, gamble, wager, chance, risk, venture, hazard 2 = interest, share, involvement, concern, investment
stale 1 = old, hard, dry, decayed ≠ fresh 2 = musty, fusty 3 = tasteless, flat, sour 4 = unoriginal, banal, trite, stereotyped, worn-out, threadbare, hackneyed, overused ≠ original
stalk = pursue, follow, track, hunt, shadow, haunt
stall VERB 1 = play for time, delay, hedge, temporize 2 = stop dead, jam, seize up, catch, stick, stop short
• NOUN = stand, table, counter, booth, kiosk
stalwart 1 = loyal, faithful, firm, true, dependable, steadfast 2 = strong, strapping, sturdy, stout ≠ puny
stamina = staying power, endurance, resilience, force, power, energy, strength
stammer = stutter, falter, pause, hesitate, stumble over your words
stamp NOUN = imprint, mark, brand, signature, earmark, hallmark
• VERB 1 = print, mark, impress 2 = trample, step, tread, crush 3 = identify, mark, brand, label, reveal, show to be, categorize
• PHRASES **stamp something out** = eliminate, destroy, eradicate, crush, suppress, put down, scotch, quell
stance 1 = attitude, stand, position, viewpoint, standpoint 2 = posture, carriage, bearing, deportment
stand VERB 1 = be upright, be erect, be vertical 2 = get to your feet, rise, stand up, straighten up 3 = be located, be, sit, be positioned, be situated *or* located 4 = be valid, continue, exist, prevail, remain valid 5 = put, place, position, set, mount 6 = sit, mellow 7 = resist, endure, tolerate, stand up to 8 = tolerate, bear, abide, stomach, endure, brook 9 = take, bear, handle, endure, put up with (*informal*), countenance
• NOUN 1 = position, attitude, stance, opinion, determination 2 = stall, booth, kiosk, table
• PHRASES **stand by** = be prepared, wait ◆ **stand for something** 1 = represent, mean, signify, denote, indicate, symbolize, betoken 2 (*Informal*) = tolerate, bear, endure, put up with, brook ◆ **stand in for someone** = be a substitute for, represent, cover for, take the place of, deputize for ◆ **stand up for something** *or* **someone** = support, champion, defend, uphold, stick up for (*informal*)
standard NOUN 1 = level, grade 2 = criterion, measure, guideline, example, model, average, norm, gauge 3 *often plural* = principles, ideals, morals, ethics 4 = flag, banner, ensign
• ADJECTIVE 1 = usual, normal, customary, average, basic, regular, typical, orthodox ≠ unusual 2 = accepted, official, established, approved, recognized, definitive, authoritative ≠ unofficial
stand-in = substitute, deputy, replacement, reserve, surrogate, understudy, locum, stopgap
standing NOUN 1 = status, position, footing, rank, reputation, eminence, repute 2 = duration, existence, continuance
• ADJECTIVE 1 = permanent, lasting, fixed, regular 2 = upright, erect, vertical
staple = principal, chief, main, key, basic, fundamental, predominant
star NOUN 1 = heavenly body, celestial body 2 = celebrity, big name, megastar (*informal*), name, luminary 3 = leading man *or* lady, hero *or* heroine, principal, main attraction
• VERB = play the lead, appear, feature, perform
• ADJECTIVE = leading, major, celebrated, brilliant, well-known, prominent

RELATED WORDS
adjectives: astral, stellar

stare = gaze, look, goggle, watch, gape, eyeball (*slang*), gawp (*Brit. slang*), gawk
stark ADJECTIVE 1 = plain, harsh, basic, grim, straightforward, blunt 2 = sharp, clear, striking, distinct, clear-cut 3 = austere, severe, plain, bare, harsh 4 = bleak, grim, barren, hard 5 = absolute, pure, sheer, utter, downright, out-and-out, unmitigated
• ADVERB = absolutely, quite, completely, entirely, altogether, wholly, utterly
start VERB 1 = set about, begin, proceed, embark upon, take the first step, make

a beginning ≠ stop **2** = begin, arise, originate, issue, appear, commence ≠ end **3** = set in motion, initiate, instigate, open, trigger, originate, get going, kick-start ≠ stop **4** = establish, begin, found, create, launch, set up, institute, pioneer ≠ terminate **5** = start up, activate, get something going ≠ turn off **6** = jump, shy, jerk, flinch, recoil
• **NOUN 1** = beginning, outset, opening, birth, foundation, dawn, onset, initiation ≠ end **2** = jump, spasm, convulsion

startle = surprise, shock, frighten, scare, make (someone) jump

starving = hungry, starved, ravenous, famished

state NOUN 1 = country, nation, land, republic, territory, federation, commonwealth, kingdom **2** = government, ministry, administration, executive, regime, powers-that-be **3** = condition, shape **4** = frame of mind, condition, spirits, attitude, mood, humour **5** = ceremony, glory, grandeur, splendour, majesty, pomp **6** = circumstances, situation, position, predicament
• **VERB** = say, declare, specify, present, voice, express, assert, utter

stately = grand, majestic, dignified, royal, august, noble, regal, lofty ≠ lowly

statement 1 = announcement, declaration, communication, communiqué, proclamation **2** = account, report

station NOUN 1 = railway station, stop, stage, halt, terminal, train station, terminus **2** = headquarters, base, depot **3** = position, rank, status, standing, post, situation **4** = post, place, location, position, situation
• **VERB** = assign, post, locate, set, establish, install

stature 1 = height, build, size **2** = importance, standing, prestige, rank, prominence, eminence

status 1 = position, rank, grade **2** = prestige, standing, authority, influence, weight, honour, importance, fame, mana (*N.Z.*) **3** = state of play, development, progress, condition, evolution

staunch = loyal, faithful, stalwart, firm, sound, true, trusty, steadfast

stay VERB 1 = remain, continue to be, linger, stop, wait, halt, pause, abide ≠ go **2** *often with* ***at*** = lodge, visit, sojourn, put up at, be accommodated at **3** = continue, remain, go on, survive, endure
• **NOUN 1** = visit, stop, holiday, stopover, sojourn **2** = postponement, delay, suspension, stopping, halt, deferment

steady 1 = continuous, regular, constant, consistent, persistent, unbroken, uninterrupted, incessant ≠ irregular **2** = stable, fixed, secure, firm, safe ≠ unstable **3** = regular, established **4** = dependable, sensible, reliable, secure, calm, supportive, sober, level-headed ≠ undependable

steal 1 = take, nick (*slang, chiefly Brit.*), pinch (*informal*), lift (*informal*), embezzle, pilfer, misappropriate, purloin **2** = copy, take, appropriate, pinch (*informal*) **3** = sneak, slip, creep, tiptoe, slink

stealth = secrecy, furtiveness, slyness, sneakiness, unobtrusiveness, stealthiness, surreptitiousness

steep[1] 1 = sheer, precipitous, abrupt, vertical ≠ gradual **2** = sharp, sudden, abrupt, marked, extreme, distinct **3** (*Informal*) = high, exorbitant, extreme, unreasonable, overpriced, extortionate ≠ reasonable

steep[2] = soak, immerse, marinate (*Cookery*), submerge, drench, moisten, souse

steeped = saturated, pervaded, permeated, filled, infused, imbued, suffused

steer 1 = drive, control, direct, handle, pilot **2** = direct, lead, guide, conduct, escort

stem[1] NOUN = stalk, branch, trunk, shoot, axis
• **PHRASES stem from something** = originate from, be caused by, derive from, arise from

stem[2] = stop, hold back, staunch, check, dam, curb

step NOUN 1 = pace, stride, footstep **2** = footfall **3** = move, measure, action, means, act, deed, expedient **4** = stage, point, phase **5** = level, rank, degree
• **VERB** = walk, pace, tread, move
• **PHRASES step in** (*Informal*) = intervene, take action, become involved ♦ **step something up** = increase, intensify, raise

stereotype NOUN = formula, pattern
• **VERB** = categorize, typecast, pigeonhole,

standardize

sterile **1** = germ-free, sterilized, disinfected, aseptic ≠ unhygienic **2** = barren, infertile, unproductive, childless ≠ fertile

sterling = excellent, sound, fine, superlative

stern **1** = strict, harsh, hard, grim, rigid, austere, inflexible ≠ lenient **2** = severe, serious, forbidding ≠ friendly

stick[1] **1** = twig, branch **2** = cane, staff, pole, rod, crook, baton **3** (*Slang*) = abuse, criticism, flak (*informal*), fault-finding

stick[2] **VERB** **1** (*Informal*) = put, place, set, lay, deposit **2** = poke, dig, stab, thrust, pierce, penetrate, spear, prod **3** = fasten, fix, bind, hold, bond, attach, glue, paste **4** = adhere, cling, become joined, become welded **5** = stay, remain, linger, persist **6** (*Slang*) = tolerate, take, stand, stomach, abide

• **PHRASES** **stick out** = protrude, stand out, jut out, show, project, bulge, obtrude ◆ **stick up for someone** (*Informal*) = defend, support, champion, stand up for

sticky **1** = adhesive, gummed, adherent **2** = gooey, tacky (*informal*), viscous, glutinous, gummy, icky (*informal*), gluey, clinging **3** (*Informal*) = difficult, awkward, tricky, embarrassing, nasty, delicate, unpleasant, barro (*Austral. slang*) **4** = humid, close, sultry, oppressive, sweltering, clammy, muggy

stiff **1** = inflexible, rigid, unyielding, hard, firm, tight, solid, tense ≠ flexible **2** = formal, constrained, forced, unnatural, stilted, unrelaxed ≠ informal **3** = vigorous, great, strong **4** = severe, strict, harsh, hard, heavy, extreme, drastic **5** = difficult, hard, tough, exacting, arduous

stifle **1** = suppress, repress, stop, check, silence, restrain, hush, smother **2** = restrain, suppress, repress, smother

stigma = disgrace, shame, dishonour, stain, slur, smirch

still **ADJECTIVE** **1** = motionless, stationary, calm, peaceful, serene, tranquil, undisturbed, restful ≠ moving **2** = silent, quiet, hushed ≠ noisy

• **VERB** = quieten, calm, settle, quiet, silence, soothe, hush, lull ≠ get louder

• **ADVERB** = however, but, yet, nevertheless, notwithstanding

stimulate = encourage, inspire, prompt, fire, spur, provoke, arouse, rouse

stimulating = exciting, inspiring, stirring, rousing, provocative, exhilarating ≠ boring

stimulus = incentive, spur, encouragement, impetus, inducement, goad, incitement, fillip

sting **1** = hurt, burn, wound **2** = smart, burn, pain, hurt, tingle

stink **VERB** = reek, pong (*Brit. informal*)

• **NOUN** = stench, pong (*Brit. informal*), foul smell, fetor

stint **NOUN** = term, time, turn, period, share, shift, stretch, spell

• **VERB** = be mean, hold back, be sparing, skimp on, be frugal

stipulate = specify, agree, require, contract, settle, covenant, insist upon

stir **VERB** **1** = mix, beat, agitate **2** = stimulate, move, excite, spur, provoke, arouse, awaken, rouse ≠ inhibit **3** = spur, drive, prompt, stimulate, prod, urge, animate, prick

• **NOUN** = commotion, excitement, activity, disorder, fuss, disturbance, bustle, flurry

stock **NOUN** **1** = shares, holdings, securities, investments, bonds, equities **2** = property, capital, assets, funds **3** = goods, merchandise, wares, range, choice, variety, selection, commodities **4** = supply, store, reserve, fund, stockpile, hoard **5** = livestock, cattle, beasts, domestic animals

• **VERB** **1** = sell, supply, handle, keep, trade in, deal in **2** = fill, supply, provide with, equip, furnish, fit out

• **ADJECTIVE** **1** = hackneyed, routine, banal, trite, overused **2** = regular, usual, ordinary, conventional, customary

stomach **NOUN** **1** = belly, gut (*informal*), abdomen, tummy (*informal*), puku (*N.Z.*) **2** = tummy, pot **3** = inclination, taste, desire, appetite, relish

• **VERB** = bear, take, tolerate, endure, swallow, abide

RELATED WORD

adjective: gastric

stone **1** = masonry, rock **2** = rock, pebble **3** = pip, seed, pit, kernel

stoop **VERB** **1** = hunch **2** = bend, lean, bow, duck, crouch

• **NOUN** = slouch, bad posture, round-shoulderedness

stop **VERB** **1** = quit, cease, refrain, put an end to, discontinue, desist ≠ start

2 = prevent, cut short, arrest, restrain, hold back, hinder, repress, impede ≠ facilitate 3 = end, conclude, finish, terminate ≠ continue 4 = cease, shut down, discontinue, desist ≠ continue 5 = halt, pause ≠ keep going 6 = pause, wait, rest, take a break, have a breather (*informal*), stop briefly 7 = stay, rest, lodge

• NOUN 1 = halt, standstill 2 = station, stage, depot, terminus 3 = stay, break, rest

store NOUN 1 = shop, outlet, market, mart 2 = supply, stock, reserve, fund, quantity, accumulation, stockpile, hoard 3 = repository, warehouse, depository, storeroom

• VERB 1 *often with **away** or **up*** = put by, save, hoard, keep, reserve, deposit, garner, stockpile 2 = put away, put in storage, put in store 3 = keep, hold, preserve, maintain, retain, conserve

storm NOUN 1 = tempest, hurricane, gale, blizzard, squall 2 = outburst, row, outcry, furore, outbreak, turmoil, disturbance, strife

• VERB 1 = rush, stamp, flounce, fly 2 = rage, rant, thunder, rave, bluster 3 = attack, charge, rush, assault, assail

stormy 1 = wild, rough, raging, turbulent, windy, blustery, inclement, squally 2 = rough, wild, turbulent, raging 3 = angry, heated, fierce, passionate, fiery, impassioned

story 1 = tale, romance, narrative, history, legend, yarn 2 = anecdote, account, tale, report 3 = report, news, article, feature, scoop, news item

stout 1 = fat, big, heavy, overweight, plump, bulky, burly, fleshy ≠ slim 2 = strong, strapping, muscular, robust, sturdy, stalwart, brawny, able-bodied ≠ puny 3 = brave, bold, courageous, fearless, resolute, gallant, intrepid, valiant ≠ timid

straight ADJECTIVE 1 = direct ≠ indirect 2 = level, even, right, square, true, smooth, aligned, horizontal ≠ crooked 3 = frank, plain, straightforward, blunt, outright, honest, candid, forthright ≠ evasive 4 = successive, consecutive, continuous, running, solid, nonstop ≠ discontinuous 5 (*Slang*) = conventional, conservative, bourgeois ≠ fashionable 6 = honest, just, fair, reliable, respectable, upright, honourable, law-abiding ≠ dishonest 7 = undiluted, pure, neat, unadulterated, unmixed 8 = in order, organized, arranged, neat, tidy, orderly, shipshape ≠ untidy

• ADVERB 1 = directly, precisely, exactly, unswervingly, by the shortest route, in a beeline 2 = immediately, directly, promptly, instantly, at once, straight away, without delay, forthwith

straight away = immediately, now, at once, directly, instantly, right away

straighten = neaten, arrange, tidy (up), order, put in order

straightforward 1 (*Chiefly Brit.*) = simple, easy, uncomplicated, routine, elementary, easy-peasy (*slang*) ≠ complicated 2 = honest, open, direct, genuine, sincere, candid, truthful, forthright, dinkum (*Austral. & N.Z. informal*) ≠ devious

strain[1] NOUN 1 = pressure, stress, demands, burden 2 = stress, anxiety 3 = worry, effort, struggle ≠ ease 4 = burden, tension 5 = injury, wrench, sprain, pull

• VERB 1 = stretch, tax, overtax 2 = strive, struggle, endeavour, labour, go for it (*informal*), bend over backwards (*informal*), give it your best shot (*informal*), knock yourself out (*informal*) ≠ relax 3 = sieve, filter, sift, purify

strain[2] 1 = trace, suggestion, tendency, streak 2 = breed, family, race, blood, descent, extraction, ancestry, lineage

strained 1 = tense, difficult, awkward, embarrassed, stiff, uneasy ≠ relaxed 2 = forced, put on, false, artificial, unnatural ≠ natural

strait NOUN *often plural* = channel, sound, narrows

• PLURAL NOUN = difficulty, dilemma, plight, hardship, uphill (*S. African*), predicament, extremity

strand = filament, fibre, thread, string

stranded 1 = beached, grounded, marooned, ashore, shipwrecked, aground 2 = helpless, abandoned, high and dry

strange 1 = odd, curious, weird, wonderful, extraordinary, bizarre, peculiar, abnormal ≠ ordinary 2 = unfamiliar, new, unknown, foreign, novel, alien, exotic, untried ≠ familiar

stranger 1 = unknown person 2 = newcomer, incomer, foreigner, guest, visitor, alien, outlander

strangle 1 = throttle, choke, asphyxiate, strangulate 2 = suppress, inhibit, subdue,

stifle, repress, overpower, quash, quell
strap NOUN = tie, thong, belt
• VERB = fasten, tie, secure, bind, lash, buckle
strapping = well-built, big, powerful, robust, sturdy, husky (*informal*), brawny
strategic 1 = tactical, calculated, deliberate, planned, politic, diplomatic 2 = crucial, important, key, vital, critical, decisive, cardinal
strategy 1 = policy, procedure, approach, scheme 2 = plan, approach, scheme
stray VERB 1 = wander, go astray, drift 2 = drift, wander, roam, meander, rove 3 = digress, diverge, deviate, get off the point
• ADJECTIVE 1 = lost, abandoned, homeless, roaming, vagrant 2 = random, chance, accidental
streak NOUN 1 = band, line, strip, stroke, layer, slash, vein, stripe 2 = trace, touch, element, strain, dash, vein
• VERB = speed, fly, tear, flash, sprint, dart, zoom, whizz (*informal*)
stream NOUN 1 = river, brook, burn (*Scot.*), beck, tributary, bayou, rivulet 2 = flow, current, rush, run, course, drift, surge, tide
• VERB 1 = flow, run, pour, issue, flood, spill, cascade, gush 2 = rush, fly, speed, tear, flood, pour
streamlined = efficient, organized, rationalized, slick, smooth-running
street = road, lane, avenue, terrace, row, roadway
strength 1 = might, muscle, brawn ≠ weakness 2 = will, resolution, courage, character, nerve, determination, pluck, stamina 3 = health, fitness, vigour 4 = mainstay 5 = toughness, soundness, robustness, sturdiness 6 = force, power, intensity ≠ weakness 7 = potency, effectiveness, efficacy 8 = strong point, skill, asset, advantage, talent, forte, speciality ≠ failing
strengthen 1 = fortify, harden, toughen, consolidate, stiffen, gee up, brace up ≠ weaken 2 = reinforce, support, intensify, bolster, buttress 3 = bolster, harden, reinforce 4 = heighten, intensify 5 = make stronger, build up, invigorate, restore, give strength to 6 = support, brace, reinforce, consolidate, harden, bolster, augment, buttress 7 = become stronger, intensify, gain strength
stress VERB 1 = emphasize, underline, dwell on 2 = place the emphasis on, emphasize, give emphasis to, lay emphasis upon
• NOUN 1 = emphasis, significance, force, weight 2 = strain, pressure, worry, tension, burden, anxiety, trauma 3 = accent, beat, emphasis, accentuation
stretch VERB 1 = extend, cover, spread, reach, put forth, unroll 2 = last, continue, go on, carry on, reach 3 = expand 4 = pull, distend, strain, tighten, draw out, elongate
• NOUN 1 = expanse, area, tract, spread, distance, extent 2 = period, time, spell, stint, term, space
strict 1 = severe, harsh, stern, firm, stringent ≠ easy-going 2 = stern, firm, severe, harsh, authoritarian 3 = exact, accurate, precise, close, true, faithful, meticulous, scrupulous 4 = absolute, total, utter
strife = conflict, battle, clash, quarrel, friction, discord, dissension
strike NOUN = walkout, industrial action, mutiny, revolt
• VERB 1 = walk out, down tools, revolt, mutiny 2 = hit, smack, thump, beat, knock, punch, hammer, slap 3 = drive, hit, smack, wallop (*informal*) 4 = collide with, hit, run into, bump into 5 = knock, smack, thump, beat 6 = affect, touch, devastate, overwhelm, leave a mark on 7 = attack, assault someone, set upon someone, lay into someone (*informal*) 8 = occur to, hit, come to, register (*informal*), dawn on *or* upon 9 = seem to, appear to, look to, give the impression to 10 = move, touch, hit, affect, overcome, stir, disturb, perturb
striking = impressive, dramatic, outstanding, noticeable, conspicuous, jaw-dropping ≠ unimpressive
string 1 = cord, twine, fibre 2 = series, line, row, file, sequence, succession, procession 3 = sequence, run, series, chain, succession
stringent = strict, tough, rigorous, tight, severe, rigid, inflexible ≠ lax
strip[1] 1 = undress, disrobe, unclothe 2 = plunder, rob, loot, empty, sack, ransack, pillage, divest
strip[2] 1 = piece, shred, band, belt 2 = stretch, area, tract, expanse, extent
strive = try, labour, struggle, attempt, toil, go all out (*informal*), bend over backwards (*informal*), do your best

stroke VERB = caress, rub, fondle, pet
• NOUN 1 = apoplexy, fit, seizure, attack, collapse 2 = blow, hit, knock, pat, rap, thump, swipe

stroll VERB = walk, ramble, amble, promenade, saunter
• NOUN = walk, promenade, constitutional, ramble, breath of air

strong 1 = powerful, muscular, tough, athletic, strapping, hardy, sturdy, burly ≠ weak 2 = fit, robust, lusty 3 = durable, substantial, sturdy, heavy-duty, well-built, hard-wearing ≠ flimsy 4 = extreme, radical, drastic, strict, harsh, rigid, forceful, uncompromising 5 = decisive, firm, forceful, decided, determined, resolute, incisive 6 = persuasive, convincing, compelling, telling, sound, effective, potent, weighty 7 = keen, deep, acute, fervent, zealous, vehement 8 = intense, deep, passionate, ardent, fierce, fervent, vehement, fervid 9 = staunch, firm, fierce, ardent, enthusiastic, passionate, fervent 10 = distinct, marked, clear, unmistakable ≠ slight 11 = bright, brilliant, dazzling, bold ≠ dull

stronghold 1 = bastion, fortress, bulwark 2 = refuge, haven, retreat, sanctuary, hide-out

structure NOUN 1 = arrangement, form, make-up, design, organization, construction, formation, configuration 2 = building, construction, erection, edifice
• VERB = arrange, organize, design, shape, build up, assemble

struggle VERB 1 = strive, labour, toil, work, strain, go all out (*informal*), give it your best shot (*informal*), exert yourself 2 = fight, battle, wrestle, grapple, compete, contend
• NOUN 1 = effort, labour, toil, work, pains, scramble, exertion 2 = fight, battle, conflict, clash, contest, brush, combat, tussle, biffo (*Austral. slang*)

strut = swagger, parade, peacock, prance

stubborn = obstinate, dogged, inflexible, persistent, intractable, tenacious, recalcitrant, unyielding ≠ compliant

stuck 1 = fastened, fast, fixed, joined, glued, cemented 2 (*Informal*) = baffled, stumped, beaten

student 1 = undergraduate, scholar 2 = pupil, scholar, schoolchild, schoolboy *or* schoolgirl 3 = learner, trainee, apprentice, disciple

studied = planned, deliberate, conscious, intentional, premeditated ≠ unplanned

studio = workshop, workroom, atelier

study VERB 1 = learn, cram (*informal*), swot (up) (*Brit. informal*), read up, mug up (*Brit. slang*) 2 = examine, survey, look at, scrutinize 3 = contemplate, read, examine, consider, go into, pore over
• NOUN 1 = examination, investigation, analysis, consideration, inspection, scrutiny, contemplation 2 = piece of research, survey, report, review, inquiry, investigation 3 = learning, lessons, school work, reading, research, swotting (*Brit. informal*)

stuff NOUN 1 = things, gear, possessions, effects, equipment, objects, tackle, kit 2 = substance, material, essence, matter
• VERB 1 = shove, force, push, squeeze, jam, ram 2 = cram, fill, pack, crowd

stuffing = wadding, filling, packing

stumble VERB 1 = trip, fall, slip, reel, stagger, falter, lurch 2 = totter, reel, lurch, wobble
• PHRASES **stumble across** *or* **on** *or* **upon something** *or* **someone** = discover, find, come across, chance upon

stump NOUN = tail end, end, remnant, remainder
• VERB = baffle, confuse, puzzle, bewilder, perplex, mystify, flummox, nonplus

stun 1 = overcome, shock, confuse, astonish, stagger, bewilder, astound, overpower 2 = daze, knock out, stupefy, numb, benumb

stunning (*Informal*) = wonderful, beautiful, impressive, striking, lovely, spectacular, marvellous, splendid ≠ unimpressive

stunt = feat, act, trick, exploit, deed

stunted = undersized, little, small, tiny, diminutive

stupid 1 = unintelligent, thick, simple, slow, dim, dense, simple-minded, moronic ≠ intelligent 2 = silly, foolish, daft (*informal*), rash, pointless, senseless, idiotic, fatuous ≠ sensible 3 = senseless, dazed, groggy, insensate, semiconscious

sturdy 1 = robust, hardy, powerful, athletic, muscular, lusty, brawny ≠ puny 2 = substantial, solid, durable, well-made, well-built ≠ flimsy

style NOUN **1** = manner, way, method, approach, technique, mode **2** = elegance, taste, chic, flair, polish, sophistication, panache, élan **3** = design, form, cut **4** = type, sort, kind, variety, category, genre **5** = fashion, trend, mode, vogue, rage **6** = luxury, ease, comfort, elegance, grandeur, affluence
• VERB **1** = design, cut, tailor, fashion, shape, arrange, adapt **2** = call, name, term, label, entitle, dub, designate

stylish = smart, chic, fashionable, trendy (*Brit. informal*), modish, dressy (*informal*), voguish ≠ scruffy

subdue **1** = overcome, defeat, master, break, control, crush, conquer, tame **2** = moderate, suppress, soften, mellow, tone down, quieten down ≠ arouse

subdued **1** = quiet, serious, sad, chastened, dejected, downcast, crestfallen, down in the mouth ≠ lively **2** = hushed, soft, quiet, muted ≠ loud

subject NOUN **1** = topic, question, issue, matter, point, business, affair, object **2** = citizen, resident, native, inhabitant, national **3** = dependant, subordinate
• ADJECTIVE = subordinate, dependent, satellite, inferior, obedient
• VERB = put through, expose, submit, lay open
• PHRASES **subject to** **1** = liable to, open to, exposed to, vulnerable to, prone to, susceptible to **2** = bound by **3** = dependent on, contingent on, controlled by, conditional on

subjective = personal, prejudiced, biased, nonobjective ≠ objective

sublime = noble, glorious, high, great, grand, elevated, lofty, exalted ≠ lowly

submerge **1** = flood, swamp, engulf, overflow, inundate, deluge **2** = immerse, plunge, duck **3** = sink, plunge, go under water **4** = overwhelm, swamp, engulf, deluge

submission **1** = surrender, yielding, giving in, cave-in (*informal*), capitulation **2** = presentation, handing in, entry, tendering **3** = compliance, obedience, meekness, resignation, deference, passivity, docility

submit **1** = surrender, yield, give in, agree, endure, tolerate, comply, succumb **2** = present, hand in, tender, put forward, table, proffer

subordinate NOUN = inferior, junior, assistant, aide, second, attendant ≠ superior
• ADJECTIVE = inferior, lesser, lower, junior, subject, minor, secondary, dependent ≠ superior

subscribe **1** = support, advocate, endorse **2** = contribute, give, donate

subscription (*Chiefly Brit.*) = membership fee, dues, annual payment

subsequent = following, later, succeeding, after, successive, ensuing ≠ previous

subsequently = later, afterwards

subside **1** = decrease, diminish, lessen, ease, wane, ebb, abate, slacken ≠ increase **2** = collapse, sink, cave in, drop, lower, settle

subsidiary NOUN = branch, division, section, office, department, wing, subdivision, subsection
• ADJECTIVE = secondary, lesser, subordinate, minor, supplementary, auxiliary, ancillary ≠ main

subsidy = aid, help, support, grant, assistance, allowance

substance **1** = material, body, stuff, fabric **2** = importance, significance, concreteness **3** = meaning, main point, gist, import, significance, essence **4** = wealth, means, property, assets, resources, estate

substantial = big, significant, considerable, large, important, ample, sizable *or* sizeable ≠ small

substitute VERB = replace, exchange, swap, change, switch, interchange
• NOUN = replacement, reserve, surrogate, deputy, sub, proxy, locum
• ADJECTIVE = replacement, reserve, surrogate, second, alternative, fall-back, proxy

subtle **1** = faint, slight, implied, delicate, understated ≠ obvious **2** = crafty, cunning, sly, shrewd, ingenious, devious, wily, artful ≠ straightforward **3** = muted, soft, subdued, low-key, toned down **4** = fine, minute, narrow, tenuous, hair-splitting

subtlety **1** = fine point, refinement, sophistication, delicacy **2** = skill, ingenuity, cleverness, deviousness, craftiness, artfulness, slyness, wiliness

subversive ADJECTIVE = seditious, riotous, treasonous
• NOUN = dissident, terrorist, saboteur, fifth

columnist

succeed 1 = triumph, win, prevail 2 = work out, work, be successful 3 = make it (*informal*), do well, be successful, triumph, thrive, flourish, make good, prosper ≠ fail 4 = take over from, assume the office of 5 *with* ***to*** = take over, assume, attain, come into, inherit, accede to, come into possession of 6 = follow, come after, follow after ≠ precede

success 1 = victory, triumph ≠ failure 2 = prosperity, fortune, luck, fame 3 = hit (*informal*), winner, smash (*informal*), triumph, sensation ≠ flop (*informal*) 4 = big name, star, hit (*informal*), celebrity, sensation, megastar (*informal*) ≠ nobody

successful 1 = triumphant, victorious, lucky, fortunate 2 = thriving, profitable, rewarding, booming, flourishing, fruitful ≠ unprofitable 3 = top, prosperous, wealthy

successfully = well, favourably, with flying colours, victoriously

succession 1 = series, run, sequence, course, order, train, chain, cycle 2 = taking over, assumption, inheritance, accession

successive = consecutive, following, in succession

succumb 1 *often with* ***to*** = surrender, yield, submit, give in, cave in (*informal*), capitulate ≠ beat 2 *with* ***to*** (with an illness as object) = catch, fall ill with

suck 1 = drink, sip, draw 2 = take, draw, pull, extract

sudden = quick, rapid, unexpected, swift, hurried, abrupt, hasty ≠ gradual

suddenly = abruptly, all of a sudden, unexpectedly

sue (*Law*) = take (someone) to court, prosecute, charge, summon, indict

suffer 1 = be in pain, hurt, ache 2 = be affected, have trouble with, be afflicted, be troubled with 3 = undergo, experience, sustain, bear, go through, endure 4 = tolerate, stand, put up with (*informal*), bear, endure

suffering = pain, distress, agony, misery, ordeal, discomfort, torment, hardship

suffice = be enough, do, be sufficient, be adequate, serve, meet requirements

sufficient = adequate, enough, ample, satisfactory ≠ insufficient

suggest 1 = recommend, propose, advise, advocate, prescribe 2 = indicate 3 = hint at, imply, intimate 4 = bring to mind, evoke

suggestion 1 = recommendation, proposal, proposition, plan, motion 2 = hint, insinuation, intimation 3 = trace, touch, hint, breath, indication, whisper, intimation

suit NOUN 1 = outfit, costume, ensemble, dress, clothing, habit 2 = lawsuit, case, trial, proceeding, cause, action, prosecution
• VERB 1 = be acceptable to, please, satisfy, do, gratify 2 = agree with, become, match, go with, harmonize with

suitable 1 = appropriate, right, fitting, fit, becoming, satisfactory, apt, befitting ≠ inappropriate 2 = seemly, fitting, becoming, proper, correct ≠ unseemly 3 = suited, appropriate, in keeping with ≠ out of keeping 4 = pertinent, relevant, applicable, fitting, appropriate, to the point, apt ≠ irrelevant 5 = convenient, timely, appropriate, well-timed, opportune ≠ inopportune

suite = rooms, apartment

sum 1 = amount, quantity, volume 2 = calculation, figures, arithmetic, mathematics, maths (*Brit. informal*), tally, math (*U.S. informal*), arithmetical problem 3 = total, aggregate 4 = totality, whole

summarize = sum up, condense, encapsulate, epitomize, abridge, précis

summary = synopsis, résumé, précis, review, outline, rundown, abridgment

summit 1 = peak, top, tip, pinnacle, apex, head ≠ base 2 = height, pinnacle, peak, zenith, acme ≠ depths

summon 1 = send for, call, bid, invite 2 *often with* ***up*** = gather, muster, draw on

sumptuous = luxurious, grand, superb, splendid, gorgeous, lavish, opulent ≠ plain

sunny 1 = bright, clear, fine, radiant, sunlit, summery, unclouded ≠ dull 2 = cheerful, happy, cheery, buoyant, joyful, light-hearted ≠ gloomy

sunset = nightfall, dusk, eventide, close of (the) day

superb 1 = splendid, excellent, magnificent, fine, grand, superior, marvellous, world-class, booshit (*Austral. slang*), exo (*Austral. slang*), sik (*Austral. slang*) ≠ inferior 2 = magnificent, superior, marvellous, exquisite, superlative ≠ terrible

superficial 1 = shallow, frivolous, empty-headed, silly, trivial ≠ serious **2** = hasty, cursory, perfunctory, hurried, casual, sketchy, desultory, slapdash ≠ thorough **3** = slight, surface, external, on the surface, exterior ≠ profound

superintendent = supervisor, director, manager, chief, governor, inspector, controller, overseer

superior ADJECTIVE **1** = better, higher, greater, grander, surpassing, unrivalled ≠ inferior **2** = first-class, excellent, first-rate, choice, exclusive, exceptional, de luxe, booshit (*Austral. slang*), exo (*Austral. slang*), sik (*Austral. slang*) ≠ average **3** = supercilious, patronizing, condescending, haughty, disdainful, lordly, lofty, pretentious
• NOUN = boss, senior, director, manager, chief (*informal*), principal, supervisor, baas (*S. African*) ≠ subordinate

superiority = supremacy, lead, advantage, excellence, ascendancy, predominance

supernatural = paranormal, unearthly, uncanny, ghostly, psychic, mystic, miraculous, occult

supervise **1** = observe, guide, monitor, oversee, keep an eye on **2** = oversee, run, manage, control, direct, handle, look after, superintend

supervision = superintendence, direction, control, charge, care, management, guidance

supervisor = boss (*informal*), manager, chief, inspector, administrator, foreman, overseer, baas (*S. African*)

supplement VERB = add to, reinforce, augment, extend
• NOUN **1** = pull-out, insert **2** = appendix, add-on, postscript **3** = addition, extra

supply VERB **1** = provide, give, furnish, produce, stock, grant, contribute, yield **2** = furnish, provide, equip, endow
• NOUN = store, fund, stock, source, reserve, quantity, hoard, cache
• PLURAL NOUN = provisions, necessities, stores, food, materials, equipment, rations

support VERB **1** = help, back, champion, second, aid, defend, assist, side with ≠ oppose **2** = provide for, maintain, look after, keep, fund, finance, sustain ≠ live off **3** = bear out, confirm, verify, substantiate, corroborate ≠ refute **4** = bear, carry, sustain, prop (up), reinforce, hold, brace, buttress
• NOUN **1** = furtherance, backing, promotion, assistance, encouragement **2** = help, loyalty ≠ opposition **3** = aid, help, benefits, relief, assistance **4** = prop, post, foundation, brace, pillar **5** = supporter, prop, mainstay, tower of strength, second, backer ≠ antagonist **6** = upkeep, maintenance, keep, subsistence, sustenance

supporter = follower, fan, advocate, friend, champion, sponsor, patron, helper ≠ opponent

supportive = helpful, encouraging, understanding, sympathetic

suppose **1** = imagine, consider, conjecture, postulate, hypothesize **2** = think, imagine, expect, assume, guess (*informal*, *chiefly U.S. & Canad.*), presume, conjecture

supposed **1** *usually with* ***to*** = meant, expected, required, obliged **2** = presumed, alleged, professed, accepted, assumed

supposedly = presumably, allegedly, ostensibly, theoretically, hypothetically ≠ actually

suppress **1** = stamp out, stop, check, crush, conquer, subdue, put an end to, overpower ≠ encourage **2** = check, inhibit, subdue, stop, quell **3** = restrain, stifle, contain, silence, conceal, curb, repress, smother

suppression **1** = elimination, crushing, check, quashing **2** = inhibition, blocking, restraint, smothering

supremacy = domination, sovereignty, sway, mastery, primacy, predominance, supreme power

supreme **1** = paramount ≠ least **2** = chief, leading, principal, highest, head, top, prime, foremost ≠ lowest **3** = ultimate, highest, greatest

supremo (*Brit. informal*) = head, leader, boss (*informal*), director, master, governor, commander, principal, baas (*S. African*)

sure **1** = certain, positive, decided, convinced, confident, assured, definite ≠ uncertain **2** = inevitable, guaranteed, bound, assured, inescapable ≠ unsure **3** = reliable, accurate, dependable, undoubted, undeniable, foolproof, infallible, unerring ≠ unreliable

surely **1** = it must be the case that **2** = undoubtedly, certainly, definitely, without doubt, unquestionably, indubitably, doubtlessly

surface NOUN 1 = covering, face, exterior, side, top, veneer 2 = façade
• VERB 1 = emerge, come up, come to the surface 2 = appear, emerge, arise, come to light, crop up (*informal*), transpire, materialize

surge NOUN 1 = rush, flood 2 = flow, wave, rush, roller, gush, outpouring 3 = tide, swell, billowing 4 = rush, wave, storm, torrent, eruption
• VERB 1 = rush, pour, rise, gush 2 = roll, rush, heave 3 = sweep, rush, storm

surpass = outdo, beat, exceed, eclipse, excel, transcend, outstrip, outshine

surpassing = supreme, extraordinary, outstanding, exceptional, unrivalled, incomparable, matchless

surplus NOUN = excess, surfeit ≠ shortage
• ADJECTIVE = extra, spare, excess, remaining, odd, superfluous ≠ insufficient

surprise NOUN 1 = shock, revelation, jolt, bombshell, eye-opener (*informal*) 2 = amazement, astonishment, wonder, incredulity
• VERB 1 = amaze, astonish, stun, startle, stagger, take aback 2 = catch unawares *or* off-guard, spring upon

surprised = amazed, astonished, speechless, thunderstruck

surprising = amazing, remarkable, incredible, astonishing, unusual, extraordinary, unexpected, staggering

surrender VERB 1 = give in, yield, submit, give way, succumb, cave in (*informal*), capitulate ≠ resist 2 = give up, abandon, relinquish, yield, concede, part with, renounce, waive
• NOUN = submission, cave-in (*informal*), capitulation, resignation, renunciation, relinquishment

surround = enclose, ring, encircle, encompass, envelop, hem in

surrounding ADJECTIVE = nearby, neighbouring
• PLURAL NOUN = environment, setting, background, location, milieu

surveillance = observation, watch, scrutiny, supervision, inspection

survey NOUN 1 = poll, study, research, review, inquiry, investigation 2 = examination, inspection, scrutiny 3 = valuation, estimate, assessment, appraisal
• VERB 1 = interview, question, poll, research, investigate 2 = look over, view, examine, observe, contemplate, inspect, eyeball (*slang*), scrutinize 3 = measure, estimate, assess, appraise

survive 1 = remain alive, last, live on, endure 2 = continue, last, live on 3 = live longer than, outlive, outlast

susceptible 1 = responsive, sensitive, receptive, impressionable, suggestible ≠ unresponsive 2 *usually with* ***to*** = liable, inclined, prone, given, subject, vulnerable, disposed ≠ resistant

suspect VERB 1 = believe, feel, guess, consider, suppose, speculate ≠ know 2 = distrust, doubt, mistrust ≠ trust
• ADJECTIVE = dubious, doubtful, questionable, iffy (*informal*) ≠ innocent

suspend 1 = postpone, put off, cease, interrupt, shelve, defer, cut short, discontinue ≠ continue 2 = hang, attach, dangle

suspension = postponement, break, breaking off, interruption, abeyance, deferment, discontinuation

suspicion 1 = distrust, scepticism, mistrust, doubt, misgiving, qualm, wariness, dubiety 2 = idea, notion, hunch, guess, impression 3 = trace, touch, hint, suggestion, shade, streak, tinge, soupçon (*French*)

suspicious 1 = distrustful, sceptical, doubtful, unbelieving, wary ≠ trusting 2 = suspect, dubious, questionable, doubtful, dodgy (*Brit., Austral., & N.Z. informal*), fishy (*informal*) ≠ beyond suspicion

sustain 1 = maintain, continue, keep up, prolong, protract 2 = suffer, experience, undergo, feel, bear, endure, withstand 3 = help, aid, assist 4 = keep alive, nourish, provide for 5 = support, bear, uphold

sustained = continuous, constant, steady, prolonged, perpetual, unremitting, nonstop ≠ periodic

swallow 1 = eat, consume, devour, swig (*informal*) 2 = gulp, drink

swamp NOUN = bog, marsh, quagmire, slough, fen, mire, morass, pakihi (*N.Z.*)
• VERB 1 = flood, engulf, submerge, inundate 2 = overload, overwhelm, inundate

swap *or* **swop** = exchange, trade, switch,

interchange, barter
swarm NOUN = multitude, crowd, mass, army, host, flock, herd, horde
• VERB 1 = crowd, flock, throng, mass, stream 2 = teem, crawl, abound, bristle
swathe NOUN = area, section, tract
• VERB = wrap, drape, envelop, cloak, shroud, bundle up
sway VERB 1 = move from side to side, rock, roll, swing, bend, lean 2 = influence, affect, guide, persuade, induce
• NOUN = power, control, influence, authority, clout (*informal*)
swear 1 = curse, blaspheme, be foul-mouthed 2 = vow, promise, testify, attest 3 = declare, assert, affirm
swearing = bad language, cursing, profanity, blasphemy, foul language
sweat NOUN 1 = perspiration 2 (*Informal*) = panic, anxiety, worry, distress, agitation
• VERB 1 = perspire, glow 2 (*Informal*) = worry, fret, agonize, torture yourself
sweep VERB 1 = brush, clean 2 = clear, remove, brush, clean 3 = sail, pass, fly, tear, zoom, glide, skim
• NOUN 1 = movement, move, swing, stroke 2 = extent, range, stretch, scope
sweeping 1 = indiscriminate, blanket, wholesale, exaggerated, overstated, unqualified 2 = wide-ranging, global, comprehensive, wide, broad, extensive, all-inclusive, all-embracing ≠ limited
sweet ADJECTIVE 1 = sugary, cloying, saccharine, icky (*informal*) ≠ sour 2 = fragrant, aromatic ≠ stinking 3 = fresh, clean, pure 4 = melodious, musical, harmonious, mellow, dulcet ≠ harsh 5 = charming, kind, agreeable ≠ nasty 6 = delightful, appealing, cute, winning, engaging, lovable, likable *or* likeable ≠ unpleasant
• NOUN 1 *usually plural* = confectionery, candy (*U.S.*), lolly (*Austral. & N.Z.*), bonbon 2 (*Brit.*) = dessert, pudding
sweetheart 1 = dearest, beloved, sweet, angel, treasure, honey, dear, sweetie (*informal*) 2 = love, boyfriend *or* girlfriend, beloved, lover, darling
swell VERB 1 = increase, rise, grow, mount, expand, accelerate, escalate, multiply ≠ decrease 2 = expand, increase, grow, rise, balloon, enlarge, bulge, dilate ≠ shrink
• NOUN = wave, surge, billow
swelling = enlargement, lump, bump, bulge, inflammation, protuberance, distension
swift 1 = quick, prompt, rapid 2 = fast, quick, rapid, hurried, speedy ≠ slow
swiftly 1 = quickly, rapidly, speedily 2 = fast, promptly, hurriedly
swing VERB 1 = brandish, wave, shake, flourish, wield, dangle 2 = sway, rock, wave, veer, oscillate 3 *usually with* ***round*** = turn, swivel, curve, rotate, pivot 4 = hit out, strike, swipe, lash out at, slap 5 = hang, dangle, suspend
• NOUN 1 = swaying, sway 2 = fluctuation, change, shift, switch, variation
swirl = whirl, churn, spin, twist, eddy
switch NOUN 1 = control, button, lever, on/off device 2 = change, shift, reversal
• VERB 1 = change, shift, divert, deviate 2 = exchange, swap, substitute
swollen = enlarged, bloated, inflamed, puffed up, distended
swoop 1 = pounce, attack, charge, rush, descend 2 = drop, plunge, dive, sweep, descend, pounce, stoop
symbol 1 = metaphor, image, sign, representation, token 2 = representation, sign, figure, mark, image, token, logo, badge
symbolic 1 = representative, emblematic, allegorical 2 = representative, figurative
sympathetic 1 = caring, kind, understanding, concerned, interested, warm, pitying, supportive ≠ uncaring 2 = like-minded, compatible, agreeable, friendly, congenial, companionable ≠ uncongenial
sympathy 1 = compassion, understanding, pity, commiseration, aroha (*N.Z.*) ≠ indifference 2 = affinity, agreement, rapport, fellow feeling ≠ opposition
symptom 1 = sign, mark, indication, warning 2 = manifestation, sign, indication, mark, evidence, expression, proof, token
synthetic = artificial, fake, man-made ≠ real
system 1 = arrangement, structure, organization, scheme, classification 2 = method, practice, technique, procedure, routine
systematic = methodical, organized, efficient, orderly ≠ unmethodical

t

table NOUN **1** = counter, bench, stand, board, surface, work surface **2** = list, chart, tabulation, record, roll, register, diagram, itemization
• VERB (*Brit.*) = submit, propose, put forward, move, suggest, enter, file, lodge

taboo NOUN = prohibition, ban, restriction, anathema, interdict, proscription, tapu (*N.Z.*)
• ADJECTIVE = forbidden, banned, prohibited, unacceptable, outlawed, anathema, proscribed, unmentionable ≠ permitted

tack NOUN = nail, pin, drawing pin
• VERB **1** = fasten, fix, attach, pin, nail, affix **2** (*Brit.*) = stitch, sew, hem, bind, baste
• PHRASES **tack something on to something** = append, add, attach, tag

tackle VERB **1** = deal with, set about, get stuck into (*informal*), come *or* get to grips with **2** = undertake, attempt, embark upon, get stuck into (*informal*), have a go *or* stab at (*informal*) **3** = intercept, stop, challenge
• NOUN **1** = block, challenge **2** = rig, apparatus

tactic NOUN = policy, approach, move, scheme, plans, method, manoeuvre, ploy
• PLURAL NOUN = strategy, campaigning, manoeuvres, generalship

tactical = strategic, shrewd, smart, diplomatic, cunning ≠ impolitic

tag NOUN = label, tab, note, ticket, slip, identification, marker, flap
• VERB = label, mark

tail NOUN **1** = extremity, appendage, brush, rear end, hindquarters, hind part **2** = train, end, trail, tailpiece
• VERB (*Informal*) = follow, track, shadow, trail, stalk
• PHRASES **turn tail** = run away, flee, run off, retreat, cut and run, take to your heels

tailor NOUN = outfitter, couturier, dressmaker, seamstress, clothier, costumier
• VERB = adapt, adjust, modify, style, fashion, shape, alter, mould

taint = spoil, ruin, contaminate, damage, stain, corrupt, pollute, tarnish ≠ purify

take VERB **1** = grip, grab, seize, catch, grasp, clasp, take hold of **2** = carry, bring, bear, transport, ferry, haul, convey, fetch ≠ send **3** = accompany, lead, bring, guide, conduct, escort, convoy, usher **4** = remove, draw, pull, fish, withdraw, extract **5** = steal, appropriate, pocket, pinch (*informal*), misappropriate, purloin ≠ return **6** = capture, seize, take into custody, lay hold of ≠ release **7** = tolerate, stand, bear, stomach, endure, abide, put up with (*informal*), withstand ≠ avoid **8** = require, need, involve, demand, call for, entail, necessitate **9** = understand, follow, comprehend, get, see, grasp, apprehend **10** = regard as, believe to be, consider to be, perceive to be, presume to be **11** = have room for, hold, contain, accommodate, accept
• PHRASES **take off 1** = lift off, take to the air **2** (*Informal*) = depart, go, leave, disappear, abscond, decamp, slope off ♦ **take someone in** = deceive, fool, con (*informal*), trick, cheat, mislead, dupe, swindle ♦ **take someone off** (*Informal*) = parody, imitate, mimic, mock, caricature, send up (*Brit. informal*), lampoon, satirize ♦ **take something in** = understand, absorb, grasp, digest, comprehend, assimilate, get the hang of (*informal*) ♦ **take something up 1** = start, begin, engage in, adopt, become involved in **2** = occupy, absorb, consume, use up, cover, fill, waste, squander

takeover = merger, coup, incorporation

tale = story, narrative, anecdote, account, legend, saga, yarn (*informal*), fable

talent = ability, gift, aptitude, capacity, genius, flair, knack

talented = gifted, able, expert, master, masterly, brilliant, ace (*informal*), consummate

talk VERB **1** = speak, chat, chatter, converse, communicate, natter **2** = discuss, confer, negotiate, parley, confabulate, korero (*N.Z.*) **3** = inform, grass (*Brit. slang*), tell all, give the game away, blab, let the cat out of the bag
• NOUN = speech, lecture, presentation, report, address, discourse, sermon,

symposium, whaikorero (*N.Z.*)
talking-to (*Informal*) = reprimand, lecture, rebuke, scolding, criticism, reproach, ticking-off (*informal*), dressing-down (*informal*) ≠ praise
tall **1** = lofty, big, giant, long-legged, lanky, leggy **2** = high, towering, soaring, steep, elevated, lofty ≠ short **3** (*Informal*) = implausible, incredible, far-fetched, exaggerated, absurd, unbelievable, preposterous, cock-and-bull (*informal*) ≠ plausible **4** = difficult, hard, demanding, unreasonable, well-nigh impossible
tally NOUN = record, score, total, count, reckoning, running total
• VERB = agree, match, accord, fit, square, coincide, correspond, conform ≠ disagree
tame ADJECTIVE **1** = domesticated, docile, broken, gentle, obedient, amenable, tractable ≠ wild **2** = submissive, meek, compliant, subdued, manageable, obedient, docile, unresisting ≠ stubborn **3** = unexciting, boring, dull, bland, uninspiring, humdrum, uninteresting, insipid ≠ exciting
• VERB **1** = domesticate, train, break in, house-train ≠ make fiercer **2** = subdue, suppress, master, discipline, humble, conquer, subjugate ≠ arouse
tangible = definite, real, positive, material, actual, concrete, palpable, perceptible ≠ intangible
tangle NOUN **1** = knot, twist, web, jungle, coil, entanglement **2** = mess, jam, fix (*informal*), confusion, complication, mix-up, shambles, entanglement
• VERB = twist, knot, mat, coil, mesh, entangle, interweave, ravel ≠ disentangle
• PHRASES **tangle with someone** = come into conflict with, come up against, cross swords with, dispute with, contend with, contest with, lock horns with
tantrum = outburst, temper, hysterics, fit, flare-up, foulie (*Austral. slang*)
tap¹ VERB = knock, strike, pat, rap, beat, touch, drum
• NOUN = knock, pat, rap, touch, drumming
tap² NOUN = valve, stopcock
• VERB = listen in on, monitor, bug (*informal*), spy on, eavesdrop on, wiretap
• PHRASES **on tap** **1** (*Informal*) = available, ready, standing by, to hand, on hand, at hand, in reserve **2** = on draught, cask-conditioned, from barrels, not bottled *or* canned
tape NOUN = binding, strip, band, string, ribbon
• VERB **1** = record, video, tape-record, make a recording of **2** *sometimes with* ***up*** = bind, secure, stick, seal, wrap
target **1** = mark, goal **2** = goal, aim, objective, end, mark, object, intention, ambition **3** = victim, butt, prey, scapegoat
tariff **1** = tax, duty, toll, levy, excise **2** = price list, schedule
tarnish VERB **1** = damage, taint, blacken, sully, smirch ≠ enhance **2** = stain, discolour, darken, blot, blemish ≠ brighten
• NOUN = stain, taint, discoloration, spot, blot, blemish
tart¹ = pie, pastry, pasty, tartlet, patty
tart² = sharp, acid, sour, bitter, pungent, tangy, piquant, vinegary ≠ sweet
tart³ (*Informal*) = slut, prostitute, whore, call girl, trollop, floozy (*slang*)
task NOUN = job, duty, assignment, exercise, mission, enterprise, undertaking, chore
• PHRASES **take someone to task** = criticize, blame, censure, rebuke, reprimand, reproach, scold, tell off (*informal*)
taste NOUN **1** = flavour, savour, relish, smack, tang ≠ blandness **2** = bit, bite, mouthful, sample, dash, spoonful, morsel, titbit **3** = liking, preference, penchant, fondness, partiality, fancy, appetite, inclination ≠ dislike **4** = refinement, style, judgment, discrimination, appreciation, elegance, sophistication, discernment ≠ lack of judgment
• VERB **1** = have a flavour of, smack of, savour of **2** = sample, try, test, sip, savour **3** = distinguish, perceive, discern, differentiate **4** = experience, know, undergo, partake of, encounter, meet with ≠ miss
tasty = delicious, luscious, palatable, delectable, savoury, full-flavoured, scrumptious (*informal*), appetizing, lekker (*S. African slang*), yummo (*Austral. slang*) ≠ bland
taunt VERB = jeer, mock, tease, ridicule, provoke, insult, torment, deride
• NOUN = jeer, dig, insult, ridicule, teasing, provocation, derision, sarcasm
tavern = inn, bar, pub (*informal*, *chiefly*

Brit.), public house, hostelry, alehouse (*archaic*)

tax NOUN = charge, duty, toll, levy, tariff, excise, tithe
• VERB **1** = charge, rate, assess **2** = strain, stretch, try, test, load, burden, exhaust, weaken

teach VERB = instruct, train, coach, inform, educate, drill, tutor, enlighten
• VERB = show, train

teacher = instructor, coach, tutor, guide, trainer, lecturer, mentor, educator

team NOUN **1** = side, squad **2** = group, company, set, body, band, gang, line-up, bunch
• PHRASES **team up** = join, unite, work together, cooperate, couple, link up, get together, band together

tear VERB **1** = rip, split, rend, shred, rupture **2** = run **3** = scratch, cut (open), gash, lacerate, injure, mangle, cut to pieces, cut to ribbons, mangulate (*Austral. slang*) **4** = pull apart, claw, lacerate, mutilate, mangle, mangulate (*Austral. slang*) **5** = rush, run, charge, race, fly, speed, dash, hurry
• NOUN = hole, split, rip, rent, snag, rupture

tears PLURAL NOUN = crying, weeping, sobbing, wailing, blubbering
• PHRASES **in tears** = weeping, crying, sobbing, blubbering

tease 1 = mock, provoke, torment, taunt, goad, pull someone's leg (*informal*), make fun of **2** = tantalize, lead on, flirt with, titillate

technical = scientific, technological, skilled, specialist, specialized, hi-tech *or* high-tech

technique 1 = method, way, system, approach, means, style, manner, procedure **2** = skill, performance, craft, touch, execution, artistry, craftsmanship, proficiency

tedious = boring, dull, dreary, monotonous, drab, tiresome, laborious, humdrum ≠ exciting

teenager = youth, minor, adolescent, juvenile, girl, boy

telephone NOUN = phone, mobile (phone), handset, dog and bone (*slang*)
• VERB = call, phone, ring (*chiefly Brit.*), dial

telescope NOUN = glass, scope (*informal*), spyglass
• VERB = shorten, contract, compress, shrink, condense, abbreviate, abridge ≠ lengthen

television = TV, telly (*Brit. informal*), small screen (*informal*), the box (*Brit. informal*), the tube (*slang*)

tell VERB **1** = inform, notify, state to, reveal to, express to, disclose to, proclaim to, divulge **2** = describe, relate, recount, report, portray, depict, chronicle, narrate **3** = instruct, order, command, direct, bid **4** = distinguish, discriminate, discern, differentiate, identify **5** = have *or* take effect, register, weigh, count, take its toll, carry weight, make its presence felt
• PHRASES **tell someone off** = reprimand, rebuke, scold, lecture, censure, reproach, berate, chide

telling = effective, significant, considerable, marked, striking, powerful, impressive, influential ≠ unimportant

temper NOUN **1** = irritability, irascibility, passion, resentment, petulance, surliness, hot-headedness ≠ good humour **2** = frame of mind, nature, mind, mood, constitution, humour, temperament, disposition **3** = rage, fury, bad mood, passion, tantrum, foulie (*Austral. slang*) **4** = self-control, composure, cool (*slang*), calmness, equanimity ≠ anger
• VERB **1** = moderate, restrain, tone down, soften, soothe, lessen, mitigate, assuage ≠ intensify **2** = strengthen, harden, toughen, anneal ≠ soften

temperament 1 = nature, character, personality, make-up, constitution, bent, humour, temper **2** = moods, anger, volatility, petulance, excitability, moodiness, hot-headedness

temple = shrine, church, sanctuary, house of God

temporarily = briefly, for the time being, momentarily, fleetingly, pro tem

temporary 1 = impermanent, transitory, brief, fleeting, interim, short-lived, momentary, ephemeral ≠ permanent **2** = short-term, acting, interim, supply, stand-in, fill-in, caretaker, provisional

tempt 1 = attract, allure **2** = entice, lure, lead on, invite, seduce, coax ≠ discourage

temptation 1 = enticement, lure, inducement, pull, seduction, allurement, tantalization **2** = appeal, attraction

tempting = inviting, enticing, seductive, alluring, attractive, mouthwatering,

appetizing ≠ uninviting
tenant = leaseholder, resident, renter, occupant, inhabitant, occupier, lodger, boarder
tend[1] = be inclined, be liable, have a tendency, be apt, be prone, lean, incline, gravitate
tend[2] **1** = take care of, look after, keep, attend, nurture, watch over ≠ neglect **2** = maintain, take care of, nurture, cultivate, manage ≠ neglect
tendency = inclination, leaning, liability, disposition, propensity, susceptibility, proclivity, proneness
tender[1] **1** = gentle, loving, kind, caring, sympathetic, affectionate, compassionate, considerate ≠ harsh **2** = vulnerable, young, sensitive, raw, youthful, inexperienced, immature, impressionable ≠ experienced **3** = sensitive, painful, sore, raw, bruised, inflamed
tender[2] **NOUN** = offer, bid, estimate, proposal, submission
• **VERB** = offer, present, submit, give, propose, volunteer, hand in, put forward
tense **ADJECTIVE 1** = strained, uneasy, stressful, fraught, charged, difficult, worrying, exciting **2** = nervous, edgy, strained, anxious, apprehensive, uptight (*informal*), on edge, jumpy ≠ calm **3** = rigid, strained, taut, stretched, tight ≠ relaxed
• **VERB** = tighten, strain, brace, stretch, flex, stiffen ≠ relax
tension **1** = strain, stress, nervousness, pressure, anxiety, unease, apprehension, suspense ≠ calmness **2** = friction, hostility, unease, antagonism, antipathy, enmity **3** = rigidity, tightness, stiffness, pressure, stress, stretching, tautness
tentative **1** = unconfirmed, provisional, indefinite, test, trial, pilot, preliminary, experimental ≠ confirmed **2** = hesitant, cautious, uncertain, doubtful, faltering, unsure, timid, undecided ≠ confident
term **NOUN 1** = word, name, expression, title, label, phrase **2** = period, time, spell, while, season, interval, span, duration
• **PLURAL NOUN 1** = conditions, particulars, provisions, provisos, stipulations, qualifications, specifications **2** = relationship, standing, footing, relations, status
• **VERB** = call, name, label, style, entitle, tag, dub, designate
terminal **ADJECTIVE 1** = fatal, deadly, lethal, killing, mortal, incurable, inoperable, untreatable **2** = final, last, closing, finishing, concluding, ultimate, terminating ≠ initial
• **NOUN** = terminus, station, depot, end of the line
terminate **1** = end, stop, conclude, finish, complete, discontinue ≠ begin **2** = cease, end, close, finish **3** = abort, end
terrain = ground, country, land, landscape, topography, going
terrestrial = earthly, worldly, global
terrible **1** = awful, shocking, terrifying, horrible, dreadful, horrifying, fearful, horrendous **2** (*Informal*) = bad, awful, dreadful, dire, abysmal, poor, rotten (*informal*) ≠ wonderful **3** = serious, desperate, severe, extreme, dangerous, insufferable ≠ mild
terribly **1** = very much, very, dreadfully, seriously, extremely, desperately, thoroughly, decidedly **2** = extremely, very, dreadfully, seriously, desperately, thoroughly, decidedly, awfully (*informal*)
terrific **1** (*Informal*) = excellent, wonderful, brilliant, amazing, outstanding, superb, fantastic (*informal*), magnificent, booshit (*Austral. slang*), exo (*Austral. slang*), sik (*Austral. slang*), ka pai (*N.Z.*) ≠ awful **2** = intense, great, huge, enormous, tremendous, fearful, gigantic
terrified = frightened, scared, petrified, alarmed, panic-stricken, horror-struck
terrify = frighten, scare, alarm, terrorize
territory = district, area, land, region, country, zone, province, patch
terror **1** = fear, alarm, dread, fright, panic, anxiety **2** = nightmare, monster, bogeyman, devil, fiend, bugbear
test **VERB 1** = check, investigate, assess, research, analyse, experiment with, try out, put something to the test **2** = examine, put someone to the test
• **NOUN 1** = trial, research, check, investigation, analysis, assessment, examination, evaluation **2** = examination, paper, assessment, evaluation
testament **1** = proof, evidence, testimony, witness, demonstration, tribute **2** = will, last wishes
testify = bear witness, state, swear, certify, assert, affirm, attest, corroborate

≠ disprove
testimony **1** = evidence, statement, submission, affidavit, deposition **2** = proof, evidence, demonstration, indication, support, manifestation, verification, corroboration
testing = difficult, demanding, taxing, challenging, searching, tough, exacting, rigorous ≠ undemanding
text **1** = contents, words, content, wording, body, subject matter **2** = words, wording **3** = transcript, script
texture = feel, consistency, structure, surface, tissue, grain
thank = say thank you to, show your appreciation to
thanks PLURAL NOUN = gratitude, appreciation, credit, recognition, acknowledgment, gratefulness
• PHRASES **thanks to** = because of, through, due to, as a result of, owing to
thaw = melt, dissolve, soften, defrost, warm, liquefy, unfreeze ≠ freeze
theatrical **1** = dramatic, stage, Thespian **2** = exaggerated, dramatic, melodramatic, histrionic, affected, mannered, showy, ostentatious ≠ natural
theft = stealing, robbery, thieving, fraud, embezzlement, pilfering, larceny, purloining
theme **1** = motif, leitmotif **2** = subject, idea, topic, essence, subject matter, keynote, gist
theological = religious, ecclesiastical, doctrinal
theoretical **1** = abstract, speculative ≠ practical **2** = hypothetical, academic, notional, unproven, conjectural, postulatory
theory = belief, feeling, speculation, assumption, hunch, presumption, conjecture, surmise
therapeutic = beneficial, healing, restorative, good, corrective, remedial, salutary, curative ≠ harmful
therapist = psychologist, analyst, psychiatrist, shrink (*informal*), counsellor, healer, psychotherapist, psychoanalyst
therapy = remedy, treatment, cure, healing, method of healing
therefore = consequently, so, thus, as a result, hence, accordingly, thence, ergo
thesis **1** = proposition, theory, hypothesis, idea, view, opinion, proposal, contention **2** = dissertation, paper, treatise, essay, monograph
thick **1** = bulky, broad, big, large, fat, solid, substantial, hefty ≠ thin **2** = wide, across, deep, broad, in extent *or* diameter **3** = dense, close, heavy, compact, impenetrable, lush **4** = heavy, heavyweight, dense, chunky, bulky, woolly **5** = opaque, heavy, dense, impenetrable **6** = viscous, concentrated, stiff, condensed, gelatinous, semi-solid, viscid ≠ runny **7** = crowded, full, covered, bursting, bristling, brimming ≠ empty **8** (*Informal*) = stupid, slow, dense, dopey (*informal*), moronic, obtuse, brainless, dumb-ass (*informal*) ≠ clever **9** (*Informal*) = friendly, close, intimate, familiar, pally (*informal*), devoted, inseparable ≠ unfriendly
thicken = set, condense, congeal, clot, jell, coagulate ≠ thin
thief = robber, burglar, stealer, plunderer, shoplifter, embezzler, pickpocket, pilferer
thin **1** = narrow, fine, attenuated ≠ thick **2** = slim, spare, lean, slight, slender, skinny, skeletal, bony ≠ fat **3** = meagre, sparse, scanty, poor, scattered, inadequate, insufficient, deficient ≠ plentiful **4** = fine, delicate, flimsy, sheer, skimpy, gossamer, diaphanous, filmy ≠ thick **5** = unconvincing, inadequate, feeble, poor, weak, superficial, lame, flimsy ≠ convincing **6** = wispy, thinning, sparse, scarce, scanty
thing NOUN **1** = substance, stuff, being, body, material, fabric, entity **2** (*Informal*) = phobia, fear, complex, horror, terror, hang-up (*informal*), aversion, neurosis **3** (*Informal*) = obsession, liking, preoccupation, mania, fetish, fixation, soft spot, predilection
• PLURAL NOUN **1** = possessions, stuff, gear, belongings, effects, luggage, clobber (*Brit. slang*), chattels **2** = equipment, gear, tools, stuff, tackle, implements, kit, apparatus **3** = circumstances, the situation, the state of affairs, matters, life, affairs
think VERB **1** = believe, be of the opinion, be of the view **2** = judge, consider, estimate, reckon, deem, regard as **3** = ponder, reflect, contemplate, deliberate, meditate, ruminate, cogitate, be lost in thought
• PHRASES **think something up** = devise, create, come up with, invent, contrive,

visualize, concoct, dream something up
thinker = philosopher, intellect (*informal*), wise man, sage, brain (*informal*), theorist, mastermind
thinking NOUN = reasoning, idea, view, position, theory, opinion, judgment, conjecture
• ADJECTIVE = thoughtful, intelligent, reasoning, rational, philosophical, reflective, contemplative, meditative
thirst 1 = dryness, thirstiness, drought 2 = craving, appetite, longing, desire, passion, yearning, hankering, keenness ≠ aversion
thorn = prickle, spike, spine, barb
thorough 1 = comprehensive, full, complete, sweeping, intensive, in-depth, exhaustive ≠ cursory 2 = careful, conscientious, painstaking, efficient, meticulous, exhaustive, assiduous ≠ careless 3 = complete, total, absolute, utter, perfect, outright, unqualified, out-and-out ≠ partial
thoroughly 1 = carefully, fully, efficiently, meticulously, painstakingly, scrupulously, assiduously, intensively ≠ carelessly 2 = fully 3 = completely, quite, totally, perfectly, absolutely, utterly, downright, to the hilt ≠ partly
though CONJUNCTION = although, while, even if, even though, notwithstanding
• ADVERB = nevertheless, still, however, yet, nonetheless, for all that, notwithstanding
thought 1 = thinking, consideration, reflection, deliberation, musing, meditation, rumination, cogitation 2 = opinion, view, idea, concept, notion, judgment 3 = consideration, study, attention, care, regard, scrutiny, heed 4 = intention, plan, idea, design, aim, purpose, object, notion 5 = hope, expectation, prospect, aspiration, anticipation
thoughtful 1 = reflective, pensive, contemplative, meditative, serious, studious, deliberative, ruminative ≠ shallow 2 = considerate, kind, caring, kindly, helpful, attentive, unselfish, solicitous ≠ inconsiderate
thrash VERB 1 = defeat, beat, crush, slaughter (*informal*), rout, trounce, run rings around (*informal*), wipe the floor with (*informal*) 2 = beat, wallop, whip, belt (*informal*), cane, flog, scourge, spank 3 = thresh, flail, jerk, writhe, toss and turn
• PHRASES **thrash something out** = settle, resolve, discuss, debate, solve, argue out, have something out, talk something over
thrashing 1 = defeat, beating, hammering (*informal*), hiding (*informal*), rout, trouncing, drubbing 2 = beating, hiding (*informal*), belting (*informal*), whipping, flogging
thread NOUN 1 = strand, fibre, yarn, filament, line, string, twine 2 = theme, train of thought, direction, plot, drift, story line
• VERB = move, pass, ease, thrust, squeeze through, pick your way
threat 1 = danger, risk, hazard, menace, peril 2 = threatening remark, menace 3 = warning, foreshadowing, foreboding
threaten 1 = intimidate, bully, menace, terrorize, lean on (*slang*), pressurize, browbeat ≠ defend 2 = endanger, jeopardize, put at risk, imperil, put in jeopardy, put on the line ≠ protect 3 = be imminent, impend
threshold 1 = entrance, doorway, door, doorstep 2 = start, beginning, opening, dawn, verge, brink, outset, inception ≠ end 3 = limit, margin, starting point, minimum
thrift = economy, prudence, frugality, saving, parsimony, carefulness, thriftiness ≠ extravagance
thrill NOUN = pleasure, kick (*informal*), buzz (*slang*), high, stimulation, tingle, titillation ≠ tedium
• VERB = excite, stimulate, arouse, move, stir, electrify, titillate, give someone a kick
thrilling = exciting, gripping, stimulating, stirring, sensational, rousing, riveting, electrifying ≠ boring
thrive = prosper, do well, flourish, increase, grow, develop, succeed, get on ≠ decline
thriving = successful, flourishing, healthy, booming, blooming, prosperous, burgeoning ≠ unsuccessful
throb VERB 1 = pulsate, pound, beat, pulse, thump, palpitate 2 = vibrate, pulsate, reverberate, shake, judder (*informal*)
• NOUN 1 = pulse, pounding, beat, thump, thumping, pulsating, palpitation 2 = vibration, throbbing, reverberation, judder (*informal*), pulsation

throng NOUN = crowd, mob, horde, host, pack, mass, crush, swarm
• VERB 1 = crowd, flock, congregate, converge, mill around, swarm around ≠ disperse 2 = pack, crowd

throttle = strangle, choke, garrotte, strangulate

through PREPOSITION 1 = via, by way of, by, between, past, from one side to the other of 2 = because of, by way of, by means of 3 = using, via, by way of, by means of, by virtue of, with the assistance of 4 = during, throughout, for the duration of, in
• ADJECTIVE = completed, done, finished, ended
• PHRASES **through and through** = completely, totally, fully, thoroughly, entirely, altogether, wholly, utterly

throughout PREPOSITION 1 = right through, everywhere in, during the whole of, through the whole of 2 = all over, everywhere in, through the whole of
• ADVERB 1 = from start to finish, right through 2 = all through, right through

throw VERB 1 = hurl, toss, fling, send, launch, cast, pitch, chuck (*informal*) 2 = toss, fling, chuck (*informal*), cast, hurl, sling 3 (*Informal*) = confuse, baffle, faze, astonish, confound, disconcert, dumbfound
• NOUN = toss, pitch, fling, sling, lob (*informal*), heave

thrust VERB = push, force, shove, drive, plunge, jam, ram, propel
• NOUN 1 = stab, pierce, lunge 2 = push, shove, poke, prod 3 = momentum, impetus, drive

thug = ruffian, hooligan, tough, heavy (*slang*), gangster, bully boy, bruiser (*informal*), tsotsi (*S. African*)

thump VERB = strike, hit, punch, pound, beat, knock, smack, clout (*informal*)
• NOUN 1 = blow, knock, punch, rap, smack, clout (*informal*), whack, swipe 2 = thud, crash, bang, clunk, thwack

thunder NOUN = rumble, crash, boom, explosion
• VERB 1 = rumble, crash, boom, roar, resound, reverberate, peal 2 = shout, roar, yell, bark, bellow

thus 1 = therefore, so, hence, consequently, accordingly, for this reason, ergo, on that account 2 = in this way, so, like this, as follows

thwart = frustrate, foil, prevent, snooker, hinder, obstruct, outwit, stymie ≠ assist

tick NOUN 1 = check mark, mark, line, stroke, dash 2 = click, tapping, clicking, ticktock 3 (*Brit. informal*) = moment, second, minute, flash, instant, twinkling, split second, trice
• VERB 1 = mark, indicate, check off 2 = click, tap, ticktock

ticket 1 = voucher, pass, coupon, card, slip, certificate, token, chit 2 = label, tag, marker, sticker, card, slip, tab, docket

tide 1 = current, flow, stream, ebb, undertow, tideway 2 = course, direction, trend, movement, tendency, drift

tidy ADJECTIVE 1 = neat, orderly, clean, spruce, well-kept, well-ordered, shipshape ≠ untidy 2 = organized, neat, methodical 3 (*Informal*) = considerable, large, substantial, goodly, healthy, generous, handsome, ample ≠ small
• VERB = neaten, straighten, order, clean, groom, spruce up ≠ disorder

tie VERB 1 = fasten, bind, join, link, connect, attach, knot ≠ unfasten 2 = tether, secure 3 = restrict, limit, confine, bind, restrain, hamper, hinder ≠ free 4 = draw, be level, match, equal
• NOUN 1 = fastening, binding, link, bond, knot, cord, fetter, ligature 2 = bond, relationship, connection, commitment, liaison, allegiance, affiliation 3 = draw, dead heat, deadlock, stalemate

tier = row, bank, layer, line, level, rank, storey, stratum

tight 1 = close-fitting, narrow, cramped, snug, constricted, close ≠ loose 2 = secure, firm, fast, fixed 3 = taut, stretched, rigid ≠ slack 4 = close, even, well-matched, hard-fought, evenly-balanced ≠ uneven 5 (*Informal*) = miserly, mean, stingy, grasping, parsimonious, niggardly, tightfisted ≠ generous 6 (*Informal*) = drunk, intoxicated, plastered (*slang*), under the influence (*informal*), tipsy, paralytic (*informal*), inebriated, out to it (*Austral. & N.Z. slang*) ≠ sober

tighten = close, narrow, strengthen, squeeze, harden, constrict ≠ slacken

till[1] = cultivate, dig, plough, work

till[2] = cash register, cash box

tilt VERB = slant, tip, slope, list, lean, heel, incline
• NOUN 1 = slope, angle, inclination, list,

pitch, incline, slant, camber **2** (*Medieval history*) = joust, fight, tournament, lists, combat, duel

timber **1** = beams, boards, planks **2** = wood, logs

time NOUN **1** = period, term, space, stretch, spell, span **2** = occasion, point, moment, stage, instance, point in time, juncture **3** = age, duration **4** = tempo, beat, rhythm, measure
• VERB = schedule, set, plan, book, programme, set up, fix, arrange

timeless = eternal, lasting, permanent, enduring, immortal, everlasting, ageless, changeless ≠ temporary

timely = opportune, appropriate, well-timed, suitable, convenient, judicious, propitious, seasonable ≠ untimely

timetable **1** = schedule, programme, agenda, list, diary, calendar **2** = syllabus, course, curriculum, programme, teaching programme

tinge NOUN **1** = tint, colour, shade **2** = trace, bit, drop, touch, suggestion, dash, sprinkling, smattering
• VERB = tint, colour

tinker = meddle, play, potter, fiddle (*informal*), dabble, mess about

tint NOUN **1** = shade, colour, tone, hue **2** = dye, wash, rinse, tinge, tincture
• VERB = dye, colour

tiny = small, little, minute, slight, miniature, negligible, microscopic, diminutive ≠ huge

tip¹ NOUN **1** = end, point, head, extremity, sharp end, nib, prong **2** = peak, top, summit, pinnacle, zenith, spire, acme, vertex
• VERB = cap, top, crown, surmount, finish

tip² VERB **1** = reward, remunerate, give a tip to, sweeten (*informal*) **2** = predict, back, recommend, think of
• NOUN **1** = gratuity, gift, reward, present, sweetener (*informal*) **2** = hint, suggestion, piece of advice, pointer

tip³ VERB **1** = pour, drop, empty, dump, drain, discharge, unload, jettison **2** (*Brit.*) = dump, empty, unload, pour out
• NOUN (*Brit.*) = dump, midden, rubbish heap, refuse heap

tire **1** = exhaust, drain, fatigue, weary, wear out ≠ refresh **2** = flag, become tired, fail **3** = bore, weary, exasperate, irritate, irk

tired **1** = exhausted, fatigued, weary, flagging, drained, sleepy, worn out, drowsy, tuckered out (*Austral. & N.Z. informal*) ≠ energetic **2** = bored, fed up, weary, sick, hoha (*N.Z.*) ≠ enthusiastic about **3** = hackneyed, stale, well-worn, old, corny (*slang*), threadbare, trite, clichéd ≠ original

tiring = exhausting, demanding, wearing, tough, exacting, strenuous, arduous, laborious

title **1** = name, designation, term, handle (*slang*), moniker *or* monicker (*slang*) **2** (*Sport*) = championship, trophy, bays, crown, honour **3** (*Law*) = ownership, right, claim, privilege, entitlement, tenure, prerogative, freehold

toast¹ **1** = brown, grill, crisp, roast **2** = warm (up), heat (up), thaw, bring back to life

toast² NOUN **1** = tribute, compliment, salute, health, pledge, salutation **2** = favourite, celebrity, darling, talk, pet, focus of attention, hero *or* heroine, blue-eyed boy *or* girl (*Brit. informal*)
• VERB = drink to, honour, salute, drink (to) the health of

together ADVERB **1** = collectively, jointly, as one, with each other, in conjunction, side by side, mutually, in partnership ≠ separately **2** = at the same time, simultaneously, concurrently, contemporaneously, at one fell swoop
• ADJECTIVE (*Informal*) = self-possessed, composed, well-balanced, well-adjusted

toil VERB **1** = labour, work, struggle, strive, sweat (*informal*), slave, graft (*informal*), slog **2** = struggle, trek, slog, trudge, fight your way, footslog
• NOUN = hard work, effort, application, sweat, graft (*informal*), slog, exertion, drudgery ≠ idleness

toilet **1** = lavatory, bathroom, loo (*Brit. informal*), privy, cloakroom (*Brit.*), urinal, latrine, washroom, dunny (*Austral. & N.Z. old-fashioned informal*), bogger (*Austral. slang*), brasco (*Austral. slang*) **2** = bathroom, gents *or* ladies (*Brit. informal*), privy, latrine, water closet, ladies' room, W.C.

token NOUN = symbol, mark, sign, note, expression, indication, representation, badge
• ADJECTIVE = nominal, symbolic, minimal, hollow, superficial, perfunctory

tolerance 1 = broad-mindedness, indulgence, forbearance, permissiveness, open-mindedness ≠ intolerance 2 = endurance, resistance, stamina, fortitude, resilience, toughness, staying power, hardiness 3 = resistance, immunity, resilience, non-susceptibility

tolerant = broad-minded, understanding, open-minded, catholic, long-suffering, permissive, forbearing, unprejudiced ≠ intolerant

tolerate 1 = endure, stand, take, stomach, put up with (*informal*) 2 = allow, accept, permit, take, brook, put up with (*informal*), condone ≠ forbid

toll[1] VERB = ring, sound, strike, chime, knell, clang, peal
• NOUN = ringing, chime, knell, clang, peal

toll[2] 1 = charge, tax, fee, duty, payment, levy, tariff 2 = damage, cost, loss, roll, penalty, sum, number, roster 3 = adverse effects, price, cost, suffering, damage, penalty, harm

tomb = grave, vault, crypt, mausoleum, sarcophagus, catacomb, sepulchre

tone NOUN 1 = pitch, inflection, intonation, timbre, modulation 2 = volume, timbre 3 = character, style, feel, air, spirit, attitude, manner, mood 4 = colour, shade, tint, tinge, hue
• VERB = harmonize, match, blend, suit, go well with
• PHRASES **tone something down** = moderate, temper, soften, restrain, subdue, play down = reduce, moderate

tongue = language, speech, dialect, parlance

tonic = stimulant, boost, pick-me-up (*informal*), fillip, shot in the arm (*informal*), restorative

too 1 = also, as well, further, in addition, moreover, besides, likewise, to boot 2 = excessively, very, extremely, overly, unduly, unreasonably, inordinately, immoderately

tool 1 = implement, device, appliance, machine, instrument, gadget, utensil, contraption 2 = puppet, creature, pawn, stooge (*slang*), minion, lackey, flunkey, hireling

top NOUN 1 = peak, summit, head, crown, height, ridge, brow, crest ≠ bottom 2 = lid, cover, cap, plug, stopper, bung 3 = first place, head, peak, lead, high point
• ADJECTIVE 1 = highest, loftiest, furthest up, uppermost 2 = leading, best, first, highest, head, finest, elite, foremost ≠ lowest 3 = chief, most important, principal, most powerful, highest, head, leading, main 4 = prime, best, select, first-class, quality, choice, excellent, premier
• VERB 1 = lead, head, be at the top of, be first in 2 = cover, garnish, finish, crown, cap 3 = surpass, better, beat, improve on, cap, exceed, eclipse, excel ≠ not be as good as

topic = subject, point, question, issue, matter, theme, subject matter

topical = current, popular, contemporary, up-to-date, up-to-the-minute, newsworthy

topple 1 = fall over, fall, collapse, tumble, overturn, totter, keel over, overbalance 2 = knock over 3 = overthrow, overturn, bring down, oust, unseat, bring low

torment NOUN = suffering, distress, misery, pain, hell, torture, agony, anguish ≠ bliss
• VERB 1 = torture, distress, rack, crucify ≠ comfort 2 = tease, annoy, bother, irritate, harass, hassle (*informal*), pester, vex

torn 1 = cut, split, rent, ripped, ragged, slit, lacerated 2 = undecided, uncertain, unsure, wavering, vacillating, in two minds (*informal*), irresolute

tornado = whirlwind, storm, hurricane, gale, cyclone, typhoon, tempest, squall

torture VERB 1 = torment, abuse, persecute, afflict, scourge, molest, crucify, mistreat ≠ comfort 2 = distress, torment, worry, trouble, rack, afflict, harrow, inflict anguish on
• NOUN 1 = ill-treatment, abuse, torment, persecution, maltreatment, harsh treatment 2 = agony, suffering, anguish, distress, torment, heartbreak ≠ bliss

toss VERB 1 = throw, pitch, hurl, fling, launch, cast, flip, sling 2 = shake 3 = thrash (about), twitch, wriggle, squirm, writhe
• NOUN = throw, pitch, lob (*informal*)

tot NOUN 1 = infant, child, baby, toddler, mite, littlie (*Austral. informal*), ankle-biter (*Austral. slang*), tacker (*Austral. slang*) 2 = measure, shot (*informal*), finger, nip, slug, dram, snifter (*informal*)
• PHRASES **tot something up** = add up, calculate, total, reckon, compute, tally, enumerate, count up

total NOUN = sum, entirety, grand total, whole, aggregate, totality, full amount,

sum total ≠ part
• **ADJECTIVE** = complete, absolute, utter, whole, entire, undivided, overarching, thoroughgoing ≠ partial
• **VERB 1** = amount to, make, come to, reach, equal, run to, number, add up to **2** = add up, work out, compute, reckon, tot up ≠ subtract
totally = completely, entirely, absolutely, fully, comprehensively, thoroughly, wholly, utterly ≠ partly
touch VERB 1 = feel, handle, finger, stroke, brush, make contact with, caress, fondle **2** = come into contact, meet, contact, border, graze, adjoin, be in contact, abut **3** = tap **4** = affect, influence, inspire, impress **5** = consume, take, drink, eat, partake of **6** = move, stir, disturb **7** = match, rival, equal, compare with, parallel, hold a candle to (*informal*)
• **NOUN 1** = contact, push, stroke, brush, press, tap, poke, nudge **2** = feeling, handling, physical contact **3** = bit, spot, trace, drop, dash, small amount, jot, smattering **4** = style, method, technique, way, manner, trademark
• **PHRASES touch and go** = risky, close, near, critical, precarious, nerve-racking ◆ **touch on** *or* **upon something** = refer to, cover, raise, deal with, mention, bring in, speak of, hint at
touching = moving, affecting, sad, stirring, pathetic, poignant, emotive, pitiable
tough ADJECTIVE 1 = strong ≠ weak **2** = hardy, strong, seasoned, strapping, vigorous, sturdy, stout **3** = violent, rough, ruthless, pugnacious, hard-bitten **4** = strict, severe, stern, hard, firm, resolute, merciless, unbending ≠ lenient **5** = hard, difficult, troublesome, uphill, strenuous, arduous, laborious **6** = resilient, hard, resistant, durable, strong, solid, rugged, sturdy ≠ fragile
• **NOUN** = ruffian, bully, thug, hooligan, bruiser (*informal*), roughneck (*slang*), tsotsi (*S. African*)
tour NOUN = journey, expedition, excursion, trip, outing, jaunt, junket
• **VERB 1** = travel round, travel through, journey round, trek round, go on a trip through **2** = visit, explore, go round, inspect, walk round, drive round, sightsee
tourist = traveller, voyager, tripper, globetrotter, holiday-maker, sightseer, excursionist
tournament = competition, meeting, event, series, contest
tow = drag, draw, pull, haul, tug, yank, lug
towards 1 = in the direction of, to, for, on the way to, en route for **2** = regarding, about, concerning, respecting, in relation to, with regard to, with respect to, apropos
tower = column, pillar, turret, belfry, steeple, obelisk
toxic = poisonous, deadly, lethal, harmful, pernicious, noxious, septic, pestilential ≠ harmless
toy NOUN = plaything, game, doll
• **PHRASES toy with something** = play with, consider, trifle with, dally with, entertain the possibility of, amuse yourself with, think idly of
trace VERB 1 = search for, track, unearth, hunt down **2** = find, track (down), discover, detect, unearth, hunt down, ferret out, locate **3** = outline, sketch, draw **4** = copy, map, draft, outline, sketch, reproduce, draw over
• **NOUN 1** = bit, drop, touch, shadow, suggestion, hint, suspicion, tinge **2** = remnant, sign, record, mark, evidence, indication, vestige **3** = track, trail, footstep, path, footprint, spoor, footmark
track NOUN 1 = path, way, road, route, trail, pathway, footpath **2** = course, line, path, orbit, trajectory **3** = line, tramline
• **VERB** = follow, pursue, chase, trace, tail (*informal*), shadow, trail, stalk
• **PHRASES track something** *or* **someone down** = find, discover, trace, unearth, dig up, hunt down, sniff out, run to earth *or* ground
tract[1] = area, region, district, stretch, territory, extent, plot, expanse
tract[2] = treatise, essay, booklet, pamphlet, dissertation, monograph, homily
trade NOUN 1 = commerce, business, transactions, dealing, exchange, traffic, truck, barter **2** = job, employment, business, craft, profession, occupation, line of work, métier
• **VERB 1** = deal, do business, traffic, truck, bargain, peddle, transact, cut a deal **2** = exchange, switch, swap, barter **3** = operate, run, deal, do business
trader = dealer, supplier, merchant, seller, purveyor
tradition 1 = customs, institution, ritual,

folklore, lore, tikanga (*N.Z.*) **2** = established practice, custom, convention, habit, ritual
traditional 1 = old-fashioned, old, established, conventional, usual, accustomed, customary, time-honoured ≠ revolutionary **2** = folk, old
traffic NOUN **1** = transport, vehicles, transportation, freight **2** = trade, commerce, business, exchange, truck, dealings, peddling
• VERB = trade, deal, exchange, bargain, do business, peddle, cut a deal, have dealings
tragedy = disaster, catastrophe, misfortune, adversity, calamity ≠ fortune
tragic 1 = distressing, sad, appalling, deadly, unfortunate, disastrous, dreadful, dire ≠ fortunate **2** = sad, miserable, pathetic, mournful ≠ happy
trail NOUN **1** = path, track, route, way, course, road, pathway, footpath **2** = tracks, path, marks, wake, trace, scent, footprints, spoor **3** = wake, stream, tail
• VERB **1** = follow, track, chase, pursue, dog, hunt, shadow, trace **2** = drag, draw, pull, sweep, haul, tow, dangle, droop **3** = lag, follow, drift, wander, linger, trudge, plod, meander
train VERB **1** = instruct, school, prepare, coach, teach, guide, educate, drill **2** = exercise, prepare, work out, practise, do exercise, get into shape **3** = aim, point, level, position, direct, focus, sight, zero in
• NOUN = sequence, series, chain, string, set, cycle, trail, succession
trainer = coach, manager, guide, adviser, tutor, instructor, counsellor, guru
trait = characteristic, feature, quality, attribute, quirk, peculiarity, mannerism, idiosyncrasy
traitor = betrayer, deserter, turncoat, renegade, defector, Judas, quisling, apostate, fizgig (*Austral. slang*) ≠ loyalist
tramp VERB **1** = trudge, stump, toil, plod, traipse (*informal*) **2** = hike, walk, trek, roam, march, ramble, slog, rove
• NOUN **1** = vagrant, derelict, drifter, down-and-out, derro (*Austral. slang*) **2** = tread, stamp, footstep, footfall **3** = hike, march, trek, ramble, slog
trample *often with* ***on*** = stamp, crush, squash, tread, flatten, run over, walk over
trance = daze, dream, abstraction, rapture, reverie, stupor, unconsciousness
transaction = deal, negotiation, business, enterprise, bargain, undertaking
transcend = surpass, exceed, go beyond, rise above, eclipse, excel, outstrip, outdo
transcript = copy, record, manuscript, reproduction, duplicate, transcription
transfer VERB = move, transport, shift, relocate, transpose, change
• NOUN = transference, move, handover, change, shift, transmission, translation, relocation
transform 1 = change, convert, alter, transmute **2** = make over, remodel, revolutionize
transformation 1 = change, conversion, alteration, metamorphosis, transmutation **2** = revolution, sea change
transit = movement, transfer, transport, passage, crossing, transportation, carriage, conveyance
transition = change, passing, development, shift, conversion, alteration, progression, metamorphosis
transitional 1 = changing, passing, fluid, intermediate, unsettled, developmental **2** = temporary, working, acting, short-term, interim, fill-in, caretaker, provisional
translate = render, put, change, convert, interpret, decode, construe, paraphrase
translation = interpretation, version, rendering, rendition, decoding, paraphrase
transmission 1 = transfer, spread, spreading, passing on, circulation, dispatch, relaying, mediation **2** = broadcasting, showing, putting out, relaying, sending **3** = programme, broadcast, show, production, telecast
transmit 1 = broadcast, televise, relay, air, radio, send out, disseminate, beam out **2** = pass on, carry, spread, send, bear, transfer, hand on, convey
transparent 1 = clear, sheer, see-through, lucid, translucent, crystalline, limpid, diaphanous ≠ opaque **2** = obvious, plain, patent, evident, explicit, manifest, recognizable, unambiguous ≠ uncertain
transplant 1 = implant, transfer, graft **2** = transfer, take, bring, carry, remove, transport, shift, convey
transport NOUN **1** = vehicle, transportation, conveyance **2** = transference, carrying, delivery, distribution, transportation, shipment, freight, haulage **3** *often plural* = ecstasy,

delight, heaven, bliss, euphoria, rapture, enchantment, ravishment ≠ despondency
• VERB 1 = convey, take, move, bring, send, carry, bear, transfer 2 = enrapture, move, delight, entrance, enchant, captivate, ravish 3 (*History*) = exile, banish, deport

trap NOUN 1 = snare, net, gin, pitfall, noose 2 = ambush, set-up (*informal*) 3 = trick, set-up (*informal*), deception, ploy, ruse, trickery, subterfuge, stratagem
• VERB 1 = catch, snare, ensnare, entrap, take, corner, bag, lay hold of 2 = trick, fool, cheat, lure, seduce, deceive, dupe, beguile 3 = capture, catch, arrest, seize, take, secure, collar (*informal*), apprehend

trash 1 = nonsense, rubbish, rot, drivel, twaddle, tripe (*informal*), moonshine, hogwash, kak (*S. African taboo slang*), bizzo (*Austral. slang*), bull's wool (*Austral. & N.Z. slang*) ≠ sense 2 (*Chiefly U.S. & Canad.*) = litter, refuse, waste, rubbish, junk (*informal*), garbage, dross

trauma 1 = shock, suffering, pain, torture, ordeal, anguish 2 = injury, damage, hurt, wound, agony

traumatic = shocking, upsetting, alarming, awful, disturbing, devastating, painful, distressing ≠ calming

travel VERB = go, journey, move, tour, progress, wander, trek, voyage
• NOUN *usually plural* = journey, wandering, expedition, globetrotting, tour, trip, voyage, excursion

traveller or (*U.S.*) **traveler** = voyager, tourist, explorer, globetrotter, holiday-maker, wayfarer

tread VERB = step, walk, march, pace, stamp, stride, hike
• NOUN = step, walk, pace, stride, footstep, gait, footfall

treason = disloyalty, mutiny, treachery, duplicity, sedition, perfidy, lese-majesty, traitorousness ≠ loyalty

treasure NOUN 1 = riches, money, gold, fortune, wealth, valuables, jewels, cash 2 (*Informal*) = angel, darling, jewel, gem, paragon, nonpareil
• VERB = prize, value, esteem, adore, cherish, revere, hold dear, love

treasury = storehouse, bank, store, vault, hoard, cache, repository

treat VERB 1 = behave towards, deal with, handle, act towards, use, consider, serve, manage 2 = take care of, minister to, attend to, give medical treatment to, doctor (*informal*), nurse, care for, prescribe medicine for 3 = provide, stand (*informal*), entertain, lay on, regale
• NOUN 1 = entertainment, party, surprise, gift, celebration, feast, outing, excursion 2 = pleasure, delight, joy, thrill, satisfaction, enjoyment, source of pleasure, fun

treatment 1 = care, medical care, nursing, medicine, surgery, therapy, healing, medication 2 = cure, remedy, medication, medicine 3 *often with* ***of*** = handling, dealings with, behaviour towards, conduct towards, management, manipulation, action towards

treaty = agreement, pact, contract, alliance, convention, compact, covenant, entente

trek VERB 1 = journey, march, hike, tramp, rove, go walkabout (*Austral.*) 2 = trudge, traipse (*informal*), footslog, slog
• NOUN 1 = slog, tramp 2 = journey, hike, expedition, safari, march, odyssey

tremble VERB 1 = shake, shiver, quake, shudder, quiver, totter 2 = vibrate, shake, quake, wobble
• NOUN = shake, shiver, quake, shudder, wobble, tremor, quiver, vibration

tremendous 1 = huge, great, enormous, terrific, formidable, immense, gigantic, colossal ≠ tiny 2 = excellent, great, wonderful, brilliant, amazing, extraordinary, fantastic (*informal*), marvellous, booshit (*Austral. slang*), exo (*Austral. slang*), sik (*Austral. slang*) ≠ terrible

trench = ditch, channel, drain, gutter, trough, furrow, excavation

trend 1 = tendency, swing, drift, inclination, current, direction, flow, leaning 2 = fashion, craze, fad (*informal*), mode, thing, style, rage, vogue

trendy (*Brit. informal*) = fashionable, with it (*informal*), stylish, in fashion, in vogue, modish, voguish

trial 1 (*Law*) = hearing, case, court case, inquiry, tribunal, lawsuit, appeal, litigation 2 = test, experiment, evaluation, audition, dry run (*informal*), assessment, probation, appraisal 3 = hardship, suffering, trouble, distress, ordeal, adversity, affliction, tribulation

tribe = race, people, family, clan, hapu (*N.Z.*), iwi (*N.Z.*)

tribunal = hearing, court, trial
tribute = accolade, testimonial, eulogy, recognition, compliment, commendation, panegyric ≠ criticism
trick NOUN 1 = joke, stunt, spoof (*informal*), prank, practical joke, antic, jape, leg-pull (*Brit. informal*) 2 = deception, trap, fraud, manoeuvre, ploy, hoax, swindle, ruse 3 = sleight of hand, stunt, legerdemain 4 = secret, skill, knack, hang (*informal*), technique, know-how (*informal*) 5 = mannerism, habit, characteristic, trait, quirk, peculiarity, foible, idiosyncrasy • VERB = deceive, trap, take someone in (*informal*), fool, cheat, con (*informal*), kid (*informal*), mislead
trickle VERB = dribble, run, drop, stream, drip, ooze, seep, exude • NOUN = dribble, drip, seepage, thin stream
tricky 1 = difficult, sensitive, complicated, delicate, risky, hairy (*informal*), problematic, thorny ≠ simple 2 = crafty, scheming, cunning, slippery, sly, devious, wily, artful ≠ open
trifle = knick-knack, toy, plaything, bauble, bagatelle
trifling = insignificant, trivial, worthless, negligible, unimportant, paltry, measly ≠ significant
trigger = bring about, start, cause, produce, generate, prompt, provoke, set off ≠ prevent
trim ADJECTIVE 1 = neat, smart, tidy, spruce, dapper, natty (*informal*), well-groomed, shipshape ≠ untidy 2 = slender, fit, slim, sleek, streamlined, shapely, svelte, willowy • VERB 1 = cut, crop, clip, shave, tidy, prune, pare, even up 2 = decorate, dress, array, adorn, ornament, embellish, deck out, beautify • NOUN 1 = decoration, edging, border, piping, trimming, frill, embellishment, adornment 2 = condition, health, shape (*informal*), fitness, wellness, fettle 3 = cut, crop, clipping, shave, pruning, shearing, tidying up
trimming NOUN = decoration, edging, border, piping, frill, embellishment, adornment, ornamentation • PLURAL NOUN = extras, accessories, ornaments, accompaniments, frills, trappings, paraphernalia
trinity = threesome, trio, triad, triumvirate
trio = threesome, trinity, trilogy, triad, triumvirate
trip NOUN 1 = journey, outing, excursion, day out, run, drive, tour, spin (*informal*) 2 = stumble, fall, slip, misstep • VERB 1 = stumble, fall, fall over, slip, tumble, topple, stagger, misstep 2 = skip, dance, hop, gambol • PHRASES **trip someone up** = catch out, trap, wrongfoot
triple ADJECTIVE 1 = treble, three times 2 = three-way, threefold, tripartite • VERB = treble, increase threefold
triumph NOUN 1 = success, victory, accomplishment, achievement, coup, feat, conquest, attainment ≠ failure 2 = joy, pride, happiness, rejoicing, elation, jubilation, exultation • VERB 1 *often with* ***over*** = succeed, win, overcome, prevail, prosper, vanquish ≠ fail 2 = rejoice, celebrate, glory, revel, gloat, exult, crow
triumphant 1 = victorious, winning, successful, conquering ≠ defeated 2 = celebratory, jubilant, proud, elated, exultant, cock-a-hoop
trivial = unimportant, small, minor, petty, meaningless, worthless, trifling, insignificant ≠ important
troop NOUN = group, company, team, body, unit, band, crowd, squad • PLURAL NOUN = soldiers, men, armed forces, servicemen, army, soldiery • VERB = flock, march, stream, swarm, throng, traipse (*informal*)
trophy 1 = prize, cup, award, laurels 2 = souvenir, spoils, relic, memento, booty, keepsake
tropical = hot, stifling, steamy, torrid, sultry, sweltering ≠ cold
trot VERB = run, jog, scamper, lope, canter • NOUN = run, jog, lope, canter
trouble NOUN 1 = bother, problems, concern, worry, stress, difficulty (*informal*), anxiety, distress 2 *usually plural* = distress, problem, worry, pain, anxiety, grief, torment, sorrow ≠ pleasure 3 = ailment, disease, failure, complaint, illness, disorder, defect, malfunction 4 = disorder, fighting, conflict, bother, unrest, disturbance, to-do (*informal*), furore, biffo (*Austral. slang*) ≠ peace 5 = effort, work, thought, care, labour, pains, hassle (*informal*), inconvenience ≠ convenience

• **VERB 1** = bother, worry, upset, disturb, distress, plague, pain, sadden ≠ please **2** = afflict, hurt, bother, cause discomfort to, pain, grieve **3** = inconvenience, disturb, burden, put out, impose upon, incommode ≠ relieve **4** = take pains, take the time, make an effort, exert yourself ≠ avoid

troublesome 1 = bothersome, trying, taxing, demanding, difficult, worrying, annoying, tricky ≠ simple **2** = disorderly, violent, turbulent, rebellious, unruly, rowdy, undisciplined, uncooperative ≠ well-behaved

trough = manger, water trough

truce = ceasefire, peace, moratorium, respite, lull, cessation, let-up (*informal*), armistice

true 1 = correct, right, accurate, precise, factual, truthful, veracious ≠ false **2** = actual, real, genuine, proper, authentic, dinkum (*Austral. & N.Z. informal*) **3** = faithful, loyal, devoted, dedicated, steady, reliable, staunch, trustworthy ≠ unfaithful **4** = exact, perfect, accurate, precise, spot-on (*Brit. informal*), on target, unerring ≠ inaccurate

truly 1 = genuinely, correctly, truthfully, rightly, precisely, exactly, legitimately, authentically ≠ falsely **2** = really, very, greatly, indeed, extremely **3** = faithfully, steadily, sincerely, staunchly, dutifully, loyally, devotedly

trumpet NOUN = horn, clarion, bugle
• **VERB** = proclaim, advertise, tout (*informal*), announce, broadcast, shout from the rooftops ≠ keep secret

trunk 1 = stem, stalk, bole **2** = chest, case, box, crate, coffer, casket **3** = body, torso **4** = snout, nose, proboscis

trust VERB 1 = believe in, have faith in, depend on, count on, bank on, rely upon ≠ distrust **2** = entrust, commit, assign, confide, consign, put into the hands of, allow to look after, hand over **3** = expect, hope, suppose, assume, presume, surmise
• **NOUN** = confidence, credit, belief, faith, expectation, conviction, assurance, certainty ≠ distrust

trusting *or* **trustful** = unsuspecting, naive, gullible, unwary, credulous, unsuspicious ≠ suspicious

truth 1 = reality, fact(s), real life **2** = truthfulness, fact, accuracy, precision, validity, legitimacy, veracity, genuineness ≠ inaccuracy

try VERB 1 = attempt, seek, aim, strive, struggle, endeavour, have a go, make an effort **2** = experiment with, try out, put to the test, test, taste, examine, investigate, sample
• **NOUN** = attempt, go (*informal*), shot (*informal*), effort, crack (*informal*), stab (*informal*), bash (*informal*), whack (*informal*)

trying = annoying, hard, taxing, difficult, tough, stressful, exasperating, tiresome ≠ straightforward

tuck VERB = push, stick, stuff, slip, ease, insert, pop (*informal*)
• **NOUN 1** (*Brit. informal*) = food, grub (*slang*), kai (*N.Z. informal*), nosh (*slang*) **2** = fold, gather, pleat, pinch

tug VERB 1 = pull, pluck, jerk, yank, wrench **2** = drag, pull, haul, tow, lug, heave, draw
• **NOUN** = pull, jerk, yank

tuition = training, schooling, education, teaching, lessons, instruction, tutoring, tutelage

tumble VERB = fall, drop, topple, plummet, stumble, flop
• **NOUN** = fall, drop, trip, plunge, spill, stumble

tumour = growth, cancer, swelling, lump, carcinoma (*Pathology*), sarcoma (*Medical*)

tune NOUN 1 = melody, air, song, theme, strain(s), jingle, ditty **2** = harmony, pitch, euphony
• **VERB 1** = tune up, adjust **2** = regulate, adapt, modulate, harmonize, attune, pitch

tunnel NOUN = passage, underpass, passageway, subway, channel, hole, shaft
• **VERB** = dig, burrow, mine, bore, drill, excavate

turbulent = stormy, rough, raging, tempestuous, furious, foaming, agitated, tumultuous ≠ calm

turf NOUN 1 = grass, sward **2** = sod
• **PHRASES the turf** = horse-racing, the flat, racing

turmoil = confusion, disorder, chaos, upheaval, disarray, uproar, agitation, commotion ≠ peace

turn VERB 1 = change course, swing round, wheel round, veer, move, switch, shift, swerve **2** = rotate, spin, go round (and round), revolve, roll, circle, twist, spiral **3** = change, transform, shape, convert,

alter, mould, remodel, mutate **4** = shape, form, fashion, cast, frame, mould, make **5** = go bad, go off (*Brit. informal*), curdle **6** = make rancid, spoil, sour, taint
• NOUN **1** = rotation, cycle, circle, revolution, spin, twist, whirl, swivel **2** = change of direction, shift, departure, deviation **3** = direction, course, tack, tendency, drift **4** = opportunity, go, time, try, chance, crack (*informal*), stint **5** = deed, service, act, action, favour, gesture
• PHRASES **turn on someone** = attack, assault, fall on, round on, lash out at, assail, lay into (*informal*), let fly at ◆ **turn someone on** (*Informal*) = arouse, attract, excite, thrill, stimulate, please, titillate ◆ **turn something down 1** = refuse, decline, reject, spurn, rebuff, repudiate **2** = lower, soften, mute, lessen, muffle, quieten ◆ **turn something in** = hand in, return, deliver, give up, hand over, submit, surrender, tender ◆ **turn something off** = switch off, turn out, put out, stop, cut out, shut down, unplug, flick off ◆ **turn something on** = switch on, activate, start, start up, ignite, kick-start ◆ **turn something up 1** = find, reveal, discover, expose, disclose, unearth, dig up **2** = increase, raise, boost, enhance, intensify, amplify ◆ **turn up 1** = arrive, come, appear, show up (*informal*), attend, put in an appearance, show your face **2** = come to light, show up, pop up, materialize

turning = turn-off, turn, bend, curve, junction, crossroads, side road, exit

turning point = crossroads, change, crisis, crux, moment of truth

turnout = attendance, crowd, audience, gate, assembly, congregation, number, throng

turnover 1 = output, business, productivity **2** = movement, coming and going, change

tutor NOUN = teacher, coach, instructor, educator, guide, guardian, lecturer, guru
• VERB = teach, educate, school, train, coach, guide, drill, instruct

twig = branch, stick, sprig, shoot, spray

twilight 1 = dusk, evening, sunset, early evening, nightfall, sundown, gloaming (*Scot. poetic*), close of day, evo (*Austral. slang*) ≠ dawn **2** = half-light, gloom, dimness, semi-darkness

twin NOUN = double, counterpart, mate, match, fellow, clone, duplicate, lookalike
• VERB = pair, match, join, couple, link, yoke

twinkle VERB = sparkle, flash, shine, glitter, gleam, blink, flicker, shimmer
• NOUN = sparkle, flash, spark, gleam, flicker, shimmer, glimmer

twist VERB **1** = coil, curl, wind, wrap, screw, twirl **2** = intertwine **3** = distort, screw up, contort, mangle, mangulate (*Austral. slang*) ≠ straighten
• NOUN **1** = surprise, change, turn, development, revelation **2** = development, emphasis, variation, slant **3** = wind, turn, spin, swivel, twirl **4** = curve, turn, bend, loop, arc, kink, zigzag, dog-leg

twitch VERB **1** = jerk, flutter, jump, squirm **2** = pull (at), tug (at), pluck (at), yank (at)
• NOUN = jerk, tic, spasm, jump, flutter

tycoon = magnate, capitalist, baron, industrialist, financier, fat cat (*slang, chiefly U.S.*), mogul, plutocrat

type = kind, sort, class, variety, group, order, style, species

typical 1 = archetypal, standard, model, normal, stock, representative, usual, regular ≠ unusual **2** = characteristic **3** = average, normal, usual, routine, regular, orthodox, predictable, run-of-the-mill

tyranny = oppression, cruelty, dictatorship, authoritarianism, despotism, autocracy, absolutism, high-handedness ≠ liberality

u

ubiquitous = ever-present, pervasive, omnipresent, everywhere, universal

ugly 1 = unattractive, homely (*chiefly U.S.*), plain, unsightly, unlovely, unprepossessing, ill-favoured ≠ beautiful **2** = unpleasant, shocking, terrible, nasty, distasteful, horrid, objectionable, disagreeable ≠ pleasant **3** = bad-

tempered, dangerous, menacing, sinister, baleful
ulcer = sore, abscess, peptic ulcer, gumboil
ultimate 1 = final, last, end 2 = supreme, highest, greatest, paramount, superlative 3 = worst, greatest, utmost, extreme 4 = best, greatest, supreme, optimum, quintessential
ultimately 1 = finally, eventually, in the end, after all, at last, sooner or later, in due time 2 = fundamentally, essentially, basically, primarily, at heart, deep down
umpire NOUN = referee, judge, arbiter, arbitrator
• VERB = referee, judge, adjudicate, arbitrate
unable = incapable, powerless, unfit, impotent, unqualified, ineffectual ≠ able
unanimous 1 = agreed, united, in agreement, harmonious, like-minded, of the same mind ≠ divided 2 = united, common, concerted, solid, consistent, harmonious, undivided, congruent ≠ split
unarmed = defenceless, helpless, unprotected ≠ armed
unaware = ignorant, unconscious, oblivious, uninformed, unknowing, not in the loop (*informal*) ≠ aware
unbearable = intolerable, insufferable, too much (*informal*), unacceptable ≠ tolerable
unborn = expected, awaited, embryonic
uncertain = unsure, undecided, vague, unclear, dubious, hazy, irresolute ≠ sure
uncertainty 1 = unpredictability, precariousness, ambiguity, unreliability, fickleness, chanciness, changeableness ≠ predictability 2 = doubt, confusion ≠ confidence 3 = hesitancy, indecision
uncomfortable 1 = uneasy, troubled, disturbed, embarrassed, awkward, discomfited ≠ comfortable 2 = painful, awkward, rough
uncommon 1 = rare, unusual, odd, novel, strange, peculiar, scarce, queer ≠ common 2 = extraordinary, remarkable, special, outstanding, distinctive, exceptional, notable ≠ ordinary
uncompromising = inflexible, strict, rigid, firm, tough, inexorable, intransigent, unbending
unconditional = absolute, full, complete, total, positive, entire, outright, unlimited ≠ qualified
unconscious 1 = senseless, knocked out, out cold (*informal*), out, stunned, dazed, in a coma, stupefied ≠ awake 2 = unaware, ignorant, oblivious, unknowing ≠ aware 3 = unintentional, unwitting, inadvertent, accidental ≠ intentional
uncover 1 = reveal, expose, disclose, divulge, make known ≠ conceal 2 = open, unveil, unwrap, show, strip, expose, bare, lay bare
under PREPOSITION 1 = below, beneath, underneath ≠ over 2 = subordinate to, subject to, governed by, secondary to
• ADVERB = below, down, beneath ≠ up
undercover = secret, covert, private, hidden, concealed ≠ open
underdog = weaker party, little fellow (*informal*), outsider
underestimate 1 = undervalue, understate, diminish, play down, minimize, downgrade, miscalculate, trivialize ≠ overestimate 2 = underrate, undervalue, belittle ≠ overrate
undergo = experience, go through, stand, suffer, bear, sustain, endure
underground ADJECTIVE 1 = subterranean, basement, lower-level, sunken, covered, buried, subterrestrial 2 = secret, covert, hidden, guerrilla, revolutionary, confidential, dissident, closet
• PHRASES **the underground** 1 = the tube (*Brit.*), the subway, the metro 2 = the Resistance, partisans, freedom fighters
underline 1 = emphasize, stress, highlight, accentuate ≠ minimize 2 = underscore, mark
underlying = fundamental, basic, prime, primary, elementary, intrinsic
undermine = weaken, sabotage, subvert, compromise, disable ≠ reinforce
understand 1 = comprehend, get, take in, perceive, grasp, see, follow, realize 2 = believe, gather, think, see, suppose, notice, assume, fancy
understandable = reasonable, natural, justified, expected, inevitable, legitimate, predictable, accountable
understanding NOUN 1 = perception, knowledge, grasp, sense, know-how (*informal*), judgment, awareness, appreciation ≠ ignorance 2 = agreement, deal, promise, arrangement, accord, contract, bond, pledge ≠ disagreement

3 = belief, view, opinion, impression, interpretation, feeling, idea, notion
• ADJECTIVE = sympathetic, kind, compassionate, considerate, patient, sensitive, tolerant ≠ unsympathetic

undertake = agree, promise, contract, guarantee, engage, pledge

undertaking 1 = task, business, operation, project, attempt, effort, affair, venture **2** = promise, commitment, pledge, word, vow, assurance

underwear = underclothes, lingerie, undies (*informal*), undergarments, underthings, broekies (*S. African informal*), underdaks (*Austral. slang*)

underworld 1 = criminals, gangsters, organized crime, gangland (*informal*) **2** = nether world, Hades, nether regions

underwrite = finance, back, fund, guarantee, sponsor, insure, ratify, subsidize

undesirable = unwanted, unwelcome, disagreeable, objectionable, unacceptable, unsuitable, unattractive, distasteful ≠ desirable

undo 1 = open, unfasten, loose, untie, unbutton, disentangle **2** = reverse, cancel, offset, neutralize, invalidate, annul **3** = ruin, defeat, destroy, wreck, shatter, upset, undermine, overturn

undone = unfinished, left, neglected, omitted, unfulfilled, unperformed ≠ finished

undoubtedly = certainly, definitely, surely, doubtless, without doubt, assuredly

unearth 1 = discover, find, reveal, expose, uncover **2** = dig up, excavate, exhume, dredge up

unearthly = eerie, strange, supernatural, ghostly, weird, phantom, uncanny, spooky (*informal*)

uneasy 1 = anxious, worried, troubled, nervous, disturbed, uncomfortable, edgy, perturbed ≠ relaxed **2** = precarious, strained, uncomfortable, tense, awkward, shaky, insecure

unemployed = out of work, redundant, laid off, jobless, idle ≠ working

unfair 1 = biased, prejudiced, unjust, one-sided, partial, partisan, bigoted **2** = unscrupulous, dishonest, unethical, wrongful, unsporting ≠ ethical

unfit 1 = out of shape, feeble, unhealthy, flabby, in poor condition ≠ healthy **2** = incapable, inadequate, incompetent, no good, useless, unqualified ≠ capable **3** = unsuitable, inadequate, useless, unsuited ≠ suitable

unfold 1 = reveal, tell, present, show, disclose, uncover, divulge, make known **2** = open, spread out, undo, expand, unfurl, unwrap, unroll

unfortunate 1 = disastrous, calamitous, adverse, ill-fated ≠ opportune **2** = regrettable, deplorable, lamentable, unsuitable, unbecoming ≠ becoming **3** = unlucky, unhappy, doomed, cursed, unsuccessful, hapless, wretched ≠ fortunate

unhappy 1 = sad, depressed, miserable, blue, melancholy, mournful, dejected, despondent ≠ happy **2** = unlucky, unfortunate, hapless, cursed, wretched, ill-fated ≠ fortunate

unhealthy 1 = harmful, detrimental, unwholesome, insanitary, insalubrious ≠ beneficial **2** = sick, sickly, unwell, delicate, crook (*Austral. & N.Z. informal*), ailing, frail, feeble, invalid ≠ well **3** = weak, ailing ≠ strong

unification = union, uniting, alliance, coalition, federation, confederation, amalgamation, coalescence

uniform NOUN **1** = regalia, suit, livery, colours, habit **2** = outfit, dress, costume, attire, gear (*informal*), get-up (*informal*), ensemble, garb
• ADJECTIVE **1** = consistent, unvarying, similar, even, same, matching, regular, constant ≠ varying **2** = alike, similar, like, same, equal

unify = unite, join, combine, merge, consolidate, confederate, amalgamate ≠ divide

union 1 = joining, uniting, unification, combination, coalition, merger, mixture, blend **2** = alliance, league, association, coalition, federation, confederacy

unique 1 = distinct, special, exclusive, peculiar, only, single, lone, solitary **2** = unparalleled, unmatched, unequalled, matchless, without equal

unit 1 = entity, whole, item, feature **2** = section, company, group, force, detail, division, cell, squad **3** = measure, quantity, measurement **4** = part, section, segment, class, element, component, constituent, tutorial

unite 1 = join, link, combine, couple, blend, merge, unify, fuse ≠ separate 2 = cooperate, ally, join forces, band, pool, collaborate ≠ split

unity 1 = union, unification, coalition, federation, integration, confederation, amalgamation 2 = wholeness, integrity, oneness, union, entity, singleness ≠ disunity 3 = agreement, accord, consensus, harmony, solidarity, unison, assent, concord ≠ disagreement

universal 1 = widespread, general, common, whole, total, unlimited, overarching 2 = global, worldwide, international, pandemic

universally = without exception, everywhere, always, invariably

universe = cosmos, space, creation, nature, heavens, macrocosm, all existence

unknown 1 = strange, new, undiscovered, uncharted, unexplored, virgin, remote, alien 2 = unidentified, mysterious, anonymous, unnamed, nameless, incognito 3 = obscure, humble, unfamiliar ≠ famous

unlike 1 = different from, dissimilar to, distinct from, unequal to ≠ similar to 2 = contrasted with, not like, in contradiction to, in contrast with *or* to, as opposed to, differently from, opposite to

unlikely 1 = improbable, doubtful, remote, slight, faint ≠ probable 2 = unbelievable, incredible, implausible, questionable ≠ believable

unload 1 = empty, clear, unpack, dump, discharge 2 = unburden

unnatural 1 = abnormal, odd, strange, unusual, extraordinary, perverted, queer, irregular ≠ normal 2 = false, forced, artificial, affected, stiff, feigned, stilted, insincere ≠ genuine

unpleasant 1 = nasty, bad, horrid, distasteful, displeasing, objectionable, disagreeable ≠ nice 2 = obnoxious, rude ≠ likable *or* likeable

unravel 1 = solve, explain, work out, resolve, figure out (*informal*) 2 = undo, separate, disentangle, free, unwind, untangle

unrest = discontent, rebellion, protest, strife, agitation, discord, sedition, dissension ≠ peace

unsettled 1 = unstable, shaky, insecure, disorderly, unsteady 2 = restless, tense, shaken, confused, disturbed, anxious, agitated, flustered 3 = inconstant, changing, variable, uncertain

unstable 1 = changeable, volatile, unpredictable, variable, fluctuating, fitful, inconstant ≠ constant 2 = insecure, shaky, precarious, unsettled, wobbly, tottering, unsteady 3 = unpredictable, irrational, erratic, inconsistent, temperamental, capricious, changeable ≠ level-headed

unthinkable 1 = impossible, out of the question, inconceivable, absurd, unreasonable 2 = inconceivable, incredible, unimaginable

untold 1 = indescribable, unthinkable, unimaginable, undreamed of, unutterable, inexpressible 2 = countless, incalculable, innumerable, myriad, numberless, uncountable

untrue 1 = false, lying, wrong, mistaken, incorrect, inaccurate, dishonest, deceptive ≠ true 2 = unfaithful, disloyal, deceitful, treacherous, faithless, false, untrustworthy, inconstant ≠ faithful

unusual 1 = rare, odd, strange, extraordinary, different, curious, queer, uncommon ≠ common 2 = extraordinary, unique, remarkable, exceptional, uncommon, singular, unconventional ≠ average

upbeat (*Informal*) = cheerful, positive, optimistic, encouraging, hopeful, cheery

upbringing = education, training, breeding, rearing, raising

update = bring up to date, improve, correct, renew, revise, upgrade, amend, overhaul

upgrade 1 = improve, better, update, reform, add to, enhance, refurbish, renovate 2 = promote, raise, advance, boost, move up, elevate, kick upstairs (*informal*), give promotion to ≠ demote

upheaval = disturbance, revolution, disorder, turmoil, disruption

uphill 1 = ascending, rising, upward, mounting, climbing ≠ descending 2 = arduous, hard, taxing, difficult, tough, exhausting, gruelling, strenuous

uphold 1 = support, back, defend, aid, champion, maintain, promote, sustain 2 = confirm, endorse

uplift VERB = improve, better, raise, advance, inspire, refine, edify • NOUN = improvement, enlightenment, advancement, refinement, enhancement, enrichment, edification

upper 1 = topmost, top ≠ bottom 2 = higher, high ≠ lower 3 = superior, senior, higher-level, greater, top, important, chief, most important ≠ inferior

upper class = aristocratic, upper-class, noble, high-class, patrician, blue-blooded, highborn

upright 1 = vertical, straight, standing up, erect, perpendicular, bolt upright ≠ horizontal 2 = honest, good, principled, just, ethical, honourable, righteous, conscientious ≠ dishonourable

uprising = rebellion, rising, revolution, revolt, disturbance, mutiny, insurrection, insurgence

uproar 1 = commotion, noise, racket, riot, turmoil, mayhem, din, pandemonium 2 = protest, outrage, complaint, objection, fuss, stink (*informal*), outcry, furore

upset ADJECTIVE 1 = distressed, shaken, disturbed, worried, troubled, hurt, bothered, unhappy 2 = sick, queasy, bad, ill 3 = overturned, upside down, capsized, spilled
• VERB 1 = distress, trouble, disturb, worry, alarm, bother, grieve, agitate 2 = tip over, overturn, capsize, knock over, spill 3 = mess up, spoil, disturb, change, confuse, disorder, unsettle, disorganize
• NOUN 1 = distress, worry, trouble, shock, bother, disturbance, agitation 2 = reversal, shake-up (*informal*), defeat 3 = illness, complaint, disorder, bug (*informal*), sickness, malady

upside down *or* **upside-down** ADVERB = wrong side up
• ADJECTIVE 1 = inverted, overturned, upturned 2 (*Informal*) = confused, disordered, chaotic, muddled, topsy-turvy, higgledy-piggledy (*informal*)

up-to-date = modern, fashionable, trendy (*Brit. informal*), current, stylish, in vogue, up-to-the-minute ≠ out of date

urban = civic, city, town, metropolitan, municipal, dorp (*S. African*)

urge VERB 1 = beg, exhort, plead, implore, beseech, entreat 2 = advocate, recommend, advise, support, counsel ≠ discourage
• NOUN = impulse, longing, wish, desire, drive, yearning, itch (*informal*), thirst ≠ reluctance

urgency = importance, need, necessity, gravity, pressure, hurry, seriousness, extremity

urgent = crucial, desperate, pressing, great, important, crying, critical, immediate ≠ unimportant

usage 1 = use, operation, employment, running, control, management, handling 2 = practice, method, procedure, habit, regime, custom, routine, convention

use VERB 1 = employ, utilize, work, apply, operate, exercise, practise, resort to 2 *sometimes with* ***up*** = consume, exhaust, spend, run through, expend 3 = take advantage of, exploit, manipulate
• NOUN 1 = usage, employment, operation, application 2 = purpose, end, reason, object 3 = good, point, help, service, value, benefit, profit, advantage

used = second-hand, cast-off, nearly new, shopsoiled ≠ new

used to = accustomed to, familiar with

useful = helpful, effective, valuable, practical, profitable, worthwhile, beneficial, fruitful ≠ useless

useless 1 = worthless, valueless, impractical, fruitless, unproductive, ineffectual, unsuitable ≠ useful 2 = pointless, futile, vain ≠ worthwhile 3 (*Informal*) = inept, no good, hopeless, incompetent, ineffectual

usher VERB = escort, lead, direct, guide, conduct
• NOUN = attendant, guide, doorman, escort, doorkeeper

usual = normal, customary, regular, general, common, standard, ordinary, typical ≠ unusual

usually = normally, generally, mainly, commonly, mostly, on the whole, as a rule, habitually

utility = usefulness, benefit, convenience, practicality, efficacy, serviceableness

utilize = use, employ, deploy, take advantage of, make use of, put to use, bring into play, avail yourself of

utmost ADJECTIVE 1 = greatest, highest, maximum, supreme, paramount, pre-eminent 2 = farthest, extreme, last, final
• NOUN = best, greatest, maximum, highest, hardest

utter[1] = say, state, speak, voice, express, deliver, declare, mouth

utter[2] = absolute, complete, total,

sheer, outright, thorough, downright, unmitigated

utterly = totally, completely, absolutely, perfectly, fully, entirely, extremely, thoroughly

V

vacancy 1 = opening, job, post, place, position, role, situation, opportunity **2** = room, space, available accommodation, unoccupied room

vacant 1 = empty, free, available, abandoned, deserted, for sale, on the market, void ≠ occupied **2** = unfilled, unoccupied ≠ taken **3** = blank, vague, dreamy, empty, abstracted, idle, vacuous, inane ≠ thoughtful

vacuum 1 = gap, lack, absence, space, deficiency, void **2** = emptiness, space, void, gap, nothingness, vacuity

vague 1 = unclear, indefinite, hazy, confused, loose, uncertain, unsure, superficial ≠ clear **2** = imprecise, unspecified, generalized, rough, loose, ambiguous, hazy, equivocal **3** = absent-minded, distracted, vacant, preoccupied, oblivious, inattentive **4** = indistinct, unclear, faint, hazy, indeterminate, nebulous, ill-defined ≠ distinct

vain ADJECTIVE **1** = futile, useless, pointless, unsuccessful, idle, worthless, senseless, fruitless ≠ successful **2** = conceited, narcissistic, proud, arrogant, swaggering, egotistical, self-important ≠ modest
• PHRASES **in vain 1** = useless, to no avail, unsuccessful, fruitless, vain **2** = uselessly, to no avail, unsuccessfully, fruitlessly, vainly, ineffectually

valid 1 = sound, good, reasonable, telling, convincing, rational, logical, viable ≠ unfounded **2** = legal, official, legitimate, genuine, authentic, lawful, bona fide ≠ invalid

validity 1 = soundness, force, power, weight, strength, cogency **2** = legality, authority, legitimacy, right, lawfulness

valley = hollow, dale, glen, vale, depression, dell

valuable ADJECTIVE **1** = useful, important, profitable, worthwhile, beneficial, helpful ≠ useless **2** = treasured, prized, precious **3** = precious, expensive, costly, dear, high-priced, priceless, irreplaceable ≠ worthless
• PLURAL NOUN = treasures, prized possessions, precious items, heirlooms, personal effects, costly article

value NOUN **1** = importance, benefit, worth, merit, point, service, sense, profit ≠ worthlessness **2** = cost, price, worth, rate, market price, face value, asking price, selling price
• PLURAL NOUN = principles, morals, ethics, mores, standards of behaviour, (moral) standards
• VERB **1** = appreciate, rate, prize, regard highly, respect, admire, treasure, esteem ≠ undervalue **2** = evaluate, price, estimate, rate, cost, assess, set at, appraise

vanish 1 = disappear, dissolve, evaporate, fade away, melt away, evanesce ≠ appear **2** = die out, disappear, pass away, end, fade, dwindle, cease to exist, become extinct

vanity = pride, arrogance, conceit, narcissism, egotism, conceitedness ≠ modesty

variable = changeable, unstable, fluctuating, shifting, flexible, uneven, temperamental, unsteady ≠ constant

variant NOUN = variation, form, version, development, alternative, adaptation, revision, modification
• ADJECTIVE = different, alternative, modified, divergent

variation 1 = alternative, variety, modification, departure, innovation, variant **2** = variety, change, deviation, difference, diversity, diversion, novelty ≠ uniformity

varied = different, mixed, various, diverse, assorted, miscellaneous, sundry, motley ≠ unvarying

variety 1 = diversity, change, variation, difference, diversification, heterogeneity, multifariousness ≠ uniformity **2** = range, selection, assortment, mix, collection, line-up, mixture, array **3** = type, sort, kind, class, brand, species, breed, strain

various 1 = different, assorted, miscellaneous, varied, distinct, diverse, disparate, sundry ≠ similar 2 = many, numerous, countless, several, abundant, innumerable, sundry, profuse

varnish NOUN = lacquer, polish, glaze, gloss
• VERB = lacquer, polish, glaze, gloss

vary 1 = differ, be different, be dissimilar, disagree, diverge 2 = change, shift, swing, alter, fluctuate, oscillate, see-saw 3 = alternate

vast = huge, massive, enormous, great, wide, immense, gigantic, monumental ≠ tiny

vault[1] 1 = strongroom, repository, depository 2 = crypt, tomb, catacomb, cellar, mausoleum, charnel house, undercroft

vault[2] = jump, spring, leap, clear, bound, hurdle

veer = change direction, turn, swerve, shift, sheer, change course

vehicle 1 = conveyance, machine, motor vehicle 2 = medium, means, channel, mechanism, organ, apparatus

veil NOUN 1 = mask, cover, shroud, film, curtain, cloak 2 = screen, mask, disguise, blind 3 = film, cover, curtain, cloak, shroud
• VERB = cover, screen, hide, mask, shield, disguise, conceal, obscure ≠ reveal

veiled = disguised, implied, hinted at, covert, masked, concealed, suppressed

vein 1 = blood vessel 2 = mood, style, note, tone, mode, temper, tenor 3 = seam, layer, stratum, course, current, bed, deposit, streak

velocity = speed, pace, rapidity, quickness, swiftness

vengeance = revenge, retaliation, reprisal, retribution, requital ≠ forgiveness

vent NOUN = outlet, opening, aperture, duct, orifice
• VERB = express, release, voice, air, discharge, utter, emit, pour out ≠ hold back

venture NOUN = undertaking, project, enterprise, campaign, risk, operation, activity, scheme
• VERB 1 = go, travel, journey, set out, wander, stray, plunge into, rove 2 = dare, presume, have the courage to, be brave enough, hazard, go out on a limb (*informal*), take the liberty, go so far as 3 = put forward, volunteer

verbal = spoken, oral, word-of-mouth, unwritten

verdict = decision, finding, judgment, opinion, sentence, conclusion, conviction, adjudication

verge NOUN 1 = brink, point, edge, threshold 2 = border, edge, margin, limit, boundary, threshold, brim
• PHRASES **verge on something** = come near to, approach, border on, resemble, incline to, be similar to, touch on, be more or less

verify 1 = check, make sure, examine, monitor, inspect 2 = confirm, prove, substantiate, support, validate, bear out, corroborate, authenticate ≠ disprove

versatile 1 = adaptable, flexible, all-round, resourceful, multifaceted ≠ unadaptable 2 = all-purpose, variable, adjustable ≠ limited

versed = knowledgeable, experienced, seasoned, familiar, practised, acquainted, well-informed, proficient ≠ ignorant

version 1 = form, variety, variant, sort, class, design, style, model 2 = adaptation, edition, interpretation, form, copy, rendering, reproduction, portrayal 3 = account, report, description, record, reading, story, view, understanding

vertical = upright sheer, perpendicular, straight (up and down), erect, plumb, on end, precipitous, vertiginous ≠ horizontal

very ADVERB = extremely, highly, greatly, really, deeply, unusually, profoundly, decidedly
• ADJECTIVE 1 = exact, precise, selfsame 2 = ideal

vessel 1 = ship, boat, craft 2 = container, receptacle, can, bowl, tank, pot, drum, barrel

vest VERB
• PHRASES **vest in something** *or* **someone** *usually passive* = place, invest, entrust, settle, confer, endow, bestow, consign ◆ **vest with something** *usually passive* = endow with, entrust with

vet = check, examine, investigate, review, appraise, scrutinize

veteran NOUN = old hand, past master, warhorse (*informal*), old stager ≠ novice
• ADJECTIVE = long-serving, seasoned, experienced, old, established, qualified, mature, practised

veto VERB = ban, block, reject, rule out, turn down, forbid, boycott, prohibit ≠ pass
• NOUN = ban, dismissal, rejection, vetoing, boycott, embargo, prohibiting, prohibition ≠ ratification

viable = workable, practical, feasible, suitable, realistic, operational, applicable, usable ≠ unworkable

vibrant 1 = energetic, dynamic, sparkling, vivid, spirited, storming, alive, vigorous 2 = vivid, bright, brilliant, intense, clear, rich, glowing

vice 1 = fault, failing, weakness, limitation, defect, deficiency, flaw, shortcoming ≠ good point 2 = wickedness, evil, corruption, sin, depravity, immorality, iniquity, turpitude ≠ virtue

vice versa = the other way round, conversely, in reverse, contrariwise

vicious 1 = savage, brutal, violent, cruel, ferocious, barbarous ≠ gentle 2 = malicious, vindictive, spiteful, mean, cruel, venomous

victim 1 = casualty, sufferer, fatality ≠ survivor 2 = scapegoat, sacrifice, martyr

victor = winner, champion, conqueror, vanquisher, prizewinner ≠ loser

victorious = winning, successful, triumphant, first, champion, conquering, vanquishing, prizewinning ≠ losing

victory = win, success, triumph, conquest, walkover (*informal*) ≠ defeat

vie = compete, struggle, contend, strive

view NOUN 1 *sometimes plural* = opinion, belief, feeling, attitude, impression, conviction, point of view, sentiment 2 = scene, picture, sight, prospect, perspective, landscape, outlook, spectacle 3 = vision, sight, visibility, perspective, eyeshot
• VERB = regard, see, consider, perceive, treat, estimate, reckon, deem

viewer = watcher, observer, spectator, onlooker

vigorous 1 = strenuous, energetic, arduous, hard, taxing, active, rigorous 2 = spirited, lively, energetic, active, dynamic, animated, forceful, feisty (*informal*) ≠ lethargic 3 = strong, powerful, lively, lusty ≠ weak

vigorously 1 = energetically, hard, forcefully, strongly, strenuously, lustily 2 = forcefully, strongly, vehemently, strenuously

vigour *or* (*U.S.*) **vigor** = energy, vitality, power, spirit, strength, animation, verve, gusto ≠ weakness

vile 1 = wicked, evil, corrupt, perverted, degenerate, depraved, nefarious ≠ honourable 2 = disgusting, foul, revolting, offensive, nasty, sickening, horrid, repulsive, yucko (*Austral. slang*) ≠ pleasant

villain 1 = evildoer, criminal, rogue, scoundrel, wretch, reprobate, miscreant, blackguard 2 = baddy (*informal*), antihero ≠ hero

vindicate 1 = clear, acquit, exonerate, absolve, let off the hook, exculpate ≠ condemn 2 = support, defend, excuse, justify

vintage NOUN (always used of wines) = harvest
• ADJECTIVE 1 (always used of wines) = high-quality, best, prime, quality, choice, select, superior 2 = classic, old, veteran, historic, heritage, enduring, antique, timeless

violate 1 = break, infringe, disobey, transgress, ignore, defy, disregard, flout ≠ obey 2 = invade, infringe on, disturb, upset, shatter, disrupt, impinge on, encroach on 3 = desecrate, profane, defile, abuse, pollute, deface, dishonour, vandalize ≠ honour 4 = rape, molest, sexually assault, ravish, abuse, assault, interfere with, sexually abuse

violation 1 = breach, abuse, infringement, contravention, abuse, trespass, transgression, infraction 2 = invasion, intrusion, trespass, breach, disturbance, disruption, interruption, encroachment 3 = desecration, sacrilege, defilement, profanation, spoliation 4 = rape, sexual assault, molesting, ravishing (*old-fashioned*), abuse, sexual abuse, indecent assault, molestation

violence 1 = brutality, bloodshed, savagery, fighting, terrorism 2 = force, power, strength, might, ferocity, forcefulness, powerfulness 3 = intensity, force, cruelty, severity, fervour, vehemence

violent 1 = brutal, aggressive, savage, wild, fierce, bullying, cruel, vicious ≠ gentle 2 = sharp 3 = passionate, uncontrollable, unrestrained 4 = fiery, fierce, passionate

VIP = celebrity, big name, star, somebody, luminary, big hitter (*informal*), heavy

hitter (*informal*)
virgin NOUN = maiden, girl (*archaic*)
• ADJECTIVE = pure, chaste, immaculate, virginal, vestal, uncorrupted, undefiled ≠ corrupted
virtual = practical, essential, in all but name
virtually = practically, almost, nearly, in effect, in essence, as good as, in all but name
virtue 1 = goodness, integrity, worth, morality, righteousness, probity, rectitude, incorruptibility ≠ vice 2 = merit, strength, asset, plus (*informal*), attribute, good point, strong point ≠ failing 3 = advantage, benefit, merit, credit, usefulness, efficacy
visible = perceptible, observable, clear, apparent, evident, manifest, in view, discernible ≠ invisible
vision 1 = image, idea, dream, plans, hopes, prospect, ideal, concept 2 = hallucination, illusion, apparition, revelation, delusion, mirage, chimera 3 = sight, seeing, eyesight, view, perception 4 = foresight, imagination, perception, insight, awareness, inspiration, innovation, creativity
visionary NOUN 1 = idealist, romantic, dreamer, daydreamer ≠ realist 2 = prophet, diviner, mystic, seer, soothsayer, sibyl, scryer, spaewife (*Scot.*)
• ADJECTIVE 1 = idealistic, romantic, unrealistic, utopian, speculative, impractical, unworkable, quixotic ≠ realistic 2 = prophetic, mystical, predictive, oracular, sibylline
visit VERB 1 = call on, drop in on (*informal*), stay at, stay with, stop by, spend time with, look someone up, go see (*U.S.*) 2 = stay in, stop by
• NOUN 1 = call, social call 2 = trip, stop, stay, break, tour, holiday, vacation (*informal*), stopover
visitor = guest, caller, company, manu(w)hiri (*N.Z.*)
vista = view, scene, prospect, landscape, panorama, perspective
visual 1 = optical, optic, ocular 2 = observable, visible, perceptible, discernible ≠ imperceptible
vital 1 = essential, important, necessary, key, basic, significant, critical, crucial ≠ unnecessary 2 = lively, vigorous, energetic, spirited, dynamic, animated, vibrant, vivacious ≠ lethargic
vitality = energy, vivacity, life, strength, animation, vigour, exuberance, liveliness ≠ lethargy
vivid 1 = clear, detailed, realistic, telling, moving, affecting, arresting, powerful ≠ vague 2 = bright, brilliant, intense, clear, rich, glowing, colourful ≠ dull
vocabulary 1 = language, words, lexicon 2 = wordbook, dictionary, glossary, lexicon
vocal 1 = outspoken, frank, forthright, strident, vociferous, articulate, expressive, eloquent ≠ quiet 2 = spoken, voiced, uttered, oral, said
vocation = profession, calling, job, trade, career, mission, pursuit
vogue = fashion, trend, craze, style, mode, passing fancy, dernier cri (*French*)
voice NOUN 1 = tone, sound, articulation 2 = utterance 3 = opinion, will, feeling, wish, desire 4 = say, view, vote, comment, input
• VERB = express, declare, air, raise, reveal, mention, mouth, pronounce

RELATED WORD
adjective: vocal
void NOUN 1 = gap, space, lack, hole, emptiness 2 = emptiness, space, vacuum, oblivion, blankness, nullity, vacuity
• ADJECTIVE = invalid, null and void, inoperative, useless, ineffective, worthless
• VERB = invalidate, nullify, cancel, withdraw, reverse, undo, repeal, quash
volatile 1 = changeable, shifting, variable, unsettled, unstable, explosive, unreliable, unsteady ≠ stable 2 = temperamental, erratic, mercurial, up and down (*informal*), fickle, over-emotional ≠ calm
volley = barrage, blast, burst, shower, hail, bombardment, salvo, fusillade
volume 1 = amount, quantity, level, body, total, measure, degree, mass 2 = capacity, size, mass, extent, proportions, dimensions, bulk, measurements 3 = book, work, title, opus, publication, manual, tome, treatise 4 = loudness, sound, amplification
voluntarily = willingly, freely, by choice, off your own bat, of your own accord, of your own volition
voluntary 1 = intentional, deliberate, planned, calculated, wilful ≠ unintentional 2 = optional, discretionary, up to the

individual, open, unforced, at your discretion, open to choice ≠ obligatory **3** = unpaid, free, willing, pro bono (*Law*)

volunteer = offer, step forward ≠ refuse

vomit 1 = be sick, throw up (*informal*), spew, chuck (*Austral. & N.Z. informal*), heave (*slang*), retch **2** *often with* **up** = bring up, throw up, regurgitate, emit (*informal*), disgorge, spew out *or* up

vote NOUN = poll, election, ballot, referendum, popular vote, plebiscite, straw poll, show of hands
• VERB = cast your vote

voucher = ticket, token, coupon, pass, slip, chit, chitty (*Brit. informal*), docket

vow VERB = promise, pledge, swear, commit, engage, affirm, avow, bind yourself
• NOUN = promise, commitment, pledge, oath, profession, avowal

voyage NOUN = journey, trip, passage, expedition, crossing, sail, cruise, excursion
• VERB = travel, journey, tour, cruise, steam, take a trip, go on an expedition

vulgar 1 = tasteless, common ≠ tasteful **2** = crude, rude, coarse, indecent, tasteless, risqué, ribald **3** = uncouth, unrefined, impolite, ill-bred ≠ refined

vulnerable 1 = susceptible, helpless, unprotected, defenceless, exposed, weak, sensitive, tender ≠ immune **2** = exposed, open, unprotected, defenceless, accessible, wide open, assailable ≠ well-protected

W

waddle = shuffle, totter, toddle, sway, wobble

wade 1 = paddle, splash, splash about, slop **2** = walk through, cross, ford, travel across

wag VERB **1** = wave, shake, waggle, stir, quiver, vibrate, wiggle **2** = waggle, wave, shake, flourish, brandish, wobble, wiggle **3** = shake, bob, nod
• NOUN **1** = wave, shake, quiver, vibration, wiggle, waggle **2** = nod, bob, shake

wage NOUN *often plural* = payment, pay, remuneration, fee, reward, income, allowance, recompense
• VERB = engage in, conduct, pursue, carry on, undertake, practise, prosecute, proceed with

wail VERB = cry, weep, grieve, lament, howl, bawl, yowl
• NOUN = cry, moan, howl, lament, yowl

wait VERB **1** = stay, remain, stop, pause, rest, linger, loiter, tarry ≠ go **2** = stand by, hold back, hang fire **3** = be postponed, be suspended, be delayed, be put off, be put back, be deferred, be put on hold (*informal*), be shelved
• NOUN = delay, gap, pause, interval, stay, rest, halt, hold-up

waiter *or* **waitress** = attendant, server, flunkey, steward *or* stewardess, servant

waive 1 = give up, relinquish, renounce, forsake, drop, abandon, set aside, dispense with ≠ claim **2** = disregard, ignore, discount, overlook, set aside, pass over, dispense with, brush aside

wake[1] VERB **1** = awake, stir, awaken, come to, arise, get up, rouse, get out of bed ≠ fall asleep **2** = awaken, arouse, rouse, waken **3** = evoke, recall, renew, stimulate, revive, induce, arouse, call up
• NOUN = vigil, watch, funeral, deathwatch, tangi (*N.Z.*)

wake[2] NOUN = slipstream, wash, trail, backwash, train, track, waves, path
• PHRASES **in the wake of** = in the aftermath of, following, because of, as a result of, on account of, as a consequence of

walk VERB **1** = stride, stroll, go, move, step, march, pace, hike **2** = travel on foot **3** = escort, take, see, show, partner, guide, conduct, accompany
• NOUN **1** = stroll, hike, ramble, march, trek, trudge, promenade, saunter **2** = gait, step, bearing, carriage, tread **3** = path, footpath, track, way, road, lane, trail, avenue, berm (*N.Z.*)
• PHRASES **walk of life** = area, calling, business, line, trade, class, field, career

walker = hiker, rambler, wayfarer, pedestrian

wall 1 = partition, screen, barrier,

enclosure **2** = barrier, obstacle, barricade, obstruction, check, bar, fence, impediment

wallet = purse, pocketbook, pouch, case, holder, money-bag

wander VERB = roam, walk, drift, stroll, range, stray, ramble, prowl
• NOUN = excursion, walk, stroll, cruise, ramble, meander, promenade, mosey (*informal*)

wanderer = traveller, rover, nomad, drifter, gypsy, explorer, rambler, voyager

wane 1 = decline, weaken, diminish, fail, fade, decrease, dwindle, lessen ≠ grow **2** = diminish, decrease, dwindle ≠ wax

want VERB **1** = wish for, desire, long for, crave, covet, hope for, yearn for, thirst for ≠ have **2** = need, demand, require, call for **3** = should, need, must, ought **4** = desire, long for, crave, wish for, yearn for, thirst for, hanker after, burn for **5** = lack, need, require, miss
• NOUN **1** = lack, need, absence, shortage, deficiency, famine, scarcity, dearth ≠ abundance **2** = poverty, hardship, privation, penury, destitution, neediness, pennilessness ≠ wealth **3** = wish, will, need, desire, requirement, longing, appetite, craving

wanting 1 = deficient, poor, inadequate, insufficient, faulty, defective, imperfect, unsound, bodger *or* bodgie (*Austral. slang*) ≠ adequate **2** = lacking, missing, absent, incomplete, short, shy ≠ complete

war NOUN **1** = conflict, drive, attack, fighting, fight, operation, battle, movement ≠ peace **2** = campaign, drive, attack, operation, movement, push, mission, offensive
• VERB = fight, battle, clash, wage war, campaign, combat, do battle, take up arms ≠ make peace

ward NOUN **1** = room, department, unit, quarter, division, section, apartment, cubicle **2** = district, constituency, area, division, zone, parish, precinct **3** = dependant, charge, pupil, minor, protégé
• PHRASES **ward someone off** = drive off, resist, fight off, hold off, repel, fend off ♦ **ward something off 1** = avert, fend off, stave off, avoid, frustrate, deflect, repel **2** = parry, avert, deflect, avoid, repel, turn aside

warden 1 = steward, guardian, administrator, superintendent, caretaker, curator, custodian **2** = jailer, prison officer, guard, screw (*slang*) **3** = governor, head, leader, director, manager, chief, executive, commander, baas (*S. African*) **4** = ranger, keeper, guardian, protector, custodian, official

wardrobe 1 = clothes cupboard, cupboard, closet (*U.S.*), cabinet **2** = clothes, apparel, attire

warehouse = store, depot, storehouse, repository, depository, stockroom

wares = goods, produce, stock, products, stuff, commodities, merchandise

warfare = war, fighting, battle, conflict, combat, hostilities, enmity ≠ peace

warm ADJECTIVE **1** = balmy, mild, temperate, pleasant, fine, bright, sunny, agreeable ≠ cool **2** = cosy, snug, toasty (*informal*), comfortable, homely, comfy (*informal*) **3** = moderately hot, heated ≠ cool **4** = thermal, winter, thick, chunky, woolly ≠ cool **5** = mellow, relaxing, pleasant, agreeable, restful **6** = affable, kindly, friendly, affectionate, loving, tender, amicable, cordial ≠ unfriendly **7** = near, close, hot, near to the truth
• VERB = warm up, heat, thaw (out), heat up ≠ cool down
• PHRASES **warm something** *or* **someone up** = heat, thaw, heat up

warmth 1 = heat, snugness, warmness, comfort, homeliness, hotness ≠ coolness **2** = affection, feeling, love, goodwill, kindness, tenderness, cordiality, kindliness ≠ hostility

warn 1 = notify, tell, remind, inform, alert, tip off, give notice, make someone aware **2** = advise, urge, recommend, counsel, caution, commend, exhort, admonish

warning 1 = caution, information, advice, injunction, notification **2** = notice, notification, sign, alarm, announcement, alert, tip-off (*informal*) **3** = omen, sign, forecast, indication, prediction, prophecy, foreboding, portent, rahui (*N.Z.*) **4** = reprimand, admonition

warp VERB **1** = distort, bend, twist, buckle, deform, disfigure, contort, malform **2** = become distorted, bend, twist, contort, become deformed, become misshapen **3** = pervert, twist, corrupt, degrade, deprave, debase, debauch, lead astray
• NOUN = twist, bend, defect, flaw,

distortion, imperfection, kink, contortion
warrant VERB 1 = call for, demand, require, merit, rate, earn, deserve, permit 2 = guarantee, declare, pledge, promise, ensure, affirm, certify, attest
• NOUN 1 = authorization, permit, licence, permission, authority, sanction 2 = justification, reason, grounds, basis, licence, rationale, vindication, authority
warranty = guarantee, promise, contract, bond, pledge, certificate, assurance, covenant
warrior = soldier, combatant, fighter, gladiator, trooper, man-at-arms
wary 1 = suspicious, sceptical, guarded, distrustful, chary 2 = watchful, careful, alert, cautious, vigilant, circumspect, heedful ≠ careless
wash VERB 1 = clean, scrub, sponge, rinse, scour, cleanse 2 = launder, clean, rinse, dry-clean 3 = rinse, clean, scrub, lather 4 = bathe, bath, clean yourself, soak, douse, scrub yourself down 5 = move, overcome, touch, upset, stir, disturb, perturb, surge through 6 (*Informal*) (always used in negative constructions) = be plausible, stand up, hold up, pass muster, hold water, stick, carry weight, be convincing
• NOUN 1 = laundering, cleaning, clean, cleansing 2 = bathe, dip, soak, scrub, rinse 3 = backwash, slipstream, path, trail, train, track, waves, aftermath 4 = splash, surge, swell, rise and fall, undulation 5 = coat, film, covering, layer, coating, overlay
• PHRASES **wash something** *or* **someone away** = sweep away, carry off, bear away ♦ **wash something away** = erode, wear something away
waste VERB 1 = squander, throw away, blow (*slang*), lavish, misuse, dissipate, fritter away ≠ save 2 = wear out, wither
• NOUN 1 = squandering, misuse, extravagance, frittering away, dissipation, wastefulness, prodigality ≠ saving 2 = rubbish, refuse, debris, scrap, litter, garbage, trash, leftovers
• PLURAL NOUN = desert, wilderness, wasteland
• ADJECTIVE 1 = unwanted, useless, worthless, unused, leftover, superfluous, unusable, supernumerary ≠ necessary 2 = uncultivated, wild, bare, barren, empty, desolate, unproductive, uninhabited ≠ cultivated
• PHRASES **waste away** = decline, dwindle, wither, fade, crumble, decay, wane, wear out
watch VERB 1 = look at, observe, regard, eye, see, view, contemplate, eyeball (*slang*) 2 = spy on, follow, track, monitor, keep an eye on, stake out, keep tabs on (*informal*), keep watch on 3 = guard, keep, mind, protect, tend, look after, shelter, take care of
• NOUN 1 = wristwatch, timepiece, chronometer 2 = guard, surveillance, observation, vigil, lookout
watchdog 1 = guardian, monitor, protector, custodian, scrutineer 2 = guard dog
water NOUN = liquid, H_2O, wai (*N.Z.*)
• PLURAL NOUN = sea, main, waves, ocean, depths, briny
• VERB 1 = sprinkle, spray, soak, irrigate, hose, dampen, drench, douse 2 = get wet, cry, weep, become wet, exude water
• PHRASES **water something down** = dilute, weaken, water, doctor, thin
RELATED WORD
adjective: aquatic
waterfall = cascade, fall, cataract
wave VERB 1 = signal, sign, gesture, gesticulate 2 = guide, point, direct, indicate, signal, motion, gesture, nod 3 = brandish, swing, flourish, wag, shake 4 = flutter, flap, stir, shake, swing, wag, oscillate
• NOUN 1 = gesture, sign, signal, indication, gesticulation 2 = ripple, breaker, swell, ridge, roller, billow 3 = outbreak, rash, upsurge, flood, surge, ground swell 4 = stream, flood, surge, spate, current, flow, rush, tide
waver 1 = hesitate, dither (*chiefly Brit.*), vacillate, falter, fluctuate, seesaw, hum and haw ≠ be decisive 2 = flicker, shake, tremble, wobble, quiver, totter
wax 1 = increase, grow, develop, expand, swell, enlarge, magnify ≠ wane 2 = become fuller, enlarge
way 1 = method, means, system, process, technique, manner, procedure, mode 2 = manner, style, fashion, mode 3 *often plural* = custom, manner, habit, style, practice, nature, personality, wont, tikanga (*N.Z.*) 4 = route, direction, course, road, path 5 = access, road, track, channel, route,

path, trail, pathway **6** = journey, approach, passage **7** = distance, length, stretch

wayward = erratic, unruly, unmanageable, unpredictable, capricious, ungovernable, inconstant ≠ obedient

weak **1** = feeble, frail, debilitated, fragile, sickly, puny, unsteady, infirm ≠ strong **2** = slight, faint, feeble, pathetic, hollow **3** = fragile, brittle, flimsy, fine, delicate, frail, dainty, breakable **4** = unsafe, exposed, vulnerable, helpless, unprotected, defenceless, unguarded ≠ secure **5** = unconvincing, unsatisfactory, lame, flimsy, pathetic ≠ convincing **6** = tasteless, thin, diluted, watery, runny, insipid ≠ strong

weaken **1** = reduce, undermine, moderate, diminish, lessen, sap ≠ boost **2** = wane, diminish, dwindle, lower, flag, fade, lessen ≠ grow **3** = sap the strength of ≠ strengthen

weakness **1** = frailty, fatigue, exhaustion, fragility, infirmity, feebleness, decrepitude ≠ strength **2** = liking, appetite, penchant, soft spot, passion, inclination, fondness, partiality ≠ aversion **3** = powerlessness, vulnerability, meekness, spinelessness, timorousness, cravenness, cowardliness **4** = inadequacy, deficiency, transparency, lameness, hollowness, implausibility, flimsiness, unsoundness **5** = failing, fault, defect, deficiency, flaw, shortcoming, blemish, imperfection ≠ strong point

wealth **1** = riches, fortune, prosperity, affluence, money, opulence ≠ poverty **2** = property, capital, fortune **3** = abundance, plenty, richness, profusion, fullness, cornucopia, copiousness ≠ lack

wealthy = rich, prosperous, affluent, well-off, flush (*informal*), opulent, well-heeled (*informal*), well-to-do ≠ poor

wear VERB **1** = be dressed in, have on, sport (*informal*), put on **2** = show, present, bear, display, assume, put on, exhibit **3** = deteriorate, fray, wear thin

• NOUN **1** = clothes, things, dress, gear (*informal*), attire, costume, garments, apparel **2** = damage, wear and tear, erosion, deterioration, attrition, corrosion, abrasion ≠ repair

• PHRASES **wear off** = subside, disappear, fade, diminish, decrease, dwindle, wane, peter out

wearing = tiresome, trying, fatiguing, oppressive, exasperating, irksome, wearisome ≠ refreshing

weary ADJECTIVE **1** = tired, exhausted, drained, worn out, done in (*informal*), flagging, fatigued, sleepy, clapped out (*Austral. & N.Z. informal*) ≠ energetic **2** = tiring, arduous, tiresome, laborious, wearisome ≠ refreshing

• VERB = grow tired, tire, become bored ≠ invigorate

weather NOUN = climate, conditions, temperature, forecast, outlook, meteorological conditions, elements

• VERB = withstand, stand, survive, overcome, resist, brave, endure, come through ≠ surrender to

weave **1** = knit, intertwine, plait, braid, entwine, interlace **2** = zigzag, wind, crisscross **3** = create, tell, recount, narrate, build, relate, make up, spin

web **1** = cobweb, spider's web **2** = mesh, lattice **3** = tangle, network

wed **1** = get married to, be united to ≠ divorce **2** = get married, marry, be united, tie the knot (*informal*), take the plunge (*informal*) ≠ divorce **3** = unite, combine, join, link, ally, blend, merge, interweave ≠ divide

wedding = marriage, nuptials, wedding ceremony, marriage service, wedding service

wedge VERB = squeeze, force, lodge, jam, crowd, stuff, pack, thrust

• NOUN = block, lump, chunk

weep = cry, shed tears, sob, whimper, mourn, lament, blubber, snivel ≠ rejoice

weigh **1** = have a weight of, tip the scales at (*informal*) **2** *often with* ***up*** = consider, examine, contemplate, evaluate, ponder, think over, reflect upon, meditate upon **3** = compare, balance, contrast, juxtapose, place side by side **4** = matter, carry weight, count

weight NOUN **1** = heaviness, mass, poundage, load, tonnage **2** = importance, force, power, value, authority, influence, impact, import, mana (*N.Z.*)

• VERB **1** *often with* ***down*** = load **2** = bias, load, slant, unbalance

weird **1** = strange, odd, unusual, bizarre, mysterious, queer, eerie, unnatural ≠ normal **2** = bizarre, odd, strange, unusual, queer, unnatural, creepy (*informal*), freakish ≠ ordinary

welcome VERB 1 = greet, meet, receive, embrace, hail, karanga (*N.Z.*), mihi (*N.Z.*) ≠ reject 2 = accept gladly, appreciate, embrace, approve of, be pleased by, give the thumbs up to (*informal*), be glad about, express pleasure *or* satisfaction at
• NOUN = greeting, welcoming, reception, acceptance, hail, hospitality, salutation ≠ rejection
• ADJECTIVE 1 = pleasing, appreciated, acceptable, pleasant, desirable, refreshing, delightful, gratifying ≠ unpleasant 2 = wanted ≠ unwanted 3 = free

weld 1 = join, link, bond, bind, connect, fuse, solder 2 = unite, combine, blend, unify, fuse

welfare 1 = wellbeing, good, interest, health, security, benefit, safety, protection 2 = state benefit, support, benefits, pensions, dole (*slang*), social security, unemployment benefit, state benefits

well[1] ADVERB 1 = skilfully, expertly, adeptly, professionally, correctly, properly, efficiently, adequately ≠ badly 2 = satisfactorily, nicely, smoothly, successfully, pleasantly, splendidly, agreeably ≠ badly 3 = thoroughly, completely, fully, carefully, effectively, efficiently, rigorously 4 = intimately, deeply, fully, profoundly ≠ slightly 5 = favourably, highly, kindly, warmly, enthusiastically, approvingly, admiringly, with admiration ≠ unfavourably 6 = considerably, easily, very much, significantly, substantially, markedly 7 = fully, highly, greatly, amply, very much, thoroughly, considerably, substantially 8 = possibly, probably, certainly, reasonably, conceivably, justifiably 9 = decently, right, kindly, fittingly, fairly, properly, politely, suitably ≠ unfairly 10 = prosperously, comfortably, splendidly, in comfort, in (the lap of) luxury, without hardship
• ADJECTIVE 1 = healthy, sound, fit, blooming, in fine fettle, in good condition ≠ ill 2 = satisfactory, right, fine, pleasing, proper, thriving ≠ unsatisfactory 3 = advisable, proper, agreeable ≠ inadvisable

well[2] NOUN = hole, bore, pit, shaft
• VERB 1 = flow, spring, pour, jet, surge, gush, spurt, spout 2 = rise, increase, grow, mount, surge, intensify

wet ADJECTIVE 1 = damp, soaking, saturated, moist, watery, soggy, sodden, waterlogged ≠ dry 2 = rainy, damp, drizzly, showery, raining, pouring, drizzling, teeming ≠ sunny 3 (*Informal*) = feeble, soft, weak, ineffectual, weedy (*informal*), spineless, effete, timorous
• VERB = moisten, spray, dampen, water, soak, saturate, douse, irrigate ≠ dry
• NOUN 1 = rain, drizzle ≠ fine weather 2 = moisture, water, liquid, damp, humidity, condensation, dampness, wetness ≠ dryness

whack (*Informal*) VERB = strike, hit, belt (*informal*), bang, smack, thrash, thump, swipe
• NOUN 1 = blow, hit, stroke, belt (*informal*), bang, smack, thump, swipe 2 (*Informal*) = share, part, cut (*informal*), bit, portion, quota 3 (*Informal*) = attempt, go (*informal*), try, turn, shot (*informal*), crack (*informal*), stab (*informal*), bash (*informal*)

wharf = dock, pier, berth, quay, jetty, landing stage

wheel NOUN = disc, ring, hoop
• VERB 1 = push, trundle, roll 2 = turn, swing, spin, revolve, rotate, whirl, swivel 3 = circle, go round, twirl, gyrate

whereabouts = position, situation, site, location

whiff = smell, hint, scent, sniff, aroma, odour

whim = impulse, caprice, fancy, urge, notion

whine VERB 1 = cry, sob, wail, whimper, sniffle, snivel, moan 2 = complain, grumble, gripe (*informal*), whinge (*informal*), moan, grouse, grizzle (*informal, chiefly Brit.*), grouch (*informal*)
• NOUN 1 = cry, moan, sob, wail, whimper 2 = drone, note, hum 3 = complaint, moan, grumble, grouse, gripe (*informal*), whinge (*informal*), grouch (*informal*)

whip NOUN = lash, cane, birch, crop, scourge, cat-o'-nine-tails
• VERB 1 = lash, cane, flog, beat, strap, thrash, birch, scourge 2 (*Informal*) = dash, shoot, fly, tear, rush, dive, dart, whisk 3 = whisk, beat, mix vigorously, stir vigorously 4 = incite, drive, stir, spur, work up, get going, agitate, inflame

whirl VERB 1 = spin, turn, twist, rotate, twirl 2 = rotate, roll, twist, revolve, swirl, twirl, pirouette 3 = feel dizzy, swim, spin, reel,

go round
• NOUN 1 = revolution, turn, roll, spin, twist, swirl, rotation, twirl 2 = bustle, round, series, succession, flurry, merry-go-round 3 = confusion, daze, dither (*chiefly Brit.*), giddiness 4 = tumult, spin

whisk VERB 1 = flick, whip, sweep, brush 2 = beat, mix vigorously, stir vigorously, whip, fluff up
• NOUN 1 = flick, sweep, brush, whip 2 = beater, mixer, blender

whisper VERB 1 = murmur, breathe ≠ shout 2 = rustle, sigh, hiss, swish
• NOUN 1 = murmur, mutter, mumble, undertone 2 (*Informal*) = rumour, report, gossip, innuendo, insinuation 3 = rustle, sigh, hiss, swish

white = pale, wan, pasty, pallid, ashen

white-collar = clerical, professional, salaried, nonmanual

whittle VERB = carve, cut, hew, shape, trim, shave, pare
• PHRASES **whittle something or someone down** = reduce, cut down, cut, decrease, prune, scale down ◆ **whittle something away** = undermine, reduce, consume, erode, eat away, wear away

whole NOUN = unit, ensemble, entirety, totality ≠ part
• ADJECTIVE 1 = complete, full, total, entire, uncut, undivided, unabridged ≠ partial 2 = undamaged, intact, unscathed, unbroken, untouched, unharmed, in one piece ≠ damaged
• PHRASES **on the whole** 1 = all in all, altogether, all things considered, by and large 2 = generally, in general, as a rule, chiefly, mainly, mostly, principally, on average

wholesale ADJECTIVE = extensive, total, mass, sweeping, broad, comprehensive, wide-ranging, blanket ≠ limited
• ADVERB = extensively, comprehensively, across the board, indiscriminately

wholly = completely, totally, perfectly, fully, entirely, altogether, thoroughly, utterly ≠ partly

whore = prostitute, tart (*informal*), streetwalker, call girl

wide ADJECTIVE 1 = spacious, broad, extensive, roomy, commodious ≠ confined 2 = baggy, full, loose, ample, billowing, roomy, voluminous, capacious 3 = expanded, dilated, distended ≠ shut 4 = broad, extensive, wide-ranging, large, sweeping, vast, immense, expansive ≠ restricted 5 = extensive, general, far-reaching, overarching 6 = large, broad, vast, immense 7 = distant, remote, off course, off target
• ADVERB 1 = fully, completely ≠ partly 2 = off target, astray, off course, off the mark

widen 1 = broaden, expand, enlarge, dilate, spread, extend, stretch ≠ narrow 2 = get wider, spread, extend, expand, broaden ≠ narrow

widespread = common, general, popular, broad, extensive, universal, far-reaching, pervasive ≠ limited

width = breadth, extent, span, scope, diameter, compass, thickness, girth

wield 1 = brandish, flourish, manipulate, swing, use, manage, handle, employ 2 = exert, maintain, exercise, have, possess

wife = spouse, partner, mate, bride, better half (*humorous*), vrou (*S. African*), wahine (*N.Z.*)

wild ADJECTIVE 1 = untamed, fierce, savage, ferocious, unbroken, feral, undomesticated, free, warrigal (*Austral. literary*) ≠ tame 2 = uncultivated, natural ≠ cultivated 3 = stormy, violent, rough, raging, choppy, tempestuous, blustery 4 = excited, crazy (*informal*), enthusiastic, raving, hysterical ≠ unenthusiastic 5 = uncontrolled, disorderly, turbulent, wayward, unruly, rowdy, unfettered, riotous ≠ calm 6 = mad (*informal*), furious, fuming, infuriated, incensed, enraged, very angry, irate, tooshie (*Austral. slang*), off the air (*Austral. slang*) 7 = uncivilized, fierce, savage, primitive, ferocious, barbaric, brutish, barbarous ≠ civilized
• PLURAL NOUN = wilderness, desert, wasteland, middle of nowhere (*informal*), backwoods, back of beyond (*informal*)

wilderness = wilds, desert, wasteland, uncultivated region

will NOUN 1 = determination, drive, purpose, commitment, resolution, resolve, spine, backbone 2 = wish, mind, desire, intention, fancy, preference, inclination 3 = choice, prerogative, volition 4 = decree, wish, desire, command, dictate, ordinance 5 = testament, bequest(s), last wishes, last will and testament
• VERB 1 = wish, want, prefer, desire, see

fit **2** = bequeath, give, leave, transfer, gift, hand on, pass on, confer

willing **1** = inclined, prepared, consenting, agreeable, compliant, amenable ≠ unwilling **2** = ready, game (*informal*) ≠ reluctant

willingly = readily, freely, gladly, happily, eagerly, voluntarily, cheerfully, by choice ≠ unwillingly

willingness = inclination, will, agreement, wish, consent, volition ≠ reluctance

wilt **1** = droop, wither, sag, shrivel **2** = weaken, languish, droop **3** = wane, flag, fade

win VERB **1** = be victorious in, succeed in, prevail in, come first in, be the victor in ≠ lose **2** = be victorious, succeed, triumph, overcome, prevail, conquer, come first, sweep the board ≠ lose **3** = gain, get, land, achieve, earn, secure, obtain, acquire ≠ forfeit
• NOUN = victory, success, triumph, conquest ≠ defeat
• PHRASES **win someone over** *or* **round** = convince, influence, persuade, convert, sway, prevail upon, bring *or* talk round

wince VERB = flinch, start, shrink, cringe, quail, recoil, cower, draw back
• NOUN = flinch, start, cringe

wind¹ NOUN **1** = air, blast, hurricane, breeze, draught, gust, zephyr **2** = flatulence, gas **3** = breath, puff, respiration **4** = nonsense, talk, boasting, hot air, babble, bluster, humbug, twaddle (*informal*), bizzo (*Austral. slang*), bull's wool (*Austral. & N.Z. slang*)
• PHRASES **get wind of something** = hear about, learn of, find out about, become aware of, be told about, be informed of, be made aware of, hear tell of

wind² VERB **1** = meander, turn, bend, twist, curve, snake, ramble, twist and turn **2** = wrap, twist, reel, curl, loop, coil **3** = coil, curl, spiral, encircle
• PHRASES **wind someone up** (*Informal*) **1** = irritate, excite, anger, annoy, exasperate, nettle, work someone up, pique **2** = tease, kid (*informal*), have someone on (*informal*), annoy, rag (*informal*), rib (*informal*), josh (*informal*), vex ◆ **wind something up** **1** = end, finish, settle, conclude, tie up, wrap up, finalize **2** = close down, close, dissolve, terminate, put something into liquidation ◆ **wind up** = end up, be left, finish up, fetch up (*informal*), land up

windfall = godsend, find, jackpot, bonanza, manna from heaven ≠ misfortune

windy = breezy, wild, stormy, windswept, blustery, gusty, squally, blowy ≠ calm

wing NOUN = faction, group, arm, section, branch
• VERB **1** = fly, soar, glide, take wing **2** = wound, hit, clip

wink VERB **1** = blink, bat, flutter **2** = twinkle, flash, shine, sparkle, gleam, shimmer, glimmer
• NOUN = blink, flutter

winner = victor, champion, master, champ (*informal*), conqueror, prizewinner ≠ loser

winning ADJECTIVE **1** = victorious, first, top, successful, unbeaten, conquering, triumphant, undefeated **2** = charming, pleasing, attractive, engaging, cute, disarming, enchanting, endearing ≠ unpleasant
• PLURAL NOUN = spoils, profits, gains, prize, proceeds, takings

wipe VERB **1** = clean, polish, brush, rub, sponge, mop, swab **2** = erase, remove
• NOUN = rub, brush
• PHRASES **wipe something** *or* **someone out** = destroy, massacre, erase, eradicate, obliterate, annihilate, exterminate, expunge

wisdom = understanding, learning, knowledge, intelligence, judgment, insight, enlightenment, erudition ≠ foolishness

wise **1** = sage, clever, intelligent, sensible, enlightened, discerning, perceptive, erudite ≠ foolish **2** = sensible, clever, intelligent, prudent, judicious ≠ unwise

wish NOUN = desire, want, hope, urge, intention, fancy (*informal*), ambition, yen (*informal*) ≠ aversion
• VERB = want, feel, choose, please, desire, think fit
• PHRASES **wish for something** = desire, want, hope for, long for, crave, aspire to, yearn for, hanker for

wit **1** = humour, quips, banter, puns, repartee, wordplay, witticisms, badinage ≠ seriousness **2** = humorist, card (*informal*), comedian, wag, joker, dag (*N.Z. informal*) **3** *often plural* = cleverness,

sense, brains, wisdom, common sense, intellect, ingenuity, acumen ≠ stupidity
witch = enchantress, magician, hag, crone, sorceress, Wiccan
witchcraft = magic, voodoo, wizardry, black magic, enchantment, occultism, sorcery, Wicca, makutu (*N.Z.*)
withdraw 1 = remove, take off, pull out, extract, take away, pull back, draw out, draw back 2 = take out, extract, draw out
withdrawal = removal, ending, stopping, taking away, abolition, elimination, cancellation, termination
withdrawn = uncommunicative, reserved, retiring, distant, shy, taciturn, introverted, unforthcoming ≠ outgoing
wither 1 = wilt, decline, decay, disintegrate, perish, shrivel ≠ flourish 2 = waste, decline, shrivel 3 = fade, decline, perish ≠ increase
withering = scornful, devastating, humiliating, snubbing, hurtful, mortifying
withhold 1 = keep secret, refuse, hide, reserve, retain, conceal, suppress, hold back ≠ reveal 2 = hold back, suppress, keep back ≠ release
withstand = resist, suffer, bear, oppose, cope with, endure, tolerate, stand up to ≠ give in to
witness NOUN 1 = observer, viewer, spectator, looker-on, watcher, onlooker, eyewitness, bystander 2 = testifier
• VERB 1 = see, view, watch, note, notice, observe, perceive 2 = countersign, sign, endorse, validate
witty = humorous, funny, clever, amusing, sparkling, whimsical, droll, piquant ≠ dull
wizard = magician, witch, shaman, sorcerer, occultist, magus, conjuror, warlock, tohunga (*N.Z.*)
wobble VERB 1 = shake, rock, sway, tremble, teeter, totter 2 = tremble, shake
• NOUN 1 = unsteadiness, shake, tremble 2 = unsteadiness, shake, tremor
woe 1 = misery, distress, grief, agony, gloom, sadness, sorrow, anguish ≠ happiness 2 = problem, grief, misery, sorrow
woman = lady, girl, female, sheila (*Austral. & N.Z. informal*), vrou (*S. African*), adult female, charlie (*Austral. slang*), chook (*Austral. slang*), wahine (*N.Z.*) ≠ man
womanly 1 = feminine, motherly, female, warm, tender, matronly, ladylike 2 = curvaceous, ample, voluptuous, shapely, curvy (*informal*), busty (*informal*), buxom, full-figured
wonder VERB 1 = think, question, puzzle, speculate, query, ponder, meditate, conjecture 2 = be amazed, stare, marvel, be astonished, gape
• NOUN 1 = amazement, surprise, admiration, awe, fascination, astonishment, bewilderment, wonderment 2 = phenomenon, sight, miracle, spectacle, curiosity, marvel, prodigy, rarity
wonderful 1 = excellent, great (*informal*), brilliant, outstanding, superb, fantastic (*informal*), tremendous, magnificent, booshit (*Austral. slang*), exo (*Austral. slang*), sik (*Austral. slang*) ≠ terrible 2 = remarkable, amazing, extraordinary, incredible, astonishing, staggering, startling, phenomenal ≠ ordinary
woo 1 = seek, cultivate 2 = court, pursue
wood 1 = timber, planks, planking, lumber (*U.S.*) 2 *or* **woods** = woodland, forest, grove, thicket, copse, coppice 3 = firewood, fuel, logs, kindling
wooded = tree-covered, forested, timbered, sylvan (*poetic*), tree-clad
wooden 1 = made of wood, timber, woody, ligneous 2 = expressionless, lifeless, deadpan, unresponsive
wool 1 = fleece, hair, coat 2 = yarn
word NOUN 1 = term, name, expression 2 = chat, tête-à-tête, talk, discussion, consultation, confab (*informal*), heart-to-heart, powwow (*informal*) 3 = comment, remark, utterance 4 = message, news, report, information, notice, intelligence, dispatch, communiqué 5 = promise, guarantee, pledge, vow, assurance, oath 6 = command, order, decree, bidding, mandate
• VERB = express, say, state, put, phrase, utter, couch, formulate

RELATED WORDS
adjectives: lexical, verbal

wording = phraseology, words, language, phrasing, terminology
work VERB 1 = be employed, be in work 2 = labour, sweat, slave, toil, slog (away), drudge, peg away, exert yourself ≠ relax 3 = function, go, run, operate, be in working order ≠ be out of order 4 = succeed, work out, pay off (*informal*), be successful, be effective, do the trick

(*informal*), do the business (*informal*), get results **5** = cultivate, farm, dig, till, plough **6** = operate, use, move, control, drive, manage, handle, manipulate **7** = manipulate, form, fashion, shape, mould, knead
• NOUN **1** = employment, business, job, trade, duty, profession, occupation, livelihood ≠ play **2** = effort, industry, labour, sweat, toil, exertion, drudgery, elbow grease (*facetious*) ≠ leisure **3** = task, jobs, projects, commissions, duties, assignments, chores, yakka (*Austral. & N.Z. informal*) **4** = handiwork, doing, act, feat, deed **5** = creation, piece, production, opus, achievement, composition, handiwork
• PLURAL NOUN **1** = factory, plant, mill, workshop **2** = writings, output, canon, oeuvre (*French*) **3** = mechanism, workings, parts, action, movement, machinery
• PHRASES **work something out** = solve, find out, calculate, figure out

worker = employee, hand, labourer, workman, craftsman, artisan, tradesman

workman = labourer, hand, worker, employee, mechanic, operative, craftsman, artisan

workshop **1** = factory, plant, mill **2** = workroom, studio

world **1** = earth, planet, globe **2** = mankind, man, everyone, the public, everybody, humanity, humankind **3** = sphere, area, field, environment, realm, domain **4** (usually used in phrase *a world of difference*) = huge amount, mountain, wealth, great deal, good deal, abundance, enormous amount, vast amount

worldly **1** = earthly, physical, secular, terrestrial, temporal, profane ≠ spiritual **2** = materialistic, grasping, selfish, greedy ≠ nonmaterialistic **3** = worldly-wise, knowing, experienced, sophisticated, cosmopolitan, urbane, blasé ≠ naive

worn = ragged, frayed, shabby, tattered, tatty, threadbare, the worse for wear

worried = anxious, concerned, troubled, afraid, frightened, nervous, tense, uneasy ≠ unworried

worry VERB **1** = be anxious, be concerned, be worried, obsess, brood, fret, agonize, get in a lather (*informal*) ≠ be unconcerned **2** = trouble, upset, bother, disturb, annoy, unsettle, pester, vex ≠ soothe
• NOUN **1** = anxiety, concern, fear, trouble, unease, apprehension, misgiving, trepidation ≠ peace of mind **2** = problem, care, trouble, bother, hassle (*informal*)

worsen **1** = deteriorate, decline, sink, decay, get worse, degenerate, go downhill (*informal*) ≠ improve **2** = aggravate, damage, exacerbate, make worse ≠ improve

worship VERB **1** = revere, praise, honour, adore, glorify, exalt, pray to, venerate ≠ dishonour **2** = love, adore, idolize, put on a pedestal ≠ despise
• NOUN = reverence, praise, regard, respect, honour, glory, devotion, adulation

worth **1** = value, price, rate, cost, estimate, valuation ≠ worthlessness **2** = merit, value, quality, importance, excellence, goodness, worthiness ≠ unworthiness **3** = usefulness, value, quality, importance, excellence, goodness ≠ uselessness

worthless **1** = valueless, rubbishy, negligible ≠ valuable **2** = useless, unimportant, ineffectual, negligible ≠ useful **3** = good-for-nothing, vile, despicable, contemptible ≠ honourable

worthwhile = useful, valuable, helpful, profitable, productive, beneficial, meaningful, constructive ≠ useless

worthy = praiseworthy, deserving, valuable, worthwhile, admirable, virtuous, creditable, laudable ≠ disreputable

would-be = budding, self-styled, wannabe (*informal*), unfulfilled, self-appointed

wound NOUN **1** = injury, cut, hurt, trauma (*Pathology*), gash, lesion, laceration **2** *often plural* = trauma, offence, slight, insult
• VERB **1** = injure, cut, wing, hurt, pierce, gash, lacerate **2** = offend, hurt, annoy, sting, mortify, cut to the quick

wrangle VERB = argue, fight, row, dispute, disagree, contend, quarrel, squabble
• NOUN = argument, row, dispute, quarrel, squabble, bickering, tiff, altercation

wrap VERB **1** = cover, enclose, shroud, swathe, encase, enfold, bundle up **2** = pack, package, parcel (up), tie up, giftwrap ≠ unpack **3** = bind, swathe ≠ unwind
• NOUN = cloak, cape, stole, mantle, shawl
• PHRASES **wrap something up** **1** = giftwrap, pack, package, bundle up **2** (*Informal*) = end, conclude, wind up, terminate, finish off, round off, polish off

wrath = anger, rage, temper, fury, resentment, indignation, ire, displeasure ≠ satisfaction

wreck VERB **1** = destroy, break, smash, ruin, devastate, shatter, spoil, demolish ≠ build **2** = spoil, ruin, devastate, shatter, crool *or* cruel (*Austral. slang*) ≠ save
• NOUN = shipwreck, hulk

wreckage = remains, pieces, ruin, fragments, debris, rubble

wrench VERB **1** = twist, force, pull, tear, rip, tug, jerk, yank **2** = sprain, strain, rick
• NOUN **1** = twist, pull, rip, tug, jerk, yank **2** = sprain, strain, twist **3** = blow, shock, upheaval, pang **4** = spanner, adjustable spanner

wrestle = fight, battle, struggle, combat, grapple, tussle, scuffle

wrinkle NOUN **1** = line, fold, crease, furrow, crow's-foot, corrugation **2** = crease, fold, crumple, furrow, crinkle, corrugation
• VERB = crease, gather, fold, crumple, furrow, rumple, pucker, corrugate ≠ smooth

writ = summons, document, decree, indictment, court order, subpoena, arraignment

write **1** = record, scribble, inscribe, set down, jot down **2** = compose, draft, pen, draw up **3** = correspond, get in touch, keep in touch, write a letter, drop a line, drop a note

writer = author, novelist, hack, scribbler, scribe, wordsmith, penpusher

writing = script, hand, printing, fist (*informal*), scribble, handwriting, scrawl, calligraphy

wrong ADJECTIVE **1** = amiss, faulty, unsatisfactory, not right, defective, awry **2** = incorrect, mistaken, false, inaccurate, untrue, erroneous, wide of the mark, fallacious **3** = inappropriate, incorrect, unsuitable, unacceptable, undesirable, incongruous, unseemly, unbecoming ≠ correct **4** = bad, criminal, illegal, evil, unlawful, immoral, unjust, dishonest ≠ moral **5** = defective, faulty, awry, askew
• ADVERB **1** = incorrectly, badly, wrongly, mistakenly, erroneously, inaccurately ≠ correctly **2** = amiss, astray, awry, askew
• NOUN = offence, injury, crime, error, sin, injustice, misdeed, transgression ≠ good deed
• VERB = mistreat, abuse, hurt, harm, cheat, take advantage of, oppress, malign ≠ treat well

X

X-ray = radiograph, x-ray image

Y

yank VERB = pull, tug, jerk, seize, snatch, pluck, hitch, wrench
• NOUN = pull, tug, jerk, snatch, hitch, wrench, tweak

yarn **1** = thread, fibre, cotton, wool **2** (*Informal*) = story, tale, anecdote, account, narrative, fable, reminiscence, urban myth

yawning = gaping, wide, huge, vast, cavernous

yearly ADJECTIVE = annual, each year, every year, once a year
• ADVERB = annually, every year, by the year, once a year, per annum

yearn *often with* ***for*** = long, desire, hunger, ache, crave, covet, itch, hanker after

yell VERB = scream, shout, cry out, howl, call out, wail, shriek, screech ≠ whisper
• NOUN = scream, cry, shout, roar, howl, shriek, whoop, screech ≠ whisper

yen = longing, desire, craving, yearning, passion, hunger, ache, itch

yet ADVERB **1** = so far, until now, up to now, still, as yet, even now, thus far, up till now **2** = now, right now, just now, so soon **3** = still, in addition, besides, to boot, into the bargain
• CONJUNCTION = nevertheless, still, however, for all that, notwithstanding, just the same, be that as it may

yield VERB **1** = bow, submit, give in, surrender, succumb, cave in (*informal*), capitulate **2** = relinquish, resign, hand

over, surrender, turn over, make over, give over, bequeath ≠ retain ≠ resist **3** = produce, give, provide, return, supply, bear, net, earn ≠ use up
• **NOUN 1** = produce, crop, harvest, output **2** = profit, return, income, revenue, earnings, takings ≠ loss

yielding 1 = soft, pliable, springy, elastic, supple, spongy, unresisting **2** = submissive, obedient, compliant, docile, flexible, accommodating, pliant, acquiescent ≠ obstinate

yob *or* **yobbo** = thug, hooligan, lout, hoon (*Austral. & N.Z. slang*), ruffian, roughneck (*slang*), tsotsi (*S. African*), cougan (*Austral. slang*), scozza (*Austral. slang*), bogan (*Austral. slang*)

young ADJECTIVE 1 = immature, juvenile, youthful, little, green, junior, infant, adolescent ≠ old **2** = early, new, undeveloped, fledgling ≠ advanced
• **PLURAL NOUN** = offspring, babies, litter, family, issue, brood, progeny ≠ parents

youngster = youth, girl, boy, kid (*informal*), lad, teenager, juvenile, lass

youth 1 = immaturity, adolescence, boyhood *or* girlhood, salad days ≠ old age **2** = boy, lad, youngster, kid (*informal*), teenager, young man, adolescent, teen (*informal*) ≠ adult

youthful = young, juvenile, childish, immature, boyish, girlish ≠ elderly

Z

zeal = enthusiasm, passion, zest, spirit, verve, fervour, eagerness, gusto ≠ apathy

zero 1 = nought, nothing, nil **2** = rock bottom, the bottom, an all-time low, a nadir, as low as you can get

zip VERB = speed, shoot, fly, flash, zoom, whizz (*informal*)
• **NOUN** (*Informal*) = energy, drive, vigour, verve, zest, gusto, liveliness ≠ lethargy

zone = area, region, section, sector, district, territory, belt, sphere

zoom = speed, shoot, fly, rush, flash, dash, whizz (*informal*), hurtle

THEMED LISTS

ACIDS

SPECIFIC ACIDS

abietic acid
acetic acid
alginic acid
aminobenzoic acid
aspartic acid
barbituric acid
benzoic acid
boric acid
butyric acid
carbonic acid
chloric acid
chloroacetic acid
chlorous acid
cholic acid
chromic acid
cinnamic acid
citric acid
crotonic acid
cyanic acid
decanedioic acid
decanoic acid
dichromic acid
dithionous acid
deoxyribonucleic acid
dodecanoic acid
erucic acid
formic acid
fulminic acid
fumaric acid
gallic acid
glacial acetic acid
glyceric acid
heptadecanoic acid
hexanoic acid
hydnocarpic acid
hydrochloric acid
hydrofluoric acid
hypochlorous acid
hypophosphoric acid
hypophosphorous
isocyanic acid
itaconic acid
lactic acid
linoleic acid
linolenic acid
lysergic acid
manganic acid
mucic acid
nitric acid
nitrous acid
nonanoic acid
octanedioic acid
oleic acid
orthophosphoric acid
oxalic acid
pantothenic acid
para-aminobenzoic acid
pectic acid
pentanoic acid
permanganic acid
phosphoric acid
phthalic acid
picric acid
platinocyanic acid
polyphosphoric acid
propanoic acid
prussic acid
pyroboric acid
pyrophosphoric acid
pyrosulphuric acid
racemic acid
ricinoleic acid
saccharic acid
selenic acid
selenious acid
silicic acid
sorbic acid
spiraeic acid (modern salicylic acid)
stearic acid
suberic acid
succinic acid
sulphonic acid
sulphurous acid
tantalic acid
tartaric acid
telluric acid
terebic acid
terephthalic acid
thiocyanic acid
thiosulphuric acid
trichloroacetic acid
uric acid

TYPES OF ACID

amino acid
carboxylic acid
dibasic acid
dicarboxylic acid
fatty acid
iodic acid
mineral acid
nucleic acid
periodic acid
polycarboxylic acid

AMINO ACIDS

alanine
arginine
citrulline
cystine
glutamine
glycine
histidine
isoleucine
leucine
lysine
ethionine
ornithine
proline
serine
threonine
triiodothyronine

AIRCRAFT

TYPES OF AIRCRAFT

aerodyne
aerostat
airliner
airship
amphibian
autogiro *or* autogyro
balloon
biplane
blimp
bomber
canard
coleopter
convertiplane, convertaplane, *or* convertoplane
cyclogiro
delta-wing
dirigible
dive bomber
drone
fighter
fighter-bomber
flying boat
flying wing
freighter
gas-filled balloon
glider
gyrodyne
hang-glider
helicopter
helicopter gunship
hot-air balloon
interceptor *or* intercepter
jet *or* jet plane
jetliner

jumbo jet
jump jet
lifting body
light aircraft
microlight *or* microlite
monoplane
multiplane
night fighter
ornithopter *or* orthopter
rotaplane
sailplane
seaplane
skiplane
Stealth bomber *or* Stealth plane
STOL
swept-wing
swing-wing
tanker
triplane
troop carrier
turbofan
turbojet
turboprop *or* propjet
VTOL
warplane
wing
zeppelin

AIRCRAFT PARTS

aerofoil
aerometeorograph
aerostructure
afterburner
aileron
airframe
air-intake
airlock
air scoop
airscrew
all-flying tail
altimeter
anti-icer
arrester
artificial horizon
astrodome *or* astrohatch
athodyd
autopilot
auxiliary power unit
basket
black box
blister
body
bomb bay
bombsight
bulkhead
cabin
canopy
cantilever
capsule
chassis
clamshell
cockpit
control column *or* control stick
cowling *or* cowl
dashboard
drop tank
ejection seat
elevator
elevon
empennage
engine
engine pod
fairing
fin
flap
flight deck
flight recorder
fuel tank
fuselage
galley
gondola
heat sink
hold
horn *or* horn balance
hydroplane
inclinometer
instrument panel
jet engine
jet pipe
joystick
keel
landing gear
landing light
launching shoe *or* launch shoe
longeron
main plane
nacelle
nose
nose wheel
Pitot tube
pod
propeller
pulsejet
pusher
pylon
ramjet *or* ramjet engine
rotor
rudder
slat
slinger ring
spinner
spoiler
stabilizer
tab
tail
tailplane
tailskid
tail wheel
trailing edge
trim tab
turret
undercarriage
waist
wing
winglet
wing tip

ALCOHOLIC DRINKS

apéritif
busera
Campari *(trademark)*
chaser
cider, cyder, *or (U.S. & Canad.)* hard cider
caudle
Cinzano *(trademark)*
cocktail
cordial
dram
Dubonnet *(trademark)*
elderberry wine
frappé
French vermouth
ginger wine
glogg
gluhwein
grog
hippocras
Irish coffee *or* Gaelic coffee
Italian vermouth
kvass, kvas, *or* quass
liqueur
malt liquor
Martini *(trademark)*
mead
mulled wine
negus
nor'wester
palm wine
posset
pousse-café
pulque
sake, saké, saki, *or* rice wine
samshu
shooter
skokiaan
slammer
snakebite
soma
spruce beer
toddy
vermouth
waragi

ALGAE

blackfish weed *(Austral.)*
bladderwrack
brown algae
carrageen, carragheen, *or* carageen
diatom

dinoflagellate
dulse
euglena
fucoid *or* fucus
green algae
gulfweed
Iceland moss
Irish moss
kelp
laver
lichen
Neptune's necklace (*Austral.*)
oarweed
phytoplankton *or* plankton
red algae
reindeer moss
rockweed
sargasso *or* sargassum
sea lettuce
sea tangle
seaweed
sea wrack
spirogyra
stonewort
wrack

ALLOYS

Alnico (*trademark*)
amalgam
austenitic stainless steel
Babbit metal
bell bronze
bell metal
billon
brass
brazing solder
Britannia metal
bronze
chromel
constantan
cupronickel
Duralumin (*trademark*)
electrum
ferrochromium
ferromanganese
ferromolybdenum
ferronickel
ferrosilicon
Invar (*trademark*)
kamacite
magnolia metal
magnox
Manganin (*trademark*)
misch metal
Monel *or* Monell metal
Nichrome (*trademark*)
nickel silver
nimonic alloy
ormolu
oroide
osmiridium
permalloy
pewter
phosphor bronze
pinchbeck
platina
platiniridium
soft solder
speculum metal
steel
Stellite (*trademark*)
sterling silver
terne
tombac *or* tambac
type metal
white gold
zircalloy

ALPHABETS

RELATED VOCABULARY

Cyrillic
hiragana
kana
kanji
katakana
Kufic *or* Cufic
Latin
lexigraphy
Linear A
Linear B
logogram *or* logograph
Nagari
Roman

ARABIC LETTERS

alif
bā
tā
thā
jīm
ḥā
khā
dāl
dhāl
rā
zā
sīn
shīn
ṣād
ḍād
ṭā
ẓā
`ain
ghain
fā
qāf
kāf
lām
mīm
nūn
hā
wāw
yā

GREEK LETTERS

alpha
beta
chi
delta
epsilon
eta
gamma
iota
kappa
lambda
mu
nu
omega
omicron
phi
pi
psi
rho
sigma
tau
theta
upsilon
xi
zeta

HEBREW LETTERS

aleph
ayin *or* ain
beth
daleth *or* daled
gimel
he
heth *or* cheth
kaph
koph *or* qoph
lamed *or* lamedh
mem
nun
pe
resh
sadhe, sade, *or* tsade
samekh
shin
sin
tav *or* taw
teth
vav *or* waw
yod *or* yodh
zayin

COMMUNICATIONS CODE WORDS FOR THE ALPHABET

Alpha
Bravo
Charlie
Delta
Echo
Foxtrot
Golf
Hotel
India
Juliet
Kilo
Lima
Mike
November
Oscar
Papa
Quebec
Romeo
Sierra
Tango
Uniform
Victor
Whiskey
X-Ray
Yankee
Zulu

ENGLISH AND AMERICAN EQUIVALENCES

English	American	English	American
aeroplane	airplane	foyer	lobby
American football	football	fringe	bangs
antenatal	prenatal	garden	yard
aubergine	eggplant	gear lever	stick shift
autumn	fall	goose pimples	goose bumps
bad-tempered	mean	ground floor	first floor
banknote	bill	hair grip	bobby pin
bat	paddle	hairpin bend	switchback
benefit	welfare	handbag	purse
bin *or* dustbin	trashcan	hessian	burlap
biscuit	cookie	high street	main street
black pudding	blood sausage	holiday	vacation
blinds	shades	indicator	blinker
bonnet (car)	hood	invigilator	proctor
boot (car)	trunk	ironmonger	hardware store
braces (teeth)	retainer	jam	jelly
braces (lingerie)	suspenders	janitor	caretaker
breve	double whole note	lawyer	attorney
broad bean	fava bean	lift	elevator
building society	savings and loan	mangetout	snowpea
burgle	burglarize	mate	friend
candy floss	cotton candy	merry-go-round	carousel
car	automobile	methylated spirits	denatured alcohol
car park	parking lot	mince	ground beef
chemist	drug store	minim	half note
chips	French fries	nappy	diaper
clothes peg	clothes pin	neat (of drinks)	straight
coffin	casket	noughts and crosses	tick-tack-toe
condom	rubber	nursery	kindergarten
cornflour	corn starch	off-licence	liquor store
courgette	zucchini	paraffin	kerosene
crisps	chips *or* potato chips	pavement	sidewalk
crossroads	intersection	pepper	bell pepper
crotchet	quarter note	petrol	gas *or* gasoline
current account	checking account	pissed	drunk
curtains	drapes	plait	braid
cutlery	flatware *or* silverware	plasterboard	dry lining
CV	résumé	plot	lot
dialling code	area code	porridge	oatmeal
dinner jacket	tuxedo	postcode	zip code
double cream	heavy cream	postman	mail man
drapery	dry goods	pub *or* public house	bar
draughts	checkers	public school	private school
drawing pin	thumb tack	purse	pocketbook
dressing gown	robe	pushchair	stroller
dummy	pacifier *or* soother	quaver	eighth note
engaged tone	busy signal	quilt *or* eiderdown	comforter
estate agent	realtor	railway	railroad
estate car	station wagon	receptionist	desk clerk
fire lighter	fire starter	reverse charge	collect
first floor	second floor	ring road	beltway
flat	apartment	roll *or* bap	bun
flick knife	switch blade	rubber	eraser
football	soccer	rubbish	trash *or* garbage

English	American	English	American
semibreve	whole note	tap	faucet
semi-detached	duplex	tarmac	asphalt
semiquaver	sixteenth note	telegram	wire
shop	store	thread	cotton
silencer	muffler	tights	pantihose
skip	dumpster	timber	lumber
skirting board	baseboard	torch	flashlight
sleeper (railway)	tie	town centre	downtown
slowcoach	slowpoke	trainers	sneakers
soft drink	soda	tram	streetcar
spanner	wrench	trousers	pants
spring onion *or* salad onion	scallion	turn up	cuff
		VAT	sales tax
state school	public school	vest	undershirt
stream	creek	waistcoast	vest
surgical spirit	rubbing alcohol	windscreen	windshield
sweet	candy		

AMPHIBIANS

axolotl
brown-striped frog (*Austral.*)
bullfrog
caecilian
cane toad (*Austral.*)
congo eel *or* snake
eft
frog *or (Caribbean)* crapaud
Goliath frog
hairy frog
hellbender
hyla
midwife toad
mud puppy
natterjack
newt *or (dialect or archaic)* eft
olm
pipa *or* Surinam toad
Queensland cane toad
salamander
siren
toad *or (Caribbean)* crapaud
tree frog

ANGELS

ANGELS

Azrael
Gabriel
Michael
Raphael
Uriel

ANGELIC ORDERS

angels
archangels
cherubim
dominations *or* dominions
powers
principalities *or* princedoms
seraphim
thrones
virtues

ANIMALS

RELATED WORDS

ant	formic
ass	asinine
bear	ursine
bee	apian
bird	avian *or* ornithic
bull	taurine
cat	feline
crab	cancroid
crow	corvine
deer	cervine
dog	canine
dove	columbine
eagle	aquiline
elephant	elephantine
falcon	falconine
fish	piscine *or* icthyoid
fowl	gallinaceous
fox	vulpine
goat	caprine *or* hircine
goose	anserine *or* anserous
gull	larine
hare	leporine
hawk	accipitrine
horse	equine
lion	leonine
lynx	lyncean
mite *or* tick	acaroid
monkey	simian
ox	bovine
parrot	psittacine
peacock	pavonine
pig	porcine
puffin	alcidine
seal	phocine
sheep	ovine
snake	serpentine, anguine, ophidian, *or* colubrine
swallow	hirundine
wasp	vespine
wolf	lupine

COLLECTIVE ANIMALS

antelopes	herd
apes	shrewdness
asses	pace *or* herd
badgers	cete
bears	sloth
bees	swarm *or* grist
birds	flock, congregation, flight, *or* volery
bitterns	sedge *or* siege
boars	sounder
bucks	brace *or* lease
buffaloes	herd
capercailzies	tok
cats	clowder
cattle	drove *or* herd
choughs	chattering
colts	rag
coots	covert
cranes	herd, sedge, *or* siege
crows	murder
cubs	litter
curlews	herd
curs	cowardice
deer	herd
dolphins	school
doves	flight *or* dule
ducks	paddling *or* team
dunlins	flight
elk	gang
fish	shoal, draught, haul, run, *or* catch
flies	swarm *or* grist
foxes	skulk
geese	gaggle *or* skein
giraffes	herd
gnats	swarm *or* cloud
goats	herd *or* tribe
goldfinches	charm
grouse	brood, covey, *or* pack
gulls	colony
hares	down *or* husk
hawks	cast
hens	brood
herons	sedge *or* siege
herrings	shoal *or* glean
hounds	pack, mute, *or* cry
insects	swarm
kangaroos	troop
kittens	kindle
lapwings	desert
larks	exaltation
leopards	leap
lions	pride *or* troop
mallards	sord *or* sute
mares	stud
martens	richesse
moles	labour
monkeys	troop
mules	barren
nightingales	watch
owls	parliament
oxen	yoke, drove, team, *or* herd
partridges	covey
peacocks	muster
pheasants	nye *or* nide
pigeons	flock *or* flight
pigs	litter
plovers	stand *or* wing
pochards	flight, rush, bunch, *or* knob
ponies	herd
porpoises	school *or* gam
poultry	run
pups	litter
quails	bevy
rabbits	nest
racehorses	field *or* string
ravens	unkindness
roes	bevy
rooks	building *or* clamour
ruffs	hill
seals	herd *or* pod
sheep	flock
sheldrakes	dopping
snipe	walk *or* wisp
sparrows	host
starlings	murmuration
swallows	flight
swans	herd *or* bevy
swifts	flock
swine	herd, sounder, *or* dryft
teal	bunch, knob, *or* spring
whales	school, gam, *or* run
whelps	litter
whiting	pod
wigeon	bunch, company, knob, *or* flight
wildfowl	plump, sord, *or* sute
wolves	pack, rout, *or* herd
woodcocks	fall

HABITATIONS

ant	ant hill *or* formicary
badger	set *or* sett
beaver	lodge
bee	hive *or* apiary
bird	nest
eagle	aerie *or* eyrie
fish	redd
fox	earth
otter	holt
pig	sty
puffin	puffinry
rabbit	warren
rook	rookery
seal	sealery
squirrel	drey *or* dray
termite	termitarium
wasp	vespiary *or* bike

MALE

ass	jack
bird	cock
cat	tom
deer	hart *or* stag
donkey	jack
duck	drake
elephant	bull
falcon	tercel *or* tiercel
ferret	hob
fowl	cock
fox	dog
goat	billy *or* buck
goose	gander
hare	buck
horse	stallion
kangaroo	buck *or* old man
lobster	cock
ox	bull
peafowl	peacock
pig	boar
rabbit	buck
reindeer	buck
ruff	ruff
sheep	ram *or* tup
swan	cob
weasel	whittret
whale	bull

FEMALE

ass	jenny		jill *(dialect)*	lobster	hen	swan	pen
bird	hen	fowl	hen	mink	sow	tiger	tigress
cat	tabby	fox	vixen	ox	cow	whale	cow
deer	doe *or* hind	goat	nanny	peafowl	peahen	wolf	bitch
dog	bitch	hare	doe	pig	sow	wren	jenny
donkey	jenny	horse	mare	rabbit	doe		
elephant	cow	leopard	leopardess	ruff	reeve		
ferret	gill *or*	lion	lioness	sheep	ewe		

YOUNG

bear	cub	falcon	eyas	owl	owlet
bird	chick, fledg(e)ling, *or* nestling	ferret	kit	ox	calf
butterfly	caterpillar, chrysalis, *or* chrysalid	fish	fry *or* fingerling	pig	piglet
cat	kitten	frog	tadpole	pigeon	squab
cod	codling	fox	kit *or* cub	salmon	alevin, grilse, parr, *or* smolt
deer	fawn	goat	kid *or* yeanling	seal	pup
dog	pup *or* puppy	goose	gosling	sheep	lamb *or* yeanling
duck	duckling	hare	leveret	sprat	brit
eagle	eaglet	herring	alevin, brit, *or* sparling	swan	cygnet
eel	elver *or* grig	horse	foal, colt, *or* filly	tiger	cub
elephant	calf	kangaroo	joey	toad	tadpole
		lion	cub	whale	calf
		moth	caterpillar	wolf	cub *or* whelp

ANNIVERSARIES

Year	*Traditional*	*Modern*	*Year*	*Traditional*	*Modern*
1st	Paper	Clocks	13th	Lace	Textile, furs
2nd	Cotton	China	14th	Ivory	Gold jewellery
3rd	Leather	Crystal, glass	15th	Crystal	Watches
4th	Linen (silk)	Electrical appliances	20th	China	Platinum
5th	Wood	Silverware	25th	Silver	Sterling silver
6th	Iron	Wood	30th	Pearl	Diamond
7th	Wool (copper)	Desk sets	35th	Coral (jade)	Jade
8th	Bronze	Linen, lace	40th	Ruby	
9th	Pottery (china)	Leather	45th	Sapphire	
10th	Tin (aluminium)	Diamond jewellery	50th	Gold	
11th	Steel	Fashion jewellery, accessories	55th	Emerald	
12th	Silk	Pearls *or* coloured gems	60th	Diamond	

ANTS, BEES, AND WASPS

Amazon ant
ant *or (archaic or dialect)* emmet
army ant *or* legionary ant
bee
blue ant *(Austral.)*
bulldog ant, bull ant, *or (Austral.)* bull Joe
bumblebee *or* humblebee
carpenter bee
cicada hunter *(Austral.)*
cuckoo bee
digger wasp
driver ant
flower wasp *(Austral.)*
gall wasp
honeypot ant *or* honey ant *(Austral.)*
honeybee *or* hive bee
horntail *or* wood wasp
ichneumon fly *or* ichneumon wasp
killer bee
kootchar *(Austral.)*
leafcutter ant
leafcutter bee
mason bee
mason wasp
minga *(Austral.)*
mining bee
mud dauber
native bee *or* sugarbag fly *(Austral.)*
Pharaoh ant
policeman fly *(Austral.)*
ruby-tail wasp
sand wasp
Sirex wasp *(Austral.)*
slave ant
spider-hunting wasp
termite *or* white ant
velvet ant
wasp
wood ant
yellow jacket

FOUR HORSEMEN OF THE APOCALYPSE

white - Christ
red - War
black - Famine
pale - Death

APPLES

biffin *(Brit.)*
Blenheim Orange
Braeburn
bramley
Charles Ross
codlin *or* codling
costard
Cox's orange pippin
crab apple
Discovery
Egremont Russet
Elstar
Empire
Fuji
Golden Delicious
Granny Smith
Greensleeves
Grenadier
Idared
James Grieve
Jonathon
Jonagold
Laxton Superb
Lobo
Lord Lambourne
Pink Lady
pippin
Prince Albert
Red Delicious
Red Ellison
Rosemary Russet
Royal Gala
russet
Spartan
sturmer
sunset
sweeting
Worcester Pearmain

TYPES OF ARCH

acute, gothic, lancet, pointed arch, *or* ogive
horseshoe arch
keel arch
Norman *or* Roman arch
gee arch
proscenium arch
Roman arch
skew arch
triumphal arch

ARCHAEOLOGY

ARCHAEOLOGICAL PERIODS

Acheulean *or* Acheulian
Asturian
Aurignacian
Azilian
Bronze Age
chalcolithic
Châtelperronian
Eneolithic
Gravettian
Helladic
Ice age
Iron Age
La Tène
Levalloisian *or* Levallois
Magdalenian
Mesolithic
Minoan
Mousterian
Mycenaean
Neo-Babylonian
Neolithic *or* New Stone Age
Old Babylonian
Palaeolithic *or* Old Stone Age
Solutrean

ARCHAEOLOGICAL TERMS

acropolis
alignment
arcade
archaeomagnetism *or* archeomagnetism
barrow
baulk
bifacial
blade
bogman
bracteate
burin
cairn
callais
cartouch *or* cartouche
caveman
celt
cirque
cist *or* kist
clovis point
core
cromlech
cross-dating
dolmen
earthwork
eolith
flake
flint
graffito
henge
hillfort
hogback
hut circle
larnax
ley line
microlith
megalith
mound
neolith
obelisk
palmette
palstave
patella
pylon
radiocarbon dating
retouch
robber trench
sondage
souterrain
stela *or* stele
stone circle
stratigraphy
tribrach
tumulus
vallum

ARCHITECTURE

ARCHITECTURAL STYLES

Art Deco
Art Nouveau
Baroque
Bauhaus
brutalist
Byzantine
churrigueresque *or* churrigueresco
classical
colonial
Composite
Corinthian
Decorated
Doric
Early Christian
Early English
Edwardian
Elizabethan
Empire
Federation *(Austral.)*
functionalism
Georgian
Gothic
Gothic Revival

Greek Revival
International Style *or* Modernist
Ionic
Jacobean
Louis Quatorze
Louis Quinze
Louis Seize
Louis Treize
Mannerist
moderne
Moorish *or* Morisco
Mudéjar
neoclassicist
new brutalist
Norman
Palladian
perpendicular
postmodernist
Queen-Anne
Regency
Renaissance
Rococo
Roman
Romanesque
Saracen
Saxon
transition *or* transitional
Tudor
Tuscan
Victorian

ARCHITECTURAL TERMS

abutment *or* abuttal
architectonic
architectonics
architectural
astylar
bolster
bracket
castellated *or* castled
cinquecento
cloistered
colossal *or* giant
composite
cradling
crenellate *or* (*U.S.*) crenelate
denticulate
diastyle
diminish
dipteral
discharge
drum
elevation
engaged
eurhythmy
fenestrated
filler
flamboyant
floor plan
floriated *or* floreated
florid
fluted
foliated
foliation
galilee
galleria
ground plan
hexastyle
high-pitched
hip
hipped
hypostyle
imbricate *or* imbricated
intercolumniation
invert
joggle post *or* king post
lanceted
lierne
lintel *or* summer
listed
loggia
member
module
Moresque
naos
order
orientation
polychromy
postiche
profile
prostyle
pulvinate *or* pulvinated
queen post
rampant
rendering
respond
return
rhythm
ribbon development
rise
rusticate
sexpartite
shaft
shafting
shell
soffit
springing, spring, springing line, *or* springing point
stilted
storey
stria
stringer, string, *or* string course
stylobate
subbase
summer *or* summer tree
supercolumnar
surbase
tailpiece *or* tail beam
trabeate *or* trabeated
tympanic
underpitch vault

ARCHITECTURAL FEATURES

abacus
acanthus
accolade
acroter
aisle
ambulatory
amphiprostyle
amphistylar
ancon *or* ancone
annulet
anta
antefix
anthemion
apophyge *or* hypophyge
apse *or* apsis
apteral
arcade
arcature
arch
architrave
archivolt
arcuation
arris
articulation
astragal
atlas (*plural* atlantes) *or* telamon
atrium
attic
baguette *or* baguet
balcony
baldachin
balk
ballflower
baluster
band
banderole, banderol, *or* bannerol
barge couple
barge course
barrel vault, tunnel vault, *or* wagon vault
base
basement
bay window
bead
beak
bed moulding
belfry
bezant, bezzant, *or* byzant
billet
binder
bolection *or* bilection
bottom house
bow
bow window
bracket
brattishing
breast
broach
buttress
caisson, coffer, *or* lacuna
calotte
canopy
cantilever
capital, chapiter, *or* cap
cartouche
caryatid
case *or* casing
casement
Catherine wheel
cavetto
ceiling
cella *or* naos
cellar
channel
chaplet
cheek
chevron *or* dancette
choir
choir loft
cinquefoil
clerestory

cloister
colonnade
columbarium
column
columniation
compass window
concha *or* conch
congé
corbeil *or* corbeille
corbel *or* truss
corbie gable
corbie-step, corbel step, *or* crow step
cordon, string course, belt course, *or* table
cornice
corona
cove *or* coving
crenel *or* crenelle
cresting
crocket *or* crochet
crossing
crown
cullis
cupola
curb roof
curtail step
curtain wall
cushion
cusp
cuspidation
cyma
cymatium
dado
decastyle
dentil
die
dogtooth
drip
dripstone, label, *or* hood mould
echinus
ectype
egg and dart, egg and tongue, *or* egg and anchor
ell
embrasure
entablature
entasis
exedra
extrados
facade
facet
fan
fanlight
fantail
fan tracery
fan *or* palm vaulting
fascia *or* facia
fascial *or* facial
fenestella
fenestra
festoon
fillet *or* listel
finial
flèche
fluting
flying buttress *or* arc-boutant
foil
footing
footstall
French windows *or* doors
frieze
frontispiece
frustum
gable
gable end
gable window
gadroon *or* godroon
gallery
gambrel
gargoyle
garret
garth
gatehouse
gazebo
glyph
gradin
griffe
groin
grotto
gutta
half landing
haunch *or* hance
headstone
headwork
helicline
hipped *or* hip roof
imperial
impost
intrados
jube
keystone, quoin, *or* headstone
lancet arch, Gothic arch, *or* ogive
lancet window
landing
lantern
leaded
loggia
long-and-short work
louvre
lucarne
machicolation
mansard
meander
medallion
metope
minaret
modillion
moulding
mullion
mutule
narthex
neck
necking *or* gorgerin
newel
niche
Norman arch *or* Roman arch
obelisk
oeil-de-boeuf
offset
ogee, ogee arch, *or* talon
ogive
onion dome
oriel *or* oriel window
ovolo, quarter round, *or* thumb
pace
parapet
patio
pedestal
pediment
pendant
penthouse
peristyle
perpend
perron
piazza
pier
pillar
pinnacle
platform
plinth
podium
predella
pylon
quad
poppyhead
porch *or* portico
portal
porte-cochere
postern
propylaeum
quadrangle
quatrefoil
quirk
quoin, coign, *or* coigne
reed
reeding
reglet
relief
respond
return
reveal
rib
ridge
rose window, rosace, *or* rosette
rotunda
roundel
saddle roof *or* saddleback
sash window
scotia
screen
scrollwork
semidome
shaft
shafting
sill
skew arch
skylight
soffit
spandrel *or* spandril
spire
splay
springer
squinch
squint *or* hagioscope
steeple
stele *or* stela
stoa
straining piece
strap work
stria
strigil
stylobate *or* stereobate
summer
taenia *or (U.S.)* tenia
tambour
tellamon
term, terminal, *or* terminus
torus *or* tore
tracery
transept
traverse
trefoil
tribune

triforium
triglyph
trophy
trumeau
turret
tympanum *or* tympan
underpitch vault
vault
veranda *or* verandah
verge
vignette
volute *or* helix
water table
web
whispering gallery
xyst

ARMOUR

armet
basinet *or* bascinet
breastplate
camail
chamfrain, chamfron, *or* chanfron
coat-of-mail
corselet *or* corslet
couter
crinet
cuirass
cuisse *or* cuish
culet
gauntlet
gorget
greave
gusset
helmet
jack
jambeau, jambart, *or* jamber
jupon
lance rest
mail
nosepiece
pavloron
poleyn
roundel
sabaton
sword belt
tasset, tasse, *or* tace
umbo
vambrace
ventail
visor *or* vizor

ART

ART STYLES AND MOVEMENTS

abstract expressionism
abstractionism
Art Deco
Arte Povera
Art Nouveau
Barbizon School
baroque
Der Blaue Reiter
Brücke
classicism
conceptual art
constructivism
cubism
Dada *or* Dadaism
De Stijl
divisionism
expressionism
Fauvism
futurism
Gothic
Impressionism
Jugendstil
mannerism
minimal art
modernism
Nabis
naturalism
Nazarene
neoclassicism
neoimpressionism
neoplasticism
op art
pointillism
pop art
postimpressionism
postmodernism
Pre-Raphaelite
realism
rococo
Romanesque
romanticism
Suprematism
surrealism
symbolism
synthetism
ukiyo-e
vorticism

ART EQUIPMENT

acrylic
airbrush
brush
canvas
chalk
charcoal
crayon
drawing paper
easel
fixative
glaze
ground
ink
lay figure
linseed oil
oil paint
paint
paintbox
paintbrush
palette
palette knife
pastel
pencil
sketchbook
spatula
spray gun
varnish
watercolour

ARTHURIAN LEGEND

CHARACTERS IN ARTHURIAN LEGEND

Arthur
Bedivere
Bors
Caradoc
Elaine
Galahad
Gareth (of Orkney)
Gawain *or* Gawayne
Guinevere
Igraine
Lancelot *or* Launcelot du Lac
Launfal
Merlin
Modred
Morgan Le Fay
Nimue
Parsifal *or* Perceval
Tristan *or* Tristram
Uther Pendragon
Viviane *or* the Lady of the Lake

PLACES IN ARTHURIAN LEGEND

Astolat
Avalon
Camelot
Glastonbury
Lyonnesse
Tintagel

ASTEROIDS

Ceres
Eros
Hermes
Hesperia
Juno
Pallas
Phaethon

ASTROLOGY TERMS

air
Ascendant *or* Ascendent
aspect
birthchart
cardinal
conjunction
cusp
Descendant *or* Descendent
earth
element
fire
fixed
horoscope
house
Midheaven *or* MC
mutable
opposition
quintile
ruling planet
satellitium
square
stars
star sign
sun sign
trine
water
zodiac

ASTRONOMY TERMS

achondrite
aerolite
aerospace
aerosphere
albedo
almucantar *or* almacantar
altitude
analemma
annular eclipse
anthelion
aphelion
apocynthion
apolune
appulse
apapsis
apsis *or* apse
asteroid
asteroid belt
astrobleme
atmosphere
aureola *or* aureole
aurora
aurora australis
aurora borealis
azimuth
barycentre
basin
binary star
black drop
black hole
blue straggler
bolide
brown dwarf
burst
cataclysmic variable
Cepheid variable
Chandrasekhar limit
chemosphere
chondrite
chromosphere
circumlunar
circumpolar
circumsolar
circumstellar
cislunar
cluster
collapsar
colour index
colure
coma
comet
companion
conjunction
constellation
cooordinate system
Copernican system
corona
cosmic
cosmogony
cosmology
crater
crescent
crust
culmination
cusp
dwarf
dynamics
eccentric
ecosphere
effective temperature
ejecta
ellipse
elongation
emersion
ephemeris
epoch
equator
escape velocity
equinox
evection
evolved star
exosphere
extinction
facula
farside
filament
fireball
flare
flocculus
galactic centre
galactic equator
galactic rotation
galaxy
giant
gravitation
heliocentric system
heliosphere
immersion *or* ingress
inclination
inequality
inertia
inferior planet
inner planet
insolation
interplanetary
interstellar
ionosphere
jet
light year
limb
lodestar *or* loadstar
luminosity
lunar
lunar eclipse
magnetosphere
magnitude
major planet
maria
mass
mass loss
mass transfer
merger
meridian
meridian passage
mesosphere
metallicity
metal ratio
meteor
meteorite
meteoroid
meteoroid stream
meteor shower
meteor storm
missing mass
molecular cloud
moonquake
moving cluster
multiple star
nadir
naked singularity
nearside
nebula
neutron star
new moon
node
north celestial pole
northern hemisphere
northern lights
northing
north polar distance
nova
nucleosynthesis
nucleus
nutation
oblateness
obliquity
observatory
occultation
octant
open cluster
opposition
orbit
orbital elements
orbital velocity
oscillating universe
outer planet
parallax
partial eclipse
penumbral eclipse
periapsis
periastron
percentre
perigee
perihelion
photosphere
physical libration
plages
planetary
planetary alignment
planetary system
planetesimal
planetoid
plasmasphere
plerion
polar axis
pole
precession
precession of the equinoxes
primary
prominence
proper motion
protogalaxy
protoplanet
protostar
Ptolemaic system
pulsating universe
pulsating variable
quadrature
quarter
quasar
quasi-stellar object
quiet

radiant
radio source
ray
reciprocal mass
red giant
red supergiant
regolith
retardation
revolution
ring
ring plain
rising
rotation
rupes
saros
satellite
Schwarzschild radius
scintillation
secondary
sextile
Seyfert galaxy
shell star
shepherd satellite
sidereal time
singularity
solar
solar constant
solar eclipse
solar spectrum
solar system
solstice
south celestial pole
southern hemisphere
southern lights
southing
south polar distance
space
spacetime
spectral type *or* spectral class
spherule
spicule
spinar
spray
star
star cloud
stellar
stellar evolution
stellar structure
stellar wind
Strömgren sphere
sublunar point
subsolar point
substellar point
sunspot
sunspot cycle
supercluster
supergiant
superior planet
supernova
symbiotic star
synodic period
syzygy
telluric line
terminator
terrestrial planet
tidal capture
tidal force
tidal friction
tide
total eclipse
total magnitude
thermosphere
train
transient lunar phenomena
triple star
tropical year
troposphere
universal time
universe
variable star
variation
velocity dispersion
vertical circle
visual magnitude
white dwarf
white hole
zenith
zenith distance

ATHLETIC EVENTS

100 metres
110 metres hurdles
200 metres
400 metres
400 metres hurdles
800 metres
1500 metres
3000 metres
5000 metres
10 000 metres
cross-country running
decathlon
discus
half marathon
hammer
heptathlon
high jump
javelin
long jump
marathon
orienteering
pentathlon
pole vault
relay
shot put
steeplechase
triathlon
triple jump
walking

REGIONS OF THE ATMOSPHERE

ionosphere
mesosphere
ozone layer *or* ozonosphere
stratosphere
thermosphere
troposphere

AVIATION TERMS

aerobatics
air corridor
air miss
airside
airspeed
air traffic control
anhedral
approach *or* approach path
attitude
automatic pilot *or* autopilot
autorotation
bank
barrel roll
batsman
belly landing
bird strike
boarding pass
bunt
ceiling
chandelle
charter flight
clearway
contact flight
copilot
crab
crash-dive
crash-land
cruise
dihedral
ditch
dive
drogue
feather
flameout
flight management systems
flight path
fly-by-wire
gate
glide
groundspeed
head-up display
holding pattern
hunt
Immelmann turn *or* Immelmann
in-flight
landing
landside
loading
loop
Mach
navigator
nose dive
overfly
overshoot
pancake landing
pilot
pitch
pitch axis
power dive
rake
redeye *or* redeye flight
reheat
roll
roll axis
runway
SBA *or* standard beam approach
scheduled flight
shockstall
sideslip
snap roll
sonic boom
sound barrier
spin
stack
stall
subsonic
supersonic
tailspin
takeoff
taxi
taxiway
trim
undershoot
vapour trail
victory roll
wide-body
wingover
yaw
yaw axis

BALL GAMES

American football
Australian Rules
badminton
bagatelle
bar billiards
baseball
billiards
boules
bowling
bumble-puppy
Canadian football
crazy golf
croquet
fives
football *or (U.S.)* soccer
goalball
golf
handball
hockey
hurling
korfball
lacrosse
netball
paintball
piggy in the middle
pinball
pocket billiards
punchball
pushball
pyramid
rounders
snooker
squash
Subbuteo *(trademark)*
tennis
volleyball

BATS

barbastelle
false vampire
flying fox
fruit bat
hammerhead
horseshoe bat
insectivorous bat
kalong
noctule
pipistrelle
serotine
vampire bat

FAMOUS BATTLES

Aboukir Bay *or* Abukir Bay	1798
Actium	31 B.C.
Agincourt	1415
Alamo	1836
Arnhem	1944
Atlantic	1939-45
Austerlitz	1805
Balaklava *or* Balaclava	1854
Bannockburn	1314
Barnet	1471
Bautzen	1813
Belleau Wood	1918
Blenheim	1704
Borodino	1812
Bosworth Field	1485
Boyne	1690
Britain	1940
Bulge	1944-45
Bull Run	1861;1862
Bunker Hill	1775
Cannae	216 B.C.
Crécy	1346
Culloden	1746
Dien Bien Phu	1954
Edgehill	1642
El Alamein	1942
Falkirk	1298; 1746
Flodden	1513
Gettysburg	1863
Guadalcanal	1942-3
Hastings	1066
Hohenlinden	1800
Imphal	1944
Inkerman	1854
Issus	333 B.C.
Jemappes	1792
Jena	1806
Killiecrankie	1689
Kursk	1943
Ladysmith	1899-1900
Le Cateau	1914
Leipzig	1813
Lepanto	1571
Leyte Gulf	1944
Little Bighorn	1876
Lützen	1632
Manassas	1861; 1862
Mantinea *or* Mantineia	418 B.C.; 362 B.C.
Marathon	490 B.C.
Marengo	1800
Marston Moor	1644
Missionary Ridge	1863
Naseby	1645
Navarino	425 B.C.
Omdurman	1898
Passchendaele	1917
Philippi	42 B.C.
Plains of Abraham	1759
Plassey	1757
Plataea	479 B.C.
Poltava	1709
Prestonpans	1745
Pydna	168 B.C.
Quatre Bras	1815
Ramillies	1706
Roncesvalles	778
Sadowa *or* Sadová	1866
Saint-Mihiel	1918
Salamis	480 B.C.
Sedgemoor	1685
Sempach	1386
Shiloh	1862
Shipka Pass	1877-78
Somme	1916; 1918
Stalingrad	1941-42
Stamford Bridge	1066
Stirling Bridge	1297
Tannenberg	1410; 1914
Tewkesbury	1471
Thermopylae	480 B.C.
Tobruk	1941; 1942
Trafalgar	1805
Trenton	1776
Verdun	1916
Vitoria	1813
Wagram	1809
Waterloo	1815
Ypres	1914; 1915; 1917; 1918
Zama	202 B.C.

BEERS

ale
barley wine
Bière de Garde
black and tan
bock beer *or* bock
boilermaker
bottle-conditioned beer *or* ale
brown ale
cask-conditioned beer *or* ale
Christmas beer *or* ale
draught beer
eighty shilling *or* eighty
export

fruit beer
guest beer
gueuze
half-and-half
heavy *(Scot.)*
home-brew
ice beer
India Pale Ale *or* IPA
Kaffir beer
keg beer
Kölsch
lager
lambic
light *(Scot.)*
light ale
mild
milk stout
nog *or* nogg *(dialect)*
pale ale
Pils
Pilsner *or* Pilsener
plain *(Irish)*
porter
Rauchbier
real ale
seventy shilling *or* seventy
shandy
shebeen *or* shebean *(Irish) (U.S.)*
sixty shilling *or* sixty
special
stingo
stout
sweet stout
Trappist beer
Weissbier
Weizenbier
wheat beer

BEETLES

ambrosia beetle
Asiatic beetle
bacon beetle
bark beetle
bee beetle
black beetle *or (N.Z.)* kekerengu *or* Māori bug
blister beetle
bloody-nosed beetle
boll weevil
bombardier beetle
burying beetle *or* sexton
cabinet beetle
cardinal beetle
carpet beetle *or (U.S.)* carpet bug
carrion beetle
chafer
Christmas beetle *or* king beetle
churchyard beetle
click beetle, snapping beetle, *or* skipjack
cockchafer, May beetle, *or* May bug
Colorado beetle *or* potato beetle
curculio
deathwatch beetle
devil's coach-horse
diving beetle
dor
dung beetle *or* chafer
elater
firefly
flea beetle
furniture beetle
glow-worm
gold beetle *or* goldbug
goldsmith beetle
goliath beetle
ground beetle
Hercules beetle
huhu
Japanese beetle
June bug, June beetle, May bug, *or* May beetle
ladybird *or (U.S. & Canad.)* ladybug
larder beetle
leaf beetle
leather beetle
longicorn (beetle) *or* long-horned beetle
May beetle, cockchafer, *or* June bug
museum beetle
oil beetle
pill beetle
rhinoceros beetle
rose chafer *or* rose beetle
rove beetle
scarab
scavenger beetle
snapping beetle
snout beetle
soldier beetle
Spanish fly
stag beetle
tiger beetle
timberman beetle
tortoise beetle
vedalia
water beetle
weevil *or* snout beetle
weevil, pea weevil, *or* bean weevil
whirligig beetle

BIBLE

BOOKS OF THE BIBLE (OLD TESTAMENT)

Genesis
Exodus
Leviticus
Numbers
Deuteronomy
Joshua
Judges
Ruth
1 Samuel
2 Samuel
1 Kings
2 Kings
1 Chronicles
2 Chronicles
Ezra
Nehemiah
Esther
Job
Psalms
Proverbs
Ecclesiastes
Song of Solomon
Isaiah
Jeremiah
Lamentations
Ezekiel
Daniel
Hosea
Joel
Amos
Obadiah
Jonah
Micah
Nahum
Habakkuk
Zephaniah
Haggai
Zechariah
Malachi

BOOKS OF THE BIBLE (NEW TESTAMENT)

Matthew
Mark
Luke
John
Acts
Romans
1 Corinthians
2 Corinthians
Galatians
Ephesians
Philippians
Colossians
1 Thessalonians
2 Thessalonians
1 Timothy
2 Timothy
Titus
Philemon
Hebrews
James
1 Peter
2 Peter
1 John
2 John
3 John
Jude
Revelation

BOOKS OF THE BIBLE (APOCRYPHA)

Tobit
Judith
1 Maccabees
2 Maccabees
Wisdom
Ecclesiasticus
Baruch
Daniel and Susanna
Daniel, Bel and the Snake
Song of the Three
Esdras
Manasseh

CHARACTERS IN THE BIBLE

Aaron
Abednego
Abel
Abigail
Abraham
Absalom
Achitophel *or* Ahithophel
Adam
Ahab
Ahasuerus
Ammon
Amos
Ananias
Andrew
Asher
Balaam
Balthazar
Barabbas
Bartholomew
Baruch
Bathsheba
Beelzebub
Belial
Belshazzar
Benjamin
Boanerges
Boaz
Caiaphas
Cain
Caspar
Cush *or* Kush
Dan
Daniel
David
Deborah
Delilah
Dinah
Dives
Dorcas
Elias
Elijah
Elisha
Enoch
Enos
Ephraim
Esau
Esther
Eve
Ezekiel
Ezra
Gabriel
Gad
Gideon
Gilead
Gog and Magog
Goliath
Good Samaritan
Habakkuk
Hagar
Haggai
Ham
Hannah
Herod
Hezekiah
Hiram
Holofernes
Hosea
Isaac
Isaiah
Ishmael
Issachar
Jacob
Jael
James
Japheth
Jehoshaphat
Jehu
Jephthah *or* Jephte
Jeremiah
Jeroboam
Jesse
Jesus Christ
Jethro
Jezebel
Joab
Job
Joel
John
John the Baptist
Jonah *or* Jonas
Jonathan
Joseph
Joshua
Josiah
Jubal
Judah
Judas Iscariot
Jude
Judith
Laban
Lazarus
Leah
Levi
Lot
Lot's wife
Luke
Magus
Malachi
Manasseh
Mark
Martha
Mary
Mary Magdalene
Matthew
Matthias
Melchior
Melchizedek *or* Melchisedech
Meshach
Methuselah
Micah
Midian
Miriam
Mordecai
Moses
Nabonidus
Naboth
Nahum
Naomi
Naphtali
Nathan
Nathanael
Nebuchadnezzar *or* Nebuchadrezzar
Nehemiah
Nicodemus
Nimrod
Noah
Obadiah
Paul
Peter
Philip
Potiphar
Prodigal Son
Queen of Sheba
Rachel
Rebecca
Reuben
Ruth
Salome
Samson
Samuel
Sarah
Saul
Seth
Shadrach
Shem
Simeon
Simon
Solomon
Susanna
Tetragrammaton
Thaddeus *or* Thadeus
Thomas
Tobit
Tubal-cain
Uriah
Virgin Mary
Zacharias, Zachariah, *or* Zachary
Zebedee
Zebulun
Zechariah
Zedekiah
Zephaniah
Zilpah

PLACE NAMES IN THE BIBLE

Aceldama
Antioch
Aram
Ararat
Arimathaea *or* Arimathea
Babel
Bashan
Bethesda
Bethlehem
Calvary
Cana
Canaan
Capernaum
Eden
Galilee
Garden of Eden
Gath
Gaza
Gehenna
Gethsemane
Golgotha
Gomorrah *or* Gomorrha
Goshen
Horeb
Jericho
Jerusalem
Judaea *or* Judea
Judah
land of milk and honey
land of Nod
Moab
Nazareth
On
Ophir
Rabbath Ammon
Samaria
Shiloh
Shinar
Shittim
Sodom
Tadmor
Tophet *or* Topheth
wilderness

BICYCLES

BICYCLE PARTS

bell
bicycle chain
bicycle pump
crossbar
handlebars
kickstand
mileometer
mudguard
pannier
pedal
rat-trap
saddle
saddlebag
stabilizer
wheel

TYPES OF BICYCLE

autocycle
bicycle
BMX
boneshaker
chopper
exercise bike
fairy cycle
mountain bike
penny-farthing
roadster
tandem
velocipede

BIOLOGY

BRANCHES OF BIOLOGY

actinobiology
aerobiology
agrobiology
astrobiology
bacteriology
biochemistry
biodynamics
biogeography
biometry
biophysics
biostatics
botany
chronobiology
cryobiology
cytogenetics
cytology
ecology
genetics
histology
microbiology
morphology
oceanography
organography
organology
palaeontology
parasitology
photobiology
photodynamics
radiobiology
sociobiology
somatology
stoichiology
taxonomy
teratology
zoology

BIOLOGY TERMS

aerobic
agglutination
albino
allele *or* allelomorph
anaerobic
anterior
asexual reproduction
assimilation
bacteria
binary fission
biomass
blood
blood vessel
bone
cell
chromosome
circulation
circulatory system
class
clone
codominance
cold-blooded
conception
copulation
cytoplasm
diffusion
digestion
diploid
division
DNA *or* deoxyribonucleic acid
dominant
dorsal
ecosystem
egg
embryo
environment
enzyme
epidermis
evolution
excretion
family
fermentation
fertilization
flower
foetus
food chain
fossil
fruit
fungus
gamete
gene
genus
germination
gestation
gland
gonad
growth
haploid
heredity
hermaphrodite
hormone
hybrid
inheritance
invertebrate
kingdom
Krebs cycle
life cycle
meiosis
menstruation
metabolism
metamorphosis
mitosis
muscle
mutation
natural selection
nitrogen cycle
nucleus
order
organ
osmosis
ovulation
ovum
parasite
pathogen
pectoral
photosynthesis
phylum
poikilothermic
pollen
pollination
pollution
posterior
predator
pregnancy
progeny
propagation
protein
protoplasm
puberty
recessive
reproduction
respiration
RNA *or* ribose nucleic acid
ribosome
root
seed
sexual reproduction
skeleton
skin
soil
species
spermatozoon *or* sperm
spore
symbiosis
translocation
transpiration
ventral
vertebrate
virus
vitamin
viviparous
warm-blooded
X-chromosome
Y-chromosome
zygote

BIRDS

accentor
amazon
amokura *(N.Z.)*
ani
apostle bird *or* happy family bird *(Austral.)*
avadavat *or* amadavat
avocet
axebird *(Austral.)*
babbler
Baltimore oriole
banded dotterel *(N.Z.)*
banded rail *(N.Z.)*
barbet
beccafico
bee-eater
bellbird *or (N.Z.)* koromako *or* makomako
bird of paradise

bishopbird
bittern
blackbird
blackcap
blackcock
black-fronted tern *or* tara *(N.Z.)*
black grouse
blackpoll
black robin *(N.Z.)*
bluebird
blue duck, mountain duck, whio *or* whistling duck *(N.Z.)*
blue grouse
blue jay
bluethroat
bluetit
boatbill *or* boat-billed heron
bobolink
bobwhite
bokmakierie
boobook *(Austral.)*
bowerbird
brain-fever bird *or* *(Austral.)* pallid cuckoo
brambling
broadbill
brolga, Australian crane, *or* *(Austral.)* native companion
brown creeper *or* pipipi *(N.Z.)*
brown duck *(N.Z.)*
brown kiwi *(N.Z.)*
budgerigar *or* *(Austral.)* zebra parrot
bulbul
bullfinch
bunting
bush shrike
bushtit
bush wren *(N.Z.)*
bustard *or* *(Austral.)* plain turkey, plains turkey, *or* wild turkey
button quail *or* *(Austral.)* bustard quail
cacique
Californian quail *(N.Z.)*
canary
Cape Barren goose
Cape pigeon
capercaillie *or* capercailzie
Cape sparrow
capuchin
cardinal *or* cardinal grosbeak
carrion crow
cassowary
catbird
chaffinch
chat
chickadee
chicken *or* *(Austral. informal)* chook
chiffchaff
chimney swallow *or* chimney swift
chipping sparrow
chough
chuck-will's-widow
chukar
cliff swallow
coal tit *or* coletit
cockatiel, cockateel, *or* cockatoo-parrot
cockatoo
cock-of-the-rock
collared dove
coly *or* mousebird
conure
coppersmith
coquette
corella
corn bunting
corncrake
cotinga *or* chatterer
coucal, pheasant coucal, *or* swamp pheasant
cowbird
crake
crane
crested tit
crocodile bird
crombec
crossbill
crow *or* *(Scot.)* corbie
cuckoo
cuckoo-shrike
cumulet
curassow
curlew
currawong *or* bell magpie
dabchick
darter, anhinga, *or* snakebird
demoiselle (crane) *or* Numidian crane
diamond bird *or* pardalote
dipper *or* water ouzel
diver
dollarbird
dotterel *or* dottrel
dove *or* *(archaic or poetic)* culver
dowitcher
drongo
dunlin *or* red-backed sandpiper
egret
emperor penguin
emu
emu-wren
fantail *or* *(N.Z.)* piwakawaka
fernbird *(N.Z.)*
fieldfare
fig-bird
finch
finfoot
firebird
firecrest
flamingo
flower-pecker
flycatcher
francolin
friarbird
frogmouth
galah *or* *(Austral.)* galar *or* gillar
gang-gang
gnatcatcher
go-away bird
godwit
goldcrest
golden oriole
goldfinch
Gouldian finch, painted finch, *or* purple-breasted finch
grackle *or* crow blackbird
grassfinch
grassquit
great crested grebe *or* loon
great northern diver
great tit
grebe
greenfinch
green leek
greenlet
greenshank
green woodpecker
grey-crowned babbler, happy family bird, Happy Jack, *or* parson bird *(Austral.)*
grey warbler *or* riroriro *(N.Z.)*
grosbeak
grouse
guan
guinea fowl
hadedah
hawfinch
hazelhen
hedge sparrow *or* dunnock
helldiver, pie-billed grebe, *or* dabchick
hen harrier *or* *(U.S. & Canad.)* marsh harrier
heron
hill myna
hoatzin *or* hoactzin
homing pigeon
honey creeper
honeyeater
honey guide
honeysucker
hooded crow
hoopoe
hornbill
house martin
house sparrow
hummingbird *or* trochilus
ibis
jabiru *or* *(Austral.)* policeman bird
jacamar
jaçana *or* lily-trotter
jackdaw
jacksnipe
Jacobin
jaeger *(U.S.)* *(Canad.)*
Java sparrow
jay
junco
jungle fowl
kagu
kaka *(N.Z.)*
kakapo *(N.Z.)*
kakariki *(N.Z.)*
karoro *or* blackbacked gull *(N.Z.)*
kea *(N.Z.)*

killdeer
kingbird
kingfisher *or* *(N.Z.)* kotare
king penguin
kiwi *or* apteryx
knot
koel *or* *(Austral.)* black cuckoo *or* cooee bird
kokako *or* blue-wattled crow *(N.Z.)*
kookaburra, laughing jackass, *or* *(Austral.)* bushman's clock, settler's clock, goburra, *or* great brown kingfisher
kotuku *or* white heron *(N.Z.)*
Lahore
lapwing *or* green plover
lark
limpkin *or* courlan
linnet
locust bird
loggerhead shrike
longspur
long-tailed tit
lorikeet
lory
lourie
lovebird
lyrebird *or* *(Austral.)* buln-buln
macaw
magpie *or* *(Austral.)* piping shrike *or* piping crow-shrike
magpie lark *or* *(Austral.)* mudlark, Murray magpie, mulga, *or* peewit
Major Mitchell *or* Leadbeater's cockatoo
makomako *(Austral.)*
marabou
marsh tit
martin
meadowlark
meadow pipit
metallic starling *or* shining starling *(Austral.)*
minivet
miromiro *(N.Z.)*
mistle thrush *or* missel thrush
mistletoe bird *(Austral.)*
mockingbird
mohua *or* bush canary *(N.Z.)*
monal *or* monaul
motmot *or* sawbill
mourning dove
myna, mynah, *or* mina
New Zealand pigeon *or* kereru *(N.Z.)*
nighthawk, bullbat, *or* mosquito hawk
night heron
nightingale
nightjar, *(U.S. & Canad.)* goatsucker, *or* *(Austral.)* nighthawk
noddy
noisy friarbird *or* leatherhead
noisy miner *or* *(Austral.)* micky *or* soldier bird
notornis
nun
nutcracker
nuthatch
oil bird *or* guacharo
oriole
ortolan *or* ortolan bunting
ostrich
ouzel *or* ousel
ovenbird
oxpecker *or* tick-bird
paradise duck *or* putangitangi *(N.Z.)*
parakeet *or* parrakeet
pardalote *(Austral.)*
parrot
partridge
peacock
peafowl
peewit
pelican
penguin
phalarope
pheasant
pied goose *or* magpie goose
pied wagtail
pigeon
pipit *or* *(N.Z.)* pihoihoi
pipiwharauroa *or* bronze-winged cuckoo *(N.Z.)*
pitta *(Austral.)*
plover
pratincole
ptarmigan
puffbird
puffin
pukeko
purple gallinule
pyrrhuloxia
quail
quarrian *or* quarrion
quetzal
racket-tail
rail
rainbow bird
rainbow lorikeet
raven
red-backed shrike
redbreast
red grouse
red-legged partridge
redpoll
redshank
redstart
redwing
reedbird
reed bunting
reedling *or* bearded tit
reed warbler
regent-bird *or* regent bowerbird
regent honeyeater
rhea *or* American ostrich
ricebird
riflebird
rifleman *or* *(N.Z.)* titipounamu
ringed plover
ring-necked pheasant
ringneck parrot, Port Lincoln parrot, *or* buln-buln *(Austral.)*
ring ouzel
roadrunner *or* chaparral cock
robin *or* robin redbreast
rock dove *or* rock pigeon
rockhopper
roller
rook
rosella
rosy finch
ruff
ruffed grouse
runt
saddleback
saddlebill *or* jabiru
sage grouse
sanderling
sandgrouse
sand martin
sandpiper
sapsucker
satin bowerbird
Scandaroon
scarlet tanager
scrub bird
sedge warbler
seriema
serin
sheathbill
shoebill
shore bird *or* *(Brit.)* wader
shrike *or* butcherbird
sicklebill
silver-eye *(Austral.)*
siskin *or* *(formerly)* aberdevine
sitella *or* tree-runner
skimmer
skylark
snipe
snow bunting
snowy egret
solitaire
song sparrow
song thrush *or* mavis
sora
sparrow
spoonbill
spotted crake *or* *(Austral.)* water crake
spotted flycatcher
spotted sandpiper *or* *(U.S.)* peetweet
squacco
starling
stilt
stint
stock dove
stonechat
stone curlew *or* thick-knee
stork
sugar bird
sulphur-crested cockatoo *or* white cockatoo
sunbird

sun bittern
superb blue wren (*Austral.*)
superb lyrebird (*Austral.*)
surfbird
swallow
swift
swiftlet
swordbill
tailorbird
takahe
tanager
tattler
tawny pippit
tern
thornbill
thrasher
thrush *or* (*poetic*) throstle
tit
titmouse
tody
topknot pigeon (*Austral.*)
toucan
touraco, turaco, *or* plantain-eater
towhee
tragopan
tree creeper
tree sparrow
trochilus
trogon
tropicbird
troupial
trumpeter
tui *or* parson bird (*N.Z.*)
turtledove
twite
umbrella bird
veery
verdin
wader *or* wading bird
wagtail
wall creeper
warbler
water rail
water thrush
wattlebird
waxbill
waxwing
weaverbird *or* weaver
weka, weka rail, Māori hen, *or* wood hen (*N.Z.*)
wheatear
whimbrel
whinchat
whip bird
whippoorwill
white-eye *or* (*N.Z.*) blighty, silvereye, tauhou *or* waxeye
white-fronted tern *or* kahawai bird (*N.Z.*)
whitethroat
whooping crane
willet
willow grouse
willow tit
willow warbler
wonga-wonga *or* wonga pigeon
woodchat *or* woodchat shrike
woodcock
wood ibis
woodlark
woodpecker
wood pigeon, ringdove, cushat, (*Scot.*) cushie-doo, *or* (*English dialect*) quist
woodswallow
wood warbler
wren
wrybill
wryneck
yellowhammer
yellowtail *or* yellowtail kingfisher (*Austral.*)
zebra finch

EXTINCT BIRDS

archaeopteryx
archaeornis
dodo
great auk
huia (*N.Z.*)
ichthyornis
moa
notornis
passenger pigeon
piopio (*N.Z.*)
solitaire

BISCUITS

abernethy
amaretti
bannock (*Scot.*)
Bath Oliver
bourbon
brandy snap
captain's biscuit
caramel wafer
chocolate digestive
cookie (*chiefly U.S.*) (*Canad.*)
cracker
cracknel
cream cracker
crispbread
digestive
Empire biscuit
fairing
farl
flapjack
Florentine
garibaldi
gingerbread man
ginger nut *or* ginger snap
graham cracker (*U.S.*)
hardtack, ship's biscuit, pilot biscuit, *or* sea biscuit
Jaffa cake (*trademark*)
langue de chat
lebkuchen
love letter
macaroon
matzo
oatcake
petit four
pretzel
ratafia
rich tea
rusk
shortbread
shortcake
soda biscuit
sweetmeal biscuit *or* digestive
Tararua biscuit (*N.Z.*)
tea biscuit
wafer
water biscuit

BLOOD CELLS

phagocytic white blood cell
erythrocyte
haemocyte
leucocyte
lymphocyte
macrocyte
microcyte
poikilocyte
polymorph
reticulocyte

BOARD GAMES

acey-deucy
backgammon
bagatelle
chequers
chess
Chinese chequers
Cluedo (*trademark*)
draughts
fox and geese
go *or* I-go
halma
kriegspiel
lightning chess
ludo
Monopoly (*trademark*)
nine men's morris
Parcheesi (*trademark*)
reversi
shove-halfpenny
snakes and ladders
solitaire
speed chess

BOATS AND SHIPS

airboat
aircraft carrier
auxiliary
banker
barge
barque
barquentine *or* barquantine
bateau
bathyscaph, bathyscaphe, *or* bathyscape
battlecruiser
battleship
Bermuda rig
boatel
brigantine
bulk carrier
bumboat
cabin cruiser
canal boat
canoe
caravel *or* carvel
carrack
catamaran
catboat
caïque
clipper
coble
cockboat *or* cockleboat
cockleshell
coracle
corvette
crabber
cruiser
cutter
destroyer
destroyer escort
dhow
dinghy
dogger
dory
dreadnought *or* dreadnaught
dredger
drifter
dromond *or* dromon
E-boat
factory ship
faltboat
felucca
ferry
fireboat
fishing boat
flatboat
flotel *or* floatel
flyboat
fore-and-after
foyboat
freighter
frigate
galleas
galleon
galley
gig
gondola
gunboat
hooker
houseboat
hoy
hydrofoil
hydroplane
icebreaker
ice yacht *or* scooter
Indiaman
ironclad
jet-boat
jolly boat
junk
kayak
keelboat
ketch
laker
landing craft
lapstrake *or* lapstreak
launch
lifeboat
lightship
liner
longboat
longship
lugger
man-of-war *or* man o' war
maxi
merchantman
minehunter
minelayer
minesweeper
monitor
monohull
motorboat
MTB (motor torpedo boat)
multihull
MY *or* motor yacht
narrow boat
nuggar
outboard
outrigger
oysterman
packet boat
paddle steamer
pink
pocket battleship
polacre *or* polacca
powerboat
proa *or* prau
PT boat
púcán
punt
quinquereme
raft
randan
revenue cutter
rowboat
rowing boat
sailing boat *or* *(U.S. & Canad.)* sailboat
scow
schooner
scull
sealer
shallop
shell
ship of the line
sidewheeler
skiff
skipjack
sloop
speedboat
square-rigger
steamboat
steamer
steamship
stern-wheeler
submarine
supertanker
surfboat
swamp boat
tall ship
tanker
tartan
tender
threedecker
torpedo boat
torpedo-boat destroyer
towboat
trawler
trimaran
trireme
troopship
tub
tug *or* tugboat
U-boat
umiak *or* oomiak
vaporetto
vedette
VJ (vaucluse junior)
warship
weathership
whaler
wherry
windjammer
xebec, zebec, *or* zebeck
yacht
yawl

PARTS OF THE BODY

Part of the body	*Technical name*	*Related adjective*
abdomen	-	abdominal
adenoids	pharyngeal tonsil	adenoid *or* adenoidal
alimentary canal	-	
ankle	talus	-
anus	-	anal
appendix	vermiform appendix	appendicular
arm	brachium	brachial
armpit	axilla	axillary
artery	-	arterial
back	-	dorsal
belly	venter	ventral
bladder	urinary bladder	vesical
blood	-	haemal, haemic, *or* haematic
bone	os	osseous, osteal, *or* osteoid
brain	encephalon	cerebral
breast	-	-
buttocks	nates	natal *or* gluteal
caecum	-	caecal
calf	-	-
capillary	-	capillary

Part of the body	*Technical name*	*Related adjective*
cervix	-	cervical
cheek	gena	genal
chest	-	pectoral
chin	-	genial *or* mental
clitoris	-	clitoral
colon	-	colonic
duodenum	-	duodenal
ear	-	aural
elbow	-	-
epiglottis	-	epiglottal
external ear	auricle *or* pinna	-
eye	-	ocular *or* ophthalmic
eyebrow	-	superciliary
eyelash	cilium	ciliary
eyelid	-	palpebral
Fallopian tube	oviduct	oviducal *or* oviductal
finger	-	digital
fingernail	-	ungual *or* ungular
fist	-	-
follicle	-	follicular
fontanelle *or* *(chiefly U.S.)* fontanel	-	-
foot	pes	pedal
forearm	-	cubital
forehead	-	frontal
foreskin	prepuce	preputial
gall bladder	-	-
gland	-	adenoid
glottis	-	glottic
groin	-	inguinal
gullet	oesophagus	oesophageal
gum	gingiva	gingival
hamstring	-	popliteal
hard palate	-	-
hair	-	-
half-moon	lunula *or* lunule	-
hand	manus	manual
head	caput	capital
heart	-	cardiac
heel	-	-
hip	-	-
ileum	-	ileac *or* ileal
inner ear *or* internal ear	labyrinth	-
instep	-	-
intestine	-	alvine
jaw	-	gnathic *or* gnathal
jejunum	-	jejunal
jugular vein	-	-
kidney	-	renal *or* nephritic
knee	genu	genicular
knuckle	-	-
labia majora	-	labial
labia minora	-	labial
large intestine	-	-
leg	crus	crural
lip	-	labial
liver	-	hepatic
loin	lumbus	lumbar
lung	-	pulmonary
lymph cell	lymphocyte	-
lymph node	-	-
midriff	diaphragm	-
mons pubis	-	-
mons veneris	-	-
mouth	-	stomatic
nape	nucha	nuchal
navel *or* omphalos	umbilicus	umbilical
neck	cervix	cervical
nerve	-	neural
nerve cell	neuron *or* neurone	neuronic
nipple *or* teat	mamilla *or* papilla	mamillary
nose	-	nasal
nostril	naris	narial *or* narine
occiput	-	occipital
ovary	-	ovarian
pancreas	-	pancreatic
penis	-	penile
pharynx	-	pharyngeal
pubes	-	pubic
rectum	-	rectal
red blood cell	erythrocyte	erythrocytic
ribcage	-	-
scalp	-	-
scrotum	-	scrotal
shin	-	-
shoulder	-	-
side	-	-
skin	cutis	cutaneous
small intestine	-	-
soft palate	-	-
sole	-	plantar
spleen	-	lienal *or* splenetic
stomach	-	gastric
tear duct	lacrimal duct	-

Part of the body	Technical name	Related adjective
temple	-	temporal
tendon	-	-
testicle	-	testicular
thigh	-	femoral *or* crural
thorax	-	thoracic
throat	-	guttural, gular, *or* jugular
thumb	pollex	pollical
toe	-	-
toenail	-	ungual *or* ungular
tongue	lingua	lingual *or* glottic
tonsil	-	tonsillar *or* tonsillary
torso	-	-
transverse colon	-	-
trunk	-	-
umbilical cord	umbilicus	-
ureter	-	ureteral *or* ureteric
urethra	-	urethral
vagina	-	vaginal
vein	vena	venous
vocal cords	glottis	glottal
voice box	larynx	laryngeal
vulva	-	vulval, vulvar, *or* vulvate
waist	-	-
white blood cell	leucocyte	leucocytic
windpipe	trachea	tracheal *or* tracheate
womb	uterus	uterine
wrist	carpus	-

BOMBS

atom bomb *or* A-bomb
bangalore torpedo
blockbuster
bouncing bomb
cluster bomb
depth charge
fusion bomb
grenade
hand grenade
hydrogen bomb
improvised explosive device *or* IED
incendiary *or* incendiary bomb
Mills bomb
Molotov cocktail
nail bomb
neutron bomb
nuclear bomb
petrol bomb
pipe bomb
plastic bomb
stun grenade
time bomb

BONES

Bone	Nontechnical names
astragalus	anklebone
calcaneus	heel bone
carpal	wrist
carpus	wrist
clavicle	collarbone
coccyx	-
costa	rib
cranium	brainpan
cuboid	-
ethmoid	-
femur	thighbone
fibula	-
frontal bone	-
hallux	-
humerus	-
hyoid	-
ilium	-
incus	anvil
innominate bone	hipbone
ischium	-
malleus	hammer
mandible	lower jawbone
maxilla	upper jawbone
metacarpal	-
metatarsal	-
metatarsus	-
occipital bone	-
parietal bone	-
patella	kneecap
pelvis	-
phalanx	-
pubis	-
radius	-
rib	-
sacrum	-
scapula	shoulder blade
skull	-
sphenoid	-
spinal column *or* spine	backbone
stapes	stirrup
sternum	breastbone
talus	anklebone
tarsal	-
tarsus	-
temporal bone	-
tibia	shinbone
ulna	-
vertebra	-
vertebral column	backbone
zygomatic bone	cheekbone

BOOKS

TYPES OF BOOK

album
almanac
anatomy
annual
anthology
armorial
A to Z
atlas
autobiography
Baedeker
bestiary
bibelot
Bible
biography
breviary
brochure
casebook
catalogue
catechism
coffee-table book
comic book
commonplace book
companion
compendium
concordance
confessional
cookery book
copybook
diary
dictionary
directory
dispensatory
encyclopedia *or* encyclopaedia
exercise book
formulary
gazetteer
gradus
grammar
graphic novel
grimoire
guidebook
handbook
hymn book
jotter
journal
lectionary
ledger
lexicon
log *or* logbook
manual
miscellany
missal
monograph
notebook
novel
novelette
novella
ordinal
peerage
pharmacopoeia
phrase book
prayer book
primer
prospectus
psalter
reader
reference book
register
road book
score
scrapbook
service book
sketchbook
song book
speller
statute book
storybook
telephone directory
textbook
thesaurus
vade mecum
who's who
wordbook
workbook
yearbook

PARTS OF A BOOK

acknowledgments
addendum
afterword
appendix
back
back matter
bibliography
binding
blurb
chapter
contents
corrigenda
cover
dedication
dust jacket *or* cover
endpaper
epigraph
epilogue
errata
flyleaf
folio
fore-edge
foreword
frontispiece
front matter
glossary
gutter
half-title
illustration
index
interleaf
introduction
leaf
margin
page
plate
postscript
preface
prelims
proem
prolegomenon
prologue
recto
rubric
running head
slipcase
spine
tail
title page
verso
wrapper

BOTANY

BRANCHES OF BOTANY

agrostology
algology
archaeobotany *or* archeobotany
astrobotany
bryology
carpology
dendrology
ethnobotany
floristics
mycology
palaeobotany
palaeoethnobotany
phytogenesis
phytogeography
phytography
phytopathology
pteridology

BOTANY TERMS

abscission
androecium
androgynous
anther
archegonium
auxin
axil
axis
berry
bulb
calyx
cambium
carpel
chlorophyll
chloroplast
corm
corolla
corona
cortex
cotyledon
cross-pollination
cuticle
dicotyledon
epidermis
filament
flower
foliation
fruit
geotropism
germination
guard cell
gynaecium
hilum
hydrotropism
inflorescence
insect pollination
integument
key
lamina
leaf

legume
lenticel
meristem
mesophyll
micropyle
monocotyledon
nastic movement
nut
operculum
ovary
ovule
palisade mesophyll
phloem
photosynthesis
phototropism
pistil
pith
plumule
pollen
pollination
raceme
radicle
receptacle
rhizome
root
root cap
root hair
root nodule
rosette
runner
sap
seed
seed capsule *or* seedcase
seed pod
seed vessel
self-pollination
sepal
shoot
spadix
spongy mesophyll
sporangium
spore
stamen
stem
stigma
stolon
stoma
style
testa
translocation
transpiration
tropism
tuber
vascular bundle
vegetative reproduction
wind pollination
xylem

BOXING WEIGHTS

Weight	*Amateur*	*Professional*
Light flyweight	48 kg	49 kg
Flyweight	51 kg	
Bantamweight	54 kg	53.5 kg
Featherweight	57 kg	
Junior lightweight	-	59 kg
Lightweight	60 kg	61 kg
Light welterweight	63.5 kg	
Welterweight	67 kg	66.6 kg
Light middleweight	71 kg	70 kg
Middleweight	75 kg	72.5 kg
Light heavyweight	81 kg	79 kg
Cruiserweight	-	88.5 kg
Heavyweight	91 kg	+88.5 kg
Superheavyweight	+91 kg	-

PARTS OF THE BRAIN

amygdala
brainstem
Broca's area
central sulcus
cerebellum
cerebral aqueduct
cerebral cortex *or (nontechnical)* grey matter
cerebrospinal fluid
cerebrum
choroid plexus
corpus callosum
diencephalon
fourth ventricle
frontal lobe
hippocampus
hypothalamus
infundibulum
limbic system
mamillary body
medulla oblongata
meninges
midbrain
myelencephalon *or (nontechnical)* afterbrain
occipital lobe
optic chiasma
parietal lobe
pineal body
pituitary gland
pons Varolli
substantia alba *or (nontechnical)* white matter
temporal lobe
thalamus
third ventricle
vermis
Wernicke's area

BREADS

bagel *or* beigel
baguette
bap
barm cake *(dialect)*
barmbrack *(Irish)*
barm cake *(Lancashire)*
batch loaf
billy-bread *(N.Z.)*
black bread
bloomer
bridge roll
brioche
brown bread, loaf, *or* roll
bun
buttery *(Scot.)*
challah *or* hallah
chapati *or* chapatti
ciabatta
cob
coburg
corn bread, corn pone, *or* Indian bread *(U.S.)*
cottage loaf
croissant
damper *(Austral.)*
farmhouse
focaccia
French bread
French stick
fruit loaf
Granary *(trademark)*
gluten bread
griddlebread
half-quartern
johnny cake
long tin
matzo, matzoh, matza, *or* matzah
muffin
naan *or* nan
pan bread *or* loaf *(Scot.)*
paratha
pitta
plain bread *or* loaf *(Scot.)*
plait
poppadom *or* poppadum
pumpernickel
puri
quartern
roll
roti
rye bread *or* rye
schnecken
soda bread
sourdough
split tin
square tin
stollen
tortilla
unleavened bread
wheaten bread
white bread, loaf, *or* roll
wholemeal *or (esp U.S. & Canad.)* wholewheat

TYPES OF BRIDGE

aqueduct
Bailey bridge
balance, bascule, *or* counterpoise bridge
box-girder bridge
cable-stayed bridge
cantilever bridge
clapper bridge
deck bridge
drawbridge
flyover
footbridge
pivot, swing, *or* turn bridge
pontoon bridge
snow bridge
suspension bridge
truss bridge
turn bridge
viaduct

SCHOOLS OF BUDDHISM

Foism
Geluk
Hinayana
Jodo
Kagyü
Lamaism
Mahayana
Nichiren
Nyingma
Pure Land Buddhism
Rinjai
Sakya
Soka Gakkai
Soto
Tendai
Theravada
Vajrayana
Zen

BUTTERFLIES AND MOTHS

apollo
argus
bag moth *(N.Z.)*
bagworm moth
bell moth
bogong *or* bugong (moth)
brimstone
brown-tail moth
buff-tip moth
cabbage white
cactoblastis
Camberwell beauty *or (U.S.)* mourning cloak
cardinal
carpenter moth
carpet moth
cleopatra
comma butterfly
copper
cecropia moth
cinnabar
clearwing *or* clearwing moth
Clifden nonpareil
codlin(g) moth
death's-head moth
drinker moth *or* drinker
egger *or* eggar
ermine moth *or* ermine
festoon
ghost moth
gipsy moth
goldtail moth *or* yellowtail (moth)
grass moth
grayling
hairstreak
herald moth
hawk moth, sphinx moth, *or* hummingbird moth
house moth
Io moth
Kentish glory
kitten moth
lackey moth
lappet moth
large white *or* cabbage white
leopard moth
lobster moth
luna moth
magpie moth
marbled white
monarch
mother-of-pearl moth
Mother Shipton
old lady
orange-tip
painted lady
peacock butterfly
peppered moth
privet hawk
processionary moth
purple emperor
puss moth
red admiral
red underwing
ringlet
silver-Y
skipper
small white
snout
speckled wood
swallowtail
swift
tapestry moth
thorn (moth)
tiger (moth)
tussock moth
two-tailed pasha
umber (moth)
vapourer moth
wave (moth)
wax moth, honeycomb moth, *or* bee moth
wall brown
white
white admiral
winter moth
yellow
yellow underwing

CAKES AND PASTRIES

almond cake
angel cake *or* angel food cake
Bakewell tart
baklava
Banbury cake
Battenburg cake
black bun
Black forest gateau
brownie
carrot cake
cherry cake
chocolate cake
Christmas cake
coconut cake
coffee kiss
cream cake
cream puff
cruller *or* kruller *(U.S.)* *(Canad.)*
crumpet
cupcake
Danish pastry
devil's food cake
doughnut *or* donut
drop scone *or* pancake *(Scot.)*
dumpling
Dundee cake
Eccles cake
eclair
fairy cake
flapjack
frangipane
French pastry
fruitcake
fudge cake
gateau
Genoa cake
Genoese sponge
gingerbread
hot cross bun
johnny cake *(Austral.)*
jumble *or* jumbal
koeksister *(S. African)*
kuchen
kuglehopf
ladyfinger *or* sponge finger
lamington *(Austral.)* *(N.Z.)*
lardy cake
layer cake
Linzer torte
Madeira cake
madeleine

marble cake
meringue
millefeuille
mince pie
muffin
pancake
pandowdy
panettone
parkin
petit four
pound cake
profiterole
queencake
rock cake
rum baba
Sally Lunn
sandwich cake
scone
seedcake
Selkirk bannock
simnel cake
singing hinny
sponge cake
stollen
swiss roll
tart
teabread
teacake
tipsy cake
torte
turnover
upside-down cake
Victoria sponge
wedding cake
yumyum

CARS

CAR PARTS

accelerator
air bag
alternator
ammeter
anti-roll bar
ashtray
automatic choke
axle
battery
bearing
big end
body
bonnet
boot
brake
brake light
brake pad
bucket seat
bulb
bumper
camshaft
carburettor
catalytic converter
chassis
childproof lock
choke
clutch
coil
connecting rod
convertible top
cowl
crank
crankcase
crankshaft
cylinder
cylinder head
dashboard
demister
dipstick
disc brakes
distributor
distributor cap
door
door handle
driveshaft
engine
exhaust
fan
fan belt
fascia
fender *(U.S.)* *(Canad.)*
flywheel
fog lamp
fuel gauge
fuse
fuse box
gasket
gear
gearbox
gear lever *or* *(U.S. & Canad.)* gearshift
generator
glove compartment
grille *or* radiator grille
handbrake
hard top
hazard light
headlight
headrest
heater
hood
horn
hubcap
ignition
indicator
jack
light
little end
lock
luggage rack
manifold
mileometer, milometer, *or* *(U.S. & Canad.)* odometer
mud flap
numberplate
oil filter
oil-pressure gauge
oil pump
parcel shelf
parking light
pedal
petrol cap
petrol gauge
petrol tank
piston
plug
points
radiator
radius arm
rear light *or* *(U.S. & Canad.)* taillight
rear-view mirror
reversing light
roof
seat
seat belt *or* safety belt
shock absorber
silencer
soft top
spare wheel
speedometer
springs
sprocket
starter
steering column
steering wheel
sump
sunroof *or* sunshine roof
suspension
tailgate
tailpipe
tank
top
torsion bar
towbar
transmission
trim
tyre
universal joint
valve
wheel
wheel brace
wheel nut
wheel trim
window
windscreen
windscreen wiper
wing
wing mirror
wing nut

CARDS

CARD GAMES

auction bridge
baccarat
beggar-my-neighbour
bezique
blackjack
boston
bridge
canasta
canfield
casino
chemin-de-fer *or* chemmy
cinch
contract bridge
cooncan *or* conquian
cribbage
duplicate bridge
écarté
euchre
faro
five hundred
gin rummy
happy families
hearts
loo
monte
nap *or* napoleon
old maid
ombre
patience
pinochle, penuchle, penuckle *or* pinocle
piquet
poker
pontoon
quinze
rouge et noir
rubber bridge

rummy
seven up
skat
slapjack
snap
solo
solo whist
spoilfive
stops
strip poker
stud poker
switch
trente et quarante
whist

BRIDGE TERMS

contract
double
dummy
east
finesse
grand slam
little slam *or* small slam
north
no-trump
redouble
rubber
ruff
singleton
slam
south
trick
trump
vulnerable
west
yarborough

POKER TERMS

ante
flush
full house
pair
raise
royal flush
see
showdown
shy
stand pat
straddle
straight
straight flush

OTHER CARD TERMS

ace
clubs
court card *or (U.S. & Canad.)* face card
cut
deal
deck
deuce
diamonds
hand
hearts
jack
joker
king
knave
queen
revoke
spades
suit
trey
wild

CARNIVORES

aardwolf
arctic fox
badger
bear
binturong
black bear
bobcat
brown bear
cacomistle *or* cacomixle
caracal *or* desert lynx
cat
see **breeds of cat**
catamount, catamountain, *or* cat-o'-mountain
cheetah *or* chetah
cinnamon bear
civet
corsac
coyote *or* prairie wolf
dhole
dingo *or (Austral.)* native dog *or* warrigal
dog
see **breeds of dog**
ermine
fennec
ferret
fox
genet *or* genette
giant panda
grey fox *(U.S.)*
grey wolf *or* timber wolf
grison
grizzly bear *or* grizzly
hog badger
hognosed skunk
hyena *or* hyaena
ichneumon
jackal
jaguar
jaguarondi, jaguarundi, *or (Austral.)* eyra
kinkajou, honey bear, *or* potto
Kodiak bear
kolinsky
laughing hyena *or* spotted hyena
leopard *or* panther
linsang
lion
lynx
margay
marten
meerkat
mink
mongoose
mountain lion
ocelot
otter
otter shrew
palm civet
panda
panther
pine marten *or* sweet marten
polar bear *or (N. Canad.)* nanook
polecat
prairie dog
puma *or* cougar
raccoon, racoon, *or* coon
raccoon dog
rasse
ratel
red fox
rooikat
sable
sea otter
serval
silver fox
skunk
sloth bear
snow leopard *or* ounce
stoat
stone marten
strandwolf
sun bear
swift fox *or* kit fox
tayra
teledu
tiger
tiger cat
timber wolf
weasel
wolf
wolverine, glutton, *or* carcajou
zibeline
zibet
zorilla *or* zorille

BREEDS OF CAT

Abyssinian
Angora
Bengal leopard
Burmese
colourpoint *or (U.S.)* Himalayan
Havana
Maine coon
Manx
Persian
ragdoll
Rex
Russian blue
Siamese
tabby
tortoiseshell
Turkish

CATTLE

BREEDS OF CATTLE

Aberdeen Angus
Africander
Alderney
Ayrshire
Belted Galloway
Blonde d'Aquitaine
Brown Swiss
cattalo *or* catalo
Charolais *or* Charollais
Devon
dexter
Durham
Friesian
Galloway
Gelbvieh
Guernsey
Hereford
Highland
Holstein
Illawarra (shorthorn)
Jersey
Kerry
kyloe
Limousin
longhorn
Meuse-Rhine-Ijssel
Normandy
Norwegian Red
Red Poll *or* Red Polled
Santa Gertrudis
shorthorn
Simmental
Sussex
Texas longhorn
Wagyu

CATTLE AND OTHER ARTIODACTYLS

addax
alpaca *or* alpacca
antelope
aoudad
argali *or* argal
ariel
axis (*plural* axises) *or* chital
babirusa
Bactrian camel
bharal
bison
blacktail
blaubok
blesbok
boar
boer goat
bongo
bontebok
brocket
bubal *or* bubalis
buffalo
bull *see* **breeds of cattle**
bushbuck *or* boschbok
bushpig
camel *or (Anglo-Indian)* oont
Cape buffalo
caribou
chamois *or* izard
chevrotain *or* mouse deer
Chinese water deer
cow *see* **breeds of cattle**
deer
dik-dik
dromedary
duiker *or* duyker
eland
elk
gaur
gayal
gazelle
gemsbok
gerenuk
giraffe *or (obsolete)* camelopard
gnu
goa
goat
goral
grysbok
guanaco
harnessed antelope
hartebeest *or* hartbeest
hippopotamus
ibex
impala
Jacob *or* Jacob sheep
karakul *or* caracul
Kashmir goat
klipspringer
kob
kongoni
kouprey
kudu *or* koodoo
llama
markhor *or* markhoor
marshbuck
moose
mouflon *or* moufflon
mountain goat
mule deer
muntjac, muntjak, *or* barking deer
musk deer
nilgai, nilghau, *or* nylghau
nyala
okapi
oribi
oryx
ox *see* **breeds of cattle**
peccary
Père David's deer
pig *see* **breeds of pig**
pronghorn
pudu
razorback
red deer
reedbuck *or* nagor
reindeer
rhebok *or* reebok
Rocky Mountain goat
roe deer
sable antelope
saiga
sambar *or* sambur
sassaby
serow
sheep *or (Austral. slang)* jumbuck *see* **breeds of sheep**
sika
springbok
stag
steenbok
tahr *or* thar
takin
vicuña *or* vicuna
wapiti
wart hog
waterbuck
water buffalo, water ox, *or* carabao
white-tailed deer
wild boar
wildebeest
yak
zebu
zo *or* zho, *or* dzo

TYPES OF CHAIR

armchair
banquette
barrel chair
bar stool
basket chair
Bath chair
beanbag
bench
bentwood chair
berbice chair
bergère
bucket seat
campaign chair
camp chair
cane chair
carver
cathedra
corner chair
curule chair
deck chair
dining chair
director's chair
dos-à-dos
easy chair
fauteuil
fiddle-back
folding chair
form
garden chair
gestatorial chair
hassock
highchair
jampan *(kneeling chair)*
ladder-back chair
lounger
milking stool
Morris chair
music stool *(office chair)*
opsitbank *(S. African)*
ottoman
pew
piano stool
platform rocker
pouf *or* pouffe
reclining chair *or* recliner
rocking chair *or* rocker
sedan chair
settle
shooting stick
stool
straight chair
súgán chair
swing
swivel chair
throne
tub chair
wheelchair
window seat
Windsor chair
Windsor rocker
wing chair

CHAMPAGNE BOTTLES

Bottle	*Capacity*	*Bottle*	*Capacity*
magnum	2 bottles	salmanazar	6 magnums
jeroboam	2 magnums	balthazar	8 magnums
rehoboam	3 magnums	nebuchadnezzar	10 magnums
methuselah	4 magnums		

CHEESES

Bavarian blue
Bel Paese
Bleu d'Auvergne
Bleu de Bresse
blue cheese *or* blue vein
Blue Shropshire
Blue Stilton
Blue Vinney *or* Blue Vinny
Bonchester
Brie
Caboc
caciocavallo
Caerphilly
Cambazolla
Camembert
canestrato
Cantal
Chaumes
Cheddar
Cheshire
chèvre
cottage cheese
cream cheese
crowdie
curd cheese
Danish blue
Derby
Dolcelatte
Double Gloucester
Dunlop
Dunsyre Blue
Edam
Emmenthal *or* Emmental
Ermite
Esrom
feta
fontina
fromage frais
Gjetost
goats' cheese
Gorgonzola
Gouda
Gruyère
Havarti
Jarlsberg
Lanark Blue
Lancashire
Leicester
Limburger
mascarpone
Monterey jack
mousetrap
mozzarella
muenster
mycella
Neufchâtel
Oka
Parmesan
pecorino
Port-Salut
pot cheese
provolone
quark
Reblochon
Red Leicester
Red Windsor
Ribblesdale
ricotta
Romano
Roquefort
Sage Derby
Saint Agur
Samsø
sapsago
Stilton
Stinking Bishop
Taleggio
Tornegus
Vacherin
vignotte
wensleydale
yarg

CHEMICAL ELEMENTS

	Symbols	*Atomic numbers*
hydrogen	H	1
helium	He	2
lithium	Li	3
beryllium	Be	4
boron	B	5
carbon	C	6
nitrogen	N	7
oxygen	O	8
fluorine	F	9
neon	Ne	10
sodium	Na	11
magnesium	Mg	12
aluminium *or (U.S.)* aluminum	Al	13
silicon	Si	14
phosphorus	P	15
sulphur *or (U.S.)* sulfur	S	16
chlorine	Cl	17
argon	Ar	18
potassium	K	19
calcium	Ca	20
scandium	Sc	21
titanium	Ti	22
vanadium	V	23
chromium	Cr	24
manganese	Mn	25
iron	Fe	26
cobalt	Co	27
nickel	Ni	28
copper	Cu	29
zinc	Zn	30
gallium	Ga	31
germanium	Ge	32
arsenic	As	33
selenium	Se	34
bromine	Br	35
krypton	Kr	36
rubidium	Rb	37
strontium	Sr	38
yttrium	Y	39
zirconium	Zr	40
niobium	Nb	41
molybdenum	Mo	42
technetium	Tc	43
ruthenium	Ru	44
rhodium	Rh	45
palladium	Pd	46
silver	Ag	47
cadmium	Cd	48
indium	In	49
tin	Sn	50
antimony	Sb	51
tellurium	Te	52
iodine	I	53

	Symbols	Atomic numbers		Symbols	Atomic numbers
xenon	Xe	54	bismuth	Bi	83
caesium *or* (*U.S.*) cesium	Cs	55	polonium	Po	84
barium	Ba	56	astatine	At	85
lanthanum	La	57	radon	Rn	86
cerium	Ce	58	francium	Fr	87
praseodymium	Pr	59	radium	Ra	88
neodymium	Nd	60	actinium	Ac	89
promethium	Pm	61	thorium	Th	90
samarium	Sm	62	protactinium	Pa	91
europium	Eu	63	uranium	U	92
gadolinium	Gd	64	neptunium	Np	93
terbium	Tb	65	plutonium	Pu	94
dysprosium	Dy	66	americium	Am	95
holmium	Ho	67	curium	Cm	96
erbium	Er	68	berkelium	Bk	97
thulium	Tm	69	californium	Cf	98
ytterbium	Yb	70	einsteinium	Es	99
lutetium *or* lutecium	Lu	71	fermium	Fm	100
hafnium	Hf	72	mendelevium	Md	101
tantalum	Ta	73	nobelium	No	102
tungsten *or* wolfram	W	74	lawrencium	Lr	103
rhenium	Re	75	rutherfordium	Rf	104
osmium	Os	76	dubnium	Db	105
iridium	Ir	77	seaborgium	Sg	106
platinum	Pt	78	bohrium	Bh	107
gold	Au	79	hassium	Hs	108
mercury	Hg	80	meitnerium	Mt	109
thallium	Tl	81	darmstadtium	Ds	110
lead	Pb	82	roentgenium	Rg	111

CHEMISTRY

BRANCHES OF CHEMISTRY

analytical chemistry
astrochemistry
biochemistry
chemurgy
cytochemistry
electrochemistry
geochemistry
histochemistry
immunochemistry
inorganic chemistry
kinetics
magnetochemistry
neurochemistry
nuclear chemistry
organic chemistry
petrochemistry
phonochemistry
photochemistry
physical chemistry
phytochemistry
radiochemistry
stereochemistry
stoichiometry
thermochemistry
zoochemistry
zymurgy

CHEMISTRY TERMS

acid
alcohol
alkali
alkali metal
alkaline earth metal
alkane
allotrope
alloy
amino acid
analysis
anion
anode
atom
atomic mass
atomic number
base
boiling point
bond
Brownian motion
carbohydrate
catalyst
cathode
cation
chain
chain reaction
chromatography
combustion
compound
concentrated
condensation
corrosion
covalent bond
crystal
crystallization
diffusion
dilute
distillation
electrode
electrolysis
electron
electrovalency
element
emulsion
equation
ester
ether
evaporation
fat
fatty acid
fermentation
fission
foam
formula
fuel
fusion
gas
halogen
hydrocarbon
hydrolysis
inert
inorganic
insoluble
ion

ionic bond
ionization
isomer
isotope
lanthanide *or* rare-earth element
liquid
litmus test
melting point
metal
metalloid
mineral
mixture
molarity
mole
molecule
monomer
neutral
neutron
noble gas *or* inert gas
nonmetal
nucleus
oil
ore
organic
oxidation
periodic table
pH
plastic
polymer
precipitate
proton
radioactivity
reaction
reagent
redox reaction
reduction
salt
saponification
saturated
soap
solid
soluble
solution
solvent
sublimation
substitution reaction
sugar
suspension
synthesis
transition metal
unsaturated
valency
van der Waals forces

CHESS PIECES

Piece	*Abbreviation*	*Piece*	*Abbreviation*	*Piece*	*Abbreviation*
Bishop	B	King's rook	KR	Queen's bishop	QB
King	K	Knight	N	Queen's knight	QN
King's bishop	KB	Pawn	P	Queen's rook	QR
King's knight	KN	Queen	Q		

CHRISTIAN DENOMINATIONS AND SECTS

Adventism
Amish
Anabaptism
Anglicanism
Baptist Church
Byzantine Church
Calvinism
Catholicism
Christadelphianism
Christian Science
Congregationalism
Coptic Church
Dutch Reformed Church
Eastern Orthodox Church
Episcopal Church
evangelicalism
Greek Orthodox Church
Jehovah's Witnesses
Lutheranism
Maronite Church
Methodism
Moravian Church
Mormons *or* Latter-day Saints
New Jerusalem Church
Orthodox Church
Pentecostalism
Plymouth Brethren
Presbyterianism
Protestantism
Quakerism
Roman Catholicism
Russian Orthodox Church
Salvation Army
Seventh-Day Adventism
Shakerism
Society of Friends
Unification Church
Unitarianism

CLOTHING

ARTICLES OF CLOTHING

apron
baldric
basque
bathing suit
bathrobe
bib and brace
bikini
blouse
body
body stocking
bodysuit
boubou
braces *or (U.S.)* suspenders
bustier
cardigan *or (informal)* cardie *or* cardy
chapeau
chaps, chaparajos, *or* chaparejos
chausses
chuddah, chuddar, chudder, *or* chador
cilice
coat
coatee
codpiece
cummerbund *or* kummerbund
dolman
dress
dressing gown
dungarees
frock
galluses *(dialect)*
gambeson
garter
gilet
glove
gown
haik
halter
hauberk
hose
housecoat
jacket
jerkin
jersey
jubbah
jumper
jump suit
jupon
kaftan *or* caftan
kameez
kanzu
kaross
kimono
kilt
kittel
leotard
loincloth *or* breechcloth
maillot
manteau
mantle *(archaic)*
mitten
muff
negligee *or* negligée
nightdress, nightgown, *or* *(Brit. informal)* nightie
nightshirt
overall
overcoat
overskirt
oversleeve
paletot
pallium
partlet
pashmina
peignoir
plaid
pullover
pyjamas *or (U.S.)* pajamas
robe
rompers
sash
sanbenito

sari *or* saree
sarong
serape
shalwar
shawl
shift
shirt
shoe
shorts
skivvy *(slang) (chiefly U.S.)*
slop
smock
sock
sporran
surcoat
sweater
swimming costume, bathing costume, costume, *or (Austral. informal)* cossie
swimming trunks *or* trunks
swimsuit
tallit
tanga
tank top
thong
tie *or (U.S.)* necktie
tights *or* hose
toga
T-shirt *or* tee shirt
tunic
undergarment
waistcoat *or (U.S. & Canad.)* vest
wrap
wrapper
yashmak *or* yashmac

PARTS OF CLOTHING

arm
armhole
armlet
bodice
buttonhole
collar
cuff
dicky
epaulette
flounce
gusset
hem
hemline
hood
jabot
lapel
leg
lining
neckline
patch pocket
pocket
seam
shawl collar
shoulder
sleeve
tail
train
waist
waistline
yoke

TYPES OF CLOTHING

academic dress
armour
baby clothes
beachwear
black tie
canonicals
civvies *or* civies
clericals
coordinates
coveralls
evening dress
fancy dress
fatigues
froufrou
Highland dress
hose
hosiery
knitwear
lingerie
livery
long-coats *or (archaic)* long clothes
millinery
morning dress
mufti
neckwear
nightclothes
nightwear
overgarments
sackcloth
samfoo
separates
skivvies *(slang) (chiefly U.S.)*
slops
sportswear
swaddling clothes
swimwear
undergarments
underthings
underwear
uniform
weepers
white tie
widow's weeds

TYPES OF CLOUD

altocumulus
altostratus
cirrocumulus
cirrostratus
cirrus
cumulonimbus
cumulus
false cirrus
fractocumulus
fractostratus
nimbostratus
nimbus
stratocumulus
stratus

TYPES OF CLUB

blackjack
bludgeon
cudgel
knobkerrie *or* knobstick
lathi
life preserver
mere *(N.Z.)*
nightstick
nulla-nulla
patu *(N.Z.)*
quarterstaff
shillelagh *or* shillala
truncheon
waddy

COATS AND CLOAKS

afghan
balmacaan
bathrobe
box coat
Burberry *(trademark)*
burnous, burnouse, *or* burnoose
cape
capote
capuchin
cardinal
chesterfield
coat dress
coatee
cope
covert coat
Crombie *(trademark)*
cutaway
dolman
domino
dreadnought *or* dreadnaught
dress coat
dressing gown
duffel coat
duster coat
fearnought *or* fearnaught
frock coat
fun fur coat
fur coat
gabardine
greatcoat
hacking coat
himation
housecoat
Inverness
jellaba *or* jellabah
Jodhpuri coat
joseph
loden coat
mac *or* mack
Mackinaw coat
mackintosh *or* macintosh
manta
mantelet
mantilla
mantle
morning coat
newmarket
opera cloak *or* opera hood
overcoat
paletot
pea jacket *or* peacoat
parka
peignoir
pelisse
peplum
poncho
Prince Albert
raglan
raincoat
redingote
roquelaure

sheepskin coat
sherwani
slicker *(U.S.) (Canad.)*
snorkel
sou'wester
spencer
surcoat
surtout
swallow-tailed coat *or* swallowtail
tailcoat *or* tails
tippet
topcoat
trench coat
ulster
undercoat
waterproof

COCKTAILS

Americano
Bellini
Black Russian
black velvet
Bloody Mary
Brandy Alexander
buck's fizz
bullshot
caudle
claret cup
cobbler
cold duck
collins
cooler
Cuba libre
cup
daiquiri
dry martini
eggnog *or* egg flip
Gibson
gimlet
gin sling
glogg
Harvey Wallbanger
highball
julep
kir
Long Island Tea
manhattan
margarita
martini
milk punch
mint julep
mojito
Moscow Mule
negroni
nog *or* nogg
oenomel
old-fashioned
orgasm
piña colada
pink gin
planter's punch
punch
rickey
Rusty Nail
sangaree
sangria
sazerac
screwdriver
sidecar
Singapore sling
sling
Slow Screw Against the Wall
snowball
spritzer
stinger *or* stengah
swizzle
syllabub *or* sillabub
Tom Collins
whiskey sour
whisky mac
white lady
zombie

COFFEES

americano
arabica
black coffee
Blue mountain
Brazilian
brown coffee
café au lait
café noir
cappuccino
Colombian
Continental
Costa Rican
decaffeinated *or* decaf
espresso
frappuccino
French roast
instant coffee
Irish *or* Gaelic coffee
Java
Kenyan
latte
macchiato
mocha
mochaccino
robusta
skinny latte
Turkish coffee
white coffee

COLLECTORS AND ENTHUSIASTS

ailurophile	cats
arctophile	teddy bears
audiophile	high-fidelity sound reproduction
automobilist	cars
bibliophile	books
brolliologist	umbrellas
campanologist	bell-ringing
cartophilist	cigarette cards
cruciverbalist	crosswords
deltiologist	picture postcards
discophile	gramophone records
fusilatelist	phonecards
herbalist	herbs
lepidopterist	moths and butterflies
medallist	medals
numismatist	coins
oenophile	wine
paranumismatist	coin-like objects
philatelist	stamps
phillumenist	matchbox labels
phraseologist	phrases
scripophile	share certificates
vexillologist	flags
zoophile	animals

COMPASS POINTS

Compass Point	*Abbreviation*	*Compass Point*	*Abbreviation*
North	N	East by South	E by S
North by East	N by E	East South East	ESE
North North East	NNE	South East by East	SE by E
North East by North	NE by N	South East	SE
North East	NE	South East by South	SE by S
North East by East	NE by E	South South East	SSE
East North East	ENE	South by East	S by E
East by North	E by N	South	S
East	E	South by West	S by W

Compass Point	*Abbreviation*
South South West	SSW
South West by South	SW by S
South West	SW
South West by West	SW by W
West South West	WSW
West by South	W by S
West	W
West by North	W by N
West North West	WNW
North West by West	NW by W
North West	NW
North West by North	NW by N
North North West	NNW
North by West	N by W

Cardinal point	*Related adjective*
north	arctic *or* boreal
east	oriental
south	meridional *or* austral
west	occidental *or* hesperidan

COMPUTERS

COMPUTER PARTS

analogue-digital converter
arithmetic logic unit *or* ALU
cartridge
case
CD-rewriter
CD-Rom drive
central processing unit *or* CPU
chip
coaxial cable
console
control key
counter
daisywheel
DDR-RAM
digital audio player
digital camera
digitizer
DIMM
disk
disk drive
disk unit
DRAM
DVD reader
DVD writer
emulator
encoder
flatbed scanner
floppy disk
graphics card
hard drive
integrated circuit
interface
joystick
keyboard
laser printer
LCD panel
line printer
magnetic tape unit *or* MTU
memory
microprocessor
modem
monitor
motherboard
mouse
MP3 player
multiplexor
optical character reader
optical disk
optical scanner
port
printed circuit board
printer
processor
scanner
screen
SDRAM
SIMM
sound card
speaker
trackball
transistor
USB port
visual display unit *or* VDU
webcam

COMPUTER TYPES

desktop *or* desktop computer
laptop *or* laptop computer
notebook *or* notebook computer
Macintosh, MacBook, *or* iMac trademark
palmtop *or* palmtop computer
PC *or* personal computer
tablet *or* tablet computer

COMPUTER TERMS

absolute address
access
access time
address
address bus
ADSL
adware
algorithm
alpha-test
analogue computer
AND gate
antivirus
applet
application program
architecture
archival storage
area
array
artificial intelligence *or* AI
ASCII
assemble
assembler
assembly language
audio response
automatic repeat
backbone
backing store
backup
bandwidth
base address
batch processing
beta-test
binary notation
bit *or* binary digit
BitTorrent *(trademark)*
black box
Bluetooth
boilerplate
bomb
boot *or* bootstrap
bottom-up processing
bpi (bits per inch)
branch instruction
broadband
buffer
bug
buggy
bulletin board
bundle
bus *or* busbar
bus master
byte
cache memory
capture
CD-Rom
character
chipset
clip art
clock
code
COM
command
command language

communications
compatible
compiler
complex instruction set computer *or* CISC
computer-aided design *or* CAD
computer-aided design and manufacture *or* CADCAM
computer-aided engineering *or* CAE
computer-aided instruction *or* CAI
computer-aided (or -assisted) learning *or* CAL
computer-aided management *or* CAM
computer-aided manufacture *or* CAM
computer-aided teaching *or* CAT
computer aided trading *or* CAT
computerate
computer-based training *or* CBT
computer conferencing
computer graphics
computer input on microfilm *or* CIM
computer integrated manufacture *or* CIM
computerize
computer science
computer typesetting
concordance
concurrent processing
condition codes
configuration
connectivity
constant
control commands
cookie
core memory
co-routine
corrupt
crash
cross assembler
cursor
cut and paste
cybercafé
cyberpunk
cyberspace
cycle
DAC
data
data bank
database
database management
databus
data capture
dataflow architecture
data processing
data protection
data structure
Datel *(trademark)*
debugging
decision support system
decision table
default
desktop
desktop publishing *or* DTP
development system
device
digit
digital computer
digital fount
digital imaging
digital mapping
digital watermark
digitize
digitized
direct-access *or* random-access storage
direct memory access *or* DMA
directory
disassembler
distributed array processor
distributed logic
dithering
document
document reader
DOS *or* disk operating system *(trademark)*
dot matrix
download
downsize
down time
dumb terminal
dump
dpi *or* dots per inch
driver
dump
duplex
EBCDIC *or* extended binary-coded decimal-interchange code
echo
ecommerce
edit
editor
EEPROM
electronic flight information systems
electronic mail *or* E-mail
electronic office
electronic publishing
emulator
encryption
error message
escape routine
exclusive OR circuit
exit
expansion slot
expert system
extranet
fail-safe
field
fifth-generation
file
file manager
filename
file sharing
firewall
FireWire
firmware
flag
flops *or* floating-point operations per second
flowchart
freeware
front-end processor
FTP *or* file transfer protocol
function
function key
fuzzy
gate
gateway
gif
giga-
gigabyte
global search
graphical user interface
graphics
greyed out
hacker
hand-held computer
handshake
hard card
hard copy
hardware
hard-wired
help screens
hexadecimal notation
high-level language
host
hot key
hotspot
housekeeping
HTML
hybrid computer
hypermedia
hypertext
icon
idle time
IM *or* instant messaging
image enhancement
incremental plotter
incremental recorder
infect
information technology
initialize
input
input device
input/output *or* I/O
install
instruction
intelligent knowledge-based system *or* IKBS
intelligent terminal
interactive
interactive video
Internet
interpreter
interrupt
intranet
ISDN
iTunes *(trademark)*
job
jpeg
key in
keyword
kilo-
kilobyte
LAN
language
lapheld
laptop
legacy
linked list
liveware
load

local area network
location
logic bomb
logic circuit
logic programming
login
log in
log out
loop
low-level language
machine code
machine learning
machine readable
machine translation
macro
magnetic bubble
mail bombing
mailbox
mainframe
main memory
malware
manager
mega-
megabyte
memory mapping
menu
menu-driven
microcomputer
microprocessor
midi
minicomputer
mobile device
module
morphing
mpeg
MP3
multiaccess
multiprogramming
multi-threaded
multi-user
NAND circuit *or* gate
network
neurocomputer *or* neural computer
node
NOR gate
notebook computer
NOT gate
object program
OEM *or* original equipment manufacturer
offline
online
open
open-source
operating system
optimize
OR gate
output
overflow
package
packet
packet-switching
palette
palmtop computer
parallel processing
parameter
parity check
parser
password
patch
patch board
PC *or* personal computer
PDA
PDF
personal computer *or* PC
piggyback
pixel
platform
plug compatible
podcast
pointer
polymorphic function
pop-up
portable
power down
power up
printout
procedure
process
program
program generator
programmable read only memory *or* PROM
programmer
programming language
program statement
prompt
protocol
query language
queue
queuing theory
random access memory *or* RAM
Random Instruction Set Computer *or* RISC
raster
read in
read out
read only memory *or* ROM
real-time processing
reboot
record
remote access
rerun
reserved word
reset
restricted users group
retrieval
RISC *or* reduced instruction set computer
robustness
routine
run
run time
screensaver
scroll
SCSI *or* Small Computer Systems Interface
search engine
sense
sequential access
serial access memory *or* SAM
serial processing
server
SGML
shareware
shell program
skinning
slide-show
smart card
software
software engineering
sort
source document
source program
spam
speech recognition
spreadsheet
sprite
spyware
stack
statement
storage capacity
storage device
store
store and forward
string
subroutine
supercomputer
SWITCH
syntax
system
systems analysis
systems disk
taskbar
teleprocessing
telesoftware
terabyte
terminal
tetrabyte
text processing
3D graphics
throughput
time out
time sharing
toggle
toolbar
top-down processing
topology
transcribe
translator
transputer
tristate
turnkey system
underflow
UNIX *(trademark)*
uptime
USB
user-defined key
user group
utility
vaccine
variable
virtual address
virtual memory
virtual reality
virtual storage
virus
visual programming
voice input
voice recognition
voice response
volatile memory
WAN
WAP
warez
webcasting
web development
Wi-Fi
wild card
window
windows icons menus pointers *or* WIMP
wireless
wizard
word
word processor
work station
World Wide Web
worm
WYSIWIG
XML

CONTAINERS FOR LIQUID

amphora
ampulla
Balthazar
barrel
bottle
can
carafe
carton
cask
coldie *(Austral.) (slang)*
decanter
firkin
flagon
flask
gourd
half-bottle
hogshead
jar
jeroboam
jug
keg
magnum
Methuselah
miniature
Nebuchadnezzar
pitcher
polypin
rehoboam
Salmanazar
screw-top *(informal)*
stubby *(Austral.) (informal)*
tantalus
tin
tinny *(Austral.) (slang)*
tube

COOKERY

GENERAL COOKERY TERMS

à la king
à la mode
antipasto
au gratin
au jus
au lait
au naturel
bake
barbecue *or (Austral. slang)* barbie
bard *or* barde
baste
batter
blackened
blanch
boil
boil-in-the-bag
braise
broth
browning
caramelize
carbonado
casserole
caterer
chafing dish
char-grill
chasseur
chef
cobbler
coddle
colander
commis
confectioner
consommé
cook
cookbook *or* cookery book
cook-chill
corned
creole
cuisine
cuisine minceur
cured
curried
custard
dice
dough
dressing
en brochette
en croute
entrée
entremets
fajita
farci
fillet
flambé
flour
fondue
fricassee
fry
fumet
garnish
gelatine
ghee
giblets
glacé
glaze
goujon
goulash
grate
gravy
grill
hors d'oeuvre
ice
icing
jardinière
jerk
julienne
knead
ladle
lard
lardon *or* lardoon
leaven
liaison
luau
lyonnaise
macedoine
marengo
marinade
marinate
marmite
mask
mash
médaillons *or* medallions
meunière
meze
mirepoix
mornay
Newburg
nouvelle cuisine
offal
oven-ready
panada
parboil
Parmentier
paste
poach
potage
Provençale
purée
ragout
rijsttafel
rise
rissole
roast
roulade
roux
royal icing
salpicon
sauce
sauté
scramble
season
silver service
sippet
smoked
soup
steam
stew
stock
stroganoff
supreme
sweat
sweet-and-sour
tandoori
tenderize
teriyaki
tikka
timbale
topping
undressed
unleavened
unsmoked
whip
wholemeal *or (chiefly U.S. and Canad.)* wholewheat
wholemeal flour *or (chiefly U.S. and Canad.)* Graham flour
yeast

CUISINES AND COOKING STYLES

balti
Cantonese
Caribbean
Californian
Chinese
cordon bleu
cuisine minceur
fast food
French
Greek
gutbürgerlich
halal
haute cuisine
home cooking
Indian
Indonesian
international
ital
Italian
Japanese
kosher
Malaysian
Mediterranean
Mexican
nouvelle cuisine
Provençal
seafood
Sichuan *or* Szechuan
tapas
Tex-Mex
Thai
Turkish
vegan
vegetarian

CRAFTS

basketry *or* basket-making
batik
calligraphy
ceramics
cloisonnage
crewelwork
crochet
decoupage
dressmaking
embroidery
flower arranging
knitting
knotwork
macramé
needlepoint
patchwork
pottery
quilling
quilting
raffia work
sewing
spinning
sugarcraft
tapestry
weaving
wickerwork

CRICKET TERMS

appeal
Ashes
bail
ball
bat
batsman
bouncer *or* bumper
boundary
bowl
bowled
bowler
bye
catch
caught
century
chinaman
cover point
covers
crease
cut
declare
doosra
drive
duck
edge
extra
extra cover
fast bowler
fielder *or* fieldsman
fine leg
follow on
four
full toss
glance *or* glide
googly
gully
hit wicket
hook
in
innings
leg before wicket
leg break
leg bye
leg slip
long leg
long off
long on
maiden (over)
mid off
mid on
mid wicket
nightwatchman
no ball
off break
off side
off spin
off-spinner
on side *or* leg side
opener *or* opening batsman
out
over
pad
pitch
pull
run
run out
seam
short leg
silly mid on
silly mid off
single
six
slip
spin
square leg
stump
stumped
sweep
swing
test match
third man
twelfth man
Twenty20
umpire *or* *(Austral. slang)* umpie
wicket
wicketkeeper
wide
yorker

CRUSTACEANS

barnacle
crab
crayfish, crawfish, *(U.S.) or (Austral. & N.Z. informal)* craw
Dublin Bay prawn
freshwater shrimp
goose barnacle
gribble
hermit crab
horseshoe crab *or* king crab
king prawn
koura *(N.Z.)*
krill
land crab
langoustine
lobster
Norway lobster
opossum shrimp
oyster crab
prawn
robber crab
sand hopper, beach flea, *or* sand flea
sand shrimp
scorpion
sea spider
shrimp
soft-shell crab
spider crab
spiny lobster, rock lobster, crawfish, *or* langouste
water flea

CUPS AND OTHER DRINKING VESSELS

canteen
champagne flute
chalice
copita
cup
demitasse
glass
goblet
mug
porrón
quaich
schooner
tankard
tassie
tumbler
water bottle

CUPBOARDS AND CABINETS

ambry
armoire
bookcase
buffet
bureau
cabinet
canterbury
cellaret
chest
chest of drawers
chest-on-chest
chiffonier *or* chiffonnier
closet
clothes-press
commode
console
Coolgardie safe
court cupboard
credence table *or* credenza
dooket *(Scot.)*
drawer
dresser
filing cabinet
étagère
garderobe *(archaic)*
highboy *(U.S.)*
larder
locker
lowboy *(U.S.)*
medicine chest
pantry
press
safe
shelf
sideboard
stand
tallboy
vitrine
wardrobe
Welsh dresser
whatnot

TYPES OF CURRY

achari
balti
biryani
bhoona *or* bhuna
chasni
dhal
dhansak
dopiaza
green thai
jalfrezi
jaipuri
karahi
kofta
korma
madras
masala
mussalman
nentara
pasanda
pathia
phal
red thai
rogan josh
tandoori
tikka
vindaloo

DANCE

DANCES

allemande
apache dance
ballroom dance
barn dance
beguine
belly dance
black bottom
body popping
bogle
bolero
boogaloo
boogie
bossa nova
boston
bourrée
branle
brawl
break dance
breakdown
buck and wing
bump
bunny hug
butterfly
cachucha
cakewalk
calypso
cancan
carioca
carmagnole
carol
cha-cha-cha *or* cha-cha
chaconne
charleston
clog dance
conga
contredanse *or* contradance
Cossack dance
cotillion
country dance
courante
czardas
Dashing White Sergeant
ecossaise
eightsome reel
excuse-me
fan dance
fandango
farandole
flamenco
folk dance
formation dance
foxtrot
galliard
galop
gavotte
Gay Gordons
german
ghost dance
gigue
gopak
habanera
haka *(N.Z.)*
hay *or* hey
Highland fling
hoedown
hokey cokey
hora
hornpipe
hula *or* hula-hula
hustle
jig
jitterbug
jive
jota
juba
kazachok
kolo
lambada
Lambeth walk
lancers
ländler
limbo
line dance
macarena
malagueña
mambo
maxixe
mazurka
merengue
minuet
Morisco *or* Moresco
morris dance
mosh
musette
nautch
old-time dance
one-step
palais glide
paso doble
passacaglia
Paul Jones
pavane
pogo
poi dance
polka
pole dance
polonaise
pyrrhic
quadrille
quickstep
redowa
reel
rigadoon *or* rigaudon
ring-shout
robot dancing *or* robotics
ronggeng
round
round dance
roundelay *or* roundel
rumba
salsa
saltarello
samba
saraband
saunter
schottische
seguidilla
shake
shimmy
shuffle
siciliano
Sir Roger de Coverley
skank
snake dance
snowball
square dance
step dance
stomp
strathspey
strip the willow
sword dance
tambourin
tango
tap dance
tarantella
toe dance
twist
two-step
Tyrolienne
Virginia reel
vogueing
volta
waltz
war dance
Zapata

GENERAL DANCE STEPS AND TERMS

chassé
choreography
dosido
glide
grand chain
keep step
in step
out of step
pas
pas de basque
pas seul
phrase
pigeonwing
progressive
promenade
rhythm
routine
score
sequence
set
shuffle
slip step
steps
time

ACADEMIC DEGREES

DEGREE

Degree	*Abbreviation*	Degree	*Abbreviation*
Bachelor of Agriculture	BAgr	Doctor of Laws	LLD
Bachelor of Arts	BA	Doctor of Letters or Literature	DLitt *or* LittD
Bachelor of Commerce	BCom	Doctor of Medicine	MD
Bachelor of Dental Surgery	BDS	Doctor of Music	DMus, MusD, *or* MusDoc
Bachelor of Divinity	BD	Doctor of Philosophy	PhD
Bachelor of Education	BEd	Higher National Certificate	HNC
Bachelor of Engineering	BEng	Higher National Diploma	HND
Bachelor of Law	BL	Master of Arts	MA
Bachelor of Laws	LLB	Master of Education	MEd
Bachelor of Letters	BLitt	Master of Laws	LLM
Bachelor of Medicine	BM *or* MB	Master of Letters	MLitt
Bachelor of Music	BMus, MusB, *or* MusBac	Master of Music	MMus
Bachelor of Pharmacy	BPharm	Master of Philosophy	MPhil
Bachelor of Philosophy	BPhil	Master of Science	MSc
Bachelor of Science	BSc	Master of Surgery	MCh
Bachelor of Surgery	BS	Master of Technology	MTech
Diploma in Education	DipEd	Ordinary National Certificate	ONC
Doctor of Dental Surgery or Science	DDS *or* DDSc	Ordinary National Diploma	OND
Doctor of Divinity	DD		

DESSERTS AND SWEET DISHES

Atholl Brose *or* Athole Brose
baked Alaska
banana split
bavarois *or* Bavarian cream
Black Forest gateau
blancmange
blintz
bombe
bread and butter pudding
cabinet pudding
cassata
charlotte
charlotte russe
cheesecake
Christmas pudding
cobbler
college pudding
compote
coupe
cranachan
crème brûlée
crème caramel
crêpe
crêpe suzette
crumble
custard
death by chocolate
duff
dumpling
Easter-ledge pudding
Eve's pudding
flummery
fondant
fool
fruit cup
fruit salad *or* cocktail
gâteau
hasty pudding
ice cream
Île Flottante
jelly *or* (*U.S.*) jello
junket
kissel
knickerbocker glory
kulfi
marrons glacés
milk pudding
Mississippi mud pie
mousse
Neapolitan ice cream
nesselrode
panocha (*U.S.*)
parfait
pashka
pavlova *or* (*Austral. & N.Z. informal*) pav
peach Melba
plum duff
plum pudding
queen of puddings
rice pudding
roly-poly
sabayon
sago
semolina
shoofly pie (*U.S.*)
shortcake
slump (*U.S.*)
sorbet
soufflé
sponge pudding
spotted dick
spumone *or* spumoni
steamed pudding
strudel
suet pudding
summer pudding
sundae
syllabub *or* sillabub
tapioca
tartlet
tiramisu
torte
trifle
tutti-frutti
vacherin
water ice
whip
yogurt
zabaglione

DIETS

Atkins diet
breatharian diet *or* inedia
cabbage soup diet
Cambridge diet
CRON-diet
dairy-free diet
detox diet
Diet Smart Plan
DASH diet
fat resistance diet
Feingold diet
Fit for Life diet
flexitarian diet
food combining diet
F-Plan diet

fruitarian diet
gluten-free, casein-free diet
GI diet
Graham diet
grapefruit diet *or* Hollywood diet
hacker's diet
halal diet
hallelujah diet
high protein diet
kosher diet
lacto-vegetarian diet
low-protein diet
macrobiotic diet
Master Cleanse diet
Mediterranean diet
Montignac diet
natural food diet
negative calorie diet
no-grain diet
Okinawa diet
Optimal diet
organic food diet
Ornish diet
ovo-lacto-vegetarian diet
Palaeolithic diet
Perricone Weight-Loss diet
pescetarian diet *or* pesco-vegetarianism
pollotarian diet *or* pollo-vegetarianism
Pritikin diet
raw food diet
rice diet
Rosemary Conley diet
Scarsdale Medical diet
sex diet
Shangri-La diet
Slimming World diet
South Beach diet
Stillman diet
Subway diet
veganism
vegetarianism
very low calorie diet *or* VLCD
weigh down diet
Weight Watchers
zone diet

DINOSAURS

allosaur(us)
ankylosaur(us)
apatosaur(us)
atlantosaur(us)
brachiosaur(us)
brontosaur(us)
ceratosaur(us)
compsognathus
dimetrodon
diplodocus
dolichosaur(us)
dromiosaur(us)
elasmosaur(us)
hadrosaur(us)
ichthyosaur(us)
iguanodon *or* iguanodont
megalosaur(us)
mosasaur(us)
oviraptor
plesiosaur(us)
pteranodon
pterodactyl *or* pterosaur
protoceratops
stegodon *or* stegodont
stegosaur(us)
theropod
titanosaur(us)
trachodon
triceratops
tyrannosaur(us)
velociraptor

THE DISCIPLES OF JESUS

Andrew
Bartholomew
James
James
John
Judas
Jude
Matthew
Peter
Philip
Simon
Thomas

DISEASES

HUMAN DISEASES

absinthism
acariasis
acne
acromegaly
actinodermatitis
actinomycosis
Addison's disease
adrenoleukodystrophy *or* ALD
aeroneurosis
agranulocytosis
ague
Aids *or* AIDS
alcoholism
Alzheimer's disease
amoebiasis
ancylostomiasis, anchylostomiasis, *or* ankylostomiasis
angina
anorexia *or* anorexia nervosa
anthracosis
anthrax
aortitis
appendicitis
apraxia
arteriosclerosis
arthritis
asbestosis
ascariasis
asthma
atherosclerosis
athlete's foot
avian flu
avitaminosis
Bell's palsy
beriberi
bilharzia
bilharziasis *or* bilharziosis
bird flu
Black Death
black measles
blackwater fever
Bornholm disease
Bright's disease
bronchiolitis
bronchitis
bronchopneumonia
brucellosis
bubonic plague
bulimia *or* bulimia nervosa
Burkitt lymphoma *or* Burkitt's lymphoma
bursitis
byssinosis
calenture
cancer
cardiomyopathy
carditis
caries
carpal tunnel syndrome
cellulitis
cerebellar syndrome
Chagas' disease
chickenpox
chin cough
chloracne
chlorosis
cholera
chorea
Christmas disease
chronic fatigue syndrome *or* CFS
cirrhosis
coal miner's lung
coccidioidomycosis
coeliac disease
cold
colitis
common cold
conjunctivitis
constipation
consumption
cor pulmonale

coxalgia
Creutzfeldt-Jakob disease
Crohn's disease
Cushing's disease
cystic fibrosis
cystitis
dead fingers
decompression sickness
dengue
dermatitis
dhobi itch
diabetes
diarrhoea
diphtheria
diverticulitis
double pneumonia
dropsy
dysentery
earache
ebola virus disease
Economo's disease
eczema
elephantiasis
emphysema
encephalitis
encephalomyelitis
encephalopathy
endocarditis
enteritis
enterobiasis
enterocolitis
epilepsy
ergotism
erysipelas
erythroblastosis
exophthalmic goitre
farmer's lung
favus
fibrositis
filariasis
fishskin disease
flu
framboesia
furunculosis
gastritis
gastroenteritis
genital herpes
German measles
gingivitis
glandular fever
glaucoma
glomerulonephritis
glossitis
glue ear
goitre
gonorrhoea
gout
grand mal
green monkey disease
greensickness
haemoglobinopathy
haemophilia
Hansen's disease
hebephrenia
hepatitis
hepatitis A
hepatitis B
herpes
herpes simplex
herpes zoster
hidrosis
histoplasmosis
Hodgkin's disease
Huntington's chorea
hypothermia
hypothyroidism
ichthyosis
icterus
impetigo
infectious hepatitis
infectious mononucleosis
influenza
iritis
jaundice
jungle fever
kala-azar
Kaposi's sarcoma
Kawasaki's disease
Korsakoff's psychosis
kuru
labyrinthitis
laryngitis
Lassa fever
lathyrism
legionnaire's disease
leishmaniasis *or* leishmaniosis
leprosy
leptospirosis
leukaemia
listeriosis
lockjaw
lumbago
lupus
lupus erythematosus
lupus vulgaris
Lyme disease
lymphoma
malaria
Marburg disease
mastitis
measles
Ménière's syndrome
meningitis
metabolic syndrome
milk sickness
motor neurone disease
multiple sclerosis
mumps
muscular dystrophy
myalgic encephalomyelitis *or* ME
myasthenia gravis
myiasis
myopathy
myxoedema
narcolepsy
necrotising fasciitis
nephritis
nephrosis
neuropathy
non-A, non-B hepatitis
non-Hodgkin's lymphoma
onchocerciasis
ornithosis
osteitis
osteitis deformans
osteoarthritis
osteomalacia
osteomyelitis
osteoporosis
otitis
Paget's disease
paratyphoid fever
Parkinson's disease
pellagra
pelvic inflammatory disease
pemphigus
pericarditis
petit mal
pharyngitis
phlebitis
phthisis
pinta
pityriasis
pleurisy
pleuropneumonia
pneumoconiosis
pneumonia
poliomyelitis *or* polio
polycythaemia
porphyria
Pott's disease
pox
presenile dementia
prurigo
psittacosis
psoriasis
purpura
pyorrhoea
Q fever
quinsy
rabies
radiation sickness
ratbite fever *or* ratbite disease
Raynaud's disease
relapsing fever
retinitis
retinopathy
Reye's syndrome
rheumatic fever
rheumatoid arthritis
rhinitis
rickets
rickettsial disease
ringworm
Rocky Mountain spotted fever
rubella
Saint Vitus's dance
salmonella *or* salmonellosis
salpingitis
sapraemia
sarcomatosis
scabies
scarlet fever *or* scarlatina
schistosomiasis
schizophrenia
schizothymia
sciatica
scleroderma, sclerodermia, *or* scleriasis
scrofula
scrub typhus
scurvy
seasonal affective disorder
seborrhoea
senile dementia
septicaemia
serpigo
serum sickness
shell shock
shingles
sickle-cell anaemia
siderosis
silicosis
sinusitis
sleeping sickness
smallpox

spina bifida
spirochaetosis
splenitis
splenomegaly
spondylitis
spotted fever
sprue
stomatitis
strongyloidiasis *or* strongyloidosis
sunstroke
sweating sickness
swinepox
sycosis
Sydenham's chorea
synovitis
syphilis
syringomyelia
tarantism
Tay-Sachs disease
tetanus
thalassaemia
thrush
tick fever
tinea
tonsillitis
Tourette syndrome
toxic shock syndrome
trachoma
trench fever
trench mouth
trichinosis
trypanosomiasis
tsutsugamushi disease
tuberculosis
typhoid fever
typhus
uncinariasis
uraemia
urethritis
urticaria
utriculitis
uveitis
vaginitis
vagotonia
valvulitis
varicosis
variola
varioloid
venereal disease
Vincent's angina *or* Vincent's disease
vulvitis
vulvovaginitis
Weil's disease
whooping cough
yaws
yellow fever

ANIMAL DISEASES

actinomycosis *or* *(nontechnical)* lumpy jaw
anbury
anthrax
blackleg
bots
braxy
brucellosis *or* undulant fever
BSE (bovine spongiform encephalopathy) *or* *(informal)* mad cow disease
bull nose
bush sickness *(N.Z.)*
canker
cowpox
distemper
dourine
foot-and-mouth disease *or* hoof-and-mouth disease
fowl pest
furunculosis
gallsickness *or* anaplasmosis
gapes
gid
glanders
grapes
hard pad
heaves *or* broken wind
laminitis *or* founder
lampas *or* lampers
loco disease
Lyme disease
malanders, mallanders, *or* mallenders
Marburg disease *or* green monkey disease
milk fever
moon blindness *or* mooneye
murrain
myxomatosis
nagana
Newcastle disease *or* fowl pest
ornithosis
pinkeye
pip
pityriasis
psittacosis
pullorum disease *or* bacillary white diarrhoea
quarter crack
quittor
red water
rinderpest
ringbone
roaring
rot
roup
sand crack
scab
scrapie
scratches
seedy toe
sheep measles
sitfast
spavin
staggers, blind staggers, *or* megrims
strangles *or* equine distemper
stringhalt *or* springhalt
surra
swamp fever *or* equine infectious anaemia
sweating sickness
sweeny
swine fever *or* *(U.S.)* hog cholera
swinepox *or* variola porcina
swine vesicular disease
Texas fever
thoroughpin
thrush
toe crack
trembles *or* milk sickness
warble
whistling
windgall

DIVINATION

METHODS OF DIVINATION

astrology
clairvoyance
crystal gazing
dice
dowsing
I Ching
numerology
palmistry
runes
scrying
sortilege
tarot
tea leaves

MEANS OF DIVINATION

ailuromancy	cats
alphitomancy	wheat or barley cakes
arachnomancy	spiders
astragalomancy	dice
bibliomancy	passages from books
cartomancy	cards
catoptromancy	mirror
ceromancy	melted wax
chiromancy	hands
cleidomancy	suspended key
crithomancy	freshly baked bread
cromniomancy	onions
crystallomancy	crystal ball
dactylomancy	suspended ring
geomancy	earth, sand, or dust
hippomancy	horses
hydromancy	water
lampadomancy	oil lamps
lithomancy	precious stones
lychnomancy	flames of wax candles
molybdomancy	molten lead
necromancy	the dead
oneiromancy	dreams
ornithomancy	birds
pegomancy	sacred pool
pyromancy	fire or flames
radiesthesia	pendulum
rhabdomancy	rod or wand
sciomancy	ghosts
tasseography	tea leaves
theomancy	god
tyromancy	cheese

BREEDS OF DOG

affenpinscher
Afghan hound
Airedale terrier
Akita
Alaskan malamute
Alpine spaniel
Alsatian *or* German shepherd
Australian cattle dog, blue cattle dog, *or* (Queensland) blue heeler *(Austral.)*
Australian terrier
Australian silky terrier *or* Sydney silky
barb *(Austral.)*
basenji
basset hound
beagle
bearded collie
Bedlington terrier
Belvoir hound
Bichon Frise
Blenheim spaniel
bloodhound, sleuthhound, *or* sleuth
blue Gascon hound
Border collie
Border terrier
borzoi *or* Russian wolfhound
Boston terrier *or* bull terrier
bouvier
boxer
briard
Bruxellois
bulldog
bull mastiff
bull terrier
cairn terrier *or* cairn
chihuahua
chow-chow *or* chow
clumber spaniel
cocker spaniel
collie
corgi *or* Welsh corgi
Cuban bloodhound
dachshund
Dalmatian *or (formerly)* carriage dog *or* coach dog
Dandie Dinmont (terrier)
deerhound
Doberman pinscher *or* Doberman
Egyptian basset
elkhound *or* Norwegian elkhound
English setter
Eskimo dog
field spaniel
foxhound
fox terrier
French bulldog
golden retriever
Gordon setter
Great Dane
greyhound
griffon
harrier
Highland terrier
husky
Irish setter *or* red setter
Irish terrier
Irish water spaniel
Irish wolfhound
Italian greyhound
Jack Russell (terrier)
Japanese spaniel
Japanese tosa
keeshond
kelpie
Kerry blue terrier
King Charles spaniel
komondor
Labrador retriever, Labrador, *or* lab
Lakeland terrier
Lhasa apso
malamute *or* malemute
Maltese
Manchester terrier *or* black-and-tan terrier
mastiff
Mexican hairless
Newfoundland
Norfolk springer spaniel
Norfolk terrier
Norwich terrier
Old English sheepdog
otterhound
papillon
Pekingese
pit bull terrier *or* American pit bull terrier
pointer
Pomeranian
poodle
pug
puli
Pyrenean mountain dog
raccoon dog *or* coonhound
retriever
Rhodesian ridgeback
Rottweiler
rough collie
Saint Bernard *or* St. Bernard
Saluki *or* Persian greyhound
Samoyed
schipperke
schnauzer
Scottish, Scotch, *or (formerly)* Aberdeen terrier *or* Scottie
Sealyham terrier
setter
Shetland sheepdog *or* sheltie
shih-tzu
Skye terrier
spaniel

spitz
springer spaniel
Staffordshire bull terrier
staghound
Sussex spaniel
talbot
terrier
vizsla
water spaniel
Weimaraner
Welsh terrier
West Highland white terrier
whippet
wire-haired terrier
wolfhound
Yorkshire terrier

DRESSES

ballgown
burka
busuuti
button-through dress
chemise
cheongsam
chiton
coat dress
cocktail dress
dirndl
gymslip
kaftan *or* caftan
kimono
mantua
maxidress
microdress
midi
minidress
Mother Hubbard
muu-muu
negligee *or* negligée
nightdress *or (U.S. & Canad.)* nightrobe
nightgown *or (informal)* nightie *or* nighty
nightshirt
overdress
peignoir
pinafore dress, pinafore, pinny (informal), *or (U.S. & Canad.)* jumper
riding habit
sack
sari *or* saree
sheath
shift
shirtdress
shirtwaister *or (U.S. and Canad.)* shirtwaist
sundress
sweater dress
tea gown
tunic
wedding dress

SOFT DRINKS

alcohol-free *or* non-alcoholic beer
apple juice
barley water
bitter lemon
Bovril *(trademark)*
buttermilk
cassis
Coca-Cola *or* Coke *(trademark)*
cocoa
coffee
cola
cordial
cream soda
crush
dandelion and burdock
fruit juice
fruit tea
ginger ale
ginger beer
grapefruit juice
herb tea *or* herbal infusion
hot chocolate
ice-cream soda
iron brew
juice
kumiss, koumiss, koumis, *or* koumyss
lassi
lemonade
lemon squash
lemon tea *or* Russian tea
limeade
lime cordial
lolly water *(Austral.) (N.Z.)*
Lucozade *(trademark)*
maté *or* mate
milk
milk shake
mineral water
nectar
orangeade
orange juice
orgeat
peppermint cordial
Perrier *or* Perrier water *(trademark)*
prairie oyster
Ribena *(trademark)*
root beer
sarsaparilla
Seltzer *or* Seltzer water
sherbet
smoothie
soapolallie
soda
soda water
spremuta
squash
sweet cider *(U.S.) (Canad.)*
tea
tisane
Tizer *(trademark)*
tomato juice
tonic
vichy water
Vimto *(trademark)*
water

DRUGS

DRUGS

acetanilide *or* acetanilid
acriflavine
allopurinol
aloin
alum *or* potash alum
amitriptyline
amphetamine, Benzedrine *(trademark), or (slang)* speed
ampicillin
amyl nitrite *or (slang)* popper
Amytal *(trademark)*
Antabuse *(trademark)*
antipyrine
apomorphine
araroba *or* Goa powder
Argyrol *(trademark)*
arsphenamine
aspirin *or* acetylsalicylic acid
atropine *or* atropin
azathioprine
azedarach
bacitracin
barbitone *or (U.S.)* barbital
barbiturate
belladonna
Benadryl *(trademark)*
benzocaine
benzodiazepine
berberine
bhang *or* bang
bitter aloes
bromal
bupivacaine
caffeine
calomel
cannabis
cantharides
carbamazepine
carbimazole
cascara sagrada
chlorambucil

chloramphenicol
chlordiazepoxide
chloroquine
chlorothiazide
chlorpromazine
chlorpropamide
chlortetracycline
chlorthalidone
chrysarobin
cinchona
cinchonine
cocaine, cocain, *or (slang)* coke *or* Charlie
codeine
contrayerva
cortisone
co-trimoxazole
crystal methamphetamine *or (informal)* crystal meth
curare *or* curari
cyclopropane
cyclosporin-A
dapsone
DET *or* diethyltryptamine
dextroamphetamine
digitalis
dimenhydrinate *or* Dramamine *(trademark)*
disulfiram
ecstasy
DMT *or* dimethyltryptamine
ephedrin *or* ephedrine
fentanyl
ganja
gemfibrozil
hashish *or* charas
hemlock
hemp
heroin *or* diamorphine
hydrocortisone *or* cortisol
hyoscyamine
ibuprofen
imipramine
indomethacin
ipecac *or* ipecacuanha
ivermectin
kaolin *or* kaoline
ketamine
laudanum
Librium *(trademark)*
LSD, lysergic acid diethylamide, *or (slang)* acid
marijuana *or* marihuana
MDMA
mecamylamine
mepacrine, quinacrine *(U.S.)*, Atebrin *(trademark)*, *or* Atabrine *U.S. trademark*
meperidine *or* meperidene hydrochloride
merbromin
mercaptopurine
mescaline *or* mescalin
methadone *or* methadon
methamphetamine
methicillin
methotrexate
methyldopa
Mogadon *(trademark)*
morphine *or* morphia
neomycin
nepenthe
nicotine
nitrazepam
nitrous oxide, dinitrogen oxide, *or* laughing gas
Novocaine *(trademark) or* procaine hydrochloride
nux vomica
opium
Paludrine *(trademark)*
paracetamol
paraldehyde
paregoric
PCP *(trademark)*, phencyclidine, *or (informal)* angel dust
penicillin
pentamidine
pentaquine
pentazocine
pentobarbitone sodium, sodium pentabarbital *(U.S.)*, *or* Nembutal *(trademark)*
pentylenetetrazol
phenacaine
phenacetin *or* acetophenetidin
phenformin
phenobarbitone
phenolphthalein
phenothiazine
phenylbutazone
phenytoin
poppy
prednisolene
prednisone
primaquine
promethazine
propranolol
Prozac *(trademark)*
psilocybin
quercetin *or* quercitin
quinidine
quinine
reserpine
rhatany *or* krameria
rifampicin *or (U.S.)* rifampin
safflower *or* false saffron
salicin *or* salicine
saloop
salts
sanguinaria
santonin
scammony
scopolamine *or* hyoscine
scopoline
Seidlitz powder, Seidlitz powders, *or* Rochelle powder
senna leaf
senna pods
squill
STP
stramonium
streptomycin
sulphadiazine
sulphadimidine *or (U.S.)* sulfamethazine
sulpha drug
sulphanilamide
sulphathiozole
sulphisoxazole
temazepam
terebene
Terramycin *(trademark)*
tetracycline
thalidomide
thiopentone sodium, thiopental sodium, *or* Sodium Pentothal *(trademark)*
thiouracil
tricyclic
turpeth
valerian
Valium *(trademark) or* diazepam
verapamil
Viagra *(trademark)*
vinblastine
vinca alkaloid
vincristine
witch hazel *or* wych hazel
wormseed
yohimbine
zidovudine *or* Retrovir *(trademark)*

TYPES OF DRUG

abirritant
abortifacient
ACE inhibitor
adjuvant
agrypnotic
alexipharmic
alkylating agent
alterative
anaesthetic *or (U.S.)* anesthetic
analeptic
analgesic
anaphrodisiac
anodyne
antagonist
antibiotic
anticholinergic
anticonvulsant
antidepressant
antidote
antiemetic
antifebrile
antihistamine
anti-inflammatory
antimalarial
antimetabolite
antimycotic
antiperiodic

antiphlogistic
antipyretic
antispasmodic
antitussive
anxiolytic
aphrodisiac
astringent
ataractic *or* ataraxic
attenuant
beta-blocker
bronchodilator
calcium antagonist *or* blocker
calmative
cardiac
carminative
cathartic
cholagogue
cimetedine
cisplatin
clomiphene
colestipol
contraceptive
convulsant
cytotoxin
decongestant
demulcent
depressant
depressomotor
diaphoretic
diuretic
ecbolic
emetic
emmenagogue
errhine
euphoriant
excitant
expectorant
expellant *or* expellent
febrifuge
general anaesthetic *or* (*U.S.*) general anesthetic
haemagogue *or* (*U.S.*) hemagogue *or* hemagog
haemostatic *or* (*U.S.*) hemostatic
hallucinogen
hepatic
hypnotic
immunosuppressive
inotropic
laxative
lenitive
local anaesthetic *or* (*U.S.*) local anesthetic
masticatory
miticide
narcotic
nervine
neuroleptic
NSAID *or* nonsteroidal anti-inflammatory drug
opiate
oxytocic
painkiller
palliative
pectoral
preventive
prophylactic
psychedelic *or* psychodelic
psychoactive
psychotomimetic
pulmonic (*rare*)
purgative
radio mimetic
recreational
relaxant
resolvent
restorative
revulsive
roborant
sedative
sialagogue *or* sialogogue
soporific
sorbefacient
spermicide *or* (*less commonly*) spermatocide
steroid
stimulant
stupefacient
styptic
suppurative
sympatholytic
sympathomimetic
synergist
taeniacide *or* (*U.S.*) teniacide
taeniafuge *or* (*U.S.*) teniafuge
tetanic
tonic
tranquillizer, tranquilliser, *or* (*U.S.*) tranquilizer
tumefacient
vasoconstrictor
vasodilator
vasoinhibitor
vermifuge, anthelminthic, anthelmintic, *or* helminthic
vesicant *or* vesicatory
vomit
vulnerary

GENERAL DRUG TERMS

absorption
addiction
addictive
adiaphorous
ana
antimonial
aromatic
arsenical
autacoid
bacterin
bioassay
bioavailability
biological
blockade
botanical
chalybeate
chemoprophylaxis
cohobate
confection
contraindicate
control group
decoction
dependency
designer drug
dosage
dose
electuary
elixir
embrocation
emulsion
endermic
ethical
excipient
exhaust
external
extract
fluidextract
galenical
glycoside
hard
hypersensitive
hypodermic
hypodermic needle
hypodermic syringe
idiosyncrasy
incompatible
inhalant
intermediate-acting
intoxicating
lethal dose *or* LD
linctus
liquor
local
long-acting
magistral
mass
median lethal dose *or* mean lethal dose
medication
menstruum
mercurial
mind-expanding
minimum lethal dose *or* MLD
mixture
normal
officinal (*obsolete*)
oleoresin
oral
overdose
over-the-counter
parenteral
pessary
placebo
positive
potentiate
prescription
proprietary
reaction
reactor
remedy
route
sensitivity
sensitize *or* sensitise
short-acting
side effect
signature (*U.S.*)
soft
spansule
specific
spirit
suppository
tincture
succedaneum
synergism *or* synergy
tachyphylaxis

tolerant
topical
trituration
unit
unofficial
vehicle
venipuncture *or* venepuncture
vinegar
wafer
wine
withdrawal

DRUG ABUSE TERMS

acid
acidhead
angel dust
blow
blow someone's mind
bombed
bong
bring down
bummer
burned
bust
buzz
Charlie
chillum
coke
cold turkey
comedown
connection
cook up
cop
crack
crackhead
crank up
dadah *(Austral.) (slang)*
dealer
do
dope
downer
drop
dry out
ecstasy *or* E
fix
freebase
gear
get off
get through *(U.S.)*
glue-sniffing
gone
goof
goofball *(U.S.)*
grass
habit
hash
head
high
hit
hooked
hop *(obsolete)*
hophead *(chiefly U.S.)*
hop up *(dated)*
hype
hyped up
jack up
jag
jellies
joint
joypop
junk
junkie
kick
kif
knockout drops
line
lit up
loaded *(chiefly U.S.) (Canad.)*
magic mushroom
mainline
make it
Man *(U.S.)*
Mickey Finn
mind-expanding
monkey *(U.S.) (Canad.)*
nail
narc *(U.S.)*
nod out
number
OD *or* overdose
opium den
pep pill
pop
popper
pot
pothead
pusher
reefer
roach
score
shooting gallery
shoot up
skin-pop
skin up
smack
smackhead
smashed
smoke
snort
snowball
solvent abuse
space cadet
spaced out *or* spaced
speed
speedball
speedfreak
spliff
stash
step on
stoned
strung out
stuff
swacked
switch on
tab
toke
toot
trip
turn on
upper
user
wasted
weight
withdrawal
withdrawal symptoms
wrap
wrecked
zonked

SNOW WHITE'S SEVEN DWARFS

Bashful
Doc
Dopey
Grumpy
Happy
Sleepy
Sneezy

PARTS OF THE EAR

ancus
auditory nerve
cochlea
eardrum, tympanic membrane, *or* tympanum
ear lobe
Eustachian tube
external auditory canal
incus
malleus
meatus *or* auditory canal
organ of Corti
oval window
pinna
round window
saccule
semicircular canals
stapes
tragus
utricle

LAYERS OF THE EARTH'S CRUST

asthenosphere
basement
continental crust
lithosphere
lower mantle
Mohorovicíc discontinuity
oceanic crust
sima
sial
transition zone
upper mantle

SPECIFIC EATING HABITS

HABIT

Habit	Food	Habit	Food
anthropophagic *or* anthropophagous	fellow humans	macrophagous	relatively large pieces of food
apivorous	bees	monophagous	only one food
cannibalistic	other members of the same species	mycetophagous	fungi
carnivorous	meat	myrmecophagous	ants
carpophagous, frugivorous, *or* fruitarian	fruit	nectarivorous	nectar
carrion	dead and rotting flesh	nucivorous	nuts
coprophagous	dung	omnivorous	meat and plants
geophagous	earth	omophagic *or* omophagous	raw food
herbivorous	plants	piscivorous	fish
hylophagous	wood	theophagous	gods
insectivorous	insects	vegan	no animal products
limivorous	mud	vegetarian	no flesh
		zoophagous	animals

ECONOMICS

BRANCHES OF ECONOMICS

agronomics
cliometrics
econometrics
economic history
industrial economics
macroeconomics
microeconomics
welfare economics

ECONOMICS TERMS

arbitration
asset
autarky
automation
balanced budget
balance of payments
balance of trade
balance sheet
bank
bankruptcy
barriers to entry
barriers to exit
barter
base rate
bear market
bid
black economy
boom
boycott
bridging loan
budget
budget deficit
building society
bull market
business cycle
buyer's market
capacity
capital
capital good
capitalism
cartel
cash
central bank
Chamber of Commerce
closed shop
collective bargaining
command economy *or* planned economy
commercial bank *or* clearing bank
commission
commodity
common market
comparative advantage
competition
conspicuous consumption
consumer
consumer good
consumption
cooperative
corporation
corporation tax
cost-benefit analysis
cost effectiveness
cost of living
cost-push inflation
credit
credit controls
credit squeeze
currency
current account
customs union
debt
deflation
deindustrialization
demand
demand management *or* stabilization policy
demand-pull inflation
deposit account
depreciation
depression
deregulation
devaluation
diminishing returns
discount
discount house *(Brit.)*
discount rate
disequilibrium
disinflation
disposable income
diversification
divestment
dividend
division of labour
dumping
duopoly
durable good
Dutch disease
duty
earned income
earnings
economic growth
economic policy
economic sanctions
economies of scale
embargo
employee
employer
employment
entrepreneur
environmental audit
exchange
exchange rate
expenditure
export
finance
financial year

fiscal drag
fiscal policy
fiscal year
Five-Year Plan
fixed assets
fixed costs
fixed exchange-rate system
fixed investment
floating exchange-rate system
foreclosure
foreign exchange controls
foreign exchange market
forfaiting
franchise
free-market economy
free rider
free trade
free trade area
free trade zone *or* freeport
freight
friendly society
fringe benefits
full employment
funding
futures market *or* forward exchange market
gains from trade
game theory
gilt-edged security *or* government bond
gold standard
greenfield investment
gross domestic product *or* GDP
gross national product *or* GNP
gross profit
hard currency
hedging
hire
hire purchase *or* HP
hoarding
holding
horizontal integration
hot money
human capital
hyperinflation
imperfect competition
import
import restrictions
income
income support
income tax
index-linked
indirect tax
industrial dispute
industrial estate
industrial policy
industrial relations
industrial sector
inflationary spiral
information agreement
infrastructure
inheritance tax
insolvency
instalment credit
institutional investors
insurance
intangible assets
intangibles
intellectual property right
interest
interest rate
international competitiveness
international debt
international reserves
investment
invisible balance
invisible hand
invoice
joint-stock company
joint venture
junk bond
labour
labour market
labour theory of value
laissez faire *or* laisser faire
lease
legal tender
lender
liability
liquidation
liquid asset
liquidity
listed company
loan
lockout
macroeconomic policy
management buy-out
marginal revenue
marginal utility
market
market failure
mass production
means test
mediation
medium of exchange
medium-term financial strategy
mercantilism
merchant bank
merger
microeconomic policy
middleman
mint
mixed economy
monetarism
monetary compensatory amounts, MCAs, *or* green money
monetary policy
money
money supply
monopoly
moonlighting
mortgage
multinational
national debt
national income
national insurance contributions
nationalization
national product
natural rate of unemployment
net profit
nondurable good
offshore
oligopoly
overheads
overheating
overmanning
overtime
patent
pawnbroker
pay
pay-as-you-earn *or* PAYE
payroll
pension
pension fund
per capita income
perfect competition
personal equity plan *or* PEP
picket
piecework
polluter pays principle
portfolio
poverty trap
premium
premium bond
price
prices and incomes policy
primary sector
private enterprise
private property
privatization
producer
production
productivity
profit
profitability
profit-and-loss account
profit margin
profit sharing
progressive taxation
protectionism
public expenditure
public finance
public interest
public-sector borrowing requirement *or* PSBR
public-sector debt repayment
public utility
public works
pump priming
purchasing power
quality control
ratchet effect
rational expectations
rationalization
rationing
recession
recommended retail price
recovery
recycling
redundancy
reflation
regional policy
rent
rent controls
research and development *or* R & D
residual unemployment
restrictive labour practice
retail
retail price index
revaluation
revenue
risk analysis

salary
sales
saving
savings bank
seasonal unemployment
self-employment
self service
self-sufficiency
seller's market
sequestration
service sector
share
shareholder
share issue
share price index
shop
shop steward
simple interest
slump
social costs
socio-economic group
soft currency
specialization
speculation
stagflation
standard of living
stock
stockbroker
stock control
stock exchange, stock market, *or (N.Z.)* share market
stop-go cycle
structural unemployment
subsidiary company
subsidy
supplier
supply
supply-side economics
surplus
synergy
takeover
tangible assets
tariff
tax
taxation
tax avoidance
tax evasion
tax haven
terms of trade
trade
trade barrier
trademark
trade union
trade-weighted index
training
transaction
trust
trustee
underwriter
unearned income
unemployment
unemployment benefit
uniform business rate *or* UBR
unit of account
unit trust
utility
value-added tax *or* VAT
variable costs
venture capital
vertical integration
voluntary unemployment
wage
wage restraint
wealth
welfare state
wholesaler
worker participation
working capital
yield

ECONOMICS SCHOOLS AND THEORIES

Austrian school
Chicago school
Classical school
Keynesianism
Marxism
mercantilism
monetarism
neoclassical school
neoKeynesians
Physiocrats
Reaganomics
Rogernomics *(N.Z.)*
Thatcherism

EDUCATION TERMS

A bursary *(N.Z.)*
academic
accredit *(N.Z.)*
accumulation
Advanced level *or* A level *(Brit.)*
adviser *or* advisor *(Brit.)*
advisory teacher *(Brit.)*
aegrotat *(Brit.)*
alumnus *or* alumna *(chiefly U.S.) (Canad.)*
assignment
assistant *(U.S.) (Canad.)*
associate *(U.S.) (Canad.)*
baccalaureate
banding *(Brit.)*
battels *(Brit.)*
B bursary *(N.Z.)*
bedder *(Brit.)*
binary
boarder *(Brit.)*
boarding house *(Austral.)*
bubs grade *(Austral.) (N.Z. (slang))*
bursar
bursarial
bursary *or* bursarship *(Scot.) (N.Z.)*
campus
campus university
catalogue *(U.S.) (Canad.)*
catchment *(Brit.)*
Certificate of Pre-vocational Education *or* CPVE *(Brit.)*
Certificate of Proficiency *or* COP *(N.Z.)*
chancellor *(Brit.) (U.S. (Canad.))*
chapterhouse *(U.S.)*
class
classmate
classroom
co-ed *(U.S.)*
coeducation
collegial
collegian
collegiate
comedown *(Brit.)*
commencement *(U.S.) (Canad.)*
commoner *(Brit.)*
Common Entrance *(Brit.)*
conductive education
congregation *(chiefly Brit.)*
continuous assessment
convocation
core subjects *(Brit.)*
coursework
crammer
credit
crib *(Brit.)*
cross-curricular *(Brit.)*
Cuisenaire rod *(trademark)*
curricular
curriculum
dean
deanery
degree
delegacy
department
detention
dissertation
docent *(U.S.)*
dominie *(Scot.)*
don *(Brit.)*
donnish
dropout
dunce
dunce cap
dux
Easter term
educate

education
educational
eleven-plus *(obsolete)*
emeritus
entry
essay
examination *or* exam
exercise
exhibition *(Brit.) (Austral.)*
exhibitioner *(Brit.)*
expel
extension
external
extracurricular
extramural
faculty
fail
family grouping *or* vertical grouping
federal
fellow
fellowship
ferule
flunk *(chiefly U.S.) (Canad. (N.Z.)) (informal)*
fresher *or* freshman
full professor *(U.S.) (Canad.)*
further education *(Brit.)*
gaudy *(Brit.)*
General Certificate of Education *or* GCE *(Brit.)*
General Certificate of Secondary Education *or* GCSE *(Brit.)*
gown
grade *(U.S.) (Canad.)*
graded post *(Brit.)*
graduand *(chiefly Brit.)*
graduate *(Brit.) (U.S. (Canad.))*
graduation
grant
grant-in-aid
grant-maintained
Great Public Schools *or* GPS *(Austral.)*
Greats *(Brit.)*
gymnasium
hall
hall of residence
headmaster *or* headmistress
headmastership *or* headmistress-ship
headship *(Brit.)*
higher *(Scot.)*
high school
Hilary term
homework
honours *or (U.S.)* honors
hood
hooky *or* hookey *(chiefly U.S.) (Canad. (N.Z.)) (informal)*
house
housefather
housemaster
housemother
imposition *(Brit.)*
incept *(Brit.)*
infant *(Brit.)*
in residence
instructor *(U.S.) (Canad.)*
internal
interscholastic
intramural *(chiefly U.S.) (Canad.)*
invigilate *(Brit.)*
invigilator *(Brit.)*
janitor *(Scot.)*
jig *(Austral.) (slang)*
junior
junior common room
key stage *(Brit.)*
lecture
lecturer
level of attainment *(Brit.)*
liaison officer *(N.Z.)*
lines
literae humaniores *(Brit.)*
LMS *or* local management of schools *(Brit.)*
local examinations
lowerclassman *(U.S.)*
lower school
lycée *(French)*
manciple
marking
master
matriculate
matriculation *or* matric
mature student
Michaelmas term
middle common room
midterm
mistress
mitch *or* mich *(dialect)*
mocks *(informal)*
moderator *(Brit.) (N.Z.)*
muck-up day *(Austral.) (slang)*
National Curriculum *(Brit.)*
Nuffield teaching project *(Brit.)*
open learning
Ordinary grade *or* O grade *(Scot.)*
Ordinary level *or* O level *(Brit.)*
Ordinary National Certificate *or* ONC *(Brit.)*
pandy *(chiefly Scot.) (Irish)*
parent teacher association *or* PTA
parietal *(U.S.)*
pass
pedant *(archaic)*
pipe *(U.S.) (slang)*
porter
postgraduate
prefect *(Brit.)*
prelims *(Scot.)*
prepositor *(Brit.) (rare)*
primers *(N.Z.) (informal)*
principal
Privatdocent
proctor *(U.S.)*
professor
professoriate
prospectus
provost
punishment exercise
reader *(chiefly Brit.)*
readership *(chiefly Brit.)*
reception *(Brit.)*
recess *(U.S.) (Canad.)*
record of achievement *(Brit.)*
recreation
rector *(chiefly Brit.)*
redbrick *(Brit.)*
refresher course
regent
registrar
Regius professor *(Brit.)*
remedial
remove *(Brit.)*
report *(Brit.)*
resit
rusticate *(Brit.)*
sabbatical
sandwich course
SCE *or* Scottish Certificate of Education
scholastic
School Certificate *(Brit.) (N.Z. (old-fashioned))*
schoolleaver
schoolman
schoolmarm
schoolmaster
schoolmistress
schoolteacher
second *(Brit.)*
self-educated
semester *(chiefly U.S.) (Canad.)*
seminar
senate
send down
senior

senior common room
session
set
shell *(Brit.)*
sixth form *(Brit.)*
sixth-form college *(Brit.)*
sizar *(Brit.)*
sophomore *(chiefly U.S.)* *(Canad.)*
sorority *(chiefly U.S.)*
speech day *(Brit.)*
sports day *(Brit.)*
stage
Standard Grade *(Scot.)*
standard assessment tasks *or* SATS *(Brit.)*
statement *(Brit.)*
stream *(Brit.)*
student teacher
subject
subprincipal
summa cum laude
summative assessment *(Brit.)*
supervisor
teach-in
term
tertiary bursary *(Brit.)*
test
thesis
transcript *(chiefly U.S.)* *(Canad.)*
transfer
trimester *(chiefly U.S.)* *(Canad.)*
Trinity term
truant
tuition
tutee
tutor
tutorial
tutorial system
union
university entrance (examination) *or* UE *(N.Z.)*
undergraduate
unstreamed *(Brit.)*
upper school
vice chancellor *(Brit.)*
visiting professor
wag *(slang)*
warden *(Brit.)*
wrangler *(Brit.)*
year

EMBROIDERY STITCHES

Arrowhead stitch
Back stitch
Barb stitch
Basque stitch
Beaded stitch
Berlin stitch
Berwick stitch
Blanket stitch
Briar stitch
Bullion stitch
Buttonhole Bar
Buttonhole Wheel
Buttonhole
Casalguidi
Cast on stitch
Catch stitch
Caterpillar stitch
Chain stitch
Chevron stitch
Chinese stitch
Closed Buttonhole
Closed Feather stitch
Coil stitch
Convent stitch
Coral stitch
Cretan stitch
Crewel stitch
Cross stitch
Crossed Buttonhole
Crossed corners
Crow's-foot
Daisy stitch
Damask stitch
Double Cross
Eyelet stitch
Feather stitch
Feathered Chain
Fern stitch
Fly stitch
French Knot
German Knot stitch
Ghiordes Knot
Greek stitch
Herringbone
Kloster stitch
Ladder stitch
Lazy Daisy stitch
Montenegrin
Open Chain stitch
Outline stitch
Pekinese
Plaited stitch
Porto Rico rose
Portuguese stitch
Post stitch
Quilt Knot stitch
Renaissance
Ribbed Wheel
Rice stitch
Roman Chain stitch
Running stitch
Russian Cross stitch
Russian stitch
Sampler stitch
Satin stitch
Scottish stitch
Scroll stitch
Sham Hem stitch
Split stitch
Stem stitch
Threaded Arrowhead
Threaded Fly stitch
Threaded Running
Twisted Chain
Twisted Lattice Band
Wheatear
Whipped Back
Whipped Chain
Whipped Fly
Whipped Running
Whipped Stem
Woven Spider's Wheel
Zigzag Chain

BRANCHES OF ENGINEERING

aerodynamics
aeronautical engineering
aerospace engineering
agricultural engineering
astronautics
automotive engineering
bioengineering
chemical engineering
civil engineering
computer-aided engineering
cosmonautics
electrical engineering
electronics engineering
environmental engineering
ergonomics
fluid dynamics
genetic engineering
geotechnics
hydraulics
mechanical engineering
mechatronics
military engineering
mining engineering
naval engineering
nuclear engineering
process engineering
production engineering
sanitary engineering
structural engineering
traffic engineering

ENTERTAINMENT

TYPES OF ENTERTAINMENT

acrobatics
aerobatics
agon
airshow
all-dayer
all-nighter
antimasque
après-ski
aquashow
ball
ballet
B and S *(Austral.)* *(informal)*
banquet
bear-baiting
bullfighting
burlesque show
busking
cabaret
carnival
ceilidh
charade
circus
cockfighting
comedy
command performance
concert
conjuring
cotillion *or* cotillon *(U.S.)* *(Canad.)*
dance
escapology
exhibition
fair
farce
fashion show
feast
fête *or* fete
film
fireworks *or* pyrotechnics
floor show
funambulism *or* tightrope-walking
gala
galanty show
garden party
gaudy
gig *(informal)*
ice show
juggling
karaoke
kermis *or* kirmess *(U.S.)* *(Canad.)*
levee
light show
magic
masked ball
masque
melodrama
minstrel show
musical
music hall
opera
operetta
pantomime
party
play
puppet show
raree show
rave
reading
reception
recital
recitation
revue *or* review
ridotto
road show
rodeo
shadow play
show
sideshow
singsong
slide show
slot machine
soiree
son et lumière
street theatre
striptease
tragedy
variety
vaudeville
ventriloquism
video game
wall of death
waltzer
warehouse party
whist drive
zarzuela

TYPES OF ENTERTAINER

acrobat
actor *or* *(fem.)* actress
artist
artiste
auguste
bareback rider
busker
chorus girl
circus artist
clown
comedian *or* *(fem.)* comedienne
conjurer
contortionist
dancer
diva
equilibrist
escapologist
exotic dancer
fire eater
fool
funambulist *or* tightrope walker
funnyman
go-go dancer
gracioso
guiser
harlequin
illusionist
impersonator
impressionist
jester
jongleur
juggler
lion tamer
magician
merry-andrew
mimic
minstrel
mummer
musician
organ-grinder
performer
prima ballerina
prima donna
puppeteer
quick-change artist
raconteur
ringmaster
show girl
singer
snake charmer
stripteaser *or* stripper
strolling player
strongman
sword swallower
tightrope walker
tragedian *or* *(fem.)* tragedienne
trapeze artist
trouper
tumbler
unicyclist
vaudevillian
ventriloquist

PLACES OF ENTERTAINMENT

amphitheatre
amusement arcade *(Brit.)*
arena
auditorium
ballroom
bandstand
big top
bingo hall
carnival
cinema
circus
coliseum *or* colosseum
concert hall
dance hall
disco
fairground
funfair
gallery
hall
leisure centre
lido
marquee
museum
music hall
nightclub
nightspot
niterie *(slang)*
opera house
social club
stadium
theatre
vaudeville
waxworks
zoo

EQUESTRIANISM

EQUESTRIAN EVENTS AND SPORTS

Ascot
Badminton
buckjumping (*Austral.*)
cavalcade
claiming race (*U.S.*) (*Canad.*)
classic
Derby
dressage
eventing
Grand National
gymkhana
harness racing
horse racing
hunt
joust
jump-off
Kentucky Derby
meeting
nursery stakes
Oaks
One Thousand Guineas
picnic race (*Austral.*)
plate
point-to-point
polo
puissance
race meeting
races, the
Saint Leger
showjumping
steeplechase
sweepstake *or* (*esp U.S.*) sweepstakes
three-day eventing
Two Thousand Guineas

CLASSIC ENGLISH HORSE RACES

Race	*Course*	*Distance*
One Thousand Guineas (fillies)	Newmarket	one mile
Two Thousand Guineas (colts)	Newmarket	one mile
Derby (colts)	Epsom	one and a half miles
the Oaks (fillies)	Epsom	one and a half miles
St. Leger (colts and fillies)	Doncaster	one and three quarter miles

HORSE RACING TERMS

accumulator
allowance
also-ran
ante post betting
apprentice
auction plate
away
blanket finish
boring
break
break away
card *or* race card
chaser
claiming race (*U.S.*) (*Canad.*)
classic
clerk of the course
clerk of the scales
colt
come in
course
daily double
dead heat
distance
dope sheet (*slang*)
draw
each way *or* (*U.S.*) across-the-board
faller
fence
filly
finish
flat
flat jockey
flat racing
flight
furlong
gate
going
green horse
handicap
handicapper
handy
harness race *or* (*N.Z.*) trotting race
head
home straight *or* (*U.S.*) home stretch
hurdle
hurdling
impost
jockey
Jockey Club
jump jockey
length
maiden
meeting
milepost
nap
National Hunt
neck
novice
objection
pacemaker *or* pacesetter
pacer
paddock
photo finish
place
plater
point-to-point (*Brit.*)
pole (*chiefly U.S.*) (*Canad.*)
post
roughie
scratch
scurry
selling race *or* plate
short head
silver ring
stakes
starter
starting post
starting price
starting stalls *or* (*U.S.*) starting gate
stayer
steeplechase *or* chase
steward
stewards' inquiry
straight *or* (*U.S.*) straightaway
stretch
sweat (*chiefly U.S.*)
sweat up
ticktack
track
trainer
turf
under starter's orders
unplaced
unseated rider
walkover
weigh in
winning post
wire (*U.S.*) (*Canad.*)
yearling

TYPES OF JUMP

brush and rails
double oxer
gate
hog's back
narrow stile
parallel poles
planks
post and rails
triple bars
wall
water jump

PARTS OF THE EYE

aqueous humour
blind spot
choroid *or* chorioid
ciliary body
cone
conjunctiva
cornea
eyeball
fovea
iris
lens
ocular muscle
optic nerve
pupil
retina
retinal vessels
rod
sclera
suspensory ligament
vitreous body
vitreous humour

FABRICS

Acrilan *(trademark)*
alpaca
armure
baize
balbriggan
barathea
barège
batik *or* battik
batiste
bayadere
beige
bengaline
bird's-eye
bobbinet
bombazine *or* bombasine
bouclé
brilliantine
broadcloth
brocade
buckskin
bunting
burlap
calamanco
calico
cambric
camlet
cavalry twill
challis *or* challie
chambray
Charmeuse *(trademark)*
cheesecloth
chenille
cheviot
chiffon
chintz
cilice
ciré
cloqué
cord
corduroy
cotton
cottonade
cotton flannel
covert cloth
crepe *or* crape
cretonne
Crimplene *(trademark)*
crinoline
cypress *or* cyprus
Dacron *(trademark)*
damask
delaine
denim
diamanté
dimity
Donegal tweed
drab
drabbet
Dralon *(trademark)*
drugget
duck
dungaree
duvetyn, duvetine, *or* duvetyne
etamine *or* etamin
façonné *or* faconne
faille
fearnought *or* fearnaught
felt
fishnet
flannel
fleece
folk weave
foulard
frieze
frisé
fur
fustian
gaberdine
galatea
georgette
gingham
gloria
Gore-Tex *(trademark)*
gossamer
grogram
gros de Londres
grosgrain
gunny *(chiefly U.S.)*
Harris Tweed *(trademark)*
hessian
honan
hopsack
huckaback *or* huck
India print
jaconet
Jacquard *or* Jacquard weave
jean
jersey
khaki
kincob
knit
lace
lambskin
lamé
lawn
leather
linen
linsey-woolsey
lisle
Lurex *(trademark)*
Lycra *(trademark)*
madras
marabou
marocain
marquisette
marseille *or* marseilles
melton
messaline
mohair
moire *or* moiré
moleskin
monk's cloth
moquette
moreen
mousseline
mull
muslin
nainsook
nankeen *or* nankin
needlecord
net
ninon
nun's cloth *or* veiling
oilskin
organdie
organza
organzine
Orlon *(trademark)*
ottoman
Oxford
paduasoy
paisley pattern
panne
paramatta *or* parramatta
peau de soie
percale
percaline
petersham
piña cloth
piqué
plush
pongee
poplin
poult *or* poult-de-soie
prunella, prunelle, *or* prunello
rayon
russet
sailcloth
samite
sarcenet *or* sarsenet
sateen
satin
satinet *or* satinette
saxony
say *(archaic)*
schappe
scrim
seersucker
sendal
serge
shag
shalloon
shantung
sharkskin
sheeting
shirting
shoddy
silesia
silk
silkaline

slipper satin
spandex
spun silk
stockinet
stroud
stuff
suiting
surah
surat
swan's-down
swanskin
swiss muslin
tabaret
tabby
taffeta
tammy
tarlatan
tarpaulin
tartan
tattersall
terry
Terylene *(trademark)*
tick
ticking
tiffany
toile
towelling
tricot
tricotine
tulle
tussore, tusser, *or* *(chiefly U.S.)* tussah
tweed
twill
velours
velure
velvet
velveteen
Viyella *(trademark)*
voile
wadmal
webbing
whipcord
wild silk
winceyette
wool
worsted

THE FATES

Atropos
Clotho
Lachesis

FENCING TERMS

backsword
bracer
carte
feint
guard
mask
octave
parade
parry
piste
prime
quarte or carte
quinte
reach
repechage
sabre
seconde
septime
singlestick
sixte
terce *or* tierce
touch
touché
volt

FIGURES OF SPEECH

alliteration
allusion
anacoluthia
anadiplosis
analogy
anaphora
anastrophe
antiphrasis
antithesis
antonomasia
apophasis
aporia
aposiopesis
apostrophe
catachresis
chiasmus
circumlocution
climax
emphasis
epanaphora
epanorthosis
exclamation
gemination
hendiadys
hypallage
hyperbaton
hyperbole
hysteron proteron
inversion
irony
kenning
litotes
malapropism
meiosis
metaphor
metonymy
onomatopoeia
oxymoron
paralipsis *or* paraleipsis
parenthesis
periphrasis
personification
pleonasm
polysyndeton
prolepsis
prosopopoeia *or* prosopopeia
repetition
rhetorical question
sarcasm
simile
spoonerism
syllepsis
synechdoche
tmesis
zeugma

FISH

TYPES OF FISH

ahi
ahuru *(N.Z.)*
alewife
albacore
alfonsino
amberjack
anabantid
anabas
anableps
anchoveta
anchovy
angelfish
arapaima
archerfish
argentine
aua *(N.Z.)*
Australian salmon, native salmon, salmon trout, bay trout *or* kahawai *(N.Z.) (Austral.)*
barbel
barracouta *or* *(Austral.)* hake
barracuda
barramunda
barramundi *or* *(Austral.)* barra *or* giant perch
bass
batfish
beluga
bib, pout, *or* whiting pout
bigeye
billfish
bitterling
black bass
black bream
black cod *or* Māori chief *(N.Z.)*
blackfish *or* *(Austral.)* nigger
bleak

blenny
blindfish
bloodfin
blowfish *or (Austral.)* toado
blue cod, rock cod, *or (N.Z.)* rawaru, pakirikiri, *or* patutuki
bluefin tuna
bluefish *or* snapper
bluegill
blue nose *(N.Z.)*
boarfish
bonefish
bonito *or (Austral.)* horse mackerel
bony bream *(Austral.)*
bowfin *or* dogfish
bream *or (Austral.)* brim
brill
brook trout *or* speckled trout
brown trout
buffalo fish
bullhead
bull trout
bully *or (N.Z.)* pakoko, titarakura, *or* toitoi
burbot, eelpout, *or* ling
butterfish
butterfish, greenbone, *or (N.Z.)* koaea *or* marari
butterfly fish
cabezon *or* cabezone
cabrilla
callop
candlefish *or* eulachon
capelin *or* caplin
carp
catfish
cavalla *or* cavally
cavefish
cero
characin *or* characid
chimaera
Chinook salmon, quinnat salmon, *or* king salmon
chub
chum
cichlid
cisco *or* lake herring
climbing fish *or* climbing perch
clingfish
coalfish *or (Brit.)* saithe *or* coley
cobia, black kingfish, *or* sergeant fish
cockabully
cod *or* codfish
coelacanth
coho *or* silver salmon
coley
conger
coral trout
crappie
croaker
crucian
dab
dace
damselfish
danio
dart *(Austral.)*
darter
dealfish
dentex
dollarfish
dorado
dory
dragonet
eel *or (N.Z.)* tuna
eelpout
electric eel
fallfish
father lasher *or* short-spined sea scorpion
fighting fish *or* betta
filefish
flatfish *or (N.Z.)* flattie
flathead
flounder *or (N.Z.)* patiki
flying fish
flying gurnard
four-eyed fish
frogfish
garpike, garfish, gar, *or (Austral.)* ballahoo
geelbek
gemfish *or (Austral.)* hake
gilthead
goby
golden perch, freshwater bream, Murray perch, *or* yellow-belly *(Austral.)*
goldeye
goldfish
goldsinny *or* goldfinny
gourami
grayling *or (Austral.)* yarra herring
greenling
grenadier *or* rat-tail
groper *or* grouper
grunion
grunt
gudgeon
guitarfish
gunnel
guppy
gurnard *or* gurnet
gwyniad
haddock
hagfish, hag *or* blind eel
hairtail *or (U.S.)* cutlass fish
hake
halfbeak
halibut
hapuku *(Austral.) (N.Z.)*
herring
hogfish
hoki *(N.Z.)*
horned pout *or* brown bullhead
horse mackerel
houndfish
houting
ice fish
jacksmelt
javelin fish *or* Queensland trumpeter
jewelfish
jewfish *or (Austral. informal)* jewie
John Dory
jurel
kelpfish *or (Austral. informal)* kelpie
killifish
kingfish
kingklip *(S. African)*
kokanee
kokopu *(N.Z.)*
labyrinth fish
lampern *or* river lamprey
lamprey *or* lamper eel
lancet fish
lantern fish
largemouth bass
latimeria
leatherjacket
lemon sole
lepidosiren
ling *or (Austral.)* beardie
lingcod
lionfish
loach
louvar
luderick *or (N.Z.)* parore
lumpfish *or* lumpsucker
lungfish
mackerel *or (colloquial)* shiner
mangrove Jack *(Austral.)*
manta, manta ray, devilfish, *or* devil ray
maomao *(N.Z.)*
marlin *or* spearfish
megrim
menhaden
milkfish
miller's thumb
minnow *or (Scot.)* baggie minnow
mirror carp
moki *or* blue moki *(N.Z.)*
molly
monkfish *or (U.S.)* goosefish
mooneye
moonfish
Moorish idol
moray
morwong, black perch, *or (N.Z.)* porae
mudcat
mudfish
mudskipper
opah, moonfish, *or* kingfish
orange chromide
orange roughy *(Austral.)*
orfe
ouananiche
ox-eye herring *(Austral.)*
paddlefish
panchax
pandora
paradise fish
parore, blackfish, black rockfish *or* mangrove fish *(N.Z.)*

parrotfish
pearl perch *(Austral.)*
perch *or (Austral.)* redfin
pickerel
pigfish *or* hogfish
pike, luce, *or* jackfish
pikeperch
pilchard *or (Austral. informal)* pillie
pilot fish
pinfish *or* sailor's choice
pipefish *or* needlefish
piranha *or* piraña
plaice
platy
pogge *or* armed bullhead
pollack *or* pollock
pollan
pomfret
pompano
porae *(N.Z.)*
porcupine fish *or* globefish
porgy *or* pogy
pout
powan *or* lake herring
puffer *or* globefish
pumpkinseed
Queensland halibut
Queensland lungfish
rabbitfish
rainbow trout
ray
red cod
red emperor
redfin
redfish
red mullet *or (U.S.)* goatfish
red salmon
red snapper
remora
ribbonfish
roach
robalo
rock bass
rock cod
rockfish *or (formerly)* rock salmon
rockling
rosefish
rudd
ruffe, ruff, *or* pope
runner
salmon
salmon trout
sand dab
sand eel, sand lance, *or* launce
sardine
sauger
saury *or* skipper
sawfish
scabbard fish
scad
scaldfish
scat
scorpion fish
sculpin *(U.S.) (Canad.)*
scup *or* northern porgy
sea bass
sea bream
sea horse
sea lamprey
sea perch
sea raven
sea robin
sea scorpion
sea snail *or* snailfish
sea trout
Sergeant Baker
sergeant major
shad
shanny
sheepshead
shiner
shovelnose
Siamese fighting fish
sild
silver belly *(N.Z.)*
silverfish
silverside *or* silversides
skate
skelly
skipjack *or* skipjack tuna
sleeper *or* sleeper goby
smallmouth bass
smelt
smooth hound
snapper, red bream, *or (Austral.)* wollomai *or* wollamai
snipefish *or* bellows fish
snoek
snook
sockeye *or* red salmon
sole
solenette
spadefish
Spanish mackerel *or* Queensland kingfish
spotted mackerel *or* school mackerel
sprat
squeteague
squirrelfish
steelhead
sterlet
stickleback
stingray
stone bass *or* wreckfish
stonefish
stone roller
sturgeon
sucker
sunfish
surfperch *or* sea perch
surgeonfish
swordfish
swordtail
tailor
tarakihi *or* terakihi *(N.Z.)*
tarpon
tarwhine
tautog *or* blackfish
tench
teraglin
tetra
thornback
threadfin
tilapia
tilefish
toadfish
tommy rough *or* tommy ruff *(Austral.)*
topminnow
torsk *or (U.S. & Canadian)* cusk
trevalla *(Austral.)*
trevally, araara *or* samson fish *(Austral.) (N.Z.)*
triggerfish
tripletail
trout
trunkfish, boxfish, *or* cowfish
tuna *or* tunny
turbot
vendace
wahoo
walleye, walleyed pike, *or* dory
warehou *(N.Z.)*
weakfish
weever
whitebait
whitefish
whiting
wirrah
witch
wobbegong, wobbygong, *or* wobegong
wolffish *or* catfish
wrasse
yellowfin *(N.Z.)*
yellowfin tuna
yellow jack
yellowtail
zander

EXTINCT FISH

ceratodus
ostracoderm
placoderm

FLOWERS

acacia
acanthus
African violet
aloe
alyssum
amaranth
amaryllis
anemone
arbutus
asphodel
aspidistra
aster

aubrietia, aubrieta, *or* aubretia
azalea
babe-in-a-cradle (*Austral.*)
begonia
betony
bignonia
black-eyed Susan
bluebell
bog asphodel
bougainvillea
burdock
Busy Lizzie
buttercup
cactus
calendula
camellia
camomile *or* chamomile
cardinal flower
carnation
celandine
Christmas cactus
chrysanthemum
clematis
clianthus
columbine
Cooktown orchid (*Austral.*)
cornflower
cotoneaster
cowslip
crocus
cyclamen
daffodil
dahlia
daisy
dandelion
deadly nightshade
delphinium
digitalis
dog rose
edelweiss
eglantine
forget-me-not
foxglove
freesia
geranium
gilliflower *or* gillyflower
gladiolus
godetia
grape hyacinth
groundsel
guelder-rose
gypsophila
harebell
heartsease *or* heart's-ease
heliotrope
hellebore
hemlock
hibiscus
hollyhock
hyacinth
hydrangea
iris
jasmine
jonquil
larkspur
lavender
lily
lily of the valley
lobelia
London pride
lotus
love-in-idleness
love-lies-bleeding
lupin
magnolia
mallow
mandrake
marguerite
marigold
marjoram
meadowsweet
monkshood
Michaelmas daisy
morning-glory
narcissus
nasturtium
old man's beard
orchid
oxeye daisy
oxlip
oxtongue
pansy
passionflower
peony *or* paeony
petunia
phlox
pimpernel
pink
poppy
primrose
primula
ragged robin
ragweed
rose
saffron
samphire
saxifrage
scarlet pimpernel
snapdragon
snowdrop
speedwell
stock
(Sturt's) desert pea (*Austral.*)
sunflower
sweetbrier
sweet pea
sweet william
tiger lily
tulip
valerian
verbena
violet
wallflower
water lily
willowherb
wintergreen
wisteria
wood anemone
woodbine
yarrow
zinnia

FLIES

antlion *or* antlion fly
aphid *or* plant louse
aphis
apple blight *or* American blight
bee fly
beetfly *or* mangold fly
blackfly *or* bean aphid
blowfly, bluebottle, *or* (*Austral. informal*) blowie
botfly
buffalo gnat *or* black fly
bulb fly
bushfly
carrot fly
chalcid *or* chalcid fly
cluster fly
crane fly *or* (*Brit.*) daddy-longlegs
damselfly
dobsonfly
dragonfly *or* (*colloquial*) devil's darning-needle
drosophila, fruit fly, *or* vinegar fly
fly
frit fly
fruit fly
gadfly
gallfly
gnat
grannom
green blowfly *or* (*Austral. informal*) blue-arsed fly
greenbottle
greenfly
horsefly *or* cleg
housefly
hover fly
lacewing
lantern fly
mayfly *or* dayfly
Mediterranean fruit fly *or* Medfly
needle fly
onion fly
robber fly, bee killer, *or* assassin fly
sandfly
scorpion fly
screwworm fly
silverhorn
snake fly
stable fly
stonefly
tachina fly
tsetse fly *or* tzetze fly
vinegar fly
warble fly
whitefly
willow fly

FOOTBALL

TERMS USED IN (ASSOCIATION) FOOTBALL

aggregate (score)
back
ballplayer
ballwinner
booking *or* caution
breakaway
cap
catenaccio
centre circle
centre forward
centre half
clearance
cross
crossbar *or* bar
corner (kick)
cut out
defender
derby
direct free kick
dribble
dummy
extra time
FA
FIFA
finishing
forward
foul
free kick
fullback
full time
goal
goal area *or* six-yard box
goalkeeper *or* goalie
goal kick *or* bye kick
goal net *or* net
goalpost *or* post
golden goal
half
halfback
half time
half way line
handball
indirect free kick
inside left
inside right
inswinger
international
kick off
lay off
left back
linesman
long ball
mark
midfield
midfielder
nil
non-league
nutmeg
offside
offside trap
onside
one-two
outside left
outside right
own goal
pass
pass-back
penalty (kick) *or* spot kick
penalty area *or* penalty box
penalty shoot-out
penalty spot
playoff
professional foul
promotion
red card
referee
relegation
reserves
right back
Route One
save
score draw
sending-off *or* ordering-off
SFA
shot
silver goal
six-pointer
six-yard line
sliding tackle
stoppage time *or* injury time
striker
square
substitute
sweeper
tackle
target man
technical area
throw in
total football
touchline
transfer
trap
UEFA
wall
wall pass
wing
winger
yellow card

TERMS USED IN AUSTRALIAN RULES FOOTBALL

Australian Football League *or* AFL
back pocket
behind *or* point
behind line
behind post
boundary
eighteen, the
field umpire
flank
footy, Aussie Rules, *or (jocular)* aerial ping-pong
follower
forward pocket
free kick
goal
goal umpire
guernsey
half-back
half-forward
handball
interchange
mark
nineteenth man
quarter
rove
rover
rub out
ruck
ruckrover
scrimmage
shepherd
shirt front
stab kick
stanza
throw in
twentieth man

TERMS USED IN AMERICAN FOOTBALL

backfield
blitz
block
center
complete
cornerback
defense
defensive back
defensive end
down
end zone
field goal
football *or* pigskin
fullback
gridiron
guard
halfback
incomplete
interception
kicker
line *or* line of scrimmage
line backer
lineman
offense
overtime
pass
play
point after
punt
punter
quarterback
run *or* rush
running back
sack
safety
scrimmage
secondary
shotgun
snap
special team
Super Bowl
tackle
tight end
touchback
touchdown
turnover
wide receiver

FRUITS

ananas
anchovy pear
apple
apricot
avocado, avocado pear, *or (U.S.)* alligator pear
babaco
banana
Bartlett pear
beach plum
bergamot pear
berry
Beurre Hardy pear
bigarreau cherry
bilberry, blaeberry, huckleberry, whortleberry, *or (Irish)* fraughan
blackberry *or (Scot.)* bramble
black cherry
blackcurrant
blackheart cherry
blood orange
blueberry
Bon Chretien pear
boxberry
boysenberry
breadfruit
calamondin
cantaloup *or* cantaloupe melon
carambola *or* star fruit
casaba *or* cassaba melon
Charentais melon
chayote
chempaduk
cherry
chokecherry
choko
citron
clementine
cloudberry *or (Canad.)* bakeapple
Concord grape
Conference pear
cranberry
custard apple
damson
date
dewberry
durian *or* durion
elderberry
fig
Galia melon
gooseberry *or (informal)* goosegog
grape
grapefruit
greengage
guava
hackberry
heart cherry
honeydew melon
jackfruit *or* jack
Jaffa orange
kiwano *(trademark)*
Kiwi fruit *or* Chinese gooseberry
kumquat *or* cumquat
lemon
lime
lychee, litchi, lichee, *or* lichi
loganberry
longan
loquat *or* Japan plum
mandarin
mango
mangosteen
May apple
medlar
melon
minneola
morello cherry
mulberry
muskmelon
nashi *or* Asian pear
navel orange
nectarine
Ogen melon
olive
orange
ortanique
papaw *or* pawpaw
papaya
passion fruit *or* granadilla
peach
pear
pepper
physalis, Cape gooseberry, *or* strawberry tomato
pineapple
plantain
plum
pomegranate
pomelo *or* shaddock
prickly pear
prune
pumpkin
Queensland blue
quince
raisin
rambutan
raspberry
redcurrant
rockmelon
salmonberry
sapota
sapodilla, sapodilla plum, *or* naseberry
saskatoon
satsuma
Seville orange
serviceberry
sharon fruit *or* persimmon
sloe
snowberry
sour cherry
sour gourd
soursop
star-apple
strawberry
sultana
sweet cherry
sweetie
sweetsop
tamarillo *or* tree tomato
tamarind
tangelo
tangerine *or (S. African)* naartje
tayberry
tomato *or (archaic)* love apple
UGLI *(trademark)*
victoria *or* victoria plum
watermelon
white currant
Williams pear
winter melon
youngberry

FUNGI

agaric
bird's-nest fungus
boletus
bracket fungus
cramp ball
death cap
dry rot
earthstar
elf-cup
ergot
funnel cap
ink-cap
jelly fungus
horn of plenty
liberty cap
mildew
milk cap
miller
mould
mushroom
puffball
rust *or* rust fungus
shaggy cap
sickener
smut
stinkhorn
sulphur tuft
toadstool
truffle
velvet shank
wax cap
wet rot
wood hedgehog
wood woollyfoot
yeast

FURNITURE

TYPES OF FURNITURE

- bedpost
- bedstead
- canopy
- cheval glass
- coatstand
- dumbwaiter
- epergne
- footstool
- girandole *or* girandola
- grandfather clock
- grandmother clock
- hallstand
- hatstand
- headboard
- lectern
- litter
- longcase clock
- screen
- tester
- trolley
- umbrella stand
- vanitory *or* vanity unit
- washstand

FURNITURE STYLES

- Art Deco
- Bauhaus
- Cape Dutch
- Edwardian
- Elizabethan
- Empire
- Georgian
- Gothic
- Greek Revival
- Jacobean
- Louis Quatorze
- Louis Quinze
- Louis Seize
- Louis Treize
- Medieval
- New Georgian
- Norman
- Puritan
- Queen Anne
- Regency
- Restoration
- Saxon
- Second Empire
- Shaker
- Tudor
- Victorian
- William and Mary

GAMES

PARTY GAMES

- blind man's buff
- charades
- Chinese whispers
- consequences
- follow-my-leader
- hide-and-seek
- I-spy
- musical chairs
- postman's knock
- Simon says
- statues

WORD GAMES

- acrostic
- anagram
- crambo
- crossword *or* crossword puzzle
- hangman
- logogriph
- The Minister's Cat *(Scot.)*
- rebus
- Scrabble *(trademark)*
- twenty questions *or* animal, vegetable, or mineral

OTHER GAMES

- bar billiards
- battleships
- beetle
- bingo *or* housey-housey
- British bulldog
- caber tossing
- conkers
- craps
- crown and anchor
- deck tennis
- dominoes
- foosball *or* table football
- French cricket
- hoopla
- hopscotch
- horseshoes
- jacks
- jigsaw puzzle
- keno, keeno, kino, *or* quino
- king of the castle
- knur and spell
- lansquenet
- leapfrog
- lotto
- mahjong *or* mah-jongg
- marbles
- nim
- noughts and crosses
- paintball
- pall-mall
- pegboard
- pinball
- pitch-and-toss
- quoits
- ring taw
- roque
- roulette
- Russian roulette
- sack race
- scavenger hunt
- shuffleboard
- skipping
- spillikins *or* jackstraws
- tag *or* tig
- tangram
- thimblerig
- tiddlywinks
- tipcat
- trictrac *or* tricktrack
- trugo
- wall game
- war game

GASES

TYPES OF GAS

- acetylene
- afterdamp
- ammonia
- argon
- arsine
- biogas
- butadiene
- butane
- butene
- Calor gas *(trademark)*
- carbon dioxide *or* carbonic-acid gas
- carbon monoxide
- chlorine
- coal gas

compressed natural gas (CNG)
cyanogen
diazomethane
diborane
dichlorodifluoromethane
electrolytic gas
ethane
ethylene
flue gas
fluorine
formaldehyde
helium
hydrogen
hydrogen bromide
hydrogen chloride
hydrogen fluoride
hydrogen iodide
hydrogen sulphide
ketene
krypton
laughing gas *or* nitrous oxide (LNG)
liquefied petroleum gas (LPG)
marsh gas
methane
methylamine
methyl bromide
methyl chloride
natural gas
neon
nitric oxide
nitrogen
nitrogen dioxide
nitrous oxide
oilgas
oxygen
ozone
phosgene
phosphine
producer gas *or* air gas
propane
radon
sewage gas
stibine
synthetic natural gas (SNG)
sulphur dioxide
synthesis gas
tail gas
tetrafluoroethene
tetrafluoroethylene
town gas
vinyl chloride
water gas
xenon

CHEMICAL WARFARE GASES

blister gas
CS gas
lewisite
mustard gas
nerve gas
nitrogen mustard
sarin
soman
tabun
tear gas
VX

GEMSTONES

adularia
agate
alexandrite
almandine
amazonite
amethyst
andalusite
andradite
aquamarine
aventurine, aventurin, *or* avanturine
balas
beryl
black opal
bloodstone
bone turquoise
cairngorm
carnelian
cat's-eye
chalcedony
chrysoberyl
chrysolite
chrysoprase
citrine
Colorado ruby
Colorado topaz
corundum
cymophane
demantoid
diamond
diopside
emerald
fire opal
garnet
girasol, girosol, *or* girasole
grossularite
hawk's-eye
helidor
heliotrope
hessonite
hiddenite
hyacinth
indicolite *or* indigolite
jacinth
jadeite *or* jade
jasper
jet
kunzite
lapis lazuli
liver opal
Madagascar aquamarine
melanite
moonstone
morganite
morion
moss agate
New Zealand greenstone
odontolite
onyx
opal
Oriental almandine
Oriental emerald
peridot
plasma
pyrope
quartz
rhodolite
rose quartz
rubellite
ruby
sapphire
sard *or* sardine
sardonyx
smoky quartz
Spanish topaz
spessartite
sphene
spinel
spodumene
staurolite
sunstone
titanite
topaz
topazolite
tourmaline
turquoise
uvarovite
vesuvianite
water sapphire
white sapphire
zircon

GEOGRAPHY

BRANCHES OF GEOGRAPHY

biogeography
cartography
chorography
chorology
climatology
demography
geology
geomorphology
glaciology
hydrology
human geography
meteorology
oceanography
oceanology
orography *or* orology
pedology
physical geography
political geography *or* geopolitics
seismology
topography
vulcanology

GEOGRAPHY TERMS AND FEATURES

afforestation
antipodes
arête
atlas
atmosphere
atoll
basin
bay
beach
canyon
cliff
climate
col
conservation
continent
continental drift
continental shelf
contour
conurbation
coombe
coral reef
core
corrie, cirque, *or* cwm
crag
crater
crevasse
crust
culvert
deforestation
delta
desert
desertification
dormitory
dyke
earthquake
eastings
environment
epicentre
equator
erosion
escarpment
estuary
fault
fell
fjord
flood plain
glaciation
glacier
glade
glen
global warming
green belt
greenhouse effect
grid reference
hanging valley
headland
ice cap
infrastructure
International Date Line
irrigation
isobar
isobath
isohyet
isotherm
isthmus
jungle
lagoon
latitude
levée
loch
longitude
longshore drift
mantle
map
meander
Mercator projection
moraine
new town
northern hemisphere
northings
North Pole
occidental
ocean
Ordnance Survey
oriental
ozone layer
permafrost
plate tectonics
pollution
precipitation
rainforest
rain shadow
reef
relief map
ridge
rift valley
rill
river basin
rivulet
salt flat
salt lake
sandbank
sand bar
sand dune
savanna *or* savannah
scree
sierra
snow line
southern hemisphere
South Pole
spit
spring
spur
stack
steppe
subsoil
suburb
tarn
temperate
Third World
topsoil
tor
tropics
tsunami
tundra
urbanization
veld *or* veldt
volcano
wadi
watercourse
water cycle
waterfall
watershed
water table
weathering
wetland
whirlpool

GEOLOGY

GEOLOGICAL ERAS

Cenozoic
Mesozoic
Palaeozoic
Precambrian

GEOLOGICAL PERIODS

Quaternary
Tertiary
Cretaceous
Jurassic
Triassic
Permian
Carboniferous
Devonian
Silurian
Ordovician
Cambrian

EPOCHS OF THE CENOZOIC ERA

Holocene
Pleistocene
Pliocene
Miocene
Oligocene
Eocene
Palaeocene

GOLF TERMS

ace (*U.S.*)
air shot *or* fresh air shot
albatross
approach
apron
back nine (*chiefly U.S.*)
backswing
bag
ball
bandit
better-ball
birdie
blade
bogey
borrow
bunker, trap, *or* (*esp U.S. & Canad.*) sand trap
caddie
caddie car
carry
casual water
chip
club
clubhouse
course
cup
cut
divot
dormie
downswing
draw
drive
driver
driving range
duff
eagle
fade
fairway
fluff
foozle
fore
four-ball
foursome
front nine (*chiefly U.S.*)
gimme

green	lag	pitch shot	sand wedge	stymie
green fee	lie	play through	sclaff	sweetspot
green keeper	links	plus fours	score	swing
greensome	local rules	plus twos	score card	take-away
grip	loft	practice swing	scratch	tee
half	long iron	pull	shaft	thin
half shot	marker	putt	shank	tiger
handicap	match play	putter	short iron	threesome
hazard	medal play	putting green	single	top
heel	medal tee	rabbit	slice	trolley
hole	midiron	recovery	slow play	waggle
hole in one	nine-hole course	rough	spoon	wedge
honour	nineteenth hole	round	Stableford system	wood
hook	par	rub of the green	stance	yips
hosel	pin	run	stroke	
iron	pitch and run	Royal and Ancient *or* R & A	stroke play	
ladies' tee	pitching wedge			

TYPES OF GOVERNMENT

absolutism	by an absolute ruler	isocracy	by equals
anarchy	absence of government	meritocracy	by rulers chosen according to ability
aristocracy	by nobility	mobocracy	by the mob
autarchy *or* autocracy	by an unrestricted individual	monarchy	by monarch
		monocracy	by one ruler
bureaucracy	by officials	nomocracy	by rule of law
communalism	by self-governing communities	ochlocracy	by mob
		octarchy	by eight rulers
constitutionalism	according to a constitution	oligarchy	by the few
		pantisocracy	by all equally
corporatism	by corporate groups	pentarchy	by five rulers
democracy	by the people	plutocracy	by the rich
despotism	by a despot or absolute ruler	pornocracy	by whores
		ptochocracy	by the poor
diarchy *or* dyarchy	by two rulers	quangocracy	by quangos
dictatorship	by dictator	slavocracy	by slaveholders
ergatocracy	by the workers	squirearchy *or* squirarchy	by squires
gerontocracy	by old people	stratocracy	by the army
gynaecocracy *or* gynarchy	by women	technocracy	by experts
hagiocracy *or* hagiarchy	by holy men	tetrarchy	by four rulers
heptarchy	by seven rulers	theocracy *or* thearchy	by a deity
hexarchy	by six rulers	triarchy	by three rulers
hierocracy *or* hierarchy	by priests	tyranny	by a tyrant
imperialism	by an emperor or empire		

THE GRACES

Aglaia
Euphrosyne
Thalia

GRAMMATICAL CASES

ablative	elative	instrumental	oblique
accusative	ergative	locative	possessive
agentive	genitive	nominative	subjective
dative	illative	objective	vocative

GRAPES USED IN MAKING WINE

WHITE WINE

- aligoté
- chardonnay
- chenin blanc *or* steen
- colombard
- furmint
- gewürztraminer
- grüner veltliner
- hárslevelü
- malvasia
- marsanne
- müller-thurgau
- muscadelle
- muscat *or* moscatel
- pinot blanc
- pinot gris, pinot grigio, ruländer, *or* Tokay-Pinot Gris
- riesling *or* rhine riesling
- sauvignon blanc
- scheurebe
- semillon *or* sémillon
- seyval blanc
- silvaner *or* sylvaner
- trebbiano *or* ugni blanc
- verdelho
- verdicchio
- viognier
- viura
- welschriesling, olasz rizling, *or* laski rizling

RED WINE

- barbera
- cabernet franc
- cabernet sauvignon
- cinsault
- dolcetto
- gamay
- grenache *or* garnacha
- kékfrankos
- malbec
- merlot
- montepulciano
- mourvèdre
- nebbiolo *or* spanna
- negroamoro
- pinotage
- pinot noir *or* spätburgunder
- sangiovese
- shiraz *or* syrah
- tempranillo
- zinfandel

GRASSES

- barley
- Bermuda grass
- blady grass, bladey grass, *or* kunai *(Austral.)*
- bluegrass
- buffalo grass
- buffel grass
- cane grass
- citronella
- corkscrew grass *(Austral.)*
- cotton grass
- couch grass *or (Austral.)* quack grass, quick grass *or* quitch grass
- crab grass
- danthonia *or* wallaby grass *(Austral.)*
- darnel
- elephant grass
- esparto
- fescue
- kangaroo grass *(Austral.)*
- maize
- marram grass
- millet
- oat
- pampas grass
- paspalum
- reed
- rice
- rye
- rye-grass
- snowgrass *(N.Z.)*
- sorghum
- spear grass *(Austral.)*
- spinifex
- sugar cane
- wheat
- wild oat
- wild rye

GUNS

- AK-47 *or* Kalashnikov
- anti-aircraft gun *or* ack-ack gun
- Armalite *(trademark)*
- arquebus
- BAR
- Big Bertha
- blunderbuss
- Bofors gun
- breech-loader
- Bren gun
- Browning
- burp gun
- carbine
- carronade
- chassepot
- chokebore
- Colt
- culverin
- derringer *or* deringer
- Enfield rifle
- firelock
- flintlock
- forty-five
- fusil
- Garand rifle
- Gatling
- howitzer
- Lewis gun
- Luger *(trademark)*
- M-1 rifle
- M-14
- M-16
- machine gun
- Magnum *(trademark)*
- matchlock
- Mauser
- Maxim gun
- mitrailleuse
- musket
- muzzle-loader
- Owen gun
- petronel
- pistol
- pom-pom
- pump gun
- Quaker gun
- repeater
- revolver
- rifle
- scatter-gun
- shotgun
- six-shooter
- Springfield rifle
- Sten gun
- stern-chaser
- sub-machine-gun
- Thompson sub-machine gun *(trademark)*
- trench mortar
- Uzi *(trademark)*
- Winchester rifle
- zip gun

HAIRSTYLES

- Afro
- beehive
- bob
- bouffant
- bun
- bunches
- buzz cut
- chignon
- corn row
- crew cut
- crop
- dreadlocks
- duck's arse *or* DA
- Eton crop
- feather-cut
- flat top
- French pleat *or* roll
- marcel *or* marcel wave
- mohican
- mullet
- pageboy
- perm *or* permanent wave
- pigtail
- plait
- pompadour
- ponytail
- pouf
- razor-cut
- shingle
- skinhead
- wedge

HATS

Akubra *(Austral.)* *(trademark)*
anadem *(poetic)*
babushka
Balaclava helmet *or* Balaclava
Balmoral *or* bluebonnet
bandanna *or* bandana
bandeau
barret
baseball cap
basinet *or* bascinet
beanie *or* beany
bearskin
beaver
beret
billycock *(rare)* *(chiefly Brit.)*
biretta *or* berretta
blackcap
bluebonnet *or* bluecap
boater
bonnet
bowler *or* *(U.S. & Canad.)* derby
broadbrim
busby
calash *or* caleche
calotte
calpac, calpack, *or* kalpak
capuche *or* capouch
castor
chaplet
cheese cutter
circlet
cloche
cloth cap
cocked hat
coif
commode
coonskin
cornet
coronet
cossack hat
crash helmet
crown
curch *or* curchef
deerstalker
diadem
Dolly Varden
dunce cap
earmuff
fascinator *(rare)*
fedora
fez
flat cap
fool's cap
forage cap
frontlet *or* frontal
Gandhi cap
glengarry
hard hat
havelock
headband
headdress
heaume
helmet
homburg
hood
Juliet cap
keffiyeh, kaffiyeh, *or* kufiyah
kepi
laurels
leghorn
liberty cap
lum-hat *(Scot.)*
mitre
mobcap *or* mob
montero
morion
mortarboard, trencher, *or* trencher cap
mutch
nightcap
opera hat *or* gibus
Panama hat
paper hat
peaked cap
petasus
Phrygian cap
picture hat
pillbox
pinner
pith helmet, topee, *or* topi
poke *or* poke bonnet
porkpie hat
sailor hat
sallet, salet, *or* salade
shako *or* shacko
shovel hat
shower cap
silk hat
skullcap
slouch hat
snood
sombrero
songkok
sou'wester *or* nor'wester
stetson
stocking cap
stovepipe
straw hat
sunbonnet
sunhat
taj
tam-o'-shanter *or* tammy *(Scot.)*
tarboosh, tarbouche *or* tarbush
tarpaulin,
ten-gallon hat
tiara
tin hat *(informal)*
tricorn *or* tricorne
toorie *or* tourie *(Scot.)*
top hat
topper *(informal)*
toque
tricorn
trilby
tuque
turban
veil
visor *or* vizor
watch cap
wimple
yarmulke

PARTS OF THE HEART

aorta
atrium *or* auricle
bicuspid valve
pulmonary artery
pulmonary vein
semilunar valve
septum
tricuspid valve
vena cava
ventricle

HERALDRY TERMS

achievement
annulet
argent
armes parlantes
armiger
armory
bandeau
bar
base
baton
bearing
bend
bend sinister
bezzant, bezant, *or* byzant
blazon
blazonry
bordure
cadency
canting arms
canton
chaplet
charge
checky
chevron
chief
cinquefoil
Clarenceux
coat armour
coat of arms
cockatrice
cognizance *or* cognisance
college of arms
compony *or* compone
coronet
couchant
crescent
crest
cross
crosslet
crown
dexter
difference
dimidiate
dormant
eagle
embattled
emblazon
ermine
escutcheon
falcon
fesse *or* fess
field
fillet
fleur-de-lis *or* fleur-de-lys
flory *or* fleury
fret
fur
fusil
garland
giron *or* gyron
gironny *or* gyronny
griffon
guardant *or* gardant
gules
hatchment
herald
heraldic *or* fetial
impale *or* empale
inescutcheon
issuant
king-of-arms
label
leopard
lion

lozenge
lozengy
Lyon King of Arms
mantling *or* lambrequin
mascle *or* voided lozenge
matriculation
moline
naissant
nombril
octofoil
officer of arms
or
ordinary
orle
pale
pall
paly
parted
party
passant
pean
pile
potent
proper
purpure
pursuivant
quarter
quartered
quartering
quarterly
rampant
rebus
regardant
roundel
sable
saltire
sejant *or* sejeant
scutcheon
semé (of) *or* semée (of)
shield
sinister
spread eagle
statant
sun in splendour
supporter
torse
tressure
urdé *or* urdée
urinant
vair
vert
voided
volant
wreath
wyvern
yale

HERBS, SPICES AND SEASONINGS

alligator pepper
allspice
aniseed
asafoetida *or* asafetida
basil
bayleaf
black pepper
borage
calendula
canella
capers
caraway seed
cardamom
cassia bark
cayenne pepper
chervil
chilli
chive
cinnamon
clove
coconut
coconut milk
coriander
cress
cumin
curry powder
dill
fennel
fines herbes
five spice powder
galangal *or* galingale
garam masala
garlic
ginger
Kaffir lime leaf
lemon grass
mace
marjoram
mint
miso
mustard
nam pla *or* fish sauce
nutmeg
oregano
paprika
parsley
peppercorn
poppy seed
red pepper
rocambole
rosemary
saffron
sage
salt
savory
sesame seed
soy sauce, soya sauce, shoyu, *or* tamari
star anise
sunflower seed
Szechuan, Szechwan, *or* Sichuan peppercorns
tansy
tarragon
thyme
turmeric
wasabi
white pepper

LABOURS OF HERCULES

the slaying of the Nemean lion
the slaying of the Lernaean hydra
the capture of the hind of Ceryneia
the capture of the wild boar of Erymanthus
the cleansing of the Augean stables
the shooting of the Stymphalian birds
the capture of the Cretan bull
the capture of the horses of Diomedes
the taking of the girdle of Hippolyte
the capture of the cattle of Geryon
the recovery of the golden apples of Hesperides
the taking of Cerberus

HINDU DENOMINATIONS AND SECTS

Hare Krishna
Saivaism
Saktas
Vaishnavism

TYPES OF HOME

adobe
apartment
bachelor apartment *(Canadian)*
back-to-back
barrack
bedsitter
black house *(Scot.)*
board-and-shingle *(Caribbean)*
boarding house
booth
bungalow
bunker
but and ben *(Scot.)*
cabin
caboose *(Canad.)*
camboose
Cape Cod cottage
caravan
castle
chalet
chateau or château
chattel house
consulate
cot *or* cote *(dialect)*
cottage
cottage flat
crannog
croft
dacha *(Russian)*
deanery
digs
doss house
duplex *or* duplex apartment *(U.S.) (Canad.)*
embassy
farmhouse
flat
flatlet
flophouse
flotel
garret
grange
guest house
hacienda
hall

hogan
hostel
hotel
house
houseboat
hovel
hut
igloo *or* iglu
inn
lake dwelling
lodge
log cabin
long house
maisonette
manor
manse
mansion
mattamore
mews *(informal)*
mobile home
motel
motor caravan
mud hut
palace
parsonage
penthouse
pied-à-terre
prefab
priory
ranch
rath *(Irish)*
rectory
rest-home
roadhouse
semi
shack
shanty
shooting box
show house
single-end *(Scot.)* *(dialect)*
slum
starter home
stately home
studio flat
tavern
tenement
tent
tepee
town house
trailer *(U.S.)* *(Canad.)*
tree house
tupik *or* tupek *(Canad.)*
vicarage
villa
whare *(N.Z.)*
wigwam

HORMONES

adrenaline *or* epinephrine
adrenocorticotrophic hormone
androsterone
antidiuretic hormone
bursicon
calcitonin
cholecystokinin *or* pancreozymin
chorionic gonadotrophin
corpus luteum hormone *or* progesterone
corticosteroid
corticosterone *or* adrenocorticotrophic hormone
cortisone
deoxycorticosterone
ecdysone
enterogastrone
erythropoietin
florigen
follicle-stimulating hormone
glucagon
gibberellic acid
gastrin
gonadotrophin
growth hormone *or* somatotrophin
insulin
interstitial-cell-stimulating hormone *or* luteinizing hormone
juvenile hormone
lactogenic hormone
luteinizing hormone-releasing hormone
luteotrophin *or* prolactin
noradrenaline
oestradiol
oestriol
oestrone
oxytocin
progesterone
parathyroid hormone
relaxin
secretin
sex hormone
somatomedin
somatostatin
stilboestrol
testosterone
thyroid-stimulating hormone *or* thyrotropin
thyroxine
trichlorophenoxyacetic acid
triiodothyronine
vasopressin

BODILY HUMOURS

black bile
yellow bile
blood
phlegm

HYDROCARBONS

alkane
alkene
alkyne
arene
cetane
cubane
cycloalkane
cyclopentadiene
cyclopropane
diene
decane
indene
isooctane
naphthalene
octane
pentane
pyrene
retene
stilbene
triptane
xylene

INSECTS

TYPES OF INSECT

apple maggot
body louse, cootie *(U.S. & N.Z.)*, *or (N.Z. slang)* kutu
bollworm
booklouse
bookworm
bristletail
cabbageworm
caddis worm *or* caseworm
cankerworm
cochineal *or* cochineal insect
cockroach
cotton stainer
crab (louse)
cricket
dust mite
earwig, *or (Scot. dialect)* clipshears, *or* clipshear
flea
German cockroach *or* *(U.S.)* Croton bug
grasshopper
katydid
lac insect
locust
louse *or (N.Z.)*

kutu
mantis *or* praying mantis
measuring worm, looper, *or* inchworm
midge
mole cricket
mosquito
nit
phylloxera
scale insect
seventeen-year locust
or periodical cicada
sheep ked *or* sheep tick
silkworm
silverfish
stick insect *or* *(U.S. & Canad.)* walking stick
sucking louse
tent caterpillar
thrips
treehopper
wax insect
web spinner
weta *(N.Z.)*
wheel bug
wireworm
woodworm

PARTS OF INSECTS

acetabulum
air sac
antenna
arista
cercus
cirrus
clasper
clypeus
compound eye
corium
coxa
elytron
endocuticle
epicuticle
exocuticle
femur
flagellum
forewing
glossa
gonopod
hamulus
haustellum
hemelytron
ileum
jaw
labium
labrum
ligula
Malpighian tubule
mandible
maxilla
mesothorax
metathorax
notum
ocellus
ovipositor
pedicel
proboscis
proleg
pronotum
prosternum
prothorax
proventriculus
pulvillus
scape
scutellum
scutum
snout
spinneret
spiracle
stigma
tarsus
tegmen
thigh
thorax
tibia
trachea
trochanter
underwing
ventriculus

MUSICAL INSTRUMENTS

accordion
aeolian harp
alphorn *or* alpenhorn
althorn
Autoharp *(trademark)*
baby grand
Bach trumpet
bagpipes
balalaika
bandore
banjo
barrel organ
baryton
bass drum
basset horn
bass guitar
bassoon
bass viol
bell
bodhrán
Böhm flute
bombardon
bongo
boudoir grand
bouzouki
bugle
calliope
carillon
castanets
celesta *or* celeste
cello *or* violoncello
cembalo
chamber organ
Chapman stick *(trademark)*
chime
Chinese block
chitarrone
cimbalon *or* cymbalon
cithara *or* kithara
cittern, cither *or* cithern
clarinet
clarion
clarsach
clave
clavicembalo
clavichord
clavier
concert grand
concertina
conga
contrabass
contrabassoon
cor anglais
cornet
cornett
cottage piano
cowbell
crumhorn *or* krummhorn
crwth
cymbal
cymbalo
didgeridoo
Dobro *(trademark)*
double bass
double bassoon
drum
drum machine
dulcimer
electric guitar
electronic organ
English horn
euphonium
fiddle
fife
flageolet
flugelhorn
flute
French horn
gittarone
gittern
glass harmonica
glockenspiel
gong
gran cassa
grand piano
guitar
Hammond organ *(trademark)*
handbell
harmonica
harmonium
harp
harpsichord
Hawaiian guitar
helicon
horn
hornpipe
hunting horn
hurdy-gurdy
idiophone
jew's-harp
kazoo
kettledrum
keyboard
kit
kora
koto
lur *or* lure
lute
lyra viol
lyre
mandola
mandolin *or* mandoline
maraca
marimba
mbira
mellophone
melodeon *or* melodion
metallophone
Moog *(trademark)*
mouth organ
musette
naker
ngoma
nickelodeon
nose flute
oboe
oboe da caccia
oboe d'amore
ocarina
octachord
ondes Martenot
ophicleide
orchestrina *or* orchestrion
organ
orpharion
oud
panpipes
pedal steel guitar
penny whistle
piano
Pianola *(trademark)*
piccolo

pipe
player piano
portative organ
racket
rebec *or* rebeck
recorder
reco-reco
reed organ
reed pipe
regal
rote
sackbut
samisen
sarangi
sarod
sarrusophone
saxhorn
saxophone
shawm
side drum
sistrum
sitar
slide guitar
snare drum
sousaphone
Spanish guitar
spinet
square piano
steam organ
steel guitar
stylophone
synthesizer
syrinx
tabla
tabor *or* tabour
tambour
tamboura
tambourine
tam-tam
theorbo
Theremin (*trademark*)
timbal *or* tymbal
timpani *or* tympani
tom-tom
triangle
trigon
trombone
trumpet
tuba
tubular bells
uillean pipes
ukulele *or* ukelele
upright piano
vibraphone
vihuela
vina
viol
viola
viola da braccio
viola da gamba
viola d'amore
violin
violone
virginal
vocoder
washboard
Welsh harp
whip
whistle
wood block
Wurlitzer (*trademark*)
xylophone
xylorimba
zither

INSULTS AND TERMS OF ABUSE

airhead
article
berk
bird-brain
bitch
blockhead
bonehead
bozo
bushpig
cabbage
charlie
cheeky monkey
chicken
chuckie
chump
clod
clot
clown
coot
cow
cretin
devil
dimwit
dipstick
divvy
donkey
doofus
dope
dork
doughnut
drip
dumb-ass
dumbo
dummy
dunce
dweeb
eejit
fathead
fool
galah
geek
git
goose
halfwit
heifer
idiot
imbecile
jerk
lamebrain
loon
mincer
minger
mong
moron
mug
muppet
nerd
nincompoop
ninny
nit
nitwit
numbskull *or* numskull
numpty
oaf
ogre
pea-brain
pillock
plank
plonker
prat
rascal
rogue
scab
scoundrel
scrubber
scutter
simpleton
slag
slapper
tart
thickhead
thicko
twerp
twit
wally
whore *or* 'ho
wimp
wretch
wuss

INTERNET TERMS

blog, blogger, *or* blogging
bookmark
broadband
browse *or* browser
chatroom
cookie
domain name
download
eBay (*trademark*)
e-book
FTP *or* ftp
Generation C
Google (*trademark*)
hit
home page
hotpsot
ISP *or* Internet service provider
leetspeak *or* 1337speak
lurk, lurker, *or* lurking
message board
netiquette
newsgroup
offline
online
podcast, podcaster, *or* podcasting
portal
RSS
search engine
search engine optimization *or* SEO
Skype (*trademark*)
spam
spoofing
surf, surfer, *or* surfing
upload
URL *or* universe resource locator
voip
VPN
Web 2.0
web address
WebBoard
webcam
webcast
web directory
weblog
webmail
webmaster
webpage
website
Wi-Fi
Yahoo (*trademark*)

INVERTEBRATES

TYPES OF INVERTEBRATE

- amoeba *or (U.S.)* ameba
- animalcule *or* animalculum
- arrowworm
- arthropod
- Balmain bug
- bardy, bardie, *or* bardi *(Austral.)*
- bivalve
- bladder worm
- blue-ringed octopus *(Austral.)*
- Bluff oyster *(N.Z.)*
- box jellyfish *or (Austral.)* sea wasp
- brachiopod *or* lamp shell
- brandling
- bryozoan *or (colloquial)* sea mat
- catworm, white worm, *or* white cat
- centipede
- chicken louse
- chiton *or* coat-of-mail shell
- clam
- clappy-doo *or* clabby-doo *(Scot.)*
- cockle
- cone (shell)
- coral
- crown-of-thorns (starfish)
- ctenophore *or* comb jelly
- cunjevoi *or* cunje *(Austral.)*
- cuttlefish *or* cuttle
- daphnia
- earthworm
- eelworm
- gaper
- gapeworm
- gastropodart
- Guinea worm
- horseleech
- jellyfish *or (Austral. slang)* blubber
- kina *(N.Z.)*
- lancelet *or* amphioxus
- leech
- liver fluke
- lugworm, lug, *or* lobworm
- lungworm
- millipede, millepede, *or* milleped
- mollusc
- mussel
- octopus *or* devilfish
- otter shell
- oyster
- paddle worm
- paper nautilus, nautilus, *or* argonaut
- pearly nautilus, nautilus, *or* chambered nautilus
- piddock
- pipi *or* ugari *(Austral.)*
- Portuguese man-of-war *or (Austral.)* bluebottle
- quahog, hard-shell clam, hard-shell, *or* round clam
- ragworm *or (U.S.)* clamworm
- razor-shell *or (U.S.)* razor clam
- red coral *or* precious coral
- roundworm
- sandworm *or (Austral.)* pumpworm
- scallop
- sea anemone
- sea cucumber
- sea lily
- sea mouse
- sea pen
- sea slater
- sea squirt
- sea urchin
- seed oyster
- soft-shell (clam)
- sponge
- squid
- starfish
- stomach worm
- stony coral
- sunstar
- tapeworm
- tardigrade *or* water bear
- tellin
- teredo *or* shipworm
- trepang *or* bêche-de-mer
- tube worm
- tubifex
- tusk shell *or* tooth shell
- Venus's flower basket
- Venus's-girdle
- Venus shell
- vinegar eel, vinegar worm, *or* eelworm
- water louse *or* water slater
- water measurer
- water stick insect
- wheatworm
- whipworm
- woodborer
- worm

EXTINCT INVERTEBRATES

- ammonite
- belemnite
- eurypterid
- graptolite
- trilobite

JACKETS

- acton
- anorak
- báinín
- banyan
- Barbour jacket *(trademark)*
- bed jacket
- biker jacket
- blazer
- blouson
- body warmer
- bolero
- bomber jacket
- boxy jacket
- bush jacket
- cagoule *or* cag
- cardigan
- combat jacket
- cymar
- denim jacket
- dinner jacket *or (U.S. & Canad.)* tuxedo *or* tux
- dolman
- donkey jacket
- doublet
- duvet *or* duvet jacket
- Eton jacket or bumfreezer
- flak jacket
- fustian jacket
- gambeson
- gilet
- hacking jacket
- hug-me-tight
- jerkin
- leather jacket
- life jacket
- lumberjacket
- Mackinaw coat *or* mackinaw *(chiefly U.S.) (Canad.)*
- matinée jacket
- mess jacket
- monkey jacket
- Norfolk jacket
- pourpoint
- reefing jacket
- sack *or* sacque
- safari jacket
- shell jacket
- shrug
- smoking jacket
- spencer
- sports jacket *or* coat
- tabard
- windcheater *or* windjammer

JEWISH DENOMINATIONS AND SECTS

- Chassidism, Chasidism, Hassidism, *or* Hasidism
- Conservative Judaism
- Liberal Judaism
- Orthodox Judaism
- Reform Judaism
- Zionism

KITCHEN EQUIPMENT

Aga *(trademark)*
bain-marie
baking tray
barbecue *or (Austral. slang)* barbie
batterie de cuisine
blender
bottle opener
bread knife
cafetiere
cake tin
carving knife
casserole
chip pan
chopping board
chopsticks
coffee grinder
coffeepot
colander
cooker
cooling rack
corkscrew
deep fat fryer
dessertspoon
double saucepan *or (U.S. & Canad.)* double boiler
egg beater *or* egg whisk
fan-assisted oven
fish slice
flan tin
food processor
fork
frying pan
grater
gravy boat *or* sauce boat
griddle *or (Scot.)* girdle
grill
ice-cream maker
icing bag
jelly bag
juicer *or* juice extractor
kettle
knife
masher
mould
ladle
lemon squeezer
liquidizer
loaf tin
mandoline
measuring jug
mezzaluna
microwave *or* microwave oven
mixing bowl
mortar and pestle
nutcracker
olla
oven
pastry cutter
peeler
pepper mill
percolator
poacher
pot
pot-au-feu
ramekin
ricer *(U.S.) (Canad.)*
rolling pin
rotisserie
saucepan
scales
sieve
skillet
spatula
spoon
spurtle
steamer
strainer
tablespoon
tagine
tandoor
teapot
teaspoon
tenderizer
timbale
tin-opener
toaster
toasting fork
whisk
wok
wooden spoon

KNITTING STITCHES

box stitch
cable stitch
diagonal rib
double seed *or* double moss stitch
fisherman's rib
garter rib
garter stitch
layette
mistake rib
moss panels
moss stitch
pavilion
rib
roman stripe
seed stitch
slip stitch
stocking stitch

KNOTS

barrell knot
bend
Blackwall hitch
bow *or* bowknot
bowline
bowstring knot
carrick bend
cat's paw
clinch knot
clove hitch
diamond knot
Englishman's tie
figure of eight
fisherman's bend
fisherman's *or* truelover's knot
girth hitch
granny knot
half hitch
hangman's knot
harness hitch
hawser bend
half-hitch
hitch
loop knot
love knot
magnus hitch
Matthew Walker
monkey fist
overhand knot *or* thumb knot
prusik knot
reef knot, flat knot, *or* square knot
rolling hitch
running bowline
running knot
sailor's knot
sheepshank
sheet bend, becket bend, weaver's hitch, *or* mesh knot
shroud knot
slipknot
slippery hitch
stevedore's knot
surgeon's knot
swab hitch
timber hitch
truelove knot
Turk's-head
wale knot
wall knot
water knot
Windsor knot

LAW

LAW TERMS

abandonee *(Contract law)*
abate
abator
abet
abeyance
able
absente reo
absolute
acceptance
accessory *or* accessary
accretion
accrue
accusation
accusatorial
accuse
accused, the
acquit
action
actionable
act of God
adjective
ad litem
adminicle
administration order
admissible
adopt
adult
advocate
advocation
affiant
affidavit
affiliate *or* filiate
affiliation *or* filiation
affiliation order
affiliation proceedings *or (U.S.)* paternity suit
affirm
affirmation
affray

agist
alibi
alienable
alienate
alienation
alienee
alienor
alimony
allege
alluvion
ambulatory
a mensa et thoro
amerce *(obsolete)*
amicus curiae
amnesty
ancient
annulment
answer
Anton Piller order
appeal
appearance
appellant
appellate
appellee
appendant
approve
arbitrary
arbitration
arraign
array
arrest judgment
arrest of judgement
articled clerk
assault
assessor
assets
assign
assignee
assignment
assignor
assumpsit
attach
attachment
attainder
attaint *(archaic)*
attorn
attorney
attorney-at-law
attorney general
authentic
authority
automatism
aver
avoid
avoidance
avow *(rare)*
avulsion
award
bail
bailable
bailee *(Contract law)*
bailiff
bailiwick
bailment *(Contract law)*
bailor *(Contract law)*
bailsman *(rare)*
ban
bankrupt
bar
baron *(English law)*
barratry *or* barretry
barrister *or* barrister-at-law
bench, the
bencher
beneficial
beneficiary
bequeath
bequest
bigamy
bill of attainder
bill of indictment
bill of sale
blasphemy *or* blasphemous libel
body corporate
bona fides
bona vacantia
bond
bondsman
breach of promise
breach of the peace
breach of trust
brief
briefless
bring
burden of proof
capias
capital
caption
carnal knowledge
cartulary *or* chartulary
case
case law
case stated *or* stated case
cassation
cause
caution
CAV, Cur. adv. vult, *or* Curia advisari vult
caveat
caveator
certificate of incorporation *(Company law)*
chamber counsel *or* counsellor
chambers
certification
certiorari
cessor
cessionary
challenge
challenge to the array
challenge to the polls
champerty
chance-medley
chancery
change of venue
charge
chargeable
cheat
chief justice
chose
circuit *(English law)*
citation
cite
civil death
civil marriage
clerk to the justices
close
codicil
codification
coexecutor
cognizable *or* cognisable
cognizance *or* cognisance
collusion
come on
commitment, committal, *or (especially formerly)* mittimus
common
commonage
common law
commutable
commutation
commute
competence
competency
competent
complainant
complaint *(English law)*
complete *(Land law)*
compound
compliance officer
composition
compurgation
conclusion
condemn
condition
condone
confiscate
connivance
connive
conscience clause
consensual
consideration
consolidation
consortium
constituent
constitute
constructive
contempt
contentious
continuance *(U.S.)*
contraband
contract
contractor
contributory *(Company law)*
contributory negligence
contumacy
convene
conventional
conversion
convert
conveyance
convincing
coparcenary *or* coparceny
coparcener *or* parcener
copyhold
copyholder
co-respondent
coroner
coroner's inquest
coroner's jury
corpus delicti
corpus juris
Corpus Juris Civilis
costs
counsel
counselor *or* counselor-at-law *(U.S.)*
count
countercharge
counterclaim
counterpart
countersign
county court
court
court of first instance
covenant
coverture
covin
criminal conversation
criminate *(rare)*
cross-examine
crown attorney *(Canad)*
crown court *(English law)*
cruelty
culpa *(Civil law)*
culprit
cumulative evidence
custodian
custody
custom
customary
cy pres
damages
damnify
dead letter
debatable
decedent *(chiefly U.S.)*
declarant
declaration
declaratory
decree
decree absolute
decree nisi
deed
deed poll
defalcate
defamation

default
defeasible
defeat
defence
defendant
deferred sentence
de jure
delict *(Roman law)*
demand
demandant
demisit sine prole
demur
demurrer
denunciation *(obsolete)*
deodand *(English law)*
deponent
depose
deposition
deraign *or* darraign *(obsolete)*
dereliction
descendible *or* descendable
desertion
detainer
determinable
determination
determine
detinue
devil
devisable
devise
devolve
dies non *or* dies non juridicus
digest
diligence
diminished responsibility
direct evidence
disaffirm
disafforest *or* disforest *(English law)*
disannul
disbar
discharge
disclaim
discommon
discontinue
discovert
discovery
disinherit
dismiss
disorderly
disorderly conduct
disorderly house
dissent
distrain *or* distress
distrainee
distraint
distributee *(chiefly U.S.)*
distribution
distringas
disturbance
dividend
divorce from bed and board *(U.S.)*
docket
documentation
Doe
domain
donee
donor
dot *(Civil law)*
dotation
dowable
dower
droit
due process of law
duress
earnest *or* earnest money *(Contract law)*
effectual
emblements
eminent domain
empanel *or* impanel
encumbrance
encumbrancer
enfranchise *(English law)*
engross
engrossment
enjoin
enter
equitable
equity
escheat
escrow
estop
estoppel
estovers
estray
estreat
evict
evidence
evocation *(French law)*
examination
examine
examine-in-chief
exception
execute
execution
executor *or (fem.)* executrix
executory
exemplary damages
exemplify
exhibit
ex parte
expectancy
expropriate
extend
extent *(U.S.)*
extinguish
extraditable
extradite
extrajudicial
eyre *(English legal history)*
fact
factor *(Commercial law)*
false imprisonment
Family Division
felo de se
feme
feme covert
feme sole
fiction
fideicommissary *(Civil law)*
fideicommissum *(Civil law)*
fiduciary *or* fiducial
fieri facias
file
filiate
filiation
find
finding
first offender
fiscal
flaw
folio
forbearance
force majeure
foreclose
foreign
foreman
forensic
forensic medicine, legal medicine, *or* medical jurisprudence
forest
forfeit
forjudge *or* forejudge
fornication
free
fungible
garnish
garnishee
garnishment
gavelkind *(English law)*
gist
goods and chattels
grand jury *(chiefly U.S.)*
grand larceny
grantee
grant
grantor
gratuitous
gravamen
grith *(English legal history)*
ground rent
guarantee
guardian
guilty
habeas corpus
hand down *(U.S.) (Canad.)*
handling
hear
hearing
hearsay
heir *or (fem.)* heiress *(Civil law)*
heirship
hereditary
heres *or* haeres *(Civil law)*
heritable
heritage
heritor
holder
homologate
hung jury
hypothec *(Roman law)*
hypothecate
immovable
impartible
impediment
imperfect
implead *(rare)*
imprescriptable
in articles
in banc
in camera
incapacitate
incapacity
in chancery
incompetent
incorporeal
incriminate
indefeasible
indemnity
indenture
indeterminate sentence
inducement
in escrow
infant
in fee
inferior court
infirm
in flagrante delicto *or* flagrante delicto
ingoing
inheritance
injunction
injury
innuendo
in personam
in posse
inquest
inquisition
inquisitorial
in rem
insanity
in specie
instanter
institutes
instruct
instructions
instrument
insurable interest
intendment
intent
intention
interdict *(Civil law)*
interlocutory

interplead
interpleader
interrogatories
intervene
inter vivos
intestate
invalidate
in venter
ipso jure
irrepleviable *or* irreplevisable
issuable
issue
jail delivery *(English law)*
jeopardy
joinder
joint
jointress
jointure
judge
judge-made
judges' rules
judgment *or* judgement
judgment by default
judicable
judicative
judicatory
judicature
judicial
judicial separation *(Family law)*
judiciary
junior
jural
jurat
juratory
juridical
jurisconsult
jurisprudence
jurisprudent
jurist
juristic
juror
jury
juryman *or (fem.)* jurywoman
jury process
jus
jus gentium *(Roman law)*
jus naturale *(Roman law)*
jus sanguinis
jus soli
justice
justice court
justice of the peace
justiciable
justices in eyre *(English legal history)*
justify
juvenile court
laches
land
lapse
larceny
Law French
Law Lords
law merchant *(Mercantile law)*
lawsuit
law term
lawyer
leasehold
leaseholder
legist
letters of administration
lex loci
lex non scripta
lex scripta
lex talionis
libel
lien
limit
limitation
lis pendens
litigable
litigant
litigation
locus standi
magistrate
magistrates' court *or* petty sessions
maintenance
malfeasance
malice
manager
mandamus
mandate *(Roman law) (Contract law)*
manslaughter
manus
mare clausum
mare liberum
material
matter
mayhem *or* maihem
memorandum
mens rea
mental disorder
mental impairment
merger
merits
mesne
ministerial
misadventure
mise
misfeasance
misjoinder
mispleading
mistrial
misuser
mittimus
monopoly
moral
moratorium
morganatic *or* left-handed
mortgagee
mortmain *or (less commonly)* dead hand
motion
moveable *or* movable
muniments
mute
naked
Napoleonic Code
necessaries
negligence
next friend
nisi
nisi prius *(History) (U.S.)*
nolle prosequi, nol. pros., *or* nolle pros.
nolo contendere *(chiefly U.S.)*
nonage
non compos mentis
nonfeasance
nonjoinder
non liquet
non prosequitur *or* non pros.
nonsuit
notary public
not guilty
novation
novel *(Roman law)*
nude
nudum pactum
nuisance
oath
obiter dictum
obligation
oblivion
obreption
obscene
obtaining by deception
occupancy
occupant
offer *(Contract law)*
Official Referee
onerous
onomastic
on, upon *or* under oath
onus probandi
open
opening
ordinary
overt
owelty
oyer *(English legal history)*
oyer and terminer
panel
paraphernalia
pardon
parol
Particulars of Claim
party
paterfamilias *(Roman law)*
peculium *(Roman law)*
pecuniary
pecuniary advantage
pendente lite
perception
peremptory
persistent cruelty
personal
personal property *or* personalty
petit
petition
petitioner
petit jury *or* petty jury
petit larceny *or* petty larceny
petty
place of safety order
plaint
plaintiff
plea
plea bargaining
plead
pleading
pleadings
portion
port of entry
posse
posse comitatus
possessory
post-obit
prayer
precedent
precept
predispose
pre-emption
prefer
preference
premeditation
premises
prescribe
prescription
presentment *(chiefly U.S.)*
presents
presume
presumption
preterition *(Roman law)*
prima facie
primogeniture
principal
private law
private nuisance
privilege
privileged
privity
privy
prize court
probable cause
probate
proceed
proceeding
process
process-server
procuration
procuratory
prohibition
promisee *(Contract law)*
promisor *(Contract law)*

proof
property centre
proponent
propositus
propound (*English law*)
prosecute
prosecuting attorney (*U.S.*)
prosecution
prosecutor
prothonotary *or* protonotary
prove
provocation (*English criminal law*)
psychopathic disorder
public defender (*U.S.*)
public law
public nuisance
public prosecutor
pupil (*Civil law*)
pupillage
pursuant
purview
quarter sessions
queen's *or* king's evidence
question
question of fact (*English law*)
question of law (*English law*)
quitclaim
quo warranto
real
real property
rebutter
recaption
receivership
recital
recognizance *or* recognisance
recognizee *or* recognisee
recognizor *or* recognisor
recorder
recoup
recover
recovery
recrimination
re-examine
reference
refresher (*English law*)
rejoin
rejoinder
relation
relator (*English law*) (*U.S. law*)
release
relief
remand
remise
remission
remit
repetition (*Civil law*)
replevin
replevy
replication
reply
report
reporter
representation (*Contract law*)
reprieve
rescue
reservation
res gestae
residuary
residue
res ipsa loquitur
res judicata *or* res adjudicata
resolutive
respondent
rest
restitution
restraining order (*U.S.*)
restrictive covenant
retain
retry
return
returnable
reverse
review
right of common
riot
rout
rule
ruling
run
salvo
saving
scandal
schedule
scienter
scire facias (*rare*)
script
secularize *or* secularise
self-defence
self-executing
sentence
separation (*Family law*)
sequester *or* sequestrate
sequestration
serjeant at law, serjeant, sergeant at law, *or* sergeant
servitude
session
settlement
settlor
severable
several
severance
sign
signatory
sine
sine prole
slander
smart money (*U.S.*)
socage (*English law*)
soke (*English legal history*)
solatium (*chiefly U.S.*)
sole
solemnity
solicitor
solution
sound
sound in
special case
special pleading
specialty
specific performance
spinster
spoliation
squat
stale
stand by (*English law*)
stand down
statement
statement of claim
state's evidence (*U.S.*)
statute law
statutory declaration
stillicide
stipulate (*Roman law*)
stranger
stultify
submission
subpoena
subreption (*rare*)
subrogate
subrogation
substantive
succeed
sue
sui juris
suit
suitor
summary
summary jurisdiction
summary offence
summation (*U.S. law*)
summing-up
summons
suo jure
suo loco
surcharge
surety
surplusage
surrebuttal
surrebutter
surrejoinder
surrender
suspension
swear
swear in
swear out (*U.S.*)
tales
tenancy
tenantry
tender
tenor
term
termor *or* termer
territorial court (*U.S.*)
testament
testamentary
testate
testify
testimony
thing
third party
time immemorial
tipstaff
title
tort
tort-feasor
tortious
traffic court
transfer
transitory action
traverse
treasure-trove
trespass
triable
trial
trial court
tribunal
trover
try
udal
ultimogeniture
ultra vires
unalienable
unappealable
unavoidable
uncovenanted
unilateral
unincorporated
unlawful assembly
unreasonable behaviour
unwritten law
use
user
utter barrister
vacant
vacate
variance
vendee
vendor
venire facias
venireman (*U.S.*)
venue
verdict
verification
verify
versus
vesture
vexatious
view
viewer
vindicate (*Roman law*)
vindictive (*English law*)
vitiate
voidable
voir dire
voluntary
voluntary arrangement

- volunteer
- voucher *(English law) (obsolete)*
- wager of law *(English legal history)*
- waif *(obsolete)*
- waive
- waiver
- ward
- ward of court
- warrant
- warranty *(Contract law) (Insurance law)*
- waste
- will
- witness
- without prejudice
- writ
- writ of execution
- wrong
- year and a day *(English law)*

CRIMINAL LAW TERMS

- acquittal
- actual bodily harm
- arson
- bailment
- battery
- burglary *(English law)*
- deception *or* *(formerly)* false pretences
- embrace
- embraceor *or* embracer
- embracery
- entry
- felon
- felonious
- felony
- force
- forgery
- grievous bodily harm
- hard labour
- housebreaking
- impeach
- indictable
- indictment
- infamous
- malice aforethought
- misdemeanant
- misdemeanour
- penal servitude *(English law)*
- perjure
- perjury
- personate
- Riot Act
- robbery
- suborn
- theft
- thief
- true bill *(U.S. law)*
- utter

PROPERTY LAW TERMS

- abatement
- abstract of title
- abuttals
- abutter
- accession
- ademption
- administration
- administrator
- advancement
- adverse
- amortize *or* amortise
- appoint
- appointee
- appointment
- appointor
- appurtenance
- betterment
- chattel
- chattel personal
- chattel real
- convey *or* assure
- deforce
- demesne
- demise
- descent
- devisee
- devisor
- dilapidation
- disentail
- disseise
- divest
- dominant tenement
- dominium *or* *(rare)* dominion
- easement
- ejectment
- enfeoff
- entail
- entry
- equity of redemption
- estate
- fee
- fee simple
- fee tail
- fixture
- freehold
- freeholder
- heir apparent
- heir-at-law
- heirdom
- heirloom
- heriditament
- hotchpot
- intrusion
- messuage
- mortgagor *or* mortgager
- oust
- ouster
- particular
- partition
- party wall
- perpetuity
- power of appointment
- reconvert
- remainder
- remainderman
- remitter
- result
- reversion
- reversioner
- revert
- riparian
- seisin *or (U.S.)* seizin
- servient tenement
- severalty
- survivor
- tail
- tenure
- transferee
- transferor *or* transferrer
- unity of interest
- vested
- vested interest
- warranty

SCOTS LAW TERMS

- advocate
- Advocate Depute
- agent
- aliment
- alimentary
- approbate
- approbate and reprobate
- arrestment
- assignation
- assize
- avizandum
- condescendence
- continue
- crown agent
- culpable homicide
- curator
- decern
- declarator
- decreet
- defender
- delict
- depone
- desert
- district court *or* *(formerly)* justice of the peace court
- feu
- feu duty
- fire raising
- hypothec
- interdict
- interlocutor
- law agent
- location
- lockfast
- mandate
- multiplepoinding
- notour
- notour bankrupt
- not proven
- poind
- poinding
- precognition
- procurator fiscal *or* fiscal
- pupil
- repetition
- repone
- sasine
- sequestrate
- sheriff officer
- thirlage
- tradition
- tutor
- wadset
- warrant sale

LITERATURE

LITERATURE TERMS

- allegory
- alliteration
- allusion
- amphigory *or* amphigouri
- Angry Young Men
- anti-hero
- antinovel
- anti-roman
- aphorism
- archaism
- Augustan
- Bakhtinian
- bathos

Beat Generation *or* Beats
belles-lettres
belletrist
bibliography
Bildungsroman
black comedy
Bloomsbury group
bodice-ripper
bombast
bowdlerization
Brechtian
bricolage
Byronic
carnivalesque
campus novel
causerie
Celtic Revival
cento
chiller
Ciceronian
classicism
coda
colloquialism
comedy
comedy of manners
commedia dell'arte
conceit
courtly love
cultural materialism
cut-up technique
cyberpunk
death of the author
decadence
deconstruction
denouement
Derridian
dialectic
dialogue
Dickensian
discourse
double entendre
drama
epic
epilogue
epistle
epistolary novel
epitaph
erasure
essay
exegesis
expressionism
fable
fabulist
faction
fantastique
fantasy
feminist theory
festschrift
figure of speech
fin de siècle
foreword
Foucauldian
Futurism
gloss
Gongorism
Gothic
hagiography
Hellenism
hermeneutics
historical novel
historicism
Homeric
Horatian
hudibrastic verse
imagery
interior monologue
intertextuality
invective
Jacobean
Janeite
Johnsonian
journalese
Joycean
Juvenalian
Kafkaesque
kailyard
kenning
kiddy lit
lampoon
Laurentian *or* Lawrentian
legend
literary criticism
littérateur
locus classicus
Lost Generation
magic realism *or* magical realism
marxist theory
maxim
melodrama
metafiction
metalanguage
metaphor
mock-heroic
modernism
motif
myth
mythopoeia
narrative
narratology
narrator
naturalism
new criticism
new historicism
nom de plume
nouveau roman
novel
novelette
novella
onomatopoeia
oxymoron
palindrome
paraphrase
parody
pastiche
pastoral
pathos
picaresque
plagiarism
plot
polemic
pornography
post-colonialism
postmodernism
post-structuralism
post-theory
pot-boiler
queer theory
realism
Restoration comedy
roman
roman à clef
Romanticism
saga
samizdat
satire
science fiction *or* SF
sentimental novel
shopping-and-fucking *or* S & F novel
short story
signifier and signified
simile
sketch
socialist realism
splatterpunk
Spoonerism
story
stream of consciousness
structuralism
Sturm und Drang
subplot
subtext
Surrealism
Swiftian
theme
theory
thesis
tragedy
tragicomedy
trope
verse
vignette

EXTINCT MAMMALS

apeman
aurochs
australopithecine
baluchitherium
chalicothere
creodont
dinoceras *or* uintathere
dinothere
dryopithecine
eohippus
glyptodont
Irish elk
labyrinthodont
mammoth
mastodon
megathere
nototherium
quagga
sabre-toothed tiger *or* cat
tarpan
titanothere

TYPES OF MANIA

ablutomania	washing
agoramania	open spaces
ailuromania	cats
andromania	men
Anglomania	England
anthomania	flowers
apimania	bees
arithmomania	counting
automania	solitude
autophonomania	suicide
balletomania	ballet
ballistomania	bullets
bibliomania	books
chionomania	snow
choreomania	dancing
chrematomania	money
cremnomania	cliffs
cynomania	dogs
dipsomania	alcohol
doramania	fur
dromomania	travelling
egomania	your self
eleuthromania	freedom

entheomania	religion
entomomania	insects
ergasiomania	work
eroticomania	erotica
erotomania	sex
florimania	plants
gamomania	marriage
graphomania	writing
gymnomania	nakedness
gynomania	women
hamartiomania	sin
hedonomania	pleasure
heliomania	sun
hippomania	horses
homicidomania	murder
hydromania	water
hylomania	woods
hypnomania	sleep
ichthyomania	fish
iconomania	icons
kinesomania	movement
kleptomania	stealing
logomania	talking
macromania	becoming larger
megalomania	your own importance
melomania	music
mentulomania	penises
micromania	becoming smaller
monomania	one thing
musicomania	music
musomania	mice
mythomania	lies
necromania	death
noctimania	night
nudomania	nudity
nymphomania	sex
ochlomania	crowds
oikomania	home
oinomania	wine
ophidiomania	reptiles
orchidomania	testicles
ornithomania	birds
phagomania	eating
pharmacomania	medicines
phonomania	noise
photomania	light
plutomania	great wealth
potomania	drinking
pyromania	fire
scribomania	writing
siderodromomania	railway travel
sitomania	food
sophomania	your own wisdom
thalassomania	the sea
thanatomania	death
theatromania	theatre
timbromania	stamps
trichomania	hair
verbomania	words
xenomania	foreigners
zoomania	animals

MARSUPIALS

agile wallaby, river wallaby, sandy wallaby, *or* jungle kangaroo
antechinus
antelope kangaroo *or* antilopine wallaby
bandicoot
barred bandicoot *or* marl
Bennett's tree kangaroo *or* tcharibeena
bettong
bilby, rabbit(-eared) bandicoot, long-eared bandicoot, dalgyte, *or* dalgite
bobuck *or* mountain (brushtail) possum
boodie (rat), burrowing rat-kangaroo, Lesueur's rat-kangaroo, tungoo, *or* tungo
boongary *or* Lumholtz's tree kangaroo
bridled nail-tail wallaby *or* merrin
brindled bandicoot *or* northern brown bandicoot
brush-tail(ed) possum
burramys *or* (mountain) pygmy possum
crest-tailed marsupial mouse, Cannings' little dog, *or* mulgara
crescent nail-tail wallaby *or* wurrung
cuscus
dasyurid, dasyure, native cat, marsupial cat, *or* wild cat
desert bandicoot
desert-rat kangaroo
dibbler
diprotodon
dunnart
eastern grey kangaroo, great grey kangaroo, forest kangaroo, *or* (grey) forester
fluffy glider *or* yellow-bellied glider
flying phalanger, flying squirrel, glider, *or* pongo
green ringtail possum *or* toolah
hairy-nosed wombat
hare-wallaby
honey mouse, honey possum, noolbenger, *or* tait
jerboa, jerboa pouched mouse, jerboa kangaroo, *or* kultarr
kangaroo *or* (*Austral. informal*) roo
koala (bear) *or* (*Austral.*) native bear
kowari
larapinta *or* Darling Downs dunnart
Leadbeater's possum *or* fairy possum
lemuroid ringtail possum
long-nosed bandicoot
mardo *or* yellow-footed antechinus
marlu
marsupial mole
marsupial mouse
mongan *or* Herbert River ringtail possum
munning
musky rat-kangaroo
naked-nose wombat
ningaui
northern nail-tail wallaby *or* karrabul
northern native cat *or* satanellus
numbat *or* banded anteater
opossum *or* possum
pademelon *or* paddymelon
parma wallaby
phalanger
pig-footed bandicoot
pitchi-pitchi *or* wuhl-wuhl
platypus, duck-billed platypus, *or* duckbill
potoroo
pretty-face wallaby *or* whiptail wallaby
pygmy glider, feather glider, *or* flying mouse
quenda *or* (southern) brown bandicoot
quokka
quoll
rat kangaroo
red kangaroo *or* plains kangaroo
red(-necked) wallaby, Bennett's wallaby,

eastern brush wallaby, rufous wallaby, *or* brush kangaroo
ringtail *or* ringtail(ed) possum
rock wallaby *or* brush-tailed wallaby
rufous rat-kangaroo
scrub wallaby
short-eared bandicoot
short-nosed bandicoot
short-nosed rat kangaroo *or* squeaker
squirrel glider
striped possum
sugar glider
swamp wallaby, black wallaby, *or* black-tailed wallaby
tammar, damar, *or* dama
Tasmanian barred bandicoot *or* Gunn's bandicoot
Tasmanian devil *or* ursine dasyure
thylacine, Tasmanian wolf, *or* Tasmanian tiger
tiger cat *or* spotted native cat
toolache *or* Grey's brush wallaby
tree kangaroo
tuan, phascogale, *or* wambenger
wallaby
wallaroo, uroo, *or* biggada
warabi
western grey kangaroo, black-faced kangaroo, sooty kangaroo, *or* mallee kangaroo
wintarro *or* golden bandicoot
wogoit *or* rock possum
wombat *or (Austral.)* badger
woylie *or* brush-tailed bettong
yapok
yallara
yellow-footed rock wallaby *or* ring-tailed rock wallaby

MARTIAL ARTS AND TERMS

MARTIAL ARTS

aikido
capoeira
Crane style kung fu
Goju Kai karate
Goju Ryu karate
hapkido
Hung Gar *or* Tiger style kung fu
iai-do
iai-jutsu
Ishin Ryu karate
Jeet Kune Do
judo
ju jitsu, jiu jitsu *or* ju-jutsu
karate *or* karate-do
kendo
kick boxing
kung fu
Kyokushinkai karate
kyudo
naginata-do
ninjitsu *or* ninjutsu
Praying Mantis style kung fu
Sankukai karate
Shito Ryu karate
Shotokai karate
Shotokan karate
Shukokai karate
sumo *or* sumo wrestling
tae kwon-do
tai chi chuan
tai chi qi gong
Ta Sheng Men *or* Monkey style kung fu
Thai boxing *or* Muay Thai
Tomiki aikido
Tukido *(trademark)*
Wado Ryu karate
Wing Chun *or* Wing Tsun kung fu
yari-jutsu

MARTIAL ARTS TERMS

Term	*Meaning*
basho	sumo turnament
bo	staff
bogu	kendo armour
bokuto	kendo wooden sword
budo *or* bushido	warrior's way
dan	black belt grade
do	kendo breastplate
-do	the way
dohyo	sumo ring
dojo	practice room or mat
gi	suit
hachimaki *or* tenugui	kendo headcloth
hakama	divided skirt
ippon	one competition point
jiu-kumite	freestyle karate competition
-jutsu	fighting art
-ka	student
kama	hand sickle
kata	sequence of techniques
katana	kendo sword
katsu	resuscitation techniques
keikogi	kendo jacket
kesho-mawashi	embroidered sumo apron
ki, chi *or* qi	inner power
kiai	yell accompanying movement
kihon	repetition of techniques
kote	kendo gauntlets
kyu	student grade
makiwara	practice block
mawashi	sumo fighting belt
men	kendo mask
nage-waza *or* tachi-waza	ju jitsu competition
naginata	curved-blade spear
ne-waza	ju jitsu competition
ninin-dori	aikido competition
ninja	Japanese trained assassin
nunchaku	hinged flails
obi	coloured belt
ozeki	sumo champion
qi gong	breath control

Term	*Meaning*
randori kyoghi	aikido competition
rikishi	sumo wrestler
rokushakubo	six-foot staff
ryu	martial arts school
sai	short trident
samurai	Japanese warrior caste
sensei	teacher
shinai	kendo bamboo sword
sifu	teacher
suneate	naginata shin guards
tanto randori	aikido competition
tare	kendo apron
te	hand fighting
ton-fa *or* tui-fa	hardwood weapon
tsuna	sumo grand champion's belt
waza-ari	half competition point
yari	spear
yokozuna	sumo grand champion
zanshin	total awareness

MATHEMATICS

BRANCHES OF MATHEMATICS

algebra
analysis
analytical geometry *or* coordinate geometry
applied mathematics
arithmetic
Boolean algebra
calculus
chaos geometry
conics
differential calculus
Euclidean geometry
game theory
geometry
group theory
integral calculus
nomography
non-Euclidean geometry
number theory
numerical analysis
probability theory
pure mathematics
set theory
statistics
topology
trigonometry

MATHEMATICAL TERMS

acute angle
addition
algorithm *or* algorism
angle
arc
area
average
axis
base
binary
binomial
cardinal number
Cartesian coordinates
chord
circle
circumference
closed set
coefficient
common denominator
common factor
complex number
concentric
cone
constant
coordinate *or* co-ordinate
cosecant
cosine
cotangent
cube
cube root
cuboid
curve
cusp
cylinder
decagon
decimal
denary
denominator
diagonal
diameter
digit
division
dodecahedron
ellipse
equals
equation
equilateral
even
exponential
factor
factorial
formula
fraction
frequency
function
graph
helix
hemisphere
heptagon
hexagon
hyperbola
hypotenuse
icosahedron
imaginary number
improper fraction
index
infinity
integer
integral
intersection
irrational number
isosceles
locus
logarithm *or* log
lowest common denominator
lowest common multiple
Mandelbrot set
matrix
mean
median
minus
mode
multiplication
natural logarithm
natural number
node
nonagon
number
numerator
oblong
obtuse angle
octagon
octahedron
odd
open set
operation
operator
ordinal number
origin
parabola
parallel
parallelogram
pentagon
percentage
perfect number
pi
plus
polygon
polyhedron
polynomial
power
prime number
prism
probability
product
proof
proper fraction
Pythagoras' theorem
quadrant
quadratic equation
quadrilateral
quotient
radian
radius
ratio
rational number
real number
reciprocal
rectangle
recurring decimal
reflex angle
remainder
rhombus
right angle
right-angled triangle
root
scalar
scalene
secant
sector
semicircle
set
significant figures
simultaneous equations
sine
slide rule
solid
sphere
square
square root

strange attractor
subset
subtraction
sum
surd
tangent
tetrahedron
torus
trapezium
triangle
union
universal set
value
variable
vector
Venn diagram
volume
vulgar fraction
x-axis
y-axis
z-axis
zero

TYPES OF MEAL

afternoon tea
banquet
barbecue *or* (*Austral.*) barbie
beanfeast
breakfast
brunch
buffet
cream tea
dinner
elevenses
feast
fish fry (*U.S.*)
high tea *or* tea
lunch *or* luncheon
picnic
smorgasbord
snack
supper
tapas
tiffin

TYPES AND CUTS OF MEAT

bacon
baron of beef
Bath chap
beef
beef-ham
black pudding
bockwurst
boerewors
bratwurst
breast
brisket
cervelat
charqui
Chateaubriand
chicken
chipolata
chitterlings, chitlings, *or* chitlins
chop
chorizo
chuck *or* chuck steak
chump
cold cuts
collar
colonial goose
corned beef
crown roast
Cumberland sausage
cutlet
devon
duck
entrecôte
escalope
fillet
forehock
foreshank
game
gammon
gigot
goose
gristle
ham
haslet
hogg *or* hogget
hough or hock
kidney
knackwurst *or* knockwurst
Kobe beef *or* Wagyu
lamb
lamb's fry
leg
lights
liver
liver sausage *or* (*esp U.S.*) liverwurst
loin
Lorne sausage, square sausage, *or* square slice (*Scot.*)
luncheon meat
médaillons
mince
minute steak
mortadella
mutton
noisette
numbles (*archaic*)
offal
oxtail
oxtongue
Parma ham
parson's nose
pastrami
pemmican
pepperoni
pheasant
pigeon
polony
pope's eye
pork
porterhouse steak
prosciutto
rack
rib
rolled lamb
round
rump
saddle
salami
salt pork
sausage
saveloy
scrag
shank
shoulder
silverside
sirloin
skirt
Spam (*trademark*)
sparerib
steak
stewing steak
sweetbread
T-bone
tenderloin
tongue
topside
tournedos
tripe
turkey
undercut
veal
venison

MEDALS

Bronze Star (*U.S.*)
Congressional Medal of Honor (*U.S.*)
Croix de Guerre (*France*)
Distinguished Service Cross (*U.S.*)
Distinguished Service Order (*Britain*)
George Cross (*Britain*)
Iron Cross (*Germany*)
Légion d'Honneur (*France*)
Legion of Merit (*U.S.*)
Militaire Willemsorde (*Netherlands*)
Purple Heart (*U.S.*)
Royal Red Cross (*Britain*)
Silver Star (*U.S.*)
Victoria Cross

MEDICINE

BRANCHES OF MEDICINE

aetiology *or* etiology
anaesthetics
anaplasty
anatomy
andrology
angiology
audiology
aviation medicine
bacteriology
balneology
bioastronautics
biomedicine
cardiology
chiropody
dental hygiene *or* oral hygiene

dental surgery
dentistry
dermatology
diagnostics
eccrinology
electrophysiology
electrotherapeutics
embryology
encephalography
endocrinology
endodontics
epidemiology
exodontics
forensic *or* legal medicine
gastroenterology
genitourinary medicine
geratology
geriatrics
gerontology
gynaecology *or* (*U.S.*) gynecology
haematology *or* (*U.S.*) hematology
hydrotherapeutics
immunochemistry
immunology
industrial medicine
internal medicine
laryngology
materia medica
midwifery
morbid anatomy
myology
neonatology
nephrology
neuroanatomy
neuroendocrinology
neurology
neuropathology
neurophysiology
neuropsychiatry
neurosurgery
nosology
nostology
nuclear medicine
nutrition
obstetrics
odontology
oncology
ophthalmology
optometry
orthodontics *or* orthodontia
orthopaedics *or* (*U.S.*) orthopedics
orthoptics
orthotics
osteology
osteoplasty
otolaryngology
otology
paediatrics *or* (*U.S.*) pediatrics
pathology
periodontics
pharyngology
physical medicine
physiotherapy *or* (*U.S.*) physiatrics
plastic surgery
posology
preventive medicine
proctology
psychiatry
psychoanalysis
psychology
radiology
rheumatology
rhinology
serology
space medicine
spare-part surgery
speech therapy
sports medicine
stomatology
surgery
symptomatology
syphilology
therapeutics
tocology *or* tokology
toxicology
trichology
urology
venereology
veterinary science *or* medicine
virology

MEDICAL PRACTITIONERS AND SPECIALISTS

aetiologist *or* etiologist
anaesthetist
anatomist
andrologist
audiologist
bacteriologist
balneologist
barefoot doctor
cardiologist
chiropodist
consultant
dental hygienist *or* oral hygienist
dentist *or* dental surgeon
dermatologist
diagnostician
dietitian
district nurse
doctor
electrophysiologist
embryologist
endocrinologist
endodontist
epidemiologist
exodontist
extern *or* externe (*U.S.*) (*Canad.*)
forensic scientist
gastroenterologist
general practitioner *or* GP
geriatrician *or* geriatrist
gerontologist
gynaecologist *or* (*U.S.*) gynecologist
haematologist *or* (*U.S.*) hematologist
health visitor
house physician
houseman
hydrotherapist
immunologist
intern *or* interne (*U.S.*) (*Canad.*)
internist
junior doctor
laboratory technician
laryngologist
matron
midwife
myologist
neonatologist
nephrologist
neuroanatomist
neurologist
neuropathologist
neurophysiologist
neuropsychiatrist
neurosurgeon
nosologist
nurse
nursing officer
nutritionist
obstetrician
occupational therapist
odontologist
oncologist
ophthalmologist
optician
optometrist
orderly
orthodontist
orthopaedist *or* (*U.S.*) orthopedist
orthoptist
orthotist
osteologist
otolaryngologist
otologist
paediatrician *or* (*U.S.*) pediatrician
paramedic
pathologist
pharyngologist
physiotherapist *or* physio
plastic surgeon
proctologist
psychiatrist
psychoanalyst
psychologist
radiographer
radiologist
registrar
resident (*U.S.*) (*Canad.*)
rheumatologist
rhinologist
serologist
speech therapist
surgeon
syphilologist
therapist
toxicologist
trichologist
urologist
venereologist
veterinary surgeon, vet *or* (*U.S.*) veterinarian
virologist

MEDICAL AND SURGICAL INSTRUMENTS AND EQUIPMENT

arthroscope
artificial heart
artificial kidney
aspirator
bandage
bedpan
bistoury
bronchoscope
cannula *or* canula
cardiograph
catheter
catling
clamp
clinical thermometer
colonoscope
colposcope
compressor
CT scanner *or* CAT scanner
curet *or* curette
cystoscope
defibrillator
depressor
dialysis machine
drain
electrocardiograph
electroencephalograph
electromyograph
encephalogram
endoscope
fetoscope
fibrescope *or (U.S.)* fiberscope
fluoroscope
forceps
gamma camera
gastroscope
gonioscope
haemostat *or (U.S.)* hemostat
heart-lung machine
heat lamp
hypodermic *or* hypodermic needle
hypodermic *or* hypodermic syringe
inhalator
inspirator
iron lung
kidney machine
kymograph *or* cymograph
lancet *or* lance
laparoscope
laryngoscope
life-support machine
microscope
nebulizer
needle
nephroscope
oesophagoscope *or (U.S.)* esophagoscope
ophthalmoscope
orthoscope
otoscope
oxygen mask
oxygen tent
pacemaker
packing
perimeter
pharyngoscope
plaster cast
pneumatometer
pneumograph
probe
proctoscope
Pulmotor *(trademark)*
raspatory
respirator
resuscitator
retinoscope
retractor
rheometer
rhinoscope
roentgenoscope *or* röntgenoscope
scalpel
scanner
skiascope
sling
sound
specimen bottle
speculum
sphygmograph
sphygmomanometer
spirograph
spirometer
splint
stethoscope
stomach pump
stretcher
stupe
stylet
styptic pencil
suture
swab
syringe
thoracoscope
tourniquet
trepan
trephine
trocar
ultrasound scanner
urethroscope
urinometer
ventilator
wet pack
X-ray machine

BRANCHES OF ALTERNATIVE MEDICINE

acupressure
acupuncture
Alexander technique
aromatherapy
autogenic training
Bach flower remedy
biofeedback
chiropractic
herbalism
homeopathy *or* homoeopathy
hydrotherapy
hypnosis
hypnotherapy
iridology
kinesiology
massage
moxibustion
naturopathy
osteopathy
radionics
reflexology
shiatsu

METALS

Metal	*Symbol*	*Metal*	*Symbol*	*Metal*	*Symbol*
actinium	Ac	chromium	Cr	hafnium	Hf
aluminium	Al	cobalt	Co	holmium	Ho
americium	Am	copper	Cu	indium	In
antimony	Sb	curium	Cm	iridium	Ir
barium	Ba	dysprosium	Dy	iron	Fe
berkelium	Bk	einsteinium	Es	lanthanum	La
beryllium	Be	erbium	Er	lawrencium	Lr
bismuth	Bi	europium	Eu	lead	Pb
cadmium	Cd	fermium	Fm	lithium	Li
caesium *or*		francium	Fr	lutetium	Lu
(U.S.) cesium	Cs	gadolinium	Gd	magnesium	Mg
calcium	Ca	gallium	Ga	manganese	Mn
californium	Cf	germanium	Ge	mendelevium	Md
cerium	Ce	gold	Au	mercury	Hg

Metal	*Symbol*	*Metal*	*Symbol*	*Metal*	*Symbol*
molybdenum	Mo	protactinium	Pa	thallium	Tl
neodymium	Nd	radium	Ra	thorium	Th
neptunium	Np	rhenium	Re	thulium	Tm
nickel	Ni	rhodium	Rh	tin	Sn
niobium	Nb	rubidium	Rb	titanium	Ti
nobelium	No	ruthenium	Ru	tungsten *or* wolfram	W
osmium	Os	samarium	Sm	uranium	U
palladium	Pd	scandium	Sc	vanadium	V
platinum	Pt	silver	Ag	ytterbium	Yb
plutonium	Pu	sodium	Na	yttrium	Y
polonium	Po	strontium	Sr	zinc	Zn
potassium	K	tantalum	Ta	zirconium	Zr
praseodymium	Pr	technetium	Tc		
promethium	Pm	terbium	Tb		

MILITARY RANKS

able rating
able seaman *or* able-bodied seaman (AB)
acting sublieutenant
admiral (Adm)
admiral of the fleet
air chief marshal (ACM)
air commodore (AC)
aircraftmen (AC)
air marshal (AM)
air officer
air vice-marshal (AVM)
branch officer (BO)
brigadier (Brig)
captain (Capt)
chief of staff (COS)
chief petty officer (CPO)
chief technician
colonel (Col)
colour sergeant (Col Sgt)
commander (Cdr)
commander in chief (C-in-C)
commanding officer (CO)
commissioned officer
commodore (Cdre)
company sergeant major (CSM)
corporal (Corp, Cpl)
drum major
field marshal (FM)
field officer (FO)
fleet admiral
fleet chief petty officer
flight engineer
flight lieutenant (Flt Lt)
flight mechanic (FM)
flight sergeant (Flt Sgt)
flying officer (FO)
general (Gen, Genl)
group captain (G Capt)
junior technician
lance corporal (L-Cpl)
leading aircraftman (LAC)
leading rating
lieutenant (Lt)
lieutenant colonel (Lt-Col)
lieutenant commander (Lt-Comm)
lieutenant general (Lt-Gen)
major (Maj)
major general (Maj-Gen)
marine
marshal
marshal of the Royal Air Force (MRAF)
master aircrew
medical officer (MO)
midshipman
noncommissioned officer (NCO)
ordinary rating
ordinary seaman (OS)
petty officer (PO)
pilot officer (PO)
private (Pte)
quartermaster (QM)
rear admiral (RA)
regimental sergeant major (RSM)
second lieutenant
senior aircraftman
senior medical officer (SMO)
sergeant (Sgt, Sergt)
sergeant major (SM)
squadron leader (Sqn-Ldr)
staff sergeant
subaltern
sublieutenant (Sub L)
vice admiral (VA)
warrant officer (WO)
wing commander

MINERALS

actinolite
agate
albite
allanite
allophane
alunite
amalgam
amblygonite
analcite *or* analcime
anatase
andalusite
andesine
anglesite
anhydrite
ankerite
annabergite
anorthite
apatite
apophyllite
aragonite
argentite
arsenopyrite
augite
autunite
axinite
azurite
baddeleyite
barytes
bastnaesite *or* bastnasite
bauxite
beryl
biotite
bismuthinite *or* bismuth glance
Boehmite
boracite
borax
bornite
braunite
brookite
calaverite
calcite
carnallite
carnotite
cassiterite
celestite *or* celestine

cerargyrite
chabazite
chalcanthite
chalcocite
chalcopyrite
chlorite
chromite
chrysoberyl
chrysotile
cinnabar
clay mineral
cleveite
clinopyroxene
cobaltite *or* cobaltine
colemanite
columbite
cordierite
corundum
cristobalite
crocidolite
crocoite *or* crocoisite
cryolite
cuprite
cyanite
datolite
diallage
diamond
diaspore
diopside
dioptase
dolomite
dumortierite
emery
enstatite
epidote
erythrite
euxenite
fayalite
feldspar *or* felspar
feldspathoid
fluorapatite
fluorspar, fluor *or* (*U.S. & Canad.*) fluorite
forsterite
franklinite
gahnite
galena *or* galenite
garnet
garnierite
gehlenite
germanite
geyserite
gibbsite
glauconite
goethite *or* göthite
graphite
greenockite
gummite
gypsum
halite
harmotome
hematite *or* haematite
hemimorphite
hessite
heulandite
hiddenite
hornblende
hyacinth
hypersthene
illite
ilmenite
jadeite
jarosite
jasper
kainite
kaolinite
kernite
kieserite
kunzite
labradorite
lapis lazuli
lazulite
lazurite
leucite
limonite
magnesite
magnetite
malachite
manganite
marcasite
margarite
massicot
meerschaum
metamict
mica
microcline
millerite
mimetite
molybdenite
monazite
montmorillonite
monzonite
mullite
muscovite
natrolite
nepheline *or* nephelite
nephrite
niccolite
norite
oligoclase
olivenite
olivine
opal
orpiment
orthoclase
ozocerite *or* ozokerite
pentlandite
periclase
perovskite
petuntse *or* petuntze
phenacite *or* phenakite
phosgenite
phosphorite
piedmontite
pinite
pitchblende
pollucite
polybasite
proustite
psilomelane
pyrargyrite
pyrite
pyrolusite
pyromorphite
pyrophyllite
pyroxene
pyroxenite
pyrrhotite *or* pyrrhotine
quartz
realgar
rhodochrosite
rhodonite
rutile
samarskite
saponite
sapphirine
scapolite
scheelite
scolecite
senarmontite
serpentine
siderite
sillimanite
smaltite
smaragdite
smectite
smithsonite
sodalite
sperrylite
sphalerite
sphene
spinel
spodumene
stannite
staurolite
stibnite
stilbite
strontianite
sylvanite
sylvite *or* sylvine
talc
tantalite
tenorite
tetradymite
tetrahedrite
thenardite
thorianite
thorite
tiemannite
topaz
torbernite
tourmaline
tremolite
triphylite
trona
troostite
tungstite
turgite
turquoise
uralite
uraninite
uranite
vanadinite
variscite
vermiculite
vesuvianite
wavellite
willemite
witherite
wolframite
wollastonite
wulfenite
zaratite
zeolite
zincite
zinkenite *or* zinckenite
zircon
zoisite

MISSILES

cruise missile
Exocet
guided missile
ICBM *or* intercontinental ballistic missile
Minuteman
MIRV *or* multiple independently targeted re-entry vehicle
Patriot
Pershing
Polaris
rocket
Scud
SLBM *or* submarine-launched ballistic missile
SLCM *or* sea-launched cruise missile
SS-18
SS-20
standoff missile
Trident
V-1, doodlebug, buzz bomb, *or* flying bomb
V-2

MONKEYS, APES AND OTHER PRIMATES

aye-aye
baboon
Barbary ape
bonnet monkey
bushbaby *or* galago
capuchin
chacma
chimpanzee *or* chimp
colobus
douc
douroucouli
drill
flying lemur *or* colugo
gelada
gibbon
gorilla
green monkey
grivet
guenon
guereza
howler monkey
indris *or* indri
langur
lemur
loris
macaco
macaque
mandrill
mangabey
marmoset
mona
monkey *or* (*archaic*) jackanapes
orang-outang, orang-utan, *or* orang
proboscis monkey
rhesus monkey
saki
siamang
sifaka
spider monkey
squirrel monkey
talapoin
tamarin
tana
tarsier
titi
vervet
wanderoo

MOTOR SPORTS

autocross
drag racing
karting
motocross
motor-cycle racing
motor racing
motor rallying *or* rallying
rallycross
scrambling
speedway
stock car racing

MUSCLES

accelerator
accessorius
adductor
agonist
antagonist
arytenoid
biceps
buccinator
compressor
constrictor
contractor
corrugator
deltoid
depressor
digrastic
dilator
elevator
erector
evertor
extensor
flexor
gastrocnemius
gluteus *or* glutaeus
levator
lumbricalis
masseter
opponent
pectoral
peroneal muscle
pronator
psoas
quadriceps
rectus
retractor
rhomboideus
rotator
sartorius
scalenus
soleus
sphincter
supinator
suspensory *or* suspensor
tensor
trapezius
triceps

MUSES

Calliope	epic poetry
Clio	history
Erato	love poetry
Euterpe	lyric poetry and music
Melpomene	tragedy
Polyhymnia	singing, mime, and sacred dance
Terpsichore	dance and choral song
Thalia	comedy and pastoral poetry
Urania	astronomy

MUSHROOMS AND OTHER EDIBLE FUNGI

black truffle
blewit
button mushroom
cep *or* porcini
champignon
chanterelle
horn of plenty
meadow mushroom
morel
oyster mushroom
puffball
shaggy ink cap *or* lawyer's wig
shiitake mushroom
straw mushroom
white truffle
wood ear mushroom

MUSIC

CLASSICAL MUSIC GENRES

ars antiqua
ars nova
baroque
classical
early music
expressionist
galant
Gothic
impressionist
minimalist
music concrète
nationalist
neoclassical
post-romantic
Renaissance
rococo
romantic
salon music
serial music
twelve-tone *or* dodecaphonic

TYPES OF COMPOSITION

air
albumblatt
allemande
anthem
aria
bagatelle
ballade
ballet
barcarole
barceuse
bolero
bourrée
canon
cantata
canticle
canzona
canzone
canzonetta
capriccio
cavatina
chaconne
chorale
chorus
concertante
concertino
concerto
concerto grosso
concertstück
contredanse *or* contradance
czardas
dirge
divertimento
divertissement
duet
dumka
duo
ecossaise
elegy
étude
fantasy *or* fantasia
farandole
fugue
galliard
galop
gavotte
gigue
grand opera
hornpipe
humoresque
impromptu
interlude
lament
ländler
lied
madrigal
march
mass
mazurka
medley
minuet
motet
nocturne
nonet
notturno
octet
opera
opera buffa
opera seria
operetta
oratorio
overture
partita
part song
passacaglia
passepied
Passion
pastiche
pastorale
pavane
phantasy
pibroch
polka
polonaise
prelude
psalm
quadrille
quartet
quintet
raga
reel
Requiem
rhapsody
ricercar *or* ricercare
rigadoon *or* rigadoun
romance
scherzo
schottische
septet
serenade
sextet
sinfonia concertante
sinfonietta
Singspiel
sonata
sonatina
song
song cycle
strathspey
suite
symphonic poem
symphony
toccata
tone poem
trio
trio sonata
waltz

POPULAR MUSIC TYPES

acid house
acid jazz
acid rock
ambient
bebop
bhangra
bluebeat
bluegrass
blues
boogie-woogie
bop
bubblegum
Cajun
calypso
cool jazz
country and western
country blues
country rock
Cu-bop
death metal
disco
Dixieland
doo-wop
dub
folk music
folk rock
free jazz
funk
fusion
gangsta rap
glam rock
gospel
Goth
grunge
hardbop
hardcore
harmolodics
heavy metal
hip-hop
House
Indie
industrial
jazz
jazz-funk
jazz-rock
jungle
mainstream jazz
Merseybeat
modern jazz
Motown *(trademark)*
Muzak *(trademark)*
New Age
New Country
New Orleans jazz
new romantic
New Wave
P-funk
pop
progressive rock
psychobilly
punk
ragga
rap
rave
reggae
rhythm and blues
rock
rockabilly
rock and roll
salsa
ska
skiffle
soul
surf music
swing
swingbeat
techno
thrash metal
trad jazz
world music
zydeco

MUSICAL EXPRESSIONS AND TEMPO INSTRUCTIONS

Instruction	*Meaning*
accelerando	with increasing speed
adagio	slowly
agitato	in an agitated manner
allegretto	fairly quickly or briskly
allegro	quickly, in a brisk, lively manner
amoroso	lovingly
andante	at a moderately slow tempo
andantino	slightly faster than andante
animato	in a lively manner
appassionato	impassioned
assai	(in combination) very
calando	with gradually decreasing tone and speed
cantabile	in a singing style
con	(in combination) with
con affeto	with tender emotion
con amore	lovingly

Instruction	*Meaning*	*Instruction*	*Meaning*
con anima	with spirit	piano	softly
con brio	vigorously	più	(in combination) more
con fuoco	with fire	pizzicato	(in music for stringed instruments) to be plucked with the finger
con moto	quickly		
crescendo	gradual increase in loudness		
diminuendo	gradual decrease in loudness	poco *or* un poco	(in combination) a little
dolce	gently and sweetly		
doloroso	in a sorrowful manner	pomposo	in a pompous manner
energico	energetically	presto	very fast
espressivo	expressively	prestissimo	faster than presto
forte	loud or loudly	quasi	(in combination) almost, as if
fortissimo	very loud	rallentando	becoming slower
furioso	in a frantically rushing manner	rubato	with a flexible tempo
		scherzando	in jocular style
giocoso	merry	sciolto	free and easy
grave	solemn and slow	semplice	simple and unforced
grazioso	graceful	sforzando	with strong initial attack
lacrimoso	sad and mournful	smorzando	dying away
largo	slowly and broadly	sospirando	'sighing', plaintive
larghetto	slowly and broadly, but less so than largo	sostenuto	in a smooth and sustained manner
legato	smoothly and connectedly	sotto voce	extremely quiet
leggiero	light	staccato	(of notes) short, clipped, and separate
lento	slowly		
maestoso	majestically	strascinando	stretched out
marziale	martial	strepitoso	noisy
mezzo	(in combination) moderately	stringendo	with increasing speed
moderato	at a moderate tempo	tanto	(in combination) too much
molto	(in combination) very	tardo	slow
non troppo *or* non tanto	(in combination) not too much	troppo	(in combination) too much
		vivace	in a brisk lively manner
pianissimo	very quietly	volante	'flying', fast and light

RANKS OF NOBILITY

RANKS OF BRITISH NOBILITY (IN ORDER OF PRECEDENCE)

royal duke *or (fem.)* royal duchess
duke *or (fem.)* duchess
marquess *or* marquis *or (fem.)* marchioness
earl *or (fem.)* countess
viscount *or (fem.)* viscountess
baron *or (fem.)* baroness
baronet

RANKS OF FOREIGN NOBILITY

archduke *or (fem.)* archduchess
boyar
burgrave
count *or (fem.)* countess
grand duke *or (fem.)* grand duchess
grandee
landgrave *or (fem.)* landgravine
marchese *or (fem.)* marchesa
margrave *or (fem.)* margravine
marquis *or (fem.)* marquise
prince *or (fem.)* princess
vicomte *or (fem.)* vicomtesse

MUSICAL NOTES AND RESTS

British name	*American name*
breve	double-whole note
semibreve	whole note
minim	half note
crotchet	quarter note
quaver	eighth note
semiquaver	sixteenth note
demisemiquaver	thirty-second note
hemidemisemiquaver	sixty-fourth note

MUSLIM DENOMINATIONS AND SECTS

Alaouites *or* Alawites
Druse *or* Druze
Imami
Ismaili *or* Isma'ili
Nizari
Shiah, Shia *or* Shiite
Sufism
Sunni
Wahhabism *or* Wahabism
Zaidi

NUTS

almond
beech nut
brazil nut
butternut
cashew
chestnut
chinquapin, chincapin, *or* chinkapin
coco de mer
dwarf chestnut
earthnut *or* pignut
hazelnut, filbert, cobnut, *or* cob
macadamia (nut), Queensland nut, *or* bauple nut
marron
peanut, monkey nut, *or* groundnut
pecan
pine nut *or* pine kernel
pistachio
quandong
walnut

OILS

EDIBLE OILS

benne, gingili, *or* sesame
butyrin
corn
cottonseed
fixed
maize
nut
oleo
olive
palm
peanut
peppermint
soya
sunflower seed
vegetable

INDUSTRIAL OILS

benzaldehyde
banana *or* pentyl acetate
bone
crude
Chinese wood *or* tung
coal
colza
diesel
drying
fuel
fusel
glutaraldehyde
gas
heavy
linseed
mineral
neat's foot
paraffin
parathion
rapeseed
rosin
shale
sperm
stand
train
turpentine
whale oil

OILS USED IN PERFUME AND MEDICINE

attar
bergamot
cajuput
camphorated
castor
chaulmoogra
citronella
clove
coconut
cod-liver
croton
eucalyptus
evening primrose
jojoba
lavender
Macassar
musk
mustard
neroli
palm
patchouli
peanut
rapeseed
sandalwood
sassafras
savin
tea tree
wintergreen
ylang-ylang

INSTRUMENTS IN A FULL ORCHESTRA

cello *or* violoncello
violin
viola
double bass
piano
harp
piccolo
flute
oboe
cor anglais
contra-bassoon
bassoon
clarinet
french horn
trumpet
tuba
trombone
timpani
gong
bass-drum
xylophone
celesta
snare drum
tubular bells

TYPES OF PASTA

agnolotti
bavette
bombolotti
bucatini
cannelloni
cappelletti
cellentani
conchiglie
ditali
farfalle
fettuccine, fettucine, *or* fettucini
fusilli
gnocchetti
gnocchi
lasagne
lasagnette
linguine
lumache
macaroni

maultaschen
noodles
orecchiette
paglia e fieno
pappardelle
penne
pipe
ravioli
rigatoni
ruote
spaghetti
spätzle *or* spaetzle
tagliatelle
taglioni
tortellini
tortelloni
tortiglioni
vermicelli
zita *or* ziti

PEOPLES

AFRICAN PEOPLES

Bantu
Barotse
Basotho
Berber
Bushman
Chewa
Damara
Dinka
Duala
Edo
Eritrean
Ethiopian
Ewe
Gabonese
Galla
Gambian
Ghanaian *or* Ghanian
Griqua *or* Grikwa
Hausa
Herero
Hottentot
Hutu
Ibibio
Ibo *or* Igbo
Kabyle
Kikuyu
Kongo
Luba
Luo
Malinke *or* Maninke
Masai
Matabele
Moor
Mosotho
Mossi
Nama *or* Namaqua
Ndebele
Negrillo
Negro
Nguni
Nuba
Nupe
Nyanja
Nyoro
Ovambo
Pondo
Pygmy *or* Pigmy
Rif, Riff, *or* Rifi
Shangaan
Shluh
Shona
Somali
Songhai
Sotho
Strandloper
Susu
Swahili
Swazi
Temne
Tiv
Tsonga
Tswana
Tuareg
Tunisian
Tutsi
Venda
Watusi *or* Watutsi
Wolof
Xhosa
Yoruba
Zulu

ASIAN PEOPLES

Adivasi
Ainu
Akkadian *or* Accadian
Amalekite
Amorite
Andamanese
Arab
Babylonian
Bakhtyari
Baluchi *or* Balochi
Bashkir
Bedouin *or* Beduin
Bengali
Bihari
Burmese
Buryat
Chaldean *or* Chaldaean
Cham
Chinese
Chukchee *or* Chukchi
Chuvash
Cossack
Cumans
Dani
Dard
Dyak *or* Dayak
Elamite
Ephesian
Ephraimite
Essene
Evenki
Fulani
Gond
Gujarati *or* Gujerati
Gurkha
Hittite
Hui
Hun
Hurrian
Igorot *or* Igorrote
Israeli
Jat
Jewish
Kabardian
Kalmuck *or* Kalmyk
Kanarese *or* Canarese
Kara-Kalpak
Karen
Kashmiri
Kassite
Kazakh *or* Kazak
Khmer
Kurd
Lao
Lepcha
Lycian
Lydian
Malay
Maratha *or* Mahratta
Mede
Mishmi
Mon
Mongol
Montagnard
Moro
Motu
Munda
Naga
Negrito
Nogay
Nuri *or* Kafir
Palestinian
Pathan, Pashto, Pushto, *or* Pushtu
Phoenician
Punjabi *or* Panjabi
Sabaean *or* Sabean
Samoyed
Saracen
Semite
Shan
Sherpa
Sindhi
Sinhalese
Sogdian
Sumerian
Tadzhik, Tadjik, *or* Tajik
Tagalog
Talaing
Tamil
Tatar *or* Tartar
Thai
Tocharian *or* Tokharian
Tongan
Tungus
Turanian
Turk
Turkmen
Uigur *or* Uighur
Uzbek
Vedda *or* Veddah
Visayan *or* Bisayan
Yakut

AUSTRALASIAN PEOPLES

Aborigine
Aranda
Dayak
Gurindji
Māori
Melanesian
Polynesian
Tagalog

CENTRAL AND SOUTH AMERICAN INDIAN PEOPLES

- Araucanian
- Arawakan
- Aymara
- Aztec
- Carib
- Cashinahua
- Chibca
- Chimú
- Ge
- Guarani
- Inca
- Makuna
- Maya
- Mixtec
- Nahuatl
- Quechua, Kechua, *or* Quichua
- Toltec
- Tupi
- Zapotec

ESKIMO PEOPLES

- Aleut *or* Aleutian
- Caribou Eskimo
- Inuit *or* Innuit
- Yupik

EUROPEAN PEOPLES

- Achaean *or* Achaian
- Aeolian *or* Eolian
- Albanian
- Alemanni
- Andalusian
- Angle
- Anglo-Norman
- Anglo-Saxon
- Aragonese
- Armenian
- Aryan
- Ashkenazi
- Austrian
- Azerbaijani *or* Azeri
- Azorean
- Basque
- Bavarian
- Belgae
- Belorussian
- Bosnian Muslim
- Breton
- Briton
- Brython
- Bulgar
- Bulgarian
- Burgundian
- Carinthian
- Castilian
- Catalan
- Celt
- Celtiberi
- Chechen
- Cheremis *or* Cheremiss
- Cimbri
- Cornish
- Corsican
- Croatian *or* Croat
- Cymry *or* Kymry
- Czech
- Dane
- Dorian
- Dutch
- English
- Faeroese
- Finn
- Ephesian
- Estonian *or* Esthonian
- Etruscan *or* Etrurian
- Fleming
- Frank
- French
- Frisian
- Gaelic
- Galician
- Gascon
- Gaul
- Georgian
- German
- Goidel
- Goth
- Greek
- Gypsy *or* Gipsy
- Hellenic
- Iberian *or* Celtiberian
- Icelandic
- Iceni
- Illyrian
- Indo-European
- Ingush
- Ionian
- Irish
- Jute
- Karelian
- Komi
- Latin
- Lapp
- Latvian
- Lithuanian
- Lombard *or* Langobard
- Lusatian
- Luxembourger
- Macedonian
- Magyar
- Maltese
- Manx
- Montenegrin
- Mordvin
- Norman
- Norse
- Norwegian
- Ostrogoth
- Ostyak
- Pict
- Pole
- Portuguese
- Provençal
- Prussian
- Romanian
- Russian
- Sabellian
- Sabine
- Salain
- Samnite
- Samoyed
- Sardinian
- Saxon
- Scot
- Scythian
- Sephardi
- Serbian
- Sicilian
- Silures
- Slav
- Slovak
- Slovene
- Sorb
- Swabian
- Swede
- Swiss
- Teuton
- Thracian
- Turk
- Tyrolese
- Ugrian
- Ukrainian
- Vandal
- Viking
- Visigoth
- Vlach *or* Walach
- Volsci
- Votyak
- Walloon
- Welsh
- Wend

NATIVE AMERICAN TRIBES

- Abnaki
- Aguaruna
- Algonquian *or* Algonkian
- Algonquin *or* Algonkin
- Apache
- Apalachee
- Arapaho
- Araucan
- Arikara
- Ashochimi
- Assiniboine
- Athabascan
- Aymara
- Aztec
- Bella Coola
- Biloxi
- Blackfoot
- Blood
- Caddo
- Campa
- Carib
- Catawba
- Cayuga
- Cherokee
- Cheyenne
- Chickasaw
- Chilcal
- Chinook
- Chippewa *or* Chippeway
- Choctaw
- Cocopa
- Comanche
- Cree
- Creek
- Crow
- Dakota
- Delaware
- Dene
- Dogrib
- Flathead
- Fox
- Haida
- Hidatsa
- Hopi
- Hupa
- Huron
- Illinois
- Inca
- Iowa
- Iroquois
- Kansa
- Karankawa
- Kichai
- Kickapoo
- Kiowa
- Kootenay
- Kwakiutl
- Leni-Lenapé
- Lipan
- Mandan
- Mapuche
- Maya
- Menomini *or* Menominee
- Miami
- Micmac
- Minnetaree

Mixtec
Mohave *or* Mojave
Mohawk
Mohegan
Mohican *or* Mahican
Moki *or* Moqui
Montagnard
Muskogean *or* Muskhogean
Nahuatl
Narraganset
Natchez
Navaho *or* Navajo
Nez Percé
Nootka
Ojibwa *or* Ojibway
Omaha
Oneida
Onondaga
Orejone
Osage
Ostiak
Ottawa
Paiute
Pasamaquoddy
Pawnee
Penobscot
Pequot
Pericu
Piegan
Pima
Powhatan
Pueblo
Quakaw
Quechua, Quichua, *or* Kechua
Root-digger
Salish
Santee
Sarcee
Sauk
Seminole
Seneca
Shawnee
Shoshoni
Shushwap
Sioux
Stonies
Susquehanna
Teton
Tlingit
Toltec
Tonkawa
Tuscarora
Ute
Wappo
Warrau
Wichita
Winnebago
Wyandot
Yaqui
Yuchi
Yuma
Yunca
Zuni

PHILOSOPHY

PHILOSOPHICAL SCHOOLS AND DOCTRINES

animism
Aristotelianism
atomism
behaviourism
Cartesianism
conceptualism
Confucianism
consequentialism
conventionalism
critical realism
cynicism
deism
determinism
dualism
Eleaticism
empiricism
epicureanism
essentialism
existentialism
fatalism
fideism
hedonism
Hegelianism
humanism
idealism
immaterialism
Kantianism
logical atomism
logical positivism
Marxism
materialism
monism
neo-Platonism
nihilism
nominalism
phenomenalism
Platonism
pluralism
positivism
pragmatism
Pyrrhonism
Pythagoreanism
rationalism
realism
scepticism
scholasticism
sensationalism
Stoicism
structuralism
Taoism
theism
Thomism
utilitarianism
utopianism

PHOBIAS

Phobia	*Meaning*	*Phobia*	*Meaning*
acerophobia	sourness	atephobia	ruin
achluophobia	darkness	aulophobia	flute
acrophobia	heights	bacilliphobia	microbes
aerophobia	air	barophobia	gravity
agoraphobia	open spaces	basophobia	walking
aichurophobia	points	batrachophobia	reptiles
ailurophobia	cats	belonephobia	needles
akousticophobia	sound	bibliophobia	books
algophobia	pain	brontophobia	thunder
amakaphobia	carriages	cancerophobia	cancer
amathophobia	dust	cheimaphobia	cold
androphobia	men	chionophobia	snow
anemophobia	wind	chrematophobia	money
anginophobia	narrowness	chronophobia	duration
anthropophobia	man	chrystallophobia	crystals
antlophobia	flood	claustrophobia	closed spaces
apeirophobia	infinity	cnidophobia	stings
aquaphobia	water	cometophobia	comets
arachnophobia	spiders	cromophobia	colour
asthenophobia	weakness	cyberphobia	computers
astraphobia	lightning	cynophobia	dogs

Phobia	Meaning
demonophobia	demons
demophobia	crowds
dermatophobia	skin
dikephobia	justice
doraphobia	fur
eisoptrophobia	mirrors
electrophobia	electricity
enetephobia	pins
entomophobia	insects
eosophobia	dawn
eremophobia	solitude
ereuthophobia	blushing
ergasiophobia	work
genophobia	sex
geumaphobia	taste
graphophobia	writing
gymnophobia	nudity
gynophobia	women
hadephobia	hell
haematophobia	blood
hamartiophobia	sin
haptophobia	touch
harpaxophobia	robbers
hedonophobia	pleasure
helminthophobia	worms
hodophobia	travel
homichlophobia	fog
homophobia	homosexuals
hormephobia	shock
hydrophobia	water
hypegiaphobia	responsibility
hypnophobia	sleep
ideophobia	ideas
kakorraphiaphobia	failure
katagelophobia	ridicule
kenophobia	void
kinesophobia	motion
kleptophobia	stealing
kopophobia	fatigue
kristallophobia	ice
laliophobia	stuttering
linonophobia	string
logophobia	words
lyssophobia	insanity
maniaphobia	insanity
mastigophobia	flogging
mechanophobia	machinery
metallophobia	metals
meteorophobia	meteors
misophobia	contamination
monophobia	one thing
musicophobia	music
musophobia	mice
necrophobia	corpses
nelophobia	glass
neophobia	newness

Phobia	Meaning
nephophobia	clouds
nosophobia	disease
nyctophobia	night
ochlophobia	crowds
ochophobia	vehicles
odontophobia	teeth
oikophobia	home
olfactophobia	smell
ommatophobia	eyes
oneirophobia	dreams
ophidiophobia	snakes
ornithophobia	birds
ouranophobia	heaven
panphobia	everything
pantophobia	everything
parthenophobia	girls
pathophobia	disease
peniaphobia	poverty
phasmophobia	ghosts
phobophobia	fears
photophobia	light
pnigerophobia	smothering
poinephobia	punishment
polyphobia	many things
potophobia	drink
pteronophobia	feathers
pyrophobia	fire
Russophobia	Russia
rypophobia	soiling
Satanophobia	Satan
selaphobia	flesh
siderophobia	stars
sitophobia	food
spermaphobia	germs
spermatophobia	germs
stasiphobia	standing
stygiophobia	hell
taphephobia	being buried alive
technophobia	technology
teratophobia	giving birth to a monster
thaasophobia	sitting
thalassophobia	sea
thanatophobia	death
theophobia	God
thermophobia	heat
tonitrophobia	thunder
toxiphobia	poison
tremophobia	trembling
triskaidekaphobia	thirteen
xenophobia	strangers *or* foreigners
zelophobia	jealousy
zoophobia	animals

PHYSICS

BRANCHES OF PHYSICS

acoustics
aerodynamics
aerostatics
applied physics
astrophysics
atomic physics
biophysics
condensed-matter physics *or* solid-state physics
cosmology
cryogenics *or* low-temperature physics
dynamics
electromagnetism
electronics
electrostatics
geophysics
harmonics
high-energy physics *or* particle physics
kinetics
macrophysics
magnetics *or* magnetism
magnetostatics
mechanics
mesoscopics
microphysics
nuclear physics
nucleonics
optics
photometry
pneumatics
quantum mechanics
quantum physics
rheology
solar physics
sonics
spectroscopy
statistical mechanics
statics
superaerodynamics
theoretical physics
thermodynamics
thermometry
thermostatics
ultrasonics

PHYSICS TERMS

acceleration
alternating current
ampere
amplifier
angstrom
anion
antimatter
atom
baryon
becquerel
Boyle's law
Brownian motion
cacion
calorie
capacitance
cathode ray
centre of gravity
centrifugal force
centripetal force
charge
Charles' law
conductor
convection
cosmic ray
coulomb
current
cyclotron
decibel
density
diffraction
diffusion
diode
direct current
Doppler effect
earth
electricity
electromotive force
electron
energy
farad
field
fission
fluorescence
force
frequency
friction
fuse
fusion
gamma ray
generator
gravity
half-life
hertz
hyperon
impetus
inductance
inertia
infrared
joule
kelvin
kinetic energy
laser
lens
lepton
luminescence
mass
matter
meson
microwave
moment
momentum
muon
neutrino
neutron
newton
nucleon
nucleus
ohm
Ohm's law
particle
pascal
Planck constant *or* Planck's constant
potential difference
potential energy
proton
quantum
radiation
radioactivity
radio wave
red shift
reflection
refraction
relativity
resistance
rutherford
semiconductor
simple harmonic motion
spectrum
static electricity
subatomic particle
super-conductivity
superfluidity
surface tension
tau particle
tension
terminal velocity
thermostat
transformer
transistor
ultraviolet
vacuum
velocity
viscosity
volt
watt
wave
wavelength
x-ray

BREEDS OF PIG

Berkshire
Cheshire
Chester White
Duroc
Gloucester Old Spot
Hampshire
Landrace
Large Black
Large White
Middle White
Pietrain
Saddleback
Small White
Tamworth
Vietnamese pot-bellied
Welsh

PLANETS

Earth
Jupiter
Mars
Mercury
Neptune
Saturn
Uranus
Venus

PARTS OF PLANTS

androecium
anther
anthophore
blossom
bract
bud
bulbil
calyx
capitulum
carpel
carpophore
catkin
caulis
clinandrium
commissure
corolla
corymb
costa
cyathium
cyme
dichasium
epidermis
filament
floral envelope
floret
foliage
fruit
gametophore
guard cell
glume
gynoecium
head
hibernaculum
hypanthium
inflorescence
internode
involucel
involucre
joint
leaf
lemma
lip
micropyle
monochasium
nectary
nucellus
offshoot
ovary
ovule
palea
panicle
pedicel
peduncle
perianth
petal
phloem
pistil
placenta
pod
pollen
pollen grain
pollinium
raceme
rachis
receptacle, thalamus, *or* torus
root
root cap
root hair
secundine
seed
seed pod
sepal
sheath
spadix
spathe
spike
spikelet
spur
stamen
stem
stigma
stoma
style
taproot
tassel
tepal
umbel
vascular bundle
xylem

POETRY

POETRY AND PROSODY TERMS

accentual metre
accentual-syllabic metre *or* stress-syllabic metre
Adonic
Alcaic
Alexandrine
alliteration
amoebaean *or* amoebean
amphibrach
amphimacer
anacrusis
anapaest *or* anapest
anapaestic *or* anapestic
antistrophe
arsis
assonance
bacchius
ballad stanza
blank verse
bob
cadence *or* cadency
caesura *or* cesura
canto
catalectic
choriamb *or* choriambus
closed couplet
common measure
common metre
consonance *or* consonancy
couplet
cretic *or* amphimacer
dactyl
dactylic
diaeresis *or* dieresis
dipody
distich
elision
end-stopped
enjambement
envoy *or* envoi
epode
eye rhyme
feminine ending
feminine rhyme
foot
free verse *or* vers libre
half-rhyme
hemistich
heptameter
heptastich
heroic couplet
hexameter
hypermeter
iamb *or* iambus
iambic
ictus
internal rhyme
ionic
jabberwocky
leonine rhyme
long metre
macaronic
masculine ending
masculine rhyme
metre
octameter
octave *or* octet
onomatopoeia
ottava rima
paeon
paeonic
pararhyme
pentameter
pentastich
perfect rhyme *or* full rhyme
Pindaric
pyhrric
quantitative metre
quatrain
quintain *or* quintet
refrain
rhyme
rhyme royal
rhyme scheme
rhythm
rime riche
Sapphic
scansion
septet
sestet
sestina *or* sextain
short metre
Spenserian stanza
spondee
spondaic
sprung rhythm
stanza
stichic
strophe
syllabic metre
tercet
terza rima
tetrabrach
tetrameter
tetrapody
tetrastich
triplet
trochaic
trochee
unstopped
verse paragraph
wheel

POETRY MOVEMENTS AND GROUPINGS

Alexandrians	imagists	Metaphysical Poets	Romantics
Decadents	Lake Poets	the Movement	Scottish Chaucerians
Georgian Poets	Liverpool Poets	Petrarchans	symbolists

POISONS

POISONOUS SUBSTANCES AND GASES

aconite	carbon monoxide	mercuric chloride	prussic acid
acrolein	coniine, conin, *or* conine	mercuric oxide	ratsbane
adamsite	curare	methanol	red lead
afterdamp	cyanic acid	methyl bromide	sarin
Agent Orange	cyanide	muscarine	silver nitrate
aldrin	cyanogen	mustard gas	sodium cyanide
allyl alcohol	digitalin	nerve gas	sodium fluoroacetate
aniline	emetine	nitrogen dioxide	stibine
antimony potassium tartrate	formaldehyde	osmium tetroxide	strychnine
arsenic *or* arsenic trioxide	hemlock	ouabain	tetramethyldiarsine
arsine	hydrastine	oxalic acid	thallium
atropine *or* atropin	hydrogen cyanide	Paraquat	thebaine
barium hydroxide	hydrogen fluoride	Paris green	tropine
benzene	hydrogen iodide	phenol	urushiol
benzidine	hydrogen sulphide	phosgene	veratrine
brucine	hyoscyamine	picrotoxin	whitedamp
cacodyl	lead monoxide	poison gas	zinc chloride
carbon disulphide	lewisite	potassium cyanide	
	lindane	potassium permanganate	

TYPES OF POISONING

botulism	fluorosis	listeriosis	ptomaine poisoning
bromism	hydrargyria	mercurialism	salmonella
digitalism	iodism	phosphorism	saturnism
ergotism	lead poisoning	plumbism	strychninism

POISONOUS PLANTS

aconite	destroying angel	manchineel	sassy, sasswood, *or* sassy wood
amanita	dieffenbachia	monkshood	staggerbush
baneberry	dog's mercury	mountain laurel	stavesacre
belladonna	ergot	Noogoora burr	thorn apple
black bryony	fly agaric	nux vomica	tutu
black nightshade	foxglove	oleander	upas
castor-oil plant	hemlock	poison dogwood *or* elder	water hemlock
cowbane	henbane	poison ivy	wolfsbane *or* wolf's-bane
coyotillo	Indian liquorice	poison oak	woody nightshade
deadly nightshade	laburnum	poison sumach	
death camass	liberty cap	pokeweed, pokeberry, *or* pokeroot	
death cap *or* angel	locoweed		

BIRDS OF PREY

accipiter	bateleur eagle	condor	falcon *or* (*N.Z.*) bush-hawk *or* karearea
Australian goshawk *or* chicken hawk	boobook	Cooper's hawk	falconet
bald eagle	brown owl	duck hawk	golden eagle
barn owl	buzzard	eagle	
	caracara	eagle-hawk *or* wedge-tailed eagle	

goshawk
gyrfalcon *or* gerfalcon
harrier
hawk
hawk owl
hobby
honey buzzard
hoot owl
horned owl
kestrel
kite
lammergeier, lammergeyer, bearded vulture, *or* *(archaic)* ossifrage
lanner
little owl
long-eared owl
merlin
Montagu's harrier
mopoke *or* *(N.Z.)* ruru
osprey, fish eagle, *or* *(archaic)* ossifrage
owl
peregrine falcon
red kite *or* *(archaic)* gled(e)
rough-legged buzzard
saker
screech owl
sea eagle, erne, *or* ern
secretary bird
snowy owl
sparrowhawk
tawny owl
turkey buzzard *or* vulture
vulture

PROGRAMMING LANGUAGES

Ada
Algol
BASIC *or* Basic
C
C++
C#
COBOL *or* Cobol
FORTH *or* Forth
FORTRAN *or* Fortran
Haskell
Java
LISP
LOGO
Pascal
Perl
PL/1
Postscript
PROLOG *or* Prolog
RPG
Simula
Smalltalk
SNOBOL
SQL

PROTEINS

actin
actomyosin
aleurone
alpha-fetoprotein
amyloid
apoprotein
avidin
calmodulin
caseinogen
conchiolin
dystrophin
factor VIII
ferritin
fibrin
fibrinogen
fibroin
flagellin
gliadin
globin
gluten
hordein
keratin
lactalbumin
lactoprotein
lectin
legumin
leptin
lymphokine
myosin
opsin
ossein
prion
properdin
ricin
sclerotin
sericin
spongin
thrombogen
vitellin
zein

PSYCHOLOGY

BRANCHES OF PSYCHOLOGY

analytic psychology
child psychology
clinical psychology
comparative psychology
developmental psychology
educational psychology
experimental psychology
hedonics
industrial psychology
neuropsychology
organizational psychology
parapsychology
psychiatry
psycholinguistics
psychometrics
psychophysics
psychophysiology
social psychology

PSYCHOLOGY TERMS

alter ego
anal
analysis
angst
anxiety
complex
compulsion
conditioning
consciousness
death wish
delusion
dementia
depression
ego
Electra complex
extrovert
fixation
Freudian slip
Gestalt therapy
group therapy
hypnosis
hypochondria
hysteria
id
inferiority complex
introvert
mania
mind
neurosis
obsession
Oedipus complex
paranoia
persecution complex
persona
personality
personality disorder
phobia
primal therapy *or* primal scream therapy
psyche
psychoanalysis
psychosis
psychosomatic
regression
repression
Rorschach test *or* inkblot test
schizophrenia
self
stress
subconscious
sublimation
superego
syndrome
trauma
unconscious

RELIGION

RELIGIONS

animism
Babi *or* Babism
Baha'ism
Buddhism
Christianity
Confucianism
druidism
heliolatry
Hinduism *or* Hindooism
Islam
Jainism
Judaism
Macumba
Manichaeism *or* Manicheism
Mithraism *or* Mithraicism
Orphism
paganism
Rastafarianism
Ryobu Shinto
Santeria
Satanism
Scientology *(trademark)*
shamanism
Shango
Shembe
Shinto
Sikhism
Taoism
voodoo *or* voodooism
Yezidis
Zoroastrianism *or* Zoroastrism

RELIGIOUS BOOKS

Adi Granth
Apocrypha
Atharveda
Ayurveda
Bhagavad-Gita
Bible
Book of Mormon
Granth *or* Guru Granth Sahib
I Ching
Koran *or* Quran
Li Chi
Lu
Mahabharata
New Testament
Old Testament
Ramayana
Rigveda
Samaveda
Shi Ching
Siddhanta
Su Ching
Talmud
Tipitaka
Torah
Tripitaka
Veda
Yajurveda

RELIGIOUS BUILDINGS

abbey
bethel
cathedral
chapel
church
convent
gurdwara
Kaaba
marae
monastery
mosque
synagogue
tabernacle
temple

RELIGIOUS CLOTHING

alb
almuce
amice
biretta *or* berretta
calotte
canonicals
capuche *or* capouche
cassock
chasuble
chimere, chimer, *or* chimar
clerical collar
clericals
coif
cope
cornet
cotta
cowl
dalmatic
dog collar *(informal)*
gremial
guimpe
habit
infulae
maniple
mantelletta
mitre
mozzetta *or* mozetta
pallium
peplos *or* peplus
pontificals
rochet
scapular
shovel hat
soutane
superhumeral
surcingle
surplice
tippet
wimple
zucchetto

RELIGIOUS FESTIVALS

Advent
Al Hijrah
Ascension Day
Ash Wednesday
Baisakhi
Bodhi Day
Candlemas
Chanukah *or* Hanukkah
Ching Ming
Christmas
Corpus Christi
Day of Atonement
Dhammacakka
Diwali
Dragon Boat Festival
Dussehra
Easter
Eid ul-Adha *or* Id-ul-Adha
Eid ul-Fitr *or* Id-ul-Fitr
Epiphany
Feast of Tabernacles
Good Friday
Guru Nanak's Birthday
Hirja
Hola Mohalla
Holi
Janamashtami
Lailat ul-Barah
Lailat ul-Isra Wal Mi'raj
Lailat ul-Qadr
Lent
Mahashivaratri
Maundy Thursday
Michaelmas
Moon Festival
Palm Sunday
Passion Sunday
Passover
Pentecost
Pesach
Purim
Quadragesima
Quinquagesima
Raksha Bandhan
Ramadan
Rama Naumi
Rogation
Rosh Hashanah
Septuagesima
Sexagesima
Shavuot
Shrove Tuesday
Sukkoth *or* Succoth
Trinity
Wesak
Whitsun
Winter Festival
Yom Kippur
Yuan Tan

REPTILES

adder
agama
agamid
alligator
amphisbaena
anaconda *or* (*Caribbean*) camoodi
anole
asp
bandy-bandy
black snake *or* red-bellied black snake
blind snake
blue racer
blue tongue
boa
boa constrictor
boomslang
box turtle
brown snake *or* (*Austral.*) mallee snake
bull snake *or* gopher snake
bushmaster
carpet snake *or* python
cayman *or* caiman
cerastes
chameleon
chuckwalla
cobra
cobra de capello
constrictor
copperhead
coral snake
crocodile
death adder *or* deaf adder
diamondback, diamondback terrapin, *or* diamondback turtle
diamond snake *or* diamond python
dugite *or* dukite
elapid
fer-de-lance
flying lizard *or* flying dragon
freshwater crocodile *or* (*Austral. informal*) freshy
frill-necked lizard, frilled lizard, bicycle lizard, cycling lizard, *or* (*Austral. informal*) frillie
gaboon viper
galliwasp
garter snake
gavial, gharial, *or* garial
gecko
giant tortoise
Gila monster
glass snake
goanna, bungarra (*Austral.*), *or* go (*Austral. informal*)
grass snake
green turtle
habu
harlequin snake
hawksbill *or* hawksbill turtle
hognose snake *or* puff adder
hoop snake
horned toad *or* lizard
horned viper
iguana
indigo snake
jew lizard, bearded lizard, *or* bearded dragon
kabaragoya *or* Malayan monitor
king cobra *or* hamadryad
king snake
Komodo dragon *or* Komodo lizard
krait
leatherback *or* (*Brit.*) leathery turtle
leguan
lizard
loggerhead *or* loggerhead turtle
mamba
massasauga
milk snake
moloch, thorny devil, thorn lizard, *or* mountain devil
monitor
mud turtle
ngarara (*N.Z.*)
perentie *or* perenty
pit viper
puff adder
python
racer
rat snake
rattlesnake *or* (*U.S. & Canad. informal*) rattler
ringhals
rock snake, rock python, amethystine python, *or* Schneider python
saltwater crocodile *or* (*Austral. informal*) saltie
sand lizard
sand viper
sea snake
sidewinder
skink
slowworm *or* blindworm
smooth snake
snake
snapping turtle
soft-shelled turtle
swift
taipan
terrapin
tiger snake
tokay
tortoise
tree snake
tuatara *or* (*technical*) sphenodon (*N.Z.*)
turtle
viper
wall lizard
water moccasin, moccasin, *or* cottonmouth
water snake
whip snake
worm lizard

RICE AND OTHER CEREALS

arborio rice
basmati rice
bran
brown rice
bulgur wheat
corn
couscous
Indian rice *or* wild rice
long grain rice
maize
millet
oatmeal
oats
Patna rice
ragi
sago
short grain rice
tapioca
wheat
wild rice

TYPES OF ROCK

andesite
anorthosite
anthracite
arkose
basalt
breccia
chalk
chert
clay
coal
conglomerate
diorite
dolerite
dolomite
dunite
eclogite
felsite *or* felstone
flint
gabbro
gneiss

granite
granodiorite
gravel
greywacke *or* (*U.S.*) graywacke
grit
hornblendite
hornfels
lamprophyre
lava
lignite
limestone
loess
marble
monzonite
mudstone
obsidian
pegmatite
peridotite
perknite
phyllite
pitchstone
pumice
pyroxenite
quartzite
rhyolite
sandstone
schist
shale
skarn
slate
soapstone
syenite
trachyte

RODENTS

acouchi *or* acouchy
agouti
beaver
black rat
brown rat *or* Norway rat
cane rat
capybara
cavy
chinchilla
chipmunk
coypu *or* nutria
deer mouse
desert rat
dormouse
fieldmouse
flying squirrel
fox squirrel
gerbil, gerbille, *or* jerbil
gopher *or* pocket gopher
gopher *or* ground squirrel
grey squirrel
groundhog *or* woodchuck
ground squirrel *or* gopher
guinea pig *or* cavy
hamster
harvest mouse
hedgehog
hopping mouse *or* jerboa rat
house mouse
jerboa
jumping mouse
kangaroo rat
kiore (*N.Z.*)
lemming
Māori rat *or* (*N.Z.*) kiore
mara
marmot
mole rat
mouse
muskrat *or* musquash
paca
pack rat
pocket mouse
porcupine
rat
red squirrel *or* chickaree
spinifex hopping mouse *or* (*Austral.*) dargawarra
springhaas
squirrel
suslik *or* souslik
taguan
tucotuco
viscacha *or* vizcacha
vole
water rat
water vole *or* water rat
white-footed mouse
white rat

RUGBY TERMS

back
back row
ball
centre
conversion
crossbar
drop goal
lock forward
loose forward
loose head
five-eighth (*Austral.*) (*N.Z.*)
flanker *or* wing forward (*Rugby union*)
forward
front row
full back
garryowen (*Rugby union*)
goalpost
half back
hooker
knock on
line-out (*Rugby union*)
mark (*Rugby union*)
maul (*Rugby union*)
number eight forward (*Rugby union*)
scrum *or* scrummage
stand-off half, fly half, *or* outside half
pack
pass
penalty
prop forward
punt
referee
ruck (*Rugby union*)
scrum half
second row
tackle
three-quarter
tight head
touch judge
try
up and under (*Rugby league*)
winger

RULERS

TITLES OF RULERS

amir *or* ameer
archduke
Caesar
caliph, calif, kalif, *or* khalif
chief
Chogyal
Dalai Lama
doge
duke
emir
emperor *or* (*fem.*) empress
Gaekwar *or* Gaikwar
Great Mogul
hospodar
imam *or* imaum
Inca
kabaka
Kaiser

khan
khedive
king
maharajah *or* maharaja
maharani *or* maharanee
mikado
nawab *or* nabob
Negus
Nizam
oba
pasha *or* pacha
Pharaoh
podesta
pope
queen
rajah *or* raja
rani *or* ranee
satrap
shah
sheik *or* sheikh
sherif, shereef, *or* sharif
shogun
stadholder *or* stadtholder
sultan
tenno
tsar *or* czar
viceroy *or (fem.)* vicereine

FAMOUS RULERS

Alexander the Great
Alfred the Great
Idi Amin
Augustus
Bismarck
Boudicca
Caligula
Castro
Catherine the Great
Charlemagne
Churchill
Cleopatra
Cromwell
de Gaulle
Edward the Confessor
Elizabeth I
Elizabeth II
Franco
Genghis Khan
Haile Selassie
Herod
Hirohito
Hitler
Ivan the Terrible
Julius Caesar
Kublai Khan
Lenin
Louis XIV
Mao Ze Dong *or* Mao Tse-tung
Montezuma
Mussolini
Napoleon Bonaparte
Nasser
Nero
Nicholas II
Pericles

SAUCES

apple
à la king
barbecue
Béarnaise
béchamel
black bean
bolognese *or* bolognaise
Bordelaise
brandy butter *or* hard sauce
bread
brown
chasseur
chaudfroid
cheese
chilli
chocolate
chow-chow
coulis
cranberry
cream
creole
cumberland
curry
custard
French dressing
fudge
gravy
hoisin
hollandaise
horseradish
ketchup
mayonnaise
Melba sauce
mint
mornay
mousseline
nam pla *or* fish sauce
orange
oyster
pesto
piccalilli
red pesto
rémoulade
Russian dressing
sabayon
salad cream
salad dressing
salsa
salsa verde
soubise
soy sauce, shoyu, *or* tamari
suprême
sweet-and-sour
Tabasco *(trademark)*
tartare
tomato
velouté
verjuice sauce
vinaigrette
white
wine
Worcester *or* Worcestershire

SEA BIRDS

albatross *or (informal)* gooney bird
auk
auklet
black-backed gull
black guillemot
black shag *or* kawau *(N.Z.)*
blue penguin, korora *or* little blue penguin *(N.Z.)*
blue shag *(N.Z.)*
booby *(Austral.)*
caspian tern *or* taranui *(N.Z.)*
coot
cormorant
fairy penguin, little penguin, *or (N.Z.)* korora
fish hawk
fulmar
gannet
glaucous gull
guillemot
gull *or (archaic or dialect)* cob(b)
herring gull
ivory gull
kittiwake
man-of-war bird *or* frigate bird
murrelet
old squaw *or* oldwife
oystercatcher
petrel
prion
razorbill *or* razor-billed auk
scoter
sea duck
sea eagle, erne, *or* ern
seagull
shearwater
short-tailed shearwater, (Tasmanian) mutton bird, *or (N.Z.)* titi
skua

storm petrel, stormy petrel, *or* Mother Carey's chicken
surf scoter *or* surf duck
takapu *(N.Z.)*
velvet scoter
wandering albatross
white-fronted tern, black cap, kahawai bird, sea swallow *or* tara *(N.Z.)*
Wilson's petrel

SEAFOOD

abalone
anchovy
Balmain bug *(Austral.)*
banana prawn *(Austral.)*
barramundi
bass
blackfish
bloater
blue cod
blue swimmer, blue manna, *or* sand crab *(Austral.)*
bonito
bream
brill
butterfish
callop
carp
catfish
clam
clappy-doo *or* clabby-doo *(Scot.)*
cockle
coalfish *or* saithe
cockle
cod
codling
crab
crayfish, crawfish, *or (N.Z.)* koura
crayfish, craybob, craydab, crawbob, clawchie, lobster, marron, *or* yabby *(Austral.)*
dab
dogfish
dorado
Dover sole
Dublin Bay prawn
eel
flounder
gemfish
grayling
Greenland halibut
haddock
hake
halibut
herring
huss
jewfish
John Dory
kahawai *or* Australian salmon
kingfish
king prawn
kipper
langoustine
lemon sole
ling
lobster
lumpfish
mackerel
marron
megrim
monkfish
Moreton Bay bug *or* shovel-nosed lobster *(Austral.)*
morwong
mud crab
mullet
mulloway
mussel
nannygai
Norway lobster
octopus
oyster
parrotfish
perch
pike
pilchard *or (Austral. informal)* pillie
pipi
plaice
pollack
pomfret
pout
prawn
queenie *or* queen scallop
rainbow trout
redfish
red snapper
roach
rockfish
salmon
sardine
scallop *or* scollop
school prawn *(Austral.)*
sea cucumber
shad
shark
shrimp
sild
skate
skipjack tuna
snapper
snoek
snook
sockeye *or* red salmon
sole
sprat
squid
swordfish
tarakihi *or* terakihi
teraglin
tiger prawn
tilefish
trevally *(Austral.) (N.Z.)*
trout
tuna *or* tunny
turbot
wahoo
whelk
whitebait
whiting
winkle
witch
wolffish
yabby *or* yabbie *(Austral.)*
yellow belly *(Austral.)*
zander

SEA MAMMALS

dugong
eared seal
earless seal
elephant seal
harp seal
hooded seal
manatee
sea cow
seal
sea lion
walrus *or (archaic)* sea horse

SEASONS

Season	*Related adjective*	*Season*	*Related adjective*
spring	vernal	autumn	autumnal
summer	aestival *or* estival	winter	hibernal *or* hiemal

SEXUAL PRACTICES AND TERMS

adultery
afterplay
algolagnia
anal intercourse, sodomy, *or* buggery
anilingus
autoeroticism
bagpiping
bestiality
bisexuality
bondage
coprophilia
cottaging
cunnilingus
felching
fellatio
fetishism
fisting *or* fist-fucking
flagellation
foreplay
fornication
frottage
heterosexuality
homosexuality
impotence
incest
lesbianism
masochism
masturbation
narcissism
necrophilia
nymphomania
oral sex
paedophilia
paraphilia
pederasty
premature ejaculation
rimming
rough trade
sadism
sadomasochism *or* S&M
safe sex
satyriasis
scopophilia
shrimping
soixante-neuf *or* sixty-nine
tribadism
troilism
voyeurism
water sports, urolagnia, *or* golden shower
zoophilia

SHAKESPEARE

PLAYS OF SHAKESPEARE

All's Well that Ends Well
Antony and Cleopatra
As You Like It
The Comedy of Errors
Coriolanus
Cymbeline
Hamlet
Henry IV Part I
Henry IV Part II
Henry V
Henry VI Part I
Henry VI Part II
Henry VI Part III
Henry VIII
Julius Caesar
King John
King Lear
Love's Labour's Lost
Macbeth
Measure for Measure
The Merchant of Venice
The Merry Wives of Windsor
A Midsummer Night's Dream
Much Ado About Nothing
Othello
Pericles, Prince of Tyre
Richard II
Richard III
Romeo and Juliet
The Taming of the Shrew
The Tempest
Timon of Athens
Titus Andronicus
Troilus and Cressida
Twelfth Night
The Two Gentlemen of Verona
The Winter's Tale

POEMS OF SHAKESPEARE

The Passionate Pilgrim
The Phoenix and the Turtle
The Rape of Lucrece
Sonnets
Venus and Adonis

SHARKS

angel shark, angelfish, *or* monkfish
basking shark, sailfish *or* *(N.Z.)* reremai
blue pointer *or* *(N.Z.)* blue shark *or* blue whaler
bronze whaler *(Austral.)*
carpet shark *or* *(Austral.)* wobbegong
cow shark *or* six-gilled shark
dogfish *or* *(Austral.)* dog shark
grey nurse shark
gummy (shark)
hammerhead
mako
nursehound
nurse shark
porbeagle *or* mackerel shark
requiem shark
school shark *(Austral.)*
seven-gill shark *(Austral.)*
shovelhead
soupfin *or* soupfin shark
thrasher *or* thresher shark
tiger shark
tope
whale shark
whaler shark

BREEDS OF SHEEP

Beulah Speckled-face
bighorn *or* mountain sheep
Blackface
Black Welsh Mountain
Blue-faced *or* Hexham Leicester
Border Leicester
Boreray
Brecknock Hill Cheviot
British Bleu du Maine
British Charollais
British Friesland
British Milksheep
British Oldenburg
British Texel
British Vendéen
Cambridge
Cheviot
Clun Forest
Colbred
Corriedale
Cotswold
Dalesbred
Dartmoor
Derbyshire Gritstone
Devon and Cornwall Longwool
Devon Closewool
Dorset Down
Dorset Horn
East Friesland
English Halfbred
Exmoor Horn
Hampshire Down
Hebridian *or* St. Kilda
Herdwick
Hill Radnor
Île de France
Jacob
karakul, caracul, *or* broadtail
Kerry Hill
Leicester Longwool
Lincoln Longwool
Llanwenog
Lleyn
Lonk
Manx Loghtan
Masham
Merino
Mule
Norfolk Horn
North Country Cheviot
Orkney *or* North Ronaldsay
Oxford *or* Oxfordshire Down
Polwarth
Portland
Rambouillet
Romney Marsh
Rouge de l'Ouest
Rough Fell
Ryeland
Scottish Blackface
Scottish Halfbred
Shetland
Shropshire
Soay
Southdown
South Wales Mountain
Suffolk
Swaledale
Teeswater
Texel
Welsh Halfbred
Welsh Hill Speckled
Welsh Mountain
Welsh Mountain Badger Faced
Welsh Mule
Wensleydale Longwool
White Face Dartmoor
Whitefaced Woodland
Wiltshire Horn

SHELLFISH

banana prawn *(Austral.)*
blue swimmer, blue manna, *or* sand crab *(Austral.)*
clam
clappy-doo *or* clabby-doo *(Scot.)*
cockle
crab
crayfish, crawfish, *or (N.Z.)* koura
crayfish, craybob, craydab, crawbob, clawchie, lobster, marron, *or* yabby *(Austral.)*
Dublin Bay prawn
freshwater shrimp
king prawn
langoustine
lobster
Moreton Bay bug *or* shovel-nosed lobster *(Austral.)*
mud crab
mussel
Norway lobster
oyster
prawn
scallop *or* scollop
school prawn *(Austral.)*
soldier crab

SHOES AND BOOTS

ankle boot
arctic *(U.S.)*
Balmoral
biker boot
blucher *(obsolete)*
bootee
bottine
bovver boot *(Brit.) (slang)*
brogan
brogue
brothel creeper *(informal)*
buskin
chopine *or* chopin
chukka boot
clog
co-respondent
cothurnus *or* cothurn
court shoe
cowboy boot
creeper *(informal)*
crowboot
deck shoe
Doc Marten *(trademark)*
espadrille
field boot
flat *or* flatty
flip-flop
football boot
gaiter *or* spat
galosh
ghillie *(Scot.)*
golf shoe
gumboot
gumshoe
gym shoe
half boot
Hessian boot
high heel
hobnail boot
jackboot

Jandal (*N.Z.*) (*trademark*)
kitten heel
lace-up
larrigan
loafer
moccasin
moonboot
mukluk
mule
overshoe
Oxford
pantofle, pantoffle, *or* pantoufle (*archaic*)
platform
plimsoll *or* plimsole
pump
racket *or* racquet
running shoe
rock boot
sabot
sandal
sandshoe
scuff
slingback
slip-on
slipper
sneaker
snowshoe
spike
stiletto
surgical boot
tennis shoe
thigh boot
top boot
track shoe
training shoe *or* trainer
veldskoen
wader
wedge *or* wedge heel
welly
Wellington boot
winkle-picker

SHREWS AND OTHER INSECTIVORES

desman
elephant shrew
mole
moon rat
shrew *or* shrewmouse
shrew mole
solenodon
star-nosed mole
tenrec
tree shrew
water shrew

SHRUBS

acacia
acanthus
arbutus
banksia
bauera
bilberry
black boy, yacca (bush), *or* yacka (*Austral.*)
blackcurrant
blackthorn
blueberry
bluebush
boronia
bottlebrush (*Austral.*)
box
bramble
briar *or* brier
broom
buckthorn
buddleia
camellia
caper
Christmas bush (*Austral.*)
clematis
coca
correa
cotton
cottonbush (*Austral.*)
cottonwood, blanket bush, tawine, tarwine, *or* tauhinu (*Austral.*)
cranberry
crowea
crown-of-thorns
daphne
dogwood
emu bush (*Austral.*)
eriostemon
forsythia
frangipani
fuchsia
gardenia
geebung, geebong, *or* jibbong (*Austral.*)
Geraldton waxflower (*Austral.*)
gooseberry
gorse
grevillea
hakea (*Austral.*)
hawthorn
heath
heather
honeysuckle
hydrangea
jasmine
juniper
kerrawang (*Austral.*)
laburnum
laurel
lilac
liquorice
magnolia
mistletoe
mock orange
myrtle
oleander
olearia *or* daisy bush (*Austral.*)
pittosporum
pituri (*Austral.*)
poinsettia
poison ivy
poison oak
potentilla
privet
pyracantha
raspberry
redcurrant
rhododendron
rose
rosemary
rue
saltbush (*Austral.*)
strawberry
tea
thyme
waratah (*Austral.*)
wax(flower)

SEVEN DEADLY SINS

anger
covetousness *or* avarice
envy
gluttony
lust
pride
sloth

SKIRTS

A-line
button-through
crinoline
dirndl
divided skirt
drop-waisted
filibeg, fillibeg, *or* philibeg
full skirt
fustanella *or* fustanelle
gaberdine *or* gabardine
grass skirt
half-slip *or* waist-slip
hobble skirt
hoop skirt
kilt
lava-lava
maxiskirt
microskirt
midiskirt
miniskirt
overskirt
pencil skirt
petticoat
puffball skirt
ra-ra skirt
riding skirt
sarong
tutu
underskirt
wrapover *or* wrapround

SNAILS, SLUGS AND OTHER GASTROPODS

abalone *or* ear shell
conch
cowrie *or* cowry
limpet
murex
nudibranch *or* sea slug
ormer *or* sea-ear
periwinkle *or* winkle
ramshorn snail
Roman snail
sea hare
slug
snail
top-shell
triton
wentletrap
whelk

SNOOKER AND BILLIARDS TERMS

baize
ball
baulk
baulkline
black
blue
bouclée
break
bricole
bridge
brown
cannon
carom *(chiefly U.S.)* *(Canad.)*
chalk
clearance
cue ball
cue extension
cue tip
cushion
D *or* d
double
draw
drop cannon
fluke
foul
frame
free ball
green
half-butt
hazard
headrail
in-off
jenny
kick
kiss
lag
long jenny
massé
maximum break *or* 147
miscue
nurse
nursery cannon
object ball
pink
plain ball
plant
pocket
pot
red
rest
safety
scratch
screw
short jenny
side *or (U.S. & Canad.)* English
snooker
spider
spot
spot ball
stun
top
triangle *or (U.S. & Canad.)* rack
white
Whitechapel
yellow

SOCKS AND TIGHTS

ankle sock *or (U.S.)* anklet
argyle
bed sock
bobby sock
half-hose
hose *(History)*
knee-high sock
legwarmer
lisle stocking
maillot
nylons
pop sock
puttee *or* putty
tights *or (esp U.S. & Austral.)* pantihose *or* pantyhose
sock
slouch sock
stay-up
stock *(archaic)*
stocking

TYPES OF SOFA

bergère
canapé
chaise longue *or* chaise
chesterfield
couch
davenport *(U.S.)*
day bed
divan
futon
lounge
love seat
settee
settle
sofa bed
squab
studio couch
tête-à-tête
vis-à-vis

SPIDERS AND OTHER ARACHNIDS

bird spider
black widow
book scorpion
cardinal spider
cheese mite
chigger, chigoe, *or (U.S. & Canad.)* redbug
chigoe, chigger, jigger, *or* sand flea
false scorpion
funnel-web
harvestman *or (U.S. & Canad.)* daddy-longlegs
house spider
itch mite
jockey spider
jumping spider
katipo *(N.Z.)*
mite
money spider
red-back (spider) *(Austral.)*
spider
spider mite
tarantula
tick
trap-door spider
vinegarroon
water spider
whip scorpion
wolf spider *or* hunting spider

SPIRITS

absinth *or* absinthe
aguardiente
applejack, applejack brandy, *or* apple brandy
aquavit *or* akvavit
aqua vitae *(archaic)*
Armagnac
arrack *or* arak
Bacardi *(trademark)*
brandy
bitters
Calvados
Cognac
dark rum
eau de vie
firewater
framboise
gin
grappa
Hollands
hooch
Kirsch *or* Kirschwasser
korn
marc
mescal
ouzo
palinka
poteen *or* poitín
raki *or* rakee
rum
schnapps *or* schnaps
slivovitz
sloe gin
taffia
tequila
triple sec
vodka
whisky
white rum

SPORTS

TEAM SPORTS

American football
association football *or* soccer
Australian Rules *or* Australian Rules football
baseball
bandy
basketball
camogie
Canadian football
cricket
curling
five-a-side football
football
Gaelic football
goalball
handball
hockey
hurling *or* hurley
ice hockey
kabbadi
korfball
lacrosse
netball
polo
roller hockey
rounders
rugby *or* rugby football
rugby league
rugby union
shinty
softball
stool ball
tug-of-war
volleyball
water polo

COMBAT SPORTS

boxing
fencing
sambo *or* sambo wrestling
savate
wrestling

OTHER SPORTS

angling *or* fishing
archery
badminton
ballooning
billiards
boules
bowls
bullfighting
candlepins
canyoning
clay pigeon shooting
cockfighting
coursing
croquet
cycling
cyclo-cross
darts
decathlon
falconry
fives
fly-fishing
fox-hunting
gliding
golf
greyhound racing
gymnastics
hang gliding
jai alai
lawn tennis
modern pentathlon
mountaineering
paddleball
parachuting
paragliding
parascending
paraskiing
pelota
pétanque
pigeon racing
pool

potholing
quoits
rackets
real tennis
rhythmic gymnastics
rock climbing
roller skating
shooting
skeet
skittles
skydiving
snooker
squash *or* squash rackets
table tennis
tennis
tenpin bowling
trampolining
trapshooting
triathlon
weightlifting

STARS AND CONSTELLATIONS

STARS

Aldebaran
Betelgeuse *or* Betelgeux
Polaris, the Pole Star, *or* the North Star
Sirius, the Dog Star, Canicula, *or* Sothis
the Sun

CONSTELLATIONS

Latin name	***English name***
Andromeda	Andromeda
Antila	Air Pump
Apus	Bird of Paradise
Aquarius	Water Bearer
Aquila	Eagle
Ara	Altar
Aries	Ram
Auriga	Charioteer
Boötes	Herdsman
Caelum	Chisel
Camelopardalis	Giraffe
Cancer	Crab
Canes Venatici	Hunting Dogs
Canis Major	Great Dog
Canis Minor	Little Dog
Capricornus	Sea Goat
Carina	Keel
Cassiopeia	Cassiopeia
Centaurus	Centaur
Cepheus	Cepheus
Cetus	Whale
Chamaeleon	Chameleon
Circinus	Compasses
Columba	Dove
Coma Bernices	Bernice's Hair
Corona Australis	Southern Crown
Corona Borealis	Northern Crown
Corvus	Crow
Crater	Cup
Crux	Southern Cross
Cygnus	Swan
Delphinus	Dolphin
Dorado	Swordfish
Draco	Dragon
Equuleus	Little Horse
Eridanus	River Eridanus
Fornax	Furnace
Gemini	Twins
Grus	Crane
Hercules	Hercules
Horologium	Clock
Hydra	Sea Serpent
Hydrus	Water Snake
Indus	Indian
Lacerta	Lizard
Latin name	***English name***
Leo	Lion
Leo Minor	Little Lion
Lepus	Hare
Libra	Scales
Lupus	Wolf
Lynx	Lynx
Lyra	Harp
Mensa	Table
Microscopium	Microscope
Monoceros	Unicorn
Musca	Fly
Norma	Level
Octans	Octant
Ophiuchus	Serpent Bearer
Orion	Orion
Pavo	Peacock
Pegasus	Winged Horse
Perseus	Perseus
Phoenix	Phoenix
Pictor	Easel
Pisces	Fishes
Piscis Austrinus	Southern Fish
Puppis	Ship's Stern
Pyxis	Mariner's Compass
Reticulum	Net
Sagitta	Arrow
Sagittarius	Archer
Scorpius	Scorpion
Sculptor	Sculptor
Scutum	Shield
Serpens	Serpent
Sextans	Sextant
Taurus	Bull
Telescopium	Telescope
Triangulum	Triangle
Triangulum Australe	Southern Triangle
Tucana	Toucan

Ursa Major	Great Bear (contains the Plough *or* (*U.S.*) Big Dipper)	Vela	Sails
		Virgo	Virgin
		Volans	Flying Fish
Ursa Minor	Little Bear *or* (*U.S.*) Little Dipper	Vulpecula	Fox

SUGARS

EDIBLE SUGARS

beet sugar	crystallized sugar	jaggery	powdered sugar
brown sugar	demerara sugar	maple sugar	panocha
cane sugar	granulated sugar	muscovado sugar	refined sugar
caster sugar	icing sugar	palm sugar	white sugar

BIOCHEMICAL SUGARS

aldose	fructose *or* laevulose	maltose	sorbose
arabinose	galactose	mannose	trehalose
deoxyribose	glucose	raffinose	triose
dextrose *or* grape sugar	invert sugar	rhamnose	xylose *or* wood sugar
	lactose *or* milk sugar	ribose	

SUITS

boiler suit	lounge suit	sailor suit	swimsuit
buckskins	Mao suit	scrubs	three-piece suit
catsuit	morning dress	shell suit	tracksuit
double-breasted suit	penguin suit	single-breasted suit	trouser suit *or* (*U.S. & Canad.*) pant suit
dress suit	playsuit	ski suit	wet suit
evening dress	pyjamas *or* (*U.S.*) pajamas	slack suit	zoot suit
G-suit *or* anti-G suit	romper suit	sunsuit	
judogi	safari suit	spacesuit	
jump suit		sweat suit *or* sweats	

THE SUPERNATURAL

PEOPLE WITH SUPERNATURAL POWERS

archimage	enchanter	magician	siren	water diviner
channeller	enchantress	magus	sorcerer	water witch
clairaudient	exorcist	medium	sorceress	white witch
clairvoyant	fortune-teller	necromancer	spaewife (*Scot.*)	witch
conjurer	hag	rainmaker	superhero	witch doctor
diviner	hex	seer	thaumaturge	witch master
dowser	mage	shaman	warlock	wizard

SUPERNATURAL CREATURES

angel	fay	hobgoblin	monster	succubus
banshee	genie	imp	ogre	sylph
brownie	ghost	incubus	peri	troll
demon	ghoul	jinni, jinnee, djinni, *or* djinny	phantom	vampire
devil	giant	kachina	pixie	werewolf *or* lycanthrope
dwarf	gnome	kelpie	poltergeist	wraith
dybbuk	goblin	lamia	sandman	zombie *or* zombi
elf	god *or* goddess	leprechaun	selkie *or* silkie (*Scot.*)	
fairy	golem	little people *or* folk	spectre	
fairy godmother	gremlin		sprite	
familiar	guardian angel			

SUPERNATURAL TERMS

abracadabra
amulet
apport
aura
black magic *or* the Black Art
charm
clairaudience
clairvoyance
cryptaesthesia
curse
divination
ectoplasm
evil eye
exorcism
extrasensory perception *or* ESP
fate
fetish
grigri, gris-gris, *or* greegree
grimoire
hex
hoodoo
incantation
invultuation
Indian sign
jinx
juju
kismet
levitation
magic circle
magic spell
magic wand
mojo
necromancy
obi *or* obeah
Ouija *(trademark)*
parapsychology
pentagram
philtre
portent
possession
premonition
reincarnation
rune
seance *or* séance
second sight
sigil
sixth sense
spell
talisman
talking in tongues, xenoglossia, *or* xenoglossy
telaesthesia
telegnosis
telekinesis *or* psychokinesis
telepathy
voodoo
wand
white magic
witching hour

SWEATERS

Aran sweater
cardigan
Cowichan sweater, Indian sweater, siwash, *or* siwash sweater *(Canad.)*
cowl-necked sweater
crew-neck *or* crew-necked sweater
Fairisle
Guernsey *(Austral.)*
hoodie *(informal)*
Icelandic
jersey
jumper
polo *or* polo neck
pullover
rollneck
skivvy *(Austral.) (N.Z.)*
slipover
sloppy joe
sweatshirt
turtleneck
V-neck *or* V-necked sweater

SWORDS AND OTHER WEAPONS WITH BLADES

assegai *or* assagai
backsword
battle-axe
bayonet
bill
bowie knife
broadsword
claymore
cutlass
dagger
dirk
épée
falchion
foil
halberd
hatchet
jackknife
jerid, jereed, *or* jerreed
knife *or (slang)* chiv
kris
kukri
machete
parang
partisan
pike
poleaxe
poniard
rapier
sabre *or* saber
scimitar
sgian-dhu
sheath knife
skean
smallsword
snickersnee
spear

TABLES AND DESKS

bar
bedside table
billiard table
breakfast bar
breakfast table
buffet
bureau
card table
carrel
coffee table
console table
counter
davenport *(Brit.)*
desk
dining table
dressing table
drop-leaf table
drum table
escritoire
folding table
gate-leg *or* gate-legged table
kitchen table
lapboard
lowboy *(U.S.) (Canada)*
nest of tables
occasional table
pedestal desk
Pembroke table
piecrust table
reading desk
refectory table
roll-top desk
secretaire
side table
snooker table
teapoy
tea table
tea trolley
traymobile *(Austral.)*
trestle table
wool table
workbench
worktable
writing desk
writing table

TEAS

Assam
bohea
camomile tea
Ceylon
Chinese tea
congou *or* congo
Darjeeling
Earl Grey
green tea
gunpowder tea
herb *or* herbal tea
Indian tea
jasmine tea
Lapsang Souchong
lemon tea
mint tea
oolong
orange pekoe
post-and-rail tea *(archaic)*
Russian tea

TELECOMMUNICATION TERMS

Blackberry
Bluetooth
e-mail
instant messaging *or* IM
MMS
mobile phone
MSN
pager
Skype
SMS *or* text messaging

TENNIS TERMS

ace
advantage
approach shot
backhand
ball
baseline
baseliner
break of serve
break point
cannonball
centre line
centre mark
chip
clay court
court
deuce
double fault
doubles
drop shot
fault
foot fault
forecourt
forehand
game
grass court
ground stroke
half-volley
hard court
lawn tennis
let
line call
linesman
lob
love
love game
match
mixed doubles
net
net cord
passing shot
racket *or* racquet
rally
receiver
return
serve and volleyer
server
service
service line
set
set point
sideline
singles
slice
smash
tie-break *or* tiebreaker
topspin
tramline
umpire
undercut
volley

TEXT MESSAGING ABBREVIATIONS AND SYMBOLS

Abbreviation or symbol	*Meaning*
A3	anytime, anywhere, anyplace
AAM	as a matter of fact
AFAIK	as far as I know
AFK	away from keyboard
al2gethr	altogether
ALrlt	all right
ATB	all the best
ATK	at the keyboard
ATM	at the moment
ATTN	attention
B	be
B4	before
BAK	back at keyboard
BBL	be back later
BCNU	be seeing you
BFN *or* B4N	bye for now
BK *or* COZ	because
BF	boyfriend
BR	bathroom
BRB	be right back
BRT	be right there
BS	bullshit
BWD	backward
BY	busy
C	see
CIAO	goodbye
CMIIW	correct me if I'm wrong
CU	see you
CUL8R	see you later
CYA	see you
EVR	ever
EZ	easy
FC	fingers crossed
FONE	phone
4	for *or* four
4EVA	for ever
F2T	free to talk
FWD	forward
FWIW	for what it's worth
FYI	for your information
GAL	get a life
G9	genius
GF	girlfriend
GG	good game

Abbreviation or symbol	*Meaning*
GGG *or* GGL	giggle
GMTA	great minds think alike
GR8	great
HAND	have a nice day
H8	hate
HD	hold
IC	I see
IDD	indeed
ILU	I love you
IMHO	in my humble *or honest* opinion
IMNSHO	in my not so humble opinion
IMO	in my opinion
IOW	in other words
IRL	in real life
IRW	in the real world
IFYWIMAITYD	if you know what I mean and I think you do
K	okay
KISS	keep it simple, stupid
KIT	keep in touch
L8	late
L8R	later
LDR	long-distance relationship
LO	hello
LOL	laughing out loud
LTNS	long time no see
LUV	love
LZ	loser
M8	mate
MSG	message
MT	empty
MTG	meeting
NE	any
NE1	anyone
Njoy	enjoy
NO1	no-one
NRN	no reply necessary
OFN	often
OIC	oh I see
PCM	please call me
PLS	please
PLU	people like us
PPL	people
PRT	party
PRW	parents are watching
Q	queue
QL	cool
QT	quiet
R	are
RGDS	regards
ROFL	rolling on floor laughing
ROFLOL	rolling on floor laughing out loud
ROTFL	rolling on the floor laughing
ROTFLOL	rolling on the floor laughing out loud
RUOK	are you OK?
SIT	stay in touch
SK8	skate
SOHF	sense of humour failure
SOM1	someone
THX *or* TX	thanks
Ti2GO	time to go
2	to, too, *or* two
2DAY	today
2MORO	tomorrow
2NITE	tonight
TTYL	talk to you later
TXT	text
U	you
U2	you too
U4E	yours for ever
UR	you are *or* your
W8	wait
WADYA	what do you
WAN2	want to
WAN2TLK	want to talk?
WB	welcome back
WK	week
WKND	weekend
WIV	with
W/O	without
WOT	what
WTG	way to go!
X	kiss
XLNT	excellent
XOXO	hugs and kisses

EMOTICONS

Emoticon	*Meaning*
:-)	happy
:-))	cheerful
:-)))	really happy
:-()	smiling with mouth open
8-)	smiling with glasses
D:-)	smiling with baseball cap
;-)	winking
:-*	kissing
:-(	sad
:'-(	crying
:-C	very sad
:-@	screaming
:-O	shocked or surprised

TIME

RELATED VOCABULARY

calends *or* kalends
civil day
civil year
day
Gregorian calendar
ides
intercalary
Julian calendar
leap year
lunar month
lunar year
month
nones
Roman calendar
synodic month
week
year

GREGORIAN CALENDAR

January
February
March
April
May
June
July
August
September
October
November
December

JEWISH CALENDAR

Tishri
Cheshvan *or* Heshvan
Kislev
Tevet
Shevat *or* Shebat
Adar
Nisan
Iyar *or* Iyyar
Sivan
Tammuz
Av *or* Ab
Elul

MUSLIM CALENDAR

Muharram *or* Moharram
Safar *or* Saphar
Rabia I
Rabia II
Jumada I
Jumada II
Rajab
Shaban *or* Shaaban
Ramadan, Rhamadhan, *or* Ramazan
Shawwal
Dhu'l-Qa'dah
Dhu'l-Hijjah

FRENCH REVOLUTIONARY CALENDAR

Vendémiaire
Brumaire
Frimaire
Nivôse
Pluviôse
Ventôse
Germinal
Floréal
Prairial
Messidor
Thermidor *or* Fervidor
Fructidor

TIME ZONES

Atlantic Daylight Time
Atlantic Standard Time
British Summer Time
Central Daylight Time
Central European Time
Central Standard Time
Eastern Daylight Time
Eastern Standard Time
Greenwich Mean Time
Mountain Daylight Time
Mountain Standard Time
Newfoundland Daylight Time
Newfoundland Standard Time
Pacific Daylight Time
Pacific Standard Time
Yukon Daylight Time
Yukon Standard Time

TOOLS

Allen key
alligator
auger
awl
axe
ball-peen hammer
beetle
billhook
bit
bitstock
bodkin
bolster
borer
bosh
brace and bit
broach
broad
burin
bushhammer
centre punch
chaser
chisel
claw hammer
clink
clippers
cold chisel
comb
comber
countersink
cradle
croze
diamond point
dibble
drawknife *or* drawshave
dresser
drift *or* driftpin
drill
drill press
drove *or* drove chisel
edge tool
eyeleteer
facer
file
fillet
firmer chisel
flange
flatter
float
floatcut file
fork
former
fraise
froe *or* frow
fuller
gab
gad
gavel
gimlet

gouger
graver
gympie *(Austral.)*
hack
hack hammer
half-round chisel
hammer
hammer drill
hob
hoe
hone
icebreaker
ice pick
jackhammer
jointer
jumper
kevel
knapping hammer
mallet
mattock
maul
mitre square
monkey wrench
nibbler
nippers
padsaw
percussion tool
pestle
pick
piledriver
pitching tool
plane
pliers
ploughstaff
pneumatic hammer
power drill
pruning hook
punch
rabble *or* rabbler
rake
rawhide hammer
ripple
rocker
rounder
router
sander
saw
sax
scorper *or* scauper
screwdriver
screw tap
scriber
scutch *or* scutcher
scythe
shave
shears
sickle
slasher *(Austral.)* *(N.Z.)*
sledgehammer
snake
slick
soldering iron
spade
spanner
spider
spitsticker
spud *or* spudder
stiletto
stylus
swage
tack hammer
tilt hammer
triphammer
trepan
trowel
wimble
wrench

TEETH

canine
incisor *or* foretooth
molar
premolar
wisdom tooth

TORTURE

INSTRUMENTS OF TORTURE

boot
brake
cat-o'-nine-tails
iron maiden
pilliwinks
Procrustean bed
rack
scourge
thumbscrew
wheel

TYPES OF TORTURE

bastinado
Chinese water torture
gauntlet
strappado
water cure
water torture

TREES

acacia
akee
alder
almond
aloe
angophora *(Austral.)*
Antarctic beech
apple
apricot
ash
aspen
balsa
banana
bangalay *or* bastard mahogany *(Austral.)*
bangalow (palm) *or* piccabean *(Austral.)*
banyalla *or* tallowwood *(Austral.)*
banyan
baobab *or* boab
bat's wing coral-tree *(Austral.)*
bay
beech
beefwood *(Austral.)*
belah, belar, billar, *or* black oak *(Austral.)*
berrigan *or* bitterbush *(Austral.)*
bimble box *(Austral.)*
birch
bitterbark *(Austral.)*
black bean *or* Moreton Bay chestnut
blackbutt *(Austral.)*
black pine *or* matai *(Austral.)*
black wattle *(Austral.)*
blackwood *or* mudgerabah *(Austral.)*
blanket-leaf *(Austral.)*
bloodwood *(Austral.)*
bonsai
boree *(Austral.)*
bottle tree *(Austral.)*
box
brazil
brigalow *(Austral.)*
bulwaddy, bullwaddy, bullwaddie, *or* bulwaddee *(Austral.)*
bunya *or* bunya-bunya (pine)
burrawang *or* zamia *(Austral.)*
butternut
cabbage tree (palm) *(Austral.)*
cacao
cadagi *or* cadaga *(Austral.)*

cajuput *or* cajeput *(Austral.)*
camphor laurel *(Austral.)*
carbeen, carbean, karbeen, *or* Moreton Bay ash *(Austral.)*
carob
cashew
cassia
casuarina *or* native oak *(Austral.)*
cedar
cedar of Lebanon
celery pine *or* celery-top pine *(Austral.)*
cherry
chestnut
cinnamon
citrus
coachwood *(Austral.)*
coco
coconut
coolabah *or* coolibah
coral tree *(Austral.)*
cork oak
corkwood *or* cork tree
cypress
date palm
deal
dogwood
Douglas fir
ebony
elder
elm
eucalyptus *or* eucalypt
eumung *or* eumong *(Austral.)*
fig
fir
firewheel tree *(Austral.)*
flame tree *or* Illawarra flame tree *(Austral.)*
flooded gum *(Austral.)*
ghost gum *(Austral.)*
gidgee *or* stinking wattle *(Austral.)*
golden wattle *(Austral.)*
grapefruit
grasstree *or* black boy *(Austral.)*
grey gum *(Austral.)*
ground ash
ground oak
guava
gum (tree)
gympie
hawthorn
hazel
hemlock
hickory
holly
hoop pine *(Austral.)*
hornbeam
horse chestnut
huon pine *(Austral.)*
ilex
ironbark
iron gum
ironwood
jacaranda
jarrah *(Austral.)*
Judas tree
juniper
karri
kauri
kentia palm *(Austral.)*
kurrajong *or* currajong *(Austral.)*
laburnum
larch
laurel
lemon
lilac
lilly pilly *or* lilli pilli *(Austral.)*
lime
lind
linden
lotus
macadamia, bauple nut, *or* Queensland nut *(Austral.)*
macrocarpa
magnolia
mahogany
mallee *(Austral.)*
mango
mangrove
manuka, kahikatoa, *or* kanuka *(N.Z.)*
maple
marri *(Austral.)*
melaleuca
mimosa
monkey puzzle *or* Chile pine
Moreton Bay fig *(Austral.)*
mountain ash
mugga *(Austral.)*
mulberry
myall *(Austral.)*
Norfolk Island pine *(Austral.)*
nutmeg
oak
olive
orange
osier
palm
papaya
paperbark
pawpaw *or* papaw
peach
pear
peppermint gum *(Austral.)*
persimmon
pine
plane
plum
pomegranate
poplar
pussy willow
quandong *or* quondong *(Austral.)*
quince
radiata pine, insignis pine, *or* Monterey pine *(Austral.)*
raffia
redwood
rivergum *or* river red gum *(Austral.)*
rosewood
rowan
sandalwood
sassafras
Scots fir
Scots pine
scribbly gum *(Austral.)*
sequoia
silky oak *(Austral.)*
silver birch
snow gum *(Austral.)*
spotted gum *(Austral.)*
spruce
stinging tree *or* gympie nettle *(Austral.)*
stringy-bark
sycamore
tamarind
Tasmanian blue gum *(Austral.)*
teak
tea-tree
umbrella tree
walnut
wandoo *(Austral.)*
wattle
weeping willow
white ash
whitebeam
wilga *(Austral.)*
willow
wirilda *(Austral.)*
witch
witch elm
yellow box *(Austral.)*
yew
ylang-ylang
yucca

VEGETABLES

ackee
adjigo *or* warran (*Austral.*)
asparagus
aubergine *or* (*esp U.S., Canad., and Austral.*) eggplant
baby corn
bean sprout
beef tomato
beetroot *or* beet
bok choy, Chinese leaf, Chinese cabbage, *or* pak-choi
broad bean
broccoli
Brussels sprout *or* sprout
butternut pumpkin
cabbage
calabrese
calalu *or* calaloo
cardoon
carrot
cauliflower
celeriac
celery
chard
chayote
cherry tomato
chicory
chive
choko
collard
corn on the cob
cos, cos lettuce, *or* (*U.S. & Canad.*) romaine
courgette *or* (*U.S., Canad. & Austral.*) zucchini
cress
cucumber
endive
fennel
finocchio
frisee
gherkin
globe artichoke
greens
horseradish
iceberg lettuce
Jerusalem artichoke
kale *or* kail
kohlrabi
lamb's lettuce *or* corn salad
leek
lettuce
marrow squash
okra, lady's finger, *or* bhindi
onion
orache
pak-choi
parsnip
pea
pepper, capsicum, *or* (*U.S.*) bell pepper
pe-tsai cabbage
pimiento *or* pimento
potato
puha, puwha, *or* rauriki (*N.Z.*)
radicchio
radish
salsify *or* oyster plant
savoy cabbage
shallot
silver beet
sorrel
Spanish onion
spinach
spring greens
spring onion, salad onion, scallion (*chiefly U.S.*), *or* syboe (*Scot.*)
squash
swede
sweet corn *or* (*chiefly U.S.*) corn
sweet potato, batata, *or* (*N.Z.*) kumera *or* kumara
turnip *or* (*dialect*) neep
vegetable marrow *or* marrow
yam

TYPES OF VEHICLE

aircraft
ambulance
articulated lorry *or* (*informal*) artic
autocycle
autorickshaw
barrow
bicycle *or* (*informal*) bike
Black Maria
boat
breakdown van *or* truck, tow truck, *or* (*Austral. slang*) towie
bulldozer
bus
cab
cabriolet
camion
camper (*U.S.*) (*Canad.*)
camper van
car
caravan
carriage
Caterpillar (*trademark*)
chaise
charabanc (*Brit.*)
chariot
coach
combine harvester
Conestoga wagon (*U.S.*) (*Canad.*)
coupé
cycle
delivery van *or* (*U.S. & Canad.*) panel truck
Dormobile (*trademark*)
double-decker (*chiefly Brit.*)
dray
dump truck *or* dumper-truck
dustcart *or* (*U.S. & Canad.*) garbage truck
estate car
fire engine
fork-lift truck
four-wheel drive
gritter (*Brit.*)
hansom *or* hansom cab
hatchback *or* hatch
hog (*informal*)
Humvee *or* (informal) Hummer
hybrid car *or* hybrid
jaunting car *or* jaunty car
JCB (*trademark*)
Jeep (*trademark*)
jet ski
jinricksha, jinrickshaw, jinrikisha *or* jinriksha
jitney (*U.S.*) (*rare*)
kart, go-cart, *or* go-kart
kibitka
komatik
koneke (*N.Z.*)
landaulet *or* landaulette
light engine *or* (*U.S.*) wildcat
limousine
litter
locomotive
lorry
low-loader
luge
milk float
minibus
moped
motorbicycle
motorbike
motorbus
motorcar
motor caravan
motorcycle
motor scooter
motor vehicle
off-road vehicle
omnibus
paddock-basher (*Austral.*) (*slang*)
panda car (*Brit.*)
pantechnicon (*Brit.*)
people carrier, people mover, *or* (*U.S.*) minivan
pick-up (*Austral. & N.Z.*), utility truck, *or* (*informal*) ute
police car
postbus
post chaise
pram
racing car
railcar
ratha
rickshaw

roadroller
road train *(Austral.)*
rocket
scooter
scout car
shandrydan
ship
single-decker *(Brit.)*
skibob
sledge *or (especially U.S. & Canad.)* sled
sleigh
Sno-Cat *(trademark)*
snowmobile
snow plough
space capsule
spacecraft
space probe
spaceship
space shuttle
sports car
stagecoach
steamroller
sulky
SUV *or* sports utility vehicle
tandem
tank
tank engine *or* locomotive
tanker
tarantass
taxi
telega
three-wheeler
tipper truck *or* lorry
toboggan
tonga
tourer *or (especially U.S.)* touring car
traction engine
tractor
trail bike
trailer
train
tram, tramcar, *or (U.S. & Canad.)* streetcar *or* trolley car
travois
tricycle
troika
trolley
trolleybus
troop carrier
truck
tuk-tuk
tumbrel *or* tumbril
unicycle
van
wagon *or* waggon
wagonette *or* waggonette
wheelbarrow

WATER SPORTS

aquabobbing
canoeing
canoe polo
diving
parasailing
powerboating *or* powerboat racing
rowing
sailing
skin diving
surfing
swimming
synchronized swimming
water polo
water-skiing
windsurfing
yachting

WEAPONS

PROJECTILE WEAPONS

ballista
bazooka
blowpipe
catapult
crossbow
fléchette
grapeshot
gun
longbow
onager
quarrel
rifle grenade
torpedo
trebuchet *or* trebucket

MISCELLANEOUS WEAPONS

biological warfare
bomb
chemical warfare
club
death ray
flame-thrower
germ warfare *or* bacteriological warfare
Greek fire
knuckle-duster
Mace *(trademark)*
mustard gas
napalm
pepper spray
poison gas

WEATHER

WEATHER DESCRIPTIONS

arctic
baking
balmy
bland
blistering
blustery
breezy
clammy
clear
clement
close
cloudy
cold
dirty
dreich *(Scot.)*
drizzly
dry
dull
filthy
fine
foggy
foul
freezing *(informal)*
fresh
hazy
hot
humid
icy
inclement
mild
misty
muggy
nippy
overcast
parky *(informal)*
perishing *(informal)*
rainy
raw
scorching *(informal)*
showery
snowy
sticky
stormy
sultry
sunny
thundery
tropical
wet
windy
wintry

WEATHER PHENOMENA

acid rain
ball lightning
breeze
cloud
cold snap
cyclone
drizzle
dust devil
dust storm
fog
freeze
gale
gust
haar *(Scot.)*
hail

heatwave
hurricane
ice
lightning
mist
peasouper *(chiefly Brit.)*
precipitation
pressure
rain
sandstorm
sheet lightning
shower
sleet
smirr *(Scot.)*
snow
squall
storm
sunshine
tempest *(literary)*
thaw
thunder
tidal wave
tornado
tsunami
typhoon
waterspout
whirlwind
wind
willy-willy *(Austral.)*
zephyr

METEOROLOGICAL TERMS

anticyclone
cold front
cyclone
depression
front
heat-island
isallobar
isobar
lee wave
occluded front
ridge
scud
synoptic chart
thermal
trough
virga
warm front

GATHERERS OF WEATHER DATA

dropsonde
meteorograph
Meteorological Office *or* Met. Office
pilot balloon
radiosonde
weather ship
weather station
weatherman
weatherwoman

MEASURING INSTRUMENTS

	Phenomenon measured
anemometer	wind velocity
anemoscope	wind direction
atmometer	rate of water evaporation into atmosphere
barograph	atmospheric pressure
barometer	atmospheric pressure
baroscope	atmospheric pressure
hygrometer	humidity
maximum-minimum thermometer	temperature variation
nephoscope	cloud velocity, altitude, and direction of movement
psychrometer	humidity
rain gauge	rainfall and snowfall
rawinsonde	atmospheric wind velocity
Stevenson's screen	temperature
sunshine recorder	hours of sunshine
thermometer	temperature
weathercock	wind direction
weather vane	wind direction
wet-and-dry-bulb thermometer	humidity
wind gauge	wind velocity
wind tee	wind direction

WEIGHTS AND MEASURES

IMPERIAL SYSTEM

Linear	*Square*	*Weight*	*Land*	*Volume*	*Liquid volume*
mile	square mile	ton	square mile	cubic yard	gallon
furlong	acre	hundredweight	acre	cubic foot	quart
rod	square rod	stone	square rod	cubic inch	pint
yard	square yard	pound	square yard	-	fluid ounce
foot	square foot	ounce			
inch	square inch	-			
mil	-	-			

METRIC SYSTEM

Linear	*Square*	*Weight*	*Land*	*Volume*	*Liquid Volume*
kilometre	square kilometre	tonne	square kilometre	cubic metre	litre
metre	square metre	kilogram	hectare	cubic decimetre	millilitre
centimetre	square centimetre	gram	are	cubic centimetre	-
millimetre	square millimetre	-	-	cubic millimetre	-

WHALES AND DOLPHINS

beluga
baleen whale
blue whale *or* sulphur-bottom
bottlenose dolphin
bowhead
dorado
Greenland whale
greyback *or* grey whale
humpback whale
killer whale, grampus, *or* orca
minke whale
narwhal
pilot whale, black whale, *or* blackfish
porpoise
right whale *or* (*Austral.*) bay whale
rorqual
sei whale
sperm whale *or* cachalot
toothed whale
whalebone whale
white whale

WHISKIES

blend
blended whisky
bourbon
corn whisky
grain whisky
hokonui (*N.Z.*)
Irish whiskey
malt *or* malt whisky
poteen *or* poitín
redeye (*U.S.*) (*slang*)
rye
Scotch
shebeen *or* shebean (*Irish*)
single malt
sour mash
vatted malt

WINDS

Wind	*Location*
berg wind	South Africa
bise	Switzerland
bora	Adriatic Sea
buran *or* bura	central Asia
Cape doctor	Cape Town, South Africa
chinook	Washington & Oregon coasts
föhn *or* foehn	N slopes of the Alps
harmattan	W African coast
khamsin, kamseen *or* kamsin	Egypt
levanter	W Mediterranean
libeccio *or* libecchio	Corsica
meltemi *or* etesian wind	NE Mediterranean
mistral	S France to Mediterranean
monsoon	S Asia
nor'wester	Southern Alps, New Zealand
pampero	S America
simoom *or* simoon	Arabia & N Africa
sirocco	N Africa to S Europe
tramontane *or* tramontana	W coast of Italy

WINES

WINES

Amarone
Asti Spumante
Bairrada
Bandol
Banyuls
Barbaresco
Barbera d'Albi
Barbera d'Asti
Barolo
Barsac
beaujolais
beaujolais nouveau
Bereich Bernkastel
Bergerac
blanc de blancs
Blanquette de Limoux
Bordeaux
Bourgogne
Bourgueil
Brouilly
Brunello di Montalcino
Bucelas
Bull's Blood *or* Egri Bikaver
Burgundy
Cahors
canary
Carema
Cava
Chablis
Chambertin
Champagne
chardonnay
chianti
Colheita Port
claret
Condrieu
Constantia
Corbières
Coteaux du Tricastin
Côte de Beaune-Villages
Côte Rôtie
Côtes du Rhône
Crémant d'Alsace
Crémant de Loire
Crozes-Hermitage
crusted port
Dão
Entre-Deux-Mers
Faugères
Fitou
Fleurie
Frascati
Fumé Blanc
Gaillac
Gattinara
Gavi
Gevrey-Chambertin
Gigondas
Grange Hermitage
Graves
Hermitage
hock
jerepigo
Jurançon
lachryma Christi
Lambrusco
Liebfraumilch
Lirac
Liqueur Muscat
Liqueur Tokay
Mâcon
Mâcon-Villages
Madeira
Málaga
Margaux
Marsala
Médoc
Meursault
Minervois
Monbazillac
Montepulciano d'Abruzzo
montilla
Moscato d'Asti
Moselle
muscadet
Muscat de Beaumes-de-Venise
muscatel
Niersteiner
Nuits-Saint-Georges
Orvieto
Parrina
Pauillac
Pessac-Léognan
Pinot Grigio
Piesporter
Pomerol

- Pommard
- port
- Pouilly-Fuissé
- Pouilly-Fumé
- Quarts de Chaume
- Quincy
- retsina
- Rhine wine
- riesling
- Rioja
- Roero
- Rosé d'Anjou
- Rosso Cònero
- Rüdesheimer
- Rueda
- Rully
- sack
- Saint-Émilion
- Saint-Estèphe
- Saint-Julien
- Saint-Véran
- Salice Salentino
- Sancerre
- Saumur
- Sauternes
- scuppernong
- sherry
- straw wine
- Tavel
- Teroldego Rotaliano
- Tokaji
- Tokay-Pinot Gris
- Valdepeñas
- Valpolicella
- Verdicchio
- Vinho Verde
- vin ordinaire
- Vino Nobile di Montepulciano
- Vosne-Romanée
- Vouvray

WINE-PRODUCING AREAS

	Country
Ahr	Germany
Alsace	France
Alto Adige *or* Südtirol	Italy
Anjou	France
Argentina	–
Austria	–
Barossa Valley	Australia
Baden	Germany
Bordeaux	France
Bulgaria	–
Burgundy	France
California	U.S.A.
Chablis	France
Champagne	France
Chianti	Italy
Chile	–
Clare Valley	Australia
Coonawarra	Australia
Côte d'Or	France
Finger Lakes	U.S.A.
Franken	Germany
Friuli	Italy
Gisborne	New Zealand
Goulburn Valley	Australia
Hawkes Bay	New Zealand
Hessiches Bergstrasse	Germany
Greece	–
Hungary	–
Hunter Valley	Australia
Languedoc	France
Loire	France
Marlborough	New Zealand
Margaret River	Australia
Martinborough	New Zealand
McLaren Vale	Australia
Mendocino	U.S.A.
Mittelrhein	Germany
Moldavia	–
Mornington Peninsula	Australia
Mosel-Saar-Ruwer	Germany
Nahe	Germany
Napa Valley	U.S.A.
Navarra	Spain
New York State	U.S.A.
Oregon	U.S.A.
Padthaway	Australia
Penedès	Spain
Piedmont	Italy
Portugal	–
Provence	France
Rheingau	Germany
Rheinhessen	Germany
Rheinpfalz	Germany
Rhône	France
Ribera del Duro	Spain
Rioja	Spain
Romania	–
Sicily	Italy
Sonoma	U.S.A.
South Africa	–
Switzerland	–
Touraine	France
Tuscany	Italy
Umbria	Italy
Valdepeñas	Spain
Veneto	Italy
Washington State	U.S.A.
Württemberg	Germany
Yarra Valley	Australia

WINE TERMS

- abbocatto
- AC *or* appellation contrôlée
- amabile
- amontillado
- AOC *or* appellation d'origine contrôlée
- aszú
- Ausbruch
- Auslese
- Baumé
- Beerenauslese
- botrytis
- botrytized
- Brix
- brut
- cream
- crianza
- cru bourgeois
- cru classé
- cuvée
- demi-sec
- dessert wine
- DOC *or* denominazione di origine controllata
- DOCG *or* denominazione di origine controllata e garantita
- dolce
- dry
- Einzellage
- Eiswein
- erzeugerabfüllung
- estate bottled
- flor
- fino
- fortified wine
- garrafeira
- grand cru
- gran reserva
- Grosslage
- halbtrocken
- Kabinett
- late harvest
- LBV *or* Late-Bottled Vintage (Port)
- malmsey
- malolactic fermentation
- manzanilla
- medium
- medium-dry
- medium-sweet
- méthode champenoise
- moelleux
- mousseux
- noble rot
- NV *or* non-vintage
- Oechsle
- oloroso
- organic
- pale cream
- passito
- pétillant
- plonk
- pourriture noble
- prädikat
- premier cru
- puttonyos

QbA, Qualitätswein bestimmter Anbaugebiet, *or* Qualitätswein
QmP *or* Qualitätswein mit Prädikat
recioto
récolte
reserva
rosé
riserva
Ruby Port
sec
secco
second wine
Sekt
sin crianza
Sigle Quinta Port
solera
sparkling wine
Spätlese
spumante
sur lie
sweet
table wine
Tafelwein
tannin
Tawny Port
terroir
tinto
trocken
Trockenbeerenauslese *or* TBA
varietal
VDQS *or* Vin Délimité de Qualité Supérieure
vendage tardive
vieilles vignes
vigneron
vignoble
vin de pays
vin de table
vin doux naturel
vin gris
vino da tavola
vintage
Weingut
Weissherbst
Winzergenossenschaft

WINTER SPORTS

Alpine skiing
biathlon
bobsleigh
curling
downhill racing
ice dancing
ice hockey
ice skating *or* figure skating
luge
Nordic skiing
Nordic walking
skating
skibobbing
skiing
skijoring
ski jumping
slalom
snowboarding
speed skating
super-G
tobogganing

SEVEN WONDERS OF THE ANCIENT WORLD

Colossus of Rhodes
Hanging Gardens of Babylon
Mausoleum of Halicarnassus
Pharos of Alexandria
Phidias' statue of Zeus at Olympia
Pyramids of Egypt
Temple of Artemis at Ephesus

TYPES OF WOOD

African mahogany
afrormosia
alerce
amboyna *or* amboina
apple
ash
assegai *or* assagai
balsa
basswood
baywood
beech
beefwood
birch
black walnut
bog oak
boxwood
brazil, brasil, *or* brazil wood
bulletwood
butternut
cade
calamander
camwood
candlewood
cedar
cherry
chestnut
citron wood
coachwood
corkwood
crabwood
cypress
durmast *or* durmast oak
eaglewood
ebony
elm
fiddlewood
fir
gaboon
gopher wood
greenheart
guaiacum *or* guaiocum
gumtree *or* gumwood
hackberry
hardwood
hazel
hemlock
hickory
hornbeam
iroko
ironwood
jacaranda
jelutong
kauri
kiaat
kingwood
koa
lancewood
larch
locust
mahogany
maple
marblewood
nutwood
oak
olive
orangewood
padauk *or* padouk
Paraná pine
partridge-wood
pear
persimmon
pine
pitch pine
poon
poplar
pulpwood
quassia
quebracho
red cedar
red fir
red gum
red oak
ribbonwood
rosewood
sandalwood
sandarac
sappanwood
sassy, sasswood, *or* sassy wood
satinwood
Scots pine
shagbark *or* shellbark
sneezewood
softwood
spotted gum
spruce
stinkwood
sumach *or* sumac (*U.S.*)
sycamore
tamarack
tamarind
teak
thorn
toon
torchwood
tulipwood
tupelo
walnut
western red cedar
white cedar
white pine
whitewood
willow
yellowwood
yew
zebrawood

SIGNS OF THE ZODIAC

Aquarius (the Water Carrier)
Aries (the Ram)
Cancer (the Crab)
Capricorn (the Goat)
Gemini (the Twins)
Leo (the Lion)
Libra (the Scales)
Pisces (the Fishes)
Sagittarius (the Archer)
Scorpio (the Scorpion)
Taurus (the Bull)
Virgo (the Virgin)

CHINESE ANIMAL YEARS

Chinese	*English*	*Years*				
Shu	Rat	1960	1972	1984	1996	2008
Niu	Ox	1961	1973	1985	1997	2009
Hu	Tiger	1962	1974	1986	1998	2010
Tu	Hare	1963	1975	1987	1999	2011
Long	Dragon	1964	1976	1988	2000	2012
She	Serpent	1965	1977	1989	2001	2013
Ma	Horse	1966	1978	1990	2002	2014
Yang	Sheep	1967	1979	1991	2003	2015
Hou	Monkey	1968	1980	1992	2004	2016
Ji	Cock	1969	1981	1993	2005	2017
Gou	Dog	1970	1982	1994	2006	2018
Zhu	Boar	1971	1983	1995	2007	2019

ZOOLOGY

BRANCHES OF ZOOLOGY

arachnology
archaeozoology
cetology
entomology
ethology
herpetology
ichthyology
malacology
mammalogy
myrmecology
ophiology
ornithology
palaeozoology
primatology
protozoology
zoogeography
zoography
zoometry
zootomy

ZOOLOGY TERMS

abdomen
aestivation
amphibian
antenna
anterior
appendage
arachnid
arthropod
biped
bivalve
carnivore
caudal
chordate
chrysalis
cocoon
coelenterate
coelom
colony
crustacean
decapod
dipteran
dorsal
echinoderm
edentate
fin
gastropod *or* gasteropod
gill
herbivore
hibernation
imago
insectivore
invertebrate
larva
lepidopteran
marsupial
metamorphosis
migration
omnivore
parenchyma
passerine
pectoral
placenta
posterior
predator
prey
primate
protozoan
pupa
quadruped
raptor
reptile
rodent
ruminant
segment
skeleton
spawn
spine
sucker
thorax
ventral
vertebrate